Aldo van Eyck
Collected Articles and Other Writings
1947–1998

Aldo van Eyck, 1947 Photo Violette Cornelius

Aldo van Eyck

Collected Articles and Other Writings 1947–1998

Edited by Vincent Ligtelijn and Francis Strauven

SUN

Contents

8 Introduction
The editors

11 **Chapter 1**
Looking back on his student years in Zurich
14 Ex Turico aliquid novum (1981)

27 **Chapter 2**
Advocate of the avant-garde in postwar CIAM (1947–1953)
32 Report concerning the interrelation of the plastic arts (for CIAM 6, 1947)
40 Intervention at CIAM 6 (1947)
42 Statement against rationalism (1951)
43 We discover style (1949)
46 On Brancusi, Sert and Miró (letter to the Giedions, 1948)
48 On the function of a UNESCO art review (letter to Giedion, 1950)
51 On the Dutch contribution (1951)
53 On the Hispano Suiza factory (1951)
56 Lohse and the aesthetic meaning of number (1952)
56 Aesthetics of Number (1953)

59 **Chapter 3**
Cobra
62 An Appe(a)l to the Imagination (1950)
64 Constant and the Abstracts (1951)
68 Corneille and the Realists (1951)
71 Corneille versus clocks (1952)
74 Corneille as a landscape painter (1952)
76 Looking back on the Cobra exhibitions (1986)
81 An evening of limbo in the Low Countries (1986)
85 Note on the experience of the elementary in the desert (1951)

86 Building in the Southern Oases (1953)
96 Spatial Colourism (1953)

99 **Chapter 4**
Playgrounds
102 Child and City (1950)
106 Lost identity, grid for CIAM 10, Dubrovnic (1956)
108 When snow falls on cities (1957)
110 After a heavy snowstorm (Student Project, St. Louis, 1961)
111 Wheels or no wheels, man is essentially a pedestrian (1962)
112 On the design of play equipment and the arrangement of playgrounds (1962)

121 **Chapter 5**
Art and Architecture in the fifties
124 On the cooperation between the arts (1955)
126 On inside and outside space (1956)
128 On garden and landscape art (1957)
131 A tribute to Carola Giedion-Welcker (1957)
136 The ball rebounds (1958)
152 Squares with a smile (1958)
159 The space behind the eye (1958)
159 On the relationship between architecture and art (1959)
160 Good morning, sculpture (1959)
162 Visser is a winged digger (1961)
164 Hello Shinkichi (1960)
169 Speech for the award of the 1962 Sikkens Prize

179 **Chapter 6**
The beginning of Team 10 and the end of CIAM
185 Statement on Habitat (1954)
186 Letter to the Smithsons on the guideline for CIAM 10 (1954)
189 Orientation, guideline for CIAM 10 (1954)

194 Nagele grid for CIAM 10 (1956)
198 Postcard to Bakema on the dissolution of Dutch CIAM (1957)
199 Talk at the Otterlo Congress (1959)
202 Is architecture going to reconcile basic values? (1961)
205 The moment of realization (1961)
208 Letter to Giedion on the dissolution of CIAM (1960)
212 About the Economist project (1961)

215 Chapter 7
The new start of Forum: The Story of Another Idea

221 The Story of Another Idea (1959)

273 Chapter 8
Forum 1959–1963: from the shape of the in-between to configurative design

279 The CIAM City and the Natural Cycles (1959)
286 Day and Night (1959)
289 Aquarium design by Jan Verhoeven (1960)
291 Between here and there, now and later (1960)
293 'There is a garden in her face' (1960)
295 Interior Art (1961)
302 Dirty linen, mostly (1960)
310 The enigma of time (1961)
312 The medicine of reciprocity tentatively illustrated (1961)
324 The fake client and the great word 'no' (1962)
327 Steps towards a configurative discipline (1962)

345 Chapter 9
Forum 1962–1963 and 1967: the Vernacular of the Heart

351 The Pueblos (1962)

371 On Rykwert's *Idea of a Town* (1963)
373 A Miracle of Moderation (1962–1967)

419 Chapter 10
The Problem of Number

422 Differentiation and unity through rhythm (1960)
423 On Blom's *Noah's Ark* (1962)
425 Discussion on the problem of number at the Royaumont meeting (1962)
440 Letter to the Smithsons after the Royaumont meeting (1962)
442 How to humanize vast plurality? (1963)
443 Tree and leaf (1965)
444 'What we are after is a new and as yet unknown configurative discipline' (1966)
447 On Christopher Alexander's *A City is not a Tree* (1968)
448 The enigma of vast multiplicity (1968–1969)
459 Who are we building for, and why? (1970)
461 The Priority Jostle (1970)
463 Fascism in a snowflake (1986)

465 Chapter 11
Interiorization

467 The Otterlo Circles (1962)
470 Built Meaning (1962)
471 Place and Occasion (1962)
472 Labyrinthian Clarity (1963, 1965, 1966, 1967)
474 The Interior of Time (1962, 1966)
476 Two kinds of centrality (1965)
477 The inner horizon in Wright's Imperial Hotel (1966)
478 On Frank Lloyd Wright's Imperial Hotel (1968)
480 The Enigma of Size (1979)
494 Transparency (1982)

499 **Chapter 12**
Contemporary architecture and traditional city
502 Why not a beloved town hall (1961)
508 City centre as donor (1970)
510 An experiment to counter urban corrosion (1971)
511 Sociocide (ca. 1971)
511 The fury of renewal (ca. 1974)
512 On breaking through monuments (1974)
514 The mute requirements (1975)
515 You can't build a thing like that for people! (1981)

527 **Chapter 13**
Polemics on postmodernism
529 Like that other gift (1976)
530 A message to Mathias Ungers from a different world (1979)
533 The Ironbound statement (1979)
537 R.P.P. – Rats, Posts and Other Pests (1981)
549 Symmetry from the bright side (ca. 1984)
550 On Codussi (1984)
552 The circle and the centre (1987)
554 And just keeping on switching between yesterday and today (1989)
555 Lured from his den (1998)

567 **Chapter 14**
On architects and other artists
570 On Le Corbusier (1960, 1961 and 1966)
571 On Loos (1965)
575 University College in Urbino by Giancarlo de Carlo (1966)
582 The Mirror Master – on Joost van Roojen (1967)
586 A propos Jan Rietveld (1971)
588 Jaap Bakema, 1914–1981, 'The Moment of Core' (1981)
590 By definition – on Lucien Lafour (1982)
594 Joop Hardy 1918–1983, autumn man between winters (1983)
597 Dylan Thomas (1986)
599 On Van Doesburg, I.K. Bonset and De Stijl (1988)
605 Unearthing the silted-up alphabet of meaningful designing – on Jan Rietveld (1990)
610 On Team 10 (1991)
622 Lucio Fontana apropos Joost van Roojen (1993)
626 On Charles Rennie Mackintosh (1993)
634 On Josep M. Jujol (1996)
637 A Superlative Gift – on Lina Bo Bardi (1997)

643 **Chapter 15**
Retro and Prospect
646 The radiant and the grim, Kassel Documenta X (1997)

650 Short biography

654 Principal projects and buildings

657 Writings by Aldo van Eyck

670 Publications on Aldo van Eyck

686 Acknowledgements

688 Editors' notes

726 Illustration credits

728 Text of lecture at INDESEM seminar 1967, Delft (registered on DVD)

738 Index

Aldo and Hannie van Eyck on a boattrip near the North Pole, ca. 1990

Introduction

This volume contains most of the articles Aldo van Eyck published in the course of 50 years, supplemented by a selection of lectures, letters, reports, interviews and notes, many of which have never previously appeared in print. Not included, however, are the explanatory notes to his projects,[1] unless they go beyond mere description and involve the formulation of ideas or theoretical views.

The texts are not presented in a strictly chronological order but are grouped into thematic clusters that correspond to the successive contexts in which Van Eyck was active and to the subjects he dealt with. The first six chapters cover his formative years and the development of his ideas up to the end of the 1950s: his participation in CIAM and his plea for grafting modern architecture back onto its avant-garde roots, his involvement in the Cobra movement and the first implementation of his ideas in the Amsterdam playground project, his critical positions in Dutch debates on art and architecture, and his role in the emergence of Team 10 out of CIAM. The three middle chapters (7–9) contain the articles he wrote for Dutch *Forum*, a review which he co-edited from 1959 to 1963: first its opening manifesto, *The Story of Another Idea*, then the unfolding of his seminal ideas in his major articles and, grouped in a separate chapter, his essays on living and building in non-Western cultures.

The subsequent chapters (10–12) cover the themes that continued to occupy him after the Forum period: the problem of building for 'the greater number', the quality of architectural space and contemporary building in historical cities. Chapter 13 bundles his criticism on the post-modern tendencies that surfaced during the 1970s. The fervour of his polemics against the repudiation of modernist ideals contrasts with the gentle tone of his appraisals of and tributes to various contemporary artists and architects which constitute the penultimate chapter. The book concludes with one of the architect's last statements on the concerns that continued to occupy him until the end of his days.

The sequence of the chapters follows the successive appearance of their subjects in Van Eyck's career, but as he was simultaneously active in several domains, they inevitably overlap chronologically. Yet we felt that the thematic grouping of the texts into clusters, each of them prefaced with an introduction to their context, renders their meaning more accessible than a strictly chronological arrangement.

As the thematic clustering meant that every chapter had to be conceived as a whole, comprising all the articles relevant to its theme, some of the texts included in *The Child, the City and the Artist* were duplicated. This applies for example to 'Steps towards a Configurative Discipline', written as a chapter for the said book, but until now only known as an article published in *Forum*. As such it could not be left out of the *Forum* section of the present book. The same goes for shorter texts such as 'place and occasion' and 'leaf and tree'. Moreover, as Van Eyck kept rewriting and touching up his texts, different versions of some of them are included.

The majority of the texts was originally written and published in English. About one third consists of translations of Dutch texts for which Van Eyck did not write an English version. The translations were made by Gregory Ball who, assisted by the editors, aimed at a way of writing consistent with the English idiom of Van Eyck.

The project to publish Van Eyck's Collected Writings, including *The Child, the City and the Artist,* was initiated by Vincent Ligtelijn and Francis Strauven in 1999. The selection, digitalisation and correction of the texts was from the beginning a joint enterprise by both editors, supported by Delft University of Technology and Ghent University. In the final stage Vincent Ligtelijn was primarily responsible for the iconographic research, the layout and the production of the DVD, while Francis Strauven took care of the introductions and the notes.

Francis Strauven

1
Looking back on his student years in Zurich

Introduction to chapter 1

Aldo and Hannie van Eyck in front of their lodgings in Froburgstrasse, Zurich, 1943

Aldo van Eyck enjoyed a rich multicultural education. He was born in Holland (in Driebergen, on 16 March 1918) but grew up in England. Son of a Dutch poet who made a living as foreign editor of the Rotterdam newspaper NRC, he was brought up in both English and Dutch. He attended King Alfred School in Hampstead and Sidcot School in Somerset, where he enjoyed a classical yet unconventional education. At secondary school he concentrated on English literature and nourished a passionate interest for symbolist poetry from Blake to Yeats. He studied architecture at The Hague Academy (1935–1938) and Zurich Polytechnic (the *Eidgenössische Technische Hochschule* or ETH, 1938–1942).

His time in Zurich, which lasted until 1946, was crucial to his personal development. He gained a sound architectural education at the Polytechnic, met Hannie van Roojen, whom he married in 1943, and was initiated into the significance of contemporary art. After finding his way into modern art through Surrealism, Van Eyck was introduced into its entire panorama by Carola Giedion-Welcker, one of the first and most original historians of the twentieth-century avant-garde.

Carola Welcker, or 'C.W.' as she liked to be called, was Sigfried Giedion's wife. While her husband deployed himself in the history of modern architecture, she concentrated on modern painting and sculpture. During her investigations into the development of the various avant-garde currents she became closely acquainted with artists such as Arp, Klee, Mondrian, Brancusi and Joyce, who made her privy to their motivations and intentions. In this way she acquired a genuine insight into contemporary art founded on the ideas of the artists themselves. At the same time she developed the original view that the various avant-garde currents – from Cubism to Dadaism, from Constructivism to Surrealism – were in fact components of one and the same movement which as a whole had brought to light a new view of the world, a 'new reality' that was to be constitutive for twentieth-century culture.

For the young Van Eyck this new world view was a true revelation, 'a real breakthrough' that would remain fundamental to his cultural outlook and architectural thinking. C.W. introduced him to the core of avant-garde thinking and put him into contact with Arp, Lohse, Vantongerloo, Giacometti, Tzara, Ernst and Brancusi. Through his personal dealings with these artists and their work he too came to know modern art from within. Like C.W. he nurtured an inclusive interest in all avant-garde currents and artists, from Cézanne to Dalí, from Miró to Mondrian. At the same time he also searched for the manifestations of the new reality in literature and science, from Joyce to Bergson. He soon started to conceive of this whole group of personalities as 'the Great Gang', a conspiracy of artists and scientists who had breached the mouldering conventions of the past in order to herald a new and inspiring view of reality, opening up exhilarating perspectives on a new culture. Van Eyck identified with 'the Great Gang' and set himself the life's work of bringing about the new reality in the field of architecture. In due course, moreover, he conceived the original view that, in spite of their apparent contradictions, all avant-garde currents were in fact based on one and the same fundamental idea, the idea of relativity.

For Van Eyck the idea of relativity, which had manifested itself simultaneously in art and science at the turn of the century, meant the revelation of the world as a reality that is not dominated by a fixed centre but where all viewpoints are of equal value. In this reality the coherence of things no longer lies in their subordination to a central principle but in their reciprocal relations. All standpoints are relative and as such coequal, and the relations between things are as important as the things themselves. The ever-recurring opposing primeval forces are not neutralized but reconciled in a cheerful and dynamic harmony.

In the story which forms the first chapter of this volume, Van Eyck looks back on his Zurich years. It was the first part of an article that appeared in a special Holland issue of the Swiss review *Archithese* (1981, no. 5). The article was written in the form of a letter to Stanislaus von Moos, the founder and editor of the review and at that time professor of architectural history at Delft Polytechnic. Von Moos had enquired about Van Eyck's student memories and his opinion of Swiss modern architecture at that time, which had been discussed in a previous issue of *Archithese* (1980, no. 2).

Carola Giedion-Welcker Photo Franco Cianetti

Ex Turico aliquid novum[1]

Article in the form of a letter, published in Archithese, *September/October 1981*[2]

Dear Stanislaus von Moos,

I have often wondered to what extent the Swiss themselves were aware of the great new things which were taking place amongst them – fermented around the Limmat[3] – even before the turn of the century. Tolerant side-line spectators or hesitant participants? Whichever, both or whatever else, Zurich, in the light of future twentieth-century thinking, was Europe's major – crucible – city!

To me the question doesn't really matter. After all, it occurred there – and was able to do so. Still, it could be an interesting question for the Swiss themselves... whence do we come – 800 years after Rütli[4] – and whither are we going? I, at any rate, benefited profoundly from those radiant traces – and the hospitality that ancient and absorbent little country granted during many – and some dangerous – years.

J.A. Brinkman and L.C. van der Vlugt, Van Nelle factory, Rotterdam, 1926–1930

J. Duiker and B. Bijvoet, Zonnestraal Sanatorium, Hilversum, 1926–1928

M. Breuer, A. and E. Roth, Doldertal flats, Zurich, 1934

How – to limit and focus the questions already brought forward – did the local architects respond to all that had flowered in Zurich? Here again, this is a question they can best put to themselves. I do know that the Neubühl architects,[5] for example, to mention the strongest and most articulate (I never got to know either Artaria or Schmidt) seemed singularly disinterested in what excited me most about the Zurich scene. Werner Moser, I recall, had two Mondrians stored away in the attic, I think, of his house, and shocked me deeply when, after an evening causerie I gave about the Zonnestraal Sanatorium and the Van Nelle Factory, he told the audience, about the latter, that those working there suffered from *'Hornhautentzündung'*[6] as a result of too much daylight (nor can I ever forget that sophisticated medical term). He said, furthermore, that his friend the architect L.C. van der Vlugt would have agreed with him, had he lived, and that my very high opinion of the building – and those of its kind – would alter as I grew older.

Well, I am older now and, had Moser (whom I liked none the less) lived, I would certainly have told him that my enthusiasm has not diminished, adding, however, that my appreciation for the Kantonsspital[7] is no longer as negligible as it used to be at the time. Although the heroic position taken by its architects vis-à-vis the site was known to me and admired, I regarded the *style* as treason – an overstatement I shall never again apply to what doesn't deserve it. Not in the face of what the Rats, Posts and other Pests (RPP) are currently perpetrating,[8] which certainly does deserve it! To return to those damaged eyes – Dr. Van der Leeuw, managing director of Van Nelle at the time, exemplary client (Bauherr) and later President curator of the Delft Institute of Technology, assured me that nobody to his knowledge had ever thus suffered due to the building's transparency.

It should be apparent by now that, bar very few exceptions, I felt no affinity with modern Swiss architecture, although the Neubühl period, albeit just before my time, could not be brushed aside. Of course, the Doldertal houses[9] and Max Bill's[10] were sources of inspiration too, but they were indeed very solitary islands in the light of Zurich's illuminating avant-garde background in the other fields. Alfred Roth, who certainly did *not* hide his beautiful – *'rouge parce que je suis jeune'* [11] – Mondrian, was the only architect I knew, bar Bill, who spoke with uncompromising enthusiasm about Le Corbusier. Roth – *salut* – was invariably busy and helpful... yes, and never on the wrong side (nor will that change). As for Bill – my mind falters a bit – even if I were to do justice to all his gifts, the chances are I would still not avoid a cyclone! So I shall leave it at that, though not without regret.

Between 1942 and 1946, when I finally returned to Holland with my wife and Swiss-born daughter (Lohse, who will enter the scene shortly, called her *'die ägyptische Prinzessin'*), I worked in many offices in order to pay the rent, keep alive and eventually start the little collection of works by artists we adore to this day. Often it was a question of drawing for competitions – mostly perspectives – but sometimes of actually designing entire entries on a 200 to 300 S.frs. *pauschal*[12] basis! These were encounters and activities not really worth remembering except those with Fischli and Stock. They, both of them, were always willing to discuss and did so in a way which was stimulating. Hans Fischli[13] loved Max Ernst and himself made very delicate haunted drypoints – I have a fine one he gave me. As I write, one more encounter comes to my mind. It was with Hans Hofmann,[14] who was not only a particularly friendly man but also something of an original – and utterly Helvetic. I cannot recall for which occasion (perhaps national?) it was, but what an undertaking! He had the Poly literally filled with trees (big ones) and plants; and the central hall turned into a lake with water plants reflecting the foliage. It was quite fantastic – all that cool leafy green within Semper's cold halls suggested warmth – even tropical shade. Who knows, the Kriers too may have liked it.

The funny thing, you know, about all those competitions I drew or designed is that some sort of prize, *Ankauf* or *Entschädigung*[15] was won each time when working for other architects in *their* manner, but never once, as soon as I started, together with Felix Schwarz, in our manner. *Herausgeflogen*[16] after the first round presumably: and to think that we never even considered entering a project if we didn't find the jury at least reasonably acceptable. The Duiker-Van der Vlugt wavelength we were on was simply not acceptable – too far out, we thought, for Zurich to tune in on!

It was around this time that something I had designed was actually executed! A room (*Turmzimmer*[17]) in a house by Hess was to be remodelled as a study for a collector of modern art.[18] Without 'touching' what existed, a new room was made within the old shell, set at a slight angle. All the elements were suspended from the rafters of the pitched roof. Both Lohse and Sigfried Giedion, whom I didn't get to know until much later owing to his absence, published it.[19] I was very proud!

Still, I was obliged to shift my intellectual attention away from the rather slim world of local architecture and look elsewhere – find other fields. My wife and I spent countless evenings and rehearsal days in the Zurich *Schauspielhaus* – backstage – as *Statisten*.[20] Dirty uncomfortable work, but exciting too: Shakespeare, Kleist, Schiller,

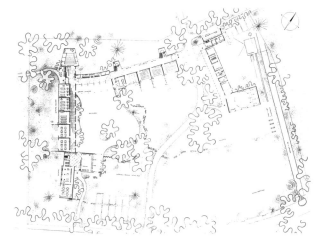

Competition project for a school, Zurich, ca. 1943 by Aldo van Eyck.

Aldo van Eyck, conversion of tower room in Löffler house, Zurich, 1944–1945.

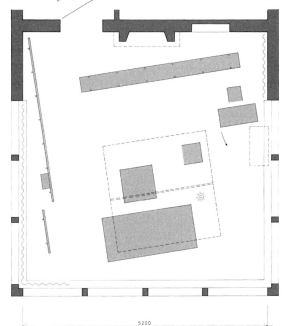

Photo Francis Strauven

Aldo als 'Leierkastenmann' in *Einen Jux will er sich machen* by Nestroy.

Composition by Yves Tanguy, 1938, oil on canvas. First painting in the collection of Aldo and Hannie van Eyck.

Ibsen, Nestroy, Brecht, Lorca, etc. etc. etc., and all those superb refugee actors and actresses just a few feet away: Parilla, Langhoff, Ginsberg, Giehse and Becker (my wife gave Maria English lessons). We got a free ticket for each performance which was then sold for us, but we used many ourselves watching other plays. I was a *Leierkastenmann*,[21] once, my wife an Amazon in *Penthesilea*,[22] and both of us *Maikäfers* in *Maikäfer-Ehe*[23] (*....eins, zwei, drei*). And how many times did I hear that strangely tense burst of laughter from the entire opera house at every '*du stecktest da einen zweiten Pfeil*'...[24]

All this of course did help to broaden my horizon, but the real breakthrough came quite suddenly and unexpectedly one afternoon after an Ovomaltine at Café Select.[25] There was a small Dalí-Tanguy-Ernst vernissage at Galerie Hans Ulrich Gasser upstairs. I was at home in those pictures the moment I saw them – doorways into another dimension (we bought a little Tanguy there and then – our first picture). A tall round-headed man with a red face and curly hair standing on end proved to be Hans Fischli (work in his office started a few weeks later). He treated himself to a small Max Ernst *Grätenwald* frottage,[26] *die Horde*. Then a voice said something, though I cannot recollect what, but it made me turn, and there in front of me stood a fantastic lady wearing a huge hat with long feathers sticking out. She began luring us, my wife and I, through those 'doorways', straight away, as it were, from the other side. The lady, you will have guessed, was Carola Giedion-Welcker or C.W. as she liked to be called.[27] Very soon after that it became clear to us that her heart and mind, like her hat, were also huge. She opened my windows – and I haven't closed them since; she tuned my strings – nor did they ever require retuning. When I re-read the letters and postcards she sent us over the years, the warm tide comes rolling in again. She loved the Great Gang and joined their Great Riot, understanding completely what *The Gang* was up to and the *Riot* was all about. Perhaps you can print, along with this letter, the little introductory speech I gave when this truly great lady came to Amsterdam in 1957 to open the big Klee exhibition in the Stedelijk Museum.[28] Carola Giedion provided nourishment for a life-time.

I was quite surprised when you told me recently that you heard me extol C.W. together with Richard Paul Lohse[29] in 1963 before a large SWB[30] audience in Zurich. Another unexpected link. As to what you heard Carola Giedion say: *'Ist ja toll, aber in dieser Kombination! Ausgerechnet Lohse, der Rationalist!'*[31] I think her surprise must have been just a half surprise, because she herself once said about Lohse: *'Ja, aber er ist eben musisch'*.[32] And look what she herself had written just a year before: *'Was jedoch Lohses Kunst über das Fundament einer bis ans letzte durchgearbeiteten Systematik und methodischen Konsequenz, zu der er sich ausdrücklich bekennt, hinausführt, beruht auf der echten poetischen Sensibilität, die ihn erfüllt'*.[33] What that implies, she then goes on to explain. I recall here what Mondrian at a Max Ernst show in New York told a journalist who was putting the usual provoking questions. This: *'Max, vous savez, il fait la même chose que moi, mais dans l'autre hémisphère'*.[34] People like C.W., Mondrian and, as you will soon see, Richard Paul Lohse react that way: *Toll!*[35] I had every reason to extol Lohse together with Carola Giedion on that occasion (and every reason to do so here again), for he is not only a superb artist – single-minded and quintessential – but also a wise man and a gentle one... immediately forgiving my simultaneous (and lasting) infatuation with both Mondrian *and* Miró saying: *'Der Aldo isch ebe-n-en halbe Holländer und en halbe Spanier – wäge dem, weisch.'*[36] (Dutch and Portuguese to be exact). Two of his paintings in particular have been in my mind as though engraved there, almost since they were made around 1946.[37] I have written and spoken about them on various occasions. Here they are: Magic even in black and white. Boundless space (in which breathing goes freely) yet firmly contained within the finite surface of two small rectangles – but what bracing rhythm – what rippling multiplication and continuity. Harmony in motion, I called it. Surely the future lies in these beautiful pictures...?

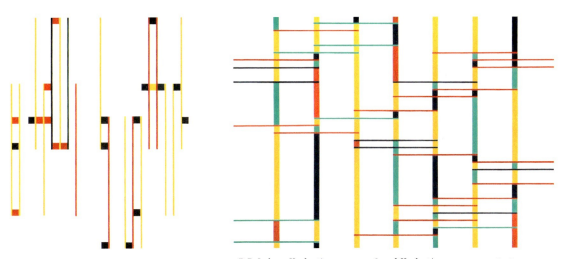

R.P. Lohse, *Konkretion I*, 1945–46 and *Konkretion III*, 1947 Both oil on pavatex

Brancusi's studio in Impasse Roncin, Paris (photo by Brancusi). Rear left, a glimpse of the column for the Gate of the Kiss; centre, on a wooden pedestal, La Sorcière (1916); next to it, l'Oiseau dans l'Espace (1923), Socrate (1922) and La Princesse X (1916); bottom right, La Négresse Blanche (1923).

The war was hardly over – in France though not yet in Holland – when I was able to go to Paris as a kind of envoy-carrier sent by C.W. and those around her. I had messages with me for Giacometti, Tzara, Léger, Braque, Pevsner, Vantongerloo, Nelly van Doesburg and for Brancusi, a weighty trunk full of roasted coffee beans, tobacco and Cognac. Having found Impasse Roncin and the door of his almost rural atelier finally opened, the trunk lock burst open and all the luxuries avalanched onto the floor in front of the great fish!

I visited Constantin Brancusi many times after that; with my wife, Felix Schwarz or alone. The last time I saw him he said, inclining his ancient head towards the light coming through the glass roof: *'Ah Henri – le seul qui attrappa la gloire.'* I sensed that he was referring to the Douanier, but didn't ask. It became apparent as he continued to talk: how Rousseau had suddenly opened a window whilst painting to let inner tension out. For us, Brancusi was the summit of what art could mean, and I'll be damned if we weren't right!

I saw a lot of Arp during my later Zurich years and, afterwards, also in Meudon; a few streets from where Nelly van Doesburg – that other fantastic lady – lived in the lovely house Theo built just before he died in 1931.[38]

Arp asked me to make a series of pen and ink drawings based on pencil sketches his late wife Sophie Täuber[39] had made: he wanted them to illuminate poems of his he wished to publish. I worried about my interpretations wherever her pencil lines were vague and ambiguous, but Arp waved my anxiety aside saying that I should regard what I was doing as cooperation – the effort of two people, not one, this time: that was how it should be in art – the way it one day will be, he said. I was flattered, eased and a lot the wiser. Arp was a fantastic guy; and Arp, the Alsatian poet, altogether incomparable – truly *alemannisch*. – 'weh, unser guter kaspar ist tot – wer trägt nun die brennende fahne im zopf, wer dreht die kaffeemühle, wer lockt das idyllische reh – auf dem meer verwirrte er die schiffe mit dem wörtchen parapluie und die winde nannte er bienenvater. weh weh weh unser guter kaspar is tot, heiliger bimbam kaspar ist tot – die heufische klappern in den glocken wenn man…' etc.[40]

Then there was Tristan Tzara, who loved signing books even if they were not his own; that was in our flat in Zurich, '*Juste ce qu'il faut de souterrain entre le vin et la vie*'[41] is what he wrote for our one-year-old daughter in the minutest of books. How well that was to fit into subsequent publications on architecture! In my wife's copy of his great poem *L'Homme approximatif*, he wrote something which teaches even *time itself* a lesson; and belongs to Max Ernst's *Intérieur de la vue*: '*L'oeil toujours neuf au retour des choses*'[42]. And on the cover of '*La main passe*', he added '*Dada reste*', and that is as it should be. Believe it or not, due to those years, Paris for me has, in a way, remained like an extension of Zurich. Going back home from there (and I went fairly often) meant going back to Zurich – full of stories to tell.

Tristan Tzara, dedication to Tess van Eyck, dated 23 November 1945, in *Sixième Cahier* of *Habitude de la Poésie* series published by Guy Levis Mano: '*juste ce qu'il faut de souterrain entre le vin et la vie*'.

Tristan Tzara's dedication of *La main passe* to Aldo van Eyck, 24 January 1946

Hans Arp, Kaspar, 1930 Plaster

Meanwhile, I must take care, don't you think, lest this issue turns into a Dutch one about the Swiss! But then, *reciprocity* belongs to my credo and there were Swiss on all sides when it took shape. One of them was Felix Schwarz[43] who, as early as 1938, introduced me to the work of those great Dutch – yes, *Dutch!* – pioneer architects L.C. van der Vlugt and Jan Duiker, of whom I had, at the time, only vaguely heard. It so happened that he had been to Holland for quite a while not long before entering the Poly (the same year I did) and had, by chance, come across the little pioneer review *de 8 en Opbouw,* which appeared every fortnight. He was by then able to read Dutch. Obviously he also went to see the actual buildings he had read about. What a revelation that must have been – and what a start. A new world of architecture opened up, founded on a new world of thought. For him first and then, though not yet as decisively – via him – for me. I say less decisively because his social and political enquiry had already begun years before – and mine... never did, to that extent!

Now, keeping the Swiss situation in mind, the main point here regarding *Das Neue Bauen* (*Het Nieuwe Bouwen*) in Holland, is that it not only moved parallel to, but actually also coincided with the De Stijl movement, i.e. with the hub of the Dutch avant-garde after 1917 as a whole, embracing *all* the various arts. Thus, the 6 De Stijl architects: Oud, Rietveld, Wils, Van't Hoff, Van Eesteren and later Van Doesburg himself, had from the very start been in close contact with the De Stijl painters: Mondrian, Van Doesburg, Van der Leck, Vantongerloo, Huszár and a little later El Lissitzky (since the group transcended frontiers). With the De Stijl poets and writers, hardly known outside Holland, there was also contact. But the horizon around these pioneer architects was wider even than that: there was *Holland Dada* (and the little review *Mécano*) around I.K. Bonset (van Doesburg's dadaist pseudonym) and Schwitters, who came regularly, carrying a big potato sack in which he collected throw-away stuff for *Merz Holland*, and wild Dada evenings with Nelly van Doesburg at the piano. Then there were the socialist poets: Herman Gorter and Henriette Roland Holst,[44] also Domela Nieuwenhuis, the great anarchist writer and leader. Thus, we see the architects joining the avant-garde fully right from the beginning.

This moving along together with the other arts in the climate of advanced social-political thought, philosophy and science, etc., continued around the review *i10*, founded and edited by Arthur Lehning, writer, political historian and the world's foremost Bakunin expert. I think it is fair to say that, whilst my contact with what I regarded as true constituent contemporary art, literature and music was direct *in and through* Zurich, my contact with parallel thought and work in architecture unfortunately was and *could not be so and was therefore necessarily indirect*. Holland, you see, was to become altogether inaccessible due to the war. This is where Felix Schwarz' little extra task begins: *Switzerland's indisputable contribution to the development of Dutch architecture*! No joking.

Now Schwarz – the Swiss-Dutch link – although unmistakably Swiss, is also like no other Swiss, in fact he is very unlike anybody and still equally unlike nobody! He is, in fact, more than less, like himself! Which is not as obvious as it sounds.

He is probably the most fringeless and accurately focused intellect that I know. Assembling himself his mental entourage – baggage – all the way, he soon evolved a way of life accordingly. Together with his late wife Lotte, their children and friends, he build a world within a world in Brüttisellen[45] – though always in immediate active contact with the world at large – no isolation ever. Felix Schwarz' undogmatic pragmatism, albeit of a questioning inclusive kind (*nüchtern*,[46] but never dessicating) has had a certain purging effect on me in so far as it pushed me towards thinking more precisely – i.e. how to spot *what is beside the point and what is not – when it is, and when it is not.*

Schwarz himself thinks too well to be able to make a building that is inappropriate – i.e. which does not *work well*. In fact, to put it another way, his buildings haven't got what they needn't have – this is my latest superslogan.[47] That already puts him on a level with the very good. More and more in recent years, I have come to think that it's all a question of the reliability which accompanies real professional compe-

Felix Schwarz's own house in Brüttisellen, 1953
Photos Felix Schwarz

tence. Schwarz' reputation as an architect is no doubt a local one: understandably, because he is the arch non-success-maker!

This brings me quite naturally, though briefly, to his oldest partner, Rolf Gutman, who contributed quietly though considerably to the formative discussions within CIAM between the Sigtuna meeting in 1952 and the one in Dubrovnic four years later. His probing exposé (with Theo Manz) apropos habitat in the light of the part-whole dichotomy – or non-dichotomy – was basic to Team 10 with which he was initially associated.[48] I elaborated extensively on the part-whole identification later during the Team 10 Royaumont meeting in 1962 to ears deaf as doornails.[49]

Between these early years in Zurich and my return to the Poly (1976–1978), there was, besides old associations extended, one new one which started not in Zurich, but in Africa in the bend of the Niger – a large landmark in one's little life! I am referring to my encounter with Paul Parin and Fritz Morgenthaler, both from Zurich, who have focused their intelligence and sensitivity combined onto psychoanalysis and anthropology, thereby increasing the depth, i.e. the true humanity of both fields reciprocally. They have written several unquestionable masterpieces, which are all available in printed form[50] (as is also the extensive illustrated essay on the house and village form of the Dogon entitled 'A Miracle of Moderation'[51], which I wrote in conjunction with them). I should like to add in this context that my incentive to reach the Dogon one day originated in Zurich where I had bought a special issue of

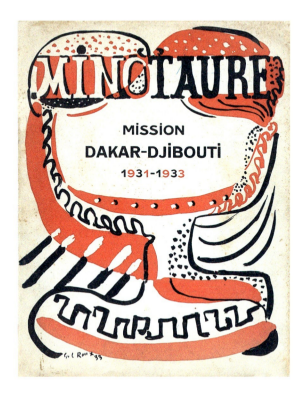

Title page of *Minotaure*, 1933, no. 2

Masked dancers from Iréli: Hunter, White Monkey and Antelopes; illustration from *Minotaure*, 1933, no. 2

Minotaure[52] containing many magnetic pictures of Ogol. When I eventually returned to Zurich to teach in 1976, I drew on this rich intermediary encounter. So instead of the saying '*Ex Africa semper aliquid novum*',[53] which every really good archaeologist will confirm! I say '*Ex Turico aliquid novum*', which I am entitled to believe whether others do or not.

Commuting back and forth every fortnight, Zurich, at first, was like a ghost town apparition in the sense that I kept brushing shoulders with the ghost of my younger self (and that of my wife) in quite odd places – which then, all of a sudden, became very tactile – awkwardly timeless though not quite like a clock ticking backwards. I always went straight up from the station; past a far too open Limmat; then that superb toy *Seilbahn*[54] with wooden cogs which I had never used before… In the Poly I was given Linus Birchler's old room just a few paces across from the entrance (same Swiss-made door handles – same feel). It all came back instantly: The way L.B.[55] used to utter 'Skopas' – his favorite Greek sculptor – in *fortissimo*, brushing his bristly dark hair forward with one rough stroke of the hand! He was a revelation, you see, whilst up north in puritanical Holland everything properly Barock was and still is contraband and therefore on the appreciation index, he, Birchler, stood there up in front pronouncing 'Balthasar' like a bugle call between Johann and Neumann and presenting Asam's Nepomuk church as something entirely *selbstverständlich*[56] – obviously beautiful. Just imagine that! Now that you are professor in the history of architecture in Holland – your task is partially defined.

2
Advocate of the avant-garde in postwar CIAM (1947–1953)

Introduction to chapter 2

Aldo van Eyck in his first lodgings at Keizersgracht, Amsterdam, 1947 Photo Violette Cornelius

After the war Aldo van Eyck settled in Amsterdam, where he was engaged by Cor van Eesteren as a designer in the Municipal Town Planning Department. Van Eesteren, formerly a member of De Stijl and since 1927 chief architect of this department, was largely responsible for the Amsterdam General Extension Plan. He was also the president of the international CIAM since 1930, and introduced Van Eyck into 'de 8', the Amsterdam CIAM group. At that moment preparatory consultations were being held for the 6th CIAM congress. The programme of this first postwar congress, which was to take place in Bridgwater, England, was subject to lively international discussion. Since its foundation in 1928 CIAM had mainly been concerned with social, economic and planning issues. In spite of the A in its name, it had largely ignored the question of architectural form and after twenty years several members were prepared for a change. Sigfried Giedion, not only the leading historian of the modern movement but also the secretary general of CIAM, aimed for a reorientation. During the war, when residing in New York, he had been reflecting on the architectural form of public buildings. Looking back on the buildings produced in the thirties, he conceived the idea that the Western world was in need of a 'new monumentality'. Modern architecture, up to then mainly concerned with primary human necessities linked to social housing, had neglected 'the eternal need of people to create symbols for their activities, for their fate or destiny, for their religious beliefs and for their social convictions'.[1] It had abandoned the field of institutional building to Beaux-Arts architecture which had everywhere produced the same kind of 'pseudomonumentality'. Giedion considered that Modern Architecture ought to counter this reactionary tendency and bring about new symbolic forms that would express the new values emerging in contemporary society. To this end architecture had to tie in with the achievements of contemporary painting and sculpture, notably the work of artists such as Arp, Miró and Leger, which he deemed emblematic of the hopes and aspirations of the postwar generation. Hence, Giedion proposed 'architecture and its relation to painting and sculpture' as a theme for CIAM 6.

At the same time, together with Gropius and Sert, Giedion took the initiative of starting a new, American, CIAM group, the CIAM

Chapter for Relief and Postwar Planning. Created in 1944 for the purpose of contributing to the reconstruction of Europe, this group put forward 'community development' as the theme of the 6th congress. Community planning, entailing the creation of neighbourhoods with their own civic centre and public facilities, was a fairly unfamiliar concept in Europe. Initiated and developed in the USA since the beginning of the century, it had remained a topical issue in progressive American town planning circles.[2] And in fact Giedion's proposal and that of the American CIAM group fitted together well. Giedion felt that architecture should again shape 'the emotional life of the community', an intention he expected to be realized through the design of new, publicly financed civic centres, conceived in the context of community planning.

When Giedion brought the American proposals to Europe, the various CIAM groups reacted in different ways. The British MARS group seemed to agree but wanted to specify the proposed issues. They preferred the planning of small towns to community planning, and instead of collaboration between architecture and contemporary art they put forward 'the impact of contemporary conditions upon architectural form'. J.M. Richards, president of the MARS group and chief editor of *Architectural Review*, was rather sceptical about the social appropriateness of a functionalist form language. Living in a country where the modern movement had scarcely taken root, he cast serious doubt on the aesthetic appeal of modern architecture to 'ordinary people'. He felt that functionalism, determined as it was by industrial production, had to be 'humanized' in some way. So the theme he proposed was 'architecture in relation to the common man'.

The Dutch group 'de 8', when informed of these proposals, promptly reacted with a counterproposal. They firmly rejected the aesthetic issues, stressing 'with the utmost emphasis that in the circumstances which prevail today in Western Europe, Eastern Europe and certainly in America as well, there is one topic that concerns all socially-minded architects and that is the problem of housing, the state of housing, the housing shortage and the concomitant task for the architect as a member of society.' And at the subsequent general meeting in Zurich (in May 1947) the Dutch delegates managed to persuade the Central CIAM Committee to place public housing higher on the agenda than problems of form and aesthetics. Eventually, it was decided that CIAM 6 would essentially be a preparatory congress for CIAM 7. It was agreed that each delegation would present a rundown of the state of affairs in their own country by reference to an eight-point scheme that had also been proposed by the Dutch. Of the eight points, only the final three related to architecture. They were preceded by 1. economic situation, 2. legislation, 3. organization, 4. technical situation and 5. social aspects. Additionally, each delegation

Photo Violette Cornelius, ca. 1957

was requested to complete a questionnaire relating to the aesthetic issues advanced by Giedion and Richards.[3]

Aldo van Eyck was introduced into the Dutch CIAM at the first postwar joint meeting of 'de 8' and 'Opbouw',[4] which took place at the end of June 1947 in the rotunda on top of the Van Nelle factory in Rotterdam, one of the high points of Dutch functionalism. During this meeting Willem van Tijen, a renowned but disenchanted functionalist, argued that the *Nieuwe Bouwen* – i.e. the modern movement – was over and done with. The windows were open and the speaker was interrupted by the noise of a passing train, giving him further occasion to criticize the openness of the building. At that very moment a robin flew in and alighted on the conference table. Referring to the bird as 'a visitor like myself', Aldo van Eyck grasped the opportunity to himself interrupt Van Tijen and make an ardent speech on the achievements of the twentieth-century avant-garde and their fundamental meaning. This intervention impressed his listeners but was not able to change the tenor of the report which the Dutch delegation were to submit to CIAM 6. So Van Eyck decided to compose a report of his own, written in two languages. The English version bore the title *Report concerning the interrelation of the plastic arts and the importance of cooperation*, the Dutch one, literally translated, *Architecture, Painting and Sculpture and their significance to the New Consciousness*. As the titles suggest, he gave an answer to the questions raised by Giedion and Richards while at the same time expressing his views on the 'new reality'.

At the Bridgwater congress Aldo van Eyck participated in committee 'III.B. Architectural Expression', where he was able to exchange ideas with Giedion, Richards and Sert. When the issue of 'architectural expression' was finally brought to the fore in a plenary meeting, it left nobody indifferent. 'It stirred the whole congress',[5] unleashing passions among supporters and opponents alike. 'To many it was virtually a solar eclipse, while to others it was the simultaneous perception of sun and moon.'[6] When Richards and Giedion had exposed their views[7] they were countered by Arthur Ling, a member of the MARS group who continued to defend prewar rationalistic planning principles. Aldo van Eyck reacted impulsively with a passionate intervention against the mechanistic attitude of rationalist planning and in favour of the imagination, the only faculty able to grasp and to shape the new consciousness. He was immediately backed by Le Corbusier, who exclaimed *'Enfin l'imagination entre les CIAM!'* and continued with a lyrical speech on *'conscience individuelle, poésie, grâce, disgrâce, émotion, art'*.

Afterwards Van Eyck summarized his intervention in a pithy statement, which Giedion incorporated in his account of the congress.[8] He formulated almost the same ideas in an article for the Dutch *Forum* review, 'Wij ontdekken stijl' ('We discover style'). Moreover, he specified his views in letters to Giedion, in his introduction to the Dutch entry at the 1951 Milan Triennale, in his discussions with Bakema and in a statement on the work of Lohse.

At first sight Van Eyck's report for CIAM 6 can be considered as offering substantial support to Giedion's plan of raising the question of architectural expression in the CIAM discussion. But in fact he proves to be quite critical of Giedion. Arguing that essential questions cannot be formulated a priori but can only result from practice, he dismisses Giedion's questionnaire as premature and irrelevant. 'Historians must be patient!' Actually, Giedion's list included questions such as: *'What do you consider could be the function of painting and sculpture in the domain of architecture? Does it have to be limited to a decorative role? Does it have to express the meaning of the building in a symbolic way? Should one of the three arts take a leading role in the cooperation? Or should painting and sculpture be involved only after the completion of the project?'*

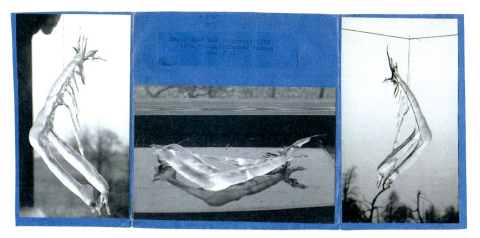

Home made greeting card from Carola Welcker to Aldo and Hannie van Eyck: 'Happy Xmas and brightest 1956 from the multiformed iceman and C.W.'.

Judging from these and other questions, Van Eyck doubted if Giedion really understood the new reality that he (Van Eyck) had been discussing with C.W. during the war. Rather than backing up Giedion, he confronts him with his wife's ideas. He puts himself forward as an ambassador of the avant-garde. He frankly asserts his faith in the new consciousness initiated by art and science at the beginning of the century and frames his report with a number of quotes by various members of the 'Great Gang', from Arp to Mondrian, from Schoenberg to Bergson.

By way of response to Giedion's questions, Van Eyck confirms architecture to be an art like the other arts and stresses the equivalence of the three plastic arts. All three have to partake independently, with their own means, in the construction of the new reality. And instead of relying on public taste or 'common sense', the arts should start from the same fundamental idea – the new reality of the avant-garde – and aspire, each in its own right, to 'the revelation of style'. Through this idea, which he reaffirms in 'we discover style', Van Eyck at once connects with the ambition of the Dutch avant-garde, from Berlage to Mondrian, to evolve an appropriate style for the twentieth century.

He explicitly appeals to Mondrian's view that 'the culture of particular form is approaching its end' and that 'the culture of determined relations has begun.' In the new culture, art will no longer represent the visible appearance of things but visualize its concealed essence, a reality of opposing but mutually related energies. Art will evolve style by harmonizing these energies into a dynamic equilibrium. And as appears more explicitly in his letters to Giedion and Bakema, Van Eyck did not consider modern art and its new reality as a purely autonomous, self-referential matter but as a reality with ethical and societal implications. As a concrete example of this, he points to the 'concrete art' of Richard P. Lohse, which appears to offer inspiring clues for overcoming 'the menace of quantity' and for shaping 'the greater number'.

Hans Arp *'L'art concret veut transformer le monde. Il veut rendre l'existence plus supportable. Il veut sauver l'homme de la folie la plus dangereuse: la vanité. Il veut simplifier la vie de l'homme. Il veut l'identifier avec la nature. La raison déracine l'homme et lui fait mener une existence tragique. L'art concret est un art élémentaire, naturel, sain, qui fait pousser dans la tête et le coeur, les étoiles de la paix, de l'amour et de la poésie. Où entre l'art concret, sort la mélancolie, traînant ses valises grises remplies de soupirs noirs.'*

Report concerning the interrelation of the plastic arts and the importance of cooperation

(for CIAM 6, Bridgwater 1947)[1]

Let us be careful not to misapprehend the true nature of a question! We shall have advanced considerably the moment we succeed in formulating really essential questions; for these result spontaneously as the essence of a problem is fully recognised. Questions that result otherwise are irrelevant. It is our business to formulate essential questions collectively, hardly to answer them. Historians must be patient! Let us avoid going against the grain; answering essential questions prematurely is putting the cart before the horse. As the questions become clearer and more precise the ensuing course becomes sounder.

That this course is by no means rectilinear is obvious; that it varies according to each individual is equally obvious. This does not imply, however, that the goal varies according to each individual, for there is only one goal, though there are several ways of getting there. Essential questions acquire shape in the course of creative activity: it seems cold-blooded to force a different sequence. Question marks are impertinent decorations. Ready-made answers are generally downright nonsense; they artificially straighten out an otherwise natural course, with the result that multitudes fly off at a tangent at the very first bend; not that they mind particularly for it seems they make a lot – a lot of money!

Arnold Schönberg *'Der Künstler tut nichts was andere für schön halten, sondern nur, was ihm notwendig ist.'*

> **Constantin Brancusi** *'La simplicité n'est pas un but dans l'art mais on arrive à la simplicité malgré soi, en s'approchant du sens réel des choses.'*

The relation between architecture, painting and sculpture is a very alluring subject indeed: let us therefore be particularly careful not to nail down details.

We shall have to decide from the very start whether we intend to use the word architecture without restriction or whether we prefer it to mean CIAM architecture in particular. As soon as we reject the former in favour of the latter – it seems obvious that we should – we are obliged to use the words painting and sculpture analogously, i.e. to accept merely those forms of expression that result from a more or less analogous creative attitude. Those who refuse to comply with this reject style in favour of limited effects, whereas limited effects should always be sacrificed in favour of style.

The revelation of style is and remains the primary object of all art.
As long as we are able to serve this primary object through cooperation with painters and sculptors all is well. As soon, however, as this becomes uncertain in a particular case it is our duty to abstain. Those that serve limited effects are merely active: those that serve style are creatively active. It requires courage to abstain from mere activity in favour of creative activity should the later prove beyond reach at a given moment. But abstinence is the hallmark of every true constructive artist.

It is style that matters for style is more than form. Without style there can be no grace: in fact what is style else but grace? A quality so illusive that we encounter it best not through form but in spite of form, as it were.[2]

Form is a medium, not an end. The difference between limited forms and elementary forms lies exactly in this distinction. The former merely tickle the primary senses, which explains their universal popularity: the latter penetrate the infinite resources of the imagination, the only faculty with which we are able to receive and transmit style or grace. Yes, to 'sense' these qualities in elementary forms calls for more than the use of the primary senses; it demands the discovery of the imagination.

> **Vordemberge-Gildewart** *'Die absolute künstlerische Gestaltung ist unvirtuos, darauf beruht ihre unpopularität.'*

Hans Arp *'Les oeuvres de l'art concret devraient rester anonymes dans le grand atelier de la nature comme les nuages, les montagnes, les mers, les animaux, les hommes. Oui! les hommes devraient rentrer dans la nature! Les artistes devraient travailler en communauté comme les artistes du moyen-age.'*

Imagination is the common denominator of man and nature.[3]

If it is to reveal itself through man as naturally as it does through nature it must be allowed to do so as directly, as unhesitatingly. Art should always take a short cut, it should resist all impurities, everything secondary to its purpose.

Art should always be natural, it should produce its own forms naturally instead of reproducing those of nature artificially.
Art should reveal the elementary whether the elementary be complex or not.
Art should reveal the mysteries of the universe or else cease to exist.
Art should be anonymous, as nature is anonymous.
Art should be liberated from the tyranny of limited forms: from the tyranny of causality; from the tyranny of metronomical time; from the tyranny of classical harmony and other static values; from the tyranny of virtuosity; from the tyranny of common sense, for common sense was always the enemy of imagination.

Although architecture answers more tangible functions, its ultimate function differs in no way from that of painting and sculpture, nor from poetry, music and religion; its object is to reveal the grace of nature through and for men. Its more tangible functions are only relevant in so far as they adjust environment more accurately to the elementary inclinations of mankind, which is no more than a preliminary to the fulfilment of the supreme object.

In discussing the cooperation of architecture, painting and sculpture the question arises as to why they gradually drifted apart; the answer is a long and tragic story. The question as to why all three drifted away from the public is also a long and tragic story – the same story no doubt. That architecture, painting and sculpture can hardly be reconciled prior to their reconciliation with the public is only partially true. To bridge the gulf between the artist and the public is to do away with the gulf. Every attempt to construct a bridge is doomed to defeat its own ends. So let this be

Hugo Ball *'Die Menschen bluten aus ihren Ästen.'*

> **Kandinsky** *'Toute époque reçoit une physionomie propre à elle seule, pleine d'expression et de force. Ainsi "hier" se transforme en "aujourd'hui" dans tous les domaines spirituels, mais l'art possède outre cela une qualité exclusive – de devenir dans "l'aujourd'hui" le "demain". Force créatrice et prophétique.'*

a warning to all those who find a sentimental satisfaction in forcing an artificial reconciliation. Only universal recognition of a single collective idea can possibly bring about the desired reconciliation.

This collective idea unites a group of architects (whether this group can be identified with CIAM at large seems problematic!) as well as several painters and sculptors, several poets and composers, several historians and scientists, several sociologists and individuals in general. In view of what has already been achieved we are justified in regarding our collective idea – the idea we call CIAM or 'Neues Bauen', which Apollinaire called 'Esprit Nouveau' and van Doesburg's Stijl group 'La Nouvelle Realité' – as the seed of a more general collective idea that may ultimately prove universally valid. The work of men like Mondrian, Arp, Rietveld and Van der Vlugt – to name a few at random – compels us to believe that we are approaching a civilisation in which gladness and brightness are a rule rather than an exception, in which – let us add this to keep alive – grace is expressed in life as it is in art.

Today, if we were able to borrow nature's dictionary, it is quite likely that we should discover under the V, as synonym for vermin, the tiny word 'man'. Yes, in the vast garden of reality we alone deserve to be regarded as vermin. Foolishly addicted to profit and common sense, man has become a ridiculous insult. His vile vanity surpasses every limit. Can the ingenuity with which he artificially tries to outstrip nature become more disgustingly tasteless? Can the ingenuity with which he equally artificially tries to outstrip his neighbours be more disgustingly diabolical? When man was allowed to choose between the making of things and the making of money he enthusiastically embraced the latter. Art became the instrument of common sense, the slave and mirror of vanity. Art and utility were torn apart as wantonly as work and responsibility. Gradually a few began to liberate themselves from this commercial nightmare; they were forced into splendid isolation, preferring the nobility of material poverty to the vulgarity of spiritual bankruptcy. The face of mankind has been shamefully disfigured: Picasso's *Guernica* shows us to what extent.

> **Hans Arp** *'Alles funktioniert, nur der Mensch selber nicht.'*

Piet Mondrian *'The culture of particular form is approaching its end. The culture of determined relations has begun.'*

Man still insanely stumbles in pursuit of material progress; all those quasi modern architects who put the wrong stress on functionalism should keep this in mind!

To insist that the wounds man has inflicted upon himself and his surroundings can be cured economically is putting the cart before the horse again. We can never correct spiritual aberration caused by 'negative' common sense by introducing 'positive' common sense, for there is no such thing as either! Common sense can never transcend common sense: there is imaginative thinking and unimaginative thinking: grace and no grace – Grace is the only cure! All those quasi socially-minded who put the wrong stress on social and economic functionalism should keep this in mind!

A new consciousness is very slowly beginning to permeate mankind: that it should have struck root in the fertile hearts of artists cannot surprise us. But not until it has broken through will nature's dictionary contain an obsolete synonym! At first sight it may seem strange that only few so far are conscious of this sanctifying current, let alone succeed in expressing it through art. The difficulty is due to the fact that it uses a language of its own, a language that of necessity is quite unintelligible as long as the basic current remains undetected. It is just as futile for an imaginary two-dimensional being to try experiencing the dimension of mass as it is futile for the unimaginative to try experiencing the dimension of this current. For not until he has discovered the only antenna really capable of its detection – the imagination – can there be any question of its language becoming intelligible and the resulting transformations becoming significant. We are convinced that this current, the recognition of which we call our collective idea, is universally latent. As soon as it approaches the brink of consciousness, more contact with its manifestations will suffice to bring it to the surface. Thus a particle of a new civilisation is born.

With this in mind who dares suggest that CIAM should not be continued? That experiment is no longer imperative? That cooperation between the arts should be fostered in order to make architecture more palatable? That ultimately compromise is not anti-cultural and anti-social?

Everything the architect, the painter and the sculptor makes must necessarily be a reflection of a collective idea if it is to be relevant to civilisation. That is why we must sacrifice everything in favour of style. Those that have failed to detect the current that is busy transforming art, language, science and even life itself invariably mistake Style for formalism and their own formalism for style! Style is the result of a collective idea; formalism of a limited idea. This current sustains our collective idea and finds its expression in style. It is naturally subject to flux: it is in fact flux itself.[4] It follows, that what is style at a given time may become formalism at the next. This process, however, is not so rapid that a continuation along the lines already followed by men of advanced insight could ever justify the general accusation that what we recognise as style is in actual fact much less.

Some architects believe that it is their divine right to protect and direct painters and sculptors! They are guilty of megalomania. Architecture, painting and sculpture are intrinsically of absolute equal importance. Then there are some architects – they usually coincide with those already mentioned – who believe it to be the duty of painters and sculptors to underline a building's function by adding symbolical representations. All these have misunderstood the significance of art entirely.

Let us never overlook the fact that we are approaching a new era and that initial work is inevitably constructive and experimental. Countless voices are trying to convince us that we have experimented long enough and that creative research work is all well and good but that the time has come 'to settle down and do some sound work'! – Fools! – That this conceited and impatient attitude has already poisoned many who were and perhaps still are CIAM members (not to mention painters and sculptors) is indeed tragic: that they should have become our most dangerous antagonists – though often in disguise – is more than tragic.

Real cooperation between the three arts hardly ensues, hocus-pocus, the moment it is thought expedient. Goodwill alone is insufficient. And yet cooperation has become a market-cry among architects. To play trio before we are able to play solo may

Henri Bergson *'Ob nun Materie, ob Geist, die Wirklichkeit erscheint als eine stete Verwandlung, sie wird oder sie entwird, sie ist nie ein fertig gewordenes.'*

Rietveld *'For the coming style that which people have in common is more important than their differences.'*

be a cosy pastime but the result is appalling, especially as soon as we are obliged to employ a completely new scale of values.

Indirect cooperation between the three plastic arts ensues as soon as a single idea pervades all three alike: direct cooperation ensues as all three independently have learnt to express this collective idea in their own media. During the last 40 years or so the indirect cooperation between the arts has been enormous, in spite of marked differences of opinion; a symptom clearly compatible with the nature of an experimental period. Cooperation in this form is imperative and should therefore be continued. We must learn to recognise the different basic problems that have occupied the advanced men of our time, from architect to poet, from astronomer to biologist, as different manifestations of one and the same current. It will help us to become more accurately conscious of the course we regard as the right one. The study of parallel phenomena is indispensable; those who thought otherwise have already gone astray.
To indulge in advanced architecture more or less unconsciously means hit and miss!

Again: the primary object of cooperation is the revelation of style: that this is no more than equivalent to the primary object of the arts independently need not worry us; it merely stresses the fact that a special function cannot possibly be allotted to cooperation unless it be one of grade.

The breach between architecture and the people whom it ultimately serves is considerable: but the breach between the two other plastic arts and the people whom they ultimately serve to no lesser degree is even more considerable. It follows that cooperation with painters and sculptors will temporarily tend to enlarge the breach between architecture and the people. This is unfortunate enough, but there is no reason why it should discourage us or cause us to waver. It has always been extremely difficult to circumvent public taste in public buildings! We have only to remember

Vantongerloo *'Nous avons besoin de l'espace pour situer les choses. L'espace dont nous ne pouvons nous passer sans toutefois le définir, est inséparable de la vie.'*

Max Jacob *'Le monde dans un homme, tel est le poète moderne.'*

what became of the Aubette in Strasbourg, perhaps the best example of cooperation so far. Let us therefore abstain the moment concessions to public taste become unavoidable, for it is the object of cooperation to achieve more, hardly less, than can be achieved independently.

During experimental stages of development such as the one we are in now it is a natural tendency to avoid dovetailing the different plastic arts too rigorously; a certain degree of independence as to spatial relations seems expedient in order to prevent the merging of one into the other.

In the course of time architecture, painting and sculpture lost sight of their most fundamental qualities; their elementary limits became hopelessly blurred. The process of reintegration must be continued at all costs, for integration and style go hand in hand. As soon as this is neglected cooperation defeats its own end.

Cooperation is a dangerous necessity: both its danger and its necessity should continually be kept in mind.

It hardly matters in the long run whether the experimental stage in the development of the coming era covers 40 or 400 years! It is obviously a fallacy to either check or stretch a stage of development artificially.

Style transcends birth and death; it is the imprint of civilisation upon nature; it is the final reward of collective consciousness.

Not until the basic current of which we have spoken has been detected universally can the reconciliation between the plastic arts and the people find fulfilment. In the meantime let us continue.

Amsterdam 1947

Eric Gill *'Holiness is not a moral quality at all, it is above and beyond prudence, it is loveliness itself, it is the loveliness of the spirit.'*

Intervention at CIAM 6, Bridgwater 1947

Unpublished manuscript, 13 September 1947[1]

A new consciousness has begun to permeate mankind.
Although this consciousness, this new approach has probably been latent for a very long time, it is only during the last 50 years or so that its nature has begun to reveal itself through the creative activity of a small group of men ranging from architect to poet and from astronomer to biologist. The immediate result of this fundamental current has been to disrupt the entire static hierarchy of values upon which contemporary existence was and still is based and which gradually – bit by bit – brought about the spiritual bankruptcy from which mankind is suffering.

CIAM is first and foremost an affirmation of a new consciousness.

It is in fact the firm belief of CIAM that the collective idea which lies behind it and which is the common determinator of all really creative contemporary activity, is latent everywhere, and that it will transform the entire aspect of existence as soon as it comes to light universally. What has already been achieved compels us to believe that we are approaching a civilisation so completely transformed that a more natural and elementary form of existence will ensue spontaneously, a civilisation in which – let us add this to keep alive – grace is expressed in life as it is in art. CIAM does not desire to give a new dress, fresh from the laundry of common sense, to outworn static values that are the basis of an outworn world. It desires on the contrary to transform this world by using a transformed language based on transformed values, values that are more flowing and elementary.

Although architecture may ensure more tangible functions, its ultimate function differs in no way from other creative activity. This is to reveal and then stimulate the current that can alone transform existence. The more tangible functions are surely only relevant in so far as they adjust an environment more accurately to the elementary inclinations of mankind. Which is no more than prerequisite to the fulfilment of the supreme object. The question thus arises whether CIAM, accepting the contemporary situation as an inevitable background to practical realisation, should nevertheless adopt a critical attitude towards this background.

Does CIAM desire to direct and control the purely mechanistic and commercial attitude of improving human environment, regarding it as a true characteristic of our time and the time to come? Or does CIAM desire to transform this attitude, i.e. to criticise the background against which it projects its activity?

What happened to the minds of man in the Age of Descartes, Giedion told us:[2] the age-old battle between common sense (static) and imagination (dynamic) was lost by the latter. Today, 300 years later, the battle is being fought again. This time common sense is going to lose. For imagination is the only common denominator between

Aldo van Eyck, Cor van Eesteren and Jaap Bakema in Bridgwater, September 1947

man and nature. It is the only faculty with which we can receive and transmit the new spirit.

Imagination is not an aim in itself that allows us to escape the infinite and marvellous reality, or to withdraw from the essence of the new spirit. On the contrary, those who lack imagination have to look for it because without the faculty of imagination they will be unable to discover the essence of the new spirit: a thing so tender and so ferocious – *une chose si tendre et si féroce*.[3]

Imagination is the essence of existence. It is never a superficial instrument for escaping natural reality, for constructing an artificial and stupid surrogate. If one refuses to accept imagination, one has to leave the world's existence to the flowers, the animals and the landscape, like 50,000 years ago. Without imagination we are decomposing corpses.

Statement against rationalism

Van Eyck's edited version of his intervention at CIAM 6, published in 1951[1]

The old struggle between imagination and common sense ended tragically in favour of the latter. But the scales are turning: CIAM knows that the tyranny of common sense has reached its final stage, that the same attitude which, three hundred years ago, found expression in Descartes' philosophy – Giedion has just mentioned its sad implications – is at last losing ground. Yes, the deplorable hierarchy of artificial values upon which contemporary existence has come to rest is beginning to totter.

A new consciousness is already transforming man's mind. During the last fifty years or so, a few – ranging from poet to architect, from biologist to astronomer – have actually succeeded in giving comprehensible shape to various aspects of its nature. They have tuned our senses to a new dimension. It is the firm belief of CIAM that the collective idea which brought us to Bridgwater from so far is the seed of a new outlook, a new consciousness, still latent today, but awaiting general recognition tomorrow. *CIAM is first and foremost an affirmation of this new consciousness*[2]. The achievement of men like Le Corbusier, Mondrian or Brancusi compels us to believe, surely, that we are indeed approaching a brighter era; one in which grace is expressed in life as it is in art.

CIAM refuses to overhaul outworn values that belong to an outworn world by giving them a new dress straight from the laundry of common sense. On the contrary, it desires to stimulate a universal revaluation towards the elementary; to evolve a transformed language to express what is being analogously transformed. No rational justification of CIAM can therefore satisfy us. Imagination remains the only common denominator of man and nature, the only faculty capable of registering spiritual transformation simultaneously and thus of significant prophecy. It is the prime detector of change. Although architecture – planning in general – answers very tangible functions, ultimately its object differs in no way from that of any other creative activity, that is, to express through man and for man the natural flow of existence.[3] The more tangible functions – those implied by the word 'functionalism' – are only relevant in so far as they help to adjust man's environment more accurately to his elementary requirements. But this, after all, is no more than a necessary preliminary. The question thus arises whether CIAM, accepting the contemporary situation as an inevitable background for practical realisation, should nevertheless adopt a critical attitude toward it and act accordingly. Does CIAM intend to 'guide' a rational and mechanistic conception of progress toward an improvement of human environment? Or does it intend to change this conception? Can there be any doubt as to the answer? A new civilisation is being born. Its rhythm has already been detected, its outline partly traced. It is up to us to continue.

We discover style

Translation of 'Wij ontdekken stijl', the first article Van Eyck published in Forum, March 1949[1]

The old struggle between imagination and reason has ended in a tragic way.

The result is disconcerting.

The triumph of reason has systematically broken every relation, disturbed every balance. A wedge has been driven between nature and man with foolish tenacity. And as for art: she was degraded into a mirror of vanity.

But we know that the tyranny of reason has reached its final stage. Therefore no rational justification of the new architecture[2] will ever satisfy us. Imagination is and remains the only faculty capable of registering the qualities of a changing worldview simultaneously. It is the eye of reality, the eye behind the eye.

A new consciousness is latent everywhere. The new architecture is first and foremost an affirmation of this fact.

During the last fifty years or so, a few – ranging from poet to architect, from biologist to astronomer – have actually succeeded in giving comprehensible shape to various aspects of its nature. What they achieved fills us with gladness and compels us to believe that we are indeed approaching a brighter era.

Woodcut by Hans Arp

Drawing by Vordemberge-Gildewart

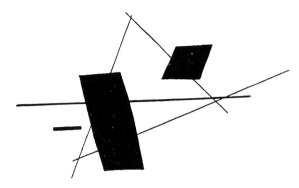

The deplorable hierarchy of artificial values upon which contemporary existence has come to rest is finally beginning to totter. A centuries-old bankruptcy is nearing its end. The new architecture lives because it knows this to be happening unavoidably. It refuses to overhaul outworn values by giving them a new dress. Those who hesitated have already gone astray.

Individual differences of accent are a matter of course. Yet nobody ought to think that our idea, albeit as mobile as the reality it sprung from, would be arbitrarily malleable.

Working magic with reality and performing tricks external to reality are two completely different occupations.

To work in a society which proves to be a negation of our collective idea in every respect demands a certain kind of perseverance. For some people spiritual isolation was a psychological burden they were not able to bear in the long run. We understand quite well that the gap between new architecture and society is a fundamental dilemma. Yet every bogus solution remains unacceptable.

Only the creative passion of the whole society can approach a complete synthesis – the sum of all relations in space and time.

Style is the reward of collective consciousness.

The new architecture stimulates a universal revaluation towards the elementary. It evolves a transformed language in order to express what was transformed correspondingly. It proceeds out of necessity and without compromise (however, a certain kind of obligingness belongs to the rules of the game).

Drawing by Sophie Täuber-Arp

Although architecture and urbanism answer very tangible functions, ultimately their object differs in no way from that of any other creative activity, that is, to express through man and for man the movement of complete reality. The more tangible functions they serve are only relevant insofar as they help to adjust man's environment more accurately to his elementary requirements. But this, after all, is no more than a necessary preliminary.

There is a tendency to regard urbanism as a more comprehensive activity than architecture. Such an attitude is uncreative. Eventually everything, from chair to city,[3] is a synthesis. The difference in the genesis of a piece of furniture, a building or an urban district lies mainly in their different relation to space and time.

The new architecture has its roots in reality: standing on the border between today and tomorrow, it is a meaningful prophesy.[4]

We are not looking for forms, we discover style. At least, that is our purpose.

> *From the exemplary to the archetypal*
> *It cannot be rushed. It has to grow, it has to grow up.*
> *And when this work happens to be in time, some day,*
> *so much the better.*
> *We still have to look for it.*
> *We have found parts of it, but not the whole thing. We don't yet have*
> *the eventual strength because we are not backed by the people.*
> Paul Klee[5]

> *Simplicity is not a goal in art but one reaches simplicity in spite of oneself,*
> *by approaching the real sense of things.*
> Constantin Brancusi[6]

On Brancusi, Sert and Miró

Letter to the Giedions, 28 October 1948

Dear CW & Prof. Pep,[1]

Oiseau, projet devant être agrandi pour remplir la voûte du ciel.[2] Gosh, I'd like to fire off to Paris & tell him he's a titan. But that's only half my secret. I'd like to fire off to god knows which polyglot South American necropolis[3] & tell Sert the opposite! What a lie, what a lie, what a tragic lie his petrol-cog-conglomeration is, what an insult to humanity, what an insult to CIAM, what lack of imagination – worse, what lack of common sense (lack of common sense, what a harsh paradox!) How miserable the whole thing has made me. He's thought of every thing yet forgotten EVERYTHING. He saw the bird & he saw the sky, but so does everybody, so why a CIAM? I thought CIAM existed because it saw the rest as Brancusi sees it, as Miró sees it. Sert told me that Miró was as a brother to him, and yet 'femme et oiseaux dans la nuit' for him, I guess, have literally remained in the dark! (You see, no architect's neon-light can penetrate such primordial night-stirrings.) 'It was falling on every part of the dark central plains, on the treeless hills, falling softly upon the Bay of Allan and, farther westward, softly falling into the dark mutinous Shannon waves.'[4] (Sert will need an army to cater for juvenile delinquency. Has he thought of that too & what about the brothel in the civic centre?)

Stacks and stacks of love. I shall attack your article, but W.[5] must be patient.

J.L. Sert and P.L. Wiener, Motor City project, 1944, for a location near Rio de Janeiro, Brazil

J. Miró, *Femme et oiseau dans la nuit*, 1945 Oil on canvas

Brancusi with *Bird in space* at the exhibition of Tri-National Art at the Wildenstein galleries in New York, January 1926

Sigfried Giedion   Paul Klee, *Vogel Pep*, 1925 Oil and watercolour on paper

On the function of a UNESCO art review

Letter to Sigfried Giedion, undated manuscript, presumably written in September 1950[1]

Dear Dr. Pep,[2]

I have an idea as to what I should like to tell you, unfortunately it's going to be rather hard to get it onto paper bang off like that, so forgive me if I'm more than abstruse. I'll start somewhere and hope UNESCO will be the end!

What is the function of art today or to what use can it be put? What is the function of a UNESCO art-review in particular?... Christ!

Collectivity (a good beginning) is not a moral asset but a primary phenomenon parallel to and no less primary than the phenomenon of individuality. When I think of 'man in equipoise' I immediately think of this dual phenomenon[3] of the relation between art, science, religion and social pattern, of how all vital art – no, everything vital and creative – results when collectivity and individuality simultaneously coincide with changing consciousness. Why not say that consciousness is the awareness of change? Now, it seems obvious that art should be the reward for such integrated consciousness, but there are two things I should like to point out that are perhaps less obvious and which I believe bear directly on what an UNESCO art review should represent. Although we are not wrong in speaking of art as being the result – or reward – of the dual phenomenon of collectivity and individuality coinciding under particular circumstances, we must remember, I believe, that in time and space cause and effect are reciprocal. I mean, however paradoxical this may sound, that creative consciousness can, during periods of spiritual transition when one aspect of existence is fading and another is latent but not yet universal, be the cause – the stimulus – of collectivity and individuality instead of vice versa. Today art has continued but the duo-phenomenon collectivity-individuality has become an universal aberration, a dual-dilemma!

Thus art today no longer represents culture, but human existence as such. Art is not one thing but next to nature everything. I mean that life (progress of human consciousness in time and space) must today be identified with art instead of art with life. Artists have succeeded in building – a comparatively small group to be sure – a bridge across which (provided the necessary sensibility is developed to discover its presence) it is possible to pass into a new consciousness. ('The era of particular form is nearing its end, the era of determined relations has begun.') The development of this creative sensibility is a prerogative not only in the pedagogic sense advocated by Herbert Read[4] in *Education through Art* but because it is the only instrument we have left with which to detect the spiritual structure of a new era – a new outlook – prior to its universal acknowledgement. There is only one guide left to us, call it imagination, call it creative sensibility. Without this third eye, everything remains

Venus of Lespugue, ca. 23,000 B.C., Haute Garonne France

Ivory, 14.7 cm

Paul Klee, Red waistcoat, 1938

Paste colour-waxed, 65 × 42.5 cm

dark. The object of education is to develop this third eye for with it we can discern what is constant in all things and what is constantly changing,[5] with it we can reject what is neither constant nor constantly changing, i.e. what is culturally irrelevant and spiritually bankrupt. (The double use of 'constant' attempts to illustrate not opposites i.e. constant and changing but a unity analogue to time-space. In fact it boils down to the same thing.) Lascaux, Brancusi, Easter Island, etc., etc., suggest eternal change through eternal constancy, that is why the constant juxtaposing of contemporary art with the earliest origins of art must be a principle in editing a UNESCO art review. This is what I want people to get hold of: that Maillart's bridges show how close together Brancusi and Mondrian are, i.e. the identity of what is constant and constantly changing. A UNESCO art review must make it clear and that is necessary because art is the only resort, the last possibility. That art today is life, because life has become a vacuum, that art is culture because culture today has gone to pot. That art is religion, because religion today has turned sour. That art is individuality because today individuality means egoism. That art is collectivity because today collectivity means nothing at all.

Perhaps it is better to say that art has temporarily replaced – or alone represents – life, culture, religion, individuality and collectivity. It must lay particular stress upon the fact that art transcends nationality as it transcends internationality, for internationality is merely a sentimental affirmation of nationality. Art is 'mondiale' not international. This is of primary importance and should be stressed again and again. It means that it should not be the object of the review to catalogue the activity of a 101 'nations'; this would be truly international. By placing immediately side by side, with the object of illustrating a universal theme, works of the most diverse races (whether 20.000 years BC or a Congo textile or a print by Klee). The justification of the existence of different patterns of culture side by side is stressed. Thus, not through sentimentality, but owing to a creative acknowledgement of what other races believe, do and make, a better interracial fellowship will ensue. Painters and sculptors have discovered the miracle of African, Indian and South Sea art.

Their admiration is creative and culturally important, not feebly dictated by ethical nonsense. Both the relativity and the splendid variety of art throughout the world must be absorbed before the wonderful similarity is really understood. The latter will bring about more than internationalism.

The review should make it clear that art is the language of continuity, the prime detector of change. It must stress from cover to cover and again and again in each number, directly or indirectly what it is that for the last 50 or 60 years has bound together certain contemporary artists, from sculptor to physicist, from poet to engineer. It must put across the nature of their collective discovery together, i.e. their creative prophecy. It must illuminate the bridge they have made, for it is the only bridge and certainly the only short-cut across the no man's land of contemporary spiritual bankruptcy.

Art proves that material progress is a very relative matter, that the African hut is more 'primitive' than the modern western house but that their art certainly is not; that Altamira man was no less a great artist than Hokusai, Picasso or Delacroix.

The accent should be placed not so much on the individual achievement as on the background and certainly more on the artist's work than the artist unless there is some particular reason. This in contrast to most other art reviews which pit one artist against another. A UNESCO review should promote creative sensibility, not individual fame, the latter takes care of itself.

Each illustration, each article should be placed against the background of contemporary thought, for it is the object of this review to show that art points the way forwards toward a healthier and more integrated era.

Sensation should be avoided. Obscurity should be avoided. Falsification through pedagogic simplification should be avoided! Internationalism should be avoided.

It should be as cheap as a newspaper and lie on the kitchen table everywhere.

It is a fundamental mistake, a sign of not really understanding the relation between one generation and the next, between younger and older, to believe that a UNESCO art review can thrive without inviting both younger and older people to participate in the preliminary discussions. It shows that not artists but critics and historians believe they can lay the foundation and that artists will do the work. Under these circumstances I am convinced the UNESCO art review will be a failure. For the artist, races and ages are no problem. If you think it important to know what I as *'nachwuchs'*[6] think, then ask me to come and explain. We are too young to be stars I suppose!

Whether star or no star I hope UNESCO is not going to promulgate a fresh batch. For it's art we want, simple art and through simple art universal fellowship.

You will know why – now – CIAM is dying, because the stars are conscious of the *nachwuchs* in an uncreative way, because they are troubling themselves like schoolmasters about their future. Believe me, art will continue nevertheless. I am sorry Dr. Pep, my admiration for you is very great indeed, but let me stop, I'll launch the attack on the CIAM hierarchy once and for all in London at the congress.

On the Dutch Contribution

Translation of 'Over de Nederlandse inzending', a statement published on the occasion of the Dutch contribution to the 9th Milan Triennale in 1951[1]

When, in the Dutch section of the Triennale, priority was given to architecture, it was because architecture was considered Holland's most substantial contribution to the birth of a new plastic language.

In the small space available, an attempt was made to show something of what one might consider the patient materialisation, in a specifically Dutch way, of an idea with universal validity.

The New Architecture in Holland is still on the same route, very much aware that what was achieved 50 years ago by Berlage, when he built the Amsterdam Stock Exchange, by 'de Stijl', and later by Van der Vlugt, Duiker and others, has not been caught up with yet, although the accent has undoubtedly shifted from the individual to the collective sphere (not always without losing sight of the former however).

1920 and 1951 are not so far apart as many people seem to think; it may take ten times thirty years to attune a new sound to the reality of everyday life, and vice versa. It is almost incomprehensible that hardly discovered creative possibilities should be applied so soon by so many in a wholly casual manner, quite contrary to the spirit from which they originated. 'The culture of particular form is approaching its end. The culture of determined relations has begun.' If the general tendency at the present points in the opposite direction, disregarding Mondrian's words, this should nonetheless be regarded as a temporary deviation – the result of impatience, of a lack of insight. Yes, today even art is in a hurry.

Architecture, and design in general, is dictated by the heart, not by the swift pencil. It should help to simplify life, never to complicate it; it should stimulate a general re-evaluation towards the elementary; reconcile what is constant and what is 'constantly' changing by uncovering their space-time identity.[2]

(In an environment such as that of Holland every man-made addition, i.e. every canal, highway, bridge, planted tree, building or signpost is an act, negative or positive, a wound or a fine determinator of space. And space in 'Paesi Bassi' is after all a primary experience. The Dutch environment offers no camouflage. It is naked and flat, often even geometrical. This no doubt helps to explain the edginess and abruptness, the stark rectangularity of most of the work shown.)[3]

What we need, at this time above all, is imagination, not fantasy.

Keeping in mind what was aimed for in Milan, Rietveld's words, chosen as the motto for the entry, speak for themselves:

'For the coming style, that which all people have in common is more important than their differences.'[4]

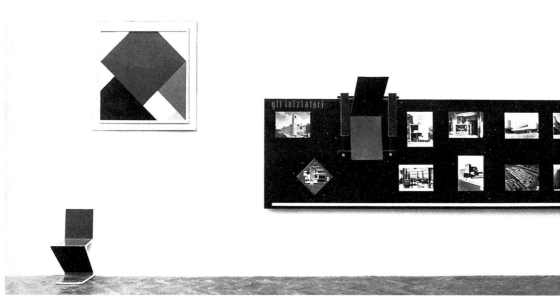

Aldo van Eyck and Jan Rietveld, Dutch contribution to the 9th Triennale of Milan, 1951

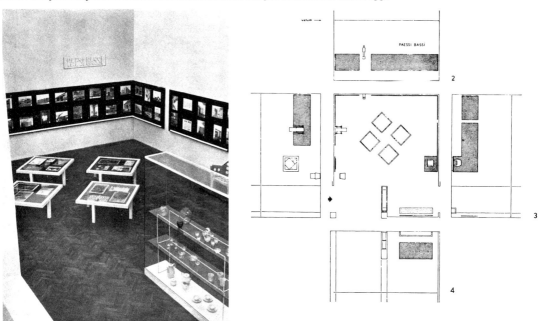

On the Hispano Suiza factory

Translation of a letter to the architects J.H. van den Broek and J. Bakema, dated 11 June 1951[1]

That conflicts arise whenever two world views – the one receding, the other approaching – clash in the reality of today is a matter of course. Such conflicts overcome everyone from time to time... to a greater or lesser extent! The truth is that one would be denying reality if one were to avoid such conflicts – after all, whoever imagines being able to act only positively today is either a pedant or an unreal being. But surely the artist whose belief it is that he must clarify the essence of the future to others through his work... and through his words (!) can scarcely willingly saddle himself (and his like-minded colleagues) with a conflict that contradicts, in the most brutal way possible, the most deeply-held principles – the structure – of that to which he hopes to 'stimulate' the consciousness of others; without at that very instant ceasing to be genuinely creative. Your acceptance of a commission such as that of which I have recently been told – a munitions factory – has placed the idea in the Netherlands in a ludicrous position – has prostituted it in the most distasteful manner. Personally, there is little so dear to me as precisely that which you have eroded by this decision (and I know that many others will think the same way about it). I shall therefore try to repair what little damage I can by publishing a letter of protest, in which I shall try to define unequivocally the boundaries of our (CIAM) responsibility as they now – today – urgently need to be defined. ... Only is perhaps capable of putting straight what CIAM has bent. Breaking publicly as threatens to become will make CIAM into what it ought to be.

The protest is appropriately illustrated and includes some quotations: it is printed in two languages and will be sent to interested people, periodicals and organisations at home and abroad. Since you are undoubtedly not the only ones among us who have accepted such assignments or have carried them out,[2] I have as far as possible composed the protest in general terms, though it was unfortunately not possible to completely avoid focusing the problem. It is not my intention to harm you or anyone else; only to repair some of the harm you have done. I am sorry if this may harm you in any way (certainly in anything other than a material nature). There is nothing to be done about it. I repeat that the protest is not primarily against the misuse you have made of your own ideals – and those of others – but against all tendencies that demonstrate that in a period of transition one is already losing sight of the essence of this transition – owing to incomprehension, impatience or material greed.

I felt the need not to surprise you in a few weeks time with the completed thing (the intention is to be ready by 7th July[3] without having written to you first. Perhaps we can talk it over. You, Bakema, have acted most inconsistently – but you will understand what I mean. It's odd, but I felt it coming from our first meeting. It's a pity you went too far – very soon in fact.

Kind regards,
A. Van Eyck

PS July, 22nd 1951

This letter has been lying on my desk for a month or so, among other reasons because of my illness. I am willing to put my intention to the two CIAM groups before going to print – although this will have to be soon. If it is decided to refrain from action because one considers that the CIAM idea and the construction of an (*a priori*) armaments factory are not incompatible – in this day and age! – all that remains to me is to address my protest to the whole group. This however strikes me as unlikely. If a better proposal emerges, I will if necessary resign myself to it. Don't forget that I do not deny the positive things you have achieved for Nieuwe Bouwen: that would scarcely be possible – but that is why your course of action is so regrettable. If CIAM cannot set an example, then no more CIAM – no more '8 en Opbouw' (and certainly no more 'cosmos', 'continuity', 'relations' and such like[4]). Do I have to armour-plate my children against a 'cosmos' of that sort... for the sake of 'continuity'? Soon the missiles will start falling. Does the 'cultural centre' have a good atomic shelter? Is the 'Venster'[5] [Window] made of shatterproof glass? How sad this all is.

Answer from Bakema

Translation of a handwritten letter by Bakema to Van Eyck, dated 26 July 1951

In the countries in and around Russia, a philosophy is growing in which 'working' is becoming the new currency. The possession of land or means of production is immoral there. The expression of this in art and architecture there is dull and hackneyed. In the countries around America, an attitude predominates in which money is the time-honoured currency. Here the common control of the means of production or land is called extremism. The expression in art and architecture here is lucid and new.

I do not know where I stand. Where do you stand? Where does CIAM stand? In Zurich 1946, Bridgwater 1947 and many other places in magazines and in meetings, I have tried to discover with regard to CIAM whether the common ground that makes cooperation possible, is ideology, its expression in art, or both.

I have been told by Rogers, Giedion, Le Corbusier, Sert: it is its expression in art that ties us! I heard this for the last time at Hoddesdon in 1951. Nor has Van Eyck ever been able to make an unequivocal statement about what CIAM is, over and above a certain collectivity in architectural expression! On the contrary, he has always occupied the topmost position in the ivory tower.

I have continually tried to keep the discussion about this going and I will continue to do so as long as there is reason. Quite certainly through the work that our firm has done and will do in future. We wish to show by 'working' what architecture can be over and above the self-gratification of the architect.

How is it that you have suddenly gone outside art and now wish to judge CIAM from that position? We assume that there must be more reason for this than a personal sense of satisfaction at bringing our firm into disrepute! ...

Two months ago the Katholiek Bouwblad has tried to do the same thing by publishing a sneering note[6] *which was passed on to me by the editors of Forum, asking for a reaction. We did not react because we understood that they wanted to hit us personally and were not picking on our architecture or only in the second place.*

Now here comes your reaction!

For a dictator who came to power by a military coup in Colombia four months ago, Le Corbusier has designed a new centre for the capital city, Bogota. The main element was the palace for this dictator. It was put up for discussion and the conclusion from Le Corbusier and Sert was: this dictator will be opposed better by means of the form of architectural and urban planning expression Le Corbusier developed than by 'doing nothing'. You may remember that Leonardo da Vinci was a strategic engineer.

All the same, you are right! ...

We feel guilty as far as to the accepting of the commission ... but we doubt whether the extend to which we feel guilty distinguishes us from others who keep silent about this feeling or do not know that feeling because they have never been placed in such a conflict in the real work situation.[7] *... Aldo, do you really think it is in accordance with your standards to involve your children in this debate? I have often thought that you are not sufficiently able to distinguish your position in Nieuwe Bouwen from Nieuwe Bouwen as a universal concept. It's a pity this had to become apparent so soon! I am only writing the latter in this form to remind you of the arrogant way you ended your letter. It has no other meaning.*

Jaap Bakema

Thoughts after a weekend discussion of the Dutch CIAM group concerning the problem of the armaments factory Hispano Suiza

Translation of a statement published in a special CIAM issue of Forum, *March 1953*[8]

For centuries, artists have been the servants of kings, popes and rich merchants. We admire the miracles they left behind. But what we crave for today is of an entirely different nature, nor do we want to approach it in quite the same way.

If we gather together all the creative moments – moments which alone need not be miracles – we may still bring about what today we have come to regard as a miracle: a world where people – less anxious – can go simply their own way, because the constructive attitude has overruled the destructive one.

Although the results of creative activity, owing to the nature of reality, can only rarely be exclusively positive, its purpose can never be but positive, exclusively positive. Today the artist is constructive, sine qua non; today he should serve everyone or no one. For him there is no question of choice because he has already chosen.

Lohse and the aesthetic meaning of number

Translation of a statement published in Forum, June 1952[1]

In search of the further principles of a new form language, the Swiss painter Lohse discovered the aesthetic meaning of number. Imparting rhythm to the similar, he has managed to disclose the conditions that may lead to the equilibration of the plural. The formal vocabulary with which man has hitherto imparted harmony to the singular and particular cannot help him to equilibrate the plural and the general. Man shudders because he believes that he must forfeit the one in favour of the other; the particular for the general; the individual for the collective; the singular for the plural; rest for movement. But rest can mean fixation – stagnation – and movement, as Lohse shows, does not necessarily imply chaos. The individual (the singular) less circumscribed within itself will reappear in another dimension as soon as the general, the repetitive is subordinated to the laws of dynamic equilibrium, i.e. harmony in motion.

Fearful of the monotony of number, repetitive elements in town planning are often needlessly combined into themes, as though the meaningful rhythmification of a repeating theme were not an even more demanding task – for the time being. The significance of Lohse's work in this process is evident.

Aesthetics of Number

Statement made at CIAM 9, Aix-en-Provence, 1953[2]

In order that we may overcome the menace of quantity now that we are faced with *l'habitat pour le plus grand nombre*, the aesthetics of number, the laws of what I should like to call 'Harmony in Motion' must be discovered. Projects should attempt to solve the aesthetic problems that result through the standardisation of constructional elements; through the repetition of similar and dissimilar dwellings within a larger housing unit; through the repetition or grouping of such housing units, similar or dissimilar; through the repetition of such housing groups, similar or dissimilar (theme and its mutation and variation).

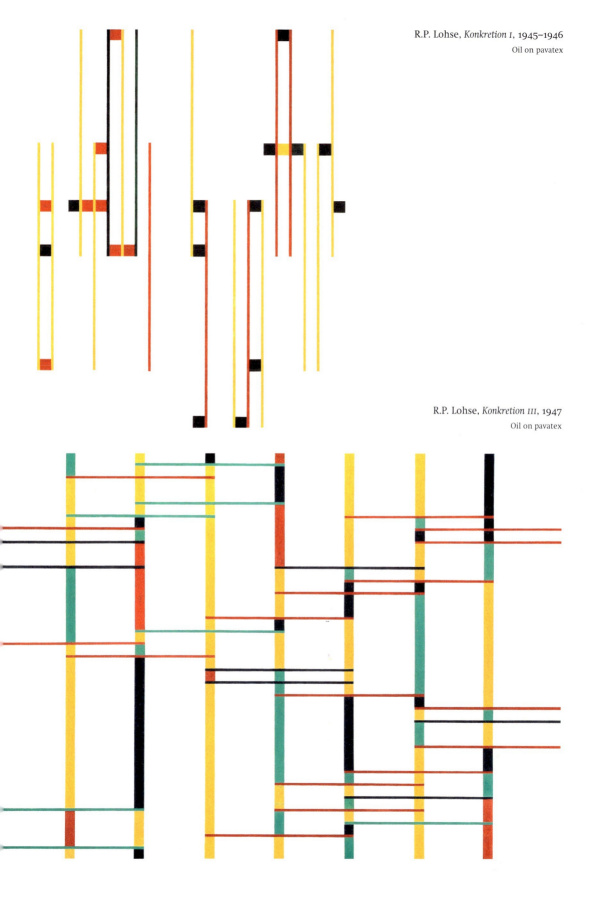

R.P. Lohse, *Konkretion I*, 1945–1946
Oil on pavatex

R.P. Lohse, *Konkretion III*, 1947
Oil on pavatex

3
Cobra

Introduction to chapter 3

Although never officially a member, in practice Aldo van Eyck may be considered one of the most active participants of Cobra.[1] Long before the Cobra artists caught the public eye, he was one of the first to acknowledge the quality and the meaning of their work. He immediately recognized their vitalist expressions as an authentic continuation of the Great Gang. In fact, despite their claim to a cultural *tabula rasa*, the Cobra artists continued to explore the surrealist regions of the new reality that had been charted by Klee and Miró. They wanted to immerse themselves as uninhibitedly as children in what they felt to be the essentials of existence: the primal forces of matter, the spontaneously felt life energy and desires, which they impulsively expressed in primitive shapes and suggestive signs. As Constant tellingly explained, they considered a painting to be 'not a construction of colours and lines, but an animal, a night, a scream, a person or all those things at the same time'.

Van Eyck was closely involved in the early development of the Dutch Cobra artists and exerted himself to promote their work and to defend them in word and deed. On their side, these artists felt strongly attracted by his erudition and his perspicacity in matters of art and literature. Soon his small flat on the third flour of Binnenkant 32 became a meeting point where Cobra painters and poets would drop in for discussions, to browse through his books on modern art or to delight in his New Orleans jazz records.

Van Eyck's most important contribution to Cobra was his layout of its two major exhibitions, in Amsterdam (1949) and Liège (1951). In these layouts he incorporated the flamboyant work of his friends, remarkably enough, into the pure geometry of De Stijl. In fact, he united their vitalist expressions with their antipode in the new reality – Mondrian's aesthetics of 'determined relations' – in order to confirm them as an integral part of that reality.

Van Eyck's first public contribution to Cobra was a manifesto in defence of Karel Appel which he launched in early 1950. Appel had obtained the commission to paint a mural in the canteen of the Amsterdam City Hall. He made a subtle composition of colour planes to which he added a few contours and spots, suggesting the gaze of hungry children such as he had seen begging along the railway lines when travelling through Germany. After its completion in April 1949 the mural was judged 'highly successful' by the appointed municipal expert committee. But Appel's *Questioning Children* had an unexpected effect on the daily users of the canteen. The civil servants were bewildered and turned violently against the mural. Deeming it 'incomprehensible' and 'tasteless', they demanded that it should be whitewashed over. And in

Party after the opening of the Amsterdam Cobra exhibition, 3 November 1949.
Aldo van Eyck is sitting in the right corner.

Entrance to the Amsterdam Cobra exhibition, 3–28 November 1949. In the background the enormous painting *Barricade* by Constant Photo J. d'Oliviera

spite of the expert committee confirming its favourable advice, the municipal executive decided in December 1949 to reject Appel's mural and to have it painted over. Van Eyck's manifesto met with much support in cultural circles and prompted the municipal executive to amend its decision. Instead of being painted over the mural was covered with a screen of lathwork and wallpaper – a covering that would not be removed until 1959.

When Appel, Corneille and Constant left the Netherlands in September 1950 to try their luck in Paris, Van Eyck kept in touch with them for a considerable time and continued to promote their work. He opened their individual exhibitions, seizing the opportunity to dwell upon the meaning of their work and to situate it in contrast to other art tendencies.[2] And in 1951 he took up the defence of his Cobra friends when their work figured as *corpora delicti* in a mock trial against modern art, organized by the conservative Dutch intelligentsia.

In the spring of that year Van Eyck and his wife also went on a journey through the Sahara with Corneille and some other friends. This journey was motivated by their common desire to become closely acquainted with the primary elements of plastic language. They expected to discover archetypal forms that, due to the extreme climate and their physical isolation, had remained, irrespective of Western civilisation, as constant as the pre-rational world-view they stemmed from.

Furthermore, after the dissolution of Cobra Van Eyck collaborated with Constant on a remarkable project. At the end of 1952 they carried out an experiment with space and colour in the Amsterdam Stedelijk Museum, proclaiming the emergence of 'spatial colourism'.

An Appe(a)l to the Imagination

Translation of a manifesto in defence of Karel Appel, launched in January 1950[1]

Amsterdam, 12 January 1950

They have got their way, Karel, the deceivers and the deceived, those who listened slyly to what you told them whilst you were still at it but then couldn't write a single decent word for their miserable newspapers; who secretly scribbled right across 'Questioning Children' in red pencil; who when counting the charity money collected for children threw away the empty tins so carelessly that your work looks like a bullet-riddled wall to one metre above the ground; all of them who chuckle uncomfortably because they are unable to discover the least trace of a story in this symbol made concrete in colour and form. They have had their way: your Questioning Children are to be destroyed. They are to be whitewashed out because they are real, because they really are questioning, because they are real Questioning Children – amid the ruins or under the trees. Congratulations, gentlemen... Karel, congratulations.

That they were not able or not allowed to arrive at any other decision, despite the whole advisory committee, shouldn't even surprise us. To the things you have forged into a visual unity, they are about as susceptible as gravel. They have lost one of their natural senses, they are missing a hormone. Go from place to place in the world, and you will see that everywhere it is precisely these people who, catastrophically for the community, seek their last chance in politics, that universal repository of the unimaginative. Everywhere – for there is not even a village in Africa where they have not pushed their way in with their bibles, booze, bad cloth and their taxes, by way of compensation to all those whom, not so long ago, they kidnapped and ferried across to the other side for auction. It is far too awful to last much longer.

They blame the child for its childishness and people for their passion. Whilst nature's cycles rankle them so sorely that they invented their own cycle, a counter-cycle: the vicious circle. For fear of freedom, they split the people and their creativity apart, because they know that the one inevitably entails the other. They desecrate the words of the saints, but do not know that the way of the saints is not their way. Yes, Karel, those who destroy your work are the heroes of an upside-down world.

They say we are 'barbarians', that we are out of our minds, that our work is 'utterly trivial'.[2]

But who is speaking to whom?

They say we are a danger to the State. There they are right. Whoever prefers the miracle of reality to the banality of illusion; the natural to the surrogate; healthy vitality to hesitant impotence; the impassioned grip to the repressed tic; the unpredictability of what is growing to the standstill of what is already complete; the

Karel Appel, *Questioning Children* (1949). Mural in the coffee room of the Amsterdam City Hall.

elementary to material perfection; whoever uses his imagination to rejuvenate himself and the community; in short, whoever has the courage and capacity to be free, is a danger to the State.

That they were unable to arrive at any other decision shouldn't surprise us at all!

Conjuring with their dried-out notions, they continue devoting themselves to the completion of their vicious monstrosity. But they do not know that the foundations are giving way because they rest on nothing, that the tyranny of reason has reached its final stage.

And us? We carry on, working magic with colour, line, space and words, because we know that it is never the conjurers who cause a metamorphosis, even though some people find amusement in their clever gestures.

But that is not enough. People want to laugh because they have to. They want to be free – the right of the bird and the fish, the stone and the star; the right that they must catch for themselves.

Karel, from those other people your Questioning Children can expect nothing.

Aldo van Eyck
Experimental Group Holland (Cobra)
Mailing address: Binnenkant 32,
Amsterdam

Constant and the Abstracts

Opening speech for the Constant exhibition at Le Canard *gallery in Amsterdam on 16 February 1951*[1]

Victor, six years old, is Constant's most loyal companion; he shares everything with him: his bread, his bed, even his palette.[2] 'Victor behaves exactly like a little Amsterdammer,' Constant wrote to me from Paris. 'He thinks it's wonderful to say '*bonsoir*' to everyone and wherever he is wants to catch a glimpse of the Eiffel Tower. But in fact the Parisians are not at all so nice. They don't like children, that's why they paint abstracts, and that's also why they slam the door when, with Victor holding my hand, I ask for a room. Yes, everything is abstract here, especially 'spontaneously' abstract. (Isn't that what they call it?) Almost everything you see here is the same empty, impersonal abstract, and the painter's reaction must out of necessity be one of the following: either giving in and sacrificing his personality to the 'art life' of Paris, or increasingly turning away from abstract art. Yesterday, Trökes[3] said to me, 'The longer I stay in Paris the more I begin to feel almost like painting a portrait.' I have never done anything else, I replied, but I feel the same disgust for this vogue for abstraction. I need something concrete, something clear, something direct.'

Considering my own distrust and irritation with it, I can well understand Constant's rejection of what currently presents itself as abstract. Because this rejection is essential both to his own work and to the development of painting as such, and the cul-de-sac it is in danger of entering. There are few things of which I am so convinced as the necessity of achieving a universal reduction of everything toward the elementary; not only the elementary in form but also, and above all, the elementary in content. When Brancusi says that *'la simplicité n'est pas un but dans l'art, mais qu'on arrive à la simplicité malgré soi, en s'approchant du sens réel des choses,'* what he means by *simplicité* is what I mean by elementary. We have come to the point where a start has to be made on elementary expression.

What has been discovered in the field of form consciousness since Cézanne, by way of Seurat, the early Cubism of 1910–1912, the dadaism of Merz and Cabaret Voltaire, *Der Blaue Reiter*, Suprematism and De Stijl movement was carried over from the realm of painting to that of architecture. So the painter is relieved of the one-sided duty (initially necessary and therefore meaningful) to suppress his need for direct expression in favour of purely formal experimentation. This duty will continue to apply to the architect for a long time to come: for the sake of man and the reality of life he will have to continue his laborious struggle with form. This is his nature and his task, but the painter has always been a very different sort of animal. He is concerned with direct and pregnant physical expression; he makes form subservient to this urge.

So anyone who, nowadays, still points accusingly at the painter for no longer wanting to fast pointlessly, because he no longer works non-figuratively, abstractly,

Constant, *War I*, 1950
Oil on canvas

idiotically or unrealistically, has his head in the sand, is a Calvinist stork, because the kiddies will appear anyway, with the whole to-do that goes with it. No artist can leapfrog the grammar of a new dimension without ceasing to be an artist, but nor can he use it without having anything essential to say. Isn't the latter much worse than the former? Anyone who paints a flowerpot because he likes the look of it is in fact a nice chap, but anyone who juggles with the essence of contemporary form because he thinks it's more agreeable, is not a nice chap but a pedant. He flaunts his progressiveness, but the world is being ruined by that sort of progressiveness! Working magic with reality and performing tricks external to reality are two completely different occupations.

It is indeed almost paradoxical that the abstract artists have come to be closer to the conjurers. That's why their work has become so meaningless, however amusing it may be to look at! It is a long time since it stimulated our imagination and our awareness of reality. It is not constructive, so does not contribute to a formal language, but is a parasite on it. They are 'truly' abstract. Not so Mondrian, Van Doesburg, Malevich, Lissitzky, Pevsner, whom they – the non-figuratives, (*Creatie* and suchlike[4]) – bring up so often as their own teachers. The things these artists found have transferred to the substance of our existence. But what does a painter, sculptor or architect do with this formal language, without a view of the new dimension from which it emerged and which it should manifest? In this case he uses the formal language as a trifle. He misuses it, performs tricks with it, not to come close to reality but to avoid it. He creates a vacuum, an arty formalism, an art which, forty years after the great clean-up, is just as sterile and alien to life as before. Without an awareness of reality, the artist is a producer of artifice, art just an arty trick. The whole artist's world is now whining that it has ended up on the periphery of society, after centuries in its midst, but society certainly does not prevent artists from working from the periphery of creativity towards its core. Or is it the case that what is peripheral remains peripheral?

The painter's task is indeed a substantial one, as Constant at least realises, and this makes his work vital and of true importance. It doesn't matter whether every painting is 'good'. (Too many 'good paintings' have been done in the Netherlands!) At last we are faced with real paintings, with real, simple, direct paintings that apply to us all but are still personal. Constant's work is real, direct, irrevocable, free of the national instinct for stylisation and ornamental lines, and has nothing to do with the stone-dead Kodachrome images of A.C. Willink,[5] who wrote in the *Vrije Volk* newspaper that Dalí should be exhibited instead of the Cobra painters. Dalí, he of all people, who claimed that blood, faeces and rotting were the three cardinal elements of existence – which Willink can only repeat. Constant has nothing to do with the idyllic national Elysium, the nasty, perfumed, illusory, ballet-scenery world of the clenched Kring[6] clique. He is concrete, just like Mondrian. He is, like Mondrian, not abstract!

The similarity to the Picasso who painted *Guernica* is not only obvious but moreover right and essential, no different from the similarity between *Guernica* and Goya. Constant is a realist, one of the very, very few; he is lyrical, despite his highly social and constructive nature; he is timid, friendly and vicious, and has as much pity on himself as on his fellow men, on whose side he stands with all his heart. He once wrote me the following about Henry Miller: 'I find him a pessimistic and anarchistic mind; his work is a harrowing witness to the attitude of bourgeois intellectuals who restrict themselves to a '*j'accuse...*', which paralyses the fighting spirit because it removes hope.' In the last litho from the superb series entitled *8×La Guerre*, it is a cat that stabs the dove of peace, not a human.

I would like to return briefly to Mondrian: 'The culture of particular form is approaching its end. The culture of determined relations has begun.' So he was no longer concerned with things themselves, but with their connections, with the relationship between one thing and another. He went so far that he was of the opinion (and it is because he succeeded in this that I admire him so) that he had to reveal this elementary relationship without the things themselves. The era of pure relationships begins: not for the things, but for the world between them.

Constant felt this too – at least in the sense that he set down before us, in the great unmoved plane of the event, the ordinary things he painted – the aircraft, the broken-down car, the broken women, the broken bicycle, the broken child – without any moralising pedestal and without any pathos. Constant's war work is prophetic, not retrospective.

For centuries, artists have been the servants of kings, popes, tyrants and vain merchants. We admire the miracles they produced, but the miracles we all yearn for now are of a completely different nature. Nor do we have to admire them in the same way. If we gather together all the creative moments – moments which alone need not be miracles – we may still bring about what today we have come to regard as a miracle: a world where it is possible to quietly drink a cup of tea without the scream of jets exercising overhead. Today the artist should serve everyone or no one.

Corneille and the Realists

Opening speech for the Corneille exhibition at Martinet & Michels gallery in Amsterdam on 7 November 1951[1]

On the occasion of Constant's exhibition a few months ago I said something about the *Creatie*[2] exhibition that had opened the day before. Constant's huge sense of reality was set in contrast to *Creatie*'s limited applications of what the major Constructivists had previously discovered. I brought up Mondrian, Malevich and Kandinsky because I think that, whatever his gifts, every abstract artist – if he wants to be concrete as they were – should be equally passionately in search of a formal language that can tell us something about the structure and the rhythm of a new world-view, of a broader, transformed reality.

I am no demagogue – at least I don't believe so – but this evening, on the occasion of Corneille's little exhibition, I am in a similar boat as I was then: almost the same boat in fact. I shall not bring up Mondrian to confront the 'Realists' who had the mayor open their show a few days ago.[3] They did not declare him their master as *Creatie* incorrectly does. Instead they printed a sort of disgusting crossword puzzle in which, alluding to Mondrian's fictional lack of eroticism, they exposed their own distasteful repressed eroticism. No, I would much rather confront them with their own gods, some of them ours too: Delacroix, Corot, Courbet, Van Gogh, Rousseau, Munch, De Smet, Permeke, Kirchner and Kruyder,[4] because just as then I believe that nowadays every realist who wants to be concrete, as they all were concrete, should tell as passionately but above all honestly about what happens in the broader reality of the imagination. I would not like, by these parallel citations, to suggest similarities that are not there.

Corneille and Constant are as different as a bird and a fish, so both as real as the air and the sea. For me, every work they paint is an extension, an intensification of reality. Which does not apply to the groups I referred to respectively with regard to their exhibition, the quasi-abstracts then, the quasi-realists now. Quasi extremes become quasi the same!

And yet this is not entirely true. I see *Creatie* as food with little taste, with few vitamins. But that is not punishable. They do not construct. They apply. They often do it well and honestly. There is still so much to discover that simply applying what has already been discovered becomes a pedantic luxury. By contrast, the realists are the worst art-makers whose work I have ever seen, including the Roland Holst chaps.[5] What they do is indigestible. For all those who have not learnt to foster their imagination so much – the deceived public – they are even poisonous.

I believe that the old conflict between universal form and personal expression, between form and content, will always exist, but that it is finally time that this conflict is enacted individually in the mind and work of each artist, and not in doctrinal groups which, tending either to the one side or the other, try to agreeably avoid this

Corneille, *Voiles Partout*, 1949 Watercolour and ink on paper

great conflict that is inherent in art: *Creatie* acting as a semi-religious association of schoolmasters, the 'realists' as a vindictive party of political interlopers. This afternoon I even caught out the realists in a little burst of honesty: '*je ne me suis pas réalisé*'. Bravo, say it, all of you: '*nous ne sommes pas réalisés*'. The example is the degeneration of Kurt Schwitters who, at the end of his life, could no longer speak normally and had descended into the state of a dribbling baby. Since when is a stroke proof of mental degeneration? I hope that Hans van Norden would be able to achieve as much as Schwitters, and will be able to die more pleasantly. Why should I care. Imitator watch your step.

After all, everyone who is genuinely creative knows that the difference between what he wants to express because of an inner need, and its direct recognisability, must somehow divide his loyalties. Some opt for what they want to express and neglect the recognisability. Others opt for recognisability but neglect what they thought

Corneille, *Ville en mouvement*, 1951 Oil on canvas

they wanted to express. These are the realists. They have nothing to tell, and therefore do not paint a cube, but a creepy sort of woman. Art has always been born out of reality, just like everything else. Reality certainly does not go back to reality just like that, abracadabra, through colour, form, space and word, unreal pocket-sized realists. Something else is needed for that. Imagination, not fantasy. It is with the imagination that Courbet, Mondrian, Schwitters, Constant and Corneille approach reality, show us real wonders that would otherwise have remained invisible. However, it is with fantasy that the realists – Engelman, Van Norden, Wijnberg, Horn – why have I remembered those names for so long? – who conjure together what their imagination cannot discover.

Reality. The imagination does not see reality as a realm that one can divide into conscious and subconscious. Corneille draws on neither, and from both, he draws on an enormous in-between realm, one whence all legends, myths, passions, birds, fish, worms, flowers, witticisms and people come, and to which they return.

Corneille versus clocks

Opening speech for the Corneille exhibition in 'Het Venster', Rotterdam, 5 January 1952[1]

Tick tock – tick tock
Tick tock – tick tock

the only difference
no difference.

Clocks are always concerned with eternity.
And so in eternity it ticks eternally.

It's hellish there.

If we were to throw all the clocks onto an enormous heap.
Then altogether trample the whole damned lot to smithereens.
Imagine
that two billion people
(including you)
were together busy trampling two billion clocks to pieces
pulverizing them
tearing them apart
smashing them ever more obsessively until not one clock goes tick-tick-tick
not a single cogwheel turns
until they are all dead
dead!!!
Only because of the sadism of eternal deficiency
here and there one pitifullygloriouslydivinely ticks every other tick
here and there a hidden cog that jolts around half-paralysed.

The true mechanocide?
The right mass-murder?

Never

Because the more the two billion clocks are smashed
the more the temperature of the two billion smashers rises
as they ever more lustily, more frenetically, more orgiastically
stamp out the ticking
until, exhausted and with not a stamp left in them
two billion stampers drop onto the shattered clocks.
But not without a billion stampers
being stamped to pulp
and another billion mutilated magnificently
by the others lies there writhing.

A proper mass-suicide?

Never

because as it becomes quieter
less movement
each of the billion exhausted stampers hears the ticking start again
softly at first
then louder
ever louder and closer.
The clocks are not dead.
Never.

A billion clocks tick in a billion bodies.
In each body a billion loud clocks are now ticking.
In the hollow of their nauseous anti-existence
there is no place for anything
only for nothing
i.e. for clocks.
Only for two billion clocks
shattered clocks which
slowly repairing themselves
penetrate from every side
unstoppable
ticking eternally
getting bigger
inescapable.
This is now eternity
the wretched eternal
the messy syrup of eternity.

Does no one ask: what has this got to do with Corneille?
So that I can answer:
nothing
absolutely nothing to do with him

Clock... what are you doing here?

Can one escape all this misery?
You expect me to say:
never
but I shan't say it.

For the billion who remain suicide is no longer possible.
They-remain-identical-to-what-they-have-stamped-to-pieces.

But there are others too
a few who were not there when the clocks were smashed
because in their bodies the heart beats
and doesn't tick
who chose the unbounded space of the temporary – do you hear
rather than the oppressive hollow of the eternal
the Christian vacuum of the empty noddle.
The movement of the temporary rather than the standstill of the eternal
temporary delight rather than eternal misery.

It is their fundamental privilege to be able to commit suicide.

There is no other reality than the reality of the imagination.
There is no ticking there
eternity just chokes there
there are no clocks.

There's no ticking in Corneille

It's all beats.

Because everything has a heart
and because one expects a heart
to beat
not tick.

Corneille as a landscape painter

Translation of handwritten notes on Corneille, c. 1952[1]

Some people approach the reality of themselves through a landscape that they paint; what is painted will not deviate so much from what they register visually but it will be transposed in their own specific way.

Others approach the landscape through their own inner reality; what is painted will deviate more from what the painter experiences visually. The painting becomes a more direct projection of its maker, whereby nature is in the first place a medium and the painter himself the subject. This is in contrast to the first sort, where the painter is in the first place the medium and nature the subject.

Works of the first sort are the most comprehensible to the viewer (Ruisdael, Hobbema, Potter). They are objective. The landscape speaks directly to the viewer through the painting and as such is immediately recognisable.

Works of the second sort are more subjective and more troublesome to understand (Hercules Seghers, Van Gogh, etc.) because the painter speaks to the viewer through the landscape. A dialogue in which mainly the painter addresses nature

Corneille, *Fish*, 1950 Oil on canvas

– in contrast to the objective kind where the dialogue is different. In that case it is mainly nature that addresses the painter. Works of this second kind are dream landscapes, landscapes of the mind.

In Corneille's case, the subjectification is complete – but not without a new and rich objectivity being born out of it. The painter today is a kaleidoscope, he himself is the purpose, and thus the kaleidoscope too. Feelings, experiences, things perceived, phenomena, in short everything he registers with or beyond his senses forms the variable glass facets of the kaleidoscope. He only really experiences them all through the kaleidoscope of himself and does so as soon as he plays with the kaleidoscope of himself. A dialogue between Corneille and the purpose-to-be, whereby the dialogue is entirely mutual. Corneille achieves self-realisation as he paints. He changes the painting and the painting changes him. Two kaleidoscopes that only work when they give each other a shove.

The boundaries between thing and thought, mind and matter, myth and reality have been abolished. Therefore a form is not a particular something because it is not something else. It is simultaneously and successively a multitude of things: bone, leaf, feather, wave, mountain, cloud, etc. Microcosm and macrocosm slide into one another. Corneille stands in the wings of existence and orders the aggregate of existing things in his own way, generating new connections between things arise so that they take on a new dimension.

Seen in this way, he is a landscape painter, because every person is himself a landscape. Painting and painter form each other's natural counterform. The kaleidoscope of complete reality coincides with that of the person of the painter. Reality takes place again and again kaleidoscopically in the painting, whereby the painter renews himself as he works. Seen in this way painting – as the ancient Chinese saw it – is a metaphysical act, no longer the making of an object.

Looking back on the Cobra exhibitions in Liège (1951) and Amsterdam (1949)

Translation of an account published in the festschrift
Niet om het even – maar evenwaardig, 1986[1]

When I saw those rooms in Liège for the first time, four days before the opening, and thought about everything I had to do, I was briefly at a loss. Deserted, immense (oversized or without measure), poorly tidied up – Belgian oddness. Tall bare walls, room after room with browning stretched jute, done years before. And then suddenly, on the vast parquet plains of these rooms, some crates filled with art! Once it had been unpacked and distributed among the rooms, it all seemed so insignificant and above all far too little. I said to Alechinsky it would all fit into two or three rooms instead of ten. '*Mais non, mon cher, ça deviendra un véritable événement avec des gens de partout.*'[2] OK, but how and with what? At the Stedelijk Museum in Amsterdam two years before, the number and size of the rooms, and the size and amount of art, differed much less from each other. What is more, most of the painters and sculptors were in attendance. In Liège, apart from Alechinsky, and later Tajiri, there was no one. So what was possible in Amsterdam was not possible here: in Amsterdam I asked Appel and Constant to paint something very big, as fast as lightning, at various points in the building to give clear articulation to the circuit. And they managed it! Appel produced a masterpiece in three days: I saw him building it up from hour to hour with no preliminary studies – a fabulous skill, tremendous effort, great vision.[3] It was the second time that year, because I had seen him at work every day on the Questioning Children in the canteen at the town hall.

In Liège anything like that was, as I have said, impossible – the painters were not there and the rooms were much larger and had less shape. The floor area was moreover well nigh endless. Having galloped kilometres back and forth for days on end we got there. With just the work itself, and with the addition only of what was necessary for an adequate presentation, it turned out to be possible to convert the void into 'space', so that the works were yet able to express themselves – and it was pleasant to spend time in these otherwise dead and uniform rooms. Of course both in Amsterdam and Liège there were people who thought that my way of organising it was fine but not objective. Strange: you never hear anyone say intelligent but subjective! Of course this 'objective' is just an illusion, because it's a matter of a temporary, fairly accidental combination of a multitude of works of art, which do not in this sense belong together (like the parts of a triptych), but appear alongside and after one another for a short time like an event. They were not made for this purpose. The assembly of works of art is artificial and that suits the art! The only thing is it cannot then occur objectively: not if one wants to arrive at an adequate solution for a specific encounter whose intention may be meaningful but is not therefore necessarily an intrinsic part of the works themselves. Similar or different,

Aldo van Eyck setting up the Amsterdam Cobra exhibition with the assistance of Tony Appel Photo E. Kokkorris-Syriër

Cartoon by Wim van Wieringen

by one painter or several, they do not simply tolerate one another when adjacent or in the same room. It is after all more than just hanging up the washing, although one does not put on the dresses and the trousers (which sometimes look pretty odd hanging next to each other) all at the same time. There is no obvious solution. Objectivity? It's a head-in-the-sand notion. All it gets you is what is falsely correct – the stupid, in other words.

Neither paintings, nor sculptures, nor people are at their best in spaces with no 'space', i.e. with no 'spatial' qualities, and therefore nor in rooms that remain 'empty' even when in fact they are not. Rooms with all the paintings at eye level, as it's called, or with their upper edges on the same line, form an incorrect horizon of their own, and the works trouble each other laterally because 'eye-level' involves only the viewer, and then imperfectly, but neither the nature nor the size of the paintings (the centre of gravity of their content), nor the nature and proportions (mainly height) of the room itself. By contrast, paintings at widely varying heights and distances from each other can together open up a completely different dimension. But to depart from the 'eye-level' principle one does have to have an eye for it; an eye for paintings and sculpture, for space and for people: the things which one after all wants to bring together! Keeping to eye-level means two things: staring and a stiff neck. In this way large and small sizes can also be brought close together instead of, as is usual, being separated, with all the small ones in small rooms and large in large. The same possibilities also arise for such items as preliminary studies, sketches, variations and so on. From this it becomes obvious that such 'categories' as prints, drawings and watercolours on the one hand, and paintings on the other, no longer need be exhibited separately (the mad hierarchy of pencil, ink, watercol-

Aldo van Eyck, layout of the Amsterdam Cobra exhibition, 1949 Photos J. d'Olivier

Aldo van Eyck, layout of the Liège Cobra exhibition, 1951 Photos Serge Vandercam (top) and Violette Cornelius (bottom)

our and oil colour only hinders appreciation of content but has still not yet been overcome).

It goes without saying that similar or different textures and structure (large or small, light, heavy, rigid, loose, dynamic, static, and so on) can also be brought into a relationship that is direct and richer in content by means of this variable exhibition technique, because it is only then that what I call balanced contrast becomes possible. What is striking here too is that people move more freely around the space. There is no longer any sign of moving from painting to painting at a more or less equal distance along the walls of the room. In this way the room remains present as a setting, and becomes a real space by the presence of what is exhibited and those who come to see it. The works thereby always determine the distance, position, order and variable movement through the rooms. Conversely, by playing this active role, the things exhibited stand out better because each particular work can isolate itself or enter into a direct relationship with another work.

So that's the walls. What about the horizontal surface – the floor? These were in part activated by using them not only to exhibit sculptures and objects, but also work that is created in a lying rather than upright position, such as drawings, lithos, etchings and gouaches. I laid them under glass on low pallets. After all, in this sort of work, 'top' and 'bottom' have a different, more relative, significance than in work conceived and created vertically.

People stand around it in a relaxed manner, forming groups in the room, seeking for themselves the 'top' as they go around the pallet from work to work, or rather, the 'top' appears in the right place as soon as one is standing in front of it.

All those backs and noses bending forward, almost against the canvas, all around the room: it's an odd sight. So crouching or sitting or kneeling to get closer to the work is a more agreeable solution. What is more, a sculpture or an object could be placed on one of these low pallets in the space between the graphic work. Sculptures can also be 'brought together' in groups.

To conclude, a general comment: always looking straight in front of you at eye-level is less self-evident (or natural) than one supposes. The only way of getting a complete experience of the space is by alternately moving the eye above or below it, meaning viewing the whole space in its height and breadth. For this reason alone, paintings and sculptures should never all be at the same height. After all, in their studios painters put paintings on the floor against the wall (except when they are very small) to look at or show them. They are also hung up high, out of reach – in safety – or to dry. In this way we see them in the space and not threaded together along a single line around an empty room.

An evening of limbo in the Low Countries

Translation of an account published in the festschrift
Niet om het even – maar evenwaardig, 1986[1]

I remember in the morass of that period – it was 1951 – an odd art evening in the Vondel Park Pavilion, organised by the International Cultural Centre.[2] On the programme was a 'Tribunal on Modern Art'. Main plaintiff: the public. Everything that should accompany such an evening of Limbo in the Low Countries was present: the court's presiding judge, lawyers, expert witnesses, the art objects that had to be condemned or acquitted and – in abundance – John Citizen's bile. Precisely what the charge was now escapes me. It was something like: it is not Art, but an expression of inability, damaging to our sense of beauty, etc.

In addition to a sculpture by Maillol and one by Zadkine (in fact it was only in the Netherlands that his work was purchased regularly) there was also Cobra work, because of course that's what it was all about.

I remember above all the exhausting 'analysis' a now legendary Amsterdam psychiatrist[3] presented. It was striking that the foundations of his diagnosis mutually undermined each other, so that it was not the indicted art objects that acquired any sort of profile, but the personal baggage of this renowned specialist. Not that it surprised me to see a psychoanalyst being so prescriptive when it came to other forms of human 'expression' than playing with faeces.

He saw a lot in Dalí, because he depicted very exactly what since Freud has seemed to emerge from dreams – recognisable illustrations. By contrast, this was not the case in the work of Appel, Corneille and Constant. Their products were indistinguishable from those of Children and Lunatics: characteristics of infantilism and regression were unmistakable. Cobra art is like a child's work and is therefore not art, or, Cobra 'art' is like the work of lunatics and is therefore not art either. Although the 'is art/isn't art' did not degenerate into proposed sanctions that evening, as an adult of healthy stock, one is taken aback by these Art = A and Art = B comparisons. Not because of their 'cultural' implications, no, but humanitarian ones, because if Art is equal to A and is also equal to B, then a by minor detour (via art, for Christ's sake!) A = B, meaning that work by Children and by Lunatics amounts to the same. I thought of all those who seek psychological support from 'experts' who are themselves not even capable of distinguishing forms of expression of such different natures from each other!

By signalling this sort of non-learning, I launched into my counter-diagnosis. Shortly afterwards I saw the hackles rise on a tall, slender erudite lady in the front row when she drew a bead on Corneille's 1949 painting *In the desert there is still place for play*, which has in the meantime become a classic. This canvas – a metre square, black from corner to corner, with all kinds of coloured things in it – was on the stage to be viewed. She told with some flair how, on her 'way' to a congress in South Africa

Corneille, *In the desert there is still place for play*, 1949 Oil on canvas

had seen with her own eyes, through the window of the aeroplane, that the Sahara is not black at all, as Corneille's painting would lead us to believe. At each climax of her indictment, with a brisk movement, she stuck a handkerchief in her mouth, which she then immediately pulled out again with a triumphant little laugh. Her listeners visibly shared her triumph. When she, as undisputed winner, had sat down again, I started my second reply with a much larger handkerchief in my mouth, because in Limbo intelligibility played not the slightest role.

I observed that airliners only fly transit over the Sahara at night, so I did not fully understand how the desert, which must after all have been as black as night down below, could possibly not have been black at that time. In my turn, I told that I, with my wife, Jan Rietveld and, *nota bene* – Corneille – had only just travelled in an old army vehicle straight across that same desert and how we had made a small discovery there that I would not like to keep from the evening's trusting audience; huge areas of the Sahara are not only figuratively, but also literally black. I was thinking of Le Plateau du Tademait, also known as *le pays de la peur*.[4] The fact that this revelation did not really explain the blackness of Corneille's indicted painting was a giveaway I granted the lovers of the literal. I then urged Dr Kekovis-Syrier – I can't bear not to mention her marvellous name – if she were to be transported through the Painted Desert in Arizona on her way to a future congress, she should do so in a car and of course in daylight, so that from then on whenever she looked at the colours in a painting she would always see that desert appear before her eyes. Lastly, I suggested to the renowned psychoanalyst of earlier in the evening to spread out a pile of mixed prints by Children, Lunatics and Cobra on a large table. I promised, by way of encouragement – but also a bit as a demonstration stunt – I would be able to sort the prints immediately according to provenance, and to make a start on it without making any further distinctions within each sort itself.

As I write, I recall the duet drawings by Arp and Sophie Taüber as well as the *Cadavres Exquis*[5] made by the surrealists. Also, not so long ago, that magnificent series of sheets by Alechinsky and Appel, painted together, and combined with poems by Claus in the book *Zwart*[6] (and years before those of Dotremont, with Jorn, Alechinsky, Corneille and Appel together).

Alechinsky and Dotremont, *Duet Drawing*, 1979. Dedication for Hannie and Aldo van Eyck in the book *Zwart (Black)*, 6 March 1979.

Hans Arp and Sophie Taüber, *Duet Drawing*, 1939
Chinese ink on paper

The unity in all these winged duos is, page by page, breathtaking – especially for those who can distinguish and are thus able to follow the interweaving of line, form and figuration with their double nature in the secured space of the thus merged new world.

When my son was still a child he too did a couple of duet prints with Appel – double children's work! – I saw them at it... now you, now me, now you again. My son disrupted – opened up – what had gone before just as precisely as Appel again and again restored the upsets – making what had gone before link up again. But from all this, and that's the point, no rigid conclusion should be drawn: in art, alchemy is variable – and does not fail eternally. Art is alchemy – childish or lunatic alchemy!

The small painting below is from a series Appel painted specially for his friends' children in 1950. Each of them went to his studio to choose one and take it home. Again the horizon is very broad – again the intelligence of a fabulous painter shines out. In that small painting (above my daughter's bed) the space was there at night too. During the day, around the colourful creatures, it is black. What a pity I did not have that whole series with me on that artistic evening in the Vondel Park; although...

Karel Appel, painting of animals dedicated to Tess van Eyck, 1949 Oil on canvas

Note on the experience of the elementary in the desert

Translation of a handwritten note, probably drafted in 1951[7]

It seems to me that when one has to do without one of life's essential accompaniments, one will experience the others more intensely; that precisely because of the lack of the one, the other is experienced more fully - that the thing which is lacked would be felt just as intensely is clear enough. Lack of water makes both water and everything that is not water clearer. The lack of something as elementary as water will cause the elementary – the origin – to be experienced more intensely. In the Sahara, one is so immersed in vastness and tininess that one begins to envisage both the phenomenon of the matter in which the visible and tangible have taken shape and the phenomenon of life in a different temporal/spatial connection; that matter, life (existence), space and time form a continuity, a simultaneous sensation. One understands why nature is not a passive backdrop for life but the agent through which man experiences this simultaneous sensation.

Aldo and Hannie van Eyck in the Tademait, Algerian Sahara, 1951

Building in the Southern Oases

Translation of the article 'Bouwen in de Zuidelijke Oasen', illustrated by Aldo van Eyck with his own photographs, published in Forum, *1953, no. 1*[1]

Mabrouk ben Hamou

The Sahara spans between two worlds: the world of Mohammed and the world of the Negro. Both in the imagination and in fact, this ocean of stone and sand is an in-between world. The inhabitants one expects to come across first in the southern part, in the Sudan, are already present in the central region, while the reverse applies to the religion of the north, for it is just as surprising to hear the cry of the Muezzin coming from a Negro along the Niger as it is to discover a Negro population of Sudanese origin as far north as Timimoun, In Salah or El Golea.

As to building, the same applies. Anyone who is acquainted with the Dingeray Beer in Timbuktu or the houses of Agades will recognize the similarity to the manner of building in the southern oases. Allah is adopted by the Negroes in a way peculiar to themselves. Both in the Sudan and in the Sahara, they have stayed faithful to their magic, their drums and their architecture.

the beginning and the approaching end of an old process:
above   –   the formation and sun-drying of adobe stones in Tamanrasset
below   –   a cracking wall

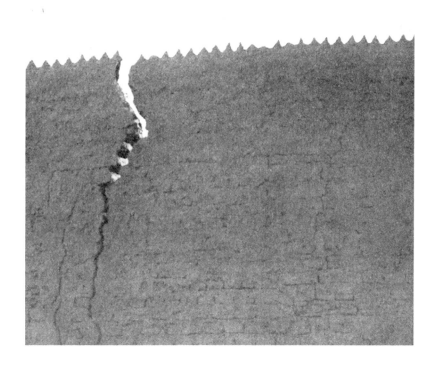

cracks in a recently built, otherwise intact house in Aoulef.

It cannot have been so very different in Ur 5000 years ago; the same laboriously fashioned bricks of sandy mud, then as now; the same sun weakly bonding and then harshly disintegrating them; the same spaces around a courtyard; the same enclosure; the same sudden transition from light into darkness; the same coolness after heat; the same starry nights; the same fears perhaps; the same sleep.

Houses in Timimoun. Boxwood stairs to a roof terrace.

In Salah: inner court of an abandoned house, partly buried under sand.

Entrance to a house in Aoulef. A heavy bolt, accessible through the round hole, closes the house.

Stairs in Timimoun

Whitewashed marabout on a square in In Salah. The phallic meaning of the pinnacles in Sudan architecture has been pointed out frequently.

The Same marabout in In Salah

One of the adjacent houses

Lonely grave in Timoudi.
the cavity intended for small offerings
contained some dates.

Marabou of Sidi Aissa in Ghardaia. Like the one at In Salah, this marabout is fascinatingly under-dimensioned. The tower is only 5 m high. Both the building and the enormous forecourt are limewashed as white as a sheet. The soot in the whole testifies to burnt offerings.

95

Spatial Colourism

Translation of Spatiaal colorisme, *1953,*
a manifesto written in collaboration with Constant[1]

As a reaction to building in the nineteenth century, when form was overwhelmed by decoration to the extent of becoming unrecognizable, the modern architect came to concentrate his attention mainly on space-form and to consider colour as secondary, as subordinate to form. The architect sees dimension, proportion and construction as the basic elements of pure space-form. The architectonic project is mainly founded on these elements, while its space is supposed to be colourless.

To carry out a project that is primarily founded on form implies from the outset a conflict, the conflict between idea and matter, between form and colour.

The architect tends to keep colour passive. He limits the number of the colours to a minimum and avoids intense colours. Yet colour is unavoidably introduced through the use of materials, through the finishing and the furnishing of space.

When added afterwards, colour forms an accidental element in regard to the project, without real constructive value for the plasticity of space. As a consequence, the enormous space-creating potential of colour is reduced to an accident and the impact of space itself is bound to remain imperfect.

When colour, a space-determining factor as important as architectonic form, is eliminated, no unity of form and colour is possible any more.

Realistic space conception is the conception of space in colour.

It goes without saying that the spatial use of colour has nothing to do with the application of colours for decorative or 'functional' purposes. Neither is the use of colour as a means of correcting an impure form or proportion through *trompe l'oeil* to be considered a plastic use of colour, because in this case form remains passive in regard to colour. Yet the use of colour as a means of correction implies an acknowledgement of its plastic value in space.

Space-form and space-colour can only form an indissoluble unity when they come into being simultaneously and from mutual relation. What holds true for painting on a flat surface also holds true for the spatial conception of colour:

Colour is nothing but the colour of form and form is nothing but the form of colour.

A spatial conception of colour thus implies more than the use of colour for the activation of architectonic space. The complete unity of form and colour, i.e. the purely plastic use of colour, brings the architect into the field of painting. Architecture will no longer first and foremost be based on abstract form elements but be conceived as a visual reality wherein form and colour are one; and painting will no longer make colour subservient to personal expression but will take part in a plan and operate directly in a plastic way.

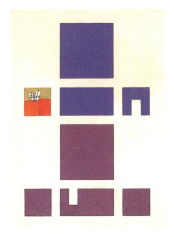

Aldo van Eyck,
Purple-Blue Room
with painting by
Constant,
Amsterdam Stedelijk
Museum, 1952

Spatial colourism, therefore, is an entirely new plastic art, with its own independent laws, and whose possibilities amply exceed those of both architecture and painting. Spatial colourism elevates schematic form to physical form and is therefore an indispensable factor in the humanization of space, in the most extensive sense of the total human habitat.

In spatial colourism the well known notion of 'colour sculpture' acquires a new meaning. In the spatial conception of colour there is no longer place for an centralized composition, nor for a 'simultaneity' of colour effects. The experience of colour sculpture is going to take place in time. Moreover, 'scale', the relation of colour quantity to human size, acquires a decisive meaning when painting exceeds the boundaries of the canvas to take up environing space.

In order to develop spatial colourism as a space conception and to realize space in colour, a close contact between painters and architects is necessary. It is important that both do not remain standing as specialists on their own demarcated field but work together as a team towards a common goal. For this goal is not the combination of architecture and painting like in the Baroque, but the surpassing of both, towards a higher organized plastic quality where colour and spatiality are unthinkable the one without the other.

Spatial colourism is not a theory but a practice.

4
Playgrounds

Introduction to chapter 4

From the time he started practising as an architect, Van Eyck was involved in an important long-term municipal project, the design of playgrounds in the city of Amsterdam.

Amsterdam had a considerable tradition of playgrounds. The city boasted several 'play-gardens' constructed by an association called the Amsterdams Speeltuinenverbond. These were fenced plots supervised by keepers and reserved for the children of the association's members. They usually contained a playing field and play apparatus such as sandpits, swings and seesaws, but being rather arbitrarily scattered around the city, they served only a limited segment of its child population. To rectify this situation the Town Planning Department resolved in 1947 to install, in addition to these closed 'play-gardens', at least one 'open' playground in every neighbourhood. These new playgrounds would be entrusted to the supervision of the general public. The initiative for the project was taken by Jakoba Mulder who headed the Design Office of the municipal Town Planning Department. She entrusted the design of the first playground to her young assistant Aldo van Eyck. It was planned for Bertelmanplein, a small public square measuring 25 by 30 metres and surrounded by housing designed in the Amsterdam School style.

Van Eyck placed a large, broad-edged sandpit eccentrically in the northern corner of the square, thereby leaving a large area for mobile play which was articulated by a group of somersault frames. He furnished the sandpit with four round stones and an arch-shaped climbing frame, and marked off the area with five benches. This modest composition of elementary forms, which was carried out in the spring of 1947, met with such favour from the local residents and the city council that the latter soon reserved a million guilders for the construction of several more such playgrounds. This was to be the start of a project which would eventually expand to cover practically every neighbourhood of the old city and every new housing estate. It was a task which was to occupy Van Eyck on and off for over thirty years. Before he received commissions to design actual buildings, it allowed him to experiment in reality with elementary forms and to evolve a personal form language.

As to these forms, he did not confine himself to the neutral elements of De Stijl. Inspired by Hans Arp, Sophie Taeuber and Brancusi as well as by primitive art, he wanted to instil the elements of his architectonic language with vital associations. The play equipment he conceived consisted of simple archetypal constructions that evoked a variety of meanings. In the first place there was the sandpit, a solid yet soft, open body that could take a variety of geometrical shapes, circle or square, a polygon with an inscribed circle or a circle with an inscribed polygon. Besides this large, encompassing form the playground usually included a number of small solid elements, cylindrical concrete blocks arranged in row or in group. They could be used as seats or as stepping stones. These solid concrete elements were contrasted with slender metal ones: the small somersault frames and the large arch. Placed in a group of three or more, the frames marked a spot or delimited the place while the primary architectonic form of the arch lent itself to a variety of uses. It was both a tunnel and a bridge, both a venue and a gymnastic apparatus.

From the outset Van Eyck refused to resort to hybrid, animal-like forms because they do not belong to the language of the city and they shut the imagination down rather than activating it. The archetypal forms do not impose a fixed function or meaning but suggest a whole spectrum of them. They offer the children the opportunity to discover things by themselves and to develop the locomotion to which they are naturally inclined.

In the course of thirty years Van Eyck designed more than 700 playgrounds. They gradually formed a continuous network of places that injected new life into the urban fabric and which the children could identify as their own territory – places where the children found due recognition as inhabitants of the city. Still, they were not the exclusive property of children. When the children went home, they did not look like deserted amusement parks. Deprived of the children's commotion, their elementary tectonic forms constituted places with a distinct urban character, places that also made sense to adults, as a point of rest or encounter. However, since the 1970s this unique urban design heritage has been treated in a particularly careless way. Most of the playgrounds were neglected, many fell prey to vandalism, were arbitrarily transformed or even demolished.

The location of the 736 Amsterdam playgrounds designed by Aldo van Eyck between 1947 and 1978
Map drawn up by Francis Strauven in 1980

Child and City

Translation of 'Kind en stad', an article published in Goed Wonen, *October 1950*[1]

This sunny stairwell designed by Jan Rietveld for a doctor's house in Ameide connects two old houses elegantly into one, despite the very limited ground area used to do so.[2]

He 'discovered' his children as he looked from the top floor down alongside the staircase. The eldest stood one floor lower, also looking down. Her little sister stood at the bottom looking straight up, her face in a shaft of sunlight. What was it she saw? Her older sister leaning over the railing, looking down from the first floor, and further up, right at the top, the half-concealed face of her father who at that moment was observing this feast of line, plane and colour, of child and sunlight, through the viewfinder of his camera, before fixing it with a tiny movement of his finger.[3]

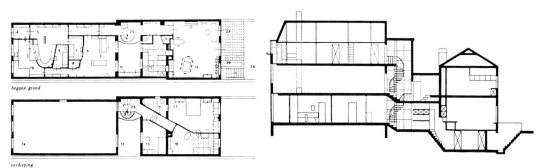

Jan Rietveld,
connection and
transformation of
two old houses into
a new one,
Ameide, 1950
Photos Nico Jesse

Perhaps it was the architecture of Jan Rietveld's stairwell that revealed once again the wonder of sun, child and perspective, or perhaps it was these things that revealed the wonder of architecture: It must have been both. The essential thing is that one actually keeps discovering the one, back and forth, in the other: only our senses would in general have to be more accurately attuned.

The photo of my daughter's bed corner illustrated here shows what architecture can do for children – and the sun for both of them. In addition, the photo of Jan Rietveld's fine staircase shows what children – unexpectedly – can do for architecture. The visual meaning of the child in architecture, but mainly in the overall image of the city, is in fact something of which people are still too little aware. It is possible that people will consider this a singular change of emphasis: however, I believe that it will hardly be possible to solve in principle the serious child/city conflict without realising that this change is essential, if the city is to acquire a positive meaning for the child.

And so I go from a staircase in Ameide to Amsterdam and its children, because here too, just as in Liège, Leeds and Karlsruhe, the solution is to be found in this sort of interaction. It's true that I have little faith in solutions, however initially well-intended, that try to locally adapt the city to the child by partially – and sometimes almost entirely – isolating them in the usual enclosed playgrounds, and withdrawing them from the living city scene. As long as there are barrel organs children will rush after them; they will continue to play hopscotch and marbles on the street and clamber up fences – as long as there are children! The new playgrounds the Department of Public Works have constructed in Amsterdam are just a worthwhile addition to all this. They are indications, deliberate indications, no more, yet this is sufficient to breathe new life into a deserted street-corner or seemingly purposeless square. In this way the child discovers its city and the city its children.

Bed corner of the architect's daughter
in his flat at Binnenkant, Amsterdam.
Photo Jan Versnel

Aldo van Eyck,
Dijkstraat playground, 1954

Climbing arch in Dijkstraat playground
Photo Louis van Paridon

'Wayward Youth'
Photo Henk Jonker

Lost identity, grid for CIAM 10, Dubrovnic 1956

☐ the problem

1

LOST IDENTITY

a city without the child's particular movement is a paradox. the child discovers its identity against all odds, damaged and damaging, in perpetual danger and incidental sunshine.

example: the child and the city

☐ symbol towards a partial solution

2

snow! the child takes over. yet what it needs is

hand in hand with whatever represents imagination unhusked the child survives edged towards the fringes of our attention, an emotional and "unproductive" quantum.

something far more permanent than snow.

amsterdam's
contribution

aldo van eyck **3**

something the city
can absorb without
losing its remaining
identity, something
meant for the child
alone and not altogether
different from the incid-
ental things the child already adapts to its
imagination and vital-
ity; something care-
fully shaped and
judiciously placed
where there is still
some room,
on innumerable form-
less islands left over
by the road engineer
and demolition worker,
on empty plots, on
places better suited
to the child than the
public watering place.
70 such places have
been adapted in this city.

the playground as core and extension of the doorstep

an appeal
to
authorities

4

he artist,

essential

ally of

he child,

s there to

essen the

onflict.

if childhood is a journey, let us see to it that

the child

the city

everywhere

the child does not travel by night.

When snow falls on cities

*English version of 'het kind en de stad',
an article published in* Goed Wonen, *October 1957*[1]

The citizen has forsaken his identity.
He has become an onlooker instead of a participant,
an isolated soul amid millions of isolated souls.

But the child withdraws from this paradox.
It discovers its identity against all odds,
damaged and damaging, fouled and fooling,
in perpetual danger and incidental sunshine.
Edged towards the fringes of collective attention, the child survives, an emotional and 'unproductive' quantum.

Look, snow! A miraculous trick of the skies – a fleeting correction.

All at once, the child is Lord of the city. The child is everywhere, rediscovering the city whilst the city in turn rediscovers its children, if only for a while.

Yet what it needs is something more permanent than snow.
Something the city can absorb without losing its remaining identity, something not altogether different from the incidental things the child adapts to its imagination and vitality, something carefully shaped and judiciously placed where there is still some room: on innumerable formless islands left over by the road engineer and the demolition worker, on empty plots, on places better suited to the child than the public watering place.

In Amsterdam 150 such places have been laid out. They became indications for play, tools for the imagination. They constitute a conscious attempt to give the child's movement a visual meaning in the image of the city. They are places where energy condenses and disperses, indications for increased community.

If childhood is a journey, let us see to it that the child does not travel by night.

The artist, essential ally of the child, is there to lessen the conflict.
He too is pushed back to the periphery of collective attention.
His function is still too decorative (he is abused and misuses himself).
His task is to bring about a plastic order.
He belongs in the centre.

Photo Violette Cornelius

After a heavy snowstorm

Brief for a 12-day student project – Washington University, St Louis, 1961[1]

Zeedijk playground in the snow Photo Ed van der Elsken

You all know what happens after a heavy snowstorm. The Child takes over – he is temporarily Lord of the City. You see him darting in every direction collecting snow off frozen automobiles. A great trick of the skies, this, a temporary correction for the benefit of the neglected child. It is up to you now to conceive of something for the child more permanent than snow – if less abundant, something quite unlike snow in that it provokes child movement without impeding other essential kinds of urban movement.

It must be conceived furthermore not as an isolated thing or isolated set of things, but as something which can be repeated at suitable places in the city. The city must be able to absorb it both aesthetically and physically; it must become part of the city's everyday fabric.

It must be elementary in that it must be respond to the child's elementary inclinations and movements (the latter does not completely cover the former) and activate his imagination. It must be able to survive the impact of city live: faulty construction, choice of materials or design inevitably go hand in hand with unnecessary danger. What you make should in the first place be attractive to children of four to eight years old. You are free as to your choice of materials. You are not bound to a particular site.

Wheels or no wheels, man is essentially a pedestrian

Statement published in Team 10 Primer, 1962[1]

As long as cities exclude particular kinds of motion that belong inseparably to urban life, their human validity – they have no other – will remain partial.

The time has come to orchestrate all the motions that make a city a city. It is somehow in the nature of cities in general and of traffic in particular to suppress certain kinds of motion which, if less insistent, are certainly no less fundamental to the idea city.

Cities today demonstrate an appallingly limited range of movement. Their rhythm is as vehement as it is monotonous.

A city, if it is really a city, has a very compound rhythm based on many kinds of movement, human, mechanical and natural. The first is paradoxically suppressed, the second tyrannically emphasised, the third inadequately expressed.

Wheels or no wheels, man is essentially a pedestrian. Whether he really wants to be, will again become, or no longer wants to be is quite arbitrary. He is! 'Side' walk indeed means just what it is! To cater for the pedestrian means to cater for the child. A city which overlooks the child's presence is a poor place. Its movement will be incomplete and oppressive. The child cannot rediscover the city unless the city rediscovers the child.

Van Boetzelaerstraat, Amsterdam, before and after the execution of Van Eyck's design in 1964.

On the design of play equipment and the arrangement of playgrounds

Translation of a lecture given at Marcanti, Amsterdam, 1962[1]

It hard to put into words what I have learnt to recognise as appropriate while designing almost 400 playgrounds in cooperation with other parties. I am aware that there is a controversy regarding the merits of 'public playgrounds' and 'enclosed playgardens'. The question of the play equipment and the architecture of play facilities is linked to this.

In a big city like Amsterdam one can only find a limited number of places that are big enough to set up an enclosed playground. These places have all been used. However, the need for places where children can play has not yet been satisfied. Years ago it was therefore our opinion that to correct this shortcoming inherent to the city we still had to find places suitable for children to play. Places that are still free and have no great commercial value. A series of forgotten spots, left over because a road takes a particular route, triangular squares lying there lifelessly. We thought we could breathe new life into them by putting a few objects there as street furniture, as an integrating constituent of the city, to which we now gave this special purpose. It turned into a long series, and these playgrounds are an essential complement to the play-gardens. In my opinion there is no need for controversy between open playgrounds and enclosed play-gardens, because I see the first as a complement to the second.

But in Amsterdam we are now in the same position as fifteen years ago: we have used up all the places in the inner city that might have been used for playgrounds. Between the playgrounds we have created a more finely-meshed network. It might be said that there is no more to be done. But despite the opposition that is to be expected, I would like to go further: I want to try to make the network even denser, by once again combing the city, this time in search of places that are just big enough for one single play apparatus. If I am able to find 500 such places, that would give us, between every two playgardens, five or six public playgrounds and in between them even more places with one or two play apparatus. The opportunity for the child to discover its own movement is an integral part of the city; the city is also a playground. The child uses everything there, everything built, everything it can crawl through and climb over. Things children are not actually allowed to play with, but with which they can play very well. I would not like to remove this opportunity altogether, nor is it possible to do so. A child will mirror itself in the city. This is inevitable, but of course leads to conflict. There is also danger everywhere and at all times. The child discovers things and appropriates them. A lamp-post is requisitioned as a play apparatus. Some things cannot cope with it. By creating things on a close-knit network throughout the city, things of which a child can say, 'That's mine,' one can localise the danger. Despite the fact that the playgrounds are very close to traffic, just a few metres from lorries, it is still safer to create them than not to. Rubbish thereby also concentrates in particular places and becomes more easily manageable. When the child plays in particular places, we know where the rubbish is and then we can clean it up.

So, our idea is to create an even finer network of single play apparatuses which the city must be able to absorb. Just as one places a bench because one wants to sit, a lamp-post because one wants to light the street, a newsstand because one wants to buy newspapers, I am putting a playdome there because children want to play.

The special thing about these playgrounds is that they do not belong exclusively to children. The city simply continues in these places, with all the dangers and disadvantages that go with it, and they are not closed off. They are meeting places, for children too, but when the child has gone to bed it's just an ordinary street again. Since there is too little parking space, they are even used for that. This is a shortcoming, but unavoidable, because the city is necessarily chaotic, however much architects and urban planners want to put everything in order. Functions conflict with each other and this may mean, to give one example, that it is not possible for children to do somersaults. So now we have, not the child misappropriating the lamp-post, but the adult misappropriating the child's play-space. The city is not a paradise, but a place of violence, full of conflicts. These things are rooted in human blood.

The playground is for everyone. At night, any play apparatus set up there becomes something different. When someone beats their rugs on it, a somersault frame is no longer a somersault frame. During the break at a girl's school, a climbing arch may provide seats for 30 girls from 15 to 17 years old, all eating their sandwiches. It has then become an aluminium hill. If one throws a tarpaulin over it, it becomes a tent. Use can also lead to misuse, and less pleasant things can happen; sometimes the big ones chase the little ones away, sometimes the whole thing is smashed.

The public playground has to be attractive as a meeting place for everyone, including adults, if its existence is to be justified. It also has to be acceptable to the city even without the movement of the child. The city has to be able to absorb the forms. For the sake of urban meaning the play apparatus have to be arranged very meticulously with regard to each other and their immediate surroundings. One must observe well the place where one wants to make a playground: where are the windows, which way do people walk, where are the front doors, can the sand from a sandpit blow inside, etc. After a few years one has gained some experience in this. You are grafting something new onto something that already exists, and if you put the wrong thing in your syringe the existing thing will react immediately. This also applies to an enclosed play-garden, but an error there does not have irrevocable consequences. It is difficult to make a play apparatus in such a way that it does not appear as an alien element in the city, and that it is acceptable in the long term. The violence of the city immediately unmasks any mistake. But the city also rewards what is meaningful, whether it was deliberate or not. There can be unexpected results, like a hill full of girls, and that is particularly nice. The child has discovered this possibility for itself, and this is a reward, a bonus for the designer.

It is my opinion that the play apparatus should be elementary in form in the sense that they satisfy movements that the child discovers anyway. Contrived ideas may be fun at a fair, which is after all temporary, but in a city we have to create the opportunity for what the child already does: tumbling, climbing, jumping. The child likes leapfrogging, so we make short pillars for that purpose. We cannot outstrip the child, we just imitate it. Fifteen years ago we still thought we had to create complicated things for play. Now we set up a simple tumbling frame, and we see the children somersaulting round it like flywheels while talking at the same time! It's a fine thing a human flywheel right there on the street. The tumbling child belongs in the city scene, just like herring carts.

My opinion is that a lot of the playground equipment you find in the catalogue is not suitable for public space, not aesthetically, and because it is not real enough. Playground equipment has to be real, just as a telephone box is real because you can phone in it and a bench is real because you can sit on it. An aluminium elephant is not real, since an elephant is meant to move, and as an object in the street it is unnatural. A child can make anything out of a simple form. If a play apparatus represents an animal from the start, the form dictates its construction so much that it puts an end to pure play. There are rods you can't stand on, sharp corners into

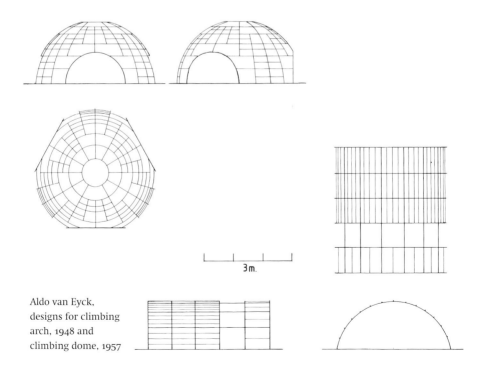

Aldo van Eyck, designs for climbing arch, 1948 and climbing dome, 1957

which your hand vanishes. An aluminium giraffe stands there odd and bored, even in a playgarden. The elementary archetypes such as the dome, igloo and arch are perfectly satisfactory because a child can sit on or under them, and can discover all sorts of things in them.

Catalogues sometimes contain some quite complicated things. There is no art in sitting down at a table and drawing all sorts of constructions. But in the course of these fifteen years we may have developed about thirty play apparatus that fit the bill well.

If we look at all the positive and negative things in the public playground, it appears that this sort of place excludes a lot of possibilities. There is no supervision there. This should not actually be necessary, since, after all, many eyes are watching and many feel they share the responsibility. In some countries this is the case, but not in ours. Unfortunately it happens all too rarely that the people in a neighbourhood help keep a sandpit or a public play area clean. You may even see ladies in fur coats letting their dogs roam there! By contrast, in the Jordaan,[2] where the population is very homogeneous, people have accepted the playground on Palmgracht as their collective property and work together to keep it clean.

Now, when I start talking about enclosed play-gardens, some of you may think I am going to say I don't understand why there has to be a fence. But that's not what I want to say at all. I am convinced that the play-garden is, or can be, essentially positive. It can be enclosed in order to guarantee from the inside the right seclusion, security, intimacy and shelter. In such cases the aim is to create an 'interior', and that is possible, even though the sky is the ceiling. But this sort of interiour is hard to achieve with a fence. A fence has the effect of keeping people away. Plants or walls are more suitable for making the playground a space of one's own. You cannot make an 'outdoor room' from a public playground, but you can from an enclosed playgarden. So the enclosure is not to keep anyone out, but for the purposes of spatiality, and to increase the possibility of proper supervision. Whether the supervision is actually good depends on the person responsible for it. Does he stay sitting in his hut or, as an adult worker, does he actively lead and stimulate?

What I am actually concerned about is whether the enclosure is justified by a greater opportunity for play inside the garden, whether in other words you succeed in making more of your play-garden, as a small world in the midst of the large. The enclosure of this particular place must bring with it an extension, intensification and enrichment of the play potential. For example, in an enclosed garden one can set up building materials and as adult occupy oneself with a group of children undisturbed. No one else can make improper use of the situation. I do not find the installation of mobile play apparatus sufficient reason for putting up a fence. I see the enclosure as a challenge to do things in the playground which one cannot do on the street. The possibilities there have been more or less exhausted, but in a playground they are almost unlimited, and I do not believe they have already been sufficiently exploited everywhere.

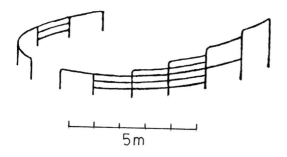

Aldo van Eyck, designs for play equipment: somersault frames, sandpits and climbing mountains
Photos by Aldo van Eyck

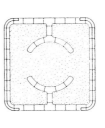

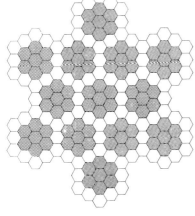
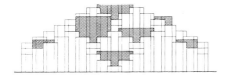

Jacob Thijsseplein
playground, 1950

Mendes da Costahof
playground, 1960

Nieuwmarkt
playground, 1968

Photo Pieter Boersma

I am a vehement opponent of current urban planning, which very much hinders spatial boundaries. Everything is made open; planners suffer from a mania for openness. Space has become so continuous that no spaces can be formed. There is one large continuous outside. In this big space there are blocks, arranged well or not, and it is in this emptiness that we move around and seek the seclusion we remember from the old city. There is also something inaccessible about the blocks themselves, and we are no longer 'received' by urban squares. We arrive abruptly at the front door, the division between the inhospitable emptiness and the inaccessible blocks. It is difficult to create an enclosed space between them. One can hardly build a wall or anything like that. It would be easier if urban planners had another concept in mind, if one created a series of enclosed, recognisable, large and small spaces: living room, street, square, indoor and outdoor spaces, instead of voids that wash around masses. The enclosed space would then already exist and all we would have to do would be to close it off. But we have to create these spaces ourselves. The fence is cold and bare, and the children play in a cage. This is not your fault. That's the way society works. The site is divided up: a rectangle for a playground, a road there, a building here. From an urban planning point of view the procedure is poor. It is difficult to create an enclosed urban space in this emptiness, not only a place where things stand, but one where a child feels at home, which it recognises as a small world amidst the big one. That is why it is so important to bring in a good designer who helps create the right environment. The atmosphere is decisive to the success of a play-garden. The designer cannot create this atmosphere only by himself, the leaders in the playground must also help to do so. But what he can do is make sure the equipment does not get in the way.

I hope I have told you a few things that differ a little from what you hear so often.

Now a very essential point. The public playground the way we make it is actually a gift from the authorities to the neighbourhood or district. This is on the one hand a fine thing, but on the other it's a pity, because in this case no justice is done to personal initiative. Here in the Netherlands there is very little opportunity to do anything on one's own initiative. It is limited to the window-sill.

In Switzerland people behave in the street as they do in their living rooms, which is a delight for the urban planner and architect, because everything is maintained by the people themselves and stays attractive. Though it does make life a little dull.

In London the people embellish the city themselves, by putting a big flowerpot out on the street, for example. People walk around it and children don't tip it over.

It is understandable that in a playgarden one wants to protect what one has made oneself by enclosing and shutting it off. For that matter, the things one makes oneself do not have to be so splendid and sound as what one receives as a present. But in fact I believe in most cases they *will* be good. So, by developing one's own initiatives, by building oneself, one ends up with a playground that accords with one's own views. You make your own mistakes and judge them yourself.

In the city one always wants everything to go increasingly along well-smoothed paths. Urban planners are scared to death of a gap or a hole. But Weesperstraat, once it was demolished, became one big play-area which not even the finest playground can match.[3] There is an incredibly big wall, which the children can daub on as much as they like. The architect feels inclined to smooth everything out. People are afraid of the unforeseen, afraid of the danger lurking around the corner, afraid of spontaneity. People do not want to accept that the city is and should be chaotic.

I read the following somewhere: 'when it's good weather play outside and when it's bad play inside'. It sounds practical, but psychologically speaking it is a limited view. If a child does not want to stay inside when it's bad weather, but has to stay inside, it remains bad weather. But if you can enjoy yourself in the playground even when it's raining, then it's no longer bad weather. And anyway, we call rain bad weather here because it rains so much. In some other countries they call it good weather. Our cities are not adapted to rain. Where there are arcades, it's pleasant to shop. In the same way, a playground can still be appealing when it rains if there's a covered play-area. That costs money, of course, but a covered play-area can in part be linked to the enclosure, so that a light construction is sufficient. On the other hand, the club building has to be attractive when it's 'good' weather too, and that is possible in a room with the right degree of openness, with a good transition from outside to inside (terraces). I find it an unnecessary restriction that a child has to play when it's good weather and do handicrafts when it's bad. And then there's snow, which is all at once good because it's a gift from heaven for the children.

Here too I again see a challenge to your enclosure. I am against putting a building inside a fence. First the fence to fend one off, and then a block that's closed too. It's better to erect the building on the public road.

The Netherlands is a flat country, but that does not make it absolutely necessary to act in a two-dimensional manner. Why would we spend twenty thousand guilders to make something utterly and totally flat? It has happened that I wanted to put some hills on one of these flat sites, but that costs money too. The ground can be banked up for dykes and bridges, so surely it can be done for children too? A small difference in height, of 1 to 1.5 metres, is sufficient to break up a large space into smaller spaces. If you stand on top of a bank 1.5 metres high, the world suddenly becomes very different. I do however understand that in a playground like that, supervision becomes a little more difficult. But we are introducing the miracle of a slope, of a valley and a hill. In this way we are anchoring our playground much more in the ground as a 'place'. A dyke is much more sculptural than a fence, in any case.

There are dozens of things like this to think up. If we create a playground well, we create a world in which man rediscovers what is essential, in which the city rediscovers the child. We must not ask the child to discover the city, without at the same time wanting the city to rediscover the child.

My intention with these words was to make a contribution, to reintroduce the child as an essential constituent of the city.

5
Art and Architecture in the fifties

Introduction to chapter 5

After his involvement in Cobra Aldo van Eyck became increasingly occupied by professional activities. He played a prominent role in the concept of the new village of Nagele, a joint project by 'de 8', and embarked on his project for the Amsterdam municipal Orphanage. But these occupations did not prevent him from continuing to foster a keen interest in the development of the arts. The museums and art galleries of Amsterdam offered plenty of opportunity for this. Especially the *Stedelijk Museum*,[1] which had been headed by Willem Sandberg since 1945, pursued a dynamic, outspokenly progressive exhibition policy. Sandberg organized comprehensive retrospectives on the great modern masters, from Picasso and Matisse to Mondrian and Miró, and at the same time endeavoured to reveal contemporary developments which he recognized as a continuation of the avant-garde. Besides the flamboyant outpourings of Cobra he repeatedly showed the abstract work of the *Vrij Beelden* and *Creatie* groups. And as he also aspired to introduce the spirit of modern art into daily life, he regularly inserted exhibitions on architecture, interior design and applied art. In due course he made the *Stedelijk Museum* into an internationally reputed centre of modern art.[2]

But Sandberg's preferential treatment of modern art was a thorn in the flesh of traditionally-minded people, the conservative artists as well as their public, and met with sharp criticism in the press. In order to counter this reaction the Dutch moderns joined forces in the *Liga Nieuw Beelden* (League of New Plasticism), an association of architects, artists, typographers and designers. Founded in 1955, this League aimed to 'prove experimentally the value of the new ideas on art and society' by organizing 'demonstrative exhibitions'[3] – an initiative that was warmly welcomed by Sandberg. In practice, most exhibitions set up by the League were tentative demonstrations of different forms of cooperation between architecture and art.

For Aldo van Eyck these exhibitions were occasions to restate and specify the ideas he had already advanced in the context of the Bridgwater CIAM Congress (see chapter 2). He reaffirmed his conviction that the individual arts would have to pass through a lengthy autonomous development before cooperation could be considered. Consistent with this view he continued, for his part, to reflect on the implications of the new consciousness for architecture and urban planning. In a short article published alongside to his Slotermeer housing project for the elderly he expressed some insights into the fundamental relationship between inside and outside he had gained in the course of the design process.

In 1957 an exhibition on the Brazilian garden designer Burle Marx offered him the occasion to develop some ideas on 'garden and landscape art'. Remarkably, he assigned plants and trees the right to an autonomous existence, considering them as organisms that should be allowed to contribute in their own right to the structure of the human environment.

The same year an exhibition on Paul Klee gave him the opportunity to present Carola Giedion-Welcker to the Amsterdam public. C.W. was invited to give a lecture and Van Eyck, who was asked to introduce her, delivered a flamboyant homage, affirming their common belief in the new reality, a 'world of metamorphosis' where 'all men are each man and each man all men, man is leaf and leaf is rock and rock is feather'.

In 1958, to celebrate Rietveld's 70th birthday, Van Eyck published two striking articles, a comprehensive one ('The Ball rebounds') in the jubilee issue of *Forum* (1958, no. 3) and a condensed one ('Squares with a smile') in *De Groene Amsterdammer*, a weekly newspaper. He expressed more specifically the appreciation he had already intimated at the 1951 Milan Triennale, but not without punctuating it with some critical notes. However, the criticism he uttered on this occasion was mainly directed at the members of the Liga Nieuw Beelden, particularly the members of the former '8 en Opbouw' groups, which had been dissolved four months before. He concluded by reaffirming his belief in the new reality, this time propounding as its foundation the idea of relativity, 'the true myth of our time'.

After the Cobra period Van Eyck also came into contact with younger and differently orientated artists. He became friends with Carel Visser, a sculptor working with elementary forms that were both geometric and biomorphic. He expressed his admiration for the young artist's work in two short articles.

At the same time he fostered a warm sympathy for the very different work of the Dutch-American sculptor Shinkichi Tajiri, who continued his own idiosyncratic course after participating in Cobra. On the occasion of his 1960 exhibition at the Amsterdam Stedelijk Museum Van Eyck dwelled upon the meaning of his work in an article written in the form of a letter.

Van Eyck had a more ambivalent attitude to Joost Baljeu, a painter whose ambition was to resume the thread of De Stijl. In 1956 he conceived the plan to edit a review called *De Stijl Continued* and asked Van Eyck to collaborate with contributions on architecture. But as Baljeu turned out to envisage this continuation as something literal, almost academic, excluding the other half of the avant-garde spectrum, Van Eyck declined the proposal. Still, by 1958 Baljeu had persuaded a group of kindred spirits from different countries to embark on a new review with a similar objective, called *Structure*.[4] When this review was awarded the Sikkens Prize in 1962, Van Eyck, being the recipient of the previous prize, was asked to introduce the new prize winners – which he did in his own, rather critical way.

J.H. van den Broek simultaneously presenting the 1960 and 1961 Sikkens Prizes, the 1960 one to Constant Nieuwenhuys and Aldo van Eyck, the 1961 one to Aldo van Eyck and Joost van Roojen.

On the cooperation between the arts

Translation of an undated typescript, obviously written in 1955[1]

1 True art is always objectivity born out of the subject (individual or collective). So it is relative. It creates a relative objectivity. The artist creates reality – whether it be harmony, fear, or something else. Mondrian is a great expressionist!

2 As soon as art is incapable of doing this, the value of the generated object is based on a purely visual effect and is thus decorative in the narrowest sense of the word. (The motifs of primitive societies appear to be decorative, but their strength derives from the fact that they are born out of the subject, a collective, socio-religious subject.)

3 Free art will always arise more strongly out of the individual subject, will become increasingly autonomous. The consequence is that it will always make greater demands on the artistry and the receptiveness necessary to experience the reality that has been created.

4 Although the value of a building, considering its direct utility, can be considerable even when, as in most cases, it does not comply with point 1, this is not the case in painting and sculpture. They have an exclusively emotional function. That is why it is only meaningful for them to participate in architecture and town planning (i.e. in the realm of generality) when their true function is respected, and when this exclusively emotional role can be complied with. They have no architectonic task to fulfil. Carried out within the framework of architecture but conceived in accordance with the essence of their art, their work can sometimes assume a substantial autonomous significance. (For example, De Stijl and Guernica, but we need not concern ourselves with these exceptions here). In essence, architecture is engaged in independently broadening its own plastic potential (the same goes for painting, etc.). This development is impeded by their combination.
The urge felt by painters and sculptors to come out of their studios is understandable in human (and economic) terms. But they thereby misunderstand their true social-psychological function, their own art, and architecture. Most painters, when they ask for walls, do not know what painting means. The same applies to architects who offer walls.

5   Since architecture fulfils both an emotional and a material function (though they can never be separated), and painting and sculpture only an emotional one, the last two will in any case have to maintain their autonomous significance in the framework of architecture. They can only really come together by letting go each other in their own essence and function.

6   When the arts come to play together it is not right to allot colour to the painter, plasticity to the sculptor and space to the architect as if they were their specific domains. Colour, plasticity and space are characteristic of all three. It goes without saying that the spatial use of colour lies within the domain of architecture. Space is not a medium for the architect, but in the best case it is a result. The painter has to take care of colour in architecture no more than the architect has to take care of the tectonics of a painting.

7   It is in the nature of technology (material progress) that it misuses the creative artist, even the industrial designer! By creative artist I also mean (and most specifically) someone like a true physicist. (After all, the theory of relativity signifies primarily a subjectification, and thus runs parallel with the development of contemporary art).

8   It is incorrect to think that free art should turn away from the subject in accordance with the continued mechanisation of existence. The opposite is true. The subjectification of art and science will develop as the standardisation of life develops. For the sake of our psychological equilibrium, art and technology apparently develop in inverse proportion. That's their natural and beneficial proportion.

Painters, sculptors and architects, remain working on the same thing in your own field. Only in this way shall we meet each other in the forum of human feeling – on the market square of civilisation.

On inside and outside space

Translation of 'Over binnen- en buitenruimte', article published in Forum, *April 1956*[1]

Like all things in architecture, openness and enclosure only matter if they can assist man in his alternating inclination towards inside and outside.

We do not exclusively breathe in, nor do we exclusively breathe out. That is why it would be so gratifying if the relationship between outside space and inside space, between individual and common space inside and outside, between open and closed (inwards and outwards) were to become the built mirror of human nature, so that man may recognize himself in its reflection. These are realities of form because they are mental realities. They are, moreover, not polar but ambivalent realities.

The dwelling and its extension outwards, the city and its extension inwards – that's our task! After all, the inside spaces and the outside spaces constitute simultaneously the interior and the exterior in which we live.

The inhabitants of the new suburbs need the city as the interior of the community just as much as people in Mediterranean countries need the piazzas and market halls where they come together daily.

Abstract and academic 'parcelling' – a hideous term for a dismal activity – of ground plans and residential areas has become a pernicious habit, which must be broken before this fat land builds itself into a state of uninhabitability.

Not the swift pencil but only the heart can help here. And who, I ask, is going to prove that imagination no longer hides in the heart?

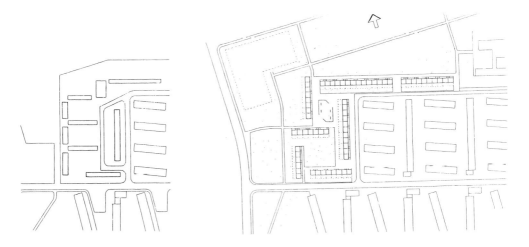

Aldo van Eyck and Jan Rietveld, housing for the elderly, Slotermeer, 1951–1954.
Left: the site plan of Public Works, right: the site plan designed and executed by the architects.

Photos Violette Cornelius

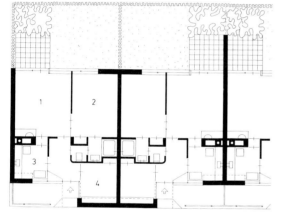

Aldo van Eyck and Jan Rietveld, housing for the elderly, Slotermeer, 1951–1954.
Left: the site plan of Public Works, right: the site plan designed and executed by the architects.

Photo Vincent Ligtelijn

On garden and landscape art

Translation of 'Over tuin- en landschapskunst',
undated manuscript of a lecture, probably given in 1957[1]

I can imagine that one might choose to do garden or landscape design for love of the material with which one has to work. For love of the soil and what all sorts of cosmic influences draw out of this soil as if by a miracle. The gardening human: someone who approaches the secret of things by being with and caring for what grows, not because he has to live from the proceeds but as a sort of spiritual handiwork; someone who shares the plant's experiences of the sun and rain, someone who flies after the bee and the butterfly to fetch and carry from flower to flower everything essential for life. Comparable in some ways – though without much similarity – to the angler, though I don't know whether the angler loves the fish very much. But you know what I mean.

There are many who are very happy in this way, though they do not give a particular shape to that which flourishes due to their devotion. An irrevocable affinity with the plant as such, with no need to involve oneself any further – only to identify with it. Others are more concerned with the result, what they achieve by their labour – the border, the lawn, the garden. They see the plant also as a building element. They make their mark on what they do; they paint with plants as their material. The plants become more or less like the paint on the artist's palette. *This is the essential moment, but its essentialness makes it dangerous.* A building element is after all nothing in itself, the paint on the palette is not yet a 'colour', but the plant is already an *autonomous form*.

Art only arises when one is engaged with plants for the sake of an overall shape. Garden and landscape design – not to mention painting flowers (think of Japan) – is for this reason a fearsomely difficult art.

If the plant is too active, only present for its own sake, there is little question of shape because the artist is too passive.

If the artist is active at the expense of his material, if he works with plants as if they were paint on a palette, if he forces them into the boundaries of his autonomous forms, then a conflict will soon arise with the plant's autonomous right to existence. An example of this is Burle Marx. Examples of the first can be seen everywhere.

Nevertheless, the task of the garden and landscape designer is to give shape to the human environment with his own means. All the gradations discussed below have to be developed within this task as a whole.

To admire the plant from close-up as an autonomous phenomenon for its own sake. Something one comes across, encounters and for which one stands still (where does this happen?).

Roberto Burle Marx, garden of the Larragoiti Hospital, Rio de Janeiro, 1957
Photo Marcel Gautherot

Plants composed into a larger entity as part of the aggregate of what one experiences visually – shrubbery, flowerbed, garden.

Plants composed into a large entity in which one no longer or hardly experiences the environment outside. A piece of man-made nature in surroundings where there is no nature – the park.

Then the plant, the tree, the flower, the grass as essential constituents of the created human environment. Not in the way this now happens as a visual accompaniment or as a correction of street and building, to fill those surfaces that remain after the street, square and building have been given their place on the urban development plan; trees as a filler for the spaces between upright walls close together or far apart. Foliage to fill in the visual gaps between the housing blocks which the urban planner has arranged and which the architect has to provide with a ground plan afterwards.[2]

What we can see in our new residential neighbourhoods has as little to do with urban planning, architecture and garden design as they have to do with the people who live there. These are of course the worst victims. When it comes to the urban planner, the architect and the garden designer, it seems to me that the last is the worst victim. Stem, foliage, flower and grass are considered decoration; they decorate the city. What is your task? To tart up the human habitat? To provide upholstery? Fellows who are allowed to put in a few things where others have coloured-in small areas between street and building with green-coloured chalk, as if they were 'green notes'?

Trees always do well somewhere or other – a typical property of trees – because they are autonomously large and beautiful, even if they are badly positioned. Imagine: splendid buildings poorly grouped with badly positioned trees – or randomly positioned and random species – a paradise compared to Nieuw West![3] The trees there will have to compensate for *everything*, if not by their careful positioning then at least by their beneficial effect as such. Just imagine that no trees had *been able* to grow in Nieuw West!

The mixing of too many species in the setting of a single form leads to visual confusion in the urban scene where people are in motion. The character and colour of a particular species, applied in large numbers, can give a place a clear character. With regard to movement in the continuous space of a city it comes down to simplicity and clarity. In the places where one spends time the group of plants itself can be varied, i.e. designed more as an entity in its own right.

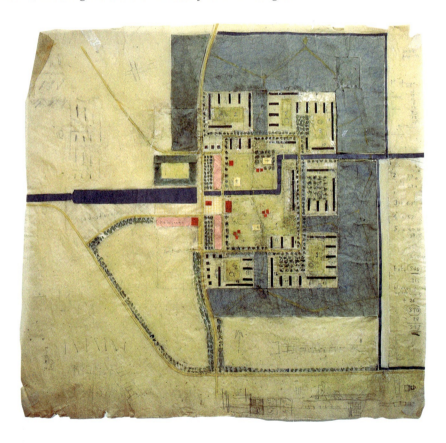

Project for Nagele, october 1953 by Aldo van Eyck.
My proposal to 'line' the communal interior space with red leaved trees was met with display by the team.
Nor was the proposed double row of trees along the ringroad ever planted. Such a tree bordered lane would have become a unifying intermedary. [A.van Eyck]

A tribute to Carola Giedion-Welcker

Speech delivered at the Amsterdam Stedelijk Museum on 8 March 1957[1]

This is going to be a very personal introduction. However, since I see no other way of arriving at the impersonal that lies beyond, I am afraid you'll have to put up with it. So here it goes:

C.W. (those that love Carola Giedion-Welcker call her so) salut!
Ordovico Viricordo – Anna was, Livia is, Plurabelle's to be.[2]

A lot has changed since we first met you – my wife and I – at the gallery Nord Sud in Zurich some time during 1942 and you oiled my hinges, first opened my window. The constituent creative products of the contemporary mind seem to have been brought out of their hiding place. Seem... for alas, what they really stand for has in the process of general acceptance been rolled out so thin as to become transparent, so diluted as to forfeit all taste.

   What we have got is a new dress... But where, I ask, is the body? A horrible masquerade. Surely, all the more tragic, since the new dress deceitfully suggests a new body; one that is missing. Again a 'façade'; and so soon. It's insufferable! The disease is ubiquitous. It has many names. In Holland, one is *'opdracht'*.[3] Legions of artists have crowded out of their ateliers into the market place – getting what they are clamouring for. Instead of producing they are reproducing, not nature this time, but something that through hazy eyes looks authentic and up to date. Yet, for those who still know better, this something is just Kandinsky with a dash of something else, e.g. Chagall or Léger; 'legall' or 'brasso'! And always Zadkine's perfume! Yes, Zadkine is what we have really got. The others, the real ones, are just his better pseudonyms! Think of it! In Holland 'the integration of the arts' is efficiently organized! You can commission such a product in either coloured lino, wood inlay, tiles, mosaic, coloured glass or one of those nice new-fangled techniques, on floor, ceiling, wall or anywhere at x florins/square metre or y% of the building sum.

   Now if it were possible to blame anybody we could do so and get it over. At any rate we cannot blame these jacks of all trades, for it is a principle of nature that jackals should subsist on what others have left. It would be unjust; the malaise is there, and we're in the boat, whether we like it or not. In the ark, if you will, parrot jack and all. And yet there is no reason to be downcast. There are one or two lighthouses still. It is their specific job to illuminate the real 'body', redefine it (whilst the imitation experts are waiting safely round the corner). Perhaps the great initiators are a little to blame themselves! At any rate the speed, intensity and thoroughness with which they tore down stifling barriers – for this is what they have done – is indeed bewildering (those that came after failed to keep up with what had already been

C.W. with James Joyce in Luzern, 1935 Photo Sigfried Giedion

done and soon ran out of breath). Yes, they tore down the barriers all right – the pioneers, the whole and holy lot – those between outer and inner reality, between object and subject, mass and space, between head, heart and abdomen; between what can be ascertained by the limited senses and that vaster reality only imagination can grasp, which transcends all barriers of space, time and matter, since these have become inextricably one.

Science has cast its determinist patina aside. The tic-tac metronomic contraption with god the father busy at the controls has run out of oil – is ready for the junk heap after a good 2000 years. From Cézanne and Seurat to Rimbaud and Bakunin. From Einstein and Bergson to Klee and Apollinaire. From Brancusi and Mondrian to Joyce and Schönberg; they among many others have left us with an expanded universe, have succeeded in detecting its rhythm, tracing its outline. Until we learn to find our way about in it, until we do so with grace benefitting from the vast metamorphosis of the spirit implied, its expanse will remain a horror vacui.

This brings me to Carola Giedion and Klee. Behind these two I shall keep in mind, if only for my own benefit, the titanic figures of James Joyce and Constantin Brancusi. Carola Giedion is one of those who have never approached the contemporary transformation of the spirit from without. Nor has there ever been anything retrospective in her approach. Never a trace of posthumous approbation. For her the death of an artist-friend – and there have been many indeed (of those who initiated the Great Riot only a handful are left) – has meant the loss of a chunk of herself. She belongs to their spiritual family, they to hers. She has loved them and understood them as brothers. Her Doldertal house in Zurich has been a stronghold surely enough. A refuge for the noblemen of the spirit in an alien world. Joyce, that great nomad, would settle down in her garden time and again and soothe his sad sad eyes. Ernst would arrive as if from nowhere without notice and usually utterly destitute. Arp came and went again and again. Schwitters, Van Doesburg, Le Corbusier, Léger, Tzara. Eluard and others, too many to mention, did the same. I never 'met' anybody there – I just came across them. It is from 'Doldertal' that I was 'sent' to Paris with a trunk full of coffee, tobacco and cognac for Brancusi shortly after armistice. I remember how the lock burst before I could even open it with due ceremony and the entire contents avalanched onto the ground at the base of the great stone fish. And, by the way, I wish you could have seen Brancusi unveiling his gleaming bird and fish. He really unveiled the timeless mystery and splendour of heaven and ocean – and seemed as amazed at the repeated sight as you would have been, gathering from

Constantin Brancusi,
Portrait of James Joyce,
1929
Carton and metal,
diameter 76 cm

the expression on his face. Let us hope that in Tîrgu Jiu his great column is still scratching laughter from the clouds.[4]

Carola Giedion never envisages time as a straight line. Eternity is no arithmetical process to her. She knows, as do the artists she is concerned with most – and Klee is certainly one of them – that change and permanence are one in time and space. She possesses something of the awareness of pre-speculative man for whom each star and each stone is a spirit; a 'thou', never an 'it'. For her, a myth is as much a concrete quantum as a milligram or millimetre. Contemporary artists have set eternity in motion. Voilà the grand old truth! The great top is spinning once more. Aeons can be measured by myths alone. Only irrelevancies pair into polarities. So let's rejoice, for there is plenty of room for evil in cyclocosm!

The vast preconscious world Klee knew so well – not through a keyhole but through actual experience – is also the world of metamorphosis. Klee went backstage jotting down what he experienced en route. Part of his vast sketchbook is now upstairs. I am convinced that the transformation of our time points towards transformation – all engulfing transformation – as first principle of reality. In such dominions all men are each man and each man all men, man is leaf and leaf is rock and rock is feather. Liffey and Irrawaddy are one and the same river. And thus there is nothing that stands between Anna Livia Plurabelle and Brancusi's fish and bird, between these and Mondrian's universe. They are the real anti-'absolute' absolutes, they contain all and exclude nothing.

Carola Giedion possessing as she does *'juste ce qu'il faut de souterrain entre le vin et la vie'*[5] has written a great deal about the creative adventure in which she participated. For her the artists she knew were windows that open onto unknown continents of the mind. Her work has not yet been collected, a fact both tiresome and sympathetic, for she dislikes the idea of burying what is essentially kaleidoscopic in a bulky volume. Her early essays on *'die Funktion der Sprache in der heutigen Dichtung'* and on Joyce can be found in *Transition*[6] and in *Der Neuen Schweizerschen Rundschau*. These belong to the first enquiries into the perplexities of word alchemy, the word-world of contemporary poetry, the primordial mutterings of Mute and Jute. The same counts for *Die Neue Realität bei Guillaume Apollinaire* published in Switzerland. A book that will throw you over, I am sure, is her *Poètes a L'écart, Anthologie der Abseitigen*. In it those poets have been brought together who lived and wrote on the outer periphery of official attention: Alfred Jarry, Charles Cros, Germain Nouveau, Paul Sheerbart – Jarry's teutonic counterpart – the German expressionists Jacob von Hoddis, August Stramm, Otto zur Linden, Lichtenstein, Hugo Ball. Hans Arp and Schwitters. And then the astounding poems by Kandinsky. Klee, Picasso, Van Doesburg and Rousseau, le Douanier. *Moderne Plastik, Elemente der Wirklichkeit, Masse und Auflockerung* first published in 1937, is a classic you probably all know. Her essays on Picasso, Klee, Schwitters, Jarry, Kandinsky, Arp, Brancusi, Delaunay, Mondrian, to mention just a few are unique.

But the time has come the walrus said etc., etc., etc.!⁷ So this is where I stop. Tonight Carola Giedion is going to let Klee do the job. It could have been one of the others, but it's Klee!

Ladies and Gentlemen,
plunge into the only reality that can save you, the reality Klee outlined in his particular way. The same reality the others have outlined in their way. C.W., I am your ambassador, you are Klee's. Klee is their's and they – all the others I have either mentioned or not – are the ambassadors of a reality unlimited not merely in time and space, for this would have no human meaning, but in essence. The full panorama.
ALLALIVIAL ALLALUVIAL.⁸
Now for the 'panaroma'.

Paul Klee, *Insula Dulcamara*, 1938, Oil on burlap

The ball rebounds

Translation of 'De bal kaatst terug', article published in Forum, *March 1958*[1]

'I am becoming primary, do you mind?' (Mondrian, 1910)[2]

Not so long ago I saw a little man racing after a tram so fast he looked as if he was trying to prove once again that the force of gravity existed no more. I'm told that this little man whose legs I could hardly make out, had just turned seventy – But what concern is this of ours?

In the beginning there was a Stijl idea – but now this genesis lies far behind us; it is forty-one calendar years since the opening words of *De Stijl* were beginning to conquer something of the meaning they implied.

'This periodical wants to be a contribution to the development of the new sense of beauty.'

Not an editor's note, not a foreword by way of justification for a new periodical, but a prodigious sentence – worthy indeed of marking the dawning of a new age. For those who are imbued with the full meaning of this 'new sense of beauty' will know that it includes the myth of our time.

And so we arrive at Rietveld with his plank-chair – just as prodigious as the sentence, not just because it made the sentence a reality at the same time but also because he managed to do this forty-one years ago (he probably did not know the actual sentence but he knew its sense.)

How do things stand with him, is he still standing? How do things stand with us, are we still standing?

Do 'we' still exist? And what about the genesis of the Stijl idea, that little sentence and the chair? Have they brought solace in the meantime? Has this salutary means had its proper effect, now that all those empty little boxes are being piled up on top of each other, dividing and intersecting, and all those red, white and blue labels have come unstuck and are being pasted onto everything vertical? – To some extent yes, of course, but I am addressing the question to those people who have been so busy with their boxes lately that one would think they had all been on a trip to the bulb-fields. (A rhetorical question, for I expect no answer.) It is not pleasant to have to say this, nor to hear it; not for the others and not for myself, nor for Rietveld, but what is currently being made – with a few exceptions – has nothing to do with the Stijl idea, or indeed with architecture at all.

In 1951 I wrote in *Forum*: '1920 and 1951 are not so far apart as many people seem to think; it may take ten times thirty years to attune a new sound to the reality of everyday life, and vice versa. It is almost incomprehensible that hardly discovered creative possibilities should be applied so soon by so many in a wholly casual manner, quite contrary to the spirit from which they originated. "The culture of particular form is approaching its end. The culture of determined relations has begun".

Gerrit Rietveld on his plank-chair in front of his workshop at Van Ostadelaan in Utrecht, 1918

If the general tendency at the present points in the opposite direction, disregarding Mondrian's words, this should nonetheless be regarded as a temporary deviation – the result of impatience, of a lack of insight. Yes, today even art is in a hurry. What we need at this time above all, is imagination, not fantasy. (Working magic with reality and performing tricks external to reality are entirely different occupations)'.[3]

   I myself would have objected if anyone had foretold that even De Stijl would be swallowed without chewing, within seven years. So now I call this haste the art of the shortest distance, with most of the participants out of breath in the comfort of a soft armchair; with Mondrian 'the candid mental defective from New York'[4] and Vincent safe and sound in our very own Dutch heaven (without Engelman however); with Appel's 'Questioning Children' in the town hall covered up by wall-paper for the past eleven years,[5] and Lucebert, winner of the Amsterdam poetry award, dressed as a king yet chased off the premises by force of truncheons before he could receive the award from the mayor;[6] with Rietveld seventy years old, and his chair forty-one; with De Stijl without style.

   How do you gentlemen feel about all this? A tiny bit embarrassed? – And what about the young generation? What do they think of this disgusting cultural bungling? What went wrong?

J.A. Brinkman and L.C. van der Vlugt, Van Nelle factory, Rotterdam, 1926–1930 Photo E.M. van Ojen

Interior of the 'bonbonnière', the rotunda on top of the building Photo E.M. van Ojen

J. Duiker and B. Bijvoet, Zonnestraal Sanatorium, Hilversum, 1926–1928

Zonnestraal's central dining hall

J.B. van Loghem, office building with warehouse, Amsterdam 1928

To him who still maintains a clear idea of a new world-view – whose vision has not been faded by the dimness of the lonely road he must travel – De Stijl is never far away, tangible yet intangible (but always vulnerable): an acute reality that seems to evaporate as soon as he thinks to have given it palpable shape, after having done his utmost. Faced with this shape even he may find himself staring after its content. But this is the fate of the strong. They, at any rate, will agree with Klee in saying: *'Wir fanden Teile dazu, aber noch nicht das Ganze. Wir haben noch nicht die letzte Kraft, denn uns trägt kein Volk.'*[7]

How to explain why this idea, in which art and life, form and essence come to unity, has been so cruelly violated? Even by those who 'propagated' the idea after its inception. For they too have done what only few are able to leave undone: to cut down that fundamental 'unity' into a series of artificial polarities. Is there to be no end to this Christian schizophrenia? In cyclocosme – within the great 'oneness' – there is even plenty of room for evil.[8]

It is indeed a highly paradoxical panorama that unfolds before Rietveld's eyes: a second foolish form-masquerade has appeared even before the first has left the stage. Poison and counter-poison prove to be equally venomous. But even Rietveld did not succeed in dissociating himself completely from this paradox – nor from the 'official entry' of De Stijl.

Fate has willed that Duiker, Van der Vlugt and Van Loghem died young, leaving Rietveld and Van Eesteren with an enthusiastic but precariously grounded following. The bridge between this following and De Stijl thus lost three of its pillars (Oud and Van der Leck being unsteady ones). Theo van Doesburg died in 1931 – a leader whose driving force, prophetic insight, intelligence and art together were of such proportions that the dream of his life, prolonged by thirty years, looms often before my eyes, for I am convinced that we would now be in a different position. It is hardly surprising that Rietveld and Van Eesteren were unable to repair the bridge on their own. Indeed this was, constructively speaking, no longer possible. How this inner loneliness eventually also diverted Rietveld from the great starting points (Van Eesteren found 'new' possibilities in CIAM) I'll discuss later. Concerning the side-track – most fateful of all – onto which urban planning has been driven as a result of the analytical *Existenzminimum* mentality,[9] see my remarks on the city as interior of the community in *Forum* 1956, no. 4.[10]

There is no doubt about the earnestness of the following that was left (except the short-of-breath, who soon resigned from 'de 8 en Opbouw' in order to sell their insecurity elsewhere – the 'commission experts' of today). The purge that they considered necessary entailed more personal sacrifices on their part than one is capable of imagining today. Yet they were concerned with something different. Their – understandable – social conviction caused them, as architects, to put the cart before the horse. They have put their aspiration to social reform above architecture, thus inevitably making architecture as an art subservient to their rational way of thinking. From this thinking – which as a matter of course was also materialistic-idealistic – originated the *Nieuwe Zakelijkheid*.[11] But the *Nieuwe Zakelijkheid* represents just one segment of the architectural circle, because it spans just one segment of the human circle. They have set out to tune those tones in the scale of life that sounded false, and to eliminate those that did not belong. But something went wrong in the way they proceeded, because they eliminated far too many tones, and tuned all the others into an equal temperament. They forfeited their hearts to 'logic' (as if that is not the most illogical thing to do), and they made no bones about their distrust of art and the artist.

Yet this distrust had very little to do with the acuteness of the anti-art, the anti-culture of Dada. In fact, their attacks concerned matters in which they themselves proved deficient. So what was nihilism in Dada became negative in them! ('Dada ist ein Narrenspiel aus dem Nichts, in dem alle höhere Fragen verwickelt sind.'[12])

Yes indeed, that logical thinking! How different from Spinoza's 'clear knowledge': 'We call that clear knowledge which comes not from our being convinced by reasons, but from our feeling and enjoyment of the thing itself, and which surpasses the others by far.'[13] The reversal of the truth that was so desperately sought after was characteristic of many of those who surrendered to historical materialism when they should have known better – especially in the 1930s, when the direct influence of the 'inspired' socialists started to wane. (Social realism – which even the Nieuwe Zakelijkheid, although contrary in form, still has a smattering of – is one example.) They were never lacking in diligence. But the dilemma of their attitude was that they all too often countered the current lack of vision with another lack of vision. Their work has been laboriously achieved, it commands much respect, and has in any case been a help in the household. Apart from that, I cannot imagine that they concerned themselves with Kropotkin and Bakunin.

'The indifference of Dada has made the bourgeoisie condemn Dada as Bolshevist, and the Communists to condemn it as bourgeois. Dada laughs'. (Theo van Doesburg).[14]

Their arguments against bourgeois behaviour were raised from all too close – from the very next room as it were. The sound did indeed penetrate the thin partition wall but was too blurred to bother the busy fixers on the other side.

They have disregarded the humour of human disorder. With an earnestness characteristic of Puritan spirits, they have repudiated every shade, every subtlety, every curl (a case of twisted logic, for when Loos links ornament to crime he means something quite different than Oud, for whom the ornament was a substitute (!) for creative impotence.[15] Loos did not speak from a position of hygienic poverty, but from the understanding that any ornament whose symbolic value has evaporated looses its tension and because of this – and only this – it detracts from the meaning of the main form).

Even so, the remaining members of 'de 8 en Opbouw' were truly creatively engaged. I remember how, apart from Van Nelle and Zonnestraal, I delighted in Kloos' Rijnlands Lyceum when pictures of this beautiful building were published in *de 8 en*

J.P. Kloos, Rijnlands Lyceum, Wassenaar, 1939, with right wing added in 1952

Interior of the wedge-shaped hall

Opbouw.[16] Their social ideal was their drive – and what a drive! Let no one make the mistake of thinking that I now scorn them for the disillusion that sooner or later had to befall them too: for it was the social ideal, distorted in the course of its fulfilment, that let them down – not the other way round. The sadness this process has inflicted on almost every thinking creature – artist or not – is immeasurable, and in many cases determined the direction of the rest of their lives. But each reacted differently to this sadness, however harsh its blow had been. (Mayakovsky and several others decided to end their lives.)

As for the architects of 'de 8 en Opbouw': they left the 'room next-door' and moved in with the neighbours.[17] Oud continued BIMming, even on the Dam, as if there had been no war in the meantime. Is he, of all people, entitled to fly at Le Corbusier as he did?[18] Van Eesteren went underground as early as 1928 in Public Works in order to implement the four functions of La Sarraz. Stam went east in order 'to put his shoulders under the cart'. Kloos remained the healthy watchdog with the raised forefinger. Van den Broek is still busy with his prologue. Salomonson and Bodon remained dedicated to cosiness. Van Tijen became a sort of nomad. Karsten moved to another creative sector. And Merkelbach followed Van Eesteren for the sake of the larger overview, to promote the new architecture on a 'broad basis'. Only Elling really retired and made a few beautiful houses near Laren.

That's where Bakema came wandering in, going over to take up his rightful position next to Rietveld and Van Eesteren. He showed himself, physically, for what he was. With unfailing energy he set to work repairing the pillars supporting the bridge. He looked back and forward and saw a lot, though even he did not see the nuances. He is both near-sighted and far-sighted. He knows that I often disagree with what he says and makes, but that's beside the point here; – it's a question of nuances. I will put down my thoughts about this artist in a separate article some time, but not in the way Van Tijen recently did.[19]

But let me not halt at the edge of the ramp (which leads to a very low plane), but descend briefly with my former 'de 8 en Opbouw' colleagues into the depths. Here, art no longer hurts, the countless numbers who reside here stay safely out of range, and have made every target hazy. They can't be killed but perish of their own accord. My 'fellow travellers', what are we going to do about the disgusting climate in which architecture has ended up? I am not even referring now to the 'buildings' but to the working climate deliberately cultivated by these puny characters, which will soon embrace even the young stalwarts if we or they do nothing about it. There is only a handful of architects left – with or without *Architecture d'Aujourdhui* – behind the drawing board. By 'architects' I certainly don't mean all those trainees of the architectural academies, who are paid a few hundred guilders a month to make and look after the designs of others, while those others quietly proceed from one committee meeting to the next, picking the material and spiritual fruits of the work that they have had little or nothing to do with, and which they would moreover never have been capable of. Is this why the Society of Dutch Architects now requires an 'aesthetic capacity for architectural draughtsmen ... equivalent at least to the level of the architecture academies'? Is this the function of architectural education: to produce architects who are and yet sneakingly are not what they are (there is already talk now of trainee periods – oh, what indolent cunning!). What we need is plenty of small, good architect's offices, each with its own architect poring over his own drawing board, doing his own work. No architecture factories. No abuse of the concept of team work. But for the time being this is an ideal that only the young – those whose talents are being abused – can realize, in a joint effort. Why don't they just flatly refuse!

But in the meantime I have reached the very depths of my descent, here the architect has become one of most obscure figures of society. Here, human conscience has handed out its arms, being an architect has made way for creative dishonesty. Here, architectural criticism has simply become impossible because nobody is able or allowed to know the hows, whys or wherefores. From the cultural dilettante the architect already was, he has now degenerated into a cultural pretender: a trend-sniffer, an idealist if required; a designer if it makes no demands on him, someone who has moreover adopted the characteristics of the megalomaniac, just as he adopts everything. Sorry, now I am seeing visions: I see people – and I see them clearly – who record precisely the mediocre in man, in order to dish up that little that can be reaped from it for the sake of man's hapiness. They are fellows whose kidneys have grown round their hearts. They tap off the noxious substances, disinfect them and package them in the white boxes they have stolen from De Stijl. To them, life is the arresting of death. With their chromium-plated fingers, they bend the cycle of nature into a long, straight pipe, through which they will soon be sucked up into bliss. Fearful of real kitsch, they make mild kitsch, a curlicue on a bare trunk. They call this bleaching treatment culture. When they draw a rectangle it's a sentimental one that looks rounded. When they draw a circle, it's a sentimental one which looks like

Gerrit Rietveld, Schröder House, Prins Hendriklaan, Utrecht, 1924
Left: interior ca. 1980 Photo Fas Keuzekamp right: exterior ca. 1925 Photo E.A. van Blitz

a square. Right angles are made obtuse by adding some extra degrees. They dislike the oval because it has two foci, the days of Baroque are over, and they themselves are out of focus. And yet (the vision is fading) they like sunlight, music, psychology and typography. They even like Rietveld when this is required. (How on earth is it possible to turn back to Rietveld by such a muddled course!)

'Der Künstler tut nichts was anderen für schön halten, sondern nur was ihm notwendig ist.' (Arnold Schönberg, *Harmonielehre*)[20]

I admire Rietveld for his artistic genius, for the magnificent things he made in the days of De Stijl (Peter Smithson exclaimed, upon seeing the house on Prins Hendriklaan:[21] 'Gosh, it's terrific, it's canonical!'). For the way he forged with his own hands a new architectural language, a language which could have evolved into what Mondrian and Van Doesburg envisaged: a liberating human habitat, an environment shaped in such a way as to prevent it at least from causing frustration. I respect him, moreover, for the way in which he has stood his ground, with varying degrees of success, in the face of a growing group of admirers who adulate him for the fact that he possesses what they don't dare possess, and, like good neurotics, flatter in him what they suppress in themselves and try to destroy in others. When a true artist gives up aiming for 'beauty' as his ultimate goal, this is not absurd for only one reason: because the final result will be 'beautiful' anyway. But that does not give everyone who calls himself an artist the right to fall back on the non-beauty principle merely to justify every mediocre product (it is not beautiful, I can hear them say, yet it is human). There had to be someone to do what they failed to do. So they turned Rietveld into a legend, their own ingenious clown. And we all know the fate of the clown, figuratively speaking, the clown who personifies the tragedy of the audience-in-the-dark so fully that, while they roar with laughter (or not) at his antics, the figure under the spotlights is grotesque and solitary. On the international level Le Corbusier plays the same role, but consciously – too consciously.

Just think of it – that it was this same clown who said: 'for the new style that which all people have in common is more important than their differences'.[22] The universality of that statement is couched in its rhythm. The way the 'teamworkers', those fanatics of normalization and industry, explain the naked words is as banal as it is incorrect. But what they expect from Rietveld is in effect that very 'difference', something else, the bizarre, the improper. No one can comply with his own legend with impunity. And it seldom happens that the reason for the formation of a legend is entirely external to the person whom the legend concerns. The reason for the legend is also inherent in him. The ball rebounds.

When Jaffé presented his dissertation[23] Rietveld addressed a significant question to him – significant, I think, because it denied the very essence of De Stijl (and the value of Jaffé's study is that it has made the elusive quality of De Stijl – that which actually determined its aesthetic – more tangible). Rietveld challenged the importance of the philosophical background disclosed by Jaffé, and held the view that De Stijl only bore upon a new formal idiom. It is curious to see this poet among architects so impervious to the poetry of the movement to which he once belonged.

Rietveld's contact with Van Doesburg and Mondrian has not been very extensive. He always believed, for instance, that according to De Stijl 'material and form are the territory of sculpture, the light-reflecting surface of the wall the territory of the painter'.[24] But this is Rietveld speaking, not De Stijl. Anyway, he calls the painter, the sculptor and the architect the 'one-sidedly sensitive to colour, plasticity and space', who all register the same aggregate of visual reality but express it in one of the three sectors in accordance with their specific 'one-sided' sensitivity. I don't believe in this. On the contrary, colour, plasticity and space have their own meaning in all three arts and belong to all three domains. There can be no collaboration between the three arts until each artist has discovered for himself the specific meaning of colour, plasticity and space in his own creative field. But then things really start to get difficult! What is more, this 'meaning' changes as soon as it is approached in a piece of work – otherwise art would long ago have arrived at a definitive solution and hence would have ceased to exist. Therefore, dear Liga Nieuw Beelden,[25] no direct 'cooperation' (let alone 'integration') for the time being. Rietveld would say, 'just leave that to the Baroque of the distant future', and he is quite right. After all: first things first. This goes for all three. But for this to happen an intensive, indirect 'collaboration' is needed. (Brrrr, what a dismal word). The difference between a painter and an architect is by no means the same as the difference between colour sensitivity and space sensitivity, or between colour and space. The same goes for sculpture, in both directions. It would be all too simple otherwise.

(Riddle: what is the difference between the relation architecture-urbanism and the relation architect-urbanist?)

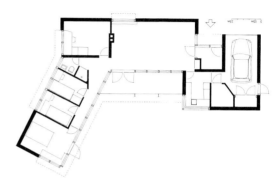

Gerrit Rietveld,
Martin Visser house,
Bergeijk, 1956
Photos Jan Versnel

However, since his Stijl period Rietveld has usually avoided active colour and has bounded his spaces with 'white'. Perhaps because he was one of the few to create space not so much by material boundaries but by the shaping of light. So it is just as well that, contrary to his own story, he did not abandon his 'light-reflecting walls' to the painter! In the presence of the ephemeral quality of light the tangibility of the wall as a wall recedes; the round column for instance, becomes a mere cylinder (in contrast to the physicality of Bakema's wall-support-slab anatomy). This often happens at the risk of the unstructural – on the verge of the insubstantial. Like Gabo's brother Pevsner, Rietveld recognises the presence of all colours in light itself, bringing the spectral phenomenon to the fore without colouring the reflecting surfaces. And yet,... a few years ago Rietveld built a house for someone with a passion for painting and graphic art, who had surrounded himself with works by Constant, Appel, Corneille and others. His artist friends left the country, and he moved to Bergeijk, where he had this house built.[26]

The ball was thrown, lovingly, to Rietveld. And see, in Bergeijk the desire for purity has actually overthrown purity. No painting can or may hang there. The occupants must make do with the aesthetics of the walls (which are mostly coloured in this case), and the paintings have had to be put in storage. Here architecture is arrogating something that is beyond its capacity, or indeed denies its existence: the meaning of pictorial expression.

Perhaps Rietveld was starting to concern himself with problems that are beyond my comprehension. But he often leaves me in the lurch, even where I *can* follow him – as in his basic living structure contained in a great architectonic gesture. In his later work, the spaces became somehow additive in relation to the whole. In themselves the spaces are relaxed and lucid, but together they no longer constitute a firm and clear idea. The relation between open and closed, wall and window, became loose. Window apertures in walls threaten to destroy those walls, tend to get stuck somewhere between hole and curtain wall. The roof is often a separate slab which projects equally on all sides, willingly following the exterior perimeter of the building-mass, and thus detracts from the expressive force of wall and volume – they both become passive. In Velp[27] a dark recessed ridge between roof and substructure has to solve the problem – but it cannot match the shadow of the roof-edge. Perhaps this is what Rietveld is actually looking for: to make a floating roof – but surely the roof does not float? Nor is the roof supported by columns. So it is a matter of *trompe-l'oeil*, to restore to the wall-planes some of the autonomy of which they were robbed by the tyranny of the projecting roof-slab.

This in fact explains why Rietveld is at his strongest when he is concerned with a single, separate space, whether or not its form is complex. Here the *periphery* of space constitutes the *matter* of its envelopment – I am deliberately putting it like this and not the other way round. Rietveld approaches the tangible, that which he must 'draw' and 'construct', by way of the intangible, by way of space and light. If the building task becomes structurally more complex and the number of individual spaces increases, this inevitably implies that the *matter* of the *periphery* of the different spaces turns into something which has its own plastic existence: as soon as one goes from one space to another – when one has to pass through the wall – there is after all physical contact. Rietveld's words 'material and form are the domain

Gerrit Rietveld
Stoop house,
Velp, 1951
Photo Jan Versnel

Gerrit Rietveld,
Sonsbeek Pavilion,
Arnhem, 1954
Photo Jan Versnel

of plasticity' thus gain a specific meaning in the light of his own work. But they also explain the absence of a tangible structure as well as the way he approaches the constructive aspect and his fondness for showing the abstract measure of one metre. People were enthusiastic about his Sonsbeek pavilion,[28] and rightly so. But in Venice[29] (a single large room) Rietveld showed splendidly what happens when he succeeds in approaching *matter* from the viewpoint of space; and not, as is usual, the other way round.

A small house in Loosdrecht[30] – I heard that Rietveld does not care for it very much! – shows what happens when he moreover succeeds in doing so from the viewpoint of exterior space, from that world of water and clouds. The treatment of the material, here conceived between interior and exterior, shows great power of expression. The curving wooden walls and the tall thatched roof are like a dome around the inhabitants. Outside is the great empty space. Bakema made some highly interesting comments on this house a long time ago in *de 8 en Opbouw*.[31] He saw what others could not yet discern.

Rietveld's work has seldom if ever been the subject of a critical study. He has been denied what every artist deserves. Uncritical adulation is foolish. People of Rietveld's stature are, by virtue of their very being, lonely. It is those who force themselves upon the lonely that cause their isolation. There was something that has kept him away from the major problems that co-determine architecture and urbanism. His anti-intellectualism certainly contributed to this. In the end this has proved to be a stumbling-block, for it is simply not enough to follow one's own nose all the time.

The greater the artistry, the greater has to be the capacity to control the proportionally wide range of feelings. In the creative process, no artist can rely only on his natural talent. To give shape to this sort of emotional matter not just once but a whole life long, it is in fact necessary that the intellect is involved in equal proportion. Using the imagination does not entail eliminating other faculties (Annie Romein-Verschoor's claim that artists have only 'limited intellects' is grotesque. Her story for A et A contained all the characteristics of the ideologically disillusioned intellectual.[32])

In Rietveld's case, his own nature and his own architecture kept each other in polar balance. This will be observed by anyone who sees or hears him and approaches his work receptively. Buffoonery and capriciousness alongside clarity and order. Sometimes – how could it be otherwise – the laughter forces its way through the seriousness; then his work gains a disarming subtlety, the prodigious becomes ordinary, the ordinary acquires a touch of wonder. This balance between the identity of the person and his work is a sensitive matter – it's *a priori* a personal matter, while architecture is *a priori* not so, or only in part. But this is a conflict that is by principle inherent in artistry and to the architect it is indeed a dilemma that must be accepted. In Rietveld's case this implies a sort of tightrope walk between the real and the unreal. Because all building are used – and as with all forms of human 'usage', they are also used up and abused. The resulting mutations pass over the subtleties which are so crucially important, they destroy them, at any rate materially. But not the idea. Behold the fate, but also the consolation of every true architect.

Still, I am convinced that Rietveld will fill me with delight again in Utrecht. He is an intimate artist. His poetry blossoms, as it were, from the security of his inner entourage. Whenever he is lured out of this warm haven into the harsh reality of the everyday world, he emerges as a benign, albeit slightly suspicious, figure. It is obvious that he would like to return as soon as possible. He has a little snake-in-the-grass with him! But surrounded by his own world, we will rediscover the greatness of the small-scale artist he is. The incessant flattery and suppressed criticism have made him vulnerable – and sometimes unscrupulous.

But I still have something I want to say about the others. For the Rietveld legend has got hold of me, too. (This weighs heavily on a critical essay – to shake off this burden completely is no mean task).

At the other end of the scale stands Van Tijen, for whom things were somewhat less complicated when he wrote that Sonsbeek 'was "built" with the means of our time, but without any refinement. No marble, no plate-glass was necessary here.' O dear, no marble!

A chameleon is a touching little animal full of surprises. But when an architect, who feels called to show his colours publicly when he senses the coming of a new colour, effectively changes colours *en plein public*, I start shivering. Van Tijen should by now be notorious for his continuously alternating rejection of and attraction to incongruous ideas. From sentence to sentence he extends his hand in order to promptly withdraw it. His praise of the ideas or work of others can only be evaluated after removing the last sentence of each paragraph, where he frenetically takes back what he just generously gave away. The one-one game he plays with Bakema is a game he has been playing for years. He will quickly lose count. I did a long time ago.[33]

To gain further insight into the twisted mental courses that are steered today in order to arrive at 'clarity', read and compare Van Tijen's *'Buitenbeentje'* (*Forum* 1953, no. 10) and *'Het bureau Van den Broek en Bakema'* (*Forum* 1957, no. 6). The following quotes illustrate the point I wish to make – they are relevant to the current situation – and that's what we are concerned with. 'When we saw those halls (of the Fokker Jet factory[34]) we all agreed that if we could use those possibilities for the benefit of our community life, we would be able, in spatial terms, to surpass Gothic.' I know I myself wanted to escape as soon as possible – but unfortunately there was no cathedral nearby! 'The Stijl exhibition in Amsterdam made a profound impression on me… One need only hold one of Van der Leck's paintings of 1917 next to the parcelling plans for Vlaardingen of 1950 to see how prophetic this manner of painting has indeed been for us.'!!! But there is worse to come. 'The shared horror of the Second World War has enormously deepened our insights into the essence of man and society.' Good heavens! What makes him think so?

Van Tijen never stops smiling at the phantoms that loom before him (unfortunately they are not only his spectres, so I shall name them): the intuitive, the instinctive, the personal, tradition and handicraft; expressionism, romanticism and classicism (the latter two fraternally united in vice, even though both of them appear to smile back alternatively), and yes! Form! But it is these very phantoms ('unphantomed' by understanding) that can free architecture from the real phantoms: the 'collective' bungling, the vegetarian mutterings about 'a viable environment for a modern democratic society', the arbitrariness of sloppy logic, the lack of true erudition. Do those who see all these phantoms think that once the architect has been divested of them – including the desire to handle the material in a craftsman-like manner and to arrive at a personal expression – they will be left with something liberating, communal, anonymous, ordinary, soundly functional and objective; with pre-fabrication and standardization; with something adopted to the 'basic needs' and socially acceptable, with team spirit?

All these nasty little clefts caused by that remorseless split-mania have to be overcome. Only the steadiness of a mechanistic-causal philosophy has managed to smash up the *unity* into a set of forced alternatives, into frustrating polarities, coldly coupled: object-subject, individual-collective, whole-part, mass-space, mind-body, good-evil and – because it concerns sinful man it is a triad – head, heart and abdomen. They are all ambivalent phenomena.

When Van Eesteren invited me, just after the war, to attend an '8 en Opbouw' meeting at Van Nelle,[35] I remember how Van Tijen had to pause when a train came past, which he seized as an opportunity to criticize Van der Vlugt for the excessive openness of his architecture, how at that same moment a bird flew in, and how that bird – a guest like me – helped me to speak up there and then. I later wrote down

M.J. Granpré Molière, P. Verhagen and A. Kok, Vreewijk Garden Village, Rotterdam, 1916–1919

my thoughts in *Forum* (1949, no. 2/3), under the title *Wij ontdekken Stijl* (We discover Style): 'The old struggle between imagination and reason has ended in a tragic way. The result is disconcerting. The triumph of reason has systematically broken every relation, disturbed every balance. A wedge has been driven between nature and man with foolish tenacity. And as for art: she was degraded into a mirror of vanity. But we know that the tyranny of reason has reached its final stage. Therefore no rational justification of the new architecture will ever satisfy us. Imagination is and remains the only faculty capable of registering the qualities of a changing world-view simultaneously, etc. During the last fifty years or so, a few – ranging from poet to architect, from biologist to astronomer – have actually succeeded in giving comprehensible shape to various aspects of its nature. The deplorable hierarchy of artificial values upon which contemporary existence has come to rest is finally beginning to totter. The new architecture has its roots in a "new reality". Standing on the border between today and tomorrow, it is a meaningful prophecy.'[36]

My conviction has in no way changed, but in the years when I was a member of 'de 8 en Opbouw' (until its recent dissolution) I felt increasingly lonely among the others. What I took for the essence of the Nieuwe Bouwen turned out to be almost the opposite of what the others saw as their aim. (Only Rietveld, Bakema and Van Eesteren often nodded to me in approval). Once again, in my opinion the fiasco of the original objective of the 'new architecture' is to be blamed on the overestimation of reason, the lack – fear even – of 'poetry'. So Molière[37] got hold of the right end of the stick after all – only his was the wrong stick. Apparently he felt helpless in the face of the new world-view he felt approaching (Vreewijk[38]), the essence of which he was unwilling – unable – to accept. Surely Molière would not deny that even the physicist struck the barrier of objective measurability, so that he cannot take another step without involving the observer – i.e. the subject – not only in his reasonings but also in his measurements and calculations.

Behold the wonder of relativity. Behold the true myth of our time. The debunking of the absolute object, the dethronement of self-sufficient entities, of the self-contained mass, of 'unassailable' matter as the only measurable reality (except energy, for this was merely the predicate of matter), of space as a *nothing* around *something*: the mere distance between A and B and C! Time – as an infinite sequence of moments, along which the entire existence moves in a rectilinear and uniform way from point-event to point-event in full obedience to the laws of causality – has finally run out.

Eternity has ceased to be an arithmetical process, nor indeed is it 'elusive', because it falls safely outside existence. Nothing falls outside existence, A myth is again as much a concrete quantum as a milligram or millimetre. The great top is spinning once more. Beginning and end meet. The deterministic patina wears off. The tic-tac metronomic contraption with God the Father busy at the controls has run out of oil. If the architects whom Molière, with a vehemence of persuasion rooted in uncertainty, incited to oppose rationalism (the 'half laid table'[39]), the new architecture, and a world without metaphysical quality – if those architects had understood what the concerns of all the arts and sciences have been for the past fifty years then they, and if not they, in any case the architects of the Nieuwe Bouwen, could have retaliated with: not we but you, dear Molière. The relativistic world-view includes transcendence, *sine qua non*. The subjectivation of measurability. Every expression that indicates the rhythm of such a world-view in art or science excludes one-sided rationalism, because it accommodates the rigid polarity between object and subject within their ambivalence. To Molière the most terrifying of all, perhaps, is mathematical evidence – the formula as blasphemy (as Galileo already knew long before). Molière and St Thomas should have been countered with St John of the Cross and Denis the Pseudo-Areopagite. Then everyone would have seen that his metaphysics – i.e. his conception of architecture – is based on the table of 1 (signor Aquino turns away).[40]

I have been rather discursive, I have said a lot of not very pleasant things, but I had no choice. I cannot imagine that people will not force their way out of this impasse and that they will no longer deny man what he deserves by virtue of his being. The conclusion is for Rietveld:

'One more thing. Let us bear this in mind always. The house for people who wish to live according to the prevailing conception already exists. We are all too familiar with it. The more complete and indestructible we make it, the more we perfect it, the less chance we have of ever overcoming it. Since we are all better off, at our best moments, sitting on a table than on a chair, or indeed need neither table nor chair, the house of the future (this is the house for you) will not and must not entirely satisfy the conception of "dwelling" that still prevails today.'[41]

Squares with a smile

Translation of 'Kwadraten met een glimlach',
article published in De Groene Amsterdammer, *17 May 1958*[1]

If one were unexpectedly to ask me what Rietveld meant to me, I would definitely hesitate, for a long time, before giving my 'architect's' answer. But I would certainly know why I was hesitating. I have rarely felt truly at home amongst architects. Like the odd man out. Everyone his opinion – they and I. There have of course been some exceptions: Van Eesteren, Bakema and Rietveld. But even the distance between them and me has remained greater than the similarities and differences would lead us to expect. No, as a species architects no longer enthral me. Now and again they are engaged in things that affect me, but usually with things that don't. Whatever the case, the architecture affects me all the more. I draw what I make and think from everything I have experienced; from what others in the past and present and everywhere have thought, made and done: the poets I meet now and met as a boy;[2] the painters and sculptors, their work, personality or both, the places I visited near and far – the Hebrides with their Celts and whisky in the winter, the Southern Sahara with its Tuaregs and Corneille in the summer.

Architects – here and now – are busy becoming uniform. The Muses have avoided them more and more – and vice versa. The stage has been reached at which the architect relates to architecture as the bookkeeper does to poetry. This seems to me an undeniable truth – an awful truth. I know of no other case where the practitioners of a such a compelling and subtle profession (I prefer to forget typographers and industrial designers completely) are surfing so easily on the outer margins of art and mind in order to cleverly 'apply' what they come across.

Architecture is a phenomenal art, but the architect is no longer an artist. That's not only an apparent paradox but the dilemma of my profession in general, the problem of a creative exchange within one's own field. With regard to the millions for whom wall, roof, door, window and city are biological necessities, it is not so much a dilemma as a tragedy, which they do not – yet – realise, because they do not know how it could be otherwise (one can leave a poor poem unread, a bad painting in the portfolio!). Why, oh why, have so many architects turned their backs on their profession – i.e. on people? After all, they certainly never had to doubt the irrevocable social usefulness of their contribution. So why do they doubt? Or have they simply become doubters? I am not exaggerating when I say that architects have largely become 'cultivated' cultural dilettantes. Many of them are additionally cultural pretenders. Like true hygienists they glorify the sun, but they think the difference between day and night is hidden in an electric switch. 'Pure' means flat; 'honest' means smooth. Fear of kitsch has led to the birth of a soft kitsch, hardly any more honest but certainly less humorous. Like real megalomaniacs they record the mediocre in man from the start, in order to dish up that little that can be reaped

Gerrit Rietveld
ca. 1960

from it for the sake of man's 'welfare'. They are fellows whose kidneys have grown round their hearts. How many of them are there who still sit at the drawing board and design things themselves? The layman would be astonished if he knew this.

So I come back to my hesitation – which in the meantime has vanished – and to Rietveld. I have never seen him as an 'architect', but as an artist as befits him. An artist who builds! This has given him a special place in the midst of the frustrated congregations who worship in him what they hardly possess or at least smother in themselves and others. The special place Rietveld occupies lies in his artisthood as such, as something exceptional in today's architects' world. But his special place as an artist amongst other artists lies solely in the special nature and degree of his artisthood. I can never rid myself of the feeling that Rietveld has become the victim of the Rietveld legend – because all those with a logical nature (is there anything less logical than that?) have tried to make him out to be a sort of brilliant fool, the way they do always and everywhere. Le Corbusier, Wright, Lorca and Dylan Thomas have at an international level had a similar role forced upon them. Nevertheless, there is no one who can comply with his own legend with impunity, not even if he himself was the source of this legend. For that matter, the reason for the formation of a legend is never entirely external to the person whom the legend concerns. He participates in it, consciously or unconsciously. In the case of Le Corbusier and Wright consciously, too consciously.

Things were different in the case of Thomas, for whom the process was not only more complex but also much more intensely interwoven with the conflicts he ultimately 'stabilised' and gave shape to in his poetry. If only for this reason, there can be no doubt about his greatness. In Rietveld's case the process was less conscious and less vehement, but creatively more essential. This is why I consider his artisthood more pure, not in terms of potency but in character. His own nature and his own architecture apparently kept each other in polar balance. This will be observed by anyone who sees or hears him and approaches his work receptively. Buffoonery and capriciousness alongside clarity and order. Sometimes – how could it be otherwise – the laughter forces its way through the seriousness. At such times Rietveld's work has an indefinable subtlety; the prodigious becomes ordinary, the ordinary acquires a touch of wonder. The balance between the identity of a person and his work is always a sensitive matter – it is *a priori* a personal matter, while architecture as such is *a priori* not so, or only partly. But this is a conflict that is by principle inherent in being an artist. For the architect this conflict implies a sort of tightrope walk between the real and the unreal. Because every building is used. Consumed and misused too, though that's inherent in all human 'use'. Every building is given a life of its own after completion. Entirely autonomous with regard to its maker. The resulting mutations pass over precisely those subtleties that are so crucially important, even if they are viable; they often ultimately nullify them. (Rietveld simply does not build in granite like the Egyptians, and the vibrating white he uses can easily be removed). Conversely, it is also true that the spatial form, which he attunes to his own being with seismographic accuracy, occasionally impedes the practice of the ordinary, rightly or not. Purity of expression will after all lose out to corrosion, at least materially. But not as an idea. Behold the fate but also the consolation of every true architect.

Rietveld is an intimate artist. His poetry blossoms from the security of his inner entourage. Whenever he is lured out of this warm haven, when, as a professional, he has to go out into the rough world outside, he emerges as a benign, albeit slightly suspicious, figure. One senses that he most wants to return, to put the vulnerable walls on his 'own territory'. He has a little snake-in-the-grass with him! At the exhibition of his work in Utrecht, surrounded by his own world, the great small-scale artist that he is will clearly appear. Of that I am sure.

Genuflections can be explained from the sentimentality characteristic of those who think mechanically. But Rietveld's work has rarely if ever been the subject of critical study. Only expressions of praise with a few anxiously formulated thoughts – always the same. Nowhere has any creative causal connection even been pointed out between the various aspects of his work.

It is clear that the lack of such a study is never advantageous to the course of the creative path, and may even blur it, unless the artist constantly tests his work against both his own inner development and that of the changing reality in which he lives. Rietveld's odd anti-intellectualism (he is the most intelligent of the architects I know in the Netherlands) did not particularly encourage this. There is something that, after the initial impulse of De Stijl, has kept him away from the major problems that have co-determined architecture and urban planning ever since. After all, an artist can't simply follow his nose. Talent will always be an instrument at the service of intellect and imagination. The greater the artistry, the greater has to be the capacity to control the proportionally wide range of feelings and force them into a form. In the creative process, no one can rely entirely on his natural talent, however enormous it may be. To give shape to this sort of emotional matter not just once but a whole life long, it is in fact necessary that the intellect is involved in equal proportion. Annie Romein-Verschoor's claim that artists have only 'limited intellects' is grotesque and in my opinion characteristic of the ideologically disillusioned intellectual.[3]

Just think of it – that it was this same fool who said: 'for the coming style that which all people have in common is more important than their differences'.[4] The marvellous universality of this sentence is couched in its rhythm. Of course, the way the 'teamworkers', the industrial and standardisation fanatics explain it is as banal as it is absurd. What is being expected from Rietveld is precisely the 'difference', something else, the improper. Expected, but not always accepted!

For a more comprehensive view of Rietveld's work in particular and the present artistic climate in general I refer to my article in the May number of *Forum*, which will be devoted entirely to him.[5] Besides the sections that I have already used here, I would like to add the following:

Rietveld's contact with Theo van Doesburg and Mondrian (according to the Angel from the Garden of Eros,[6] 'the candid mental defective from New York'!) has not been very extensive. He has for example always continued to take the view that for De Stijl 'material and form are the territory of sculpture, the light-reflecting surface of the wall the territory of the painter'.[7] But this is Rietveld through and through, not De Stijl. Anyway, he calls the painter, the sculptor and the architect the 'one-sidedly sensitive to colour, plasticity and space', who all register the same aggregate of visual reality but express it in one of the three sectors in accordance with their specific 'one-sided' sensitivity. I don't believe in this. On the contrary, colour, plasticity and space have their own meaning in all three arts and belong to all three domains. There can be no collaboration between the three arts until each artist has discovered for himself the specific meaning of colour, plasticity and space in his own field, their meaning with regard to the dimension in which he works. But then things really start to get difficult! What is more, this 'meaning' changes as soon as it is approached in a piece of work – otherwise art would long ago have arrived at a definitive solution and have disastrously ceased to exist (the dream of the standardisation-prefabrication boys). Therefore, I would say, dear Liga Nieuw Beelden,[8] no direct cooperation for the time being. Rietveld would say, 'leave that to some future final phase, to a future Baroque – we are only just starting'. He would be right. First move our own business on a bit, independent of each other. Our great-great-grandchildren will deal with 'integration'. Why such haste? No art that's out of breath; no short-winded art, please. The difference between a painter and an architect is of a completely different kind from that between colour sensitivity and space sensitivity, colour and space. The same goes for sculpture, in both directions. It would really be all too simple otherwise. Anyway, how many painters, sculptors and architects who mess around together for X% of the building costs (it's called *'opdracht'*,[9] a commission!) are respectively colour, sculpture and space-sensitive? Not to mention leaving out the word 'respectively'.

However, since his Stijl period Rietveld has usually avoided active colour and has bounded his spaces with 'white'. Perhaps because he was one of the few who created space, not so much by material boundaries but by the shaping of light. So it is just as well that, contrary to his own story, he did not abandon his 'light-reflecting walls' to the painter! In the presence of the ephemeral quality of light the tangibility of the wall as a wall recedes; the round column for instance, becomes a mere cylinder (in contrast to the physicality of Bakema's wall-support-slab anatomy). This often happens at the risk of the unstructural – on the verge of the insubstantial. Like Gabo's brother Pevsner, Rietveld recognises the presence of all colours in light itself, bringing the spectral phenomenon to the fore without colouring the reflecting surfaces. Rietveld is a master in the use of colour for plastic-spatial correction. This explains why he is at his strongest when concerned with a single, separate space, whether or not its form is complex. Here the *periphery* of space constitutes the *matter* of its envelopment – I am deliberately putting it like this and not the other way round. Rietveld approaches what is tangible, that which he actually has to 'draw' and 'construct' by way of the intangible, by way of space and light. If the task now becomes more complex, in the sense that the number of spaces increases, this inevitably implies that the matter of the periphery of the different spaces becomes something – must become something – that has its own physical, and thus plastic, existence. As soon as one goes from one space to another – when one has to pass through the wall – there is after all physical contact. In this way, Rietveld's words, 'Material and form are the territory of plasticity', do indeed have meaning, from the point of view of his own work at least. But they also explain the absence of a tangible structure, the additive of the individual spaces – all relaxed and clear – with regard to the whole. People were enthusiastic about his Sonsbeek pavilion,[10] and rightly so. But in Venice[11] (a single large room) he showed splendidly what can happen if he succeeds in approaching the material with which he has to build from the viewpoint of space, and not, as is usual, the other way round. A small wooden house in Loosdrecht[12] – I heard that Rietveld does not care for it very much! – shows what can happen when if, in addition, he succeeds in doing so from the viewpoint of exterior space, from this world of water and clouds. The handling of the material, here conceived between inside and outside space, shows great power of expression. The house has an obsessive simplicity and plastic quality. The curving wooden walls and the high thatched roof are like a dome around the inhabitants. Outside is the great empty space.

Gerrit Rietveld, Netherlands Pavilion at the Biennal Giardini in Venice, 1954 Photo Jan Versnel

Photo Cas Oorthuys

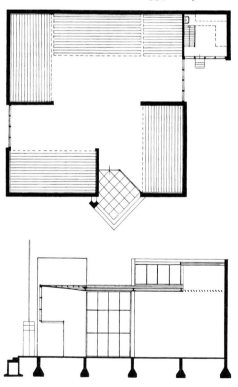

High dining room Photo Marijke Küper, 2005

Low sittingroom with original lay-brick fireplace and floor existing of thin oak discs laid in blue grano Photo 1941

Gerrit Rietveld, Verrijn-Stuart Summerhouse, 1941, situated in the middle of the Loosdrecht Lakes, Breukelen St. Pieters.

Design sketches, 1940–1941

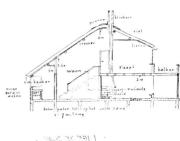

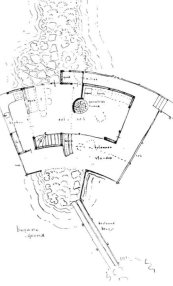

Photo 1941

The space behind the eye

Translation of 'de ruimte achter het oog', undated statement, probably written in 1958[1]

There has been so much palaver about the spatial impact of colour that there is little colour to it and no space left for the impact! It is as though reason can no longer cope with vision and our eyes no longer perceive what eludes reason – and that's quite a lot.

The impact of colour does not result from visibility, it merely presupposes it. That we 'see' colour is no more than a matter of fact – the same goes for space. 'Without light no colour' is therefore a statement that bears on nothing but itself. The converse statement 'without colour no light' on the other hand, is of an altogether different order, for it bears on the human being who is able to 'see' even without light. We know colour present, here, there, now, then, soon. We remember colour, long for colour, dream colour. In the space behind the eye there is always colour.

On the relationship between architecture and art

Translation of Van Eyck's response to an inquiry published in Forum, *1959, no. 6[1]*

With regard to architecture and art:
1 as cooperation: possible and desirable (but not yet)
2 as synthesis: possible but **not** desirable
3 as integration: **not** possible and thus **not** desirable either
In the 1st case: synthesis is possible
In the 2nd case: cooperation is possible
The 3rd case: is theory, but art is practice.
Integration = impotence.

Good morning, sculpture

Translation of 'Dag beeld', article published in De Groene Amsterdammer, *2 May 1959*[1]

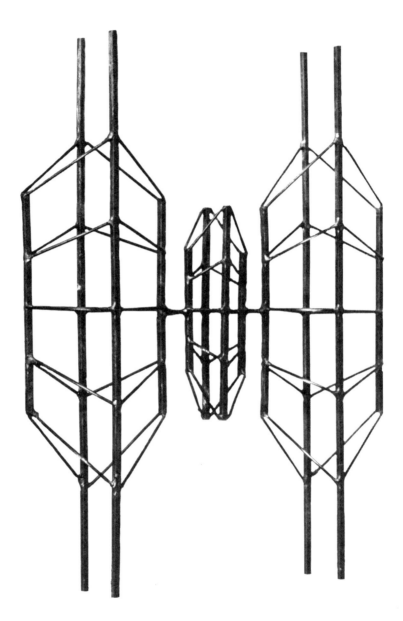

Carel Visser, *Family*, 1955 Welded iron

There have been times, before man started to think metronomically, when he was able to distinguish himself from everything else not exclusively by having a personality, because impersonal was (and still is) nothing, not the things, not the animals, not man, nor the things he made, nor the materials from which he made them. In remote parts of the world this is to varying degrees still the case. The aggressive contrast between myth and measure, between a reality that can be sensed intuitively and an intellectually analysed reality did not yet exist there and at that time. But today everything is different: the community has reluctantly handed over to the artist alone, pushed away to the margins of the attention, the task of yet revealing something of what is indefinable.

In the meantime science has started to measure its measurements against the subject, which is why our salvation lies in relativity – nowhere else. Although the sun and moon are circles while a circle has long since ceased to be a sun or moon – not even a face with a smile as every child sees it – it is still the artist's breathtaking task not to perform tricks with forms that gratify the senses but to work magic with form in order to conjure up shapes that catch the imagination by their immanent personality (not that of their maker). Which touch the heart, not the eye, because who is still going to prove that imagination no longer hides in the heart?

I have had the privilege of, in addition to my own family, having at home one made of iron so as to clarify its essence.

This can never do any harm. From direct experience I therefore consider Carel Visser, who saw the opportunity to weld it together, to be one of the rare birds who actually fulfils the task shirked by the community. He flies and he catches. From pieces of iron he conjures up shapes that can breathe, that can stand, lie, walk, sleep; that talk and sometimes mate. He proves that iron is capable of this too; that even iron can be soft, at least for those who are prepared to digest it.

If he were to make a ball or a circle – perhaps he rules out this possibility – it would be as warm as the sun, or reveal the wonder of the far side of the moon because, I have to get this off my chest, the moon is flat, even though people attempt to unmoon it by means of a rocket.

In the Stedelijk Museum I recently discovered a new 'ism' – not non-formal, of course not, but 'figurative' was printed neatly on a board. There's the inverted inverted for you. It's all too incredible. Anyone who is receptive to sculpted associations will sooner or later meet Carel Visser's iron people, being two big ones with a small one between them. And then, instead of asking whether there are still sculptors (a frustrated question whether it concerns sculptors, painters, poets or architects), reply: at least sculptures are still made, not 'abstract' but real, that do not misuse the space they occupy.

Visser is a winged digger

Statement published in Forum, *April-May 1961*[1]

Visser is a winged digger.
He carries the earth with him into space,
and brings space down to earth.
It is as if the struggle with nature is overcome
the moments he takes off and alights.
Earth and air; space and body; motion and rest; cell and crystal:
immutability and transience are gathered into his artifacts.
That he should talk to birds in steel and teach lines to fly
astonishes neither man nor bird.
One bird – two birds; one form – two forms;
twin bird form; twin form; flight.
What more significant object
could sustain congenial entry and departure?
Precision of contact between the tips of wings –
and all at once the trembling vault of space between bodies:
open for the next moment – in the warmest place.
The egg's interior – anticipation of new flight.

Carel Visser, *Birds,* 1954 Pencil on paper

Carel Visser, *Two Birds,* 1954 Welded iron

Hello Shinkichi

Article in the form of a letter written on the occasion of a Tajiri exhibition at the Amsterdam Stedelijk Museum, April 1960[1]

This is to tell you, though not without a feeling of shame, that I haven't got you down on paper yet! Still, if you don't mind me being as right as I am wrong, I'll jot down what comes to my mind here and now. So here it goes.

Some artists – wish I could think of a more magic word for the blokes – give my harp strings the right twang. Most don't, and that's obvious. Of those that do, I can usually name the chord sooner or later, i.e. detect for myself the approximate whereabouts of my... let's call it centre of gravity, which means I've strolled through the right door – discovered another landscape. You know – the sensation of new clarity and the kind of dizziness that goes with it – wonderful thing. That's it: the real magic of art. This 'dooring-in', this homecoming – it's all part of mating, I suppose. You revolve – feel enveloped while you migrate, move in while you move out; get what I mean. You 'return', which means you escape.

But let me get back to those that strum chords I cannot name (only a few of those around and you're one of them), weird soft chords with shifting undertones that annihilate mental gravitation altogether. It's like running after a shadow – like discovering a self-portrait in a kaleidoscope that works without jerking. Still, one can best get to know the stars by trying to catch them – better anyway, than by spying at them through a telescope. However, whether the spirit finds or forfeits gravitation, whether it is gained or resolved, the 'dooring-in', the homecoming, the mating is there again, although I can't picture the nature of the door I pass through, the home I entered or the mate I found.

I suppose by now you've hitched on to what I'm getting at? I don't know whether magician is the right word for you – Wait, I know what you are – Holy Primrose: you're a cross between a wizard and a witch no one can catch – a cross between both and a bat. Do you like bats? I let one go during French at school. The whole class quaked as if they were being pitched through the doors of hell (it was a Quaker school) by a horde of devils, until the bat fluttered and bumped itself into a coma, fell on the floor and was still. It looked smaller and softer than before and more human than my classmates – it palpitated whereas they were breathless.[2]

This anecdote brings me to the first time we ran into each other – Amsterdam, 1949. I was trying to hang the first International Exhibition of Experimental Art[3] – the one that made the lowlands feel very low – when a crate was hauled into the museum (the same wonderful museum you're showing in now). More stuff, I thought – didn't know if you were around because we hadn't met. I remember as if it was yesterday the emergence of a pile of woodshavings and a mass of plaster fragments with wires sticking out. Looked like a heap of wrecked angels to me. I left the spot and went on coping with the others: later I discovered you eyeing the rubble with

Shinkichi Tajiri, *Torso, Head, Angel no. 1, Spectre no. 1* and *Hybrid*, leftover bronze, 1958–1959 on show at his 1960 exhibition in the Amsterdam Stedelijk Museum.

incredible calm. At the opening the wreckage had vanished; what had gone into the crate was there again as if by magic.

In Liège, two years later, what happened proved that there must have been an omen hovering over the first smash. Everything was larger in Liège – the cold neoclassic halls, the crates and the heap of wrecked angels! While I spent days running from one void hall to the next with huge canvases – and the artists after me – you seemed to shrink bit by bit as the shattered beings took shape again, grew and grew and regained their two-metre spooky stature. I still regard this as a triumph of creative single-mindedness; a human triumph, no less – you grew in the process of shrinking. Amid the nervous helter-skelter, Shinkichi manipulating wire and fresh plaster with astounding dexterity, reassembling, goading back into form what seemed irretrievably lost. Days on end: silent, concentrated and alert.

 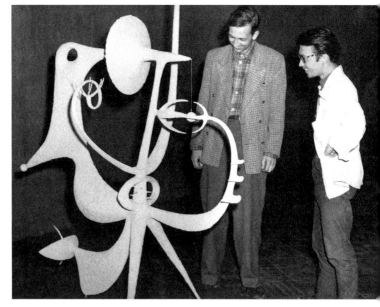

Sculptures by Tajiri at the Liège
Cobra exhibition, 1951: *Family Group,* 1949, and in the background, *Bird,* 1950
Photo Violette Cornelius

Tajiri with Constant watching *Bird*
Photo Serge Vandercam

Perhaps I'm catching hold of the witch's broomstick after all. There was something in those bits, Shinkichi; you weren't just repairing. You were coaxing the debris with such determination, fondling the fragments as fragments in a way you wouldn't have done with plaster yet unformed. You were giving birth this time, discovering your true material, spelling the letters of a vast alphabet. Ever since, you've been spinning the fabric of a wonderful fairy tale, telling the world of things yet untold. It's the story of junk – the epic splendour of what has been cast away, thwarted, bruised, spat upon, trampled underfoot. The story of what has lost purpose or never had any. You were orchestrating betrayed man-soiled matter that had lived a life and acquired a personality in the process. You continued what had been started before, smashing the hierarchy of 'noble material' and the frozen obsolete languages allied to them by incorporating matter with an already determined form: determined either consciously – the keys, cogs, scissors, blades, screws and nails – or by chance, the spilt bronze from the foundries of your last period. A dialogue with things acquiring being.

What Schwitters meant by Merz was by no means the same as what the early Cubists meant by their collages. 'Ein Spiel mit den schäbigen Ueberbleibseln', as Hugo Ball[4] put it in 1916, referring to Dada, doesn't cover Picasso's statement of 1935, *'L'artiste est un réceptacle d'émotions venues de n'importe où, du ciel, de la terre, d'un morceau de papier, d'une figure qui passe, d'une toile d'araignée. C'est pourquoi il ne faut pas distinguer entre les choses. Pour elles il n'y a pas des quartiers de noblesse'.*[5]

Dada incorporated the associative vehemence of what has been 'thumbed' by man reflecting his little doings (reminds me of the Robber Symphony and the

Beggar's Opera⁶). The collages of the Cubists are more gentle, Latin not Teutonic, more an extension of aesthetic sensibility in its own right. Schwitters alone perhaps avoided the pitfalls of both: the political overtones of the former and the new formalism waiting around the corner in the case of the latter. And yet, together with the Surrealist method adapted from Lautréamont of provoking a casual meeting of two alien realities with a third, alien to both, causing a shudder of unprecedented poetry (when the liaison comes off) – the ground was covered all right programmatically. But these three parallel approaches will remain only partially valid unless they are caught under a larger common denominator and explored; and that Shinkichi is exactly what you've succeeded in doing. Yes, explored… for it's the exploration that matters in art, getting closer to the shifting centre by extending the spiral of the mind.

Damn, there's nothing beyond the spiral, since it's always expanding, reaching outward and inward. There's nothing else we can know – nothing else knowable. You can bump up against all the gods and blessed saints there have been within a pretty limited horizon, I swear.

The way you handle keys and screws, opens the door onto a reality beyond all gods. Gods surely are the invention of contracted man. Man is his own spiral. If he plays the game he can double or triple the windings. This is his adventure. There's nothing outside the spiral – beyond the spiral is the spiral. The transcendental begins where man leaves his gods behind. We've got all there is to heaven and hell down here without one or the other. It's all there in what you, Shinkichi, refashioned into something rich and strange.

By the way, what you told me about the small bronzes that preceded the things you've been doing with the scraps from the foundries has set me longing for an intrinsically inverted architecture. You see, I'm always coping with material in order to get to grips with that which transcends material – space. So you cut the negative form – the space – in soft porous brick, then pour in the bronze and let it solidify – think of it – into space. The bronze creeps into its own skin, creeps into the crevices secretly – flaunting the supremacy of mass's tyrannical frontier.

You were telling me about the plastic language you were evolving. I'm aware of the inner logic of what you said. It approaches the roots of language, of expression through language, better still of expression through the creation of language. Language makes us while we make it. The process is reciprocal and therefore endless.

Art, as we know it, is still too far removed from the language idea – get what I mean – which I hope is what you mean! I believe in the coincidence of method and motive. It just isn't a question of putting the cart before the horse or the horse before the cart. Things are just different in art. It's a different kind of transport – the vehicle is self-powered and forms its own cargo, it moves everywhere and within itself. That's art, that's man, that's reality, that's the holy trinity!

The metal junk you piled up along the banks of the Seine in 1951, resurrected into a horde of unsavoury warriors ready to rape Paris, is now menacing other regions.

You brought us face to face with the principle of aggression, that's certain. It's there in all your work. The scratched countenance of the mind, the forked shadow edging in, the split pelvis of the earth... Hieroglyphs of agony, undeciphered. Hope I'm pretty close to the meaning.

Then came your 'scorched earth' reliefs (1954). Shinkichi parrying the next onslaught, extending the dignity of man's last defence against himself into wrought iron, into wrought iron marked with colour. Charred, torn, grated, bleeding surfaces. Tormented landscapes with the caves of maternity closed from within to avert violation and ensure survival. We know now that the principle of art and 'scorched earth' go hand in hand and why this must be so.

You came to Holland in 1956 with Ferdi,[7] a wizard herself, and I seldom saw you. Twice you called, and both times left a tiny, neatly labelled sculpture as a memento of some new mystery. What's on the label is a mystery to many. I know it's a mystery to you as well. Let me get them. F + S = X, X = Giotta Fuyo Tajiri, 6 June 1957, Amsterdam. That's what's on the earlier one. The other one has Ryu Vinci Tajiri, 25 April 1959, Amsterdam, written on the back – tokens of birth.

Voilà the essence of your latest work – the essence of the coloured paper balloons you wanted the children of Amsterdam to send up to illuminate our pale skies, but the police would not allow.

No longer death in life as before, no longer the solitary warrior's sword-penis piercing life into death, but life and death united in growth and change. Foliage that precedes and antecedes consciousness. Left-over bronze from the foundry welded elsewhere into new life. Night and day embracing in twilight. Metal shadows... muttering, withering, germinating... but still fierce.

By the way, my son wants to see the magnificent racing car you constructed for Giotta, he hasn't seen it with the body painted and the exhaust pipes.

Speech for the award of the 1962 Sikkens Prize

Translation of a speech held in the Amsterdam Stedelijk Museum, on 3 November 1962

Ladies and gentlemen artists and art-makers,

In 1960 and 1961, together with Constant and Joost van Roojen I was awarded the Sikkens Prize.[1] It was a pleasant surprise for us – it was also pleasantly paradoxical. Cooperation in art ensues from the relationship between the artists as people; not between the arts as categories. It is, as Constant rightly said, practice, not theory: a creative dialogue – or duel – between particular people in a particular place at a particular time. I think theoretical similarities are less essential than is generally supposed. Similar natures or having things in common is an illusion that is all too often attached to cooperation as a condition. Artists are simply not pathfinders; the paths of art are too imponderable, as are personal paths. The dialogue, or duel, comes about or does not come about. Apparent similarities between people who are cooperating may be just as much a hindrance as a condition. Constant and I, for example, exploited our differences – and they are indeed far from apparent! After all, Constant is a new Babylonian.[2] I would not like to meet great numbers of them on this earth. But we certainly need constants, because without them nothing changes.[3]

Joost van Roojen, mural on the engine hall of the Eerbeek paper factory, 1962
Photo Aldo van Eyck

Aldo van Eyck and Joost van Roojen, Zeedijk playground, Amsterdam, 1956 Photos Har Oudejans

Constant, New Babylon project, *Spatiovore* and *Sector Contructie*, 1958–1960   Photo Victor E. Nieuwenhuis

Photo Bram Wisman

Things are completely different when it comes to Joost van Roojen. Not so much about the world has to change in order to reach a result with him. He is more like an old Babylonian. He lets the same old stars always tell a new story, and therefore never talks about a new or different star system. A society full of such old Babylonians might well bring a lot of new things into being! Because those who rediscover sooner or later always discover the new. That which is constant and constantly changes does not form an opposition in time and space, but is time-space. (As I say this I am thinking of Van Woerkom, who, like me, expects a great deal from relativity!) Anyway, I went on very well with both Babylonians. I always try to rediscover and to meet constants in a specifically new way.

The fact that the previous winner always hands over the prizes at these award ceremonies can create thorny problems, mainly for these predecessors. For this reason the Sikkens Prize has in any case become a lively award. Let me start by saying that I have little trouble agreeing with the jury's choice, though this is certainly not the case with every cornerstone of the winners' mental construction. To limit myself to Baljeu and Van Woerkom: as one example, they consider what I built along the Amstelveenseweg to be 'a grouping of regressions'![4] I can't bid against a judgement like that!

What I want to say here mainly amounts to objections of principle. But – now listen, art critics – in art the dialogue-duel only comes about when it starts from a profound mutual appreciation; Personally I actually object to the five prizewinners just as much as I appreciate their presence in the world of art. I see myself as the reverse of an art critic, and that is because I have always been engaged in art itself and with the people who bring it into being! Which is what art critics generally don't do, hence the wretchedness art criticism has run into. With a few rare exceptions, art critics and art historians are today's art villains. They are stuck on art with the wrong organs. They are bedbugs – you can't flatten them because they are already flat!

Therefore I prefer to address myself to my fellow-artists, opponents and prize-winners. My criticism is a general one and does not concern the kind of work they make, but certain basic intentions, insofar as they have become accessible in the well-wrought magazine *Structure* – the actual winner.[5]

Art does not exclude, but includes. However, as to what the artist does or does not include he is freer than a bird (so he must in the first place be able to fly!). However, it is so that what is included has to come out again as art; it should never disintegrate art. Art always means a broadening limitation, never a narrowing generalisation.

Fortunately not too many roads lead to Rome, but there are countless ways one can come to an understanding with the kaleidoscope of reality. The chosen route certainly does not become more direct because it is, for example, straight (rectilinear) or rectangular. Nor does it become more easily passable – this is what it's all about – by breaking up the roads one has not taken. In the first place it isn't possible anyway, and in the second place it weakens every sense of the kaleidoscopic. Rectilinear or rectangular, this line of thought somehow appears to be twisted. An infinite number of things can happen in art, but never the abolition of the kaleidoscopic. There's no Don Quixote who can manage that. It is pointless, hopeless and actually negative to clarify a specific sort of clarity, brightness and exactness by polemically muddying other kinds of clarity, brightness and exactness, i.e. approaching these other kinds in the light of the one chosen kind. It is odd that artists want to cut off each other's paths in this way, in the opinion that one wonder excludes the other. In fact wonders tolerate each other particularly well, since they are all accommodated in that huge kaleidoscope of reality. For this reason I would like to ask the founder and editor of *Structure*, Joost Baljeu, thinking of his booklet *Mondriaan or Miró?*,[6] 'Why

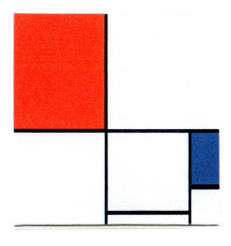

P. Mondrian,
Composition A,
1932 Oil on canvas

J. Miró, *Personages and Dog before the Sun*,
1949 Oil on canvas

Mondrian *or* Miró? Are the two of them too much for us? After all, Mondrian and Miró – whom Baljeu puts forward as ambassadors of two apparently contrasting worlds – were in the first place both partisans in the same great riot and against the same outworn hierarchy of values. With his plastic imagination Miró fascinatingly breached the suffocating fossilisation that makes any form of metamorphosis impossible (Is it a dog? Miró: Yes. Or is it a goose? Miró: Yes. Or is it a child? Miró: Yes.). He breached the bastions behind which every phenomenon entrenches itself in isolation, made a myth again more tangible than a millimetre or a second, and thus in his own way discovered the 'interior of seeing'. In this way everything ends up back in man, like the animals in Noah's ark. '*Le monde dans un homme, tel est le poète moderne*', said Max Jacob.[7] In his neo-plasticism, Mondrian broke splendidly through the smothering fossilisation of a world where the one closes itself off from the other. In this universality all the contraries were put in balance. They freed themselves from the rigid bastion of their 'particular' form and restrictive meaning in order to enter into reciprocal, i.e. 'pure', relationships with each other. In Miró the world was made relative within one man, in Mondrian man was made relative within the world. Now, the first would be inconceivable without the second, and *vice versa*.

That is why I say Mondrian *and* Miró; precisely for the sake of a world where relativity (the mild gears of reciprocity) makes metamorphoses possible again, because surely it is precisely just such a time-space continuum that Baljeu is concerned with? This sort of continuum includes metamorphosis as a first principle, because otherwise there can be no continuum regarding both the meanings and the shape of things, and that is what it is all about.

Pathology versus pataphysics[8]

In one quite exciting issue of *Structure*, Baljeu writes: 'art is not philosophy' and he is right. Some pages further on, Jean Gorin writes, and he too is right: 'all true art expresses a philosophy'. Still further on, Charles Biederman, surely one of America's profoundest, and hence most *isolated* artists, writes the following: 'The new or second phase of western art is non-Aristotelian. It reveals and exemplifies the infinite creative fecundity of nature. The main spring of man's highest inspirations remains grounded in the instinctual. But it is not, and cannot be, that of the primitive, unless one is content with the only available substitute for it – the pathological.'[9]

Now to dissociate the instinctual from the 'instinctual' of the primitive, that is to say to associate the 'primitive' indirectly with the 'pathological' – through substitution – is a very, very determinist thing to do. Something that shocked me, coming

Joost Baljeu, *F 0*, 1956 Painted wood

Jean Gorin, *Study for a small house with neo-plastic colours*, 1927 Ink and gouache on paper

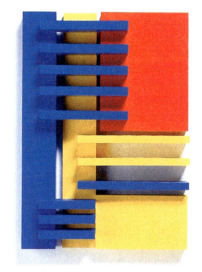

Charles Biederman, *Work no. 9A*, 1937
Painted wood

Dick van Woerkom and Joost Baljeu, *Model of a studio apartment*, 1959 Painted wood

as it does from a non-determinist thinker like Biederman, for it is Biederman after all who claims that the first or Aristotelian era of western art is closing. He thus not only qualifies the pathological and the primitive as set categories which they simply are not, but thereby also disqualifies them – the usual unfortunate consequence of categorisation. Alfred Jarry, not long ago, proposed the real alternative: not the pathological but something utterly anti-categorical: the pataphysical.[10] But then, you see, Jarry was superbly non-deterministic – in this alone he was by instinct categorical! He was in fact one of the first and only complete relativists. I mention all this because Biederman's argument, in a sense, supports Baljeu's 'Mondriaan or Miró' and all the others Miró is supposed to represent – all those nice pataphysical ones!

Baljeu, Van Woerkom and spatial continuity

So, now to our colleague Van Woerkom: he too is engaged in time-space, that means in our time! But since he thinks this can only be achieved by means of rectangular, parallel horizontal and vertical planes arranged perfectly square to each other (each with its own colour), I believe he will overshoot both this sought-after 'spatial continuity' as well as this 'time-space unity'.

Architecture is about both continuous and discontinuous space, so it's also about fully or partly enclosed spaces; spaces of which not 'the six' but x planes 'are seen to move around a core'. I would say: 'seen but not only seen' because architecture is not a purely visual matter. After all, it involves more senses than just the eye! It is about the eye behind the eye, and in the first place about equivalence and simultaneity and not about spatial continuity in such a literal sense.

Relativity presupposes the involvement of the subject – and thus the full presence of man, not just his eyes. Space therefore is (and means) the experience of it. It is the built counter-form of the mind. I do not believe, like Van Woerkom, that a cylinder, a segment of a sphere or a curved wall, a space or form that rests within itself, or the use of natural materials, are hostile to architecture; but it is hostile to architecture to *a priori* exclude such things when the project requires them. Contemporary architecture has so often slipped away into 'spatial continuity' that space or continuity turn out to be out of the question. Just emptiness with no one on either side – gaps through which the the mind blows away.

What I actually want to say is that it is all interior art! 'Making it inside' in the right way, even if it is outside. Architecture should be the greatest enemy of alienation. It is therefore a continuous discussion with the outside, with being-outside-oneself, and with unbounded space. Yes, the notion of space coincides with the appreciation of it. That is why I like to use the word 'place', and see both the house and the city as a bunch of places. Van Woerkom deals with these things in his own way, and unfortunately there are now very few architects who do that. He knows that I cannot find the places that people deserve between his coloured surfaces.

Against the integration of the arts

Let me touch on just one more topic before I lose the five scrolls. I distrust the current need for an integration of the arts, because it is connected with the supposition that it will ultimately culminate in a sort of total art, an all-embracing shaping into which the three so-called plastic arts would fuse, while ceasing to exist in their own right. If paradise on earth has to be like that, then I'm going to make a pact with the devil right now, so that things can remain as they are.

To those who are of the opinion that painting, sculpture and architecture are either already, or will in the future be, indefensible as creative categories, I say: they are not categories but phenomena, not temporary categories but enduring phenomena. One can integrate categories, though it is not worthwhile, but not phenomena: they exist in parallel and tolerate each other. They can manifest themselves together, side by side. However, as soon as they merge they lose their autonomous identity, but then there will certainly be no form of expression that encompasses all-three-plus-life-too, no super-art, only a pseudo-art that no longer encompasses anything. Yes, rather the worlds of the individual arts than the sham world of this sort of super-art! The individual arts draw the variable outline of a world of wonder, while a super-art would only eject the wonders from the world.

They are and remain three phenomenal realms. Anyone who prefers a super-art to the arts, the impersonal to the personal, sham integration to creative identity, is an ostrich, an infra-tinkerer, diligently working on the superfluous. In the meantime I remain loyal to the ordinary artist and the existing fields of art. I distrust those who do not feel at home in any field because they are afraid of the specific nature of the huge space there! Even though they move skilfully along the false borderlines they themselves have drawn. Talk about the art of safe and artistically fairly lucrative tightrope-walking! In the Netherlands there are hundreds of them. They make anything with everything, wherever you like, for x guilders per square metre or y% of the total building costs.[11] They are all clever conjurers who are at a loss amongst the magicians and therefore want to break all the magic wands! But please understand, this in no way applies to this afternoon's prizewinners.

We also know the other story: architect, space is for you; sculptor, plasticity is for you; painter, colour is for you – in this great whole! Hocus pocus – and there goes autonomous painting, there goes the autonomous sculpture, there goes autonomous space! Of course we are waiting for the super-dish, the pot in which everyone sociably stirs together, but which is never ready to eat. In any case, the 'integrationists' behave like new heroes, because they think that with their theories they have managed to wipe out the others who really can do something – the real painters, sculptors and architects.

Colour, plasticity and space are to be found in every true painted work, in every true sculpted work and in every constructed space. The painter, sculptor and architect are always working with colour, plasticity and space in accordance with their own nature and the nature of their aim and means. Colour, plasticity and space are the material, goal and reward in all three plastic arts. If a painter works in the framework of a building, he creates colour, plasticity and space there in a painterly manner. Architecture is in any case not the Alma Mater of the arts. However, the environment we live in could be the field of work and the workplace for all the arts, because without being shaped by colour, plasticity and space, the environment is not liveable, nor is it without the specific dimension of what colour, plasticity and space mean to the painter, the sculptor and the architect in the light of their own specific field.

Mondrian's vision

Mondrian saw in the distant future a world in which art, rather than being a separate phenomenon, would be absorbed into the shape of life itself.[12] As if this world, so soon after his death, was already emerging, his vision is already being misused as an argument against all those who, on the basis of human paradox, are working in one or other expressionist or surrealist way, or at any rate in a 'non-figurative', i.e. not literally 'abstract' way. I distrust this polemical exploitation of Mondrian's vision as much as I am able to remain loyal to the vision in the light of Mondrian himself. The beauty of Mondrian's work transcends its means. Mondrian is great in spite of his 'planes, lines and blocks'. They smile, just like the spaces created by Rietveld, the grandfather of this prize. It is not about the opposition between horizontal and vertical as such, nor is it a matter of the white, black, grey, red, blue or yellow, but about the way all these things speak of a very special dimension. Not the fourth, but Mondrian's dimension! Its universality lies in the wonderful results. The fact that this is so borders on the incredible. He brought the universal within reach, for it has become what he made of it. Ten years before Mondrian found his 'Stijl' tools and started his long wrestle with them, he said to Til Brugman: 'I am becoming primary, do you mind?'[13] Wonderful. Incredible! Here is the only 'integration' art enters into, that of the artist and his art.

He managed to give plastic expression to equilibrated ambivalence. As if he understood that he would never be able to really dance very well with the girls (which he equally liked to do), he ventured into his most marvellous painting: *Victory Boogie Woogie*. Mondrian was an angel if ever there was one. But this is certainly not the reason why Jan Engelman, high above Utrecht in his Garden of Eros, called Mondrian 'the candid mental defective from New York'.[14] I don't actually have anything against Utrecht, but nevertheless I occasionally think, 'Wipe Utrecht off the map and just keep Rietveld'.

6

The beginning of Team 10 and the end of CIAM

Introduction to chapter 6

During the fifties substantial transformations took place in architectural thinking. As functionalism grew into a settled practice, it met with increasing discontent in the very core of the Modern Movement. Within CIAM many younger members aspired to a less analytical, more integrated approach. In due course they initiated a dissident movement that would result in the creation of Team 10 and eventually in the dissolution of CIAM .[1]

Having been the first younger member to raise a critical voice in post-war CIAM at the Bridgwater congress in 1947, Aldo van Eyck did not reappear on the international CIAM scene until five year later. Prevented by illness, he had been unable to participate in CIAM 7 and 8. In 1952 he was delegated by *de 8 en Opbouw* to the interim congress at Sigtuna, near Stockholm, which was meant as a preparation for CIAM 9. The CIAM Council had decided that CIAM 9 would be devoted to framing a *Charte de l'Habitat*, a document intended as a sequel to the *Charter of Athens*. But at the Sigtuna congress the notion of habitat turned out to be a source of discord. Whereas the older generation saw 'habitat' simply as a synonym for 'habitation', the younger understood it in a broader, ecological sense, as a complete human settlement for a whole community – that is to say, not only a collection of dwellings but a housing structure interwoven with all its necessary communal facilities. It was in the discussion of this issue that the split between the generations became apparent.[2]

At CIAM 9, which took place at Aix-en-Provence in 1953, this split fully burst open. The tone of the discussion was set by a number of radical younger members who challenged established CIAM thinking: Georges Candilis, Jaap Bakema, Aldo van Eyck and Rolf Gutman who had already attracted attention at earlier congresses, and four Britons who were just entering the CIAM scene: Alison and Peter Smithson, Bill Howell and John Voelcker. These 'angry young men' and one woman shared an aversion to the current analytical/functional mentality of CIAM and discovered they had an attitude in common. Instead of the prevailing approach in terms of four functions (dwelling, work, recreation and circulation), they perceived and wanted to conceive human environment in terms of interrelations. They ignored the congress agenda and advanced a number of new topics. The Smithsons proposed to replace CIAM's functional hierarchy by a 'hierarchy of human associations'. Bakema argued for the structuring of new neighbourhoods into housing units or 'visual groups'. Candilis, who was involved in large housing projects in North Africa, raised the question of 'habitat for the greater number' and drew attention to the importance of the age-old patterns of habitat that persisted in the medinas as well as in the shanty towns the people built themselves. Tying in with these themes, Van Eyck expounded his 'aesthetics of number'.[3]

After CIAM 9 the Dutch and British young guard arranged a meeting in Doorn (near Utrecht) in order to recapitulate and to define their position. The outcome of this meeting, which took place at the end of January 1954, was a 'Statement on Habitat', a short declaration that introduced the new approach. It advanced the concept of 'human association' as a first principle and reduced the four functions to aspects of the habitat to be studied. Town planning had to be approached not in terms of functions but as a hierarchy of different levels of association, corresponding to different types of community characterized

Proclamation of the death of CIAM at the end of the Otterlo Congress, 1959, by Peter and Alison Smithson, John Voelcker, Jaap Bakema, and below, by Aldo van Eyck and Blanche Lemco.

by 'varying degrees of complexity'. The hierarchy contained four levels of association – 'detached buildings, villages, towns and cities' – and was illustrated in a diagram inspired by the 'valley section' of the Scottish town planner Patrick Geddes.[4] Each level of association had to be approached as a specific 'ecological field' in which habitat takes a specific form. Remarkably, the notion of 'relation' does not show up in the text. It appears to have been substituted by the notion of 'association', a terminological shift that is symptomatic of the initial and lasting misunderstanding between the Britons and the Dutch.[5]

Retrospectively, the Doorn meeting can be considered as the first Team 10 meeting, held in anticipation of its official formation, which took place at the next CIAM Council meeting in Paris five months later.[6] There the organization of CIAM 10 was placed in the hands of a small group of 'senior youngers, volunteering for this task'. The group consisted in the first instance of Bakema, Peter Smithson, Candilis and Gutman, and was later expanded to include Aldo van Eyck, Alison Smithson, W. Howell, J. Voelcker and S. Woods. This ' CIAM 10 Committee' was entrusted with the task of organizing a congress that would once again be devoted to habitat. It had to produce a synthesis of the material available about habitat and would invite the participants to submit projects for an 'ideal habitat', i.e. a habitat designed in the full consciousness of the social and climatic conditions but not influenced by existing legislation or economic pressures.

But in fact Team 10, as the Committee soon came to be known, dedicated itself in the first place to formulating a guideline for CIAM 10, a set of instructions in which they propounded their views and tried to stimulate CIAM 10 participants to see and present their projects in the same light. Still, the production of this text was far from straightforward. It demanded many a team meeting and soon gave rise to manifest discord.

The initial versions of the instructions were chiefly the work of the Smithsons. They began with a critique on the blurring of conceptual standards in post-war CIAM – 'We of the youngers received a shock at Aix, in seeing how far the wonder of the *Ville Radieuse* had faded from CIAM' – and urged the participants not to hide behind vague theories or diagrams but to commit themselves as architects, i.e. with clearly articulated architectural projects. In accordance with the directives of the Council, they asked for projects of 'ideal habitat' at a particular place and at that particular moment, 'uncompromised by existing arbitrary laws and restrictions, in attempt to reach a moment of truth'. These projects should no longer be set out in elaborate analytical grids but should 'be presented in the most digested form to bring out their unique characteristics'. They were to be condensed into four small panels:

1. Identification image (a characteristic photograph or drawing depicting the context and the concept),
2. Development Pattern (situation and general layout),
3. Development Type (typical plan, section and elevation),
4. Significant Fragment (an image which sums up the project, with an explanation of how the project contributes to the aim of the congress).

How the congress was to examine these mini grids was explained in the terms of the Doorn declaration and its associated valley diagram. The six standing CIAM committees (Urbanism, Aesthetics, Education, Building Techniques, Social Aspects, Legislation) would be replaced by four new 'working parties', each for one of the proposed levels of association. Each party would, instead of focusing on a single aspect of all projects, apply itself to an integral study of all projects at its given level of association. The four working parties were expected to deduce 'general and practical laws, archetypes, universals, trends etc.' from the material presented, thereby providing a basis for the 'observations and resolutions' the Council had asked for.

The Dutch team members agreed with this document, but after its third draft had been discussed in a joint meeting with Le Corbusier and Giedion, they felt it to be rather reductive as to the ideas that had already been advanced in the course of the team meetings. Bakema sent the Smithsons a list of twenty points, expounding the ideas he wanted to see incorporated in the 'instructions', notably the idea of global life defined in terms of relationships between man and things, and the question of identity in the course of growth and change. Aldo van Eyck wrote an elaborate commentary in which he proposed some major adjustments and changes. He pointed out the desirability of an historical introduction explaining why Team 10 denounced the prevailing CIAM approach, and what it expected from the new approach it presented. In, particular he proposed to draw the participants' attention to three problems: the greater reality of the doorstep, time as a positive factor in design, and the aesthetics of number.

Although the Smithsons wrote to Bakema that they had received 'excellent comments from Aldo', they only casually incorporated some of the Dutch ideas into their next version of the 'Instructions'.[7] So Van Eyck decided to rework the instructions in order to articulate his and Bakema's views properly. He wrote a new introduction in which he stressed the new generation's awareness of significant relations, connecting these with the aspirations of the twentieth-century avant-garde, the 'culture of determined relations' announced by Mondrian. He maintained the approach of the 'hierarchy of human associations' which had been accepted in Doorn, summarizing it under the title 'the ecological approach', but he prefaced it with the three new points of view which he had explained in his letter.

Bakema fully agreed with Van Eyck's new version. In his capacity as secretary of Team 10 he duplicated it and sent it to all Team 10 members, the members of the CIAM Council and several other members in the Netherlands and abroad. The British reacted promptly and fiercely. They declared to be 'completely bewildered' by the Dutch initiative, 'unable to understand why we are now confronted with a document which only vaguely resembles what was agreed at our four meetings, and which, where we understand it, we disagree with.' And although they averred that they had carefully studied the text in question, they did not find it worthwhile even to criticize it: 'because we feel that the author of the new sections of the document has very largely missed the point of last year's work.' They insisted emphatically that the introduction should be limited to the 'common factor' which was agreed upon at the Doorn meeting.[8]

In response Van Eyck edited a new version. He omitted the three points of view which he had introduced and put them in an appendix, a 'Dutch supplement' – this entirely in agreement with Bakema, who informed the English that if, in their opinion, Team 10's common approach had been specified too much by the three questionable points, the Dutch would like to submit these points to the congress on their own behalf. This is what finally happened, albeit after many a skirmish.[9]

At the Dubrovnic congress CIAM effectively split into two factions. The older generation continued to devote itself to the compilation of a *Charte de l'Habitat*. Team 10 and their kindred spirits went their own way. The grids submitted were hung in accordance with the scale levels of the Doorn diagram and discussed by four working parties, which focussed respectively on 'cluster' (or 'organic unity'), 'mobility', 'growth and change' and 'urbanism as a part of habitat'. The Smithsons presented five instances of cluster, on different scale levels. Bakema showed the large urban projects by *Opbouw*, from Pendrecht to Alexanderpolder. Van Eyck had prepared two grids, one on the Amsterdam playgrounds, the other on the Nagele project he had developed as a member of a joint team of *de 8* and *Opbouw*.

In parallel with the discussion of the projects, many arguments went on about the future of CIAM. They had been provoked by a message from Le Corbusier and a declaration by Van Eesteren. In a letter to Sert, Le Corbusier had expressed his opinion that 'the metamorphosis of CIAM 1956 should be based on the new generation: those of 40 years in 1956, the only ones qualified to act in the new phase of CIAM, turned to the solution of the problems posed by our times'. As he later clarified in a message to the congress, he considered them the 'only ones capable of feeling actual problems personally, profoundly, the goals to follow, the means to reach them, the pathetic urgency of the present situation. They are in the know. Their predecessors no longer are, they are out, they are no longer subject to the direct impact of the situation.'[10] He thus urged the young guard to make a new start under the name of CIAM II, in clear distinction to their predecessors, whom he proposed labelling CIAM I.

Van Eesteren went a step further and expressed the undisguised view that CIAM should simply be abolished. In his view CIAM, which was originally a spontaneous, informal meeting of people who aspired to a common goal, had become unnecessarily institutionalized over the years. It had lost its dynamic character and subordinated its proper work to its formal structure. But now that the original dynamism seemed to be reviving among the younger CIAM members, they ought be allowed to proceed free from of all institutional ties; and 'the constitution of CIAM should regard its specific task as ended'.[11] In fact, due to the statutory reforms made in Bridgwater, CIAM had a growing number of members who were eager to attend the congresses, hundreds of 'observers' who did not come to present or do any work but to be spectators and gape at the famous veterans. Hence, the final discussions at the Dubrovnic congress turned into the decision to abolish the organizational hierarchy of CIAM, leaving the national and regional groups to their own autonomy. The idea was to reduce CIAM to its original format of a congress with a limited number of participants. This decision had a devastating effect on the national CIAM groups. The Dutch group, which had been among the best organized and most active, wound up its activities within a year – a process in which Aldo van Eyck played an active role. He was convinced that after dissolution 'the worthwhile contacts will be re-established automatically and perhaps one or more new groupings of people who want something in common will arise in a year or two'.[12]

After Dubrovnic the majority of the older CIAM guard continued trying to stay at the helm to preserve the continuity of CIAM, but the younger contingent became increasingly irritated by this paternalism and aimed to shake themselves free as quickly as possible. The next steps in this direction were taken in late August 1957 at a final meeting in La Sarraz. There it was decided to dissolve all former CIAM groups and to start a new organization under the name 'CIAM: Research Group for Social and Visual Relationships'. The selection of the limited group of new founding members was entrusted to a small coordinating committee which consisted of Bakema, Rogers, Roth, Voelcker and Wogenscky. After two years of preparation this committee did indeed convene a working congress of forty-three delegates. This congress, which took place in Otterlo in September 1959, turned out to be a particularly exciting event, with memorable contributions by Ernesto Rogers, Giancarlo de Carlo, Aldo van Eyck and Louis Kahn. Team 10 came into full bloom. Ignoring their internal divergences, the Team 10 members came to the fore

Aldo van Eyck with Blanche Lemco, José Coderch, John Voelcker, Alison Smithson and Oskar Hansen at the Otterlo congress, 1959

as a firm and solidary group. Relieved of the tutelage of the old guard, they candidly discussed and exchanged views with some thirty kindred spirits of their own generation. The CIAM structure of permanent commissions was entirely brushed aside. All discussions took place in plenary sessions, coordinated by Bakema.

At the conclusion of the congress, Team 10 resolved to continue its activities yet decided to stop doing so under the name of CIAM. In other words, the Team 10 members resigned from CIAM; and since they constituted the last vital force within the thirty-one-year old organization, this act meant its certain demise.

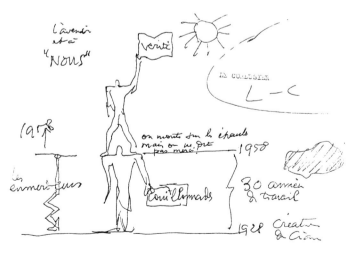

Acknowledging the reception of the Otterlo book with a letter to the publisher, dated 5 July 1961, Le Corbusier wrote: *'Je suis content de voir la ligne de conduite adoptée par les gens d'Otterlo. Il faut que chaque génération prenne sa place à l'heure utile'*, a statement he illustrated with the present drawing.

Statement on Habitat

Doorn declaration, drawn up on 31 January 1954 by J. Bakema, H. Hovens Greve, P. Smithson, J. Voelcker, A. Van Eyck and Van Ginkel[1]

1. La Charte d'Athènes proposed a technique which would counteract the chaos of the nineteenth century, and restore principles of order within our cities.
2. Through this technique the overwhelming variety of city activities was classified into four distinct functions which were believed to be fundamental.
3. Each function was realized as a totality within itself. Urbanists could comprehend more clearly the potential of the twentieth century.
4. Our statement tries to provide a method which will liberate still further this potential.

As a direct result of the 9th Congress at Aix, we have come to the conclusion that if we are to create a Charte de l'Habitat, we must redefine the aims of urbanism, and at the same time create a new tool to make this aim possible.

Urbanism considered and developed in the terms of the Charte d'Athènes tends to produce 'towns' in which vital human associations[2] are inadequately expressed. To comprehend these human associations we must consider every community as a particular total complex.

In order to make this comprehension possible, we propose to study urbanism as communities of varying degrees of complexity. These can be shown on a Scale of Association as shown below:

We suggest that the commissions operate each in a field not a point on the Scale of Association, for example,
isolated buildings
villages
towns
cities.

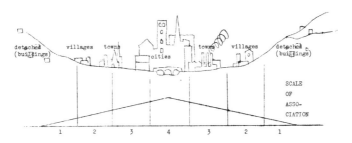

This will enable us to study particular functions in their appropriate ecological field. Thus a housing sector or satellite of a city will be considered at the top of the scale, (under City, 4), and can in this way be compared with development in other cities, or contrasted with numerically similar developments in different fields of the Scale of Association. **This method of work will induce a study of human association as a first principle, and of the four functions as aspects of each total problem.**

Letter to the Smithsons on the guideline for CIAM 10

Undated manuscript, obviously written shortly after 20 September 1954[1]

Dear Smithsons,
just a few remarks:

AIM

To examine projects for *ideal* human habitat etc.
I don't follow your idea that there should be no conclusions a priori. I agreed here with the old chaps in Paris that some document must be the result of our work. The document has a vital task to fulfil, it must be written. We agree on this in Holland.

NEW WORKING METHOD

We should remind the members of the method of work followed at Aix and prior to Aix (a commission for each aspect of the total habitat object – social, aesthetic, economic etc. – instead of a commission for each kind of habitat object on the scale as a totality). You should state why this analytical method complied with the spirit of the Athens Charter (four functions as opposed to multiple functions in associations – see Doorn) and explain why this method will never get us beyond the surface. Then a sentence to explain why the suggested method will bring out what we are looking for.

In explaining your scale of associations, I should do so a bit more elaborately. Your Doorn story about comparing projects numerically different but at the same point of the scale, and contrasting projects numerically equal at different points of the scale should be added, it was very clear.[2] Perhaps you could add too the comparison of projects numerically equal at the same point of the scale but each under different climatic, economical or social conditions.

Perhaps it could be good to add a special commission for tropical countries.

In your 'draft framework' you state that commissions should 'not force a predetermined philosophy onto any project' (fetch a mirror!). Agreed, but we don't want to dig & dig & dig & find next to nothing of what we are looking for as at Aix. Therefore it would be wise to ask participants beforehand to pay particular attention to the following problems. Perhaps you could put it like this:

We should like to ask those intending to submit a project to CIAM 10 to bring out clearly both in the contents and in the way of presentation some aspects which seem to us of fundamental significance (this in order to avoid at the congress such statements being made as: this or that is of great importance and should be studied by architects).
We want to study these at Algiers:[3]

a projects should manifest – in architectural terms – the real desire to overcome curbing polarities that actually don't exist, i.e. individual-collective, material-emotional, part-whole, permanency-change, inside-outside. These are ambivalent. They are not dualistic, nor are they polarities. This fact should be expressed everywhere in the plans.
b The projects should give form both to what is constant and to what is constantly changing. In the reality of time and space there is no dualism. (Use of the same word 'constant' and 'constantly' in order to link seeming polarities. Introduce a sentence on 'change' in basic Smithson here!)
  Bakema's point is important.[4] Buildings should withstand the onslaught of time and changing reality without losing their identity or obstructing the possibility of acquiring a new identity.
  Time as a positive factor in plastic expression in architecture.[5] In order to avoid man spending his life pushing down walls that need not have been there.
c Bakema's points 4, 5 and 6 (5 is excellent[6]). We must rediscover the faculty with which to distinguish between what is elementary or permanent to man and what is arbitrary or temporary to man (or not even that – just permanently arbitrary!). This is important as it stresses the need for imaginative thinking in architecture to discover what is and what just is not. We hope therefore that the projects will demonstrate a greater awareness of the manifold activities, desires, needs and frailties of man: *the greater reality of the doorstep*, your Aix story.[7]

The mesh of the four functions lets through most of what goes to make life.

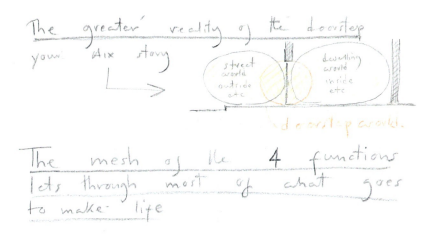

Fragment of Van Eyck's handwritten letter

d   Projects should attempt to solve some of the aesthetic problems resulting from the multiplication of units (structural units, housing units etc.). The grouping of units (elements) into theme. The variation and repetition of groups (theme, element, variation). The laws of Harmony in Motion (dynamic harmony next to static harmony) should be discovered in order to compel quantity into order – real order, aesthetic order – not regimentation.

RECAPITULATION
Participants should be asked to bring out clearly in their projects:
a   the ambivalence rather that the polarity of:
    individuality-collectivity;
    material-emotional (spiritual);
    part-whole;
    permanency-change.
b   Time should be introduced creatively (flexibility of construction, structure and plan).
c   Eye for manifold aspects, i.e. all that happens on the doorstep and the expression of this in architecture.
d   Aesthetic problems resulting from repetition, *the* aesthetic problem of our time.

That's all. Please introduce a, b, c and d somehow.
Participants must know what there bloody will be up this time. No holy Harlow stuff this time. Why not say so in advance!

So long,
A. van Eyck

Orientation

Van Eyck's alternative version of the guideline for CIAM 10, written in October 1954[1]

> *The culture of particular form is approaching its end,*
> *the culture of determined relations has begun.*
> Mondrian[2]

There need be no difference of opinion as to the role CIAM has played in the past. Focusing its attention on urbanism first and foremost it desired – and succeeded – to evolve a technique for urbanism, capable of counteracting the forces that disfigured the places in which we live; capable of restoring basic principles of order.

The overwhelming variety of city activities were classified into four fundamental functions. Each of which was conceived more or less as a totality in itself. In this way architects and urbanists were able to comprehend more clearly the positive potential of the twentieth century (Charte d'Athènes).

The highly analytical approach CIAM adopted went hand in hand with a particular kind of social consciousness, with an undiminished belief in progress, the very nature of which called for confidence in the possibilities of science and technique on the one hand, suspicion of the possibilities of art and aesthetics on the other (functionalism).

Since the war, however, we have become more and more aware that if urbanism and architecture are really to meet man and not to miss him, a profounder approach will be imperative. There can be no doubt as to the fundamental validity of the Athens Charter (as a necessary preliminary). It is not the contents that demand essential change today, but the spirit in which it is employed.

Already at Bridgwater a plea for imaginative thinking was made. Since then a new aesthetic consciousness has been winning ground. Urbanism is now in the process of becoming an art dependent upon and unthinkable without form – the distance between urbanism and architecture is diminishing.

It became clear to us at Hoddesdon (CIAM 8) that it was exactly those aspects (forces) that elude classification into either of the four functions that make the core of a city stand for so much more than its centre (civic centre) – the word core was indeed well chosen to express this shift of accent.

In other words it became clear that what actually goes to the making of life falls through the mesh of the four functions; lies, in fact, beyond the narrow scope of analytical thinking. In imaginatively relating the four functions to each other it should prove possible to express what has hitherto eluded 'conscious expression'.

The chief result of Aix (CIAM 9) was the spontaneous recognition by several younger groups of a mutual outlook. What had been fermenting took on shape and was contained in some of the work presented, as well as in what was said standing round it, i.e. a greater awareness of *significant relations* and the necessity of giving expression to these relations – this greater reality as it were – in terms of planning, i.e. *in terms of form*. In fact form came forward as a direct and positive factor, the tool with which we can specifically establish the kind of order an imaginatively planned environment can bestow on man and society as a framework for fuller life (a tool furthermore for the effective use of which we accept complete responsibility).

In order to get beyond the surface, now that we are faced with the actual construction and reconstruction of human habitats, greater comprehension and creative use of the forces of human association must be made since these are the very basis of every built form.

ORGANISATION

With the encouragement of the council, entr'acte meetings were held by a group of younger CIAM members at Doorn (Holland), London and Paris. The object was to discuss:

a Why urbanism conceived in terms of the Athens Charter tends to produce habitats in which vital human associations are inadequately expressed.
b Why the commission system employed so far had failed.
c In what way the difficulties implied above should be overcome.

It was agreed that the projects presented at the next congress should be *ideal projects* aimed at solving issues insufficiently recognised hitherto, yet vital today.

It was furthermore agreed that the existing commissions should be dropped, since they had not only proved inadequate (fruitless) but are in every way incompatible with the real content of CIAM.

Instead we propose a different, more ecological approach. At CIAM 10 attention should be focussed on:

1 vital issues bearing directly on the total subject of Habitat design; issues which nevertheless each contain all the aspects hitherto segregated into the existing commissions, and:
2 the study of each Habitat project presented in the light of its particular – unique – context as well as in the light of the particular kind (degree of complexity) of the community to which it belongs, i.e. in the appropriate field on the scale of Association as shown below.

A housing sector of a city will be considered at the top of the scale (under city 4) and can in this way be compared with analogous developments in other cities or contrasted with numerically similar developments in different fields on the scale of Association.

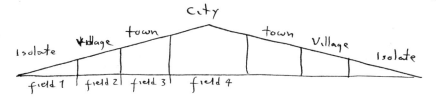

Why city-town-village-isolate?

The traditional association hierarchy is expressed in the words City, Town, Village and Isolate which are symbols – image entities – that stand for a much more complex series of relationships than can be expressed by 'large group, group, small group, single dwelling', which imply simply numerical accumulations. Although they may be mutating it is important to retain them as starting points as they are whole things and particular things and it is as whole things in *a network of related whole things* that we wish to consider the problem of Habitat. The words, the entities, may change. At CIAM 10 we may put our finger on this change and find new patterns of association.

This method of work will induce a study of human association as a first principle and of the four functions as basic aspects of each total problem.

At the Council meeting in Paris the group previously mentioned was charged with the task of preparing the framework of CIAM 10.

FRAMEWORK

Juste ce qu'il faut de souterrain entre le vin et la vie.
Tristan Tzara[3]

A The greater reality of the doorstep

We must rediscover the faculty with which to distinguish between what is permanent and essential to man and what is arbitrary, what *is* and what is *not*. Realising that what is constant and constantly changing is ambivalent in time and space. We must develop a greater awareness of significant relations, as well as the capacity to stimulate their expression through form. The new human habitat should reflect and stimulate the primary contact between man and man, between man and thing – what we call 'the greater reality of the doorstep'. We should manifest in architectural terms our desire to overcome the curbing polarities from which we are still suffering:
– individual-collective;
– physical-spiritual;
– internal-external;
– part-whole;
– permanence-change.

The time has come to recognise them as duo-phenomena.

In view of the above we propose that CIAM 10 should study the problem of the dwelling along the following lines. (One working party adequately subdivided.)
1. the dwelling as such, the homestead of the family constituting the smallest collective entity.
2. the relation between the dwelling and its exterior space – individual and collective.
3. the relation between the dwellings within a larger housing unit.
4. the relation between these larger housings units.
5. the degree of integration within the housing sector, housing group or larger housing unit, of the other major urban functions.
6. the degree of differentiation of the different basic types of dwellings within a larger housing unit, within a group of such housing units, within a housing sector.

1 – 6 Always in terms of design!

B L'habitat pour le plus grand nombre – the Aesthetics of number

In order that we may overcome the menace of quantity now that we are faced *with l'habitat pour le plus grand nombre,* the aesthetics of number, the laws of 'Harmony in motion' must be discovered. Projects should attempt to solve the aesthetic problems that result through the standardisation of constructional elements; through the repetition of similar or dissimilar dwellings within a larger housing unit, through the repetition and grouping of larger housing units (theme), similar or dissimilar in type, through the repetition of such housing groups.

In view of this we propose that special attention should be focussed on the following problems: (one working party adequately subdivided)
1. repetition of dwellings and structural elements within a larger housing unit (technical implications);
2. repetition and grouping of such larger housing units;
3. repetition (and variation) of such housing groups;
4. aesthetic implications of A.6.

C Growth and change

The introduction of 'time' as a positive factor in plastic expression. Architecture and planning must loose something of their finite character. Habitat should be planned and constructed so as not to resist their own spontaneous development (the development of those they serve). To resist change is to loose identity. This counts both for those the Habitat serves as for the Habitat itself.

One working party adequately subdivided should study the following issues:
1 growth and change within the dwelling (flexibility);
2 growth and change within the larger housing unit;
3 growth and change within the housing sector;
4 structural and constructional implications;
5 implications of B 1, 2, 3.

D **The ecological approach** (already specified)

The study of each Habitat project presented in the light of its particularly – unique – context as well as in the light of the particular kind (degree of complexity) of community to which it belongs, i.e. in its appropriate field of association.
   One working party with sub-parties for each field of association and a final party for relations between these fields. Each party should contain members from each of the parties A, B and C.

1 The isolate human habitat
2 in the village
3 in the town
4 in the city
5 conclusions 1, 2, 3 and 4.

The manner in which the problems mentioned under A, B, C and D can best be divided for study is a matter of further discussion. It seems probable that the experience gained through the study of A, B and C will help in the final study of D so that the working parties could be regrouped after working on A, B and C in order to study D. (One for each field of association with a final working party to relate what has been discovered by each).
   Each party or sub-party should have a chairman, whose job it is to see that discussions run smoothly. It is not his job to force his personal opinion on the working party. (This in contrast to the past).

Nagele grid for CIAM 10

Grid prepared by Van Eyck on behalf of 'de 8' for CIAM 10 at Dubrovnik, 1956[1]

Panel 1

- **physical and plastic content**
  a large territory claimed form the sea, man made – geometric – visually unlimited windswept. a territory adjusted to the changing mode of agricultural production. problem: a space for approx. 2500 people to live in, visually limited – plastically defined – protective.
- **social content**
  old land: local farm-hand has his dwelling not in the village but on the farm. he is tied to the farmer and depends on an uncertain and scanty livelihood upon hand and horse. small spare time enterprise to make ends meet. socially he is of course hardly integrated.
  new land: field labourer selected from all over the country, has his dwelling in the village. he is no longer tied to the farmer and depends for a regular livelihood upon the machine and science. he adapts himself to the new scale of life but retains his former religious faith, is socially already well integrated.
- **problem**
  new village primarily a home for field labourers. core and housing zone develop simultaneously. in contrast to prevailing village forms there need therefore be no schism between the core and the surrounding housing zone. the entire village should be the expression of unity.

Panel 2

- total area of territory in the process of being claimed from the sea: 220.000 ha.
- area N.E. Polder: 48.000 ha.
- ca. 1600 agric. farms, area 40.000 ha.
- future population N.E. Polder: ca. 40.000
- Nagele population: ca. 2500.

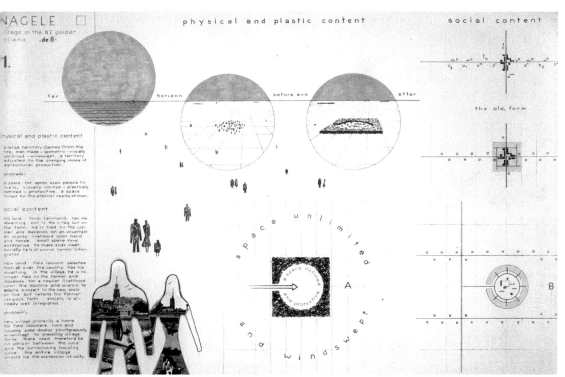
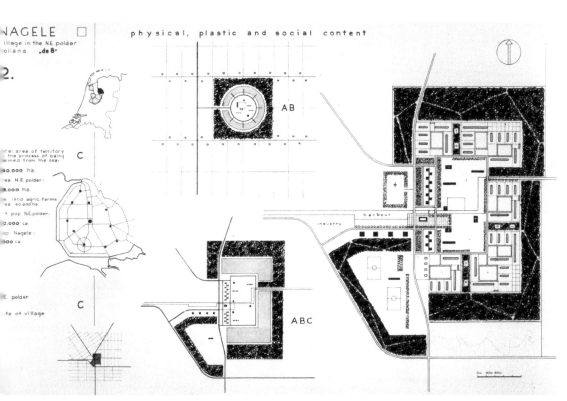

NAGELE

village in the N.E. polder
holland „de 8"

3.

D relation
dwelling — core,
relation
district — core,

some places of contact
with those from beyond
the village.

E relation
indiv. dwelling – dwelling group,
relation
group — central green,
relation
central green — polder,

aspect of ascending
dimensions.

F relation
central green — wood,
relation
dwelling group — dwell. group

groves where children
play and parents meet,
lead to the wood.

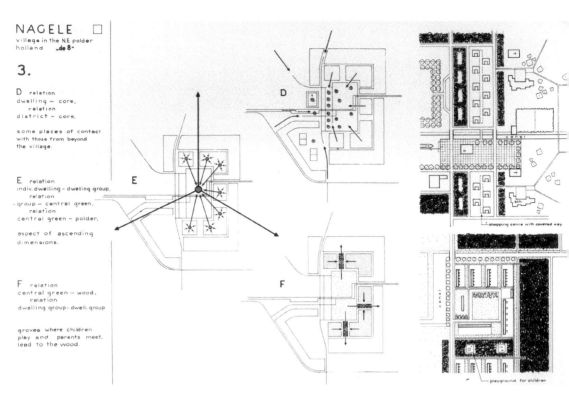

shopping centre with covered way

playground for children

NAGELE

village in the N.E. polder
holland „de 8"

4.

G a large central green,
groves, woods and places for
fun, repose and seclusion;
these rather than the
rigidity of the vast polder
or the „streets" of the usual
village form.

H a central green and en-
circling dwellings: perhaps
a contribution towards
unity inspite of spiritual
discrimination.

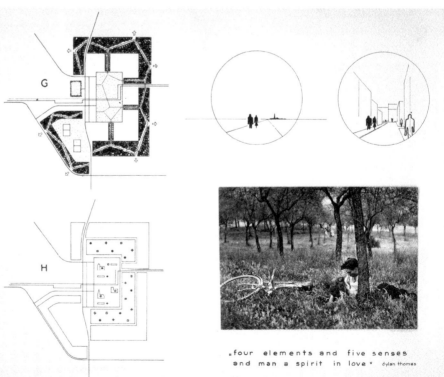

"four elements and five senses
and man a spirit in love" dylan thomas

Panel 3

D relation dwelling – core
   relation district – core
   some places of contact with those from beyond the village
E relation individual dwelling – dwelling group
   relation group – central green
   relation green – polder
   aspect of ascending dimensions
F relation central green – wood
   relation dwelling group – dwelling group
   Groves where children play and parents meet lead to the wood

Panel 4

G a large central green, groves, woods and places for fun, repose and seclusion; these rather than the rigidity of the vast polder or the 'streets' of the usual village form
H a central green and encircling dwellings: perhaps a contribution towards unity in spite of spiritual discrimination

'four elements and five senses and man a spirit in love'
Dylan Thomas

Postcard to Bakema on the dissolution of Dutch CIAM

Handwritten postcard in Bakema archives dated 19 February 1957

For that reason alone,[1] 'our consciousness as a group' has become a burden; for that reason alone I would like to recover a different 'consciousness' – sprung from a different 'us' – not a burden but a stimulus … a *delight*. Voilà – let's wrap up the whole business and start again, let's strike a new note. Realizing De Stijl (i.e. staying dynamic) is a good starting point. Accepting the positive-negative, the yes-no, the light-dark, inside-outside etc. as a totality and visualizing this in what we have to make. Isn't that enough? I no longer take to those social boy-scouts with their good deeds and sloppy forms. (So how can I still consider them social?)
We have to be negative. neg. neg. negative.
N e g a t i v e !
That's good – positive and, if you like, social.

New earth, new plants, new weeds. We really should be new-old again.

Talk at the Otterlo Congress

Transcription of Van Eyck's talk on 11 September 1959[1]

I should like to start with the question of Euclidean and non-Euclidean space. There was a period in history in which the mind of man functioned and thought according to what we now call a Euclidean or classical way of thinking. On the other hand, round about the end of the last century, a non-Euclidean form of perception has been evolved. We see non-Euclidean aspects in Rimbaud and we see non-Euclidean aspects in Cézanne. We see it gradually starting in science and art, in physics and anthropology, in painting and poetry: a new and different conception – another way of thought – another language. And what is wonderful about this non-Euclidean thinking – this non-Euclidean language – is that it is contemporary. It is contemporary to all difficulties, social and political that our period poses to man. In each period we require the specific language that corresponds to our problems.

So, we have two different views of the world, Euclidean and non-Euclidean. But man himself is never either Euclidean or non-Euclidean, he is just man. Our problems are also those of eternal man – of archaic man. We are after all just archaic people. We do nearly all the same things that people did nearly 60,000 years ago. Man just remains the same.

What I want in architecture personally, is passionately to do the old. Because I believe that the moment you rediscover the old primordial principles of human nature, you discover something new. Because rediscovery always means to discover something new. It's just a constant rediscovery of eternal truth, which you translate into architecture, and that is the eternal truth of the ways of man. Man is always the same, in all places on earth and in all times. He has the same mental equipment, he just uses it and reacts differently according to his cultural or social background.

I put those archaic images in the right hand circle to remember that there have always been men, women and children, living in a kind of society. They represent constants in space and time, constants that constantly change. The yellow circle on the left shows three historical images. First, as a symbol of non-Euclidian thought, a contra-construction by Van Doesburg. It stands for the new dynamic concept of space. And, as I said, we must use this language created in our time to solve the human problems of our time. To do otherwise would be contradictory – it would be like using the machine in the wrong way. It's impossible. It's just logic, absolute logic, that you use the language – the spirit – of the period in order to solve the problems of the period. But the circle contains two other images which stand for other basic human values. They represent the wonder of Euclidian order. They correspond to man's fundamental desire for enclosure. Man breathes in and out. There is no man on earth who can breath either in or out. You go out and you go in – you have a closed and an open space. Man breathes in and out. It's simply fundamental that

Aldo van Eyck arguing at the Otterlo congress

John Voelcker, Alison Smithson and Oskar Hansen viewing Van Eyck's 'Otterlo Circles'

man does both – he always will. Somehow we have seen in modern architecture a certain desire to open up a house in such a way that it only breathes out and it never gets the chance of breathing in.

That's why I went to the Sahara, to rediscover enclosure in its archaic, absolute form. It was a tremendous experience. Thus I asked myself what I wrote here: *Is architecture going to reconcile basic values?* In each culture, as a result of the geographic, climatic, cultural or religious circumstances, certain aspects of man are exaggerated. In other countries, other aspects of man are expressed more clearly, but they are all aspects which are universally human. This is not a question of history. I am thinking of it in the sense of the *musée imaginaire* introduced by Malraux: a concept intended to enrich the knowledge of man – not the knowledge of architecture but the knowledge of man. We have to find out who and what we are.

Who am I? What am I? Who are you? If I don't know that, then I can't build a roof over my head. What I have been doing for years – it's my hobby almost – is to simply (I won't say study, I'll say enjoy) enjoy just the way people have lived and behaved in all ages and in all times, and this has saved me, I believe, from eclecticism. It's not a matter of eclecticism, it's a matter of finding out, not how they make a kitchen in Japan or how they make a kitchen in Africa, but how a man and a woman and a child eat in Japan and how they eat in the Sahara. I am not going to try to make a kitchen so that you can eat as they do in Japan or as they do in the Sahara, but merely to represent the fundaments of what it is about, not a bedroom, but sleeping. And this simply hangs in your head and you've sort of come into contact with the reality of what we are trying to do today – not making a bedroom, not organizing space – just making a habitat for people to live in, with the problems of today.

In the twentieth century the world has become very small. We have the possibility of travelling to the remotest places with ease. Japan is now very near. It is possible for us to discover different cultures and by so doing enrich ourselves, not by copying, not by eclecticism, but by more deeply understanding the mystery of man. It is that which I find important. It is not a question of history when I study a house

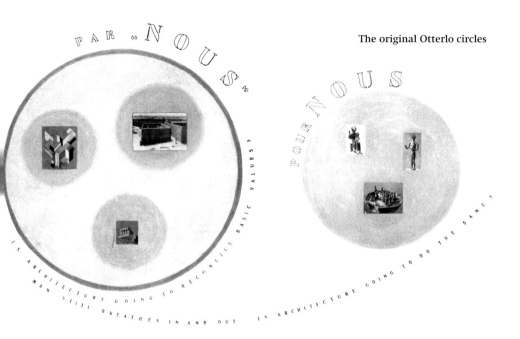

The original Otterlo circles

In the left circle
A contra-construction of Van Doesburg's *Maison Particulière* (1923)
The Temple of Nike at the Athens Acropolis (424 B.C.)
Houses at Aoulef in the Algerian Sahara

In the right circle
Three bronze age sculptures
A Sardic statuette of a sitting woman with child
An Etruscan statuette of a standing man
A Cypriot burial gift, a round dish containing a little community of people

in Ur or a Greek house from the period of Pericles. I only want to see, to enjoy the marvel of a house which is truly human, for each time I see a house which is truly human, of whatever period, I am enriched. It's not a question of form but a question of human content.

Now I'm going to switch over to the concrete job.

W.H. Lovett:[2] I thought from reading the correspondence I received that the conference would be devoted primarily to the explanation of concrete projects and not the architects' individual philosophy.

Alison Smithson: Aldo is not stating his individual philosophy, he is stating our philosophy – the philosophy of the group.

Van Eyck: Honestly, I can't explain this building until I have said that. You see, I haven't ironed this things out completely because I wanted to make the whole thing a mixture of concreteness and abstraction; of philosophy and building. Otherwise I could have hung up this building on the whole wall – there is such a lot of it. I just took a few photographs as a symbol – perhaps some of you will be seeing it in reality.[3]

Is architecture going to reconcile basic values?

*The **1959** talk at the Otterlo Congress edited by Van Eyck in **1961***[1]

There was a time not so long ago when the minds of men moved along a deterministic groove; let's call it a Euclidian groove. It coloured their behaviour and vision, what they made and did and what they felt. Then some very keen men, with delicate antennae – painters, poets, philosophers and scientists most of them – jumped out of this groove and rubbed the deterministic patina off the surface of reality. They saw wonderful things and did not fail to tell us about them. Our unbounded gratitude is due to them: to Picasso, Klee, Mondrian and Brancusi; to Joyce, Le Corbusier, Schoenberg, Bergson and Einstein, to the whole wonderful gang. They set the great top spinning again and expanded the universe – the outside and the inside universe. It was a wonderful riot – the cage was again opened.

But society still moves along in the old groove, making only sly use of what these men discovered; worse still, applying on a purely technical, mechanical and decorative level, not the essence but what was gleaned from it in order to give the pretence of moving more effectively, but in reality moving securely and profitably along the old circumscribed groove. We know all this. But do we also know that architecture has been doing the same for the last 30 years?

A damnable truth this. When are architects going to stop fondling technique for its own sake – stop stumbling after progress? When are they really going to join the riot and stop gnawing at the edges of a great idea? Surely we cannot permit them to continue selling the diluted essence of what others spent a life-time finding. They have betrayed society in betraying the essence of contemporary thought. Nobody can really live in what they concoct, although they may think so.

Now what is wonderful about this non-Euclidian idea – this other vision – is that it is contemporary; contemporary to all our difficulties social and political, economic and spiritual. What is tragic is that we have failed to see that it alone can solve them. Each period requires a constituent language – an instrument with which to tackle the human problems posed by the period, as well as those which, from period to period, remain the same, i.e. those posed by man – by all of us as a primordial being. *The time has come to gather the old into the new; to rediscover the archaic principles of human nature.*

To discover anew implies discovering something new. Translate this into architecture and you'll get new architecture – real contemporary architecture. Architecture is a constant rediscovering of constant human proportions translated into space. Man is always and everywhere essentially the same. He has the same mental equipment though he uses it differently according to his cultural or social background, according to the particular life pattern of which he happens to be a part. Modern architecture has been harping continually on what is different in our time to such an extent even that it has lost touch with what is not different, with what is always essentially the same. This grave mistake was not made by the poets, painters and sculptors. On the contrary, they never narrowed down experience. They enlarged and intensified it; tore down not merely the form barriers as did the architects, but the emotional ones as well. In fact the language they evolved coincides with the emotional revolution they brought about. The language architects evolved, however, and this after the pioneering period was over, coincides only with itself and is therefore essentially sterile and academic – literally abstract. We must evolve a richer tool – a more effective approach – to solve the environmental problems our period poses today. These problems will not remain the same, but they concern the same man, and that is our cue.

Is architecture going to reconcile basic values? In each culture there are things universally valid which for some reason or other – climate, tradition, taboos – are emphasized whilst others are subdued. Man suffers in many ways from these restrictions; from what is over-emphasized at the cost of what is omitted and often forgotten. Now, surely, what is peculiar in a culture – what gives it the colour – does not necessarily have to depend on what is omitted and what is not. It can depend on how things are combined instead of on what things are omitted or overstressed. Today we can travel to the remotest places, and if we can't, we can buy a paperback and bring them close. We can meet 'ourselves' everywhere – in all places and ages – doing the same things in a different way, feeling the same differently, reacting differently to the same. *(The Otterlo circles: see p. 201)*

The three little photographs united in the first circle are symbols not of conflicting aspects, but of partial aspects. I have been in love with all three for years, with the values divided between them. I can't separate them any more, I simply can't. They complement each other, belong together. Add 'San Carlo alle quattro Fontane' – not just to avoid the trinity – and we can start reconciling them – the essence, not the form – in an endless sequence of possibilities that will really fit man. This is our job: *'par nous pour nous'* and by 'for us' I mean each man and all men; one man and another man, the individual and society (a dual phenomenon that cannot be split into conflicting polarities – hence the second circle). I have invented a slogan to link the two circles because I think the time has come for us to see to it that they coincide: *Man still breathes both in and out; when is architecture going to do the same?*

The time has come moreover to avoid the pitfalls of eclecticism, regionalism and modernism, for these are utterly false alternatives – three kinds of short-sightedness that continually alternate. Thus, redoing Palazzo Vecchio's tower all the way up in Milan, with the aid of inverted flying buttresses and syncopated windows, strikes me as an exercise hardly worth taking.[2] It is annihilating instead of reconciling the basic principles I mentioned a moment ago, allowing the one to destroy, instead of enhance, the other. Of course this was not the objective, but it is there in the object made.

L. Belgiojoso, E. Peressutti, E. Rogers, *Torre Velasca*, Milan, 1959

We simply cannot breathe only one way – we can hold our breath for only a very short time. Modern architecture has been trying hard to breathe only out without breathing in – and that is just as stifling a thing to do as the opposite – at any rate the result is the same. You can't open up unless you enclose. You can't just split dual phenomena into polarities and alternate your loyalty from one to the other without causing despair. It is hard to avoid doing this entirely but we can at least avoid turning it into a human principle by splitting what is virtually unsplittable into a set of artificial absolutes. It is a devilish disease causing breaking point tension everywhere. I regard it as the major hobby of society – in spite of the wonderful effort made by art and science to flout society's genuine love of schizophrenia.

There is one more thing that has been growing in my mind since the Smithsons uttered the word 'doorstep' at Aix.[3] It hasn't left me ever since. I have been mulling over it, expanding the meaning as far as I could strech it. I have even gone so far as to identify it as a symbol with what architecture means as such and should accomplish. *To establish the 'inbetween' is to reconcile conflicting polarities. Provide the place where they can interchange and you re-establish the original dual phenomena.* I called this *'la plus grande réalité du seuil'* in Dubrovnic. Martin Buber calls it *'das Gestalt gewordene Zwischen'*. You can't translate that because the equivalent of 'Gestalt' is missing in both English and French. Take an example: the world of the house with me inside and you outside or vice versa, there is also the world of the street – the city – with you inside and me outside or vice versa. Get what I mean: two worlds clashing, no transition. The individual on one side, the collective on the other. Between the two, society in general, throws up lots of barriers, whilst architects in particular are so poor in spirit that they provide doors two inches thick and six foot high (flat surfaces in a flat surface – of glass as often as not). Just think of it: 2 inches or 1/4 of an inch if it is glass) between such fantastic phenomena – hair-raising, brutal – like a guillotine. Every time we pass through a door like that, we are split in two – but we don't take notice any more. Is that the reality of a door? What then, I ask, is the greater reality of a door? Well, perhaps it is the localized setting for a wonderful human gesture: conscious entry and departure. That's what a door is; something that frames your coming and going, for it is a vital experience not only for those that do so but also for those encountered or left behind. *A door is a place made for an occasion that is repeated millions of times in a lifetime between the first entry and the last exit.* I think that is symbolical. And what is the greater reality of a window? I leave that to you.

For 30 years architects have been providing the outside for man even on the inside. But that is not their job at all. Architecture means providing inside for man even outside – and that goes for urbanism as well. We must also stop splitting the making of a habitat into two disciplines – architecture and urbanism. Why? That's a long story. A house must be like a small city if it's to be a real house; a city like a large house if it's to be a real city. In fact, what is large without being small has no more real size than what is small without being large. If there is no real size, there will be no human size.

If a thing is just small or just large we can't cope with it. The same goes for many and few, small and many – large and many, small and few. The thought processes in planning cannot be divided on the basis of part-whole; small-large; few-many; i.e. into architecture and urbanism.[4]

The moment of realization

Talk at the conclusion of the Otterlo Congress edited by Van Eyck in 1961[5]

The wonderful thing about architecture is that it is an art – just that. The terrible thing about architects is that they are not always artists. Worse yet, they are semi-artists (and that is the last thing they should be) comfortably engaged in something super. But architecture is neither a semi- nor a super-art. It is an art – simply that.' I think we are beginning to understand this again – and that is a crucial thing in itself.

For almost half a century architects have been tampering with the principle of art, squeezing it into the jacket of semi-science (not science, oh no – semi-science – applied). I mean technique and the kind of rubbish that clings to technique – progress, weak mechanical thinking; grovelling naturalism; sentimental social thinking (antiseptics compared with the other arts). Compared with science, architecture and especially urbanism, have made a very poor show. Far from expanding reality as the others have done, architects have contracted reality – sidetracked the issue of contemporary creativity. You all know how suspicious architects have been of the few exceptions that defy measurement in grams or millimetres, and fall through the coarse mesh of the four functions, and are therefore regarded as contraband (hence all the graphic surfaces with hollowness on both sides, and everybody a nobody on either side). Heavens, that we should have been fooled so long. Architecture is an art, and we are not going to twist it into something else because we can't live up to what it is, we are not going to redefine it – so as to make it fit neatly round a lack of creative potential. Modern architecture has been dishonest, with a halo of honesty more often than not. If it were a reaction against falsity, which it was supposed to be, why was art rejected instead of falsity? It wasn't the pioneers that started flirting with science but the hordes that came after the next generation, who flirted with what they imagined science to be. You can't really fall in love with what science really is without somehow falling in love with what art really is (perhaps you can, but I personally can't see how).

We know again that we never perceive until we conceive. What we discover through a microscope or telescope is kaleidoscopic – the projection of the mind. You see, there is no longer a conflict between science and art (there is between technique and both). There has been a lot of suffering through split loyalty, but that should be over by now. If architecture is an art (an art-science or science-art like all art and science), let's not add or subtract anything from it; let's not postpone coming to terms with the art process any longer. We must come to terms with the machinery of art.

Infinitely more important that the confrontation with the end products presented here in Otterlo, is the confrontation with the art process – possible non-art process – which made them what they are in each case. We will get closest to what is wrong or right in each – what's wrong or right with us – by following the trail of the creative process, getting to know the alchemy of the design realization. That is our job, to shed light on the moment of realization within this process: whether it took place at all and whether it took place at the right moment during the process. We have not only got the thing made, we have got the man that made it here too, so let's tackle him: the way he did it. A hitch in the process means a hitch in the product. Where in the process did the hitch take place and why? The why and where are important. It means getting close to the subject – the man – that made the object; listening to the dialogue between him and what he was making. That means we must commit ourselves – or go home.

Now, if we think a project is the gradual crystallization of an idea, in the sense that the idea ensues smoothly as a reward once the factual data have been adequately related, we are wrong. It is the moment of realization that counts in the art process – Kahn has already referred to it – and it doesn't just follow because you have done your homework well. No! The process is not as mechanical as that, nor is it as naturalistically functional. You may have to start like that, but you won't meet what you are after anywhere along the route. You'll have to jump sooner or later, you'll have to risk it. That is the moment of realization – the jump, the risky jump. It is really tragic when you think the way architects and urbanists still fail to creep out of their determinist straight jackets; still fail to really participate in the contemporary world of art; still cling to mother nature as if unable to walk without her. Now, in order to be natural in architecture, we must depart from nature. It is in the nature of art that it should be different from nature. Of this I am certain. We are not concerned with the way nature does the trick. Art has its own kind of logic. It looks illogical beside nature's logic, but so does nature's logic look illogical beside that of art – beside that of man. Hence the conflict and the fear to risk the jump. Nature has

G. de Carlo, housing in Matera, 1956–1957

R. Erskine, project for an arctic city, 1958

a process of realization quite its own. You can learn something from it but you can't copy it. Nature's products seem accurately composed; seem to fit into a big scheme well enough, but the over-abundancy is staggering – the waste! We are concerned with art, not nature (think of what would happen if nature imitated art!).

The moment of realization is what is crucial in the realization process. Of course there is nothing wrong in discussing the whole process as long as we know we can't get to the other side without jumping. No arbitrary stop-gap-whim is going to bridge the gap. The art is in the jumping: how you take off, when, and where. Without the jump there will be no architecture – good or less good; just buildings and cities – bad or worse.

Looking back at Erskine's contribution, or Polonyi's, for instance, both follow the natural lead a long way, relating the factual realities that were relevant into coherent stories – urban life in the tundra; mass lake and lakeshore recreation in Hungary. Both stories are exciting (Erskine's was a masterpiece), but the ultimate design concepts evolved demonstrate that the natural story-making process can never be extended in a straight line beyond the story into architecture with no noticeable transition as it seems to be effected in nature. The realization process can cling to the story until the story ends; can grow with it, coincide with it, but there won't be any architecture without the crucial jump. Intuition can make you do the right jump long before the story ends. I have the feeling that both Erskine and Polonyi are still clinging faithfully and a bit fearfully to their respective stories. But they seem well prepared for the jump. I suggest that many projects took a side-track instead of jumping. We must not mistake one for the other. I believe Rogers did. So did de Carlo. It is obvious de Carlo can jump, but he side-tracked before the moment came, slipped into the wrong groove. At any rate, the houses he showed failed to become Calabrian houses for Calabrians, which is the only thing they ought to have become. It is the hiatus, the crucial pause, the gap which necessitates jumping. Otherwise you are forcing people to live in a gap instead of in a house. That is what's tragic about not jumping – millions of people surviving in millions of gaps. The function of architecture is to overcome hollowness, so let's jump – let's all of us jump.

Letter to Giedion on the dissolution of CIAM

Undated manuscript, obviously written shortly after 10 December 1960[1]

Dear Pep,

I saw your document some days ago. It will of course be published as you wish. The difficulty is that the facts stated are exact enough, inexact is the light the document sheds on them. We'll reply to the document in print therefore and hope it won't cause any more ill feeling.[2]

You may be right about the majority, but not a single one objected to the document you quote in Otterlo when it was read and put before the meeting. In fact all consented. You see, Pep, there's the weakness. The majority disliked us but did nothing – contributed no ideas – talked about membership, membership, membership – the old Prof. Schütte and Co story.[3] Our not very gentle method got rid of them (Schütte and Co can't breathe alone – they need the plumes of CIAM). That killed CIAM *as it was*. At Aix we all – I mean the future Team 10 group – wanted CIAM but CIAM without the bad perfume. CIAM stuck to its bad perfume like a maniac and the council – especially the old members – behaved very, very badly towards us; wanted to hand over but supervise.[4] It was tyranny all right, dressed as sloppy democracy. You gave us Roth and Rogers along at Dubrovnic – now I ask you. No Pep, to get rid of the bad odour we had to get rid of the body – not the idea necessarily. This we did – If CIAM can stand up again without this particular bad odour – fine. If people want it they must do it, for it is a great, great pity a wonderful CIAM is not there at the moment. I don't know whether it's going to be wonderful though should it continue in whatever form. Not until an idea carries it, not until it can stand on its own feet, will collaboration with the old generation (not the middle generation) again be possible. Unless you people want to prolong your grip beyond its limits and necessity, which I somehow feel is what you want – and at the same time don't want. Sert said in Philadelphia that our job is to substantiate, enrich, make more subtle, fill with more humour the fundamentals found (and there ready for use) by your generation. Now this is *not* the thing *your* generation must tell *us*, but vice versa. We like to word our own respect, we're not dumb. I think it's true that we learnt how to fly from you people. Stop shouting this around all the time. We can fly ourselves now, with you perhaps. Now that we can fly we don't want to do so in quite the same way (we're men not birds) as you taught us, but we're thankful for what you all did. Yet we're not sure you taught us to fly in the right way, nor are we sure that you taught us to fly in the right direction. I for my part know that both the method and route were wrong. Not only in the light of today but also in the light of yesterday. The story of modern architecture – let alone urbanism – is terrifyingly weak, hollow, rational and abstract if you compare it to the avant-gardism in other creative fields of art and science – it follows the 20th-century political story more than the spiritual-creative one. Architecture and urbanism especially have simply sidetracked the main issue of constituent contemporary thinking. Their approach was mechanical – naturalistic – idealistic and deterministic (Artaria, Schmidt, Steiger, Roth, Van Eesteren, Forbat etc. etc.) Just the wrong people shouting the wrong story. You've simply got to stop sticking to this story. You, Pep, know how weak it is. That has got nothing to do with what you and C.W. have been after for a lifetime.

CIAM extended the inherent weaknesses of the Bauhaus climate – teutonic, stale, didactic derivative – instead of its strength. I was laughed at when I mentioned Schlemmer and Klee at Bridgwater. Only Moholy and Breuer (atrocious architect) and Herbert Bayer were allowed. And no Mies, oh no, no Mies! Too near De Stijl, and the Bauhaus hates De Stijl because it got what it stood for first hand from Van Doesburg and some Russians passing by.

The facts, the facts. I ought to put the whole thing straight one day in a long article with an encyclopaedia of facts and proofs – that is what I ought to do. But I don't think I actually will unless the old lie is continued. Why, Pep, this lie?

For years C.W. – still, though she perhaps doesn't believe it, our supreme friend – she's the embodiment of an idea CIAM never succeeded in making its own, never understood – but for a few.

Ask yourself why I don't believe in the philosophy of CIAM whilst I do believe in the philosophy of all the arts combined into one story. That, Pep, is not my deficiency. I really know what twentieth-century creative thought is about. It's the deficiency of CIAM that the philosophy which ties the rest into one magnificent story is hardly recognizable in CIAM. And look at the tragic results all over the world.

Thousands of millions of people living in uninhabitable modern habitats and urban quarters. Come to Amsterdam and you'll witness the utter desolation due partly to weak adaptation but due also to the inherent insufficiency of the CIAM background. You know this, and yet.

Another teasing but fundamental remark: Why wasn't the CIAM climate such that C.W. would have liked to come – could have been one of its great members? Why? Why? Ask yourself that. And why – you brought this up and rightly so – didn't Barbara Hepworth want to participate in Bridgwater?[5] Same reason. Why? because of those damnable spiritual dilettantes called architects – those professional know-nothing-know-alls. Because the wrong people ooze out of society and become architects. The right people become poets even if they become bad ones – the same goes for painters. CIAM was so afraid of art that it fell in love with pseudo-science, i.e. bad applied science – technique. The poverty is ghastly, the executed results are worse than nineteenth-century chaos, for that had the benefit of being chaos – human chaos – and now we have chaos regimented. Open space? You mean hollowness inside and out, with man single and collective nowhere, a nobody on both sides. CIAM split fundamental dual phenomena into arbitrary polarities as all the fools still do from pulpit, council rooms and governments, and this is the very thing the great creative

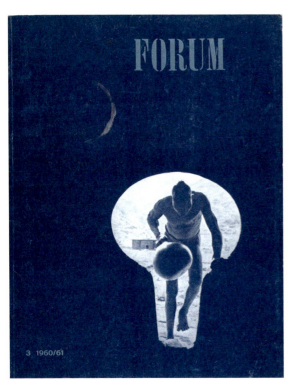

Door-window issue of Forum (August 1960), cover and start of Van Eyck's prose poem on the in-between.

gang to which CIAM ought to have belonged did not do. They redefined in thousands of poems, paintings, sculptures, ideas and formulas the unity of such polarities. The outside-inside spatial continuity story is a farce. Without appreciation of the value of extending the outside into the inside spiritual world, i.e. in the mind, head, heart and abdomen of man and society, the greater reality – neither outside nor inside – means nothing at all, boils down to abstract rubbish. Not with Corbu, but how I had to listen to Van Eesteren objecting to him year in year out, to Van Tijen, to all these semi-creative boy scouts. I was sick of it, really sick of it. If you help those that need CIAM to extend this bad thin philosophy (to grab what is already secondhand!!!) you'll have me against you with all the vehemence I'm capable of – with all my memory for facts.

Dear Pep, this is *not* a threat. As for the Gropius remark,[6] it was printed only in the 60 odd copies for Otterlo. I changed it on my own accord for the final print. I didn't want to be unkind personally. I hate that. But as much as I love the pioneers in whatever field, I loathe the side of Bauhaus that leaked into CIAM, and Gropius is the symbol of this side. That's why I struck at him – he represents the tyranny of dullness, mediocrity, non-creativity, pseudo-humanity – he's too afraid of evil. Besides his educational inheritance is a bad one – worldwide in a diluted form (thank goodness) but as bad as the dogma propounded is bad. Bad because it's a fraction of the story – and a fraction is just no story.

Now that we've got rid of all the 'members', taken their medal away, the time has come to shake hands and continue. Instead you go and write this document. Very understandable but you're hitting the wrong people, those it's worth while working with to continue the idea (first bring it up to the level where the poets and painters put it 40 years ago).

Now all we can do is reply with the whole story which it would have been better not to do. Still it's better not to do it, provided a modus can be found (notice there was no attack on you or Corbusier in the *Forum* number I edited and for which I wrote the text [7] – on the contrary).

I'm not a Judas but I'll shine light on the faces, on the Judases that kept architecture and urbanism (CIAM) from being part of the great spiritual movement of our time; that are responsible indirectly for the new desolation people live in. Responsible only in so far as they kept on hammering the idea into society long after its incompleteness was apparent in thought and realization. (A bit of Amsterdam – a new bit – is now planned exactly the same as the pre-war horror. No attempt was made to evolve beyond. Every attempt was subdued. Like Gropius, Van Eesteren is a despot though not enough people have noticed.)

And so let me end. As editor, I'll wait until I have some sort of reply from you – personal reply of course – I'm no demagogue like Bill, though you may think so (they strike with lies, if I have to I'll do it with the truth).

Dear Pep – we ought to have a good time someday together in Doldertal with C.W. and you. Talk it all over, forget what's only worth forgetting. Remember what's worth remembering and carry on. You've got no enemy in me at all. Did you like the door-window number of Forum and my English text 'There's a garden in her face'?[8] Send us a nice article for printing, one that will show that we are one family – better than all this bickering (we won't meet on that score).

Love to C.W. a thousand million times. Best wishes from all of us for yourself.

About the Economist project

Undated letter to the Smithsons, probably written shortly after 5 July 1961[1]

I have been thinking a lot about the Economist complex – especially after having seen Stirling's work at his office. These people all have a style which maybe will become threadbare. Your Economist is of a different order because what you 'are' is larger that what you can 'do' – ever do. That's as it should be always. It's a prerogative – a basic principle of art. 'Designing' entails no risk – you're safe. 'Invention' entails risk and no safety. I think it is a marvelous plan. The inbetween place – the actual door – will become one. It should be by means of the different treatment of the three elements & Boodles, i.e. by means of structural interval in relation to the dimension of the three elements (four actually). This is absolutely fundamental – proves that you can't split architecture and urbanism. You see, the three elements as *'volume dans l'espace'* are inconceivable without the detail invention. The elements are as it were reciprocally familiarized with the *participant*. He wouldn't be one if it wasn't so, he would just be a *spectator*, he would be excluded instead of included. The intermediary place would not be a place but a space for this very reason, i.e. abstract – hollow if you like. 'Urbanistically' conceived spaces always are hollow.

I walked down St. James Street, it's all going to be just right – Boodle's will become a twentieth-century reality too.[2] Detail the piazza surface beautifully – it's as important as the surfaces of the buildings – in fact piazza and building are one. This I think is very important – I mean the paving. Detail every bit – and do it better than the Seagram plateau. Every slab is wrong there: where they meet the flight of steps, the water and the columns, everywhere. If you succeed, I'll not be angry with Mies any more. You'll have mitigated my discontent, and furthermore grasp why I'm right on this score.

London was great – it's a metropolis for people, they 'live' there. An enormous village symphony.

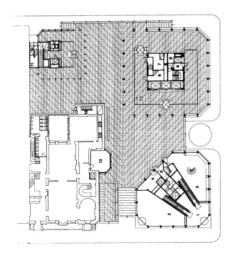

Ground floor

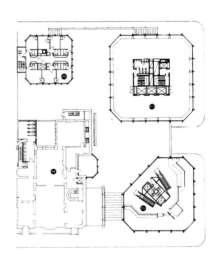

First floor

Alison and Peter Smithson, Economist Building, London, 1959–1964

The Economist Building and the historic Boodles' club building with its new bay coming together Photo Francis Strauven

7

The new start of Forum: The Story of Another Idea

Introduction to chapter 7

A session of the *Forum* editorial team, from left to right: unknown person, Schrofer, Van Eyck, Hardy's back, Bakema with Hertzberger lying on the foreground.

Forum was a Dutch architectural review that had already existed for some time. It had been founded in 1946 by the old *Architectura et Amicitia* ('A et A') architectural society in order to establish a common platform for the different tendencies in Dutch architecture, from the traditionalists of the Delft School to the modernists of CIAM. But in the course of the fifties the traditionalists, urged by the general spread of industrial building techniques, grew towards modernism so that the differences gradually faded. Holland saw the development of a kind of standard idiom that made the old polemics seem superseded. As a result, *Forum* became the podium for well-disposed reviews by architects writing fraternally about one another's work. Displeased by this state of affairs, the board of *A et A* decided to entrust the review to a younger and more dynamic editorial team which included, besides Bakema and Van Eyck, the architects Dick Apon, Ger Boon and Herman Hertzberger, art connoisseur Joop Hardy and graphic designer Jurriaan Schrofer.

Van Eyck found himself in the company of kindred spirits who valued and welcomed his views. Hardy and Schrofer belonged to his circle of friends. Both had a broad cultural horizon and held a non-hierarchical world-view. Hardy nurtured a strong interest in all forms of art, from primitive sculptures to the contemporary avant-garde, from Renaissance palaces to interiors of vernacular dwellings, and cultivated his own *'musée imaginaire'* in the form of extensive photographic archives.[1] Schrofer was averse to the rigid schemes of modern typography and considered all graphic components, text as well as images, to be equivalent so as to develop a meaningful dialogue between them. Bakema, Van Eyck's life-long ally and sparring partner, was the only institutionally-oriented member of the team. Being the head of one of the Netherlands' most prestigious firms, he depended on large commissions and regular consultations with various authorities. Owing to his experience with large scale projects, he was prone to rather pragmatic views. Beyond the basic ideas Bakema shared with Van Eyck, their points of view remained polarized. They actually formed the main poles in the editorial team, and it was in the field of force between them that the Forum ideas emerged and took shape. The younger members, Apon and Hertzberger, initially looked up to Bakema as much as to Van Eyck, but in the event were to side with the views of the latter.

For Van Eyck the invitation to join the new editorial team came at the right moment. The ideas he had been pondering in the course of the Team 10 discussions and his design experience had ripened and he was eager to have at his disposal an apt vehicle for expressing them. In fact, it was in *Forum* that he was to develop his key concepts and to publish his major articles. Together with *The Child, the City and the Artist*, which was written in the same period, his *Forum* articles constitute the substantial core of his writings. They also amount to a large volume of text which, for the sake of comprehensibility, is spread over three chapters in this edition: in the present chapter the opening manifesto, in the next the development of his key concepts, from the shape of the in-between to configurative design, and in the third 'the vernacular of the heart', i.e. life and building in archaic cultures which Van Eyck considered an evocative source of inspiration for contemporary design.

The first issue by the new editorial team, *'Het verhaal van een andere gedachte'* (The story of another idea), was launched in September 1959. Composed by Van Eyck, it was an elaborate manifesto that struck home. It opened with a downright assault on established modern town planning – particularly the established planning practice in the Netherlands which boasted a firm tradition of rational organization and efficient implementation. The Dutch town planners were plainly held responsible for the country's rush into uninhabitability. *'Seldom have our chances been greater. Seldom has a craft thus failed and a profession thus sunk below the level of the need.'* Looking for the causes of this plight, the author[2] situated its roots forthrightly in CIAM thinking, which developed 'the theoretical foundation upon which urbanism consciously or unconsciously rests'.

After this polemic introduction the 'story' begins with a critical overview of pre-war ideas, based on a selection of characteristic quotes from the first five congresses – a selection which, remarkably enough, had been made by Giedion in order to point out the achievements of CIAM.[3] Yet Van Eyck highlights the technocratic tenor of these texts by contrasting them with quotes from poets and artists of the same period. This assessment is followed by 'the story of another idea' proper, a comprehensive account of the new approach that emerged within and in opposition to post-war CIAM. It starts in 1947 with the contribution by the young Dutch delegates to the Congress of Bridgwater: Bakema, who moved to amend the aim of CIAM 'to satisfy man's emotional and material needs' by adding 'to stimulate man's spiritual growth'; and Aldo van Eyck himself who urged CIAM to abandon its narrow rationalism and identify itself with the new consciousness of the twentieth-century avant-garde. The Congress of Bergamo (1949) is skipped, but the story goes into all the more detail on the introduction of the 'core' concept at the Congress of Hoddesdon (1951): the Mars Group who introduced it, Giedion who defined it in sociological and historical terms, and Bakema explicitly connected it with the relation concept

– 'That is the moment of "core"; the moment in which we become aware of the fullness of life by experiencing relationships of whose existence we were unaware.' The long quotation from Giedion makes it clear that the author far from underestimates the part played by the older generation in the origin of 'the other idea'. Giedion, who had taken the initiative in steering post-war CIAM in a new direction, did not define 'core' in the usual functionalistic terms but as the expression of a democratic form of community. He pointed out that the Greek agora, one of the original manifestations of 'core', in no sense had a utilitarian or commercial function but was purely a place of urban meeting, the place where the citizens could feel themselves to be a community.

The story continues with the interim congress of Sigtuna, not to concern itself with the discussion on the *Charte de l'Habitat*, but with the often overlooked contribution by Gutmann and Manz: their conception of habitat as a structure of *Beziehungen* (relations) that ought to be actualized at every level in clearly articulated spaces, *das Gestalt gewordene Zwischen* (the in-between that has taken shape).

The story goes most comprehensively into the congress of Aix-en-Provence (1953): the Smithsons, who specified the concept of relation with their notions of 'identity', 'human association' and 'appreciated unit'; and the French CIAM groups whose North African studies radically widened CIAM's horizon by raising the problem of building for the greater number while drawing attention to the traditional habitat in 'primitive' societies. Especially the North African studies were wholly after his own heart. He felt that nothing in the whole course of CIAM had been more compelling than the confrontation with the problems and values of these 'foreign and humble civilizations'.

Aix is followed by the formation of Team 10, which introduced the concept of 'human association' as a primary principle into the Doorn declaration (1954). The story does not breathe a word about the rifts that plagued the Team from its inception, but closes with the Congress of Dubrovnic (1956) where the Smithsons advanced the 'cluster' concept and agreed with Aldo van Eyck about the importance of 'identifying devices' at every urban level of association, while Bakema and Voelcker delved into the issues of change and growth.

So *The Story of Another Idea* offered a personal, passionate, yet almost complete historical account of the emergence of Team 10 out of CIAM – more complete than the one composed later by Alison Smithson, who decided to ignore all contributions to Team 10 thinking before 1953. In the course of the story, the 'other idea' appears as a broadly founded and bountiful version of the Team 10 idea. If the general Team 10 idea, common to all members, can be summarized as the view that the essence of a city or an urban district, i.e. what determines its identity, cannot be understood in terms of functions but should be approached in terms of relations, this view acquires a very specific meaning in the 'other idea'. Van Eyck considered these relations to be rooted in history, in age-old patterns of life, in the philosophy of Martin Buber and in the aesthetics of the avant-garde. He identified them with 'the culture of determined relations' announced by Mondrian. This view has consequences that fall entirely outside the framework of British Team 10 thinking: the return to the elementary, the reflection on life patterns in archaic cultures, a non-hierarchical and non-deterministic way of thinking, and in particular the three themes that had been barred from Team 10's 'Instructions' for CIAM 10: the 'shape of the in-between', time as a factor in town planning and the shaping of number. It was precisely these themes that were to determine the course of the new *Forum*.

By way of conclusion, the 'other idea' is illustrated by five Dutch projects that are all devoted to the last of the above three themes. Four of these projects are the major CIAM studies carried out by Opbouw, namely Pendrecht I and II, and Alexanderpolder I and II, that show a persistent effort to master the greater number by developing housing units of successively increasing differentiation. The final example is a project by Piet Blom, one of Van Eyck's former students at the Amsterdam Academy. Van Eyck thus fully acknowledges the contribution by Bakema and the Rotterdam CIAM group to the deveopment of the 'other idea', but surprisingly he also considers that their endeavour reached its culmination in a project by an Amsterdam student. Van Eyck indeed accords Blom's design a particularly important place in the development of contemporary town planning and does not refrain from stating this explicitly. He makes no less an assertion than saying that this project presages a new design approach that is to reunite architecture and town planning – an approach that *'will inevitably lead to a dignified human habitat, one which will look more like an organized kasbah than one would be inclined to believe today'.*

The 'story' – its carrying text – was originally written and published in Dutch while the quotes, which form its subject matter, appeared in their original language, whether English, French, German or Dutch. So it constituted a multilingual document for the participants of the Otterlo congress among whom it was distributed. The present English version was composed on the basis of a slightly shortened translation Van Eyck made himself in 1961, when he was visiting professor at Washington University in St Louis. The text was completed with the translation of the passages left out of the Dutch original. For the sake of clarity the quotes are distinguished by margin lines.

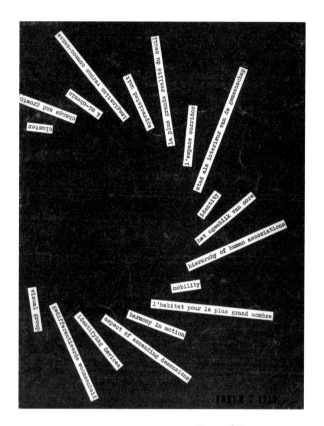

Cover of Forum 1959–7 with The Story of Another Idea (het verhaal van een andere gedachte).

het verhaal van een andere gedachte

Photo George Rodger

The Story of Another Idea

Qu'il nous est difficile

Aerial view of the new Slotermeer district, Amsterdam

Pavement trattoria in Rome

Photo Carel Bl

> To pose the question of modern habitat implies posing the question of the art of living today. Does this art still exist?
>
> [Le Corbusier, CIAM 9 Aix-en-Provence, 1953[1]]

This tentative manifesto is both an end and a beginning. Let us begin the beginning with two observations.

1. that the western world[2] is racing towards uninhabitability; a reality which somehow fails to penetrate consciousness until breath becomes very short.
2. that architects and urbanists, whose very right of existence presupposes imagination and the constructive application of its potential, have even contributed towards making the western world less rather than more habitable; a paradox that is gradually beginning to gnaw.

Seldom have our chances been greater.
Seldom has a craft thus failed and a profession thus sunk below the level of the need.

> Between a way of life based on the constructive forces of art and science and a way of life based on governmental laws and regulations, a barrier has been thrown up, causing both a waste of ideas and a waste of human activity. The time has come to recognize once again the absolute necessity of reintroducing the power of imagination into the organization process of society.
>
> [Bakema, CIAM 10 Dubrovnic, 1956]

One asks oneself how it became possible that man today is no longer able to create the very thing the great gift of consciousness should enable him to create: an environment in which he can recognize himself and assure his survival without forfeiting his identity.

> **Feeling that you are somebody living somewhere**
> [Peter Smithson]
>
> We are living, as you know, in an age which is essentially technological, not really a scientific age. You've got to dig extraordinarily deep to find any philosophy at all dominating technological development.
>
> [Dr. G. Scott Williamson,[3] CIAM 8 Hoddesdon, 1951]

This tentative manifesto attempts to set your feelings in motion – your feelings also as to what responsibility means. The barrier of which Bakema spoke is there. But architects and urbanists have, beyond a shadow of doubt, erected another barrier between themselves and the very thing they are supposed to accomplish; between themselves and their constructive ability on the one hand, between this ability and society on the other. They have furthermore been drawn towards a bog of complacency and arbitrary activity into which they have sunk, disregarding both their constructive ability and the unspoken need of society.

> Hand in hand with whatever represents imagination unhusked, the child survives, edged towards the periphery of collective attention – an emotional and specifically unproductive quantum. Hand in hand, therefore, with the child, the artist too, survives on the periphery of collective attention, another emotional and 'unproductive' quantum. His function is still decorative (he is misused and therefore tends to misuse himself). To participate in the production of imaginative order is his job. Essential allies, both child and artist have but one true place: the centre.
> [Aldo van Eyck, CIAM 10 Dubrovnic, 1956]

The time has come to focus our full attention on the plight in our respective countries. The time has come to commit ourselves again, to crawl out of the depths and face light. From CIAM meeting to CIAM meeting, frozen ideas and methods were tediously forced to make way for more vital and adequate ones.

What happened within CIAM must happen everywhere. As a stimulant, extracts from what was said and written during CIAM meetings – for the most part by those who demonstrated CIAM's inadequacy – follow along with linking comments. They demonstrate a different way of thinking: a different method of approach and hence a different concept of architecture and urbanism, one that can more adequately cope with today's specific problems, one that breaks away from a concept that has led (in a derivative and administrative form quite unworthy of the original limited concept) to the dilemma of many of the most representative new towns in Europe.

> CIAM was founded when the creative period was virtually over and its aim was to popularize the concepts of the pioneers for predominantly social reasons. Such an activity needed formal organization to systematize the intuitions of the pioneers and give the movement authority. Everything has so changed since the nineteen twenties that the solutions evolved at that time are no longer valid and we are forced once again to rethink our attitude and to invent new forms and new techniques.
> [Alison and Peter Smithson,[4] 1957]

CIAM undoubtedly succeeded in evolving the theoretical foundation upon which urbanism consciously or unconsciously rests. Disregarding inevitable misinterpretation and misuse, what was evolved, though valid to a limited degree at the time, has today proven substantially inadequate. It is now no more than a still frequented obsolete shrine. Its aftermath has become destructive – a tragic reality unworthy of its heroic heydays.

> The fruits of the decade 1928–1938 seem colossal not only in architecture built but in the popularizing of an urban programme. It was inevitable that such a programme when stripped of its imagery should result in the banalities of much post-war planning.
> [John Voelcker,[5] Architects' Yearbook, 1957]

We are still concerned with the difficult step (a truth we cannot sidestep)
from reaction to action,
from theory to reality,
from idea to realization.

Revaluating what CIAM achieved between 1928 and 1938 will help to clarify an important issue: to what extent the ideas and methods evolved departed from the negative. The deplorable situation CIAM attempted to tackle may account for this, but it cannot justify it – painters, sculptors, poets, composers and scientists, etc. (along with a few architects) showed greater insight. The products of their creative activity have proven valid because they constituted a basic renewal. That architects and urbanists should alone have sidetracked the message of the others is deplorable and unfortunately not quite forgivable – these 'others' were very close at hand![6]

It was not 'la ville radieuse' that penetrated the 'office' of the town planning 'officer' but 'die funktionelle Stadt'.[7]

Not the 'liberated dwelling' but 'the dwelling for the existence minimum' became the model. CIAM squinted, that is certain, with one eye it saw the past and exaggerated its darkness and squalor, with the other the future and believed it saw light and soaring progress. Technocratic eyes are always weak whichever way they look, whether they squint or not, they discern neither star nor cloud.

In order to demonstrate the thinness of the old doctrine, a few typical extracts, chosen from pre-war CIAM statements by some of the authors who were responsible for them,[8] follow:

La Sarraz 1928

> The idea of modern architecture implies a connection of the phenomenon of architecture with that of general economy.
> Urbanism is the organization of the functions of collective life.
> The proportions between the surface for habitation, planted surface (sports included) and the surface for circulation are dictated by economical and social conditions. The determination of the population densities establishes the necessary classification.

> The technical means of today, which are expanding continually, are the very keys of urbanism. They imply and propose a total transformation of existing legislation. This transformation should move parallel to technical progress.
> It is the destiny of architecture to express the orientation of the epoch. Works of architecture must be subsidiary to the present time.
> [From La Declaration de La Sarraz,[9] 1928]

How meagre, compared to:

> **All art, irrespective of the period in which it appears, can be called modern, as soon as harmony, the essence of beauty, appears in complete accordance with the intrinsic ways of art.**
> [Theo van Doesburg,[10] 1918]

The La Sarraz statements are both blatantly limited and embarrassingly hollow. The poverty of thought is incredible – it is clear that the kind of urbanism that followed from these slim ideas can claim little real human credit. Realization has proven this beyond doubt all over the world.

Frankfurt 1929

> **Existence minimum**
> In accordance with the future's heavy stress on individual life within society and the justifiable demand of the individual to isolate himself temporarily from the world around him, the following ideal prerogative must be postulated: Every adult should have his own room, if only small. The minimal dwelling which results from such a postulate will fulfil its factual minimum based on function and meaning: the standard dwelling.
> [Gropius, 'The social principles of the minimal dwelling for urban industrial population',[11] CIAM 2 Frankfurt, 1929]

It is clear that this – although well meant – tends to lead to a new kind of slum dwelling – extended, more efficient and more hygienic, no doubt, but still a slum dwelling!
The well known CIAM publication, 'The Dwelling for the Existence Minimum', has therefore certainly proven attractive to all those indulging in speculative housing as well as to administratively minded urbanists! To define a minimum cell is one thing – to define a liveable minimum cell in multiplicity quite another!

The wrong choice

In Dessau, Bauhaus students were for a time torn between clearly unequal alternatives: listening to Gropius and listening to Theo van Doesburg in his hotel room. Eventually both 'master' and 'pupil' followed the latter. His radiant personality and the soundness of his thought made this inevitable, though he was never accepted personally, remaining peripheral as a trespasser – one of the many nasty weaknesses of Bauhaus. CIAM succumbed to these same weaknesses – it adhered to Gropius, the dullest character who ever aspired to fame,[12] preferring to listen to the Bauhaus doctrine – diluted rationalized Van Doesburg rather than to Van Doesburg himself. (He died in 1931, three years after CIAM was founded!) That CIAM should have chosen Bauhaus instead of De Stijl and what it really stood for is significant indeed. CIAM wagered on dogma instead of on constituent ideas; on material progress instead of on relativity; on the international instead of on the universal; on technology rather than on art; on Moholy Nagy instead of on Mondrian. (Klee, Kandinsky and Schlemmer, of course, are great in spite of Bauhaus! It is surprising that they survived there at all.) In Bridgwater, first reunion of CIAM after the war, at Gropius' request the entire meeting stood in silence for Moholy, who had died between 1937 and 1947. The meeting seemed oblivious of the fact that a legion of pioneers – poets, painters and sculptors as well as many others had died during the same period.[13] This emotional restriction was hardly sympathetic to the idea of a new post-war beginning. It demonstrated once more CIAM's loose and casual affinity to a great spiritual movement.

Brussels 1930

> The Congress has studied the application possibilities of low, medium and high-rise housing. It maintains that experience on the subject of low and medium rise housing (4–5 floors) is at present sufficient to judge the validity of these types of construction. (A hair-raising statement this. AvE)
> Although low housing types have proven to be very uneconomical, especially during the first stages of their application, they have been constructed in great number following the demand posed by authorities. During the period of intense development of large cities, medium-rise housing became more current, moreover, as a result of private speculation: in fact, compared with low housing it permits a great exploitation of every kind. As regards high-rise housing, we have the experience of the United States, but this experience only concerns high-rise flats for rent.
> The Congress maintains that this form of housing could lead to the solution of the problem of the minimum dwelling – without thereby proving that this form is the only desirable one.

> It is therefore necessary to continue examination of all the possibilities contained in high-rise housing and to study all their efficacy on executed types even if obstacles of a financial and sentimental order as well as obstacles due to regulation oppose them.
>
> [*Rational Housing*, CIAM 3 Brussels, 1930]

Basing their opinions almost entirely on a negative attitude concerning the validity of low and middle-rise housing, they came to regard high-rise elements as the right solution for low cost minimum housing. It is obvious that Le Corbusier's *Ville Radieuse* has a much richer meaning.

Athens 1933

> The city is only a part of an economic, social and political whole which constitutes the region.
> Life flowers according to the degree in which the two contradictory principles that govern human personality – the individual and the collective – come to terms.
>
> The keys of urbanism are contained in the four functions.
> 1   to dwell
> 2   to work
> 3   to recreate (free time)
> 4   to circulate
>
> [*La Charte d'Athenes*,[15] CIAM 4, 1933]

Individualism and collectivism envisaged as contradictory polarities, on the contrary, cause loss of human personality, i.e. split personality. Contradictory principles cannot come to terms unless the idea of contradiction is entirely forsaken; unless they are envisaged as ambivalent principles which together form a basic dual phenomenon. There is no such thing as reconciliation based on false premises. A negative concept of individualism can only lead to an arbitrary and purely abstract concept of collectivism. CIAM forsook architecture and art in favour of urbanism and industrial production for this very reason. Subordinated from the former, the latter surely has no meaning.

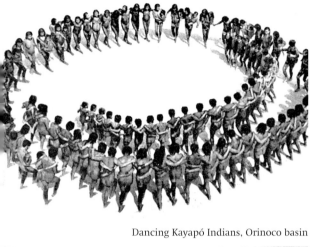

Dancing Kayapó Indians, Orinoco basin

Cypriot burial gift, ca. 2100 BC

Nuer, Nile basin

Individual and community are ambivalent.
Joined with one another they form one dual phenomenon.

Et toute la chaleur [Jules Supervielle]

Paris 1937

A city constitutes part of an economic, social and political entity. Along with this comes directly the complex psychological and biological activities of the individual and the collective. Their development depends on:
a geographic and topographic factors: water and land, nature of soil, climate.
b economic factors: resources of the region and natural or artificial relationship with its environment at large.
c political factors: administrative system.

[*Logis et loisirs*, CIAM 5 Paris, 1937]

The technocratic eye did not see that

The full understanding does not dwell in separate rooms but in the structure of the world. It is matched by a thought that is not active in separate and split truths but in a meaningful coherence whose organizing power lies in its combinatory potential.

[Ernst Junger, *Das abenteuerliche Herz*,[16] 1929]

Still, there need be no difference of opinion with respect to the meaning of CIAM for the development of architecture and urbanism. Focusing its attention almost entirely on the problems of urbanism, CIAM made the world aware of the sorry plight cities were in as a result of thoughtless speculative enterprise and random development. It succeeded in evolving a preliminary technique with which it was able to canalize the destructive forces, which have caused cities to become what they are today. A technique which by means of some very general principles was able to establish some kind of urban order. In order to achieve this, a highly analytical approach was adopted, the very nature of which we today, in the light of the much wider approach taken by those dedicated to the creation of a constituently twentieth-century concept of science, art and society in other fields, find it very difficult to account for. The enormous multiplicity of urban activities was reduced to four functions: the Athens Charter's four keys to urbanism. Each of these was distorted in such a way as to become an absolute. This distortion, however, was successful in as much as it threw light on aspects of the positive potential of the 20th century. This highly analytical and mechanically rational approach went hand in hand with a certain kind of social consciousness. An unbounded belief in the promise of material progress; a naive trust in the constructive possibilities of technology along with an equally naive distrust of the constructive possibilities of art, was part and parcel of CIAM's mental make-up (functionalism, Neue Sachlichkeit) i.e. a misinterpretation of 'form follows function'.

Already in Bridgwater, where CIAM came together for the first time since 1937, a few made a vehement plea for imagination. Since then a different approach to the problems of today has been slowly breaking through. The resistance within CIAM was initially very great indeed. Although this resistance slackened during CIAM's final phase, it is true to say that CIAM was unable to regenerate itself by absorbing positively the impact of a new generation (nor was it able to listen to the warnings of Le Corbusier and Giedion).

The distance between architecture and urbanism is shrinking. **Revaluation of the meaning of both will soon cause them to coincide on a multitude of qualitative levels. Distinction on a single quantitative level has proven utterly inadequate (beyond the limited scope of theory).**

The Bridgwater Congress decided on the following non-committal restatement of aims:

> **The aim of ciam is to work for the creation of a physical environment that will satisfy man's emotional and material needs,**

though not before Bakema had induced the congress to add:

> **and stimulate man's spiritual growth.**

The aggressive schism between emotional and material needs was mitigated and their 'satisfaction' reconciled in the higher dimension of 'stimulating' spiritual growth. What was added (as if it were an afterthought) would alone have been sufficient of course.

Bridgwater saw architecture as an 'art' hesitatingly appearing on the horizon of CIAM! The other arts entered the scope of CIAM's hitherto limited attention (and began to seduce the puritans!) and the end of their expulsion drew closer. **Many regarded this as an eclipse – a few (among them some of the new generation and, of course, Giedion) as the simultaneous reality of moon and sun!**

> The old struggle between imagination and common sense ended tragically in favour of the latter. But the scales are turning: CIAM knows that the tyranny of common sense has reached its final stage, that the same attitude which, three hundred years ago, found expression in Descartes' philosophy – Giedion has just mentioned its sad implications – is at last losing ground. Yes, the deplorable hierarchy of artificial values upon which contemporary existence has come to rest is beginning to totter.
> A new consciousness is already transforming man's mind. During the last fifty years or so, a few – ranging from poet to architect, from biologist to astronomer – have actually succeeded in giving comprehensible shape to various aspects of its nature. They have tuned our senses to a new dimension. It is the firm belief

of CIAM that the collective idea which brought us to Bridgwater from so far is the seed of a new outlook, a new consciousness, still latent today, but awaiting general recognition tomorrow. **CIAM is first and foremost an affirmation of this new consciousness.** The achievement of men like Le Corbusier, Mondrian or Brancusi compels us to believe, surely, that we are indeed approaching a brighter era; one in which grace is expressed in life as it is in art.

CIAM refuses to overhaul outworn values that belong to an outworn world by giving them a new dress straight from the laundry of common sense. On the contrary, it desires to stimulate a universal revaluation towards the elementary; to evolve a transformed language to express what is being analogously transformed. **No rational justification of CIAM can therefore satisfy us.** Imagination remains the only common denominator of man and nature, the only faculty capable of registering spiritual transformation simultaneously and thus of significant prophecy. It is the prime detector of change. Although architecture – planning in general – answers very tangible functions, ultimately its object differs in no way from that of any other creative activity, that is, to express through man and for man the natural flow of existence. The more tangible functions – those implied by the word 'functionalism' – are only relevant in so far as they help to adjust man's environment more accurately to his elementary requirements. But this, after all, is no more than a necessary preliminary. The question thus arises whether CIAM, accepting the contemporary situation as an inevitable background for practical realization, should nevertheless adopt a critical attitude toward it and act accordingly. Does CIAM intend to 'guide' a rational and mechanistic conception of progress towards an improvement of human environment? Or does it intend to replace or transform this conception? Can there be any doubt as to the answer? A new civilization is being born. Its rhythm has already been detected, its outline partly traced. It is up to us to continue.

[Aldo van Eyck, CIAM 6 Bridgwater, 1947]

The inadequacy of the old analytical approach became very apparent during he next congress in Hoddesdon in 1951. It became clear that it was just the functions which elude classification within the rigid grid of the four functions that make the concept of 'core' so much richer than the concept 'civic centre.' **In other words, it became apparent that the things which endow a city with real urbanity – that make it a city – fall through the coarse mesh of the four functions. It became clear that they lie beyond the narrow scope of rational and analytical thinking.**

> At the Seventh Congress (Bridgwater) the four elements of Town Planning were considered. Dwelling, Work, Cultivation of Mind and Body, Circulation. There is, however, another element which is quite distinct, it is, in fact, the element which makes the community a community and not merely an aggregate of individuals.

An essential feature of any true organism is the physical heart or nucleus, what we have here called the CORE.

For a community of people is an organism, and a self-conscious organism. Not only are the members dependent on one another, but each of them knows he is so dependent. This awareness, or sense of community, is expressed with varying degrees of intensity at different scale-levels. It is very strong, for example, at the lowest scale level, that of the family. It emerges again strongly at five different levels above this, in the village or primary housing group; in the small market centre or residential neighbourhood; in the town or city sector; in the city itself, and in the metropolis, the multiple city. At each level the creation of a special physical environment is called for, both as a setting for the expression of this sense of community and as an actual expression of it. This is the physical heart of the community, the nucleus, THE CORE.

[CIAM 8 Hoddesdon, 1951, Mars Group Invitation and Proposal]

The agora

We first studied Priene and the Greek cities of the fourth and fifth centuries BC. Immediately the sociological question was raised: what was the relation between the plan of the city and its social life? And immediately we were plunged into this curious experiment of Greece – I guess the most exciting mankind ever experienced – this sudden awakening of the individual mind and behind it this enormous background of oriental and Egyptian tradition.

The gridiron system is absolutely an oriental invention – there is no doubt about this. This is clear not only from the recent discoveries in the valley of the Indus, but above all in the work of the only Egyptian revolutionary, the Pharaoh Aken-Aton who about 2,700 B.C. built within 25 years a city on the Nile, Tel-el-Amarna, which is absolutely on a gridiron system. But the Greek gridiron system by Hippodamus is something completely different from the gridiron system of Aken-Aton (and completely different from the gridiron system of Manhattan). In both Egypt and the culture of the Near East the gridiron system had as its centre either the palace of the king or the temple. In Greece it was completely different. Here the focus of the gridiron was the *agora*, the gathering place of the people.

What is the *agora*? It is now known that at the beginning the *agora* was, above all, the gathering place of the people and not just a market. It was in the 5th century BC, with increasing trade and wealth, that the *agora* became more intermingled with commerce.

An *agora* is nothing else than an open space – a square – surrounded loosely by simple buildings for public use. In the Hellenistic period the *agora* came to be bounded by simple standardized elements – columns, porticos and an entablature – forming the *stoa*, a covered way protected against rain and sunshine, and

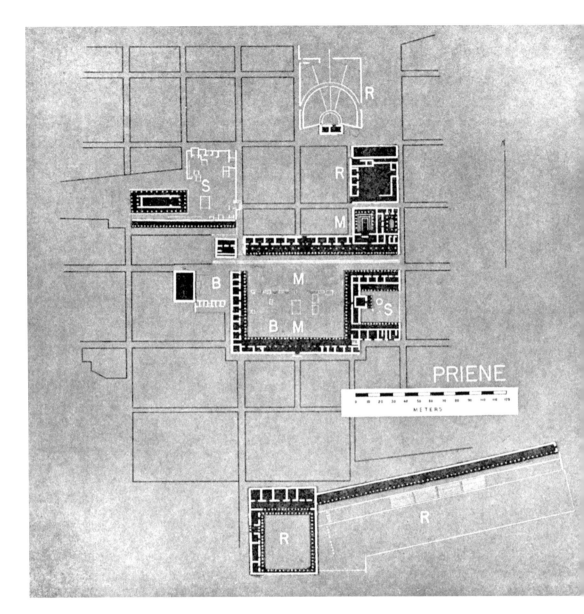

Priene plan
An agora is nothing else than an open space
– a square – (surrounded in the later period) by
standardised elements, with colums, porticos and
an entablature. Sociologically it is interesting that
there were no buildings on the agora. The agora
was pure.

serving above all as a meeting place for the formation of public opinion. Sociologically, it is interesting that no buildings faced directly onto the *agora*. The public buildings – prytaneum, buleuterium, etc. – were in close contact with the *agora*, but behind the *stoa*. The *agora* was only for the community, not for the Council, not for somebody else: only for the people and exclusively for the people. The *agora* was pure. We know that there was a Temple on the *agora* at Athens, but the *agora* at Athens is not very good. We must look at the small places like Priene in Asia Minor.

Priene, which is one of the best examples to study because it is the best excavated, is very interesting for its lack of direct relation between effect and cause – here as in so many other cities the final status of the *agora* only came when the Greeks had lost their liberty. *Agoras* were made at the time of Alexander or later, very few before. But the idea of the *agora* is inherent in the democratic conception of the Greek life.

In the Greek cities there is a clear classification. Monumentality is only for the Gods. The Acropolis was never a gathering place. First it was the quarters of the king, then, when he was eliminated, it was the quarters of the Gods. There were the Temples. Then there is the *agora*. A community place: well defined, very nicely done, but very simple. Then the private life. By the law of Athens the citizen who had too big a house was chased out of the city. Private life was very humble. These three degrees – first the Gods, then community life and then private life – were never made with such clear distinction. Even in the mediaeval period there was an intermingling of the different functions.

And now let me finish by answering the question I put at the beginning. There is certainly a relationship between the social structure of a city and the physical structure – or the urban form – of its Core. But one must issue a warning that this is not always literally true.

It was so easy before. In the old days – even in the nineteenth century – history was simple, and so was physics. Effect and cause in history; effect and cause in psychology.

It was the physical sciences that first abolished this rule, and to-day we are forced to recognize that the relation between the Core of the city and the social structure of the city is not at all so simple and so rational as we once thought. It does not always obey the law of effect and cause.

Let me finish with one example. It is a tragic example. I speak of the Capitol at Rome of Michelangelo. The Capitolina area occupies one of the hill-top sites of the ancient city of Rome. It is composed of a complex of the square itself (which is not a real square but more a trapezoid), a broad ramped stairway (the *Cordinata*) and three buildings (the Senatorial Palace or town hall in the background, the *Palazzo dei Conservatori* on the right and the Capitolina Museum on the left).

> The architectural composition of the Capitolina can be rapidly summarized as a comprehensive development in depth: – piazza, stairway and then the relation with the old medieval city of Rome.
>
> In 1530 the city-republic of Florence lost its independence to the Medici despot, Cosimo the First. As you will know, Michelangelo came from an old Florentine family and, in 1534, he left Florence for ever and spent the remaining thirty years of his life in voluntary exile in Rome. Here he gave concrete reality to what he had derived from his youthful democratic experiences in Florence. Here, in the Rome of the Counter-Reformation – a Rome in which there was no freedom and no democracy! – Michelangelo's Capitol (a very perfect expression of the core) was a symbol of the vanished liberties of the medieval city republic that he held in his heart. It was, at the same time, a memorial to the tragic dreams of its creator.
>
> The lack of imagination usually shown today (though there are a few exceptions) in our attempts to devise new city centres – new city cores – is invariably excused on the grounds that we no longer have a way of life that is possible to express. What Michelangelo has mirrored in his Area Capitolina is the baffling irrationality of historic events and the enigmatic omission of any direct relation between effect and cause.
>
> **Once more we realize that a great artist is able to create the artistic form for a phase of future social development long before that phase has begun to take tangible shape. This is our task today.**
>
> [Giedion, 'Historical Background of The Core',[17] CIAM 8 Hoddesdon, 1951]

A space set apart

> For in truth, the most accurate definition of the *urbs* and the *polis* is very like the comic definition of the cannon. You take a hole and wrap some steel wire tightly around it and that's your cannon. So the *urbs* or the *polis* starts by being an empty space. The forum, the *agora*, and all the rest are just a means of fixing that empty space, or limiting its outlines. The *polis* is not primarily a collection of habitable dwellings, but a meeting place for citizens, a space set apart for public functions. The city is not built, as is the cottage or the *domus*, to shelter from the weather and to propagate the species – these are personal, family concerns – but in order to discuss public affairs. Observe that this signifies nothing less than the invention of a new kind of space, much more new than the space of Einstein. Till then only one space existed, that of the open country, with all the consequences that this involves for the existence of man. The man of the fields is still a sort of vegetable. His existence, all that he feels, thinks and wishes for preserves the listless drowsiness in which the plant lives. The great civilizations of Asia and Africa were, from this point of view, huge anthropomorphic vegetations. But the Greco-Roman decides to separate himself from the fields, from Nature, from the geo-

botanic cosmos. How is this possible? How can man withdraw himself from the fields? Where will he go, since the earth is one huge unbounded field? Quite simple: he will mark off a portion of this field by means of walls which set up an enclosed finite space over against amorphous, limitless space. Here you have the public square. It is not, like the house, an 'interior' shut in from above, as are the caves which exist in the fields. It is purely and simply the negation of the fields. The square, thanks to the walls which enclose it, is a portion of the countryside which turns its back on the rest, eliminates the rest and sets up in opposition to it. This lesser rebellious field, which secedes from the limitless one, and keeps to itself, is a space *sui generis* of the most novel kind, in which man frees himself from the community of the plant and the animal, leaves them outside and creates an enclosure apart which is purely human, a civil space.
[J. Ortega y Gasset, The Revolt of The Masses (1930), quoted by J.L. Sert,[18] CIAM 8 Hoddesdon]

We all try to say how one should build the core. It is just as important not to destroy such cores as we have. I speak of the Piazza San Pietro in Rome: a very important place, where one could sit down – with something behind one – and look at a very important monument (St. Peters Cathedral). Now this beautiful core has been completely destroyed because the sense of enclosure has been destroyed – and this is the worst thing one can do to a core.
[Peressutti, CIAM 8 Hoddesdon,[19] 1951]

I am absolutely of the opinion of Peressutti. But you know Carlo Fontana made a scheme for the Piazza San Pietro in about 1590 which was never carried out. It is characteristic that the Baroque approach was quite different from Fascism. Instead of a great opening with avenue obelisks, he opened the area slowly – just for humble shops to serve the pilgrims who were standing around. His scheme shows that a core can be opened without destroying the place but it needs talent and this it seems Fascism does not possess.
[S. Giedion's answer[20]]

Hearth

The first principle is that the underlying main force that one meets with in biology at every turn is a tendency to fullness or wholeness. Then there is another principle, which I think is substantiated completely, that is that the human organism is not the individual, as we have considered in the past. The individual is mere part of that organism.
The organism is the whole, with the family as its nucleus. You can visualize it as a sort of cell – a sort of socioplasm – constituting the home; and in the centre dominating it, this nucleus of the family enclosed in their house, which is really

an enclosure around their hearth. It's the hearth that matters, not the house. There's been a tremendous stress on the housing of the hearth. But the hearth itself is a lively, living protoplasm, probing in every direction, attempting to creep out into the broader avenues of society.

The principle of the 'Family-in-its-Home', then, is a fundamental one. It is the 'core' for human development. The smallest living human 'whole' is this family embedded in its own bit of the environment which it has specified, or made its own – by familiarity. It can be closely local, or it can be world-wide in its excursion.

[Dr Scott Williamson,[21] CIAM 8 Hoddesdon, 1951]

The moment of core

If we speak of the core as an expression of life, I immediately ask myself "Why this title?" Is there also in our cities the possibility of a core as an expression of death? For example, can a cemetery be a core?

Some months ago I was walking in the cemetery of Asplund's crematorium in Stockholm – in this wonderful composition of trees, grass, halls, flowers, hills, rocks and living and dead people. Several people were there: they went there to remember their dead. I think in this cemetery there is a core – though a core of a special kind. It is a place where the isolation of life from death has been altered into a wonderful relationship.

A few days before, in Aulanko in Finland, we were waiting in front of an old wooden building – waiting until we could take a sauna, the Finnish steam-bath. Six persons where waiting there, sitting together. We asked them how to take a sauna, and why do the Finnish people bath in this way. We then talked about so many things that we almost forgot to go in at all! I assure you a Finnish steam-bath can be an element of a core.

Yesterday Corbusier explained how in every private house there is a core. In the early days around the hearth; in our days, or in the coming days perhaps round the television-screen? Or around the mechanized kitchen?

What I ask myself is, at what moment can we really speak of core – the core that we can plan in architecture and town planning.

Perhaps the answer is this: There are moments in our life in which the isolation of man from things is destroyed: at that moment we discover the wonder of relationships in men and things. That is the moment of Core: the moment we become aware of the fullness of life by the experience of relationships whose existence we did not know.[22]

The developments of science have made it clear that the things we see in nature and culture are not really there. Every day we discover that the only thing that exists is relationship, and perhaps we can even say that the goal of human life is to become aware of the governing principles of a full life. This seems to me to be the reason why, in the development of spatial conceptions in architecture and town planning, we speak so often of continuity in space.

For us in ciam the relations between things and within things are of greater importance than the things themselves.

One can express this awareness of relationships, and one can also predict how they will be.

In CIAM people come together who like to predict. We are a fighting group and in the Dutch group I think it was Van Eesteren who said that we have today to anticipate the day of tomorrow. Perhaps that is why we are now discussing the core. We feel a lack of the core in society, and we know that we need it in order to be really free and happy.

[Bakema, CIAM 8 Hoddeson,[23] 1951]

The word 'core' in the sense we are using it, does not mean merely the centre of the urban agglomeration, nor the busy heart of the city traffic or economic activity: sometimes it may be united with these areas, but the core includes other elements, often of imponderable nature.

The essence of the Core is that it is a rendezvous. Its situation and contents may be planned or spontaneous; drawn from history or from some isolated accident; derived from the convergence of activities or as a refuge against such activities. Whatever the cause, the Core should give both the impression of freedom of movement and also a release from loneliness or boredom; an atmosphere of general relaxation, of participation in a spontaneous and impartial performance, a touch of the warmth of human kindness, a possibility of new encounters and – at the same time – a recovery of civic consciousness. It is in this meeting place for pedestrians that the human scale and values may be re-established within the public domain.

The Core is a civic landscape: it enhances contemporary life by providing unlimited resources of enjoyment of the interplay of emotion and intelligence.

Many old cities have lost their former cores through changes in the location of activities or people: some newer cities have never had cores of any consequence: if new towns are built without cores they will never become more than camps.

The expression of the Core must interpret the human activities that take place there: both the relations of individuals with one another, and the relations of individuals with the community. **Only full development of both these relationships can safeguard the dignity of individual life.**

Photos Ed van der Elsken

Core – stage for the spontaneous expression of the public

The Core must express a human geographical focus either already in being or desiring an outlet. Its function is to provide opportunities – in an impartial way – for spontaneous manifestations of social life. It is the meeting place of the people and the enclosed stage for their manifestations. It is also the safety valve for any emergent expressions. Here spontaneous activities, whether momentary or expressing a decisive outpouring of emotion, again become possible.

The people must be given a means by which they express their feelings or give vent to spontaneous reactions. It is these spontaneous expressions that will give a vitality to modern society. It will not find this in universities or professional organizations, but there in the Core, where an idea can suddenly gush forth – free, independent, creative, large or small, the visible and touching witness of a new society which has begun to balance what it is with what it might become.
['A Short Outline of the Core',[24] CIAM 8 Hoddesdon, 1951]

In spite of a general broadening of attitude within CIAM, due to the activity of a minority, it developed into an unwieldy international institution. On the one hand a very large body of 'members' – colourless and passive; on the other, a certainly dedicated council, neither colourless nor passive, but closed and conservative. The presence of a group of angry young men made itself felt. Their number grew from congress to congress. Van Eesteren is replaced by José Luis Sert, a man indeed more suited to 'consolidate' CIAM than his predecessor.

> CIAM was originally a spontaneous gathering of people who wanted to achieve a mutual aim. During this period no constitutions were necessary. Since then this dynamic character has been lost and the form of CIAM became static so that the essential work that had to be done became subordinate to a too formal structure.
> [Van Eesteren in a talk with Merkelbach, Van Eyck and Bakema, message sent to CIAM 10 Dubrovnic,[25] 1956].

After Hoddesdon CIAM is virtually 'governed' from Harvard. With the exception of the minority group from which 'Team 10' evolved after Aix-en-Provence, everybody seemed to be convinced of the necessity of compiling a Habitat Charter and presenting this as a guide to the world.

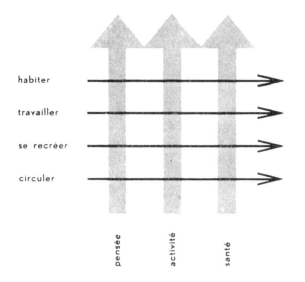

The interim congress of Sigtuna, Sweden, failed to bring CIAM nearer to the charter, but it did bring it closer to the real problems. Wogensky's suggestion to confront the four functions of the Athens Charter with *'pensée – activité – santé'* in their widest connotation, certainly gave the four functions a more relative meaning, made them less abstract and absolute.

Applied to man, the word Habitat embraces all the aspects of his taking possession of land and space in order to organize them in terms of his biological, sociological and spiritual life.

It is necessary here to insist on the double aspect – concrete and abstract – of the Habitat. On the one hand the word points towards something material made of materials which issue from the organization which we wish to give to our Habitat. On the other hand it points towards something which is abstract: the idea we have of Habitat; the conception we evolve of it; the way in which we think of it.

We therefore ask all CIAM groups indulging in preparatory work for the next congress to tackle primarily concrete problems and submit concrete examples. We ask all groups, furthermore, not to lose sight of the abstract – the idea – of which the Habitat, from a concrete angle, is but the material expression.

Our studies and our critical analyses must be led by investigation of the quality and relationships – reciprocal and multilateral – of the part and the whole.

We declare that the Habitat cannot be dissected into distinct parts but that it is an organized structure; that modification of each part modifies the whole.

We declare that the Habitat is not static, but that it is in perpetual mobility according to the mobility of man and society. Its organization is subject to continuous renewal.

We declare that it is not static, but that there exists between it and man a perpetual play of action and reaction. Man reacts to the Habitat as the Habitat reacts to man, contributing towards conditioning him and, in consequence, making of him what he really is.

[Wogensky, Van Eyck, *et al.*, Report of the Commission on the theme of CIAM 9, CIAM Sigtuna, 1952]

The ideas introduced by Rolf Gutman and Theo Manz as to the inadequacy of the analytic approach were impressive – though for many they spoke a very unfamiliar language!

> **Art is neither the impression of natural objectivity, nor the expression of soulful subjectivity; it is work and witness to the relation between the *substantia humana* and the *substantia rerum*, the in-between that has taken shape.**
> [Martin Buber, Urdistanz und Beziehung,[26] 1951]

At its early congresses CIAM investigated the different functions of the human settlement, going through all levels of the architectonic-urbanist field, from the minimum dwelling to regional planning. As Bottoni stated in his *'Constatations et resolutions'* for the 8th congress, CIAM 'has almost exhausted the principal themes related to the technique of modern architecture and urbanism', and has thereby largely contributed to the knowledge, the clarification and the solutions of these problems.

It appeared to be necessary to investigate first and foremost the technical-functional aspects of the separate problems, and to do this in a successive and additive way. Only this procedure seemed to offer a safeguard for a clear understanding, a precise investigation and a concrete solution of the building task. At the 8th CIAM congress in Hoddesdon it became clear that in the case of complex problems the sole analytical investigation of individual and sub-functions cannot produce any comprehensive result. The discussion of the theme of 'core' has shown that, although the integral parts of the 'core' can be acknowledged and defined, their mere sum does not yet constitute the essence of 'core design'. Therefore the final resolutions did not appear to be conclusive in every respect and further elaboration of the theme did prove to be desirable. The reason for the not altogether satisfying result probably lies in the fact that the problem of 'core' is one of those that cannot be grasped in an isolated form and that essentially avoid any analytical method of investigation, carried out from a merely technical-functional point of view.

For the 9th congress, to be held in 1953, the theme chosen is the drawing up of a 'Charte de l'habitat'. So the question arises of the direction and the sense in which this theme has to be formulated, interpreted and developed. It implies a questioning of the purpose of this work, and also of the sense and utility of the result. This theme could be specified in the sense that the notion of 'habitat' includes, as a subproblem, the function of 'dwelling' in the human settlement.

It is necessary to acknowledge that the isolation of individual problems and their separate treatment can only produce inadequate values, the sum of the individual parts but not a whole. The human settlement must be conceived as a synthesis, as a whole and as a unity, as the formation of our whole living space. This forma-

> tion must neither be understood as a amassment of equalized individuals in the collectivist sense, nor as an unrelated juxtaposition of individuals. The human settlement should rather correspond to a lively community based on a twofold relation of its members: the mutual relation of the individuals and the relation of the individuals to the whole.
>
> The 'Charte de l'habitat' should postulate the shaping principle of the human settlement, in which the community itself takes shape. Function, technique and emotion alone cannot produce the valid form. Only on the basis of a knowledge of the existential form of the community, appropriate to man as such, can the settlement arrive at a suitable shape, at a specific concept of space and at architectonic form. 'Art is neither the impression of natural objectivity, nor the expression of soulful subjectivity; it is work and witness to the relation between the *substantia humana* and the *substantia rerum*, the in-between that has taken shape.' (Martin Buber, *Urdistanz und Beziehung*)
>
> [Gutman and Manz, Considerations on the Essence of the Theme,[27] CIAM Sigtuna, 1952]

Some participants already implicitly introduced the notion of Change and Growth by pointing to the meaning of time in architecture and urbanism.

> **It is imperative that we recognize the problems of simultaneity and temporal mutation. CIAM is the affirmation in architectural terms of a new concept of time.**
>
> [Aldo van Eyck,[28] CIAM Sigtuna, 1952]

> **We are faced with the necessity of creating a structure or forms that are able to develop in time without losing their structure or form. These structures must, both following their inception and during their further growth, continue to form a whole and maintain the coherence among their parts. The failure to do so will lead to self-destruction.**
>
> [Wim van Bodegraven,[29] CIAM Sigtuna, 1952]

The idea of housing for the largest number is underlined with relentless fervour by French members working in North Africa.[30] The accent has shifted significantly from the badly housed European industrial population (CIAM 2 – existence minimum, functional city) to the universal problem of the roofless world paupers at last. Along with this decisive shift of attention came the interest in the magnificent and inspiring qualities of 'primitive' societies and their cultures.

> **And Jesus said to him, 'Foxes have holes, and birds of the air have nests; but the Son of Man has nowhere to lay his head'.**
>
> [Matthew[31] VIII: 20]

> The Habitat of tomorrow will be a Habitat for everybody whereas that of yesterday was concerned with a few. The right of habitat is a universal one and is valid for all men.
> [Eccochard and Wogensky, CIAM Sigtuna, 1952]

> It is to be remembered that 3/4 of this globe's population is not able to benefit from the function of Habitat. The congress of Aix-en-Provence must proclaim **The Right of Habitat for all**.
> [Emery, Algiers, CIAM Sigtuna,1952]

The congress of Aix-en-Provence was a turning point. Whilst CIAM continued to become more institutional, the renewal of thought continued. Some of the Grand Old Man did not stand in opposition to the aspirations of the new generation. It is in the nature of Le Corbusier's personality and genius that he should have supported the potential of the younger generation. His continual regenerative capacity and great humanity lifted CIAM beyond its limited scope from the very beginning. He was CIAM's barely understood banner. His 'rationalism' was fused with both mystery and crystal clarity – a reality none of his germanic CIAM colleagues managed to live up to, and all too often even suspiciously counteracted. Nor do we today desire to minimize for a second Giedion's message. He spoke about matters of the mind in the light of relativity again and again – to all but a few deaf ears.

> **Above all, life must continue and the leaves of spring must unfold in front of the leaves of the preceding autumn which fold silently and sometimes fall.**
> [from a letter by Le Corbusier to Bakema[32]]

As a result of the study of the plans submitted at the congress, the inadequacy of the old 5-commission system became clear. These 5 commissions: urbanism, social problems, synthesis of the arts, technology and construction, legislation and administration – focused their attention on the problems inherent in the plans. Parts and part aspects were extracted and disproportionately enlarged, others – the greater part – completely eluded the insensitive antennae of the separate commissions and remained out of their grasp. Synthesis, the supposed reward for 'sound' analytical classification, did not appear since the classifications were not sound but pseudo. Blanche Lemco and especially John Voelcker contributed some very essential thinking. Alison and Peter Smithson – apocalyptically loaded – appear on the scene, also Howell with his gigantic moustache and Candilis, the burning Greek, with a slightly less gigantic moustache, and Shadrach Woods, often inspiringly silent. J. Bakema and Aldo van Eyck found no difficulty in shaking their hands. The natural human association based on compatible conviction that led to Team 10 and its later extension grew at Aix-en-Provence.

Man's identity

The most urgent problem next to food and health is the provision of dwelling.
The dwelling is the unit of habitation whether it be for single persons old or young, married couples old and young, families with children etc.
Technically we are to be asked to build millions of dwellings. It must be stressed that this is not a numerical problem alone. The multiplication of dwellings is limited by several conditions – sociological, economical, geographical, political and plastic.
Any architectural or town planning proposals which ignore these conditions and do not give **man his identity,** fail to meet the requirements of **life.**
This identity is to be found in the dwelling itself – in the residential unit – in the community unit – in the town and in the region – in other words, in all stages of multiplication.
Since La Sarraz CIAM has found tools by means of which it became possible to analyze functions such as work, living, circulation and recreation. CIAM also mastered the technique for attacking the chaos of the nineteenth century and the problems resulting from it. The central problem of our time still remains the provision of dwellings for millions of people. Architects must accept this challenge as their first priority, and their technical language has to be enriched for man to fulfil his material and spiritual needs. True development in town planning can therefore only take place by the interaction of architects and town planners with the people, which must be a continuous process.

Visual group
The need is felt for a further differentiation of functions, as, for example, between the dwelling and the residential unit. This element may be called the visual group, which is an essential element of neighbourliness. The articulation of such visual elements will help to preserve man's identity in spite of the great numerical extension of the problem. The architect has a special task in the creation of this element in order to give it plastic expression. Architects and planners will help mankind to find its identity on earth by humanizing space required for man's needs.

Belonging
Man may readily identify himself with his own hearth, but not easily with the town within which it is placed. 'Belonging' is a basic emotional need – its associations are of the simplest order. From 'belonging' – identity – comes the enriching sense of neighbourliness. The short, narrow street of the slum succeeds where spacious redevelopment frequently fails.
the eye is a sure measure of human scale.
What can be seen at one glance is immediately recognized as an entity.

Hence the importance of recognizing the visual group within the neighbourhood.

But where the neighbourhood has first a functional basis (e.g. the support of the school), the visual group has first an emotional basis. (Although its significance may be reinforced by providing a functional element within it, e.g. a playground). Whereas the distance to school is but a functional consideration, the more important aspects of planning are to give security and to see a limit to a small world – because it is derived from a basic human need, common to all men from infancy to old age.

[Bakema, Lemco, Van Ginkel, Voelcker, *et al.*, Report urbanism, CIAM 9 Aix-en-Provence, 1953]

Appreciated unit

The aim of Urbanism is comprehensibility, i.e. clarity of organization. The community is by definition a comprehensible thing. And comprehensibility should also therefore be a characteristic of the parts. The community sub-divisions might be thought of as 'appreciated units'.

An appreciated unit is not a 'visual group' or a 'neighbourhood', but a part of a human agglomeration. The appreciated unit must be different for each type of community… For each particular community one must invent the structure of its sub-division. This is the key problem of habitat.

[A. & P. Smithson, CIAM 9 Aix-en-Provence, 1953]

1. There should be a basic programme for the dwelling in terms of the activities of the family, considering them separately, and in association with each other. **The house.**

2. We should then consider the first point of contact outside the dwelling. Here children learn for the first time of the world outside the home, and here are carried on those adult activities which are essential to everyday life, for instance shopping, making minor repairs, posting letters, cleaning the car or exercising the dog. **The street.**

3. Outside the street people are in direct contact with the larger range of activities which give identity to the community. Such communities can be based on workplaces, although new forms of transport offer new possibilities of identity. Free choice is essential. **The district.**

4. Districts in association generate the need for a richer scale of activities, which in their turn give identity to the ultimate community. **The City.**

In most cases the grouping of dwellings does not reflect any reality of social organization, rather they are the result of political, technical and mechanical expediency.

Although it is extremely difficult to define the higher levels of association, the street implies a physical contact community, the district an acquaintance community, and the city an intellectual contact community.

This hierarchy of association can be expressed in the following way:

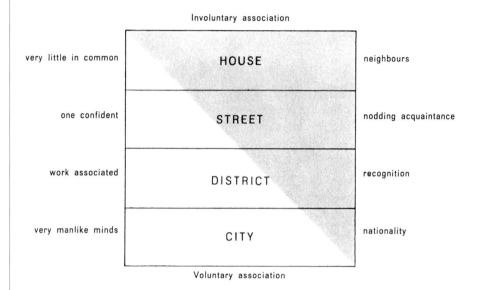

We are of the opinion that we should construct a hierarchy of human associations which should replace the functional hierarchy of the Charte d'Athènes.
The architect-urbanist is one of the few people who, so far, has not been totally isolated and sterilized by specialization – it is in the nature of his work that he cannot be. There are two developments possible, that we shall cease to exist and fall back into the undefined chaos of contemporary life, or that we shall rediscover and transform the particular techniques which identify us as differentiated and therefore active individuals within the community.
We are primarily concerned with problems of form and we need, immediately, to develop techniques which enable us to transform our experience as social beings into the plastic expression of architect-urbanists.

[A. & P. Smithson, W. & G. Howell, 'Report of the English Group', Commission 6, CIAM 9 Aix-en-Provence, 1953]

Urbanist and architect or architect-urbanist

At Aix it became quite clear that a reassessment of what architecture and urbanism really mean with regard to each other was a first priority. Both extracts already point to this. Light is cast on the putrid spot: the arbitrary relation between two 'professions'. It became clear that the creative field in which architects and urbanists find themselves active could not be defined quantitatively.

The splitting of the total scale of association into two disciplines is artificial, inadequate and consequently cannot cope with the problems posed by our time. Reality and actual realization have proved this beyond a shadow of doubt. Between house and city lies a single creative field that cannot be split according to degree of complexity, i.e. according to the ideas part-whole, small-large, few-many, or any other idea of quantitative specialisation. The urbanist is an unreal invention of the late twenties born from the essential one-sidedness of the architect (his failure to live up to what a twentieth-century architect must be if he is to solve the problems the twentieth century sets) and the idea that a non-art 'scientific' approach was necessary. Departing from a negative concept of art (understandable if art had not entered a new dimension since Cézanne demonstrated its constructive potential – in which case this would have been justifiable) CIAM shook hands with what they thought science was. It shook hands with a 19th-century ghost since science also had moved into another – the same – dimension. The artists knew this all along! How is this blindness of architects to be explained? Their association with just those artists was very direct. (An active early CIAM member[33] kept some Mondrians in his attic!) There, face to face with the sickness of cities stood the new-born urbanist – stillborn urbanist – like a quack physician. His integrity, however, was as great as his shortsightedness. He evolved a method of diagnosis, concocted some medicine, but failed to see that neither diagnosis nor medicine can do more than alleviate at best the organism's sickness – neither can extend the life of an organism from without beyond its lifespan or bring to life again what is dead. The particular human artefact called city cannot be healed, it can only regenerate. It is hard to separate the urbanist – or the limited architect for that matter – from the abstractly academic infill-pattern-maker using urban ingredients and ideas that were already obsolete the moment they were conceived. In the light of the above the meaning of Bakema's formula becomes quite clear.

> **Architecture by planning**
> **Planning by architecture**
> [Bakema 1956]

Bakema, Smithson, Voelcker and van Eyck were for this very reason continually pondering the idea of an architect-urbanist or urbanist-architect – i.e. an 'architect' of a new sort. That the job ahead of us was one that demanded a different approach and a different kind of man was put forward more vehemently from year to year. Yet there were many other essential matters that entered the general consciousness at Aix-en-Provence. The congress at Aix was indeed both a turning point and the beginning of breaking-point tensions.

The aesthetics of number

> 'In order that we may overcome the menace of quantity now that we are faced with *l'habitat pour le plus grand nombre*, the aesthetics of number, the laws of what I should like to call 'Harmony in motion' must be discovered. Projects should attempt to solve the aesthetic problems that result through the standardisation of constructional elements; through the repetition of similar and dissimilar dwellings within a larger housing unit; through the repetition or grouping of such housing units, similar or dissimilar; through the repetition of such housing groups, similar or dissimilar (Theme and its mutation and variation).'
> [Aldo van Eyck, CIAM 9 Aix-en-Provence, 1953]

> In search of the further principles of a new form language, the Swiss painter Lohse discovered the aesthetic meaning of number. Imparting rhythm to repetitive similar and dissimilar form, he has managed to disclose the conditions that may lead to the equilibration of the plural and thus overcome the menace of monotony. The formal vocabulary with which man has hitherto successfully imparted harmony to the singular and particular cannot help him to equilibrate the plural and the general. Man shudders because he believes that he must forfeit the one in favour of the other; the particular for the general; the individual for the collective; the singular for the plural; rest for movement. But rest can mean fixation – stagnation – and multiplicity, as Lohse shows, does not necessarily imply monotony. The individual (the singular) less circumscribed within itself will reappear in another dimension as soon as the general, the repetitive is subordinated to the laws of dynamic equilibrium, i.e. harmony in motion.
> [Aldo van Eyck, 1952]

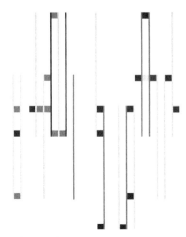

R.P. Lohse, *Konkretion I*, 1945–1946

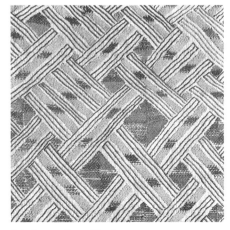

Bakuba textile, raffia, Congo

We shall meet each other half way

In the whole course of its development CIAM probably never experienced anything more compelling than its confrontation with these 'foreign and humble' countries. Faced with the frail vestiges of archaic man, CIAM acknowledged, albeit too late, the simple grandeur of an integrated society – the simple magnificence of the right gesture and the right gait. Voilà, extremes in equilibrium – zeal and resignation, control and passion, happiness and distress, love and hate – human metabolism, the right blood circulation, the intact pattern.

Voilà – 'the moment of core'

> Qu'il nous est difficile
> De trouver un abri
> Même dans notre cœur
> Toute la place est prise,
> Et toute la chaleur.
>
> [Jules Supervielle[34]]

There must have been a time when man's mental equipment was different from what it is now, when it was evolving from a condition similar to that found among the higher apes. That period lies far behind us and no trace of a lower mental organization is found in any of the extant races of man. So far as my personal experience goes and so far as I feel competent to judge ethnographical data on the basis of this experience, the mental processes of man are the same everywhere, regardless of race and culture, and regardless of the apparent absurdity of beliefs and customs. Some theorists assume a mental equipment of primitive man distinct from that of civilized man. I have never seen a person in primitive life to whom this theory would apply. There are slavish believers in the teaching of the past and there are scoffers and unbelievers, there are clear thinkers and muddleheaded bunglers: there are strong characters and weaklings.

The behaviour of everybody, no matter to what culture he may belong, is determined by the traditional material he handles, and man, the world over, handles the material transmitted to him according to the same methods.

[Franz Boas,[35] 1927]

1 Contemporary architecture has also been involved in the great process which has expanded our civilisation – confined as it was until now to a few centres within the western hemisphere – so that it now covers all regions and people of the world.

2 These other centres are in the process of forming themselves within the framework of the contemporary world. Through contact with 'primitive' and ancient cultures, architecture today has broadened its outlook and approach. It has become more profound.

3 Our approach and attitude to foreign civilizations is humble. We no longer envisage primitive society from the point of view of technical development. We know how to trace, even in the shanty towns, the last vestiges of an equilibrated civilization. Its forms teach us how to deal with the specific social, territorial and cosmic conditions which confront it. Here, we know social and aesthetic imagination form a complete unity.

4 A low 'primitive' standard of living by no means implies a primitive aesthetic standard. **A house in the Cameroon has more aesthetic dignity than most of our prefabricated houses.**

5 We detect in the cultural life of the west a weakening of a purely rational attitude. On the other hand, the desire of 'primitive' people to acquire our scientific methods and productive ability **is about to meet us halfway.**

6 'Primitive' architecture, approached in the right way, has become a symbol directly reflecting a way of life which comes to us across the ages, leaving profound marks on human and cosmic conditions. What contemporary painters (sculptors, musicians and poets no less, A.v.E.) have shown us during the last 40 years (Gauguin left for Tahiti almost a century ago! A.v.E.) – that the most direct methods of expression are to be found in primitive and prehistoric art – is now, in view of the present urgent need for realization, becoming a new possibility of imparting depth to architecture.

7 **We must confirm that owing to this kind of approach, aesthetic and social imagination have become inseparable.**

8 We have understood that modern technical methods can very well be combined with traditional materials and methods. In order to comply with the material demands of 'primitive' man one need only supply a structural framework so that his inborn ability to form and transform architecture is not destroyed.

9 **Western man has the obligation to give the necessary implements, but the people themselves will complete the work according to their own vital standards.**

[Giedion, Van Eyck, *et al.*, 'Attitude vis-à-vis des Données Naturelles et des Civilisations Archaïques', report commission 2: 'Rôle de l'esthétique dans l'habitat', CIAM 9 Aix-en-Provence, 1953]

Fifty years too late!

That this attitude should have entered CIAM is gratifying. That it did not do so in 1928 when CIAM was founded is, to say the least of it, disconcerting. After all, painters, sculptors, musicians and poets had shaken hands with the archaic peoples of Africa, Asia, America, the South Seas and prehistoric times half a century earlier. They did so from a profound inner need. And behold, at Aix tired CIAM inclined its haughty head, recognizing at last the lost conditions of creativity. It understood that technical ingenuity guided by a limited artistic and social sense is not enough to produce real architecture. That CIAM should have also missed the real meaning of constituent contemporary thought, about which Van Eyck spoke at Bridgwater six years earlier, is due to the same short-sightedness. To say that this wider attitude became general at Aix would be to exaggerate. It was merely put before the meeting by both the new generation and Giedion. It failed, however, to transform the self-assured minds of most participants, even at Aix. It sounded like music to a few and gave them new hope.

Differentiation of types

Integration of urban functions

The Rotterdam group under the guidance of Bakema demonstrated an entirely different approach to several very urgent problems.

a Differentiation within a fairly small repetitive group of varied basic housing types with the object of reintegrating from place to place different kinds of families as well as all age groups, from young to old. This of course is an idea diametrically opposed to the common practice based on analytical segregation into large sequences containing a single type: i.e. either low, medium or high-rise elements each containing apartments of the same kind and size and based on either one or the other of the known and obsolete access methods, plan and section. The fact that various kinds of families (also choice within the same kind) and all ages participate within a small area not only affords a much less sterile and limited scale of association but also overcomes the monotony caused by the endless repetition of a single basic type within a sector and the arbitrary and abrupt scale transition between one sector and another containing altogether different housing elements – different in meaning, size and open space interval. All stages of family life between childhood and old age, therefore, are represented.

b Integration of not merely the four functions, which CIAM abstracted and pulled apart, but also of those that fell through the coarse mesh of the over-rational method adopted before. In the first place those which CIAM expelled from the residential sector so that one function need no longer hinder the other – again, of course, a negative approach, albeit based on real negative examples. It is obvious that urban realities should not mutilate each other, obvious enough, but they should always interact from place to place and enhance each other. This implies greater complexity and variety of urban activity within any small urban area (no matter how small).

[Bakema and Opbouw, explanatory note to Alexanderpolder project, 1953]

The imponderable qualities

There is also a need for spaces with which to identify – in correlation with the spaces for the four determined functions – all those other functions which are difficult to classify but which nevertheless belong to urban reality. The imponderable qualities.

[CIAM 9 Aix-en-Provence 1953, Commission 2, Rôle de l'esthétique dans l'habitat]

These, surely, are the true ingredients. The four others acquire meaning – each of them – not only in terms of each other but in terms of just these imponderable qualities. The idea residence (house), work, communication (traffic) and recreation (free time) is so closed a concept that it does not allow either of them to coincide with the other – absolutes cannot shake hands; they have no flavour so they cannot absorb the flavour of another absolute, they only appear to be what they circumscribe. In the light of their abstractness and meaninglessness the 'imponderable' things they defy naturally 'seem' imponderable, but these are the very things that are not abstract but very concrete. The whole thing is based on false premises – an artificial paradox born from one-track mechanical thinking. It is the function of art and hence of architecture to make the imponderable tangible, to manifest its concrete reality. But in order to live up to this ultimate function a greater sensibility for detecting **associative meaning** is necessary on the part of the architect-urbanist. If architects and urbanists are becoming obsolete it is surely in the first place because they are too insensitive to the real concrete human qualities that make a house a house and a city a city. Society needs a more sensitive sort of architect-urbanist, a sort that is not merely less impervious to the kaleidoscopic subtleties of urban reality than the sort that thrives today, less inclined to generalization and social sentimentality, but one that is supremely aware of the poetic multiple meaning of whatever it deals with and endowed with the ability to prepare for this multiple meaning's manifestation through whatever it conceives.

> **Not the swift pencil but the heart only can help here and who, I ask, is going to prove that imagination no longer hides in the heart?**
> [Aldo van Eyck 1954]

The reactions after Aix-en-Provence were anything but lukewarm. In Doorn (Holland), London and Paris there were small spontaneous gatherings. Their object was to pave the way for another approach to our task as well as a richer form of human association between architects in general, though in the first place between those few who thought in a more or less similar way about the problems confronting architecture and urbanism today. The result of these gatherings was the Doorn report, and the spontaneous formation of Team 10, the group which, though not quite in its present form, was at last asked to prepare the next CIAM congress – to be held in Dubrovnik, Yugoslavia, according to its basic ideas.

CIAM Meeting, January 1954, Doorn

Bakema, Van Eyck, Van Ginkel, Hovens Greve, Smithson, Voelcker

Statement on Habitat

1. La Charte d'Athènes proposed a technique which would counteract the chaos of the nineteenth century, and restore principles of order within our cities.
2. Through this technique the overwhelming variety of city activities was classified into four distinct functions which were believed to be fundamental.
3. Each function was realized as a totality within itself. Urbanists could comprehend more clearly the potential of the twentieth Century.
4. Our statement tries to provide a method which will liberate still further this potential.

As a direct result of the 9th Congress at Aix, we have come to the conclusion that if we are to create a Charte de l'Habitat, we must redefine the aims of urbanism, and at the same time create a new tool to make this aim possible. Urbanism considered and developed in the terms of the Charte d'Athènes tends to produce 'towns' in which vital human associations are inadequately expressed. To comprehend these human associations we must consider every community as a particular total complex. In order to make this comprehension possible, we propose to study urbanism as communities of varying degrees of complexity.

These can be shown on a Scale of Association as shown beside:

We suggest that the commissions operate each in a field not a point on the Scale of Association, for example: isolated buildings* / villages / towns / cities.

This will enable us to study particular functions in their appropriate ecological field. Thus a housing sector or satellite of a city will be considered at the top of the scale, (under City, 4), and can in this way be compared with development in other cities, or contrasted with numerically similar developments in different fields of the Scale of Association. **This method of work will induce a study of human association as a first principle, and of the four functions as aspects of each total problem.**

[Doorn Statement, 31 January 1954]

---

* These fields are sufficiently finite for general purposes but there may be new forms of association, new patterns of community which replace the traditional hierarchy.

Team 10

Alison and Peter Smithson
John Voelcker
William Howell
Candilis
Bakema
Aldo van Eyck
Rolf Gutman
Woods

> We of the youngers received a shock at Aix, in seeing how far the wonder of the 'Ville Radieuse' had faded from CIAM.
> CIAM X must be a participants Congress. Each architect is asked to appear project under his arm, ready to commit himself. **Today we each recognize the existence of a new spirit. It is manifest in our revolt from mechanical concepts of order and in our passionate interest in the complex relationships in life and the realities of our world.**
> CIAM X must make clear that we as architects accept the responsibility for the creation of order through form. We accept the responsibility for each act of creation, no matter how small. We must find the means of realizing in architecture the idea of a cosmos continuously in change, **inconceivably complex, yet at each moment exquisitely finite.**
>
> ### Aim of Congress
> The Council meeting in Paris decided that the theme of CIAM X should be *'Problèmes de l'Habitat: Première proposition CIAM, Constatations et Résolutions'*, and that the work presented should take the form of projects for ideal human Habitat. These projects are to be prepared by the Groups, each recognizing and exploiting the reality of their various situations.
> We are seeking the ideal habitat for each particular place at this particular moment, uncompromised by existing arbitrary laws and restrictions, in an attempt to reach a moment of truth. In the preparation of their projects, groups should use whatever methods they consider necessary to arrive at a solution, for example: collaboration with engineers, anthropologists and specialists of all kinds. But it must be emphasized that we are only interested in the outcome of this collaboration – architecture, not in diagrams of relationships or analytical studies. We are working as architects and at this Congress for Architects.
> [Team 10, guideline for CIAM 10,[36] 1954]

Dubrovnic 1956

Those present at Dubrovnic – there were very many – split into two groups and the fate of CIAM was thereby sealed. A smaller group including the older generation, some founders and most of the council members, busied themselves entirely with the preparation of a large representative publication to commemorate 25 years of CIAM activity.

The study of all the habitat plans submitted – for the most part the work of the younger generation and presented according to the precise method evolved by Team 10 – was left to the quantitatively larger rest! After the congress all the plans were packed in crates for the benefit of the smaller group and sent to America – material for teaching at Harvard?
The end of CIAM obviously lurked in this highly paradoxical and immoral act.

All projects were studied by four groups working in close contact according to the four chosen aspects:
cluster / mobility / growth and change / urbanism and habitat

Some of the conclusions arrived at follow here.

> ### Cluster
> The word 'cluster' meaning a specific pattern of association, has been introduced to replace such words as house, street, district, city, or isolate village, town, city, which are too loaded with historical overtones. Any coming together is cluster. Cluster is a sort of clearing-house term during the period of creation of new types.
> [A. and P. Smithson]
>
> ### Identifying devices
> The problem of cluster is one of developing a distinct total structure for each community, and not one of sub-dividing a community into parts.
> To relate the parts of a community into a total cluster, a new discipline must be developed.
> We must find ways of weaving new units into the whole cluster so that they extend and renew the existing patterns.
> At all levels of community identifying devices are necessary, but at the city scale the community cannot be made comprehensible without something particular to city.
>
> **There is a tendency to change from small cellular units of cluster which are used additively, to the creation of a major structural element, increasing the scale in order to make it more comprehensible.**

The anonymous people are the true realizers of Habitat through private and collective initiative. They constitute the actual client of the architect working in the field of Habitat. But the anonymous people will remain a passive client until a Habitat consciousness is developed. [Albini]

To work in the light of the time concept demands a new creative discipline. Open the concept of time and you will discover its different applications along the total scale from the teacup to the city.
[A. van Eyck]

Principle of renewal

A possible discipline for the mutation of the community is the **irritant principle of renewal.** Example – the Amsterdam playgrounds.
[A. & P. Smithson, Albini, Van Eyck *et al.*, commission B4 Cluster, CIAM 10 Dubrovnic, 1956]

Honfleur harbour, France

Identifying devices – natural or man-made – hill, tower, river, harbour, cathedral, sea-side, agora, etc.

Mobilité physique and Mobilité d'Esprit.

The problem at any scale level or in any of the terms in which it is studied, can be looked at in two ways.
We have so far defined the following parts of the problem of mobility.
The pattern of circulation must be comprehensible. Examples of obviously comprehensible patterns: gridiron plan – main-street town or village – seaside town; this suggests the ability to give meaning to movement of a large feature – natural or man-made, a hill, a tower, a river. (Compare identifying devices).
We have briefly discussed the way in which the creation of a new thing in an old situation can change and revitalize the old. Additions to existing towns and villages always have the possibility of enriching the whole, but too often they are meaningless, and detract from what was there before.
[From report commission B5, Mobility, CIAM 10 Dubrovnic, 1956]

1 **Ecological**
Mobility as an element in the changing environment in which man lives.
2 **Anthropological**
Mobility as it affects man. Here we can be helped by all the techniques which study man – social, economic, psychological, cultural, etc. This contains the study of mobility as an expression of man's spirit, and of man's reaction to the environment as he moves through it.
3 **Technological**
A study of all the techniques which facilitate mobility – road engineering, transport, prefabrication etc.
[R. Pietilä, contribution to report commission B5, Mobility, CIAM 10 Dubrovnic, 1956]

Change and growth

Statements
Change, an essential aspect of Habitat.
Creation, construction, use, destruction; these phases form an organic unity.
The architect-urbanist observes the accelerating tempo of life, and he remembers that the lifespan of the individual remains constant. To maintain the relationship between lifespan and life-tempo through the built forms of Habitat is the direct responsibility of the architect-urbanist.
The architect-urbanist knows that an evolution from ownership of habitat to use of habitat is essential.
The architect-urbanist observes a trend towards the reduction of the use of materials in building and an increase in the labour of building – designing, fabricating, transporting, erecting and replacing.

The architect-urbanist must face the total, ever-changing and complex problems of habitat by developing the method of his discipline.

Needs
To develop habitat through built elements which, at every stage, have their own identity.
Each stage in the development must be a complete expression of habitat.
To respond to the accelerating tempo and extending space of the situation.
To facilitate the right of people to move or to remain in one place. (Choice of habitat).
To build for *'le plus grand nombre'*. This is still the critical problem of the situation.
To transform and re-animate existing expressions of habitat; on the land, in village, town and city.
To find means which will stimulate the spontaneous expression of identity among individuals and among groups.

Proposals
The architect-urbanist must develop a discipline (analogous to that of the road-engineer or bridge-builder) through which he may control the size and growth of habitat. Through this discipline he must realize built elements which are, in themselves, complete expressions of habitat, and yet, because of their size and their content, they may become interdependent elements of the whole.
The architect-urbanist must realize elements of reference ('signs' of identity), through which people who are moving may experience a sense of location in the world.
The architect-urbanist must provide, among other elements, elements which can be changed by individuals and by groups in order that they may express creatively their separate identities.
The architect-urbanist must interpret, select and integrate in plastic form the results of scientific investigation which may enhance the condition of existing habitat (automation, mass communication, the automobile), or extend the possible geographical location of habitat.
The architect-urbanist must interpret specific expressions of existing habitat and make building elements, whether simple units or complex groups, which will not only satisfy the immediate requirements for which they are designed, but will also imply, through their form, the reorientation of the existing habitat which surrounds them.
The precept of the 'Master Plan' must be superseded by the concept of building elements which are both total, achieved, plastic expressions and, at the same time, instruments of research into the development of the specific habitat.

The architect-urbanist must make the public authorities aware of their responsibility to promote building experiments. For the public authorities, and no longer the individual, have the power to initiate and finance such experiments (Hansa Viertel). For example *'L'Unité d'Habitation'*, experiment promoted by the French Minister of Public Works, Claudius-Petit.

The architect-urbanist must re-establish the power of his discipline so that his active participation in the affairs of the community is equal to that of the economist and politician of the present time.

[Bakema, Voelcker, *et al.*, Report commission B6, Growth and Change, CIAM 10 Dubrovnic, 1956]

La rue corridor a disparu avec la Charte d'Athènes. Maintenant c'est l'espace corridor qui doit disparaître.[37]

[Candilis, CIAM 10 Dubrovnic, 1956]

Indeed! More was lost than gained. Today life is more dignified in a medieval city than in one of the new towns.

Images
1930 The frame building and the multilevel high-rise city, images which contained a complete urban system.
Compared with:
1950 Random images drawn from many sources containing single ideas which, one by one, contribute to change and extend the experience of space.

Programme
1930 To popularize the already established style of the modern movement – Didactic.
Compared with:
1950 The search for a plastic system which reciprocates and extends in architectural form existing ecological patterns.

Method
1930 To categorize the general situation and to develop it through the dialectical manipulation of the categories made.
Compared with:
1950 The empirical observation of particular situations and development through the architectural expression of those unique patterns observed within them.

Technique
1930 To replace existing buildings and cities with new categorically formulated elements.

Compared with
1950 The time-conscious techniques of renewal and extension derived from the recognition of the positive ecological trends to be found in every particular section.

Results
1930 Prototype buildings and master plans each charged with the full 'international' urban programme. Irrespective of location – Didactic.
Compared with:
1950 Building in unique situations. The elements articulate and resolve the ecological patterns, and provide instruments of research into the possible development of each location.
[John Voelcker]

We are facing the task of creating inhabitable cities in a land that is already almost uninhabitable. True interiors for the community, so that every individual can know who and where he is, and so that the sheltered mind can once again warm the houses, streets and squares.

This unequivocally means the overthrow of *l'espace corridor*. Of scattering unusable dwelling forms around in space. Of every amorphous-additive housing mush. Of arbitrary-sentimental groupings of domestic elements into pointless pseudo-courtyards. Of the cerebral fission of urban functions and their inorganic absolutization. The subduing of large number and small size. Of the 'small' in general.

The overthrow of the numerous senseless regulations and their petty application; of the commission disease; of the official town planning and housing agencies' uncreative tinkering; of the craving for authority and comfort which appear to be so characteristic of today's architects.

Reunification of architecture and urbanism into one discipline.
A task for a more complete kind of man.

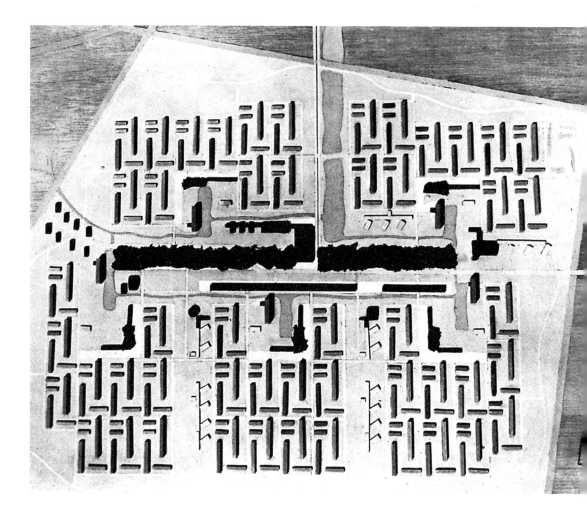

Pendrecht 1949[38]

Repetition of a great number of small housing units. Hardly susceptible of differentiation.

Housing units barely susceptible of mutual variation, visually or plastically.

Very fine dwelling surface texture.

Limited recognizability, only through articulation into subclusters.

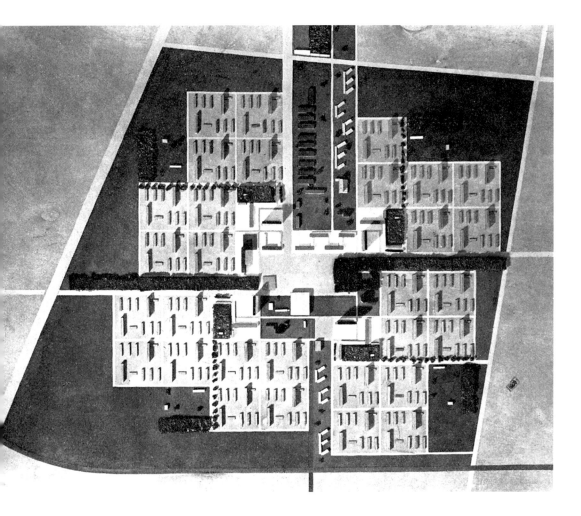

Pendrecht 1951

Repetition of a smaller number of greater housing units. More susceptible of differentiation.

Housing units still barely susceptible of mutual variation, visually or plastically.

Less fine dwelling surface texture.

Increased recognizability through enlargement of the housing units and reduction of their number.

Organic articulation into four subclusters.

A pre-parcellation by the town planner is hardly possible any more, because the main structure results from the dwelling texture, i.e from the quality of the cells.

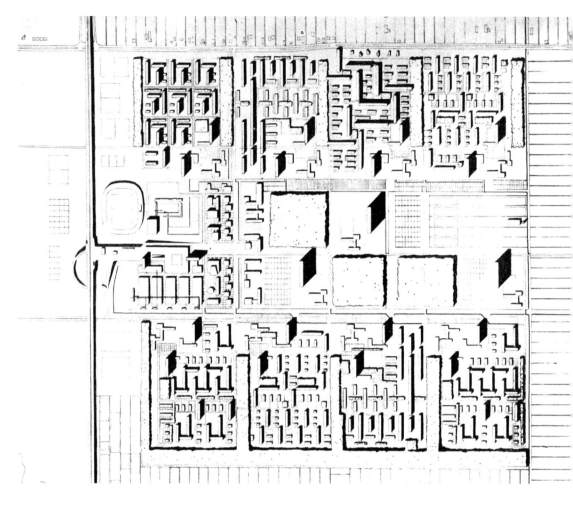

Alexanderpolder 1953

Repetition of a small number (8) of large housing units (which coincide, so to speak, with the subclusters), highly susceptible of differentiation. Owing to the increasing autonomy of the large housing units the recognizability of the whole improves, while the surface texture within the housing units gets finer again, causing a decreasing recognizability within the housing units.

The dividing of the whole into two parts in order to bring in the large scale of the polder counteracts the desired unity.

Aside from the higher elements and schools, the architects can develop separate housing units. Drawback: eight housing units and eight housing spheres whose differences have no social basis.

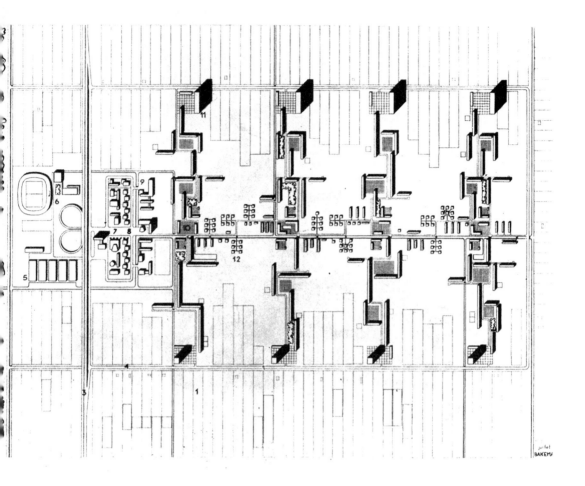

Alexanderpolder 1956
Repetition of only four large housing units, highly susceptible of differentiation. Good visual and plastic variability.
Overall recognizability due to very large size and small number of housing units.
Strong coherence while the surrounding space penetrates on all sides. All dwellings are in contact with the large polder space: yet the whole remains resting within itself. The resulting unity is partly based on the aesthetics of number: four housing units centrally linked into one settlement, and two times three space intervals bring about a clear structural shape. Decrease in size and densification of texture towards the centre without loss of recognizability.
Space scale
Exterior spaces within the separate housing elements
Enclosed exterior spaces within the four housing units
Variable green spaces between the housing units
Polder space
All together exemplifying the idea of ascending dimensions

Here the pre-parcellation by the town planner as well as the architect's little ground plan have been surmounted.

When the dwellings within the housing units link up together more closely, when they eventually merge and partly or entirely cease to be separate bodies – see the project by Blom – the replacement of both architecture and urbanism by a new discipline that encompasses both, becomes a necessary condition.

And to conclude: this approach will inevitably lead to a dignified human habitat, one which will look more like an organized Kasbah than one would be inclined to believe today.

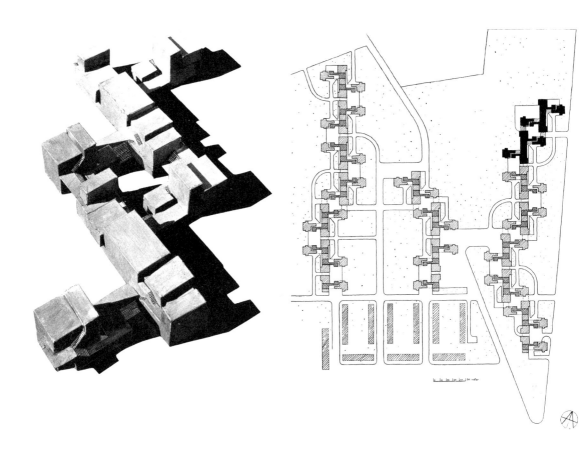

Piet Blom, 'the cities will be inhabited like villages' (1958)
An urban design project for a section of the new Amsterdam Slotermeer neighbourhood.[39]

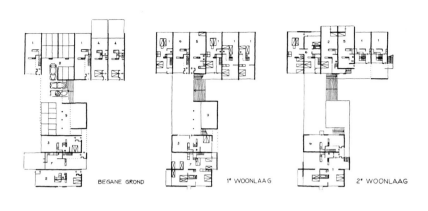

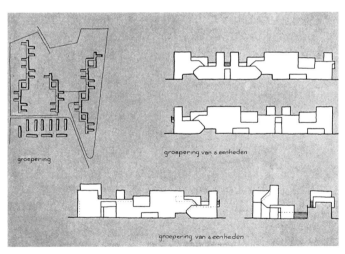

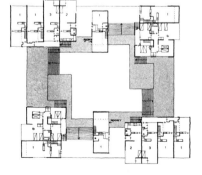

Vers une Casbah organisée...

Maandblad voor architectuur en gebonden kunsten, opgericht door het Genootschap „Architectura et Amicitia" in samenwerking met de Koninklijke Maatschappij tot Bevordering der Bouwkunst Bond van Nederlandsche Architecten B.N.A. - Orgaan van het Genootschap A. et A.

Veertiende jaargang No 7 (september 1959)

Redactie

D. C. Apon
Aldo van Eyck
J. B. Bakema
G. Boon
Joop Hardy
Herman Hertzberger
Jurriaan Schrofer, typografische vormgeving

Redactie secretariaat: Academie van Bouwkunst Waterlooplein 67 Amsterdam.

Voor de ondertekende artikelen dragen de schrijvers verantwoordelijkheid, ook wanneer het leden van de redactie betreft. Overname van artikelen, foto's en tekeningen is slechts geoorloofd met toestemming van redactie en uitgever en dan nog slechts met bronvermelding.

Voor advertenties wende men zich tot de uitgever

„FORUM" verschijnt met 12 nummers per jaar

Abonnementsprijs / 24.— per jaar, franco per post bij vooruitbetaling te voldoen
Voor België Frs. 400.—
Prijs van dit nummer / 2.50/B.frs 40.—

Uitg. en adm.: G. VAN SAANE, Keizersgracht 546 Postbus 1170 Amsterdam-C. Tel. 36186-34613

FORUM

8
Forum 1959–1963: from the shape of the in-between to configurative design

Introduction to chapter 8

The new editorial team that took charge of Forum from 1959 to 1963 produced some twenty issues, including a 'posthumous' one in 1967: a rather limited but particularly substantial output that was to be of seminal importance to architectural thinking. And although most of the editors contributed in a notable way, there can be no doubt that the calibre and the purport of the review mainly resulted from the input by Aldo van Eyck. He set the tone, initiated the major themes and wrote the most significant articles. His fellow team members fully identified with most of the themes he had advanced in The Story of Another Idea. Actually, they were keen to take up these themes, to explore their further implications and to interpret them in their personal way. But paradoxically, due to their very keenness, Van Eyck soon felt prompted to stand back, at least for a while.

Van Eyck had proposed to devote the second issue to a theme he had only touched upon briefly in The Story of Another Idea: time as a positive factor in town planning. His idea was to consider town planning in the light of the natural cycles, namely day and night, the four seasons and the various stages in the life of man. The subject was discussed in numerous meetings and gave rise to various ideas, from limiting the theme to 'day and night' to taking it as a platform for all the other themes, so as to turn the whole issue into a second manifesto that would specify the common intentions of the team members. Van Eyck's original proposal was inundated and the discussion ended in deadlock. A way out was found by Hardy who succeeded in persuading his friend Lucebert to stand in as a guest editor. The result was the so-called 'day and night' number (ultimately not the second but the fourth issue), which consisted

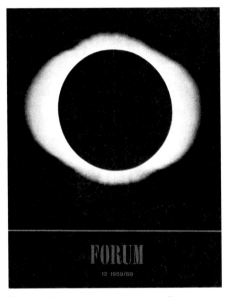

Cover of the 'day and night' issue of Forum, December 1959

of an experimental poem on the complexity of urban life, interspersed with a selection of nocturnal and diurnal city views selected by Hardy. At the beginning of the discussion Van Eyck had prepared an outline proposal including a draft on the day and night cycle. The present chapter starts with a selection of sketches from this declined proposal.

In the meantime the second issue had actually been devoted to the in-between, a theme that preoccupied Van Eyck for years. He had also discussed it at length in the editorial meetings but in the event he had left it to Hardy and Hertzberger, who produced the 'threshold and encounter' issue.

So Van Eyck first limited himself to some minor contributions. Only after a year did he return to the fore with an essential statement. He wrote a kind of prose poem in which he worded his views on the in-between in a condensed and telling way. Heading it with a verse by the seventeenth-century poet Thomas Campion, *'There is a garden in her face'*, he published it in the so-called 'door and window' issue. The Dutch version ran over 10 pages and was illustrated with various images selected by Hardy. He also wrote an English version which was included at the end of the issue. But remarkably, the two versions turn out to be quite different. Apparently the two languages inspired him to evolve different lines of thought. So, for a better understanding of this key text we included a more literal translation of the Dutch original.

In this prose poem Van Eyck introduced several new concepts: the idea of conceiving architecture as a 'counterform of human reality' – or in the Dutch version, as the 'counterform of the mind' – the mutual identification of house and city and the specification of space and time as 'place' and 'occasion'. Moreover, reversing Campion's interpretation of the human face in terms of a garden, he conceived architecture 'in the image of man', as an artefact endowed with human features and attitudes, as an organism capable of breathing in and out.

These notions and images evoke multiple meanings, and although this was no doubt Van Eyck's intention, it is no less interesting to understand the meanings he had in mind himself. He explained them in a lecture entitled 'Interior Art', which is published here for the first time.

The new *Forum* series provoked numerous critical reactions, both in the general and the professional press. After one year the review published a special 're(d)action' issue, bundling a number of press comments and the responses of six editors. In his article *'overwegend vuile was'* (dirty linen, mostly) Van Eyck reacted to various criticisms and dwelt upon the statements received from Rietveld and Oud.

In regard to architectural form, *Forum* initially took a rather indeterminate, open-ended course. The projects that were published as 'illuminations' of the 'other idea' ranged from Hansen's Auschwitz monument to the Smithsons' terraced crescent housing, from Erskine's Polar City to Voelcker's Zone Project. Still, at the conclusion of *The Story of Another Idea* Van Eyck had argued the necessity of a new approach that would reunite architecture and urbanism into 'one discipline'. What he actually had in mind was the 'configurative' approach with which he had himself been experimenting in the Nagele village project and the Amsterdam Orphanage.

In the Orphanage he was realizing the first major synthesis of his ideas. It consisted of a number of dwelling units based on a single theme and worked out in elementary, both geometric and biomorphic forms. The units developed like the themes of a fugue and were interconnected through articulated in-between areas, thus offering a small-scale demonstration of the 'aesthetics of number'. For all their expressive appearance, the units did not withdraw into a self-sufficient autonomy but joined in order to configure gently articulated places. And as Van Eyck explained in 'The Medicine of Reciprocity', the article he wrote to present the Orphanage in *Forum*, he deliberately intended the building to be a realization of his view on relativity. He conceived it as a small city, as a cluster of elements whose coherence did not lie in their subordination to a dominant principle but in their reciprocal relations. In this context he now advanced a concept he had been brooding on for a long time, the concept of the 'dual phenomenon'.[1] By 'dual phenomenon', or 'twin phenomenon' as he was soon to rename it, Van Eyck meant a unity of two opposites which are reconciled into complementary halves that reinforce each other so as to form a dynamic whole. It constituted his basic type of the non-hierarchical, purely reciprocal relation, his primary material for the construction of the 'new reality'.

As the Orphanage took shape, it appeared like a modern version of a traditional settle-

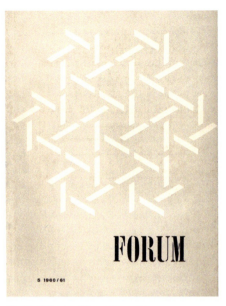

Cover of Forum, May 1960–1961

Cover of Forum, June/July 1960–1961

ment, as a prototype of a new kind of urban fabric that offered a compelling alternative to the rationalist housing in the new urban extensions. While still under construction, the building appealed greatly to the younger generations of Dutch architects, in the first place Van Eyck's former students. One of them, Piet Blom, adopted the configurative principle as early as 1958 when still a second year student at the Amsterdam Academy of Architecture. He gave it concrete form in a small urban design project called 'the cities will be inhabited like villages'. Van Eyck highly appreciated this plastically evocative project and recognized it as an outstanding actualisation of his ideas. He included it in his presentation at the Otterlo congress and gave it a place of honour at the conclusion of *The Story of Another Idea*. In the years to come Blom went on to achieve a number of other urban projects that displayed an increasingly complex, fugue like structure.

These projects, and Van Eyck's Orphanage, which were published in *Forum* shortly after each other,[2] brought the configurative idea to the centre of editorial discussion, a discussion that induced Van Eyck to specify his views. He first formulated his configurative vision at the end of his contribution to the 're(d)action' issue ('Dirty linen, mostly') and expounded it two years later in a comprehensive essay entitled 'Steps towards a Configurative Discipline'. With the term 'configurative' Van Eyck adequately summarized his new approach – a 'configuration' denoting the organisation of various elements into a coherent figure, within which these elements themselves acquire a new meaning.[3] He endeavoured to implement this notion, derived from Gestalt Theory, in architecture and urbanism. After proposing it as an alternative to the prevailing housing developments, he extended it to the scale of the whole city. It became his answer to the problem of designing new urban structures for 'the greater number', or more specifically, the problem of designing new towns, a topic that had been under discussion in CIAM since the early fifties and was being tackled by various Team 10 members, notably Bakema, Candilis and Tange.

'Steps towards a Configurative Discipline' was both included as a chapter in *The Child the City and the Artist* and published in the so-called Pueblo issue of *Forum* (August 1962). Composed by Van Eyck and Hertzberger, the Pueblo issue was partly intended as a reaction to Bakema who had exposed his way of dealing with 'the greater number' in the previous issue. Bakema had raised the problem that the majority of Dutch housing was produced for anonymous clients, i.e. without any personal contact between the architect and the client – a situation that tended to result in standardized, uniform housing forms. In order to tackle this problem and to meet the 'variety of housing wishes of the masses' he divided the building process into a 'support' and 'detachable units'. The fixed support would be equipped with the necessary common facilities and constructed by the community, whereas the individual detachable units would be left to 'the ensuing personal building initiatives, which, in their turn, could make architecture the expression in space of the variations in human behaviour'.[4] Bakema illustrated this idea with an original example: the Palace of Diocletian at Split, 'an emperor's house' transformed into 'a town for 3000 people'. His photographs and sketches showed his fascination with the interaction between the sixteen-century-old 'support' and the highly varied 'detachable units' that the inhabitants had added since the Middle Ages. But when in conclusion he demonstrated how to implement this concept in contemporary practice, he came up with an anticlimax. He narrowed down the idea of 'growth and change' to a single dwelling type in the low-rise zone of his neighbourhood unit (the traditional single-storey house between parallel party walls) and failed to draw any consequence from his Split story as to the form of the support, the large, general form that determines the identity of the settlement as a whole.

As a reaction Van Eyck opened the Pueblo issue with a quite explicit title: 'the fake client and the great word "no"'. He frankly rejected the prevailing rationalist production system of housing and overtly urged his colleagues to withdraw from participating in it. He asserted that 'building for the anonymous client' in the Netherlands amounted to building for a fake client, i.e. a narrow-minded administrative apparatus that ignored the very nature of the contemporary building task. He stressed that this task was thoroughly different from the one architects were used to in the past, 'different in that it concerns – at last – the immediate environment of each man and all men; different also in that it is numerically vast (for today the architect is the ally of everyman or no man).' In the past the housing of 'the greater number' had rarely if ever been assigned to architects. In pre-industrial societies people used to build their houses themselves, with or without the help of the craftsman in their midst. And they mostly managed to achieve adequate forms of habitat. They created villages and towns that were attuned to their way of life and expressed their identity. Archaic cultures all over the world display a wonderful variety of vernacular architecture that belongs among the most valuable but also the most ignored constituents of the world's built heritage. The quality of these 'humble miracles' is a result not only of their inhabitants being closely involved in the building process but also of their sharing a generally assumed world-view. As opposed to this tradition, the twentieth century architect is saddled with the task of building for large quantities of people whom he does not know and who are denied any participation in the design process. Moreover, they find themselves in a plural society that is drifting in undetermined directions, in search of its form. This awareness raises the uncomfortable question: 'if society has no form, can architects build the counterform?'

The configurative approach is meant as a way out of this conundrum. Starting from the mutual identification of house and city

Van Eyck proposes to develop a new kind of urban fabric based on a structural similarity between part and whole; more specifically, to conceive urban components on the basis of a ground pattern that can be multiplied into a cluster of a similar pattern – in such a way that their identity is not impaired but confirmed and enriched in the very shape of the cluster they compose. In the same way these clusters should be combinable into a larger cluster in which their identity is again recovered and intensified. Van Eyck evokes the image of a complex, 'polyphonic' and 'multi-rhythmic' fabric, structured like a fugue and including room for common facilities and 'identifying devices' at every level of association. In the formulation of this vision Van Eyck was again inspired by a project by Blom, a large-scale urban plan called 'Noah's Ark'. Van Eyck felt that Blom had succeeded in overcoming the hierarchy between large and small, part and whole, and contrasted his project polemically to Kenzo Tange's megaform concept.

Following on 'Steps towards a Configurative Discipline' Van Eyck published an account of his journey to the American Pueblo Indians in whose settlements he recognized a kind of archaic prefiguration of the configurative idea. He saw them as a proof of man's ability to deal with number and to bring about in built form a convincing reconciliation of the individual and the collective, part and whole. What particularly appealed to him in the Pueblos was their articulation of individual dwelling components within clear and expressive megaforms. In the *Forum* issue the Pueblo article is directly linked to 'Steps towards a Configurative Discipline'. In this edition the choice of clustering the articles thematically resulted in the Pueblo article being incorporated in the next chapter.

From 1961 'the other idea' became effectively identified with configurative design. Apart from some contributions by Bakema, all the projects published henceforth in *Forum* were characterized by the new approach,[5] which soon was to be improperly labelled 'structuralism'.[6]

The CIAM City and the Natural Cycles

Translation of a sketch proposal for an unpublished issue of Forum, *late 1959*

When life in the city is projected onto the phenomenon of day and night, it throws the inadequacy of rectilinear thinking into the correct light – it brings the cyclical to the fore, out of the darkness, and with it the wonder of metamorphosis – the kaleidoscope of imagination…

It is the right projection because one encounters everything – even the four functions – and rediscovers a lot that had seemed to have been forgotten and banished, expired and evaporated. The things that are familiar take on a new face: summer and winter, sun, rain, wind, moon, storm, ice and snow, light and dark.

Between day and night: twilight: threshold of the day, between summer and winter, spring and autumn: thresholds of the year, between rain and sun: the rainbow, between one and the other: everything, between yourself and another: everyone, between yesterday and tomorrow: now, between young and old: one's own time, one's own age.

Simultaneous perception of the sun and moon: the eclipse.

The street also takes on new substance: going home and to work, the human movement, his natural gait.
The door: a welcome. The window: the appearance on the other side.
The square: the community's living room, stage for urban life. The park because one can make love there.
No refuges, because why would one have to take refuge?

Four elements and five senses and man a spirit in love
Dylan Thomas

Where did go the face,
the moon,
the eye, the ear,
the answer,
the smell, the song, the star?

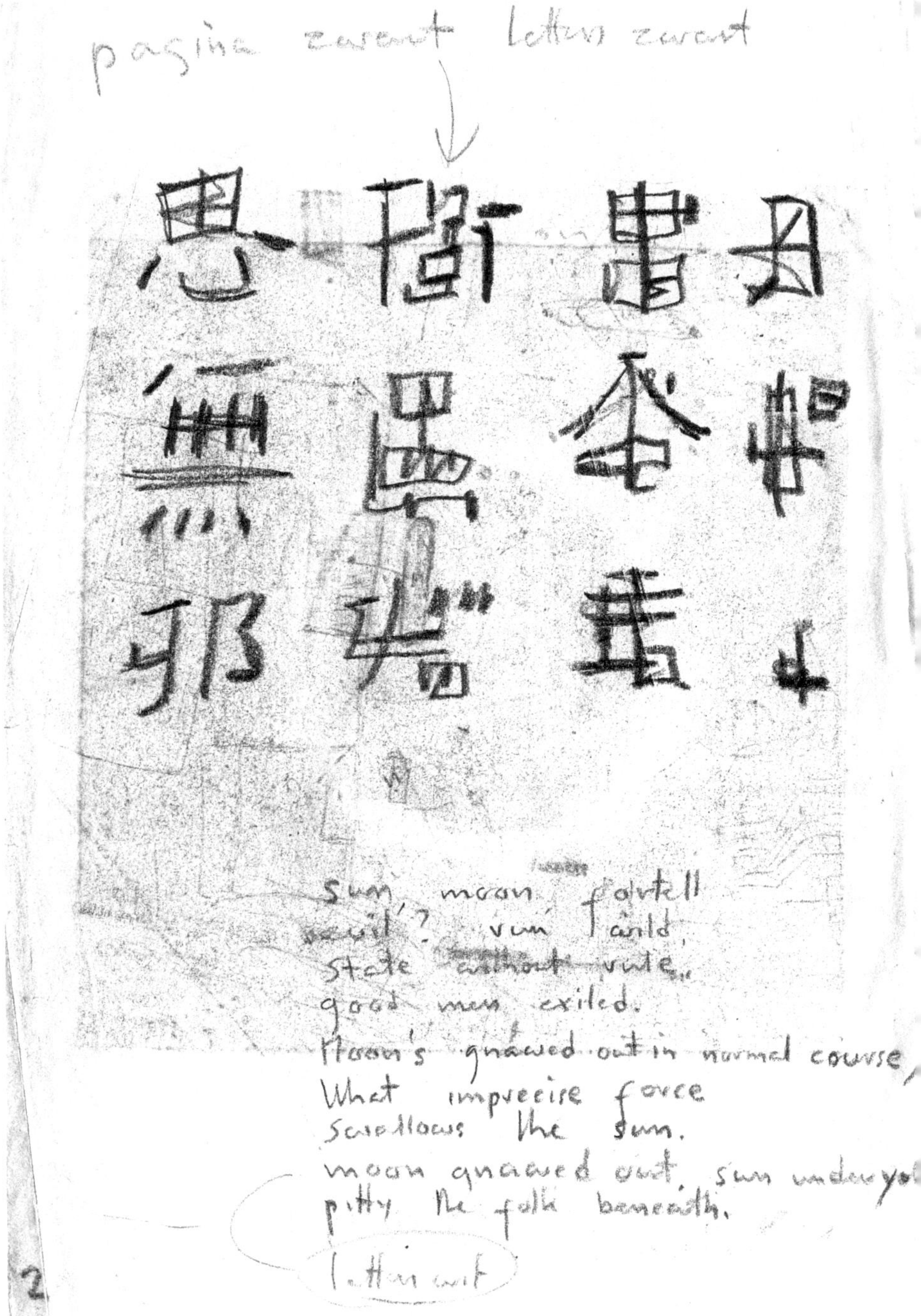

Sun, moon, foretell
Evil? run wild,
State without rule,
Good men exiled.
Moon's gnawed out in normal course,
What imprecise force
swallows the sun?

Ezra Pound

The CIAM City

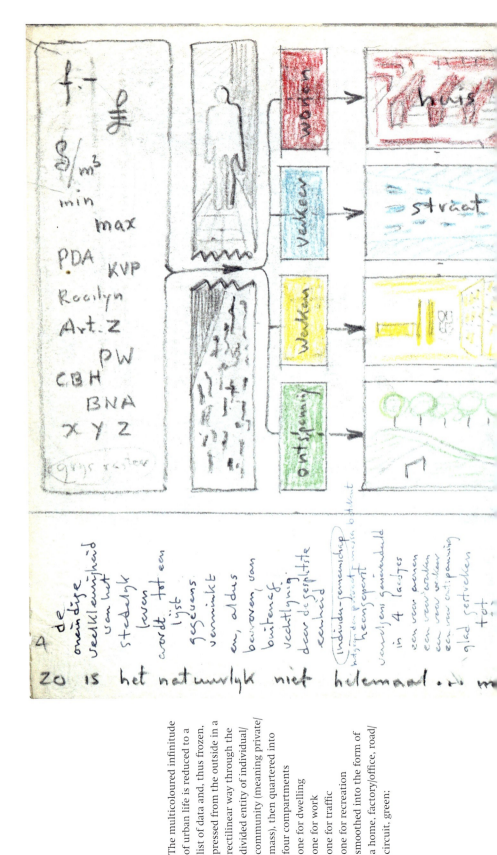

What does this sort of skeleton have to do with a human habitat? Nothing but a world full of emptiness.

What does it offer man? The loss of his identity. What does it make man into? A spectator, solitary amidst 1000 solitaries.

The multicoloured infinitude of urban life is reduced to a list of data and, thus frozen, pressed from the outside in a rectilinear way through the divided entity of individual/community (meaning private/mass), then quartered into four compartments
one for dwelling
one for work
one for traffic
one for recreation
smoothed into the form of a home, factory/office, road/circuit, green;

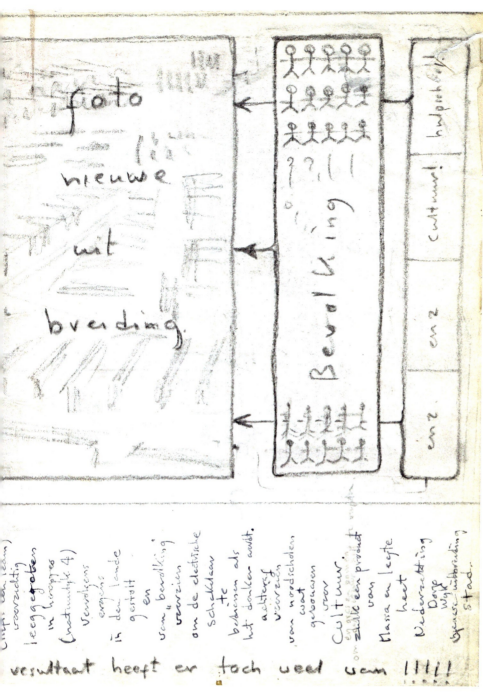

carefully poured out into piles (4 of course) on a drawing board in a cool office by a 'professional' (preferably a team); then coagulated somewhere in the country and provided with 'population' to operate the electric light switch when it gets dark; afterwards supplied with emergency schools, a few buildings for culture and some grass and trees, so as not to forget nature. This sort of product of mass and emptiness is called Settlement, Village, Neighbourhood, Urban Extension.

Of course, it's not entirely like this, but the result comes rather near to it!

The Development of the Western City

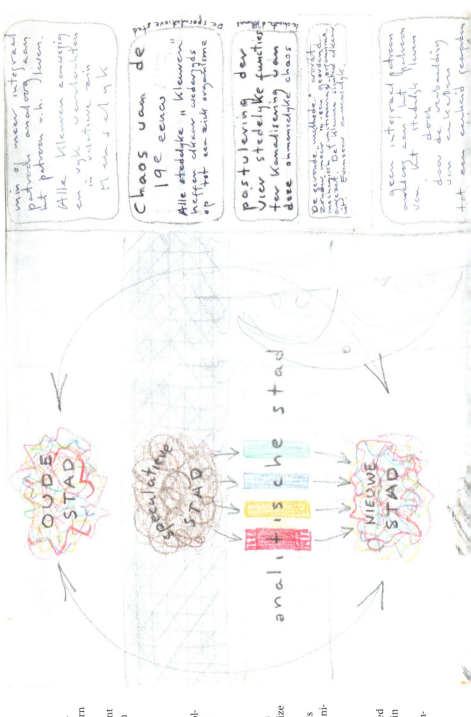

The old city

More or less integrated pattern analogous to the pattern of life.

All urban colours are present and abundantly interwoven in a relative sense.

The speculative city

In the chaos of the nineteenth century all urban colours cancel each other and produce a sick organism.

The analytical city

CIAM postulates four urban functions in order to canalize the inhuman chaos.

The adopted method results straight away into a mechanically split environment.

The new city

The imagination of a limited group will bring about again an integrated pattern through a new abundant interweaving of all colours.

Cyclic Thinking

'sun man and moon man' in the middle circle, circumscribed by the 'dual phenomenon individual-community' and 'the imagination – cyclic thinking'.

'Man breathes both in and out. Why do our new cities not breathe?'

Day and Night

Translation of an unpublished article drafted for the 'day and night' issue of Forum, *late 1959*[1]

Switch on the stars before the fuses go!

In earlier times – and also where our technical society has had little influence – the natural cycles and the elements that go with them, as well as all the uncontrollable forces, were a challenge to man, both physically and mentally, individually and collectively. It goes without saying that the notion of raising oneself above them did not even arise. It was a question of holding one's own, of safeguarding one's existence.

Ingenuity played a major part but could neither avoid nor neutralise the forces that both threatened life and made it possible. It was a challenge, one that determined everything. Man deliberately reacted to this challenge in accordance with the nature of the environment in which he had to survive and in accordance with his attitude to these forces and their mysterious causes. He did this, and here and there still does it, in many different ways. He made sacrifices to influence these forces. Ritual and prayer had a direct functional sense. In short, man created a technique for existence in which the physical and mental were woven into a single whole. He developed a homogeneous pattern of socio-religious and economic behaviour that enabled him to grasp the forces that formed the reality of the place he was born in. He was able to absorb them, to subjugate them to a certain extent, sometimes even resist them, influence and explain them. Quite apart from the question of whether he incidentally or locally succumbed or triumphed, he ultimately succeeded in holding his own by tremendous effort and dedication. Above all, he was able to do this with astounding precision. It is not we in our era, but they in theirs who acted with great precision, because there was no margin for error.

But nowadays everything is different. We have moved forward – yes, that's what it's called. We have overcome the margins – and created an immense margin around ourselves, at least in the sense that we are abundantly able to safeguard our existence (but not all, of course). The slums have almost gone, at least in a material sense. Whereas at one time everything had a meaning – when everything was 'you' and nothing 'it' – everything was charged, and now everything is discharged – everything is 'you'-less, everything is 'it', everything has become a thing. That's why I say: switch on the stars before the fuses go. We now live safely in the backstreets of the mind. It's paradoxical, this. Because human ingenuity has after all finally achieved what it rightly wanted – space beyond the subsistence level. And see, now that the age-old burden of the insurmountable and the inescapable has been lifted – we have secured the space – we discover that we can no longer fly, that we are flapping around in the most absurd cage ever invented: the illusory freedom exacted from nature with obsessive industry. Now that our existence has been amply safeguarded, the womb has gone – our origin and our goal. We have shot away the space – that is the one thing we still do with drastic precision and seriousness. We no longer live afflicted and supported by the cycles but in spite of the cycles, the elements notwithstanding. Now that we could enjoy their glory we have lost the receptiveness to their meaning. We have become lost in the margin we have won, wandering in the awful cavity between the material and the mental, instead of in their indivisible space. The seasons are still there – night and day too – and also rain, lightning, wind, snow, sun, stars, cold, heat, youth and old age – we notice something of them at most – yet they are gone. When we read about a natural disaster in New Zealand, Persia or Catalonia, we are shocked and look at the bank account number and feel wings growing on our backs. The seasons, the elements, youth and old age are impediments. Even the sun, yes, even our beloved sun, is becoming a hindrance because there is no space to say 'good day!' to the sun (after all, the sun causes traffic problems). Nature is vanishing from our consciousness along with the cycles – what we retain are trees, grass and plants, and antibiotics to protect them against nature and at the same time to contaminate them, to denaturalise them, to make them into a gift – tree, flower, bush – stopgaps to give uninhabitable places of residence the appearance of naturalness. Trees, grass, flowers, bees, butterflies and birds represent our bad conscience – not nature, don't imagine that. Our cities are no longer cities (with or without trees) because nature is no longer nature, because we have become rectilinear and uniform, and have a square heart. We are no longer winged diggers – cyclical beings. If we carry on like this, our country will become a no man's land, neither city nor nature. When it comes to our cities, bad weather really is bad weather. Because a fine day now means bad weather too, as soon as millions – rightly – wish to enjoy it.

Anyone who was to project today's city onto the background of the natural cycles, both the minor – day and night – and major – the four seasons – and also onto the background of the various stages in the life of man, would obviously come to the conclusion that not the slightest creative attention was paid to these cycles. It is only in the light of the natural cycles and elements that it becomes clear just how much the urban functions of dwelling, working, traffic and recreation have become absolute, frozen and abstracted from each other. It also becomes apparent just how much the presence of insubstantial light was presupposed in the design of new urban extensions (because forms are simply invisible without light). In fact visibility is very much taken for granted, has been separated from the notion of light, and light from its source. The result is that the visual effect has become too all-determining. There is no question of a real city, not even a real daytime city, nor of a real rainy-day city, sun or moon city, snow city or springtime city.

The time has come to conceive the places we live in, in the light of the positive potential hidden in the natural cycles. Only then we will discover the positive potential hidden in technique and ingenuity. It is not a matter of fighting, neutralising or eliminating with the aid of technique or form the inherent or supposed negative forces that the cycles undoubtedly include. Elimination is not creation. Involving nature positively in a city means a positive expression of the natural cycles (not just taking them into account): the seasons, the elements, the weather – constant and constantly changing.

We have to accept rain as rain, wind as wind, snow as snow, night as night, and make something of them so that the city-dweller, who is at most only marginally or negatively aware of these phenomena, can live, i.e. can be a citizen.

It is not only geometry and the standard functions with their coarse meshes, not only house, garden, street, green strip, etc., or concrete, steel, glass and everything else in the building catalogue, but that which is not in there, that which is part of the cyclical reality in which we live: rain, storm, snow, spring, stars, winter, sun, clouds, ice, moon, the child and old people, these and the huge number of other things are the materials with which architecture in its broadest sense makes something for the community. A city is not a life-sized model that has to be 'populated'. When we say 'city', surely we mean the people who live there?

Neither the cycles nor the elements are always comfortable. We have to become aware once again of the value of the meaningfully uncomfortable, reasonably adapted, to avoid the fall of the pseudo-comfortable. We should not neutralise nature with the aid of technique and form, but intensify it.

Aquarium design by Jan Verhoeven

Assessment of a student's project made in 1958 and published in Forum, *July 1960*[1]

A design that really approaches the essence of the problem set, obviously nourished by a direct awareness of just those subtle relationships that are best experienced through the medium of art – in this case architecture.

The scheme succeeds in reconciling the world of the fish with that of man – no easy task! – and demonstrates that an aquarium can be more than a diverting peep-show – a good thing unless we are to assume that the fishes, visitors themselves, peep at us whilst we peep at them.

If the visitor is at all susceptible to associations he will be able by means of fish and architecture to experience the phenomena of the sea, the river and lake as such. To have achieved this without resorting to juxta-architectural means certainly deserves credit. From the meniscus – strange line of demarcation – the structure winds downwards pyramidically into water as it winds pyramidically upwards into air. Both water-depth and airspace have been indicated plastically and will affect the visitor each time the meniscus is passed diagonally. He witnesses increasing darkness as he descends, increasing light and airiness as he ascends. Man and animal; warmth and coldness; land, air and water; light, little, half-light and darkness: phenomena that can be appreciated in association.

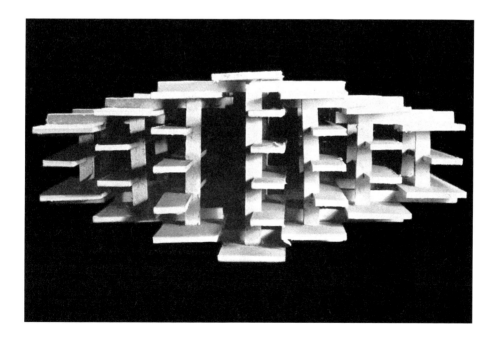

Then there is the way the visitor enters and leaves this tectonically controlled play with the elements. He enters and leaves analogously, for coming and going are ambivalent, just as air and water, light and darkness, inside and outside are ambivalent.

The problem of left, right and centre here touches on the problem of equilibrium – i.e. the real problem of symmetry!

J. Verhoeven, Aquarium design, 1958

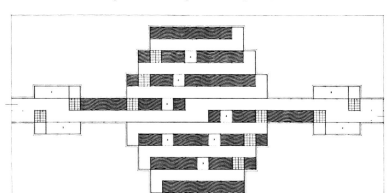

Upper floors plan

Lower floors plan

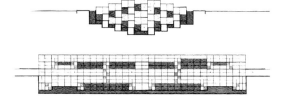

Cross section and longitudinal section

Between here and there, now and later

Translation of Van Eyck's Dutch text for the 'door and window' issue of Forum, *August 1960*[1]

'There is a garden in her face'
Thomas Campion[2]

The mind reaches between here and there, now and later, between one man and another.
But not just like that. Because in between are the physical things which man makes for himself with the aid of tools, materials and intelligence, giving them a more or less ordered place.
Does the mind penetrate this matter? Does it reach another, the other side, a following moment?
(For all those who do not shun the paradox of the right answer this has been written.)
Space went astray in the void, and so did the mind, along with space. Both are searching a common place, but they cannot find it.

Provide that place

make a welcome of each door

and a face of each window

(both of them with a warm 'insight' and a good 'prospect').

Start with this, for the own realm of the mind is the realm of the in-between – the real wealth of architecture.

Make of each window and each door a place,
a bunch of places of each house and each city.
Make also of each house a small city and of each city a large house.[3]
Build the counterform[4] of the mind for each man and all man,
since they no longer do it themselves.

Senmut[5] made what he was commanded to make: a habitable house of granite for a single dead queen. Are the sons of Senmut today unable to make what they are requested to make: habitable places for the millions that live, but are no longer able to fashion their own houses with mud – no longer forced to drag granite.

Architects and urbanists have become true specialists in the art of organizing the meagre.

Whoever does not shun the paradox of the right answer knows that the result draws very close to crime.
Whoever attempts to catch the secret of space in a mindless void will construct the outline of emptiness and call it space.
Whoever attempts to meet man in a mindless void will speak with his echo and call this a dialogue.

Man still breathes both in and out. When is architecture going to do the same?

Between one man and all man, the one and the other, between here and there, now and later, lies the in-between realm, the home of the mind.

The countenance of a window.
The welcome of a door.

Prospect to space

'There is a garden in her face'

Thomas Campion[1]

Van Eyck's English version of the previous text in Forum, *August 1960*[2]

Space has no room and time not a moment for man.
He is excluded.
In order to 'include' him – help his homecoming – he must be gathered into their meaning
(man is the subject as well as the object of architecture).

Whatever space and time mean, place and occasion mean more.

For space in the image of man is place and time in the image of man is occasion.

Today space and what it should coincide with in order to become 'space' – man at home with himself – are lost. Both search for the same place but cannot find it.

Provide that place.

Is man able to penetrate the material he organizes into hard shape between one man and another; between what is here and what is there; between this and the following moment? Is he able to find the right place for the right occasion?

No – So start with this: make

a welcome of each door
a face of each window.

Make of each a place, a bunch of places of each house and each city (a house is a tiny city, a city a huge house).

Get closer to the centre of human reality and build its counterform – for each man and all men, since they no longer do it themselves.

Senmut[3] made what he was commanded to make: a habitable house of granite for a single dead queen. Are the sons of Senmut today unable to make what they are requested to make: habitable places for the millions that live, but are no longer able to fashion their own houses with mud – no longer forced to drag granite.

Architects and urbanists have become true specialists in the art of organizing the meagre.

The result draws very close to crime.

The time has come for another sort

Whoever attempts to solve the riddle of space in the abstract will construct the outline of emptiness and call it space.

Whoever attempts to meet man in the abstract will speak with his echo and call this a dialogue.

Man still breathes both in and out. When is architecture going to do the same?

Interior Art

Translation of a talk given at the Royal Academy of Art in The Hague on 6 February 1961[1]

Man breathes both in and out: never just out – never just in. This is not simply a commonplace. He stands alone among millions; one isolated man among countless isolated men. He has excluded himself, shut himself out.

Man has lost himself in the expanding universe of which Bakema spoke. Man has lost his identity, he looks at life as if through a keyhole. He spies on himself through the keyhole, he is on the other side of himself. Of course he tries to coincide with himself, to be secure, to be at home with himself and thus also at home with others, with another.

What did the architects concoct to meet this feeling of isolation, both individual and social? Did they ever mind dealing with the mind?

To meet, to mind. That's what it's all about!

How, when we build, can we contribute to the rediscovery of the mind, to housing the mind? The mind extends between here and there, now and later – in the sense of both time and space – between a man and another man; or at least it should. But not just like that, because in between are the physical things, countless physical things that man makes for himself with the aid of materials and tools, intelligence and techniques, giving them a more or less ordered place all around us. We are fettered amongst all these material things.

My question is: is the mind able to get through this matter?

Does the mind reach another one, the other side, in the following moment?

No! Space – our beloved space, the reward for building – went astray in the void, and with space the mind too. They are both searching for a common place, but they cannot find it.

So do not talk about space anymore, but provide that place!

The word I want to talk about is *place*. Because look, the word 'space' has become a sort of academic conjuring word. It means everything and therefore nothing. It is precisely this 'space' in which the mind went astray, and this space has been absorbed into the void along with the mind. One might construct the outline of the emptiness and call this space!

We have reached the point in architecture where we have even succeeded in constructing the outline of a void in which we peek from one cavity to another through a keyhole. We have been engaged in constructing something in which it is only good to breathe *out*. You can do that once and then you suffocate. Conversely, you can also just breathe *in*, and you will suffocate then too. Anyone who tries to meet a human in a mindless void will speak only to his echo and call this a dialogue.

In the mindlessness of the void that we call 'space', you can only talk to your echo and not even with any other. There is no dialogue.

It is all a matter of creating a place. And why do I use the word 'place' instead of 'space'? Because space in the image of man is place.

Space is an abstraction. It is only when we see space as a place where it's good to be that we have included man in the concept of space. So you could call space in the image of man 'place'.

Time is just as abstract as space – the notion of time, and so you might say that time in the image of man is an event. An occasion.

So, if we take an example of this: a table is not a table space. I cannot categorise a table as a space. I can of course say that I made it so that it occupies a spatial (there's that word again – it's enough to spoil your appetite) position in the space – that means that we choose whether it stands on four legs at the corners – and is therefore a block – or on one leg in the middle and therefore more or less floats, always relative to that academic notion of 'space'.

But the table and the original idea of space in which this table stands are reconciled as soon as you speak of a 'place'. The place where you eat, where you spend time, eat and eat together. It is an event. It is a place that is created for an instant, a moment, for an occasion, for a dialogue between yourself and the food and between yourself and the others with whom you are eating. If you look at it this way, the dining room does not become the room with a table where you spoon in food, but a place where you do one of the most essential things, together.

Do not talk about space, provide that place.
Make a welcome of each door.

And when I say 'make a welcome of each door,' I mean: **Make a place of each door.**

Because between the first time and the last time we go in or out through a door – when we are sacked and filed away – between the one time and the other we come in thousands of times and go out thousands of times.

Door – place – doorstep – score for coming and going, for staying, spending a short time – meaning for lingering too (architecture should encourage lingering). Going out means coming into another world, because outside and inside are essentially the same – seen in this way, the same. So it is not a matter of seeing the door as a necessary evil for getting through a wall that separates one room from another – such a thin thing a few centimetres thick with a threshold a few centimetres wide.

The area between here and there, between me and the other side of the door – that is a much more wonderful thing. That is the moment when you leave the one and see the other again. In the case of a door it does not matter whether it is 'spatial' or well proportioned. *Who* is on the other side of this door?

Have a look at how doors are made. How often one stays lingering with the handle in one's hand, remaining hesitating on this threshold, that place that is actually not a place, with very nervous movements of the sole of the shoe on that thin threshold, not knowing exactly whether we ought to stand on the one side or the other, not knowing whether we want to go away or not. This door does not give any shape at all to this human moment, when one does not simply want to go straight from the one side – like through a trapdoor or a guillotine – to the other. The 'in-between' that this is all about is a most essential thing.

What do we now see happening in modern thinking, what has happened in all these 25 years?

Modern thinking has wanted to abolish boundaries. Arbitrary boundaries.
It has wanted to abolish limitations.
It has wanted to abolish the barrier between the one reality and the other, between seemingly split realities.
It has demolished the barriers between apparent polarities, it has wanted to reunite the split unity of inside and outside, of individual and community, of the perceptible reality and the reality that is no longer sensorily perceptible, that can only be captured by the imagination.

In the newspaper that was lying opposite me on the train, I read a section on 'whether scientists have become sufficiently involved with literature'. It was a survey. The question was put to several professors, mainly astronomers and physicists. Professor Zernike answered that he had always had a great aversion to literature, possibly unjustly, because literature concerns itself with things that cannot be measured and he has always been engaged specifically in things that can be measured.
   I have to say I don't know what the Nobel Prize is awarded for, but I would in any case never give it to anyone who thought that in science things are measurable! Measurable à la Zernicke. Anyone occupied with what is measurable is not engaged in science, but in applied science. And of course you can do a great many worthwhile things with that, like making atom bombs and extra moons!

In fact there is no barrier between the myth and what is measurable. After all, measurable doesn't mean that you can measure something in centimetres, kilos, guilders and dollars, does it? This has no meaning whatsoever as far as measurability is concerned. It doesn't have anything to do with measure or right-size. We try to give shape to the place between here and there, between this and the following moment, between inside and outside. These are things that cannot be 'measured'. They are things where the mind can feel at home if we gauge instead of 'measure'.

So what I have asked is: is the mind able to penetrate this matter?

Can it get through all the matter we build, through all the barriers we erect between one human and another. Does the mind get through that? I don't think so.

That's why I say:
Make a welcome of each door.
Make a countenance of each window.

If one thinks in depth about the 'window' one will not quickly run out of ideas. So what is the phenomenon of a 'window'? *This* window is completely different from an opening to let in light, it is also different from an opening for a view, to be able to enjoy a view. So that's why I say:

Make a countenance of each window with a warm view in and a good prospect and just forget the view out.

In addition, make of each window and each door a place where it is good to be and, here it comes: **make a bunch of places of each house and each city.**

Furthermore, I would like to say: make a small city of each house and a huge house of each city.

This is another way of saying what Bakema said: 'architecture by planning and planning by architecture'. I just wanted to touch on it here because it may cover the wretched controversy between architecture and urbanism. You could extend it and say that there is controversy between interior architecture and architecture. But this is not true – definitely not.

In essence it is the controversy between the part and the whole; the profession that is occupied with the part and the profession that is occupied with the whole. But part and whole are inseparable.

And when I say 'make of each house a small city and of each city a huge house', what I want to do is dialectically destroy – break – the quantitative hierarchy between the large and the small, between part and whole, between one human and a number of humans.

So what I would like to say is that the time has come to look at architecture from an urban planning point of view and urbanism from an architectonic point of view, whereby one is not allowed to choose the one half of the sentence or the other, but only experience them together.
Unity and multiplicity.

Now, as a matter of fact, we do know or feel what a single person signifies and what the distance is between ourselves and ourselves, at least to a certain extent. But – and this is the great tragedy of our time – the distance between one person and another escapes us (it has also vanished into this emptiness). The distance between one person and another, the distance between an individual and the group, is staggering.

This means that we no longer even know what 'a number of people' is, what 'number' means; what a 'group' (or a plurality of people) means.

And yet we have to create an environment for great number – a fiasco for urban planning.

You can see for yourself how often architecture succeeded in making one single house, or a number of 'single' houses. They are not 'grouped'.

The phenomenon of the single house, of the successful single house, of the successful single building. There are countless examples of it. But there are virtually no examples whereby our society – of which we, as architect, interior architect or urban planner, are a part – has succeeded in creating a number of houses in such a way, grouping them in such a way, that they are inhabitable by several people, not just by an individual.

So apparently we are able to approach the singularity of a building, and the aesthetics of the singular. But as soon as we are faced with number, every architect, urban planner, community and authority stands with two left hands. We are able to make one single thing, and maintain the identity, the personality, of one such single thing. But as soon as this same thing is conceived in repetition, in one or other strange way it loses its personality, its identity, and this is of course tragic.

Is this because we have not yet discovered the aesthetics of number? The visual laws of 'harmony in motion', the aesthetics of the plural? Or is this because **we simply no longer know what a number of people is**, because after all, the one covers the other.

Is it not possible to conceive of a unit in such a way that it can be repeated while maintaining its identity? To conceive of a basic unit that, when multiplied into a group, generates a larger unit with a stronger identity which reinforces the basic unit's identity? In this way one could develop a city that is just as organic as an exemplary house. But strangely enough, when planning authorities have to deal with large urban areas, they mostly resort to an infill procedure; a purely additive procedure.

We have no idea what a plural number of people means; our present society is characterised by plurality, by repetition, we know that, but we do not know exactly what and why something is repeated, that's for sure. One is just daily confronted with the fact that it is so, but one does not know the means by which to force the plural into order, human order, that is not the 'order' of monotony nor of regimentation, but an order in which unity is only conceivable by way of diversity and diversity only by way of unity. I mean diversity in the urban planning sense – not urban planning in the narrow sense of the word, but in the sense of the total environment of the community, which brings out the specific colours, range of colours, that makes every individual what he is, and does not subdue the colours as happens now, reducing them to a series of muddy tones. That is the negative concept of number.

We still don't have a grip on the aesthetics of number. It is not a sort of calculator method. I don't believe it is necessary to tell you that we have yet to discover the first rudimentary beginnings, the fundamental principles for grouping. I mean the creation of themes from countless related elements: not only architectonically formal themes but themes that also have content, in the sense that they fit around a group of people. It is not a question of the mere multiplication of a number of ingredients.

So in fact I would just like to link up to the notion of the interior: I believe that modern architecture has been fanatically engaged in making the inside into an outside.

Architecture has never been the creation of the outside – even if it is inside! – but always the creation of the inside, even if it is outside.

Architecture is the creation of the interior for the individual, for a smaller group, for a larger group or for the whole community. A city is the interior of the community. It is the complex living room of the community. At the same time the city is the continuation of clothing. It starts with the naked body, then protective layers are gradually added for all sorts of reasons: shirt, trousers, jacket, wall, roof, street, square, city. Everything is included in the continuation of the clothing, in the fullest sense of the word. And now the question is: can one as an architect provide the clothing for a community? Is it actually true that the architect is able to create this continuation of the clothing, this living room the community organises so that the mind can be housed?

Has the architect ever been asked this?

No, never, hardly ever.

The architect has been asked to create a single building. It may be a king, priest or warlord, who asked a building for a single purpose. It may also have been a villa for an individual, for a powerful figure.

You have all heard of Senmuth, one of the first architects, whose name is known as such. Senmuth accomplished what was asked of him. He made an 'inhabitable' house of granite for a single dead person, Queen Hatseput. Now, what I wonder is, is it such a terrible burden for the descendants of Senmuth to make what is now asked of them? An inhabitable place for all the living! The living who no longer drag the granite and who no longer let themselves be whipped either, but who, on the other hand, have lost the gift of themselves producing the continuation of their clothing using mud and their own hands, in their own, now perished houses.

A lot is said about Greece, Rome and Egypt; a lot is said about Roman houses. These are a question of rather difficult reconstruction. There are a few in Pompeii – the lava saw to that and if that had not happened they would have perished too. They were all as transitory as everyday human things. The people themselves built these houses, a clothing of the mind, the interior of the community.

Only the large singular buildings – temples, palaces, etc. – were created by 'architects' and in durable materials.

The question is, 'Can one ask an architect alone – or else as part of a team of specialists – to build a city for the community, where it is warm, where it is good to be, where one can actually live, where it is not just a matter of holding one's own in spite of everything, but where you can actually live – where one really has the feeling of being a proper human being.

I don't know.

What I would like to say is: **don't talk too much about 'space', but build the counterform of the mind.**

When you build the counterform of the mind, you are in any case to some extent meeting the human desire to put on a pullover that 'fits' nicely, in which you feel comfortable, that is not too heavy, looks pleasant, is warm, everything at once. The city should be able to put on the community like a pullover.

But if you look at the outfit the community pulls over its head to make sure it feels a bit comfortable and looks good! Awful!

When you see what sort of agitated people walk – shuffle – along the streets. You notice it yourself when you are in an old city somewhere, where nothing is directly linked to our era – that's why millions escape to the Mediterranean Sea: that's where the last remnants are, not so much of an old world, but of people.

You notice there that the pavements are made so wide that it is worth walking on them. So that it is worthwhile noticing how you walk, to see whether your shoes look good. You walk there to see and be seen.

You suddenly feel you are a king.

It's true you have to pay for it, but if there are not too many other kings you really have the feeling of having rediscovered human dignity. Not in someone else, just in yourself!

There the pavement is a welcome, just as a door should be a welcome. A pavement there is more than a strip that enables you to go as quickly as possible from one place to another following the traffic.

I can't talk all afternoon about architects, urban planners, interior architects and industrial designers (I certainly shouldn't forget them!), and everything they have done wrong. We have already been engaged for 20 years in the art of organising the meagre. Now we have to put and end to it!

Dirty linen, mostly

Partial translation of Van Eyck's contribution to the 'reaction issue' of Forum, *November 1960*

Dionysus shivers – Apollo tipsy

Some surprise at finding it in my letter-box; opened it without expecting much; read it not without interest; and laid it aside with mixed feelings – the February 1960 issue of *Katholiek Bouwblad*.[1] I will not argue that the contents do not merit ample attention – the same incidentally goes for Marius van Beek's comments about *Forum* in *De Tijd* some time ago.[2] Could it be time to start building some sort of bridge?[3] There are reasons and conditions now that didn't exist before. Whether these reasons are sufficient to make a start right now is a question that hinges on the first. Whether it would be passable depends on the 'construction'; on the constructive possibilities; on whether proper attention is paid to the enormous disparity in soil conditions on either side (structural engineering can do a lot but not everything). The one thing both sides have in common at least is the gap between them.

That classicism and romanticism, tyranny and liberation alternate constantly in cultural-historical terms, that this should be an inevitable consequence of splitted man's eternal conflict with himself, strikes me as one of those unsubtle, makeshift dialectical constructions which abound in popular science; but they are also to be found elsewhere. To equate classicism with the Apollonian: 'the clear serenity of the ordering mind, the marble temple etc.'; romanticism with the Dionysian: 'the beating heart, ecstasy, yearning, dreaming and longing for warmth etc.' means to presuppose, all too much I think, the absence of an ordering mind among the romantics and the absence of a beating heart among the classicists. Things are not, altogether, quite as simple as that.

So how does this awkward handle fit into the blunt axe in the case of Borromini and Neumann, Hölderlin and Keats? And how in the case of Pierro della Francesca and Brunelleschi, Corneille and Couperin? Incidentally, calling Kropholler and Kromhout[4] Romantic in the Dionysian sense certainly does not do an injustice to them – but it certainly does to the meaning of Romanticism! And what about the architects of the Nieuwe Bouwen, did they really sit on Apollo's lap? Was not his motto, carved on his headquarters in Delphi –'no superfluity'? i.e. no superfluity of clarity, either? – This seems highly unlikely to me. It is as if only the Greeks were wise enough to eventually welcome the god of wine to Olympus too, to give him a place of honour next to Demeter.

The Lost Negro

Van Tijen[5] – that benign Mephisto (sometimes I think 'the malevolent Samaritan', but he's welcome to thinking that of me) – is certainly allergic to saints. In my article about Rietveld 'The ball rebounds'[6] he found no fewer than '8' ('no doubt one for each original member', as he wrote me irritably).[7] Yet there weren't eight of them, only two – one for Molière and one for me.[8] Van Tijen – and I demand an answer to this question – where did you get the other six from? How did you get it into your mind to smuggle saints?

But let's come to the point. Unlike the *Katholiek Bouwblad*, van Tijen has a holy fear for the Romantics. Understandably so, for he makes them out to be really terrible (of course it's all interconnected). Just because of his old courage he divorces himself from those whose 'opinion' he seeks to – or rather seems to – interpret: those who mutter, grumble, whisper, but who leave the actual saying to him.

Van Tijen is truly an opponent – an opponent even when he is not (this is hard to make out). Neither he nor we can do anything about this. Nor is this necessary, for he is, at least in his own special way, still one of us. And neither he nor we nor those people who regard him as their spokesman, can do anything about this either. Van Tijen, what you write about that Negro in Mozambique is all very well, only you didn't run into him in *Forum* but in the *Katholiek Bouwblad*.[9] A slight topographical shift, that's all! Ah well, as you see, inaccuracy and 'clarity' can get along very well indeed at times.

Eagle or Sparrow

What Rietveld says, almost casually, about the 'Day and Night' issue – except for the reference to Chicago, which is completely irrelevant as far as I'm concerned – gives me the feeling that he could have said very constructive things about the other issues too. It is a great pity that he hasn't done so, for he formulates the intentions of the 'day and night' issue exceptionally well (I think even Van Tijen would agree): 'Yet such an issue can give a strong incentive to all those planners who don't succeed in designing suburbs, contemporary living environments, which are just as attractive as the old situations, so that they can unburden the old city centres.'[10]

It is because Rietveld does not want to commit himself to agreeing or disagreeing with *Forum* that his reaction is disappointing. This doesn't get him any further, nor us, nor the reader. On the contrary, by just adding a few more remarks as he puts it, he has needlessly obscured our intentions. I suspect that Rietveld will get quite a shock when he realizes just how little his 'few more remarks' differ from those of so many others, and I really can't imagine him feeling at home with those non-committal minds with whom he thus appears to associate himself. Why did Rietveld keep insisting that he has never even read Mondrian? Why is it so difficult for those few Stijl men who are still left to express their ideas about De Stijl in a relaxed way, about their own creative contribution, and that of others? They just don't seem to have the energy any more. Not Oud, not Van Eesteren, not Vantongerloo, not Rietveld (nor indeed Van der Leck, for that matter). It's all quite exhausting.

But regardless of whether Rietveld did or did not read Mondrian, the fact remains that the Stijl eagles that he, at any rate, created will never become Stijl sparrows.[11] They deserve unconditional respect. As for 'setting the clock back': that indeed won't help. Whether it would do any good to stop the clock altogether is a question that I am loath to ask Rietveld – and I would never have raised it if he himself had not provoked it by his hardly constructive and quite unjustified remarks. I really don't see what grounds he can have for saying that we are setting the clock back. So long as Rietveld's squares smile we will keep our pinches of salt ready for when he gets down to writing (which he is extremely good at, as it happens, only this time he was obviously not in the mood).

Oud's illumination[12]

Oud sent us the design reproduced here, from 1917, to illustrate the Casbah idea.[13] There is much, very much to be said about this famous design in the light of Oud's relationship to the Stijl group and his lonely explorations of the horizon of our time – now and then visible, now and then out of sight. But I would like to refer the reader in the first place to what Oud himself wrote in the Bauhaus book *Holländische Architektur* on this subject.

It is not difficult to imagine life there on a summer's day or evening, between inside and outside, between living room and street. The plastic periphery of the housing block (or indeed the plastic periphery of the street space) can be truly 'peopled'... lived in. One would have the feeling of being both inside the dwelling and in the street area, instead of behind a façade or street wall. The inhabitable exterior spaces are 'there' from the very outset: nowhere are they later additions. Especially the strongly projecting terraces with the narrow access steps between them are a delight, because they extend the atmosphere of the home outwards to the street, and bring the street atmosphere closer to the home. That the Casbah idea is in line with the doorstep idea is evident here too. Oud was at the time aware of issues that are now, a good thirty years later, gaining central importance. But the difference between Oud's vision at that moment and ours of today is evident! He was involved in the design of the independent, large housing block – struggling with it, trying to pry it loose from the flat plane of the façade. But he was not concerned with the relationship between *several* blocks. The fugue-like character of his plan ends just there where we want it to continue: i.e. it ends before the large housing block is generated, for his theme can only be continued to a very limited extent and it can hardly be brought to a satisfactory conclusion (let alone be repeated) without losing

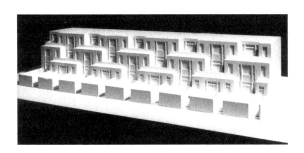

J.J.P. Oud, Strandboulevard project, Scheveningen, 1917

its identity. One needs to know more about the other side of the block to be able to judge whether repetition would result in a street area that is just as rich as the front leads one to expect.

A constructive reaction

Hammel, Klunder and Witstok[14] are right: the projects published in *Forum* don't all illuminate the words equally well. Still, it's a pity that this enthusiastic triumvirate often fails to notice the glimmer of light where it actually shines. At the CIAM congress in Aix en Provence, for example, Voelcker's contribution impressed a lot of people.[15] I am sure H., K., and W. will seldom have occasion to see the very problems they are concerned with so well thought-out in a study project (by three architects of their own generation).

The selected projects are indeed intended as illuminations if not of the whole concept in any case of certain aspects. The urbanism project H., K., and W. sent us as a possible example is, if I am not mistaken, partly intended as a critique of the Kennemerland plan. But it can't possibly serve as such – and therefore not as an example or illustration either – because it doesn't counter the basic concept underlying the Kennemerlandplan with any ideas that are not already outdated by this plan. The value of their study project, as far as I'm concerned, is their way of dealing with dwelling forms as such. But they don't deal with interrelationships. How different from the Kennemerland plan, whose great asset is that it is actually based on this interrelationship while the designers deliberately chose as their point of departure, for the time being, conventional dwelling types, albeit in an improved form.

Not surprisingly, P. Blom's plan (at the conclusion of *The Story of Another Idea*) did not fail to draw the attention of the designers. But I don't think they fully grasped the essential meaning of both the Kennemerland plan and this plan: that both contribute to a greater understanding of the problems faced by urbanism – not to mention the enormous possibilities that would arise if the basic ideas contained in each were united. See the comments on the Alexanderpolder project, at the end of *The Story of Another Idea*.[16] In his preliminary sketches for this project (in 1952!) Bakema too pointed in the direction of such a possibility.[17]

The Kennemerland and Alexanderpolder plans can be understood as follows: Few very large housing units with highly differentiated dwelling possibilities, reaching into the total space of the environment like long sensitive fingers, and allowing the space (nature) between them to penetrate into the collective core of the residential area – in such a way as to match the scale of the housing units. Living at the top, in the space at the tips of the fingers, here finally gains the meaning that this form of dwelling deserves, while the traffic, now led past the dwelling towers, is beneficial to life in the core.

For reasons of immediate practical expedience, these plans were deliberately based on the dwelling types which are nowadays current in The Netherlands. With-

Hammel, Klunder and Witstok, housing project in Westpolder extention plan, Papendrecht, 1960

in the large housing units – especially in the 1956 Alexanderpolder plan – the disposition of housing elements generates differentiated smaller exterior areas which, being visually related to the larger areas between the housing units, constitute a meaningful link between living-room (with outdoor extension!) and the total space of the environment. This plan can be carried out within the present-day limits of architecture and urbanism as different complementary disciplines (since it is based on current dwelling types).

Unlike these two plans, Blom's plan is not based on current dwelling types in The Netherlands, nor on architecture and urbanism as two separate disciplines. By overcoming these two – mutually causal – evils, by crossing the frontier of established practice but not – and I want this to be absolutely clear – of what is plausible, Blom's project demonstrates[18] that it must be possible to design richly varied dwelling cells which do not loose their specific identity through repetition, but on the contrary, actually acquire a richer identity in the larger housing unit generated by their repetition. Each cell has the potential (while maintaining its own identity) to generate larger units with an identity of their own and which in turn enrich that of the individual cells. And these larger housing units, which are similarly varied – have in turn the potential to generate, by means of repetition and connection, even greater housing units which again enrich the identity of the component units, and so on.

The identity, the personality as it were, of the smallest component – its form and dwelling potential – is embraced and intensified in that of the larger one. This is why we are in favour of enlarging the dwelling units – but only if they originate from such a process. The numerical stages of multiplication – conceived simultaneously not consecutively – cannot acquire real significance until they coincide with the individual-community configuration (fuel for the entire process but also recipient of the generated warmth). To achieve this end, more is needed than a fugal configuration of dwellings. No less important for the identity of a habitat are the other requirements necessitated by every multiplicity of dwellings, each greater number of people. So it is not merely a question of repeating cells in such a way that at each stage a significant configuration emerges from the process of multiplication, for this is possible only if, at each numerical stage, the identity of the intermediary configuration is generated by the spontaneous assimilation of the community provisions needed from stage to stage.

With regard to the shape – the configuration – of a habitat, this means that the identity of the whole must be latently present in the component parts, while the identity of each component must continue to exist in the whole. The habitat thus becomes the counterform of the complete individual-community configuration, with individual and community being more than part and whole: they constitute each other's ingredient. Both form and counterform can only derive from each other in time and space (man may just as well be regarded as the counterform of his habitat as the other way round, for he is both the destination and the substance of the city).

I proceed from the idea of dwelling, in the sense of 'living' in a house, in order to arrive at the idea of living, in the sense of 'dwelling' in a city, fully aware that this is only possible if I proceed simultaneously from the idea of dwelling in the sense of 'living' in a city in order to arrive at the idea of living in the sense of 'dwelling' in a house. It is this reciprocity as well as the ambivalence of part and whole that I was referring to when I said: 'Make a bunch of places of each house and every city – make of each house a small city and of each city a large house', implying the essential relativity of 'large' and 'small'. Being humane means being both large and small.

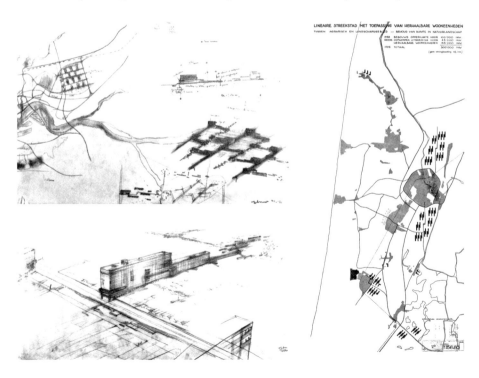

J. Bakema, conceptual schemes for the 1953 Alexanderpolder project

J. Bakema, conceptual scheme for Kennemerland project, 1957–1959

J. Bakema, Kennemerland project, site plan for the urban extension of Alkmaar, 1957–1959

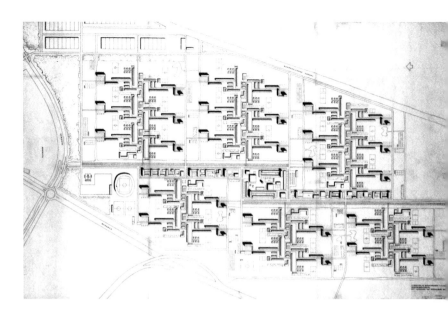

Axonometric view of a housing unit

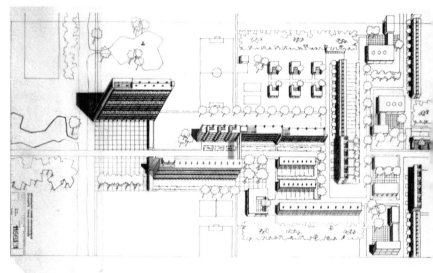

Photomontage of the project in the landscape

Monotony arises where both are missing, where the meaning of both is obscured by 'quantity' and 'measurement' (not size). The large without the small, the small without the large, loses all size. 'The cities will be inhabited like villages' (Blom, at the conclusion of *The Story of Another Idea*). 'This approach will inevitably lead to a dignified human habitat, one which will look more like an organized casbah than one would be inclined to believe today.'

The concept of 'ordered casbah' (the evocation and challenge are included in the apparent paradox) can only be grasped when it is understood that the coupling of the concept of ordering and the concept of casbah presupposes a revaluation of both concepts. Indeed, to see the two values as cancelling out each other's content in order thus to 'invalidate' the new meaning generated by the coupling (Van Eesteren!) betrays a very restricted kind of logic.

It is in fact the trap set by this kind of pseudo-logic – the urge to disconnect – that has side-tracked town planning. The 'ordered casbah' concept was chosen as an image in order to define the ultimate limit towards which the fugal ordering process outlined above can but need not lead. Nor are the form-associations that Blom's plan evokes necessarily contained in the term 'ordered casbah'. Why do people always concern themselves with: what does it look like, and not with: what is it?

And this brings us, in view of the above explanation, back to the plan of Hammel, Klunder and Witstok, who provoked it. High and low volumes can only be placed in open space in this way – as plastically contrastive elements – if the forms are basically simple (certainly as far as high-rise buildings are concerned, for these cannot extend too plastically *beyond* the periphery of the volume without forcing construction and proportion). However, it is possible, while remaining *within* the periphery, and for the sake of a richer dwelling potential, to hollow out the volume plastically to quite a large extent, without detracting from the construction or proportions of the building as a whole (Hansa Viertel apartment building, by Van den Broek and Bakema, Stokla. Dwellings in Geneva, by Le Corbusier). But the nature of the dwelling units designed by H., K., and W., shows that the architects wanted to avoid this kind of smooth volume for the very sake of this richer and more varied dwelling potential – and rightly so, only with some reservations about high-rise building, therefore.

So their design has turned out to be ambivalent. For the complex plasticity of their dwelling units obviously points to the necessity of arriving at a richer aesthetic of the plural, of developing a fugal skill in order to serve simultaneously the relationship between individual and community and the ensuing relationship between part and whole. The Kennemerland plan proves that it is indeed possible, starting out from conventional dwelling types, to arrive at a structure for a habitat that is richer both in form and content. That, conversely, starting out from dwelling types as proposed in H., K. and W.'s plan but making use of essentially additive-abstract and therefore academic parcelling practices, could yield a richer structure, is at any rate contradicted by the result achieved.

The enigma of time

Translation of a text written in 1961 after a visit to Duiker's Zonnestraal sanatorium[1]

We sail on open water – we are somewhere between one beginning and another beginning (we call this sailing on open water the Present).

Our direction and future are pointed out by the constellations, i.e. we allow ourselves to be led by our senses.

We know where we are sailing (but will we get there?) and why we set sail (the right distance is needed for this).

We occasionally pick up provisions in the ports of the past that border the open water, take strength from the dishes we sought and need. It does us good to stay longer than we are accustomed in the port we have here entered, because it is a very special port.

Believe it or not, we met the riddle of time there.

It is an old harbour, but not as old as the battered quay would lead us to suspect. What is more, there are so many provisions lying there that we feel inclined to stay and not set sail again. How did they get here? Where did they come from? Why is this quay, of all places, so battered? We ask ourselves these questions.

It is as if we have reached our goal, so abundant are the provisions for the future on this battered quay. Have we found the future? Have we really encountered it, on this battered quay, in this harbour that is not very old? The open water, which apparently has so brutally sinned against the quay, has at any rate suddenly disappeared! Dream without a present – the enigma of time.

It is certain that we have here learnt a lot (perhaps it would be better to say: started to suspect)... that time passes the present by – actually skips over the present, while the past – here alongside this battered quay – meets the future (talk about miracles!), which means that we shall from time to time find the quays of the future in the harbours of the past (harbours live from their quays) ... that the present becomes tangible by assaulting the future in the past; as a result of the wounds it leaves on the face of the past (they are the concealed eyes of the past, which see the future) ... lastly, that we shall after all leave here again (the open water lures us) with plenty of provisions on board and strengthened by what we saw – alongside this battered quay in this harbour that is not very old: the reflection of the future on the mutilated face of the past – Zonnestraal.

J. Duiker and B. Bijvoet, Zonnestraal Sanatorium, Hilversum, 1926–1928

The medicine of reciprocity tentatively illustrated

Introductory article to the publication of the Amsterdam Municipal Orphanage, in Forum, *April-May 1961*[1]

> *Juste ce qu'il faut*
> *de souterrain*
> *entre le vin et la vie*
> Tristan Tzara

This building is a house, a particular house as all houses should be within the framework of a certain generality. Peopled, it provides a home for approximately 125 children of all ages between a few months and 20 years who have no other home, i.e. nobody willing, suitable or able to take care of them properly. Poverty, illness, imprisonment, death etc. of parents or foster parents, neglect, and irresponsible treatment are the most frequent causes for a child's stay. A house, therefore, for the unprotected child with a short and a long term function: a home for those temporarily unprotected – often for only a few weeks – as well as for those who would otherwise be permanently unprotected. The latter are often in a very sorry state, and demand extreme care in order to make good what has previously befallen them – an objective sometimes beyond reach. Still, the children are not cut off from society, for they go to the same kinder-gardens and schools in the city as other children do, have the same jobs, follow the same courses, or go to the same clubs. There are between 30 and 40 working on the staff; 12 live on the premises.

Since the pattern structure of the house derives from, covers, and thus also sustains specifically the particular daily life pattern evolved for its inmates, it follows that its flexibility or adaptability, whilst permitting development of this pattern, is such that it cannot adequately cover and sustain a daily life pattern or group structure that varies fundamentally from the one the pattern-structure of the house derives from. Extreme flexibility of this kind would have led to false neutrality, like a glove that becomes no hand because it fits all hands. A harrying reality this that many flexophiles, I assume, will prefer to disagree with! A great problem none the less.[2]

Open space requirements pointed towards a site just outside the city's abrupt south-west periphery. It lies a few hundred yards south of an enormous stadium along the highway from Amsterdam to the national airport Schiphol and this city's only large recreation area a mile south. The site content is simple and emphatic; exciting in that it includes many of the great motions that belong to the metropolis of to-day. Places near and far are present here, for there is always traffic moving north-south on the road and diagonally overhead in the air. Thousands gather in the stadium from time to time from all over the country for international matches. And when the weather is good thousands more pass by on foot or on bicycles on their

Aldo van Eyck, Amsterdam Municipal Orphanage, 1955–1960
Photo P. Goede

The domed roofscape and its construction
Photo Aldo van Eyck

Photo J.J. van der Meyde

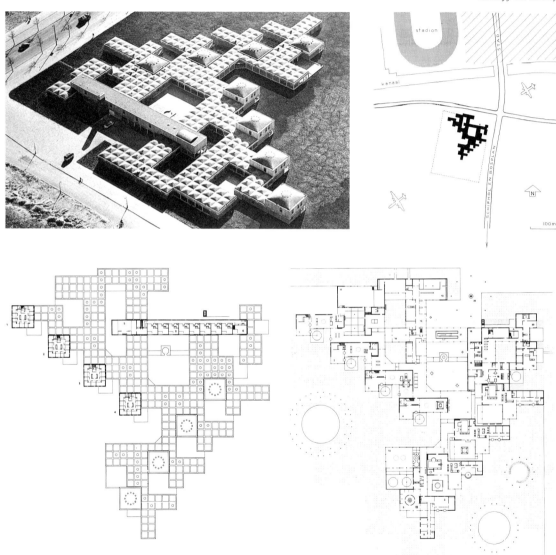

Amsterdam Municipal Orphanage, 1955–1960,
general views and plans

Photo Aldo van Eyck

way to the recreation area. Fifty thousand packed together in a huge oval cheering, and quite close, lots of little domes with children underneath them, protected, chattering, laughing. People flying overhead in planes watch both pass below – lots of domes in a multiple pattern, and a single oval – a little less little now.

The plan attempts to reconcile the positive qualities of a centralized scheme with those of a decentralized one avoiding the obvious pitfalls that cling to both: the concentrated institutional building that says, 'get into my bulk up those steps and through that big door there', with children heaped up close around a well-oiled service machinery on the one hand; on the other, the loosely knit additive sprawl of the false alternative to which contemporary planning still sentimentally adheres (a number of small scale elements for individual groups strung along traffic space of an even smaller scale connecting them with some marked larger scale communal elements). The hard heart of the former is indeed softened in the latter, but even so fails because the blood coagulates in the arteries or is diluted covering the long distance.

The plan attempts to provide a built framework – to set the stage – for the dual phenomenon[3] of the individual and the collective without resorting to arbitrary accentuation of either one at the expense of the other, i.e. without warping the meaning of either, since no basic dual phenomenon can be split into incompatible polarities without the halves forfeiting whatever they stand for.

As the plan took shape the problem of reciprocity imposed itself time and again. The very nature of the project pointed to the necessity of resuming the revaluation of the real relationships unity-diversity, part-whole, large-small, many-few, inside-outside, open-closed, mass-space, constancy-change – a revaluation started a few generations ago but today almost forgotten. I started from the conviction that these are all dual phenomena that lost each other when they were forced apart into conflicting polarities and false alternatives. As work progressed, what took shape began to verify the old forgotten truth: that diversity is only attainable through unity; unity only through diversity; that unity and diversity are each other's mirror image. The imagination is the mirror where conflicting polarities regain their lost reciprocity; the configurated place is where they are reconciled and welcome the mind.[4]

There are, of course, many ways of dealing with unity and diversity. The one chosen here was, first, to allow the various elements to form a dispersed complex pattern. Then, to draw them together again by imposing a single structural and constructional principle throughout and introducing a device with an unquestionable

Photo P.H Goede

Photo Aldo van Eyck

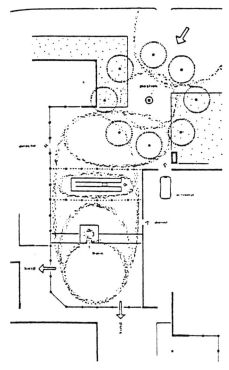

Scheme of the entrance sequence and two opposite views of the central courtyard

Circular seat on the central courtyard Photo Louis van Paridon

human content – the internal street. Although all spaces, irrespective of their function and span, were subjected to a single principle, through their place, sequence and subtreatment as well as through their relation to each other, the whole and the site-content, each of them got the specific meaning it demands within the total context, general plan pattern and constructional idiom. I hope that in its final form the architectural reciprocity unity-diversity and part-whole (closely linked dual phenomena) to some extent cover the human reciprocity individual-collective.

Still there are two more dual phenomena likewise closely linked to those just mentioned which still elude adequate translation into planning – a twin set: large-small and many-few. The irreconcilable polarities – false alternatives – into which they are split cut no less brutally across the gaunt panorama of urbanism today. Failure to govern multiplicity creatively and humanize number by means of articulation and configuration (the verb 'to multiply' should coincide with the significantly nonexistent verb 'to configurate') has led to the curse of most new towns. The mere fact that habitat planning is arbitrarily split into two disciplines – architecture and urbanism – demonstrates that the principle of reciprocity has not yet opened the deterministic mind to the necessity of transforming the mechanism of the design process. As it is, architecture and urbanism have failed to come to terms with the essence of contemporary thinking. Inseparably linked as all basic dual phenomena are, a few were extracted from the rest and mal-digested – those already mentioned (part-whole, unity-diversity, large-small, many-few) as well as others equally significant (inside-outside, open-closed, mass-space, change-constancy, motion-rest, individual- collective, etc.). Disregarding the inherent ambivalence in each one of them, one half of each was warped into a meaningless absolute (part, diversity, small, outside, open, space, change, motion, collective), and twisted in such a way as to become 'a new town'. Hence 'spatial continuity', 'constructive flexibility, 'structural interpenetration', 'human scale', and more of that kind of music!

The time has come to conceive of architecture urbanistically and of urbanism architecturally (this makes sensible nonsense of both terms), i.e. to arrive at the singular through plurality, and vice versa. As for this home for children, the idea was to persuade it to become both 'house' and 'city'; a citylike house, and a houselike city. I arrived at the conclusion that *whatever space and time mean, place and occasion mean more, for space in the image of man is place and time in the image of man is occasion.* Split apart by the schizophrenic mechanism of deterministic thinking, time and space remain frozen abstractions (the same goes for all the bitter halves mentioned). Place and occasion constitute each other's realization in human terms. Since man is both subject and object of architecture, it follows that its primary job is to provide the former for the sake of the latter. Since furthermore place and occasion imply participation in what exists, lack of place – and thus of occasion – will cause loss of identity, isolation and frustration. A house, therefore, should be a bunch of places, and the same applies no less to a city.

Make a configuration of places at each stage of multiplication, i.e. provide the right kind of places at each configurative stage, and urban environment will again become liveable. Cities should become the counterform of man's reciprocally individual and collective urban reality. It is because we have lost touch with this reality – the form – that we cannot come to grips with its counterform. Still it is better to acknowledge the sameness of architecture and urbanism – of house and city – than to continue defining their arbitrary difference, since this leads us nowhere – i.e. to the new town of today!

It would take us too far to demonstrate how creative thinking has since the turn of the century been engaged in breaking down the walls between incongruous polarities, for this is the drift of whatever has been achieved by the creative minds of our time, from poet to scientist, from painter to anthropologist, from architect to psychologist, from philosopher to composer. In science many such polarities were reconciled in a higher dimension: space and time, energy and matter, rest and movement, micro- and macrocosm, conscious and unconscious, etc. This was only possible through the acknowledgment of relativity. Relativity implied the recognition of role of the subject in science. As a result, the 'objective' realm of science is no longer diametrically opposed to the 'subjective' realm of art. Subject and object have cheerfully merged together. In art similar polarities were reconciled in the same higher dimension – in form, colour, sound, word, space and movement: dream and reality, organic and inorganic, mind and matter (all of them constituting together the foundation for metamorphosis), time and space, rest and movement, etc.[5]

Whilst constituent contemporary art, science and philosophy etc. have joined hands wonderfully for half a century reconciling split polarities through reciprocal thinking – tearing down the stifling barriers between them – architecture, and urbanism especially, have drifted away, indulging paradoxically in arbitrary application of what, after all, is essentially based on relativity and thus misunderstood. In the light of what the other creative fields have managed to evolve – a relaxed relative concept of reality – what architects and urbanists have failed to do amounts to treason. All the more so since what is done is done and cannot be torn down again (nobody is forced to look at a bad painting. read a bad poem, or listen to bad music).

To return to this house and how is was saved from becoming a bad house. It seemed best to anchor the children's large house-little city to the street, i.e. to the public sphere, there were they enter and leave it, by introducing a large open square as a transition between the reality outside and that inside. It is an in-between domain leading the trail gradually in stages, helping to mitigate the anxiety that abrupt transition causes, especially in these children. Leaving home and going home are often difficult matters; to go in or out, to enter, leave or stay, sometimes painful alternatives. Though architecture cannot do away with this truth it can still counteract it by appeasing instead of aggravating its effects. It is human to tarry. Architecture should, I think, take more account of this. The job of the planner is to provide built homecoming for all, to sustain a feeling of belonging – hence, to evolve an architecture of place – a setting for each subsequent occasion, determined or spontaneous.

There are eight departments, each marked by one of the large cupolas in which the children live in age groups – they leave, and new ones arrive too often to allow mixing all ages within a group. Yet this grouping is by no means a curbing hierarchy, for all departments, service spaces and rooms for special activities give onto a large interior street in such a way as to invite the children to mix and move from one department to another, visiting each other. This interior street is yet another intermediary – there are many more. In fact the building was conceived as a configuration of intermediary places clearly defined. This does not imply continual transition or endless postponement with respect to place and occasion. On the contrary, it implies a breakaway from the contemporary concept (call it sickness) of spatial continuity and the tendency to erase every articulation between spaces, i.e. between outside and inside, between one space and another. Instead, I tried to articulate the transition by means of defined in-between places which induce simultaneous awareness of what is significant on either side. An in-between place in this sense provides the common ground where conflicting polarities can again become dual phenomena. For thirty years architecture – not to mention urbanism – has been providing outside for man even inside (agravating the conflict through attempting to eliminate the essential difference). Architecture (sic urbanism) implies the creation of interior both outside and inside. For exterior is that which precedes man-made environment; that which is counteracted by it; that which is persuaded to become commensurate by being interiorized.

Since the interior street is an intermediary place, I wanted the child's behaviour and movement in it to remain as vigorous as they are outside. No sudden curbing of spontaneity this side of a narrow doorstep; no living-room manners here. So, the materials used in this interior street differ in no way from those used outside. The constructional elements have not changed face or put on soft delicate slippers. Inside the child is like the child outside – the same child – with a roof over its head instead of the sky. The electric lighting, moreover, is like street lighting in the sense that the child moves from illuminated place to illuminated place via comparative darkness. No lux meter was allowed to prove the advantages of an even distribution of light. Darkness outside demands reduction of dimensions inside. Then there are the courtyards – patios; all of them different exterior rooms strung along the interior street accessible from it as well as from the departments between which they lie. They also form intermediaries – reconciling the movement of the traffic rushing by outside to the child inside. I think it is wrong to see these as incompatible realities; they can meet wonderfully as long as the right form is found for a right relationship.

All external and internal walls, as well as all major elements built within their enclosure terminate at column height. The space between here and the roof is either occupied by horizontal precast reinforced concrete architraves – intermediary ele-

The chamfered corners of the internal street give additional articulation to the internal corner columns of the 'architectural order'.
Photo Aldo van Eyck

ments that either bind and enclose, whilst extending the walls upwards and the roof downwards – or is filled in with glass. Sometimes it is left open. The walls envelop interlock and open up consecutively. Within the actual departments of the groups the walls are plastered and there is more active colour (patches of red and violet here and there throughout) as well as a gamut of smaller elements built within the main structure. But the architraves and cupolas continue. In the interior street, the walls are like those outside – rough, brown and powerful, like the outside of a coconut; whilst in the departments they are white, smooth and softer, like the milky inside of a coconut. Two kinds of protection – a winter coat with a soft silky lining on the inside close to the body, heavy rough tweed on the outside where it touches the world – the elements and other people. Since concrete, brick and white surface do not sparkle – and something always should – there are lots of tiny mirrors embedded in concrete slabs and some large ones in the street floor that distort for the sake of laughter. All of them jewels, and cheap at that.

The cupolas – eight large ones cast in situ and 336 small ones precast, all of light-weight concrete – transform an endless flat roof into a landscape willing to receive the elements; for rainfall gathers along the horizontal channels between the hillocks which cast oblique shadows when the sun is low (rainbow weather is the most effective). The cupolas at the same time assist the part-whole, small world – large world, unity-diversity idea. They continually shift one behind the other. As one moves the building moves within itself. But it remains part of a larger world all the time. A small world in a large world, a large world in a small world, a house like a city, a city like a house; a home for children, a place were they can live rather than survive – this at least is what I intended it to be.

Different views and places in the interior street

Photo J.J. van der Meyden

Photo Louis van Paridon

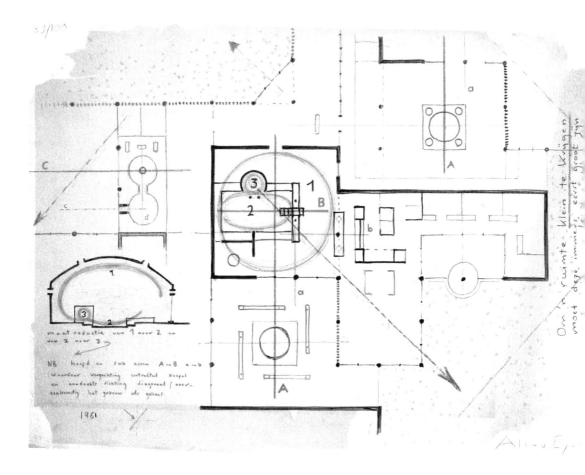

Plan and diagrams of spaces
1 space turned in on itself, with strong periphery
2 compelling centrality relieved by excentric places; also, double reduction of size
3 shift of attention by offsetting sub-axes
4 combining 1, 2 and 3 results in outward-directed attention

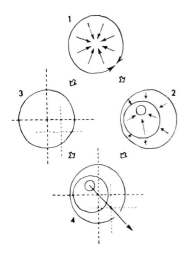

Dwelling unit for 4–6 age group

Little mirrors in the kitchen draining board

The fake client and the great word 'no'

Article published in Forum, *August 1962*

Architects were the allies of kings, popes and tyrants. We marvel at the miracles they left behind. But the miracles for which we crave today are not the same miracles, nor need we marvel at them in quite the same way. If we gather together all creative efforts – efforts which alone need not be miracles – we may still bring about what today we have come to regard as a miracle: cities of which we can say, without exaggerating, that they are really habitable places – for every citizen.

Today the architect is the ally of every man or no man.

We shall have to make habitable places of our sick cities before it is too late. We know this and we forget this, as we choose, whilst the borderline of the uninhabitable lies just ahead. We are certainly catching up with it at an alarming pace. Mine, for instance, is a tiny, flat, open and appallingly crowded country. We must therefore act quickly and at least dispel the excessive stupidity for which there is really no room.

In the meantime architects continue to occupy themselves with matters, which, although not foreign to our time, are often clearly foreign to the constructive task they should set themselves, which is simply this: to provide the urban 'interiors' society needs; the built counterform of its dwindling identity.

To those architects who are still inclined to believe that all this has nothing to do with 'The Story of Another Idea' I can only say: go and take another walk in one of the new towns – as an outsider, guiltily implicated. It seems to me that any idea concerning the architect's task which may be lodged in their heads will soon make way for another. And then the story begins – but not until then. Architects and urbanists have become true specialists in the art of organizing the meagre. The result draws very close to crime. The time has come for another sort. It seems to me, furthermore, that the making of a habitable place for all citizens – and this implies another sort of place – is also another sort of task. In order to accomplish the indispensable union of architecture and urbanism within a single discipline a severe revaluation of what both really stand for is a preliminary prerequisite: for the sake of the task and its inherent limits.

The first step – the very first – is really very simple, because as soon as all decide – having had another good look at one of the new towns – never to go in for that kind of thing again, a new era will have begun for our faltering cities; and for those who took the right decision, a new and fuller task.

When I say, 'go build the counterform of human association for each and for all', I know this opens the door to a terrifying paradox, for those who are to live there no longer build it themselves and we who must do so instead are not yet able to. It is because the 'first step' of which I spoke is still shunned, that the terrifying question the paradox encloses – 'can it be built without those for whom it is meant?' – remains unanswered.

If society has no form, can architecture build the counterform?

So little attention is accorded to the creative potential of the countless millions and what they made for themselves through the ages in humble multiplicity – what I wish to call the vernacular of the heart. Not merely because it has perished along with the people who fashioned it, but because one still esteems almost exclusively the less ephemeral more enduring accomplishment of exceptionally endowed individuals, or a particular ruling minority. The proud monuments still speak for themselves and for those who conceived them, whilst the houses and streets where the countless millions once lived their daily lives have crumbled away and are mute.

The architect has always been concerned with single buildings or a complex of single buildings. These were always particular buildings, commissioned by particular members of society. The humble multitudes, those that moved about in the countless little houses and streets, were never his clients. His attention was never directed towards them – sometimes indirectly, but in such cases his client was certainly another, like himself, socially and emotionally an alien. No, yesterday's multitudes – today's 'anonymous client' – contrived what they needed and regarded as good within the narrow scope and uncertain conditions which prevailed. True, they called upon an array of craftsmen from their midst, but their affinity to them was direct – direct also their affinity to the humble miracles which resulted – they extended their own specific behaviour into built form.

Senmut, the Egyptian, made what he was commanded to make: a habitable 'house' for a single dead queen.[1] Are the sons of Senmut today unable to make what they are requested to make: habitable places for the millions that live, but are no longer able to make their own houses with mud and sticks, no longer whipped as they drag the queen's granite?

Can architects meet society's plural demand? Can they possibly substitute the present loss of vernacular and still build a city that really is a city? – a liveable place for a very large multitude of people. Vernacular was always able to cope with limited plurality in former times. How are people to participate in fashioning their own immediate surroundings within a conceived overall framework? You see, when one says 'city' one implies the 'people' in it, not just 'population'. I've said this before.

These are the first problems confronting the architect-urbanist today. And what have we got? Architects everywhere, sitting lucratively on the lap of the particular client (as if nothing has changed since Hatschepsut's tomb was robbed) or ludicrously on the ambiguous lap of some government body – the fake 'anonymous client' of today!

But surely our primary task is a different one, different in that it concerns – at last – the immediate environment of each man and all men; different also in that it is numerically vast, for today the architect is the ally of every man or no man. But the task is still handed to us by the wrong client, reaching us hopelessly garbled. It is left to the muttering multitudes to make the best of the inferior absurdities which are then handed to them – to inhabit not as 'people' but as 'population'.

It is true, of course, that we face the real task our period sets with two left hands. Yet between the real task and the real client – the silent passive one in whose name the false one trespasses 'democratically' – a monstrous barrier of administrated pusillanimity has been thrown up behind which the majority of architects and urbanists have chosen to hide.

Architects, see to it that the erroneous and feeble gets what it deserves – just this: NO! For the constructive potential of this great word is still there for the service it can render.

Steps towards a configurative discipline

Article published in Forum, *August 1962*

'Open up that window and let the foul air out.'
Jelly Roll Morton[1]

Architecture – planning in general – breathes with great difficulty today. Not because of the erroneous obstacles society casts in its way, but because architects and planners refuse to extend the truth that man breathes both in and out into built form. The breathing image epitomizes my conception of twin phenomena – we cannot breath one way, either in or out. As to what Jelly Roll cried: which window and what foul air? The 'window' is relativity and the 'foul air'… well, it is what exudes from the aggressive halves into which twin-phenomena are brutally split by some disease of the mind which, in our particular part of the world, has been devoutly cultivated for 1962 years!

Right-size

I am again concerned with twin phenomena; with unity and diversity, part and whole, small and large, many and few, simplicity and complexity, change and constancy, order and chaos, individual and collective; with why they are ignobly halved and the halves hollowed out; why too they are withheld from opening the windows of the mind!

As abstract antonyms the halves are rendered meaningless. As soon however as they are permitted to materialize into house or city their emptiness materializes into cruelty, for in such places everything is always too large and too small, too few and too many, too far and too near, too much and too little the same, too much and too little different. There is no question of right-size (by right-size I mean the right effect of size) and hence no question of human scale.

What has right-size is at the same time both large and small, few and many, near and far, simple and complex, open and closed; will furthermore always be both part and whole and embrace both unity and diversity.

No, as conflicting polarities or false alternatives these abstract antonyms all carry the same luggage: loss of identity and its attribute – monotony. Monotony not merely in the sense of uniform because, as I have already said:

If a thing is too much and too little the same, it will also be too much and too little different. Right-size will flower as soon as the mild gears of reciprocity start working – in the climate of relativity; in the landscape of all twin phenomena.

The amorphous and additive character of all new towns – their heterogeneous monotony – is the immediate result of the complete absence of right-size. Those urban functions which were not forgotten were compartmentalized. The actual building elements were subsequently arranged academically according to a trivial infill habit, and the open space between them is so casually articulated and emptied of every civic meaning that they loom up like oversized objects, pitilessly hard and angular, in a void (what Candilis justly calls 'espace corridor').

Within the tyrannical periphery of such objects there is no room for emotion; nor is there any in the resulting emptiness between these objects. Emptiness has no room for anything but more emptiness. All urban ingredients curdle, all urban colours clash. Just planned wasteland.

The devaluation of various abstract antonyms

Now the object of the reciprocal images contained in the statement: *make a bunch of places of each house and every city; make of each house a small city and of each city a large house*, is to unmask the falsity which adheres to many abstract antonyms: adheres not merely to small versus large, many versus few, near versus far, but also to part versus whole, unity versus diversity, simplicity versus complexity, outside versus inside, individual versus collective etc. etc. It seems to me that these reciprocal images furthermore upset the existing architect-urbanist hierarchy. It is what I wanted them to do – gladly.

To proceed from the idea of dwelling, in the sense of 'living' in a house, in order to arrive at the idea of living, in the sense of 'dwelling' in a city, implies proceeding simultaneously from the idea of living, in the sense of 'dwelling' in a city, in order to arrive at the idea of dwelling, in the sense of 'living' in a house. That is as simple and involved as it actually is!

When I say, therefore, *make a welcome of each door and a countenance of each window: make of each a place, because man's home-realm is the in-between realm - the realm architecture sets out to articulate*, the intention is again to unmask false meaning and to load the meaning of size with what right-size implies! As soon as the equilibrating impact of the in-between realm – extended so that it coincides with the bunch of places both house and city should be – manifests itself in a comprehensibly articulated configuration, the chances that the terrifying polarities that hitherto harass man's right composure may still be reconciled, will certainly be greater.

It is still a question of twin phenomena; a question of making the in-between places where they can be encountered, readily mitigating psychic strain. What is direly needed is a dimensional change both in our way of thinking and working which will allow the quantitative nature of each separate polarity to be encompassed and mitigated by the qualitative nature of all twin phenomena combined: the medicine of reciprocity.

First approach to a configurative discipline

Commenting on some housing projects by Piet Blom published in *Forum,* I stressed the fact that these projects did not depend on current types of housing, since the latter have amply proved their own obsolescence, especially in a larger context[2]. Nor do these projects depend on the current narrow views of what inside and outside, individual and public space mean; nor for that matter on the frozen quartet of functions and the foolish severing of urbanism from architecture into two conflicting disciplines. They successfully demonstrate the validity of a way of thinking and a corresponding design process which I have advocated for many years.

By liberating oneself of the abject burdens mentioned above, by crossing the frontier of established practice – though not of what is plausible – and making constructive use of the kind of capacity rejection of the obsolete precludes if new valid forms are to replace it, it is now possible to invent dwelling types which do not lose their specific identity when multiplied,[3] but, on the contrary, actually acquire extended identity and varied meaning once they are configurated into a significant group.

What is essentially similar becomes essentially different through repetition instead of what is but arbitrarily 'different' becoming arbitrarily 'similar' through addition (a universal city-molesting sickness).

Each individual dwelling possesses the potential to develop, by means of configurative multiplication, into a group (sub-cluster) in which the identity of each dwelling is not only maintained but extended in a qualitative dimension that is specifically relevant to the particular multiplicative stage to which it belongs. Whilst the resulting group is, in turn, fortified in the next multiplicative stage by a new identity which will again enrich that which precedes it.

As it is, all hitherto adopted methods impoverish whatever limited identity a preceding numerical stage may possess as such. In fact the absurd truth of it is that the identity of a dwelling, if it has any at all, is at present almost invariably such that it is incapable of surviving the very first repetitive stage, i.e. that of the single block! This demonstrates that the established design mechanism is unable to cope with plurality; that it deals with the wrong singular in a basically wrong – additive – way.

It is of course true that the plural must first acquire meaning in human terms if it is to be guided by the still unexplored aesthetics of number. But the reverse is equally true. We simply cannot embark on one without the other – they are both part and parcel of the same problem.

The identity of a smaller cluster – its intrinsic 'gestalt' in human terms, i.e. its real 'dwelling' potential – is embraced and intensified in that of the larger one which grows out of it through further repetition, whilst the identity of the larger cluster is latently present in the smaller one. This, of course, points towards the meaning of unity through plurality and diversity; diversity through unity and configurative similarity, but also towards the need to articulate both interior and exterior space clearly and consistently, since only their complete ambivalent accordance can ultimately constitute the sequences of places that must accommodate the occasions which real urban existence calls for.

This is why I propose so emphatically not only a far greater comprehensibility at all stages of multiplication but also a radical enlargement of scale in the sense of far greater configurative compactness. Furthermore, a greater audacity of form and articulated place-clarity within a closely-knit compound rather than an amorphous texture of inevitably oversized items (oversized however measurably insignificant!) additively arranged in space-emptiness.

But it is also why I propose a greater urbanity, since this implies a far closer meshing of all urban functions, aspects and kinds of human association. A far greater affinity towards their interdependent multi-meaning on the part of the architect is a first condition. Hence the city-like nature of a house and the house-like nature of a city. No configurative stages of multiplication – simultaneously rather than consecutively conceived – can acquire real significance until they coincide to some extent at least with the illusive configuration of the individual and the collective. Fuel for the entire process as well as recipient of the engendered warmth.

To achieve this end, more is required than a fugal configuration of dwellings. We must indeed proceed from this but we must also proceed from more than this. Why, is apparent enough, since it is those functions that every plurality of people requires in order to exist within an urban cluster in a fashion and degree of urbanity pertinent to it, which must further identify each configurative stage.

We must do all that can be done in our field to make each citizen know why it is good to live citizen-like in a city built for citizens, for a city is not a city if it is just an agglomeration for a very large 'population' – a meaningless accretion of quantities with no real room for anything beyond mere survival.

Coincidence of urban identity and dwelling configuration
It is a question of multiplying dwellings in such a way that each multiplicative stage acquires identity through the significance of the configuration at that stage. I say, through the 'significance' of the configuration in order to make it clear that it is not merely a matter of visual form, since this alone would be purely academic, but of significant content transposed through structural and configurative invention into architecture. Each multiplicative stage should therefore achieve its appropriate identity by assimilating spontaneously within its structural pattern those public facilities this stage requires and which inseparably belong to it.

The important question here is, therefore, how to identify the part in terms of the whole, i.e. what can identify it beyond the multiplicative stage reached. How is one to comprehend whether the cluster one resides in is self-contained and independent, or a dependent configurative part of a larger cluster?

To put it in general terms: by what means can the degree of 'urbanity' (literally used as derived from 'urban'), that belongs to the particular complexity and scale of a given urban entity, be identified throughout – i.e. become significantly comprehensible in terms of what it actually is?

It seems to me that at each multiplicative stage large elements that have a wide specifically civic meaning or city-forming potential, beyond that of the immediate public requirements the stage calls for locally, should be included within its configuration.

On a city level these elements are so manifold that if meaningfully localized in a framework of urban reference they could help to impart a specific urban identity to each sub-area – a different one, moreover, in each case. Such decentralization of the civic possibilities that belong to a large city would impart city-like identity evenly instead of concentrating it in one or a few centres. It would, at any rate, counteract the kind of urban congestion through overpressure, which of course goes hand in hand with suburban anaemia as its equally nefarious counterpart, and impute fuller urban context to the sub-areas beyond their specifically local context. Each citizen would thus 'inhabit' the entire city in time and space. (See John Voelker's Zone project [4], in *The Child, the City and the Artist*, pp. 206–207)

It may sound paradoxical but decentralization of important city-scale elements will lead to a greater appreciated overall homogeneity. Each sub-area will acquire urban relevance for citizens that do not reside there. The urban image – awareness of the total urban cluster – is then no longer represented by strictly personal place-reference, different for each citizen, and a centre common to all, but, apart from such personal place-reference, by a gamut of truly civic elements more or less equally distributed and relevant to all citizens. As I have already suggested, such elements will bring varied specific identity to each sub-area. They will, moreover, induce citizens to go to parts of the city otherwise meaningless to them.

How obsolete the accepted ingredients with which most city plans and housing projects are additively concocted really are, especially in this century, is demonstrated by the schemes which have tentatively succeeded in re-estimating the meaning of many if not yet all urban ingredients and inventing new forms and ideas for them by means of one single simultaneous configurative discipline. Those housing projects, which are real sources of inspiration today, have evolved new dwelling types, new methods of access; communication and integrating public facilities through a single complex constructive and sequential discipline. All these matters coincide in that they constitute part of each other's immediate counterform and are contained in each other's embracing periphery. The house, for instance, is thus also part of the street, whilst the street, reinterpreted, is included in the house in that it is not necessarily exterior to it in the limited sense – nor for that matter are external living spaces. All ingredients are redefined and closely meshed.

The vehemence of vast plurality

Provided the dimension of a given cluster is fairly small, whether independent or part of a larger urban complex, the suggested configurative process could no doubt bring about the required overall comprehensibility. In city scale clusters or entire cities, however, the forces and the movements which result from these forces – the vehemence of vast plurality – are so great that functional and emotional conflicts ensue with which even the sequential configurative process I have referred to cannot fully cope. This is due to the heaping up of quanta which, even if they may one day be so interadjusted as to become compatible, confront us today in all their apparent discrepancy as irreconcilables which the citizen can no longer respond to positively, but which together, nonetheless, belong to the essence of the citizen's environment.

The accumulative nature of cities today is such that the forces which cause it and the movements which ensue cannot be canalised adequately in time and space by any of the ideas and methods hitherto accepted by urbanists whether in the CIAM tradition or not.

Amorphous texture versus comprehensible structure
Nor will the configurative process manifested in the outstanding schemes already referred to, which deal with the grouping of a large though still limited number of dwellings and the public facilities this number requires, suffice, unless the 'infrastructures' are so conceived that identity is maintained locally as well as throughout the entire city-compound. If this fails, what we shall end up with will, in spite of the desired opposite, again become an amorphous additive texture instead of a comprehensible configurative structure; a mere arrangement, still, of some urban components instead of a meaningful configuration of all urban components in the right association.

Locally, the configurated sub-areas will, no doubt, be richer and more habitable by virtue of the same fugal process of thinking that brought about the housing schemes mentioned. A great advance indeed – but the vastness of the urban areas covered and the numerical problems that go with it can well cause the successful establishment of identity during the initial stages of multiplicative configuration to be discontinued during the further ones, so that textural incomprehensibility instead of structural comprehensibility will again result.

It is not my intention to devaluate what has been gained so far by reciprocal thinking and the configurative design process that goes with it. The process is certainly the right one; it must only be extended because, as yet, it has the numerical limits I have just dealt with. But they can be resolved if new structural devices are invented that have urban validity for all citizens and impose a clear, large, and comprehensible overall framework on the whole urban entity within which the smaller numerically limited configurations are integrated and acquire overall specifically urban identity. These large structural devices may be the 'infrastructures' about which the Smithsons have thought a great deal; they may be the 'megastructures' which have also occupied the minds of Tange, Maki, Ohtaka, and Kurokawa.[5] An inspiring scheme for a total and very compact habitat on which Piet Blom is at the moment working – it will be published in a forthcoming number – attempts to integrate the smaller and larger urban components by means of a single configurative discipline, proving tentatively that this is certainly possible.[6]

Without such large identifying structures the vehemence of the forces and movements that belong to a city – and make it a city – cannot but assault the identity meaningful configuration may have acquired within it. Whilst it is certainly possible to guide repetition through the initial stages of multiplication – the schemes already published demonstrate this effectively – it is not possible to maintain, extend, or augment identity through any number of stages by continuing the fugal process beyond the stages it can cope with. Whether it will be necessary to subordinate it from the start to a large structural service framework (Tokyo Bay plan), or whether the configurative process can become so rich that it incorporates all components, including the most intimate, as Blom's new plan (albeit for a much smaller cluster) attempts, is a question of crucial importance. I, for my part, do not believe that these two concepts are incompatible. On a vast metropolitan scale, at any rate, their integration seems inevitable. The configurative discipline already discussed should at all costs be extended and enriched as far as possible.

The necessity to uncover the still hidden laws of numerical aesthetics – what I call harmony in motion – was already brought forward in our first *Forum* issue. Failure to govern multiplicity creatively, to humanize number by means of articulation and configuration, has already led to the curse of the new towns! They demonstrate how the identity of the initial element – the dwelling – has hardly proved able to survive even the very first multiplicative stage – those in Holland are terrifying examples of organized wasteland. The fact is that in most cases the initial elements had no identity to lose, anyway!

The aesthetics of number[7]

We have forgotten most of what there is to know about the aesthetics of the single thing, whilst we know little yet about the aesthetics of multiple things. The capacity to impart order within a single thing – to make it rest within itself – is unfortunately no longer ours and that is a terrible thing; we cannot do without classical harmony. The capacity, however, to impart order to a multiplicity of things is as unfortunately not yet ours either, and that is a terrible thing too, for we cannot do without harmony in motion.

In order that we may overcome the menace of quantity now that we are faced with *l'habitat pour le plus grand nombre*, the aesthetics of number, the laws of what I should like to call 'harmony in motion' must be discovered. Projects should attempt to solve the aesthetic problems that result through the standardization of constructional elements; through the repetition of similar and dissimilar dwellings within a larger housing unit; through the repetition or grouping of such housing units, similar or dissimilar; through the repetition of such housing groups, similar or dissimilar (theme and its mutation and variation), as I put it in Aix-en-Provence. We must continue the search for the basic principles of a new aesthetic and discover the human meaning of number. We must impart rhythm to repetitive similar and dissimilar form, thereby disclosing the conditions that may lead to the equilibration of the plural, and thus overcome the menace of monotony.

The formal vocabulary with which man has hitherto successfully imparted harmony to the singular and particular cannot help him to equilibrate the plural and the general. Man shudders because he believes that he must forfeit the one in favour of the other; the particular for the general; the individual for the collective; the singular for the plural; rest for movement. But rest can mean fixation – stagnation – and multiplicity does not necessarily imply monotony. The individual (the singular) less circumscribed within him(it)self will again appear in another dimension as soon as the general – the repetitive – is subordinated to the laws of dynamic equilibrium, i.e. harmony in motion.

Having suggested that it is due both to the great area covered and the quantitative aggression of the forces vast plurality entails which tend to invalidate the configurative articulation of repetitive elements beyond the first stages of multiplication, it is obvious and reasonable to suggest that identity beyond these first stages – real city identity – can only be established by the very quanta which tend to obstruct the sequential process half way. With this in view, it is clear that large city-forming attributes – other than circulation – must be introduced stage by stage in the whole configurative process to impart localized full-city identity, whilst bold infrastructures must generate a framework within which all configurative stages of multiplication – i.e. not merely the initial ones – become meaningfully comprehensible. Failure to govern mobile quanta through infrastructures will make it impossible for cities to become more than vast disorganized accretions that frustrate the very needs they are meant to provide for.

It is all too often claimed that the great metropolis defeats its own ends in principle! This, of course, is the kind of sentimental loose thinking that stands in the way of any solution that proves the opposite.

Urban transmutability

If it were possible to comprehend a city as a complex with a certain finality, or as a determined mechanism geared to a kind of urban existence which is fairly constant in time and space – subject only to either slow gradual change or to sudden mutations at very long intervals – it would perhaps also be possible to rely on the extended configurative discipline. But a city is no such thing – no longer at any rate. Nor am I prone to speak instead of a city as an organism, since this suggests quite predictable 'natural' change and growth according to fixed inherent impulses and external forces.

The 'organic' image of a city is therefore as false and misleading as the mechanical one. Without wanting to be nasty, both sprout from the same sentimental and rational type of mind; a type, moreover, that is invariably addicted to technological advance for its own sake, and all too common among architects and urbanists. A city, however, is a very complex artefact and, like all artefacts, fits no pseudo-biological analogy. It is a man-made aggregate subject to continual metamorphosis to which it either manages or fails to respond. Accordingly, it is either transfigured or disfigured. Our experience is founded on the latter, our hopes on the former – that is the plight we are in now. But we know this much, that transfigurative potential implies enduring and dynamic identity; lack of it: disfigurement, loss of identity and paralysis.

A city is only transmutable as a whole if its components are also transmutable. One change can effect, delay, or check another change, but this does not alter the fact that each component is subject to change of some kind. Transmutations seldom coincide in time and degree nor are they affected at the same tempo. Such incongruity is simply the spontaneous outcome of urban life. It is a reality that must be accepted and understood.

A city is chaotic and necessarily so. One can no more rule this truth out than one can rule out the eternally incongruous desires of man. The manifold functions of a city must be adequately organized in the light of all aspects of mobility, not for the sake of subduing the chaotic element they incur, for this is happily as impossible as it is undesirable, but in order to avoid their reciprocal elimination (functional paralysis), mechanical stagnation, and the human distress implied.

Are we such fools as not to realize this? All these nefarious properties do not exude from either order or chaos as such but from the mismanagement of both. Order and chaos form yet another twin phenomenon which, if split into incompatible polarities, turns both halves into a twin-negative. Now architects and urbanists today are addicted to this splitting mania. Their particular nature seems to make them as wary of chaos as they are willing to bestow order.

One cannot eliminate chaos through order, because they are not alternatives. Sooner or later it will dawn upon the mind that what it mistook for order is not really order, but the very thing that causes the stagnation, paralysis, and distress falsely attributed to chaos. It will also dawn upon the mind that what such 'order' is supposed to dispel – chaos – is quite a different thing from the negative effects brought about in trying to do anything so foolish.

Chaos is as positive as its twin sister order.

It is clear that the time has come to reconsider the entire configurative process in the light of the many aspects mobility embraces in order to discover new spatial, structural and constructive possibilities for our cities.

Kenzo Tange, referring to his Tokyo Bay plan, says: *'The spatial order in cities will doubtless become richer in content as time goes on. It will come to include not only spaces of an orderly but free, non-ordered spaces as well.'* He adds: *'We must seek order in freedom and freedom in order. It is by relating these two extremes that we will create a new spatial organization for contemporary cities.'*[8]

As fully as the order-freedom reciprocity appeals to me, as little can I cope with order and freedom as extremes which they only are as long as they are negatives (insofar as the chaotic element is here rightly implied in the word freedom). Since there must always be some kind of space between the alleged extremes, a distinguishable borderline between ordered and non-ordered space is unthinkable. They are not separate categories that can be locally provided for.

The fulfilment of a great desire – the metropolis

A lot has been written about circulation – its mechanical and numerical connotations. It is still too often handled in the abstract, as one of many urban functions. But circulation cannot be fully understood in terms of function – that is why we have hitherto failed to come to terms with it. Transportation is a particular aspect of communication, communication a particular aspect of mobility in general. Now mobility is not merely an aspect of city life, it is of the very essence of human association, whilst cities in principle are meant to provide the framework for human association in its most complex and varied form.

Cities tend to become more magnetic, and consequently larger and larger as the web of association is intensified and its range extended. I say it this way and not the other way around because it is important to comprehend the expanding city in the light of man's basic desire to communicate, i.e. from a positive human need, and not from statistical, economical and technological inevitability in an impersonal hence negative sense. I believe it is because this quantitative attitude still prevails that the prospect of urban expansion seems terrifying instead of gratifying, and the solutions ubiquitously proposed so functionally inadequate and contrary to the growing communicative need of the citizen.

There is one more question Tange's excellent exposé of the Tokyo plan poses. I should like to deal with it here briefly because it immediately concerns the argument of the present essay. He says:

'The speed and scale of contemporary life call for a new spatial order in cities. Nevertheless man himself continues to walk in steps of a meter or so and we are still surrounded by the unchanging human scale. Furthermore, whereas the life-cycle of large-scale constructions is growing longer, the life- cycle of our houses and the articles we use in daily activities is gradually growing shorter. This fact results from our ever-increasing reliance upon manufactured goods and from our tendency to take up new things and discard them more and more rapidly. Individuality, freedom, and spontaneity form an ever-strengthening antithesis to the control of technology. Man desires more and more to exercise his own individual choice in matters that concern houses, gardens, streets and plazas. There are then two conflicting extremes – the major structures which have a long life cycle and which, while restricting individual choice, determine the system of the age, and the minor objects that we use in daily living which have a short life cycle and which permit the expression of free individual choice. The gap between the two is gradually growing deeper. The important task facing us is that of creating an organic link between these those two extremes and, by doing so, to create a new spatial order in our cities.'[9]

Some basic objections to this concept, which I underline fully, have been thus formulated by Fumihiko Maki and Masato Ohtaka in an essay on 'Group Form'[10]:

'Tange's megaform concept depends largely on the idea that change will occur less rapidly in some realms than it will in others, and that the designer will be able to ascertain which of the functions he is dealing with fall in the long cycle of change, and which in the shorter. The

question is, can the designer successfully base his concept on the idea that, to give an example, transportation methods will change less rapidly than the idea of a desirable residence or retail outlet? Sometimes the impact and momentum of technology become so great that a change occurs in the basic skeleton of social and physical structure. It is difficult to predict to which part of a pond a stone will be thrown and which way ripples will spread. If the megaform becomes rapidly obsolete, as well it might, especially in those schemes which do not allow for two kinds of change cycle, it will be a great weight about the neck of urban society. The ideal is not a system, on the other hand, in which the physical structure of the city is at the mercy of unpredictable change. The ideal is a kind of master form which can move into ever new states of equilibrium and yet maintain visual consistency and a sense of continuing order in the long run. Inherent in the megastructure concept, along with a certain static nature, is the suggestion that many and diverse functions may beneficially be concentrated in one place. A large frame implies some utility in combination and concentration of function. That utility is sometimes only apparent. We frequently confuse the potential that technology offers with a kind of compulsion to use it fully. Technological possibility can be sanguinely useful only when it is a tool of civilized persons. Inhuman use of technological advance is all too frequently our curse. Optimum productivity does not even depend on mere concentration of activities and workers.'

Paul Goodman says in *Communitas*[11]: *'We could centralize or decentralize, concentrate population or scatter it. If we want to continue the trend away from the country, we can do that; but if we want to combine town and country values in an agrindustrial way of life, we can do that. … It is just this relaxing of necessity, this extraordinary flexibility and freedom of choice of our techniques, that is baffling and frightening to people. … Technology is a sacred cow left strictly to (unknown) experts, as if the form of the industrial machine did not profoundly affect every person.'*

Technology must not dictate choices to us in our cities. We must learn to select modes of action from among the possibilities technology presents in physical planning. If the megastructure concept presents the problems outlined above, it also has great promise.

Motive, means and end in confusion

I have nothing against the megaform concept; on the contrary, this essay is a plea for a configurated megaform, i.e. for the city as a single complex megaform in which the conflicting extremes, about which Tange speaks, are not resolved, however, by 'creating an organic link,' but are simply not accepted as conflicting categories. Were it not for the fact that Tange seeks order in freedom and freedom in order, what are now but doubts as to some albeit vital implications with regard to motive, means, and end would have become real objections.

I would contend that it is primordially man's nature as a social being to seek immediate intercourse with his fellow men and participate as an individual in the doings of society at large. This is in fact as much a consequence of consciousness as of man's specific ability to evolve the means, technological and economical, with which he manages not merely to survive physically but, beyond that, to frame more effectively all the shades of human intercourse he seeks. As soon as his physical survival is secured – a stage as yet only reached in a small part of the world – what lies beyond survival as such becomes paramount – and, one would imagine, well within reach.

This is my point of view: once this stage has been reached I think one can say, without looking for reservations which can easily be construed, that ultimately man tends to move towards large cities simply because he wants to, and that he does so because it is his nature to gather and communicate in as varied a way as possible. It is not merely because he must, in that impersonal economical factors or systems of production necessitate him to do so, since this is no longer true.

We cannot solve the problem of the expanding metropolis if we continue to approach it negatively. That the metropolis 'explodes' instead of expanding naturally – I am thinking among other things of the suburban disease – is based on an existing negative status quo. Even if the vicious circle qualities are evident, we must start from the simple positive truth that cities expand because man today is drawn towards them for intrinsically human reasons – because the desire to communicate and participate is a primordial attribute of consciousness. In order to accomplish this end he has developed technological and economical means with which – quite apart from whether or not these succeed or fail – to accomplish the terrific human clustering his desire for complex association demands. That there is an emotional chasm between the way the increased speed and scale this desire causes manifests itself, and the desire itself, is evident enough, but this is no reason to disparage either the ultimate human validity of the great metropolis or the increase in speed and scale of contemporary life which has, of course, in many ways unfortunately developed in a way both arbitrary, impersonal and hence inhuman.

I do not like proverbs but one is certainly putting the cart before the horse when one suggests that man must adapt himself mentally and emotionally in order to accommodate himself to his own artefacts because he fails to build them as a means towards an end he fundamentally desires.

Technology and economics are servants of man's desire to achieve kinds of human association beyond those which survival necessitates (in the light of his hobby of making bombs and rockets I cannot help adding: so I would like to think!). If instead they have become the very tyrants that frustrate this great desire, so much for that; this should never be allowed to alter the right relation between motive, means and end.

Herein lies the danger of labelling the two conflicting extremes major structures and minor objects, as Tange does, since the minor objects are always the end, in that they appertain to daily living, whilst the major structures (must they determine the system of the age?) are the means (the servant), in that they are conceived to help the end accord with the desire. It seems strange, therefore, that Tange calls minor what I would call the major end.

As long as architects desire to create a new spatial order for our cities, because they not only desire to bridge the great 'gap', but because they think it is these 'major structures which, while restricting individual choice, determine the system of the age,' they will not fully succeed, because this concept is founded on false premises – on a technological slant – albeit a different one from that which infected CIAM for so long. This is also why the whole concept of 'open' versus 'closed' society or 'open' versus 'closed' form, cherished by astute architects today, is, in my opinion, untenable and erroneous. I detect in Tange's intellectual excursions into the realm of social, economical, aesthetic and historical criticism, with which he attempts to fortify the open-versus-closed-form concept, a continuation of the same overestimation of technology and productive progress for their own sake which also infected the minds of so many architects and urbanists of the previous generation. A 'closed' concept, to use Tange's word just once!

In view of Japan's incredible technological development and its formidable impact on an enormous impoverished population, Tange's attitude is very understandable. His audacious Tokyo Bay plan could only have been conceived in a country confronted with such terrific plurality. The Smithsons also attribute major importance to the structures that must be invented to identify a city as a city, but they very wisely use the term 'infrastructure'! It must be remembered that their Berlin and London circulation schemes came after many years of thinking about association in the sphere of the intimate 'minor structures' that concern the spaces, houses, and articles we use in our 'daily activities.' The danger that the Smithsons will put the cart before the plodding horse is therefore so small that there is still hope for Team 10! Their concept of motive, means and end, it seems to me, is sound, simple and safe, – 'open' if I may use that word as well, just once!

To return to the problem of mobility and how it affects the configurative discipline for which this essay makes a plea. A city's effective transmutability depends on whether the various aspects of urban mobility have been structurally recognised. I mean by the various aspects of mobility everything which appertains to urban movement, growth, and change. This includes so many things that they cannot be listed (as long as they are appreciated!). Yet it is important here to point to a few primary aspects:
– the sensorial and emotional impact of urban environment on the citizen as he moves through it in general – the nature of this impact in the light of the different ways and speeds the citizen moves from one place to another and what he experiences en route;
– mutations of use, aspect and functional potential due to the natural cycles, small and large – the seasons (including weather), night and day, age-phases of the human being;

- the relation between the nature and the tempo of the different phases of human life and the overall nature and tempo of urban life – and the way the latter changes;
- change of dwelling, neighbourhood or city with regard to the individual or a particular group of citizens (the right and the desire for such change is increasing, whereas the possibilities are decreasing!);
- furthermore all mutations in size, quantity, place, kind, form and function of all urban components – the incongruity as to speed, time, extent and place of one mutation in relation to others.
(See also Dubrovnik report on Mobility, in *The Story of Another Idea*, p. 258–260.)

I am prone to suggest that our cities will not be able to exist in time and space unless all these aspects are supported by the configurative discipline which is being evolved to re-establish and perpetuate their identity for the sake of the purpose cities stand for... because it is so blatantly obvious.

And yet, when Willem van Bodegraven read an essay[12] he had written on urbanism and the time factor to the Dutch CIAM group in 1952, the reaction of the older generation was such that it is perhaps best forgotten. *'We are faced with the necessity of creating a structure or forms which are able to develop in time without losing their structure or form. These structures must, following their inception and during their further growth, continue to form a whole and maintain the coherence among their parts. The failure to do so will lead to self-destruction.'*

This means that the identity of the whole should be latent in the components whilst the identity of the components should remain present in the whole. It does not imply, however, that these identities need or should remain constant in the face of mutations. On the contrary, it is exactly this potential to change face without losing it which cities must acquire in order to fulfil their purpose in space and time: the provision of places where vast numbers of people can live, benefiting liberally from all the varied forms of human association and activity large cities can best furnish.

A city should embrace a hierarchy of superimposed configurative systems multilaterally conceived (a quantitative not a qualitative hierarchy). The finer-grained systems – those which embrace the multiplied dwelling and its extension – should reflect the qualities of ascending repetitive configurative stages as has already been put forward. All systems should be familiarized one with the other in such a way that their combined impact and interaction can be appreciated as a single complex system – polyphonic, multi-rhythmic, kaleidoscopic and yet perpetually and everywhere comprehensible. A single homogeneous configuration composed of many subsystems, each covering the same overall area and equally valid, but each with a different grain, scale of movement, and association potential. These systems are to be so configured that one evolves out of the other – is part of it. The specific meaning of each system must sustain the meaning of the other. Structural qualities must contain textural qualities and vice versa – in terms of consecutive place-experience, structure and texture must be ambivalent, for only then can wrong emphasis of the structural and amorphousness of the textural be avoided, i.e. the reciprocal meaning of small and large, many and few, part and whole, unity and diversity, simplicity and complexity, be established and right-size guaranteed.

The large structures (infrastructures) must not only be comprehensible in their own right, they must above all – this is the crucial point – assist the overall comprehensibility of the minutely configured intimate fabric which constitutes the immediate counterform of each and every citizen's everyday life. They must not only be able to absorb reasonable mutations within themselves but also permit them within the intimate smaller fabric they serve. Reasonable mutations should be possible without loss of the identity of that which changes; of that which is immediately effected by it, or of the whole; without one reasonable change hindering or invalidating another reasonable change.

Flexibility and false neutrality

Take the flexophiles, for example. They have turned flexibility into yet another absolute, a new abstract whim. The tendency to desire great neutrality for the sake of extreme transmutability is as dangerous as the prevailing urban rigidity from which this tendency springs as a reaction. Significant archetypal structures should have enough scope for multi-meaning without having to be continually altered. Beware of the glove that fits all hands and therefore becomes no hand. Beware of false neutrality.

Identifying devices

In our first Forum number we referred to the need for new 'identifying devices' brought forward by Team 10 at Dubrovnik in 1956. Without these a house will not become a house, a street not a street, a village not a village, and a city not a city. They should be structurally bolder and far more meaningful than those which satisfy architects and urbanists today. They must, above all, be of a higher order of invention, so that the congeniality and human immediacy of the small, intimate configuration can become of a higher order through them.

Make a bunch of places of each house and each city, for a city is a huge house and a house a tiny city. Both must serve the same persons in different ways and different persons in the same way.

At a city level many closely-related identifying devices will be necessary to establish a rich scale of comprehensibility. Identifying devices can be artefacts – new or historical – or given by nature and more or less intensely exploited. In the past it was often a church, a palace, a great wall, a harbour, a canal, an important street or square – often, too, a river, valley, hill or seafront. Many of these are still valid beyond their visual impact.

We know this well enough, but I am not so sure if we are sufficiently aware of the fact that it is those identifying devices – call them images – which not only articulate visually but also frame civic association between people, i.e. which still possess direct physical meaning and still bear witness to this day by day, which remain in our memory most persistently. They articulate places for simple occasions in which we are able to participate directly. I need not name them since everybody has found his own – and more than can ever be listed. They make continents your own. Yet although the human validity of such places is recognized again and again, as soon as they are reencountered, the wonderful effect they have is sorrowfully forgotten the moment architects and urbanists grab a pencil. But we cannot continue to exploit old identifying images – those we have inherited – passively without impunity. They cannot possibly survive continual molestation nor can their identity be maintained unconditionally.

The time has come to invent new significant identifying devices that perpetuate in a new way the essential human experiences the old ones provided for so well. At the same time those new ones must provide for equally essential experiences the older ones no longer provide' for or never did.

Voilà the meaning of the examples that follow. In each case an evocative image was chosen from the past to put its essence across. The previous number showed how people, supported by the colossal remains of a Roman palace, built and modified continually from age to age an entire city within them, against them, on them and between them. The present number shows the wonderful 'houses' – each like a small city – which Pueblo Indians of the South West built for themselves. They were built by free men of their own volition and for their own benefit. They memorize the lives of the people – not of kings – for they had no kings. They are of the people, by the people and for the people.

Split and the pueblos

The Split and the Mesa Verde images demonstrate magnificently to what extent the right exploitation of large given structural elements can help to identify a fairly small habitat. In the case of the former it was the enormous ruin left by the Romans; in the case of the latter the enormous cavities in the cliffs. The Chaco Pueblos of New Mexico demonstrate, in contrast to those already mentioned, to what extent a large structural form, conceived and built stone by stone by the people themselves, has resulted in large structures as emphatically comprehensible as the topographical setting to which they respond. I refer to the majestic all-enclosing walls, the terraced 4 to 5 storey houses they support and the central ceremonial plaza they surround. The structural, spatial and constructive potential one single element can offer a very small cluster, should, I believe, help to shed light on the necessity to invent other new structural elements for our rigid and amorphous cities.

Both Split, Mesa Verde and the Pueblos of the Chaco Canyon and the Rio Grande area, furthermore, clearly demonstrate what I mean by unity through diversity and diversity through unity; the ambivalence of large-small and many-few (the way the one determines the other); the individual and the collective as a twin phenomenon; and the mutation potential within a fixed indestructible element.

It is also clear, with reference to the structural mobility, that in each case the people, relying on the simple means usually at their disposal for simple home-building, could not only build both more compactly and higher because of the great constructive support the ruins, the cavities and the built walls offered, but were also able to effect continual modifications and additions according to need without impairing the clarity and the adequacy of the whole. A truly wall- and rock-fast support and protection against the wild elements, endless space and menacing enemies.

Diocletian's Palace in Split

An incriminating misinterpretation

Having allowed these images to speak to the imagination, I suggest that the reader should turn once more to the final page of our first *Forum* number, *The Story of Another Idea*. Having furthermore discovered, on this final page, two pictures of Taos Pueblo, he will now perhaps no longer stumble over the words *'vers une casbah organisée'* printed there in large letters. I tried to make it clear (in *Forum* 1960–61, no. 4, p. 154), that this word-image calls for a revaluation of the meaning of the word organized and the word Casbah in terms of their junction; that is why Van Eesteren is wrong when he suggests that the one excludes the other, rendering the image useless. The image shows the ultimate limit towards which the configurative discipline, set forth in this essay, can lead as to density and meshing of functions – *can* but *need not* lead. The secondary form associations the word casbah calls up are quite arbitrary and have nothing to do with the main issue.

Cliff Palace, Mesa Verde   Photo Vincent Ligtelijn

Pueblo Bonito in Chaco Canyon
Reconstruction drawing by H.H. Nichols

It is however incriminating enough that such sentimental associations were able to blur the essential meaning of the word-image. Incriminating with regard to the intellectual feebleness of these readers! The word-image as such has nothing to do with what they and others thought fit to label 'casbahism'.

343

9
Forum 1962–1963 and 1967
The Vernacular of the Heart

Introduction to chapter 9

Van Eyck's interest in 'other', non-western cultures dated from his Zurich years. Paradoxically it originated from his passion for modern art. He discovered African art in *Minotaure*, the surrealist review which explored the layers of the unconscious through modern art and science as well as in 'primitive' cultures. The second issue (1933, no. 2) was entirely devoted to an ethnological expedition across Africa undertaken by Marcel Griaule. It comprised a number of pictures showing utensils and cult objects, including Dogon masks that appeared to be closely akin to modern sculpture. Breton and his friends held the conviction that contemporary art was rediscovering the primary elements of universal visual language, the morphemes of a plastic *Ursprache* that had survived down the millennia within a number of archaic cultures. In the publications of the Surrealists Van Eyck soon gained access to other archaic cultures, first those of the Pacific and then those of the American Indians. As he became familiar with their art and architecture, he reckoned their cultural production to be an essential component of the human heritage, as important as the classical and the modern patrimony of Western culture. He held that so-called primitive cultures were just as sophisticated as Western culture, particularly as regards cultural production, such as language and art. Being allergic to its disparaging tone, he never used the term 'primitive' in connection with this art and architecture but characterized it as 'the Vernacular of the Heart'. In the course of time he also built up a large collection of archaic art, including sculptures and ornaments, pottery and textiles, as well as an extensive library.

Within the broad anthropological horizon he gradually explored, there were two cultures which inspired him with special interest: the Dogon of the south of what was then French Sudan and the Pueblos of New Mexico. These appear to be two different and geographically remote cultures but on closer examination they prove to have more than one fundamental feature in common. They are both archaic cultures that have succeeded in upholding their original identity. Both have managed to stave off external influences and resist the civilizing pressure of East and West in the course of their development. But this was only at the cost of an isolated existence in a barren, naturally inhospitable place. In the one case their settlements cling to the rocky precipices of Bandiagara, and in the other they are surrounded by the near-desert of the American South-West: situations in which things they consider essential are stripped of every accidental and hence stand out all the more clearly. They both constitute non-hierarchically structured societies: societies that lack a central authority but live in a scattered network of small urban settlements where their actions are governed by a shared social and religious view of life.

Van Eyck travelled to the Pueblos in December 1961, at the end of his term as a visiting professor at Washington University in Saint Louis. After visiting Mesa Verde, Chaco Canyon and the Rio Grande area, he stayed for some time in Taos, where he made contact with the inhabitants and was allowed to witness the deer dance, a major religious ceremony. He also explored the Pueblo culture by reading anthropologists such as John Collier, Stanley Stubbs, Ruth Benedict, Margaret Mead and Ruth Underhill. Back in Amsterdam, he did not take long to report on his findings. Intended as a complement to 'Steps towards a Configurative Discipline' (see chap-

Zuñi amulet, reproduced in larger format in order to be incorporated in a seat of Van Eyck's Sonsbeek pavilion, 1966.

ter 8, p. 327), it became a rather factual introduction with an illustrated overview of the most remarkable Pueblo settlements.

The article on the Dogon turned out to be a longer-winded affair. He visited Dogonland almost two years earlier than the Pueblos but, due to various circumstances, the publication he devoted to it did not appear before 1967. Van Eyck travelled with his wife Hannie to the Dogon in the early spring of 1960. Soon after arriving in Bandiagara, they made the acquaintance of Paul Parin and Fritz Morgenthaler, two Swiss psychoanalysts who were engaged in research into the personality structure of the Dogon. Possessing a profound knowledge of the mythology, rites and symbolic language of this culture, they introduced the Dutch visitors into the Dogon world and put them in touch with a number of local inhabitants. The close acquaintance with the Dogon, the concrete experience of their everyday life and rituals, the first-hand confrontation with the evocative form language of their houses, shrines and meeting places, was an experience that made a profound impression on Aldo van Eyck. The archaic views he found among 'these astounding people' seemed to accord with certain ideas he was pondering at that time.

Back in Amsterdam, he set out to compose a special *Forum* issue on the Dogon, for which he requested the collaboration of Parin and Morgenthaler. They both wrote an essay, Parin a general introduction to Dogon culture, Morgenthaler an account of a walk with a local inhabitant revealing the Dogons' identification of house with village and *vice versa*. After receiving their essays in May 1961, Van Eyck started a lively correspondence with Morgenthaler, asking for specifications on several topics, notably on the relationship between house, village and region in Dogon culture. And although Morgenthaler declared that he fully agreed with Van Eyck's intuitive views on this matter, he was rather reticent to provide concrete examples to illustrate the point. Remarkably, he did not refer to the writings of Marcel Griaule who revealed the mutual identification of house, village and region to be a basic principle in the Dogons' world-view, but tried to answer Van Eyck's questions on the basis of the socio-psychological insights he had acquired during his field work.

But when Van Eyck thereupon discovered the post-war writings of Griaule and his school[1] by himself, he underwent a shock of recognition. The Dogons' view of the world as a structure of interlocking analogous organisms conceived 'in the image of man', their identification of house with village, house with inhabitant, almost literally corroborated the organizational principle he had developed in the Nagele project and the

The cover of the first issue, published in 1959 by the new Forum team showed a fanning bundle of the major Team 10 topics constituting the 'other idea':
visual group – differentiated housing unit – identifying devices – aspect of ascending dimensions – harmony in motion – l'habitat pour le plus grand nombre – mobility – hierarchy of human associations – the moment of core – identity – the city as the interior of the community – l'espace corridor – la plus grande réalité du seuil – appreciated unit – imagination versus common sense – à mi-chemin – change and growth – cluster.

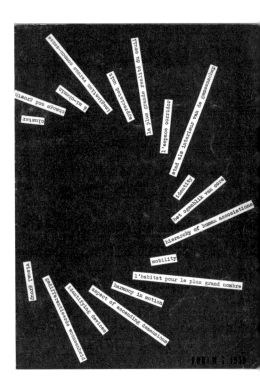

Orphanage: the coherence of part and whole founded on structural similarity. It goes without saying that the discovery of this archaic precedent gave Van Eyck substantial support in the formulation of his configurative view. He was also greatly impressed by the crucial role of the twin relationship in Dogon thinking, notably its equilibrating meaning both in their cosmology and their daily life. Hence his renaming of his 'dual phenomena' as 'twin phenomena' in 1962.[2]

The Forum issue was planned to appear in 1963, but as the architect members of the editorial team were increasingly absorbed in professional activities,[3] the issue was delayed. In fact the team only succeeded in publishing three issues in 1963. Considering this state of affairs, the board of A et A deemed the editorial team to be running out of fuel and decided to discharge it. Forum was handed over to a new team, headed by N.J. Habraken. Still, after discussion it was agreed that the resigning team would be welcome to publish its last issue later on. This intention would indeed be implemented, albeit not before four years had elapsed.[4]

In July 1967 the former editorial team issued its last number,[5] featuring a set of configurative student projects, Hertzberger's Amsterdam students' house, Van Eyck's Sonsbeek Pavilion and his Dogon story. This Forum edition of the Dogon story was quite different from the one written for *The Child, the City and the Artist*.[6] Van Eyck published the articles by Parin and Morgenthaler in their original German version, embedded in an essay of his own. In this essay he now not only relied on the accounts of his Swiss friends but also on the post-war writings of Marcel Griaule and his school. Whereas formerly he appeared somewhat uncertain about his perception of the Dogons' mutual identification of house, village and region, he now plainly asserted it.

Van Eyck published his essay in Dutch but also wrote a concise translation for the Eng-

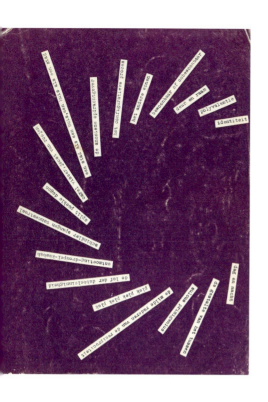

The cover of the last *Forum* issue, issued in 1967 by the previous editorial team, showed an inverse fanning bundle composed of the ideas developed in the review during the period 1959–1963: day and night – the shape of the in-between – sulcus primigenius – the mild gears of reciprocity – place place place place – in praise of ambivalence – encounter-threshold-kasbah – schindler spangen zonnestraal – split pueblo dogon – carel visser, joost van roojen – a city as a house, a house as a city – the anonymous client – the configurative discipline – the other way of housing – habitable or inhabitable – door and window – polyvalence – identity.

lish insert added to the *Forum* issue. The same year he enlarged this English version for publication in *Via*, a student review of the Graduate School of Fine Arts at the University of Pennsylvania.[7] Thus the complete English version of his Dogon story, including a translation of the essays by Parin and Morgenthaler, appeared in *Via1 – Ecology in Design*, issued in 1968.

In the meantime the last 1963 Forum issue had been devoted to a rather unusual subject that could be understood as a specific case of 'the vernacular of the heart'. It consisted of a comprehensive and substantial essay on the structure of the ancient Etruscan town, written by a then completely unknown author called Joseph Rykwert. Invited as a guest editor by Van Eyck, Rykwert published 'the idea of a town',[8] a well-wrought archaeological-philological study in which he substantiated the idea that the design of the classical Roman city was not based on functional or utilitarian principles, but was primarily intended to express a world-view. He explained how the ancient Romans tried to harmonize their cities with cosmic reality by conceiving them as a reflection of the whole universe. Structuring the city on the basis of *cardo* and *decumanus,* and the balanced implantation of institutional buildings on both sides of these intersecting axes was meant as a way of re-enacting and reconciling the cosmic opposites. In conclusion, Rykwert raised the question of whether contemporary town planning could again be based on cosmology. Considering that contemporary cosmology had not yet succeeded in forming a clear picture of the universe, he suggested modern town planning should look elsewhere for 'some ground of certainty', namely 'in the constitution and structure of the human person'. Linking up with this line of thought, Van Eyck expressed the opinion that the form of the new urban environment should be based on the ambivalent nature of man.

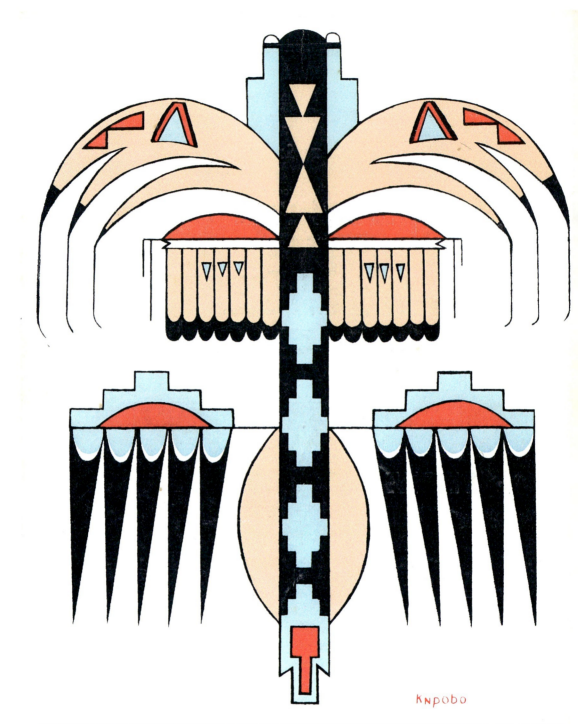

FORUM VOOR ARCHITECTUUR EN DAARMEE VERBONDEN KUNSTEN - NR. 3 1962

The Pueblos

Article published in Forum, *August 1962*

Some time ago both Bakema and myself have journeyed consecutively to New Mexico to submit ourselves to the impact of the Pueblo phenomenon.

In spite of the fact that the Indians maintain an extremely reserved attitude towards anybody who, anthropologist or layman, asks too detailed questions concerning their social institutions, religious ceremonies and village structures, or desires to take photographs, I was permitted to take some of Taos and collect relevant data. However, it was forbidden to take photographs of the high terraces or of the entire village population gathered on all terrace levels, from the lowest to the highest, to witness the great deer dance; a great sight, for Taos was all at once transformed into an enormous stadium. It represented the ultimate social and religious function of the great structural form evolved.

The elderly of Taos refuse unconditionally the introduction of electricity within the pueblo precincts, whereas Picuris, one of the smallest communities, is the first to have permitted archaeologists to dig a trench down into one of their ancient refuse mounds. Had the pueblos not shown such stubbornness towards the exterior world, nothing of their culture would have existed today. In view of the proximity of influences which in most places in the world have proved irresistible, the degree to which the Indians have managed to preserve their own pattern of culture is indeed miraculous. It points to a specific frame of mind, which is very rare. Prior to contact with Western civilization the Pueblo Indians resisted that of the Spaniards for centuries – and that is saying something! They have taken from other cultures what they needed in order to improve their precarious existence, absorbing it in their own fashion.

As to the material here published: that concerning the prehistoric pueblos, which I visited this winter in the Chaco and Rio Grande area, was especially collected for this publication by Mr. Charlie R. Steens, regional archeologist for the National Park Service in Santa Fe. We are extremely grateful to him for responding to the request so willingly and to Mr. Manten for preparing graphically the survey and reconstruction drawings of the various ruins for publication.

Last but not least, I wish to thank Knpobo (Cradle Flower), daughter of Duh Thlawa (Elk Chief) of Taos, for the beautiful cover design. She was willing to explain some but not all – for that is never allowed – of the symbols it contains.

For 1500 years the Pueblo Indians have inhabited the American 'South-West': an immeasurable semi-desert carved out by canyons and defined in space by strangely shaped mesas (table-mountains). During this long period they were able to maintain

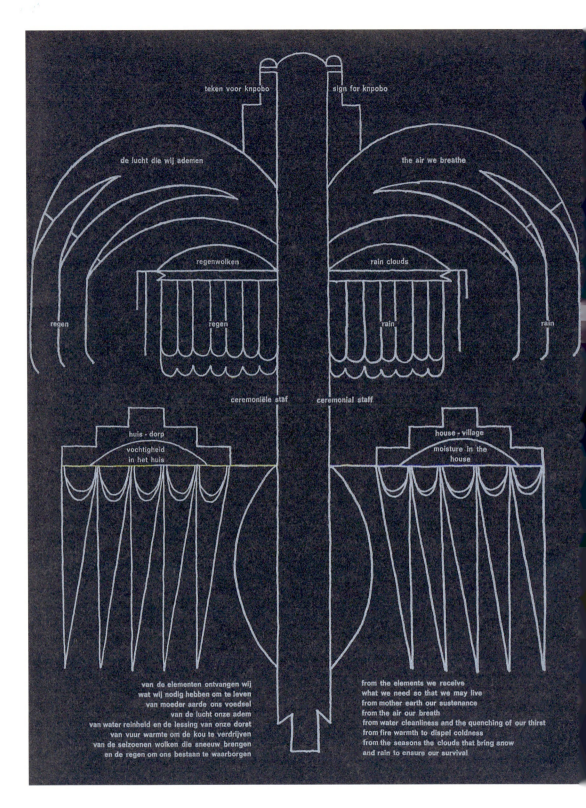

themselves with unequalled perseverance as peace-loving farmers in an almost completely barren region – in spite of all influences and threats from outside, although these caused them to move again and again within the area.

At the time of their greatest cultural prime (1100–1300) the Aztec empire had not yet been formed, while that of the Incas had only just come into being. Of these great cultures little more than what the people made has remained beside a great number of Spanish records. But the Pueblos – about whom the Spaniards report little, for there was no gold to be found! – are still there today, their culture more or less intact. They still look after their little plots of land and live on the same meagre crops, corn, beans and squash. They hunt as they have always done; still make and paint beautiful pots; and from their kivas still dedicate full spiritual attention to the supernatural powers, especially those that bring rain. The Pueblos have never accepted central authority. Each community is still self-governed.

In view of the proximity of bellicose nomadic tribes and – since the 16th century – Spaniards and Americans (with their proselytism), the social and religious steadfastness of the Pueblo Indians is baffling.

Economically and technically the Pueblos have always succeeded in adopting innovations introduced by others to improve their precarious existence: new plants, making adornments of silver and – later on – some live-stock. But they always assimilated the new without affecting the essence of their pattern of culture. This does not alter the fact, however, that the compact settlements developed by Pueblo Indians for their closed communities are quite autochthonous. They greatly impressed the Spanish conquerors, for they called these Indians after their villages 'pueblos' ('pueblo' being the Spanish for 'village').

Casteñeda, the chronicler of Coronedo's expedition of 1590, wrote about a pueblo he had visited: 'It is square and is built on a big table rock with a spacious inner-court in which there are many kivas. The houses are all identical and four stories high. One can walk high over the village without being bothered by impeding streets. On the first stories there are terraces that go round. They look like balconies and the people can shelter underneath. The lowest houses have no doors, but instead people use ladders, which they pull up, like a drawbridge. In this way they reach the terraces, which are situated on the inside of the village. Because the house-doors open onto the higher terraces, these serve as streets.'

The question as to the factors which led to such pattern of culture arises, of course, for it distinguishes itself fundamentally from all other Indian cultures, and therefore also from that of the nomadic tribes who shared the same area with them. The Pueblos have never known central authority. Each pueblo is governed as an autonomous community, there is no question of a ruling minority. Each has its own dialect, belonging to one of four different linguistic groups: Tanoan, Karesan, Zuñian, and Shoshonian.

built for the people of the people by the people

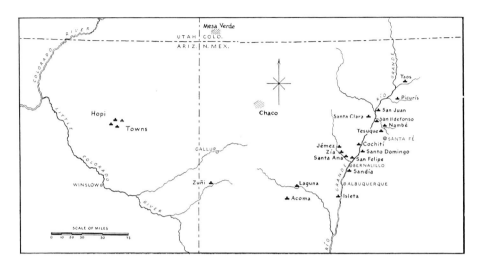

Taos Pueblo Photo A. van Eyck, winter 1961

With the exception of the great – though temporary – retreat of the Spaniards from the entire area in 1680, the Pueblos waged no war amongst themselves – although they were often obliged to defend themselves against intruding tribes.

From an ecological point of view it is certainly possible to find causal factors that partly account for the particular character of this specific pattern of culture, but it is impossible to provide an all-explicit explanation.

In order to survive as agriculturists in such desiccated areas, concerted action was always necessary, resulting in great social and religious homogeneity. Hunters and makers of negotiable goods can maintain themselves as nomads in small bands, i.e.

to some extent individually, although they too have to act collectively if it is a question of hunting on large herds.

The mere possibility of rendering the Nile, for example, more serviceable through combined initiative, led, in accordance with the enormous scale of such an enterprise, to an extremely homogeneous and enduring society, though for that very reason centrally governed. In the barren area where the Pueblo Indians settled, however, the possibilities of irrigation, or of collecting small quantities of rainwater in reservoirs, were not so great that such a centrally controlled initiative was ever called for. In this enormous semi-desert the possibilities of constructive correction as such were modest – unlike the Nile basin. The extent, therefore, but not the intensity of the collective effort was also modest.

According to Stanley Stubbs, such a way of life, firmly organized and founded on a highly complex texture of religious and social conceptions and customs, led, as a matter of course, to urbanity. He writes: 'It was essential for control, as well as for protection, to keep all members of the group in close and rather confined contact', adding: 'The concern of the Indians is not for personal advancement and easy living, but rather for conscious integration and participation with the group in its ceremonial striving for supernatural assistance in gaining a living in a harsh environment, and for mutual protection of numbers.'[1]

How did these exceptional small city-like communities develop?

Before the early 14th century the ancestors of the present-day Rio Grande, Zuñi and Hopi Pueblos inhabited the elevated semi-desert area that today is called 'The Four Corner Country' (because of the central border-crossing between the states Colorado, Utah, New Mexico and Arizona). During this long period the Pueblos remained agriculturists. They grew corn, gourds for their squash and later, after the 6th century, also beans. As for their houses, many hundreds of years had to pass before the marvellous miniature cities built between the 10th and 13th centuries in the Mesa Verde and Chaco areas were evolved.

During the 6th and 7th centuries they generally built pithouses, for the greater part on the mesa tops in the immediate vicinity of their fields. These dwellings, completely or partly underground, housed but a single family and formed hundreds of small village-units, irregularly grouped. Characteristics of the later ceremonial rooms or kivas were, in rudimentary form, present in these pithouses.

The Indians were very skilled in making beautiful baskets – hence the name 'Basketmakers'. During this period they began to make pots, so that henceforth they could prepare (hence also grow) beans. Along with other innovations the bow and arrow came into use. There was a large increase in population.

The 8th and 9th centuries saw a steady development: aboveground houses, in long curved rows, came into existence. In front of these there were deep underground spaces which, step by step, acquired the character and function of kivas. During the 10th and 11th centuries it was mainly the construction of the houses that improved. Instead of adobe (a good mixture of clay and sand that dries up very

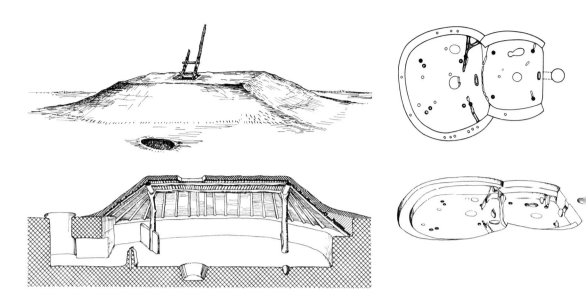

Pithouses (Mesa Verde area)
Example of a pithouse as they were made everywhere in the 'Four Corner' area by the 'Basketmakers', during the 6th and 7th centuries. Each of them accommodated but one family. Spread across the mesa tops in irregular groups, they formed hundreds of small village-units Drawings by G. Manten

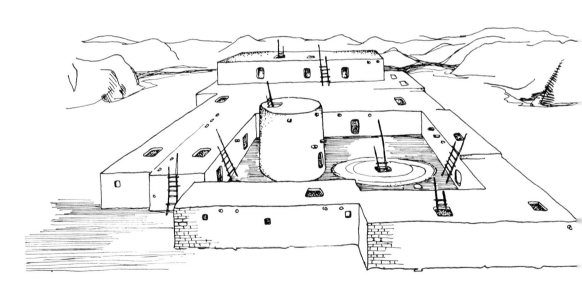

Sun Point House (Mesa Verde area)
Just before, but also during the Great Pueblo Period, many units of this kind were built. The kiva acquired its classical form and came to be situated within the closed group of houses. The tower, connected underground with the kiva, occurs frequently. This fact, together with the general concentration of the units in a few favourably situated areas, indicates a greater threat by nomadic tribes Drawings by G. Manten

White House Ruin in Canyon de Chelly Photo Vincent Ligtelijn

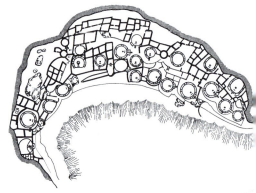

Photos Vincent Ligtelijn

Cliff Palace (Mesa Verde area)

This pueblo, built in a rock cavity, is the largest of the many pueblos in the Mesa Verde area. There were about 200 rooms – built, as usual, stepwise and four stories high – and 23 kivas. The apartments were mainly used as rooms for sleeping and storage, while daily life took place in the courts and on the roofs.

The entire pueblo is built of stone covered with a layer of adobe. Presumably this little-city-in-the-air was only inhabited during the 13th century and then all of a sudden deserted as the result of a series of disastrous droughts (1275–1299 according to the tree ring-calendar!) and threats from nomadic tribes. The present-day descendants of these nomadic tribes – the Navajos – who still live, widely scattered, in this desert area to-day, still talk about the Anasazi, the ancient people, with great reverence.

hard without cracking) reinforced with vertical wooden poles, they began to build walls of natural stone in adobe mortar. At first the pieces were large and crudely modelled, with a rich filling of adobe in between. Later however, various kinds of horizontally stratified masonry were developed. The kiva approached its classical shape, but continued to be built outside the group.

During the 12th and 13th centuries the Pueblos reached the summit of their astounding civilisation. This period is therefore known as The Great Pueblo Period. Their painted pots are among the most beautiful ever made and adorn the museums lucky enough to have them, whilst the form of dwelling that then developed soon reached an unparalleled homogeneity. This period saw the concentration of very many small villages, scattered over the many mesa tops, into a far smaller number of large units close to each another. Presumably this took place for defensive reasons. The kivas multiplied and came to be situated in the central square, completely enclosed by houses.

In the Mesa Verde area, however, a fast migration to the steep precipices took places where, in enormous, high and often almost inaccessible cavities, complete villages were built. Earlier, in the Chaco area, the great pueblos illustrated below came into being.

Then something of crucial importance for the whole further development took place: in fairly quick succession the Pueblo Indians moved away in groups, southwards and eastwards, leaving their towns and fields behind for ever. Most of them settled in the far more fertile Rio Grande area in New Mexico. Only the Zuñi and Hopi settled once more in a semi-desert area, far away from the others, where they are still living today. (Oraibi, one of the Hopi pueblos, is the oldest settlement in America to be inhabited without interruption by one and the same community.)

There has been much speculation as to why the Pueblos left the area where they had been living for more than a thousand years. Although illness and threats by hostile tribes provide possible reasons, one today tends to accept as the most important cause the fact that the entire Four Corner Country rapidly became drier. At that time small rivers were still running through what is today a desert; there was still sufficient rainfall also to enable people to make a very hard living. As for the Mesa Verde area in Southern Colorado, it is an established fact that the last quarter of the 13th century was a period of extreme drought (tree-ring calendar).

However, there is no sign whatsoever of any cultural decline; the Pueblos departed during their greatest period. Everything points to a quick and well organized exodus – no trace of any violence or hastened departure has been found in the great ruins in the Mesa Verde and Chaco areas.

This was more than 600 years ago. Today the Indians still inhabit the new regions they found. Their crop – though a bit more extensive – is still based on corn, beans and squash; they still live in small autonomous communities, remaining faithful to their ancient customs and religious ceremonies.

Pueblo Bonito, Chaco Canyon Photo Vincent Ligtelijn

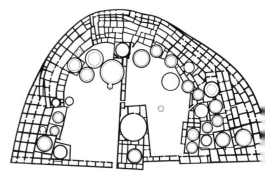

Reconstruction drawing and groundplan by H.H. Nichols

Pueblo Bonito is the largest of the 12 pueblos built close together in Chaco Canyon – the greatest distance between the outermost is only 8 miles. In contrast with the natural backing of the rock cavities in the Mesa Verde area, in which the holes for the floor-beams are still to be seen, we here see an enormous uninterrupted curved wall, 60 ft. high and 700 ft. long, within which more than 600 rooms (app. 1200 inhabitants) were built descending stepwise from five stories to one story in the middle. There are, furthermore, 20 kivas large and small shielded within this wall. If one takes into consideration the fact that the number of stones, neatly hewn and worked up, is about 50 million while tens of thousands of poles were needed for the roofs, that only part of the community were able to occupy themselves with the fetching, hewing and masoning of all these stones; and furthermore that nobody stood watching them whip in hand (they knew of no such thing as forced labour), then one will realise what a humble community can achieve Photo Elisabeth Zulauf Kelemen

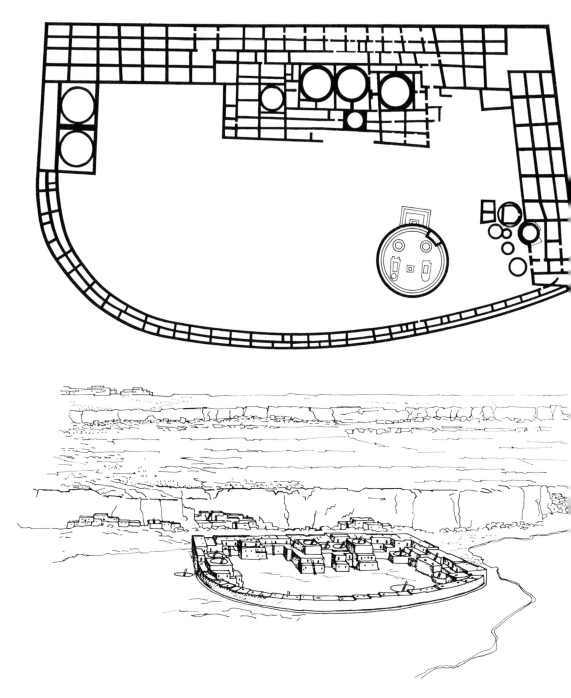

Chettro Kettle, one of the largest pueblos of this area. The great kiva has a diameter of 60 ft. The total length of the enveloping wall, still partly standing, is a good 900 ft.

Aztec Ruin, New Mexico.
Interior of reconstructed Kiva.

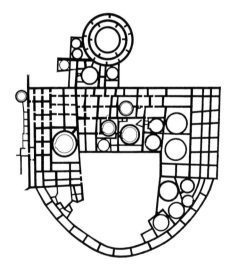

Pueblo Arroyo, approximately 300 yards from Pueblo Bonito, is a far smaller settlement.

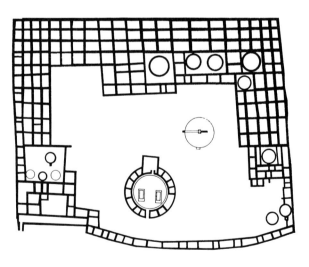

Aztec Pueblo. South of Mesa Verde, in quite a different prehistoric pueblo area, we find this rectangular settlement. The name 'Aztec ruin' is very deceptive, because the pueblos have nothing to do with the culture of the later Aztecs of Mexico.

Photo Vincent Ligte

Ruin of Tyuonyi Pueblo in Friyolas Canyon. This prehistoric pueblo, situated in the Rio Grande area, was already deserted when, towards the end of the 16th century, the Spaniards settled there. Two kivas (dotted) and the part left blank have not yet been investigated. Against the cliff, higher up, the houses; originally four stories high. Note holes for beams.

Photo Aldo van E

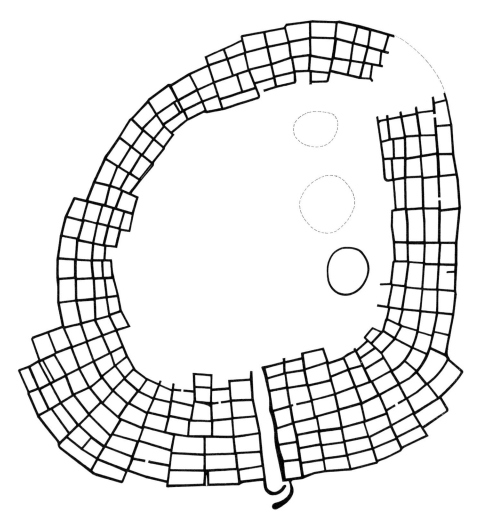

Plan and reconstructed model of Tyuonyi Pueblo

Kiva ladder Photo Aldo van Eyck

Tsankawi Pueblo. There is a striking similarity between these prehistoric pueblos and present-day Taos. Although the houses of Tyuonyi as well as those of Tsankawi encircle a central square, the enormous completely closed walls that characterize the Chaco pueblos are missing. The houses therefore mount stepwise in both directions. In the Rio Grande area too, people were forced over and over again to build new villages and desert the old ones as a result of fires, floods, a serious drought or hostile nomadic tribes. The enormous number of village ruins that have been found are an indication of this and not, as one might think, of a great increase in the population during the centuries before the arrival of the Spaniards. This makes even more astonishing the enthusiasm with which again and again – perhaps even more than once during a single lifetime – these small agricultural communities brought themselves to build such great structures.

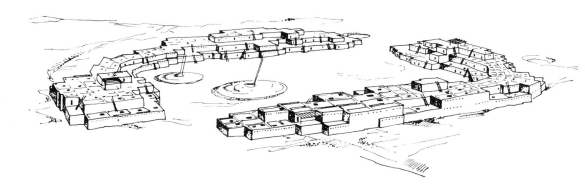

Taos Pueblo

Taos Pueblo, on the foreground ovens for baking ritual bread

Bent can lids to direct rainwater
Photos Aldo van Eyck

Protruding corner of the wooden post and beam construction

Taos Pueblos Photo Aldo van Eyck

The present-day pueblos, Rio Grande, Zuñi and Hopi areas

Of the approximatively 80 pueblos that the Spaniards came across in this area, 28 remain today. A few of the villages inhabited are very old (Oraibi and Acoma, for instance, have been inhabited uninterruptedly by the very same community ever since the 12th century while others date from the 13th or 14th century). Quite a few, such as Taos (Tua), Santo Domingo (Kina) and San Filipe (Katishtya), were rebuilt later either on the same site or nearby. While the Zuñi, Acoma and Hopi pueblos, built on high mesas, are made of stone, all the others in the Rio Grande area are of adobe. Originally the adobe was applied layer after layer, that is to say a wet layer over one already hardened (as if a house were an enormous pot). It was the Spaniards who introduced the shaping in wooden moulds and drying in the sun of adobe bricks, but this constructive improvement did not entail a change in the form of the houses as such.

For a thousand years, the building of compact city-like entities for communal living, 2, 3, 4, and even 5 stories high, receding stepwise over the entire depth of the house, has been characteristic of all pueblo communities.

The factors leading to this exceptional way of living have already been mentioned. Although the enormous enveloping walls do not recur in the new areas where the pueblos settled after the great migration, the other characteristics are maintained. The roof of a lower house not only serves as the entrance to the house built over it and recedes over the full depth of it, but also as the outdoor living-space of the latter, and so on. During the warm seasons much of the ordinary daily life of the women takes place there – the drying of corn and vegetables, the storage of firewood, pottery and often also the cooking.

The many dark inner rooms resulting from this pyramid-like form of living were used mainly as store-rooms and sometimes for the safe-keeping of ceremonial objects. In former days these dark spaces were also used as rooms for sleeping during the cold winter months. The highest roof was always communal or served, as it still does in Taos today, as a place from where to proclaim matters of importance.

The house-doors one encounters in all pueblos today were not yet there fifty years ago, and certainly not at ground level. That is why the number of ladders, so characteristic of the pueblos, used to be far greater. In order to enter a house, one climbed an 'outside ladder', and, having arrived on the roof terrace, descended by way of an 'inside ladder' through a rectangular opening in the terrace – this is why we see so many rectangular trap-doors with ladder poles sticking out obliquely (often only one pole). 'Go up and down the ladder' in Zuñi means as much as 'come inside'.

During ceremonies the roofs are used as public galleries. The special possibility that this form of habitation offers spectators is certainly of great importance in view of the central significance and the frequency of these ceremonies. During the great dances the houses that are grouped round the central square look like hills entirely made up of standing human beings, for the latter cover the greater part of the low walls.

The building-sequence was as follows. First channels were dug and, by way of foundation, filled with stones or adobe. A few rooms, connected by low, often T-shaped doorways, were raised at the same time. Although these rooms usually have an area of 12 × 15 ft. (determined by the limited length of available beams), the height varies; thus the ultimate height of the terraces also varies. Against, and also on top of this nucleus new apartments were built successively.

While all houses are coated regularly on the outside with a new layer of adobe, they are whitewashed with home-made wall paint on the inside. In the old days furniture was mainly built-in, that is to say it consisted of niches or projecting additional forms of adobe. Originally the openings in the roofs also served as smoke-holes.

Like many other things, house-building is a ceremonious matter for the pueblos. Ruth Underhill writes on this subject: 'House-building is a matter for prayer and offerings, just as planting is. If it were a Hopi house – at least a ground-floor house – there would have been prayer feathers placed under the corner stones. Then the lines where the walls were to be would have been marked out with food crumbs, sprinkled to the sound of an ancient house-building song. When the walls were up and the roof in place, more food crumbs would have been sprinkled along the rafters, to "feed" the house and bring health to those within it. Finally, some soft feathers would have been tied to one of the beams as an offering to the great Beings. Every November, at the Hopi New Year, the householder would renew this prayer for safety, which was as valuable to him as an insurance policy to modern owners of real estate. Other pueblos had various different ways of blessing the house. Zuñi held, and holds still, a great midwinter feast called the Shalako. Eight Zuñi men volunteer to build big new houses each year to receive the masked gods which then visit the town. A man and his wife have to call on all their relatives to help build the new house and pay them with food while they work. Then gods dance in it all night and give it their blessing. This is the way most houses in Zuñi are built and thus the whole town is a dedicated place, the actual home of the gods.'[2]

On Rykwert's *Idea of a Town*

Translation of Van Eyck's introduction to the prepublication of The Idea of a Town *in* Forum, *1963, no. 3*

'The story of Another Idea' is the name we gave to our first number four years ago. Since then other numbers have received other names. Each tells the 'story' in quite a different way (as stories should be told), but the 'idea' prevails from number to number. Sometimes a significant image from distant places and ages is called upon to give perspective: Diocletian's palace in Split, the Pueblos of New Mexico, the arenas of Arles and Lucca, the Etruscan town, the villages of the Dogon.

The present issue owes its name to Joseph Rykwert's beautiful treatise which is published here for the first time.

'The idea of a Town' fits in and around 'The Story of Another Idea' with such ease that no justification for its inclusion is necessary. However, it is not unlikely that its major implications, though nowhere overemphasised, will gratify some and gall others. The opening paragraphs, at any rate, leave the reader in no doubt as to the nature of what he is in. For if he ventures beyond them, they make it clear straight away that towns confound every comparison with natural phenomena. They do not grow, in fact.

Cover of *Forum*, 1963, no. 3, showing a curved labyrinth reproduced from a coin of Knossos, 5th century BC.

Sand drawings done by natives of New Hebridean Islands, illustration to Rykwert's discussion of mazes

The town, Joseph Rykwert reminds us, is an artifact – 'an artifact of a curious kind, compounded of willed and random elements, imperfectly controlled. If it is like any piece of physiology at all,' he adds, 'it is more like a dream than anything else.' A man like Klee, of course, would have had no difficulty with that, but it is a far cry indeed from the clockwork notions which many of his architect-contemporaries, and those who still parrot them today, fostered so diligently. It is, above all, nearer the truth.

Joseph Rykwert delves into the past with all the necessary precision and humility. As he does so, as the initial furrow is cut and the bronze plough is carried over the places where the gates are to come, as each event discloses a multitude of meanings and ancient words flower again, light falls on the present, for time is rendered transparent. Yes, as the idea of the town opens up we encounter ourselves contained within it.

If we, today, are unable to read the entire universe and its meaning off our civic institutions as the Romans did – loss or gain – we still need to be at home in it; to interiorize it; refashion it in our own image – each for himself this time. To discover that we are no longer Romans and yet Romans still, is no small thing.

Finally, as we read the closing paragraphs, the 'ground of certainty' which our time can still neither find nor face – call it shifting centre or lost home – momentarily reveals its whereabouts. 'It is no longer likely that we shall find this ground in the world the cosmologists are continuously reshaping round us, and so we must look for it', Rykwert concludes, 'inside ourselves, in the constitution and structure of the human person'.

This much is certain: The town has no room for the citizen – no meaning at all – unless he is gathered into its meaning. As for architecture; it need do no more than assist man's homecoming.

The identification of town and cosmos[1]

Rykwert shows how the Etruscans identified the familiar and tangible world of house, town and region with the intangible cosmic world which nobody knows but which gives life to all and assures survival. The Etruscan citizen felt only safe and at home in the world when he had made his town into a small scale version of that world which otherwise would have been immeasurable, unexplicable and inaccessible, and therefore mentally threatening. He brought closer the universe, he rendered the cosmos surveyable and gave it a human measure. In short, he made the world into an inhabitable place, bringing inside what was outside.

A Miracle of Moderation

Bundle of articles, including essays by Paul Parin and Fritz Morgenthaler, written between 1961 and 1967, published in 1967–68 and illustrated with photos made by Van Eyck in 1961[1]

'It cannot have been so very different in Ur 5,000 years ago: the same laboriously fashioned bricks of sandy mud, then as now, the same sun weakly bonding and then harshly disintegrating them; the same spaces around a courtyard; the same enclosure; the same sudden transition from light into darkness; the same coolness after heat; the same starry nights; the same fears perhaps; the same sleep.'

I remember with what difficulty I managed to get that paragraph on paper. It accompanied a series of photographs I made in 1951 and 1952 in the central Sahara.[2] One house; several houses; a village; a door; some steps; a place for offerings and a fascinatingly undersized marabout; also a boy smiling at you from the page, then as now. 5,000 years! 15 years! These are long periods indeed.

Meanwhile I still incline towards the immutable. Nor has my affection for those silent desert villages diminished. It is a spleen from which nothing can estrange me; some kind of affinity I have no wish to define, though I do wish something of their gentleness would enter our own sad environments.

At the time, I was unable to get beyond the Hoggar mountain range, 2,500 kilometres south of Algiers. Timbuktu, in any case, was still another 1,500 kilometres or so away – no distance, really, for a fable-city! All the more reason to talk *en route*, with those travelling with me, about the distant Niger and the cliffs of Bandiagara where the Dogon live.

I had come upon Marcel Griaule's account of the Dogon in *Minotaure* (Mission Dakar-Djibouti 1931–1933) during the war.[3] The illustrations I knew by heart. Thus, for years to come, Ogol was just round the corner.

Later in Paris and elsewhere I searched for more material concerning the houses and villages of the Dogon, but with little success. Although much has been written about these astounding people (they are among the greatest sculptors of the world), too little is devoted to their building activity as a contribution in its own right, whilst the same few photographs are used again and again from publication to publication.

I decided, therefore, to venture out myself and make up for this unfortunate lack. The photographs published here form a selection from the many I took in the early spring of 1960.[4]

When I arrived in Ogol, Dr Parin and Dr Morgenthaler had been there for months probing the Dogon personality structure.[5] Their presence was a great surprise, for without their knowledge and interpretive ability much that occurred would have remained incomprehensible. And a great deal did occur: the funeral rites for the chief hunter, as well as the Dama for the deceased chief of the mask cult, kept us on our feet for days and nights.

Both scholars enjoyed the confidence of the villagers. This helped me to get to know not only the houses and villages I had admired for so long, but their builders also. This I regard as a special privilege. Beyond that, both were so kind as to write essays to augment my own and sustain with relevant data some of my ideas. I was thus able to avoid trespassing into their field further than was strictly necessary. I mean that one cannot respond to built form if one is unable to respond to its users and builders. When this is no longer possible, which it may well be, we know we are dealing with archaeology.

Subsequent discussion and correspondence with Dr Parin and Dr Morgenthaler has clarified many problems that concerned me very much at the time; problems which one is inclined to solve on one's own, thereby often unintentionally misinterpreting data gleaned to support a personal concept. My preoccupation with archaic cultures, however, has made me wary of this.

The kind of awareness the Dogon image wishes to kindle can help us to gather the meaning of certain prerogatives into the scope of our mental orbit again.

It should also enable us to judge them with humility and, if necessary, 'depart' from them consciously. Yet there are perils lurking behind any desire to open the

Dogon boy with self-made spectacles

mind to the kind of image chosen here. If we attempt to transfer too directly what we have become aware of again into a construed opinion, thereby freezing the meaning of it through arbitrary influence or ready-made definition, we will not only blunt the acquired awareness but also lame the formative potential this awareness would, without such false exploitation of data, be able to guide. We must, in fact, keep nourishing this awareness; allow it to embrace the dormant meanings it detects, assimilates, and carries with it – apprehended though left significantly undefined. Finally, architect-urbanists must see to it that those meanings which are of lasting human value are silently and unobtrusively contained in what they conceive, and not overemphatically or superficially transferred. The fulfilment of art – hence of architecture also – rests in its potential to perpetuate awareness as such. It does not define or freeze into static form what the artist – or society, for that matter – becomes aware of, it merely represents this as an apprehended or reapprehended aspect of human reality. It perpetuates in time and space 'undefined' meaning, nourishing in turn the awareness which detected it in the first place. Defining dormant meaning through form rather than allowing it to slumber in form is giving the lie to art, molesting the meaning – its repose and continuity. The meaning is gutted and awareness checked.

I am inclined to think that what we perceive is guided by what we conceive. But what we perceive tends to warp what we conceive (and vice versa) if either is grafted too inflexibly on to the other or their coincidence is claimed too ostensibly, so as to leave no play for still hidden meaning slumbering in what is perceived as well as in what is conceived. To force conception and perception (concept and the data found to support it) to coincide completely is to contract rather than to extend the meaning of either. The poetry lies in the persistence of scope – scope for undefined and latent multimeaning.

The Dogon People (1)
by Paul Parin

The population of the Dogon today numbers about a quarter of a million. In terms of the natural bases of existence (soil condition, climate, flora, and fauna), in appearance, and in their daily life, the Dogon differ little from their close neighbours, the Peuhl and the Bambara, or even from the Bantu far to the south. Their economy, family structure, political organization, customs, and religion are typical in the Sudan south of the Sahara. Yet it is no contradiction to say that they have developed a way of life which distinguishes them from any other people, in Africa or elsewhere.

They live in the steppe region south-west of the bend in the Niger River at Timbuktu, in some 700 small communities strung along the great falaise of Bandiagara, an escarpment which stretches about 200 kilometres north-east to south-west. The cliffs rise to a rocky plateau 200–300 metres above an arid plain wrinkled with sandy hills. On the irregular surface of the plateau, on ledges and among the rock-strewn slopes at the foot of the cliff, and scattered into the plain lie the compact villages, singly or in small groups. From a distance the houses and granaries appear to be part of the rocky cliff, like greyish-yellow crystal growths, barely distinguishable from the surroundings.

It is not known whether the Dogon came here from 'Mande' in the 10th or in the 14th century, and Mande itself would seem to designate no definite land; the word means 'place where the king lives'. The Dogon came, in flight or in migration, to found their people anew, perhaps after the fall of the kingdom where, one tradition says, they were serfs of the Emperor Keita. Each family and each village still traces its history from one of the four tribal fathers who brought the four original tribes into the region. So sharp is the mythico-historical consciousness of these people that their coming, which we have been unable to pinpoint in time or place, has remained alive in their minds. They have never forgotten the former inhabitants of the land, who fled at their coming and yet whose mythical descendants are still considered the actual owners of the land. They call them the Tellem, a name which they also give to the wooden statuettes and other artifacts left by 'those who were here before us' and found today in caves and in Tellem granaries and shrines that remain. The Dogon ascribe strong magic power to the statuettes, the Europeans high artistic value.

The Dogon God Amma, who created everything living, made first of all the earth, that was then his wife. He slept with her, but the first act of creation failed, because Amma's member hit against his wife's, the clitoris, the termite hill that projected up from the earth. Amma tore out the hill, circumcising his wife, and the earth gave in gently to her master. From the turmoil of this first act of creation arose Yurugu, the desert fox, who brought into the world menstrual blood and incest, and the Promethean theft of the first word of God.

Yurugu came from his mother's womb before his time because of his incestuous wishes, and thus lost his feminine twin Yasige, who remained in the womb. Yurugu committed incest by stealing his mother's fibre skirt and danced with joy on the roof of the house of heaven; the tracks left by his dancing feet are the first word of God which came to man, the word from dance. Today the diviners consult Yurugu, the first, fallen son of God. They mark off a place near the village, and in the evening scatter food for him. In the morning they read from the tracks in the sand Yurugu's secret wisdom, which he has stolen from God, who alone knows the future.

Soon Amma slept with his wife anew, and the rain, his holy seed, soaked into the earth and made her fruitful. In the second creation she bore the twinpair Nommo, feminine and masculine, the ideal pair, who with the water brought the second word of God to the world. The Nommo have delicate, wavy limbs without joints, like snakes, and a green coat (the plant cover of times to come), and they covered the naked mother with a fibre skirt. Words damp with Nommo's breath became interwoven with the fibres. The fertilization by rain, the quickening of all things by water, continues today when, moist with breath, speech flows from between the teeth of men and rushes into the ear, stimulating; it happens when the thread runs from the shuttle between the threads of the loom, guided by the teeth of the comb. The second act of creation could limit evil, but not wholly remove it from the world. From then on the principle of Yurugu, the restless seeker and thief, has worked in opposition to happiness and harmony with the divine. Yurugu is night, dryness, infertility, and death. Everything that loves is like Yurugu searching for the lost twin Yasige, only in loving union will he find again the happy exchange of the twinpair.

The great cliffs of Bandiagara from above and below. Note the ancient Tellem built forms in horizontal recesses of the cliff just above the village of Narni.

Nommo is day, moistness, fertility, and life. For success in an undertaking, a person consults Yurugu through a diviner, and then makes an offering at one of the altars of life, that have their power from Nommo.

Then Amma moved to the third act of creation. This time he formed from clay eight Nommos, four double-beings – the first mythical generation of mankind, the immortal ancestors. In their destinies and in those of their 80 offspring, the five mythical generations, are revealed all of the possibilities of people living today. Each Dogon family therefore includes in principle five generations with 80 individuals.

The seventh of the first mythical generation is the most perfect, because the number seven contains 3 and 4, the masculine principle (penis and testicles) and the feminine (four labia). Over a rainbow to earth God sent the seventh Nommo, who went with a granary – containing all the creatures and stones, all the skills and customs of man – and carried in the snakelike arms an iron hammer. The granary landed hard on the earth, and the arms of the Nommo broke and formed joints, making arms suited for work. Immediately Nommo began hammering on an anvil. The clanging accompanying the first work, ringing from the first smithy, is the third word of God: the present language of the Dogon. The seventh Nommo is called the teaching Nommo for giving man good council and for showing him what to do with the animals and plants and arts that spread from the granary through the world.

The Dogon came to the cliffs without herds, and because of the lack of grazing land they have become planters. They build on bare rock so the dwellings will have good foundations, and so that no arable land will go to waste; new fields can be established only where the bushland is cleared or soil laboriously transported in baskets and surrounded with rows of stones to keep it from being washed away.

In the hot and dry season of the year, from March to June, they patch their houses with a mixture of clay and water so they will be watertight at the coming of the first rains in June, when the entire population celebrates the sowing feast. In October they harvest the eight kinds of staple crops, mostly cereals, which stand between them and starvation and are stored in their mud granaries. The largest and by far the most productive fields are held by each of the Dogon Ginnas. A Dogon, even though he is part of one household, thinks of himself as a member of a larger, patrilocal family composed of many households and founded by one of the original tribal fathers from Mande. Whether this genealogy is biologically accurate is difficult to determine, and not too important. This extended family is called a Ginna, a word which also means 'great house'. This usage is much like ours when referring to the House of Hapsburg or the House of the Medici. Speaking of a Ginna, one may mean both the extended family and the large house in which the Ginna Bana (oldest living member of the family) lives with his wives and children. When the last Bana of one generation dies, the oldest of the generation of sons inherits the position, and after him his next oldest brother. ('Brothers' are not, here, only the sons of one father, but also all cousins within the family.) When a successor moves into the Ginna, the younger members are promoted in the family hierarchy and change dwellings then, too.

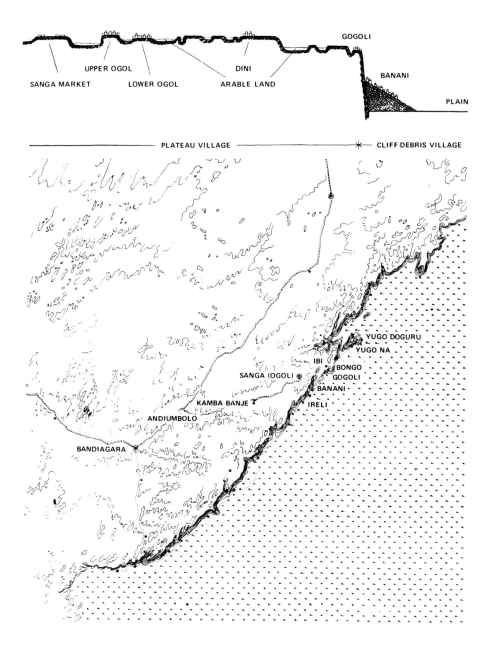

Map of Dogonland and section. There are two main village types: the plateau type (Upper and Lower Ogol, Bongo, Andiumbolo, etc.), often built from edge to edge on elevated tablelike rock masses, and the cliff-debris type (Banani, Ireli, Yugo Doguru, etc.). The latter form a long, almost continuous chain and are built on the fallen rocks at the foot of the great cliffs. The plain type villages are not numerous and are of more recent origin. The emphatic transition from the rocky plateau above to the vast plain of Gondo to the southeast 600–900 feet below has deeply affected both the life and history of the Dogon.

Banani

In earlier times the fields were taken care of in order, beginning with the land of the oldest member of the family. In many villages today the family works the fields of the Ginna together for four days of the week; the youngest married men, who by tradition still have no claim to land of their own, are given charge of some by the Bana, to be worked as they want. On the fifth day, market day, which corresponds to our Sunday, the older members of the family may work their own fields, those passed down from father to son and from mother to daughter. The crops from them are stored in personal granaries, of which all Dogon men and women have at least one. And in these fields, after the harvest of the cereals, they plant and tend their second crop, onions which grow in the cool, dry season from October to March.

Most of the onion harvest, in the form of crushed and dried balls, is exported. They are nearly the only (and the most important) product the Dogon can exchange for cash, thus the possession of cash is for the most part individual rather than collective, complementing the cooperative yield of their economic autarky. The production of onion balls probably gained impetus at first from the imposition of a head tax by the French colonial authorities earlier in this century. The Dogon expected from the beginning that each family member would come up with his own tax money. Now the Dogon and their neighbours pay their taxes to the Republic of Mali.

In studying the way of life of these people, or seeing one of the achievements of their culture, their villages or dwellings, we are brought to realize that our Western culture is only a special case among innumerable possibilities that man has developed. Many of their techniques are simpler than ours. For some universal human problems they seem to have found better solutions than we have. Individuals are better adjusted and more content; there is less conflict and hostility among them. Some other problems, such as health care and the production of necessary goods, have been solved less successfully.

The material and spiritual phenomena of Dogon life correspond to each other so well that it is almost impossible to describe them with our words that tend to divide and classify. They see even the most commonplace object as part of an all-embracing system. The beautiful woven basket which the Dogon woman uses to carry grain and onions on her head, and as a unit of measure, has a square bottom and a round rim; the cosmos is represented by the basket inverted: the sun is round and the heaven above it is square. The heavenly granary in which the Nommo brought to earth all the animals, plants, and kinds of grain has the form of the inverted basket, as do the granaries in which the Dogon store up their food through the long months between harvests. The use of a granary or basket of some other form would disturb the relationship of sun and heaven and affect the annual rains. The granaries would remain empty, and the continuity of the creation with the present generation would be upset. We are accustomed to designating as 'primitive' cultures those in which the material life, such as the economy, and the spiritual, such as religion and the psychological make-up of individuals (formed through traditional upbringing) are in an independent system of manifestations in which they correspond to each other relatively well; we often contrast the symbolic-magical mode of thought with the empiric-logical.[6] The 'correspondences' become more comprehensible as expressions of symbolic thought if one imagines the participative nature of each symbol, which is at the same time the one and the other (for us a flag is as much a piece of cloth as it is also the country).

The efforts of Europeans to achieve greater happiness in life through the accumulation of money, or through good deeds to have a better life in the hereafter, seem just as illogical to the Dogon as their attempts to bring water by magic seem to us.

In the whole steppe-region of Africa, water is scarce and defines the 'being and consciousness' of those who live there. During the part of the year when the nomads of Mauritania must stay near the water holes with their valued herds, their freedom is limited by an order which permits all to still their thirst. The one-dimensional water hole with the dense pack of animals, usually scattered along the horizon, has given the nomads a system of justice, based on the right to have an animal draw out buckets of water for a certain number of days, and a tribal morality.

Yet in the life of the Dogon, who dip their water from the water holes among the rocks of Bandiagara, the same lukewarm, reddish-yellow and turbid liquid has a meaning different from that it has for other people, even since mythical times. In the flight of migration from Mande, the Dogon ancestors could remain to build houses and found families only where there was water to be found, often hidden in rock crevices or in pools in the low brush. Nangabanu was thirsty, it is said. A crocodile came near him; he followed the animal to the riverlike pool where it lived with others, and there, with that much water, Nangabanu founded Bandiagara – the only large settlement in the land of the Dogon, today their capital. The inhabitants revere the crocodile as a tribal father. Friendship binds them to the animal; none ever harms a Dogon, and no Dogon kills one.

The animal of the water, the life in the water, has remained bound up with the life of the family. In many of the Ginnas the original founder of the family lives on in the form of a turtle. At night when it creeps out of its hiding place, it finds under the family altar its nourishment (as do the spirits of the ancestors, who visit the sacred spot). Millet meal with water is offered – water, which sustains, creates, and binds together. When a wife finally leaves her father's house after the birth of a second or third child to live with her husband, she is said to have drunk water with him.

At birth and death the family drinks nourishing millet-water together. The elders in council, the men in the market, and all the guests at a feast drink beer, the fermented 'strong' water, which is also taken when people build a house together, begin the planting, or finish the harvest. The water of the Dogon is there so that they can propagate, exercise their skills, drink and speak, take and give. It means the fruition, beginning, and strengthening of the family; it means clothing, understanding, and manners. It is to communicate with God through his seed, and through his breath, which brings the word. Thus everything is due to water. Its use can never be limited by a system of rights; one gives water to strangers as a gesture of hospitality, and all the children of a family have a natural and equal claim to it, just as to life itself, through their ancestors, from God.

With this attitude toward their water may be connected the fact that the Dogon, who otherwise show many technical skills – who can build ingenious houses and weave strong cloth – go about the management of their most important material in a 'primitive' way. Using small gourd shells, they ladle water into large clay pots and take them into the yards of houses, or out to water the fields. Except for this simple way of distributing water, they know none of the other techniques that are found in West Africa. Those who could increase and store up water – the substance closest to God – have, for the Dogon, taken on an aura of superhuman wisdom and power. Professor Griaule, the ethnologist who studied the Dogon for many years, convinced the French authorities to build dams there in some appropriate places. This act raised him to the status of the founding forefathers of the people. When the news that he had died in Paris reached them, his soul was taken up among the spirits of the dead through the ritual of the Dama, so that his life-force or Nyama would benefit the living among 'his' people. The people of Sanga, where Professor Griaule often stayed, built a grave for him near the fields that were 'created'. The French researcher has entered into not only their history but also Dogon myth.

It is in the mask cult and the dance of the masks itself that the most important part of the spiritual and social life of the Dogon people is found. In its dealing with the phenomenon of death, their society has created an institution which draws it together again and again, structures and refreshes it, one in which it finds its most characteristic expression. The death ceremonies, and particularly the Dama, a masked dance for the termination of a period of mourning, distribute the life-force of the deceased among the living, while the soul – liberated from both life and death – is admitted among the immortal ancestors. (In some cases, though, the dead have a harmful force which must be kept away through special ritual.) In a symbolic funeral procession the masks first go to get the deceased from the house where he used to live. They accompany him to the land of the immortal ancestors, to Mande of origin and destination; then they return, winding back through the hills to the village streets. They begin there the dance through which the beneficent Nyama they have brought back is distributed. Thus the strength of their dead renews and protects the living.

Unlike people of other religious convictions, the Dogon expect of the hereafter no compensation through a better life. They find their life not bad, and learn in their well-ordered world that one is immediately rewarded for goodness, and that one soon pays for doing wrong and need not trail it with him after death.

The paradise of the Dogon, where the deceased reside, looks like Dogonland itself. The villages are like those in which the living dwell, the rich are rich, the poor are poor. All live with their families, planting millet and onions as they did on earth. In the dry brush the same trees stand, though the fruits they bear are more beautiful in colour, more lustrous, so that the dead can tell they are in paradise and no longer in the land of the Dogon.

Paul Parin – The Dogon People (1)

Design Only Grace; Open Norm; Disturb Order Gracefully; Outmatch Need

There is no limit to what the Dogon basket can hold, for with its circular rim and square base, it is at once basket and granary; at once sun, firmament, and cosmic system; at once millet and the forces which cause millet to grow.

It seems to me that people for whom all things are so much one thing that one thing can also be all things carry this essential unity within themselves. Even Dogon paradise falls within this unity insofar as it resembles the land of the living in everything except the fruits of the baobab tree which are more lustrous so that those in paradise may recognize where they are. Everything prevails – not even the hardships of life on earth are mitigated in Dogon afterlife. They too prevail. Nothing is discontinued: in paradise the Dogon is satisfied as he was on earth!

In order to be at home in the universe, man tends to refashion it in his own image, accommodate it to his own dimension. Constructed enclosure was hitherto seldom sufficient. There was always the limitless exterior beyond – the incomprehensible, intangible and unpredictable – harassing man's right composure, shaking whatever 'ground of certainty', to use Joseph Rykwert's phrase, he was able to find. So his cities, villages and houses – even his baskets – were persuaded by means of symbolic form and complex ritual to contain within their measurable confines that which exists beyond and is immeasurable: to represent it symbolically. The artefact – whether small or large, basket or city – was identified with the universe or the power or deity representing the cosmic order. It thus became a 'habitable' place, comprehensible from corner to corner, familiar and tangible. Mystery was thus rendered at least partly accessible. The transcendental was brought within reach: with the Zuñi Pueblos, the great Shilako dance in each house just after completion before it is inhabited – thus the entire village actually 'becomes' the house of the gods.

Those who agree with Joseph Rykwert[7] that 'the ground of certainty', without which no inner equipoise is possible, must now be discovered within the 'structure and constitution of the human person', i.e. in the interior of the mind and no longer outside it, will probably find it more meaningful to identify the city with the dream than to identify it with the exterior universe. Whilst the latter, I think, is no longer either possible or desirable, the former is singularly suggestive, since it points towards an 'interiorization' of the mind – an 'interior' universe, at once kaleidoscopic, metamorphic, and chaotic, in the way – this is my point – cities are kaleidoscopic, metamorphic and chaotic – and necessarily so.

The transcendental begins where man leaves his gods behind – this side of the beyond. We no longer need the *cardo* and the *decumanus* to feel at home in the universe, but we need to be 'at home' nonetheless. That is why it is no small thing to discover that we are indeed Romans no longer, yet Romans still.[8] Rykwert's suggestion that a town, if it looks like anything physiological at all, looks more like a dream than anything else, is suggestive in many ways. For it is in the nature of dreams that things – all things – escape from the rigid meanings assigned to them, cross their own frontier, merge, and are significantly reshuffled; that absolutes and quantitative antonyms (false polarities) – this concerns me especially – are deflated and rendered meaningless; and, finally, that order and chaos, continuity and discontinuity, the determinate and the indeterminate, are gratifyingly united.

Both the Pueblos and the Dogon tell us, each in a different way, that right-size is not a quantitative matter at all. They reveal once again that what large and small, many and few, far and near, part and whole, unity and diversity, simplicity and complexity, etc., etc., mean in a qualitative and relative sense, depends on what they mean in terms of each other, i.e. as a linked sequence of twin phenomena. In a valid solution – whether it is a Pueblo or a Dogon village, all these qualities are simultaneously present. Each acquires something of the meaning of the other and is enriched by it – given perspective. This is what I call right-size. It is also what the large house-little city image is meant to suggest. With regard to false physiological analogies, I find the currently quantitative leaf-house or tree-city analogies as meaningless as I find the qualitative leaf-tree or house-city identifications meaningful – i.e. endowed with multimeaning (see note on Christopher Alexander's 'A city is not a tree').[9]

Whilst in Africa, I discussed the large house-little city image with Dr Parin and Dr Morgenthaler, and was very excited when they told me that the various aspects of the Dogon reality could probably support the image's validity. The essays they wrote show that this supposition was not unjustified.

There are indeed some combined physical and mental problems which the Dogon in particular have managed to solve remarkably well. I am referring in the first place to the way they are able to release from moment to moment inner tensions

These photographs (above and next two pages) are of the main open space in Upper Ogol. The first was taken in the morning, the others in the afternoon of the same day during an important Dama, the great masked ceremony which terminates a period of mourning, divides the Nyama or life-force of the deceased among the living, and releases the spirit from life and death so that it can be received by the immortal ancestors.

Although women and children are forbidden to watch a Dama – its very essence excludes this – they are seen here standing on the roofs in large numbers doing so! All at once a masked figure dances past the houses bordering the open space with great leaps, emitting fierce noises and throwing gravel up at those watching on the roofs. Screaming, terror stricken, the latter disappear immediately.

The conflict is resolved magnificently at once on both levels, the cosmic and the human. The terrifying figure who scares the women and children away actually belongs to the Dama and fulfils this particular dance function. The cosmic equipoise is thus quickly restored. But the human one also, for soon the transgressing spectators, having regained the right composure, reappear on the roofs and proceed to watch the Dama below as if nothing had occurred. They are neither forcibly prevented from doing so nor are they punished for it. Instead, in order to safeguard the houses bordering this particular open space from collapsing under the weight of so many women and children watching what they should not watch, but still 'need' to watch, they are built more firmly than those elsewhere in the village. The extra material this requires is furnished by the village. Just think of it!

The mastery with which the Dogon are able to restore equipoise when it is disturbed is breathtaking. Their sense of reality is such, so it seems, that merely to 'maintain' equipoise becomes insufficiently constructive – a non-inclusive and arbitrary procedure which fails to respond to the reality of the cause of the disturbance and its possible validity, in human terms or otherwise. This creative ability to re-establish equipoise on whatever level it may have been disturbed (cosmic, social, or psychic), points to a frame of mind both generous, perceptive and functional. Tensions are quickly mitigated and conflicts reasonably resolved. As to the women and children watching the Dama: that the Dogon are concerned not only with the consequence of their transgression (disturbance of the cosmic order) but also with the understandable desire of the transgressors to witness the Dama and the mental stress (disturbance of the individual's inner equipoise) which would result were they not to do so – is revealed by the contribution of the extra building material to reinforce the houses bordering the open space.

by means of a mental process which to us, who are wont to accumulate and even nourish grinding remnants left over from former human contact (allowing them to disturb our inner composure and distort our subsequent behaviour), must seem like a miracle.[10]

The Dogon rely on an all-pervading framework which embraces every facet of their existence, material, emotional and transcendental. Such frameworks are so intricate, complete and self-contained that they may tend to leave little scope for the individual whose mental structure, though moulded by them to a large extent, nonetheless never coincides fully. Not so with the Dogon, for they include within the intricate, closely knit fabric of their system a gratifying kind of scope (flexibility) which permits circumstantial and incidental modification without transgressing against the system's generative and protective potential, infringing on its essence, or damaging the individual's psychic structure. The Dogon adhere to their system with great accuracy, but never rigidly. This accuracy is due to an astounding responsiveness which enables them to resolve immediately both the conflicts which beset the community at large and the intimate ones which weigh on the individual.

The miraculous vision of paradise to which I have already referred epitomizes the Dogon mind, and also reveals extraordinary mental relaxation. People able to reward a life of great hardship with a vision of afterlife so moderate must in truth be essentially satisfied with the reality they were born into. What measurable grandeur! What sanity!

Basket – House – Village – Universe

by Aldo van Eyck

Building both house and village implies inaugurating a microcosm in which life is perpetuated – hence the various rituals which accompany the building process from stage to stage. There is no categorical conflict between those prerogatives which have a physical and those which have a metaphysical basis, since the natural and the supernatural, or the material and the spiritual, do not constitute impregnable or conflicting categories. What is true of the Dogon basket is also true of the Dogon house and the Dogon village; their symbolic meaning is likewise extraordinarily expansive. I am not exaggerating when I say that all the material objects, from the smallest to the largest, which support daily life are charged with extra meaning and are identified in stages with the totality of creation. A sequential pattern of identification expanding and, finally, corresponding with the universal order. About these stages Marcel Griaule, to use his own words, says that each stage of the process represents the whole, whilst a series of material avatars leads from the world itself to smaller and smaller groupings – district, village, village-section, homestead. He speaks of *'emboîtements successifs'* progressing from man to cosmos in which every stage contains the whole. His daughter, G. Calame-Griaule, who is also a leading

Upper Ogol

Lower Ogol

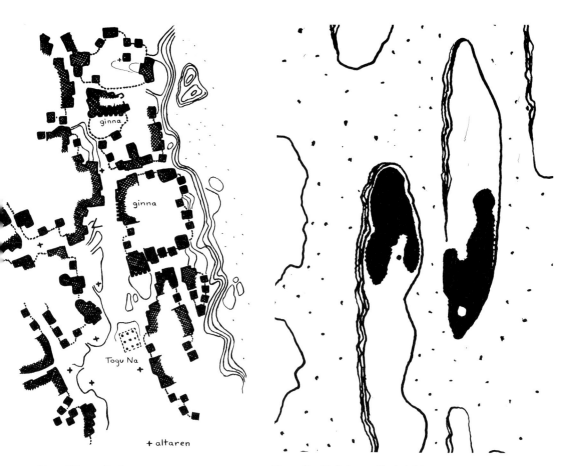

Plan of Upper Ogol   Upper Ogol left, Lower Ogol right

Dogon specialist, affirms that the cosmos projected in a human scale reveals an essential humanism.[11]

But let me glean more relevant data concerning symbolic meaning from the two Griaules. I must condense what they say, in places partly in my own words. The house is built in the image of man: the actual place where the cooking is done represents the respiratory organ and is always situated there where a fruit of the *nonô* plant (*nonô* = perpetual) is walled-in during the building process, whilst the kitchen itself is the head. The entrance represents the vulva (the cooking place lies in the axis: kitchen – central living space – entrance). I should like to remind the reader of the Pueblo Indians, whom I admire as I do the Dogon and about whom I have written a companion essay.[12] As with the Dogon, marking the plan of a house on the ground calls for complex rituals. Such rituals are continued at different stages throughout the entire building process. Ogotemmêli, the old blind Dogon sage, called this: the imprint of the house's image which commences. It is also the universal arch descended from the heavens to reorganize creation. The four main spaces grouped around the principal one are the four ancestral couples (these, together with the animals, plants, minerals and Nommo, constitute the universal arch).

The Ginna or family patriarch's house is Nommo in human form. Also a man lying on his right side procreating. The different heights of the roofs over the rooms express the diversity, Griaule says, of the beings which issued from the ejected seed. Each part of the house is thus an original being germinating and growing from its genitor. The whole plan of the house, furthermore, is contained in an oval. It again represents the universal arch from which all space, all living beings, and everything has emerged.

There are definite symbolic proportions for all buildings based on the male number three and the female number four. Thus a normal house is 6 × 8 paces, i.e. twice the male number multiplied by twice the female number. The Ginna is double this. A granary belonging to a man is 6 (i.e. 2 × 3) × 6, a granary belonging to a woman is 4 × 4. The numbers three and four prevail, even in clothing![13]

Now for the villages. Not only are they anthropomorphic like the house, but, to follow Griaule, each part or section of them is a complete or separate entity and, so far as possible, must be laid out on the same pattern as the whole. Thus individual families are fitted into a grouping which itself is a unity. The village, like the house, is the projection of the universe in the form of a man lying on his back in a north-south direction. Smithy and Togu Na are his head; the two menstruation huts standing outside the village precincts are his hands; the main shrines, his feet; whilst the various Ginna situated around the village centre are his chest and stomach.[14]

What excites me especially with respect to the village is the fact that they are generally built in pairs. The same goes for the districts. Since I am deeply concerned with twin-phenomena, the principle of twin-ness – *gémelliparité* – which runs right through the entire Dogon cosmology, manifesting itself at every scale level can, therefore, hardly fail to excite me! A rare sense of equipoise pervades the life and doings of the Dogon and epitomizes their specific genius. It seems to me that it could well be nourished by this principle of twin-ness, the one sustaining the other reciprocally.

Theoretically, the in-between space formed by such twin villages should be round the way the sky is round – like the rim of the Dogon basket. The Lébé shrine situated there is the sun, whilst the various Binu shrines in the two villages are the stars.[15] The space between an Upper and Lower district is marked by a public meeting place, in the village where the Hogon, the district chief, lives.

What Marcel Griaule says about the villages as seen from above is extremely relevant here. He describes how the roofs shining in the sun and the shadows cast on the ground resemble hillocks of cultivated land casting shadows into the hollows. Moving down in scale, the '80' niches of the Ginna and the checked black-and-white Dogon blanket reveal the same pattern. Thus the settlement where people dwell close together is a representation both of man himself and of the layout of the fields

Ogol, doorway to a yard

Upper Ogol. The plateau type villages are built to the very edge of flat rock masses.

Ogol. People have always been able to cope with the single house – or a limited multiplicity of houses.

outside the walls; a way of calling to mind the fact that the processes of germination and gestation are of the same kind.

I will conclude with what Griaule has to say about the territorial organization of the Dogon and the Hogon. It accords with the idea that the world developed in the form of a spiral. The fields are laid out in such a way that they represent the world in miniature. In principle they form a rectilinear spiral around three ritual fields, one for each of the basic cults. First, nearest the centre, come the fields belonging to the kin groups. These are followed by those belonging to individuals. Sacrifices are offered in the shrines situated along the spiral, starting with the one nearest the centre. The actual process of cultivation and the way the Dogon labour in the fields

extends the symbolic meaning of the spiral layout into symbolic action – in accordance with it.

The Hogon priest, the district chief, Griaule says, is the personification of the universe and the regent of Nommo on earth. In consequence, all his material attributes and all the prerogatives attaching to his function represent the qualities and movements of the cosmic mechanism. He controls the cosmic rhythm. Thus his daily life is set against a background which presents the world in miniature and in reference to which his ceremonial acts and movements symbolize the motive power which animates the world.

The Dogon People (2)
by Fritz Morgenthaler

The daily life of the Dogon is concerned with the gathering of necessary goods. As settled planters, they plan and adjust the course of their labours according to the laws of nature. They naturally expect rain to come at the right time and hope for a good harvest. Their requirements are basic ones, as are the satisfactions they seek from life. They live through their disappointments, gaining from them practical understanding to alleviate their troubles. The work is hard, but the return is generally such that they can live without great hunger – also such that they cannot amass wealth. Yet the Dogon are neither melancholy nor apathetic people; even though they do not expect a better life – or know 'longing', as understood by Western civilization – they are largely content and at their ease.

Psychic tensions arising from contact with fellow men are not of lasting consequence with the Dogon, and so they hardly ever experience the pressure of dammed up feelings that can find expression in hoping and longing. Tension will usually be discharged at the point of its origin and without delay, distributed, and cleared in a common transaction. This can succeed to a high degree, because for

each emotion, each disturbance, and all impulses a material or spiritual response lies ready to facilitate abreaction, without disturbing the external or internal order that defines their world.

In the hot hours at noon, by a small river that runs near Andiumbolo, we art resting in the shade of a tree. An old man appears wearing a large straw hat. At a little distance from us he stops and stands for a time – then he comes closer and greets us in his language. It is a long greeting whose rhythm and intonation convey the earnestness of a tradition. At the same time, it holds a cheerful invitation to reply. It is a greeting like a dialogue, or a canon, whose complete structure calls for a matching response. We answer the greeting, but as our answer is without form and spirit, we try to make up for the obvious shortcoming with some gestures. The old man smiles. One of us has just finished a mango and throws the stone away. The Dogon comes over quickly, picks it up, and begins a story without words. We will plant the stone, here, and a mango tree will grow up; people will sit in its shade and pick fruits from its branches to eat. With these gestures the man has completed the greeting we failed to carry out properly. He got something from us, the mango stone, and with it has made something whole and appropriate as a response; the tree. Now he stands there laughing, seeing that we have been able to follow him. The greeting that is such comprehensive contact between Dogon is well done with the foreigners too. He drops the stone and goes his way.

That was Bai, the village chief of Andiumbolo. He has gone for people from the village now, so we may come in contact with one another.

In another village I spend quite a while looking for Amba, a young man with whom I have arranged to meet. After many detours, I finally find him in a remote onion garden. We greet each other, and our conversation follows:

'I was told in the village that you were working in a garden on the other side of the hill'.

'That's where my garden is.'

'But you are working here and not in your garden.'

'Today I'm helping my little brother harvest the onions. He is going to help me finish my house.'

'Are you building a house?'

'I was away for four years, and when I came back I married. Now I'm building a house so I can live there with my wife.'

'The people in the village showed me your house, the last one before the rocks.'

'I was there this morning. It's my big brother's house.'

'Do you live, there?'

'No, I live with my father.'

'Why did they tell me that your big brother's house is your house?'

'I sleep there with my wife. In the morning she goes back to her father's house.'

'Do you have children yet?'

'No, that wouldn't work. First the house has to be finished. Then my wife will have children, and I will take them in.'

'Most Dogon wives stay with their father until the third child is born. Then they live with their husband in his house.'

'Yes, of course. When a woman bears a child she naturally returns to her father.'

'Even when you have finished your house?'

'Of course. When a child is born, the mother returns to her father.'

'Then why do you have to finish your house before your wife can have a child?'

'You will see the house I'm building now. Then everything will be clear to you.' He looks down at the ground and shakes his head. 'A wife can't have a child as long as the house isn't finished. It just doesn't happen that way.'

'Is the big brother whose place you sleep in with your wife also married?'

'He's married, and his wife has two children. She and the children live with her father.'

'Had he built himself a house before his wife had her first child?'

Amba leans over toward me and taps me on the shoulder. 'Now you understand the Dogon. The big brother's house will be there for the younger brothers when they want to sleep with their wives.'

The substance of our conversation seemed quite simple at first. A young Dogon builds a house, takes in his wife, and starts a family. Then it emerges that the new house is not simply intended for the immediate family, but is placed at the disposal of younger brothers for years to come. Amba thereby gains a new position in the community of the village. He becomes a 'big brother', and that involves his being a mature man with responsible functions. Only then can he too have his own children. The social meaning, still more the whole experience of being a father, is divided into two matching parts in Amba's mind, two parts which are inseparably correlated and yet do not overlap. As big brother, he has the social role of father to all those younger, for whom he becomes an example. As procreator, he secures himself the offspring who will care for him when he is old. For his own children, though, other big brothers will in turn become more important than he. Then just as father and big brother match each other, so do the building of a house and the act of procreation, the house and the child – not symbols of each other, not just comparable parts of a whole, but one and the same, like the square basket with the round opening that is at once basket, granary, and cosmos. In such continuity of psychic experience appears the wholeness of the Dogon culture.

> 'Would you like to come and see my house?' We get up and go back to the village. Amba's house on the edge of the market place is square and has a small anteroom. There is no roof yet.
> 'You have a very fine house. There are no windows.'
> 'White people put windows in their houses. We Dogon don't do that. When the roof is up, the house will be dark inside.'
> 'Why should it be dark?'
> 'Anybody who wants light can go outside. In the house it should be dark. It's better that way.'

The wholeness of this culture is also reflected in the words of Dommo, a man of forty from the village of Andiumbolo: 'Everyone here is satisfied. Everyone is content with things as they are.' With a sweep of his hand he indicates the landscape before us. 'When one can work and have a good harvest, there is enough to eat. Then there are holidays, and we go around to the other villages. There is something to drink and a lot of talk with everyone, and then it is time to go home again.'

When I ask Dommo for his opinion about why the white people are not always as content, he can't think of an answer and explains my question to the chief of the village. He considers for a moment, and then Dommo translates his words.

'White people think too much and then do many things, and the more they do, the more they think. And then they earn a lot of money, and when they have a lot they worry that the money could get lost and they would have no more. Then they think more and make still more money, and never have enough. Then they never have any peace again. So it is that they are not happy.'

The ease in this culture is present in the words that Dommo speaks. It is a kind of ease that can forego hoping and longing.

Then comes the day Dommo is with me in the car as we drive by the market place of Andiumbolo. Some children there wave to us. We pass the great rock where the road drops down steeply, and the gentle, hilly landscape gives an impression of distinct loneliness. Far and wide not a village is in sight, as all of them lie hidden to us. We drive on to the great festival of the masks at Kamba Banje, the only village that can be seen from the road, sitting on a rock about 60 metres high. From up there, after a climb, one has a completely different view of the land. What seemed gentle ridges are now terrace-like rock formations with jagged crests of glistening basalt.

Dommo stands there like a king considering the castle grounds. He motions me to look across the wide land into the distance where we see the masks dancing to the village – they come nearer now. On the way to the village open space where the great dance will take place, I stop and, captivated, stand looking into a small yard, over the mud wall where it has been damaged and is low enough for me to see. 'Leave it – come on!'

The tone is severe. But in the way Dommo says it, the Dogon cheer rings through, even more compelling. Immediately I leave behind the strange sight in the yard and follow after him.

There is great commotion in the village open space. The dance of the masks begins, and I lose sight of Dommo in the crowd. One may see the masks when they are alive and dancing, but the lifeless masks are taboo. They are put away in caves, to be visited by the initiates in the mask cult only, at night and in secret. I was looking at a dark-red, barrel-shaped mask behind that mud wall. It stood there motionless and enigmatic, one side still faintly lit by the sinking sun. The upper part of the mask tapered like the roof of a cylindrical house, and bore a small head with trunklike finery.

The masked dance nears its climax in the open space. Now moving slowly and deliberately, the barrel-shaped mask appears – and then again from the other side. The dance takes on a particular quality. To the rhythm of the drums the mask moves itself in a circle, rocking up and down. All at once the dancer in it crouches and the 'mask house' is left frozen. The structure, sturdily built, rests on the ground now just as I caught it a short time ago in a forbidden glimpse. But already it has continued its dance.

Dommo says right at my side. 'That's the elephant. He appears only in a few villages, and only once in a while.' The 'elephant' embodies motion and rest together like no other mask. He dances and stays still – then he dances again, and so on. There is no stop, no end of motion without its continuing again immediately. So death too is only a phase. It begins during life, and life still goes on after death. Nothing may ever come completely to an end – something always follows.

Dommo found it hard to bring together his divided feelings toward me in conversation, so one day he took my hand and led me over high rocks up to Andiumbolo. Stopping at the entrance he said, 'This is my village.' He spat, took my hand again, and said, 'I want to show you my house.'

The village is on a rocky hill. From here one sees far into the valley below, to the river, and across the fields to another hill and the twin village of Goloku.

It happens to be the very image of Banani against the cliffs which has been in my mind ever since I saw a photograph in an issue of *Minotaure* during the war. From a distance – see photo of Narni – the villages blend so wonderfully into the environment to which they belong that they are almost invisible. But contrast can be equally wonderful, as any Cycladic island village shows. The sister picture on the right shows a man standing next to his huge-small granary.

Banani is a good example of a cliff-debris type village. Each man and each woman possesses one or more personal granaries. Unlike the blacksmith and the weaver, the builder is not a specialised professional. Each man builds his own house assisted by the male members of the large family to which he belongs, and those of his neighbourhood. Building is thus a collective undertaking, though houses are personal property.

Banani. Granaries around a courtyard.

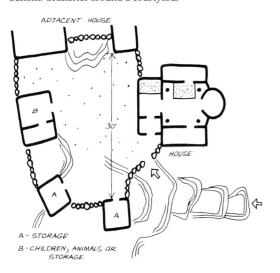

A - STORAGE
B - CHILDREN, ANIMALS OR STORAGE

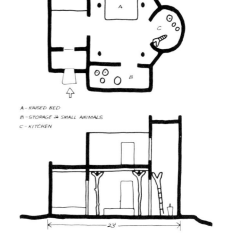

A - RAISED BED
B - STORAGE & SMALL ANIMALS
C - KITCHEN

Banani. Note the ancient Tellem structures in the horizontal crevice.

Banani-type house

Yugo Doguru. dwelling of the Hogon priest. Note entrance at lower right and ancient granaries (probably Tellem).

Andiumbolo is larger than one would think looking up from the foot of the hill. A few houses stand just at the verge of the rocky slope. They are surrounded by a mud wall, and there are small trees in some of the yards. Further back in the village is a larger open space. Here Dommo points out the shade-roof (Togu Na), under which the old men like to rest, and 'also the young,' as he says. 'I'll show you my house now,' he says again and draws me on. The narrow, winding streets we pass through are shaped by the mud walls that enclose yards. The houses are in these yards, and along the yard walls stand the granaries built up on posts, as if on stilts, and bearing pointed thatched roofs. We meet three men, and Dommo introduces us. They greet me like an old acquaintance – Bai has spread the story about the white people under the tree.

The three men join us. I am no longer sure where we are headed, and Dommo explains. 'We are going to the village chief's house. He's my uncle, my mother's brother.' The house of the village chief is larger than

The small brought about by the large

Yugo Doguru is the Mecca of the Dogon people because the grave of the first ancestral Dogon is situated there. It is the privilege, furthermore, of the male elders of this sacred place to order the advent of the Sigi every 60 years – the great masked celebration which constitutes the renewal of the entire Dogon people. The manner in which the houses, granaries and yards are adapted and modified owing to the gigantic rocks which lie scattered over the site is revealing. The sacredness of this particular site left no alternative than to build there. As a reward for coping with the difficulties this brought with it, however, many shaded places resulted under and between the rocks and buildings, which are absent in villages elsewhere, built as they are on more regular and 'suitable' sites.

What this really implies is of crucial importance, since it points towards the old truth that what is just large without embracing what is small at the same time has no right-size in terms of human appreciation and will hence remain inaccessible. Thus right-size is the gratifying reward of magnitude approached as a twin phenomenon. This includes, of course, the interdependence of many and few, far and near; part and whole, simplicity and complexity, unity and diversity, inside and outside, open and closed, change and constancy, movement and rest, and finally, the individual and the collective – their simultaneous presence as an essential prerequisite if environment is to mean what we wish it to mean. The ingredients we need lie still dormant in what I personally wish to call Labyrinthian Clarity, for in its inclusive ambiguity and scope for multimeaning, it is nourished by and nourishes all twin phenomena together. Labyrinthian Clarity exemplifies a frame of mind as well as what issues from it, a climate in which all false partitions inevitably fall down.

Yugo Doguru. Cliffs sheltering ancient granaries.

Yugo Doguru. In the background the great plain of Gondo several hundred feet below.

Yugo Doguru,
a sacred place

all the others. There are two front doors, and around them 22 rectangular niches have been fashioned in the wall. Various useless items lie in the niches: a broken gourd shell, a few rusty pieces of metal, even two eggs. In a matter-of-fact way Dommo says, 'Birds nest in there.' He shows no awareness of the significance of the niches, that they are supposed to represent the 80 immortal ancestors from the third mythical generation.

After the greeting, and after Bai has offered me some Konjo, I remind Dommo that it is late and I have to go back soon. 'Yes, of course,' he says, 'but let's go to my house.' He chooses a way we haven't taken yet. We come to some houses with small towers, and I stop. Large stones, whitened with a coating of dried millet paste, lie around in the yard. They are altars, at which someone has made an offering. An old crippled man makes his way among the stone blocks. Dommo does not greet him – he pulls me away as if he is afraid I will speak to the old man. 'That is the house of the Hogon priest of Andiumbolo. Come on, we have to hurry. We are going to my house now.'

Again Dommo seems to change direction. He stops before a large mud wall and knocks on the closed gate there. 'This is my uncle's house.' After I ask, surprised, whether we are going to his house or not, I learn that this is the Ginna, the 'big house' of the family, where Dommo's paternal uncle lives, the family elder, or Bana. In the dark vestibule I almost step on the children and women sitting everywhere. Dommo says, 'My father isn't here.' meaning the Bana. His immediate father has been dead for a long time. We continue through the narrow streets and reach once more the open space with the Togu Na.

I turn for home, and Dommo asks, disappointed, 'Don't you want to see my house? I don't live where we just were – when my wife is working in the fields or is sick and can't cook, I eat in the big house. I'm home, here.' So we walk into a yard near the entrance to the village. It is the place where, more than an hour ago, Dommo said he wanted to show me his house.

Dommo's house has two doors. A small mud wall, really an extension of the house, divides the yard, as if in halves. In the yard are three granaries – two near the entrance for Dommo and his first wife, the third in the rear of the yard for his second wife. Standing next to each other are the two women, who greet us. Dommo says, 'My father lived here. He also had two wives. When he died I took over the house. I've been here for fifteen years with my first wife, and for a while my second wife has been living in the other house, that used to be empty.'

Dommo's wish to show me his house took us in turn to the council-place of the elders, to the village chief's place, to the priest's, then to the place of the family elder, and just at last to his own dwelling. To each of these places he is bound by a quite definite part of his sense of 'being home'. So it is in this culture that a house is never sold, for one calls a house the people living there.

Fritz Morgenthaler – The Dogon People (2)

Some Comments on a Significant Detour

Although it is true that only a particular kind of society conditions the particular kind of emotional place-affinity Dommo has towards the various 'houses' he passed or entered with Dr Morgenthaler before finally entering the house he shares with his first wife and children, it would be wrong to suggest that only an all-encompassing framework can condition the kind of multilocated attachment (web of emotional place-affinity) which is required before one can really say: my house is my village (city), my village (city) is my house, or when I say village (city) I imply the people living there.

The emotional identification of house and village (city) need not of course depend on such collectively conditioned place-attachment, but the idea as such stands out

Ogol. Tugu Na, a place where the village elders gather to rest and discuss all things appertaining to the life of the community, religious, social and economic.

A Ginna

Ogol. Each village has several such houses (Ginna) in which a family patriarch lives with his wives and unmarried sons and daughters. Other members of the family live in small houses of the normal type close around the Ginna. Note the niches (never 80!) which represent the primordial descendants of the four ancestral couples of the Dogon people.

Ogol. A priest's house. Many libations are poured over the façade and shrines from the roof.

Ogol. Konjo, indigenous beer, waiting for those who come from afar to participate in the Dama. Note the bubbling fermentation.

clearly enough. Nor does the emotional identification of either house or village (city) with the people living there necessarily require an attachment so immediate that a house, for example – as is the case with the Dogon – cannot be sold.

If that were so, my desire to conceive of a house as a small city and a city as a large house would be abstract, in the sense that it would be an altogether unattainable objective. I can visualize a culture which is not negatively indeterminate but positively so, because it strives primarily to stimulate the personal self-realization of the individual according to his own personal idea. This in turn would provide the true ingredient that goes to the fulfilment of the multicoloured entity that society – hence also the city – should be. The house-like city with city-like houses (build-

ings), gratifyingly comprehensible and chaotic; homogeneous and kaleidoscopic at the same time (I call this labyrinthian clarity).

What would have conditioned another man's route through Andiumbolo (with the same object of showing a visitor his house) to differ from Dommo's is not a different kind of emotional attachment, but a similar kind accorded to a different (perhaps partly the same) sequence of houses and places. Their actual location differs from one Dogon to another according to the way he is linked to the community (its total framework). I do not wish to suggest for a moment that Dommo is not emotionally linked to other places, houses, or people for strictly personal reasons – in this, of course, he differs from no man. But they were simply not incorporated in his route, leading from place to place (each of which was his 'own house' in a particular way) until he finally returned to the place

A tree constitutes a shady place – a place also for what the Dogon calls a 'special stone'. Children play a kind of checkers there.

Grinding stones, kept near to jars of water near the entry to the house. On these stones fresh ears of corn are crushed, yielding a liquid (associated with the male seminal fluid) which is carried to the left of the entry and poured on the shrine of the ancestors.

from where the detour had started and entered the house he shares with his wife and children (his 'own' in that particular respect).

The fact that the same collectively rooted reasons cause each Dogon to be linked emotionally to a different network of houses and places within his village (so that for each individual within the village community the village is also 'his' house) does not imply that because in the city of today the strictly personal reasons are different from individual to individual, linking each to a network of places (strangely enough often the same), his city cannot be 'his' house also. With the Dogon, the emotional house-village-region relationship constitutes a reality the entire community is aware of, whereas with us such a relationship is a thing each individual is aware of for strictly personal reasons. With the Dogon what is essentially similar becomes emotionally differentiated from person to person. With

A shrine of Ogol

us what is superficially dissimilar tends to become emotionally stereotyped from person to person. Now, without having to resort to the former it is obvious that the latter is a sad alternative. Surely what is essentially dissimilar can be embraced in what is essentially similar from person to person, establishing the real scope for differentiation.

There are as many Londons as there are Londoners, as many Parises as there are Parisians (as many too as there are Londoners going to Paris!), yet London is not Paris.

A village (town or city) is not just one bunch of places; it is many bunches at the same time, because it is a different bunch for each inhabitant. Consequently there are many Andiumbolos. This means that a village can be identified with each villager individually but also with all the villagers collectively. What implications!

If and how far an identification similar to that of house and village is tenable for village and region has occupied me a great deal. To illuminate this question adequately in terms of the Dogon, Dr Morgenthaler says, would lead us beyond the scope of this publication. I can, however, quote from what he wrote me on the subject.

'The five-day week of the Dogon is grouped vicariously around the market day of the individual village, the Sunday-market day falling on a different day in each village group. A travelling Dogon could thus, theoretically, experience every day of the week as Sunday-market day. For this is the day when people get together; the day people sense that all Dogon villages belong together. Then there is another thing: that the Dogon feels well and happy only when he is in Dogonland, in the region within which his village lies amongst the other villages. However, it is probably true that his village, within the region and country where it lies, also belongs to the 'entire world order' and that it can be replaced by means of corresponding experiences. He will thus not merely feel himself at home in his village among other villages, in the region and country to which it belongs, but will actually *be* there when he recounts a fable to a fellow Dogon in foreign territory. The difference between the Dogon and us is not that we are unable to remember similar representational images or to transmit them to others in order to feel at home in a foreign land; no, the difference lies somewhere else. With us such images are fantasies. We tend to look at them hoping that they will conjure up what we miss, whereas, by means of the process referred to above, the Dogon transmits what *is* and not what he misses, because, in fact, he misses nothing.'[16]

Thus the direct emotional affinity to house, village, or region – reciprocally identified – is so complete, reaches so deep psychically that, for the Dogon at least, it irrevocably includes the identification of all three with those who live there (a space is the appreciation of it – a building, that same building entered); this is why a house cannot be sold.

Is it, I ask, in terms of ourselves, still a prerogative that we must rely on place-affinity of a kind thus collectively rooted, in order to really know that when we say house or city we actually imply the people living there, i.e. ourselves; imply that *we* are that city or that house? I would not like to think so. Yet something else will have to persuade us – condition us again – to identify both house and city, in fact environment in general, with the people living there, and to act accordingly.

It is futile to continue freezing abstract notions into poor organized shape, calling this 'human environment' and then just go whistling for 'population'. Environment is for *people*. That is the least obvious thing I could possibly have said. If society has no comprehensible form, can it acquire a counterform which is human?

Beyond feeling lost outside one's own region (or estranged even within it) there should still be some reasonable alternative. A man at home wherever he happens to be carries his roots with him, is himself his own house, inhabits his own inner space – and his own time. He will also be able to inhabit, as it were simultaneously, all the places to which he is emotionally linked in memory and anticipation, but also through mental association.

However, this requires a frame of mind quite different from the one we have burdened ourselves with in our respective societies. It also requires another kind of environmental behaviour; in fact a different kind of environment altogether. The one will have to sustain the other – assuming that a habitable world is what we have in mind!

Impervious to the spirit of ecology, society at large behaves with insanity instead of grace, like a half-wit with two left hands. A far cry indeed from the way the Dogon tend the natural morphology of their environment.

'Everything functions, only man himself does not,' Arp once said. As it happens, our dealings with the landscapes of the world (and the mind) are such that, assessing the achievement of our civilization in terms of the effects – and there is every reason to do so – Arp is proved right. Disregard the delicate intricacies of the limitless microcosm; trespass into the limitless macrocosm and frighten the angels; mess up the Mississippi and the Mekong in between.

If that is what is desired, it can soon be fulfilled (there is a limit even to the limitless) and we shall get what we are looking for: mediocosm, limitless mediocosm. It will no longer be necessary to cross-identify all things from basket to universe in order to achieve some ground of certainty within appreciated mystery, for the identity of each thing and all things will have been levelled. Man falling in line with entropy at last.

Yes, and paradise will be just like mediocosm. Nothing will be different in any way, except toothpaste, which will be smoother and softer and more refreshing, so that those in paradise may know that they are no longer in mediocosm.

Hurry, switch on the stars before the fuses go.

Gogoli, and the market place in Ogol. 'The Dogon believes twins are the universal symbol of happiness and perfection. The principle of twinness, inherent in their highest ideas, is present in many everyday affairs. In the marketplace the buyer and seller are "twins", for the things they exchange "match" each other. The market is the most important meeting place. One goes there to drink beer, and over good beer to exchange words of friendship and understanding.'[17]

10

The Problem of Number

Introduction to chapter 10

District unit scheme forming the basic structure of Piet Blom's *Noah's Ark* project, 1962.

When Van Eyck formulated his configurative approach[1] he relied not only on his own design experience but also on projects by his former student Piet Blom, in particular 'Noah's Ark', a vast urban project that Blom did in 1962 for his finals at the Amsterdam Academy of Architecture. Covering an interurban extension between Amsterdam and Haarlem, it was conceived as an urban structure for a million inhabitants, articulated into seventy neighbourhood units. These units, each of which occupied sixty hectares, were based on a complex geometrical theme consisting of two superimposed motifs: a centripetal square and a centrifugal windmill pattern. This theme provided, as it were, the germ of an immense crystalline organism which developed over five levels of association, with the centripetal and centrifugal pattern appearing alternately as 'served' and 'serving' spaces.[2] The resulting urban structure displayed a particularly consistent fugal quality: a spatial fabric of interlocking clusters, large and small, part and whole, that were all based on the same geometrical theme; an urban fabric that provided spatially interlaced zones for almost every imaginable urban function, which, in addition to housing, also included offices, 'temples', theatres, clinics, and cultural and leisure facilities.

At the first larger meeting of Team 10 that took place in 1962 at the Royaumont Abbey near Paris, Van Eyck, who had not received any commissions since the Amsterdam Orphanage, was not able to present new projects of his own. He decided to expound his configurative view and to illustrate it with projects made by two of his former students: 'Under Milk Wood' by Hans Tupker[3] and 'Noah's Ark' by Piet Blom. Van Eyck's talk and the two projects, notably Blom's, elicited the most diverse, indeed extreme, reactions. The Team 10 members were astonished by Blom's systematic and complex geometrical fabric. Some expressed their admiration, others were critical, deeming it an all too literal visualisation of an idealistic thought pattern. The sharpest reaction came from the Smithsons, who found that Van Eyck had misled his students, had alienated them from the true foundations of modernism. Alison Smithson found that the complex interlacing would in practice amount to a pre-programming of all functions and activities, to a generalized control by everyone of everyone and thus to a loss of privacy. And, apparently irritated by the recurrent swastika-like motif in Blom's design, she disparaged it as 'completely dogmatic and German' and as 'completely fascist'.

Van Eyck was far from indifferent to this assault. He felt radically repudiated by those he had hitherto regarded as kindred spirits.

Their rejection shook his belief in the approach he had patiently developed for ten years. And when Blom learned about the allegation of his project being 'fascist', he was quite thrown off balance. As the rumour of the Smithson's verdict spread in Amsterdam, he felt pursued by it. Driven to despair, he ended up by destroying the whole 'Noah's Ark' project. This traumatic course of events caused a rift between Van Eyck and Blom. Blom went his own way. He did several more interesting configurative projects but eventually endeavoured to evade his configurative systematics in fantastic constructions such as the 'housing forest' in Helmond. Van Eyck gradually took a certain distance from configurative design. While remaining fundamentally convinced that it was the appropriate way to deal with the problem of number, he began to harbour doubts about the concrete forms this approach had produced up to then. When he broached the subject in lectures, at congresses in Auckland (1963) and Perth (1966), he voiced a growing scepticsm. When in 1968 he was invited to take part in the 14th Milan Triennale, which was entirely devoted to the problem of *'il grande numero'*, he did not present a project but expressed his pessimistic vision in a particularly grim installation. In the accompanying statement he noted that Western civilisation, contrary to most traditional cultures, proved to be unable to deal with the problem of number.

One year later, when invited to participate in the experimental PREVI housing project near Lima in Peru, Van Eyck did not design a configurative structure but developed a clustering of cells based on the way of building and living in the *Barriadas*, the self-built settlements which he acknowledged to be an authentic form of contemporary vernacular. In a note to his project ('Who are we building for and why?') he expressed the opinion that the development of the *Barriadas* should not to be thwarted by imported concepts. He felt that the Peruvian people clearly expressed their needs and aspirations in their settlements. He expounded his understanding of these aspirations and the way they were ignored by Western welfare consultants at a colloquium in Delft ('The Priority Jostle').

In the meantime the conflict over 'Noah's Ark' casted a dark shadow on the already strained relations between Van Eyck and the Smithsons. On several occasions he invited them to withdraw their allegation, but apparently they never realized the full consequences of their assault. As late as 1986 Van Eyck expressed his disappointment at this state of affairs in a short notice, published in the festschrift *Niet om het even*.

Aldo van Eyck discussing the problem of number in Auckland, New Zealand, 1963.

Piet Blom at work in his attic studio at Kuipersteeg, Amsterdam.

Differentiation and unity through rhythm

Extract from an article on the Nagele schools, published in 1960[1]

Differentiation and unity through rhythm and sub-rhythm – an old story a little forgotten. As I have said before, if we are to overcome the menace of quantity faced with the terrific problem of habitat for the greatest number, we shall have to extend our aesthetic sensibility: uncover the still hidden laws of what I have called Harmony in Motion – the aesthetics of number. Quantity cannot be humanized without sensitive articulation of number.

The relation between visual perception and duration approaches that between sound perception and duration in music as soon as numbers can no longer be articulated 'vertically' (e.g. $12 = 4 \times 3$ or 3×4) in the classic sense. Rhythm, sequence and theme variations must become part and parcel of architecture and planning. Quantity cannot be humanized without a sensitive articulation of number. The space between classrooms and entrances has become qualitatively more than the shortest distance between both, more than an economical no-man's land between imposed alternatives, i.e. movement and sound outside, rigidity and silence inside (oh horror!). Instead of this it has become an in between province, a true doorstep by way of which the exhilarating world outside penetrates the school physically (it is not enough to let glass do the job). This 'in between province' continues into the classrooms in the form of open cloakrooms. These, however, belong to the classrooms also since they have the same height as these and share the same rectangular ceiling.

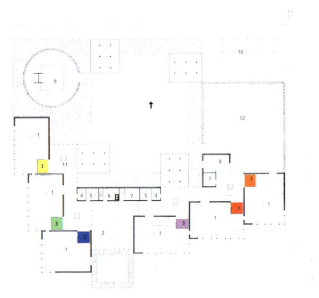

Aldo van Eyck, plan of Nagele School, 1955

On Blom's *Noah's Ark*

Translation of a manuscript, undated but obviously written in 1962[1]

Blom's plan is the result of an enviable fugal capability. Its basic figure is not simply a formal or mental motif in the abstract sense, but a germinal shape that has the rare potential to assimilate in the course of its growth – its fugal development – precisely those things which by nature it needs at each stage in order to enable the implementation of the next stage. The identity of each stage reveals itself likewise in the next stage, and does not exist without both the previous and the following stages. The specific identity of each stage always confirms not only the identity of the germinal shape but also always reveals itself in the subsequent stage.

The words 'stage', 'growth', 'development' and 'subsequent' are not used here primarily in their literal, temporal sense. The analogy with music does not altogether hold because the plan did actually not come about through the development of a basic motif in the course of time, but rather through the simultaneous projection of all the stages of its fugal development. (Music would only be a series of sounds if it were not able to free itself from the tyranny of a purely consecutive perception of the purely auditory. It is only its auditory sensory registration that is consecutive).

I say this because it is important to make it clear that the fugal basic motif, or its urban equivalent, the germinal shape of the urban structure to be developed, is none other than – could be no other than – the actually experienced you-me relationship – the experienced reality of the relation between individual and community. Since this is a twin-phenomenon – the identity of the individual only exists if the identity of the community exists, and vice versa – the stages of development can only be experienced simultaneously and can only actualize themselves simultaneously. Regarding the shape of a city, this means not only that the reality of the whole must 'be present' in each constituent part, while the identity of each constituent part must 'remain' present in the whole (giving the identity of the whole its specific dimension), but that it must also be so for all configurations and constituent parts (intermediate configurations) that simultaneously define the overall configuration and thereby determine the value of both constituent part and whole. So the city is the counterform – and thus in a certain sense identical to – the total human configuration, where individual and community are more than constituent part and whole, where they are rather each other's constituent parts. Form and counterform, and the shape of both, can only originate from each other. Since man is the form and it is he that makes the counterform, he will only be able to do this if he knows his own identity. The circle is extremely vicious because the identity of the community is just as elusive as that of the individual. The essence of the artist is that he always gropes for this elusive thing and in so doing comes closer to it. Blom has now succeeded in coming closer to the elusive. He has succeeded in uncovering something of this creative process of approaching. It is as if he has been given access to the great score from which it is so hard for all of us to draw the right sounds for composing a habitable city.

What is wrong with the architect and urban planner that makes him unable to do this, i.e., why does he remain, even now, an architect or an urban planner? – while in fact he simply isn't! To return to the music analogy (it's a matter of the difference in dimension between sound and music, between the successive hearing of sounds and the simultaneous experience of a composition), architects and urban planners appear to register successively. What they register at each moment is independent from what they have just heard and what they are just about to hear. What they heard is already made nonexistent by hearing, and therefore no longer has any significance. The planner knows only *that* he hears (and often badly – but that's a question of good or bad hearing!), but not *what* he hears, because this only exists by means of what he has heard and will hear. Of course he should not register things successively but experience and conceive them simultaneously. Only then would he know what he is hearing.

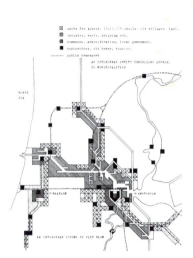

Photo and drawing (below right) by Cecile De Kegel

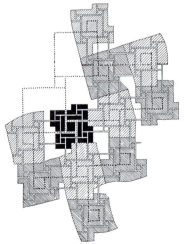

Discussion on the problem of number at the Royaumont Meeting, September 1962[1]

Proceedings summarized from the original transcript of the meeting's tape recordings[2]

I don't know if you have read or heard of this very simple image which I have put forward, the story of the house as a small city and the city as a large house. I want that to be the basis of all I think in terms of architecture. The large house-little city image provides scope for multi-meaning. It seems to me, moreover, that it creates a climate in which the four terms – house, city, small, large – released from the bondage of their definition, can encounter each other liberally. The image is, of course, ambiguous and consciously so. It would not have the necessary scope otherwise, nor would it be an image. I will confess here that the nature of its ambiguity is of a kind I should like to see transposed to architecture – built ambiguity – for it provides the kind of clarity that does not render invisible what is 'also' there – what is equally true – what is simultaneously present. It is above all the kind of ambiguity which pervades the in-between realm, for the in-between realm includes, never excludes. It is the home for twin phenomena; therefore a home where a man can tarry (a man who can do that is a relaxed man), where he can encounter himself without anguish and discover himself well-prepared to meet another man. The in-between realm is a frame of mind. The kind of architecture which ensues from it, represents it and transmits it. It transfers what it receives. It is therefore that I identify architecture with the in-between realm. I see no other human point of departure than this: to dedicate our creative ability to the imaginative articulation of the in-between realm by means of construction, to construct ambiguity. To my mind that is what architecture is – what environmental planning is in general. How to do this is not the subject of this talk; it eludes both definition and method. My subject is the frame of mind I personally identify with the in-between realm and hence with architecture.

Now, the large house – little city image is an in-between realm image. Through multilateral identification it persuades the limited connotation that has settled on the idea 'house' to open up. Reciprocally it opens up the conceptual limitations that weigh heavily on the idea 'city'. But it has more in store, for by identifying a human microcosm with a human macrocosm, it dethrones an array of absolutes, unmasks the fraudulent countenance of construed polarities.

My continual concern with relativity (the in-between realm is a kind of personal translation) should be attributed to the way it discloses the malignant artificiality of polarities enshrined as absolutes; also to the way it renders subjective and emotionally valuable, though not in weights and measures, what was hitherto abstract. Einstein, de Broglie, Planck, Bohr, Heisenberg and others have made it quite clear that, ultimately, we cannot measure what cannot be related to ourselves.

It is not my intention to suggest that there is no difference between house and city, between part and whole, simplicity and complexity, small and large, many and few, individual and collective etc., nor that the values which appertain to their difference are of arbitrary importance. There would be no meaning gained by their reciprocal identification if this were so, for it is fruitless to identify what is equivalent. I am concerned with ambivalence not with equivalence. No Hegelian implications should be searched for therefore, on the contrary, it should be understood that they are for once categorically absent. I am not concerned with the unity of opposites. I do, however, suggest that the time has arrived to adjust the mind to the essential sameness of house and city with regard to their human meaning, in order to come to terms with what really differentiates them with regard to each other.

The twin-image I am dealing with (house-city) has enough scope and is sufficiently ambiguous to rally the assaults of stratified logic aimed at it by compartmental minds. The sameness of house and city – of all the twin-aspects the image embraces – dwells in another dimension to that in which their alleged difference is miserably cloistered. Both are a bunch of places for human beings. As such, both constitute place, both are bunches of places for human beings. Does it take us any further to say that one is much larger than the other, has more places, more aspects, is a more complex bunch? I find it far more evocative to say: 'well, they are all for the same human beings, so if they are right – possess right-size and hence human size – they will be as simple and complex as the species they provide for, regardless of whether the bunch is small or large, whether there are many places to the small one or few to the large one and vice versa.' So their alleged differences have brought us nowhere. 'Styled' as they are by a faulty design mechanism and a false 'design' attitude, which, exploiting their alleged difference, fails to adjust itself to the fact that their essential sameness and essential difference result simultaneously, each from both the twin-aspects the twin phenomena part-whole, small-large, many-few, simplicity-complexity etc. embrace. I say 'each' because qualitatively a house is in each case as subject to either of the twin-aspects as a city is.

The term 'human scale' is fired back and forth whenever architects meet – it spices their discussions without gain or loss. It has even outlived the once cherished term 'organic' which is understandable! For this is but a sentimental makeshift. As soon as 'human scale' is defined it begins to mean what organic tries to mean and loses its meaning in groveling naturalism – the inevitable counterpart and ally of mechanical rationalism. Used to identify non-rectangular, non-geometric or non-angular architecture, the word 'organic' is particularly preposterous. It's a side-step.

Size and number mean nothing without reference, to that all will agree. But there is little agreement as to the nature of this reference, beyond that it should accord with the measure of man! Now this is what I mean. Something may be appreciated as too small because it is small in the wrong way or not small enough in the right way. There may be too few of them, which may again imply too small in the wrong way or too many which, once more, may imply too small in the wrong way. Similarly, something may be too large because it is large in the wrong way or not large enough in the right way, it may be too large because there are too few or too many of them in the wrong way – i.e. not enough in the right way.

Objects may elude right-size, which includes right-number, because they are the same in the wrong way or not different in the right way. The difference may be too small or too large, small and large in the wrong way (differences may be too few or too many – few or many in the wrong way). You can go on like that for ages, you see. I do that purposely until you simply do not know anymore what far and near, small and large, complexity and simplicity mean.

In order to demonstrate the idea of ascending dimension and degree of complexity from house to city as a natural sequence towards an integrated entity, the tree analogy is sometimes put forward.[3] The object of this analogy is, of course, to suggest the 'organic' relationship between the smallest part – via intermediary stages each with an increasing degree of complexity – and the whole. It furthermore attempts to show the inadequacy of a too analytical and mechanically additive approach. Now, while in principle I am not prone to relying on comparison with natural phenomena when dealing with human artefacts, because it tends to be misleading, I am altogether against analogies as such since they are not only misleading but false. The one in question is no exception and, had it not suggested an image to me, likewise based on the tree, I would not have mentioned it here. Needless to say an image is quite a different thing from a mere analogy. The tree image the tree analogy suggested, may, however, further assist understanding of the large house-little city image. As it is, the tree analogy, apart from the fact that it fails to transcend the limits of analogy as such, is a naturalistic rather than a 'natural' one. It confounds both biology and architecture, both the relation house-city and the essence of a tree. Had it also taken account of the fact that a tree grows from seed to maturity and is subject to birth and death; that new trees ensue from it; that it has systems from root to leaf and leaf to root by means of which it is able to live, that it is furthermore also subject to seasonal transformation, it may have provided an analogy not altogether arbitrary in that it could still have shed some light on the qualitative meaning of small-large, many-few, part-whole, simplicity-complexity, unity-diversity and change-constancy. But it did not. Yet, suffering the weakness of incompleteness which adheres to all analogies, I do not think it could have shed full light on the multi-meaning of the twin phenomena mentioned. Analogies compare directly instead of identifying indirectly through what one may call poetic association.

Now, as soon as one identifies what a tree represents visually with what it represents beyond that (i.e. its visual reality with its life reality), one arrives at an image capable of identifying what a city represents as a visual reality with what it represents beyond that – with the people that live there, i.e. its life reality. The tree image succeeds simultaneously in identifying what a house represents as a visual reality with what it represents beyond that – with the people that live there, which is its life reality also, as it is the life reality of a city.

The tree analogy fails altogether here, because it departs from the leaf (house) as a part and leads up to the entire tree (city). Direct analogy leads nowhere, neither to the idea tree nor to the idea city, neither to the idea leaf nor to the idea house. A tree can no more be conceived as a sequence of individually definable components gathered in ascending dimension and composite complexity to form an integrated whole than a city can. That is to say a tree conceived in terms of leaves, twigs, branches, limbs, trunk, entire tree is no more a tree than a city conceived in terms of houses, streets, quarters, centre, entire city is a city (in terms of elements, groups of elements, larger groups and a well-related total thing).

The dimensional and quantitative leaf-tree sequence is therefore as lifeless as its false analogy, the house-city sequence. The full reality of both leaf and tree, house and city transcends all the qualitative connotations such a mechanical approach to the real problem of ascending and descending dimension of number and degree of complexity may provide and lies far beyond the limited meaning of part-whole which the analogy expounds.

A tree is tree from leaf to root, across the seasons, from seed to lifeless trunk – upwards and downwards, inwards and outwards.
That is to say, tree is leaf and leaf is tree. City is house and house is city.
Take any 'part' and there is the 'whole'. Take the 'whole' and behold the 'part'.
Whole is part and part is whole, provided each is identified with what it needs in order to be house or tree, city or leaf – moisture, air, sap, people and people's activities, emotions and associations.
It is the multiple meaning within the image that matters in each case – the multiple meaning of the ambiguity within the image which is not there in the analogy.
By saying tree is tree and leaf is leaf, you say a tree is a tree because it is also a large leaf.
A leaf is a leaf because it is also a small tree. A city is a city because it is also a large house.
A house is a house because it is also a small city.
Say tree, leaf, large leaf, small tree. Say leaves or leaves on a tree. Say a few leaves still or many leaves soon, Say leafless tree.
You can say this tree when my child grows up and that tree when I was young.
You can say one tree, lots of trees, all sorts of trees, trees in the forest.
You can say forest, you can hear a lot: lost, dark, owl's hoot, toadstool, squirrel, tiger, timber.
You can say apple tree, apple orchard, apple pie. You can go on with that thing for ages.

Here is another thing. To proceed from the idea of dwelling in the sense of living in a house in order to arrive at the idea of living in the sense of living in the city, implies simultaneously that you proceed from the idea of living in the sense of dwelling in the city in order to arrive at the idea of dwelling in the sense of living in a house.

I have turned that another way. What is small without being large is neither small nor large and what is large without being small is neither small or large. Only what is large and small has the right size.

Now this project ('Noah's Ark' by Piet Blom): this is the first time I've seen someone so concerned with anxiety – not with the facts that go into making a city but with his anxiety about cities – and he's made a drawing out of it. The idea is that this is a diagram of a process of mind, it is not a city. It is a diagram of a process of mind by which he approached the phenomenon of a city of one million of people. He tried to arrive at something which is completely undetermined. You will not find a street, a house, a shop, a road or anything like that directly placed. He didn't even define the roads – they can be anywhere. It's conceived like a kaleidoscope, and you can't stop a kaleidoscope and say: 'now I have got you.' Still, you've got to try and have a catalyzer in order to get to terms with the way the kaleidoscope works. So he chose two images, he has taken two forms: a square and a star. These are just two forms that are absolutely juxtaposed in character, sort of embedded in the same shape. One is centripetal, the other centrifugal. (The two forms are both incomplete, they have both been amputated. Here you can seen the first step of indeterminacy in his method of thinking.) You can put these forms on top of each other, either the black one on the red one, or the red one on the black one. You see, he says now that, irrespective of multiplication, irrespective of whether we are concerned with house or city, we are only concerned with that which makes it necessary to live, irrespective of whether it is one person or a million. That is to say, you have the idea of living and you have the idea of the servicing of it: the means and the end. Now, means and end in confusion is a thing we see a lot. The whole story of major structure being the symbol of our time and the minor structure which is the intimacy of ourselves, being the minor, seems to me preposterous. But there is no hierarchy here, you see. One of these shapes – it doesn't matter which – represents that which serves and the other represents that which is served. We tend to make a schism between the living and that which serves the living. But he doesn't do that. You see, he has those two shapes, one black, one red, but when they are superimposed, they intersect and partly cover each other. They are not conflicting realities because there is a large region where they coincide. Now these two forms constitute the urban structure on every scale of the city. Now, apparently he starts the usual way: the city, the larger city district, the smaller quarter and the neighborhood. You can go up here until you get some polyurban city, and you can go down there until you get a house. But in fact this hierarchy is continually contradicted by being reversed at every level. He starts with the living at city scale, giving it the shape of a huge star. This star is superimposed on the huge square of the main road system. On the next level, the four housing districts are conceived in the form of squares, while the road system takes the form of the star. In this case the star is the one that does the servicing while the square is the housing. The places where they intersect are both. And on the following level, you see the opposite, the star with the servicing being a square.

You could ask: why haven't we got this drawing in yellow for the city, in blue for the next stage, and the next stage green, etc. It is just the point of this drawing to show that this is impossible. You see, you could put a magnifying glass on any part of this thing. And maybe this degree of complexity will be there or not. If you asked where the centre is, he'd say it doesn't matter because anywhere within this structure of served and serving, he makes as many drawings of the square served by the star, as of the star served by the square.

This drawing is about the fundamental question of means and ends. He refuses to juxtapose served and serving. He keeps on covering them with two fundamental forms: one that can embrace and one that can expand, in all stages of multiplication. He has no data to say why the centre should be here or there, or why there would be no small neighborhood here. It is absolutely undetermined where either of these degrees of complexity and size would take place. Now you ask where the streets are – and it's so obvious that he says: wherever they want to be. Because these are no plans, this is a region. In the plans he's going to do now, he will define the place of traffic and communication. It will be just where service and living intersect. On the scale of the village it may be a bicycle shop or the post office, at the higher level it may be a station. At a particular stage, the station becomes the service reality and at a very small scale it may be the telephone booth. It is absolutely undetermined.

If you took the biggest map you could buy of a city, the biggest scale they make – the biggest possible scale – perhaps 6 inches to the mile, 1:2500 – and you put it all together in a big map so it would be as big as a house and then you made a photograph of it – wouldn't it be that?

Discussion

Smithson: Yesterday you were knocking John Voelcker for using precisely the same technique on a minute scale. John chose an element.

Van Eyck: I wasn't knocking the element. I was telling him why it doesn't work.

Smithson: Now tell us why yours works.

Alexander: In your opinion it is not complicated enough to look at a tree as a grouping of small elements into large elements and those large elements into larger elements and so on. Now I don't understand why you think that is a bad way to look at a tree. But never mind about that. Why is this something else than such a grouping? You began by saying that this was going to be something slightly more complex.

Van Eyck: You're not quite right – because the configuration of the smaller part and the larger part is similar. There is quite a different reality in the tree, and the twig is so different from the trunk.

He succeeds in making a drawing which doesn't have a symbol. He doesn't assign a little symbol to the leaf, and another one to the twig, in order to add them into a tree structure – add them very cleverly, bringing the computers around to make it work. He doesn't do that.

Voelcker: I am with you on the distinction between the analogy and the unit. What I think here is that you have associated the unit, which I accept, with a change in situation, in spite of the fact that you are trying to relate the image to a thought process. By nature we have thought in terms of very extreme poles. They are not necessarily extreme, they are relative to our experience. The ideal method of thought is that they become identified – the house with the city. What we're concerned with – with the city and with the house – is reducing this polarity, letting it bounce off – then by extension of our experience, to the extent that we can reduce the polarity within our experience. You are trying to put an idealistic thought pattern into a built thing. It's an image of an image.

Van Eyck: The aspect of ascending dimensions. The leaves, twigs, branch, etc., till you get the whole tree. Increasing degree of complexity, increasing degree of size. That was the analogy I was talking about. I agree that he does make these steps of multiplication, and that they seem rigid. So he calls for red to green, from green to blue, from yellow to pink. But he hasn't specified whether this is a house or this is a neighborhood or this is a city. It ascends and it is always for the same people. All I can say is that I believe that his project is a translation of the tree-leaf or house-city image. I have to sit down at a table for about half a year and see whether I can identify that image more clearly for myself, with the ascending dimensions, the question of service and living, and all the questions which we discussed this morning. This is the first step to that end.

Smithson: Whether we think the tree business is a viable thing – the leaf and the big tree – what you are postulating is a sort of a mental technique to deal with something else. It doesn't illuminate the basic statement any more. It's just another demonstration.

Alexander: You know damn well that a tree is not a big leaf – that it is useless in that respect to bring the parallel image.

Van Eyck: I'm sorry for you. The poetic reality of what you do is discarded if you think a tree is not a leaf. You are trying to put a tree on a weighing scale and a leaf on a weighing scale in order to determine the difference. I know that a leaf is a leaf and a tree is a tree, too! As long as you can identify them you can understand their difference. ...

This man (Blom) who is also a poet and a painter, identifies with Amsterdam. He was born in the city, the son of a grocer, and has never left it. He sleeps under bridges and knows everything about the city. The only thing he doesn't know is just what it is. What he calls Amsterdam is this, the old centre. To the left you see Haarlem, and he knows as well as anybody does that Amsterdam and Haarlem are going to grow into one city very soon. The solid blocks in-between are the existing villages. He has taken a bicycle and gone all over this area to study all these existing agglomerations. After some calculations he discovered that they are all ten to fifteen thousand people. Not only that, back in Amsterdam he discovered that most of its quarters also consist of ten to fifteen thousand people. It led him to believe that this is a kind of optimal size for a community. And in this drawing he wanted to prove that the city is as large as its largest part, or that, in terms of human emotion, it can never be larger than its largest part. ...[4]

You see, this man is supremely naïve. He has the kind of supreme intelligence which naïve people have. Kahn has something of that. Somehow he has the idea of being able to conceive a whole world, in which he can tell you in his terms about everything, about drinking a cup of tea, about Botticelli, which Kahn loves doing. It's his (Blom's) dream of society. He has imagined for himself a form of society. He has his idea what the school teacher is, what the prostitute is, and where they should be. He's got all this thought out in his mind and now he's got that form. It may be not real but he has succeeded in simultaneously – not additively – composing all these feelings and emotions and quanta, all small and big sizes in that sense, into one thing that's both small and large, in the same way that you'd do when you build a house. When we design a house we all somehow find one image which catches the enormous complexity of the entirety – getting up in the morning, or hating somebody, or feeling warm or feeling cold, or liking to see a white wall, or wanting to go on the balcony, or cooking, or eating... Somehow you find a formula for it, an image. And if it's somehow there you say it's a nice house. But the moment it becomes a city you can no longer do it. I think it's exciting to acknowledge in a plan like this (of course, it is rigid, a rigid configuration of his dream) if he managed to grasp the complexity of the city simultaneously, just like when we make a house.

Wewerka: May I say something? When I saw that first I felt my heart knocking, you know. I feel excited that it's something... I mean the whole thing, it's a town, it's one thing. In Paris you have the big underground, which is one big system with entrances and exits, and it functions. And there are the quay buildings on the river Seine which are endlessly long and have a very special structure. And there is a funny point, because sometimes the underground structure and the quay structure meet. Maybe the question is stupid, but do you think that the framework we are looking for – which in theory is very clear, and I never saw such a rich approach – do you think that before someone started to put two pieces of wood together there was a formal aspect? Do you think that? How is it possible to make something like that in a town where people live. I don't believe it. I don't know why.

Christopher Dean: This particular pattern seems to be common to all these students and perhaps others too. In Holland geometrical patterns seem to predominate. I am wondering why.

Van Eyck: Why don't you look in a geometry book? Architecture is never anything but geometry, even if you come to a form like Ronchamp. It's still geometry.

Colin St John Wilson: But there is a difference between the geometry of this (Blom's project) and the geometry of that (Pueblo Bonito in New Mexico, also shown by Van Eyck) which has a differentiated quality. It can change. In the project all small things are conditioned by one form, aren't they? And I should imagine he has chosen this geometry because it is an unconditioned one.

Van Eyck: Blom has a whole story about the purposeful incompleteness of his project. There are a few lines written here:
'A place for rest in a restless city, not a rest house in a restful region. An oasis within the metropolis. There was a tension and the direct menace of existence in experience, having been cut off from the earth and its sources that offer such subsistence in a widest sense.
We desire a safe place, however, to comprehend and live with the danger.
We must express ourselves citizen-like about the security and danger of which we are an inexplicable part.'

So you see, we must express ourselves within city life, find ourselves, realize ourselves in terms of security and the danger of which we are an inexplicable part. Therefore, no illusory living space! – Damn you, architects. Damn you, urbanists. Damn myself. Because the illusory living space does not exist anyway. Space must be conquered. Our world includes both order and a new kind of chaos. That chaos is our living space. It is the desert of freedom, the desert of danger in which we first confront ourselves. Personal spaces ensue in that desert which is the twin-sister of order, created by that order. So the only objective of order in our time is to create that form of chaos in which we find place. This is the wonderful new desert where men and women find new living space – space to be. And thanks to this desert, life in natural environments and garden cities has lost all meaning.

Bakema: (commenting on another project by Blom, the Pestallozzi Village he entered for the Prix de Rome competition of 1962) Thinking about how in a room two beds could be placed together, he came to a pattern for a house, and from that he came to a pattern of four houses together, and so on.. And the result was that the place with the bed was not only felt as your own environment but simultaneously a moment where you could feel that there was a total complex where the other moments were. That was the reason I thought this is a man who has the capacity to see a certain number in a way that the number in itself is something, but while being the smallest part of this number, you can feel the total number. You can feel the total thing because it is in the smallest part. This man has the capacity to accept great number, and simultaneously, to enable those who constitute great number to get out of their anonymity.

At a certain moment we found each other in our concern for identity. We realized that the extensions of large cities and the new towns were done in a way that a simple man was no longer able to identify himself in the totalness of the big town. By splitting the whole thing in functions we lost the feeling that the totalness is made by the identity of the whole being based on the identity of the smallest element. So I have the feeling that one of the reasons for our protest was that the reason of architecture was lost. And the reason of architecture for me is very simple: that we make shelter for people that we have to protect against something. But simultaneously – and that is the thing – we must identify man in terms of space from which a piece is taken to be a shelter.

Now I will speak about my doubts about this plan. After overcoming the splitting of the functions we have reached a stage where we see again the total thing. And the reason why we like to interrelate buildings is that we want to create an environment that man can identify with in totalness. The point is, if I'm living somewhere here (pointing to a particular spot in the plan), can I still identify myself in totalness? That is really my doubt about what he is doing here.

Van Eyck: Let us be honest about it. The simultaneous or aerial view of the total complexity of this thing is like the aerial view of any city. And you must not think that he has specified everything. He has specified quality. This thing is 'the Mother of the City'. You also must not forget that Blom devised many different types of houses within this one system. Every man has his external living space of a large size. On the second street level, the sun penetrates into these balconies, and there can be a relationship between somebody standing on this balcony and somebody walking in that street. He has made a kind of archetypal house, a kind of shell in which different partitions can be made. So there is a lot of variability in this type. That's all we can do. We can find a building which has all these things we like so much: people entering the balcony, talking to somebody from the balcony, talking to somebody down in the street; the way the children are given access to their playspaces.

Bakema: I mean it this way. Each house has, let us say, very good conditions and you can play on the balcony and you have contact with the street where people go, etc. The point for me is the total statement he made. Everybody will have these very good conditions but as to the way in which these conditions are interrelated, it is not so easy to find out what he means. The way in which these conditions are interrelated, is that an event, which in itself is an identifying thing?

Van Eyck: There are different spheres of intensity. You just walk and suddenly the atmosphere is different. There are people shopping and there are all kinds of activities. And when the same street enters into this other thing, the sphere of urbanity changes again.

Alison Smithson: Listen Aldo, does any of that matter? What worries me is that it all goes north, east, south, west, and just keeps repeating.

Peter Smithson: I think it's the exact opposite of what we are looking for. We're looking for systems which allow things to develop as they need to develop without compromising each other. Here you have a system which takes absolutely literally the concept that the city is a big house; but the city is not a big house. It's impossible to deal with the functions in a house in the same terms as you have to deal with the functions in a city. It is a completely false analogy, a false image. I think you have misled this boy. I really do. I think you have abrogated your responsibility to define what you mean by a city as a big house.

Van Eyck: This project is not the only possible interpretation of that image, maybe it is not my interpretation of it. The image of identifying the house with the small city and the city with the large house is an image of which I have given no interpretation myself, except in the orphanage and the Jerusalem project.

Bakema: My first feelings about this project were that many things are happening here. Then comes the second thing: will I have the right to be there alone or together in the way I should like. When I look at it, I have the feeling that this multiplicity is a wonderful thing, but suddenly there comes a doubt and I think: 'Hey, that's well organized for me: where I have to be alone and where I have to be together. And that's why Alison mentioned the Gestapo,[5] of course, not thinking about the police but about the spirit in which it is ordered for you.

Van Eyck: If there are a million people in the city, in your terms, that would mean that there are a million cities, not one. There are as many cities as there are people that live in it. How are you going to do that?

Alison Smithson: Maybe that's we are after.

Van Eyck: Still, in the end you either have an amorphous thing or you risk it.

Peter Smithson: I'll risk it. We have to clarify. Therefore we will take perfectly ruthless segregations as one of the tools. Certain people, notably Le Corbusier, were able to take these tools and extract a certain poetry, particularly because they were dealing with fragments. Now if you take what the other people did, Ernst May or Van Eesteren e.g., they took these tools and applied them with the ruthlessness of mechanism, you might say. Today we say these tools are inadequate because they don't give us the freedom for things to develop together so they become something. Nor do they give the freedom that a thing can change and still have a structure – a structure you can't imagine now because it's in time – a structuring device which can develop into a structure and yet the parts have their own validity. But I really think that this scheme is back into a Ledoux situation where the thing has got no visibility except a geometrical one.

Wewerka: Aldo, this is a fantastic thing, a fantastic world, an atmosphere, but…

Alison Smithson: Aldo, explain why you brought this ruddy scheme. Why should we struggle with this guy's brain?

Van Eyck: Alison, who do you think you're talking to? You're not talking to Lovett. Always talk in the right dimension. Talk in the dimension of the thing you have in front of you. Otherwise you cannot talk.

Alison Smithson: This is completely dogmatic and German – completely fascist. Explain why you brought it.

Guedes: Isn't it terribly important that Blom has called this thing 'the Ark of Noah'? That he feels for him there is some salvation in it?

Peter Smithson: Can you say that you support him for another reason than to make us angry?

Van Eyck: It's frightfully simple. I brought it because I thought you would enjoy it and find it interesting, negatively or positively you would sort of get outside it, or red hot or angry but whatever happened, it would induce discussion.

Colin St John Wilson: I enjoyed it. Aldo, did you bring this kaleidoscope as a means of action? It isn't a plan, is it? It's a sort of image about a lot of things.

Van Eyck: Let me say it this way. Let us take a painter, Miró. The moment Miró paints and does his life's work, everything in reality changes. That is not to say that Miró himself bewitches reality, but he changes it by having existed as an artist – he has changed the reality of everything. Since Miró, a moon is a different thing. It is always like that with art. As to the question of rigidity, let's say we may suddenly understand fascism, it doesn't matter, it's up to you. That is the freedom. I think this thing is in that sense a work of art. It's not a question of quality. It's an absolute, immediate confrontation of somebody with himself in terms of his environment, and the expression of that could have been a poem. In this case, he turned himself into an architect. And the reactions you all have to it justify his making it in terms of the absolute confusion in which we are – confusion, not chaos. I'm a bit disappointed, honestly, that what to me is a configuration of liberty, which I find in its kaleidoscopic quality, you people seem to see as a geometric pattern. I very much enjoy his concept of liberty and I find it extremely inspiring that there is somebody who in his heart is so free – free because he's so disciplined – that his form of freedom should be labeled fascism. That is for me exceptionally important. It justifies the whole reason for my bringing it here. And not only that. If you look at the geometry, it's just like the alphabet and the words in a dictionary. The 24 letters and the words are in the dictionary but poetry is something beyond the dictionary. You have regarded every poem as nothing else but a compound of letters and words – but you have just missed the poem. If you can't get the multi-meaning out of the structure of the words and their associations, it is just a blank.

Woods: Aldo, do you honestly think that is poetry in the sense that it illuminates our life in some way today? Do you really think that this is poetry?

Van Eyck: Uh huh.

Woods: Then there is no point in talking about this any more. We are talking about different poetry.

Voelcker: This is an interesting form in that it is concerned with methodology, with a method which, in point of fact, we have discussed. It's a question of mathematical addition and geometrical addition.

Some extracts from the final discussion

Alison Smithson: Could we start off tonight – which is a sort of summing up – by asking Coderch to say, in English, what he said to Candilis, because I didn't quite understand it.

Coderch: I found his plan (Toulouse-le-Mirail) to be impossible. It's like trying to make a baby in two weeks. To plan one house takes me more than six months. I don't understand how he, on his own, could be able to make all those houses.

Bakema: I don't know very much about Spain, but I think there are many people who need other houses.

Coderch: The thing I can say is that in Spain the houses are built historically. I don't know why. As I can't understand how to do it, that's why I asked Candilis.

Alison Smithson: Why I asked you to say it again is that it seemed to bring a criticism very appropriate at the moment, the question of moral responsibility – the position that Team 10 has always taken – for what to build. On this point, I would like to take up again that business of this scheme that Van Eyck brought to this meeting; because I think this scheme could have happened if Le Corbusier had never been, and only if Van Doesburg or Van der Leck or somebody had been. Van Eyck, we know, has always been the strongest critic of CIAM, yet we build absolutely on the foundation that Le Corbusier and CIAM laid for us and I feel it is a terrible thing that Van Eyck hasn't made this boy see what we all believe in Team 10. He said he asked the boy if he would like to build it. 'Yes' said the boy, he would build it just like that, Van Eyck told us without comment. Now he must make this boy understand about Le Corbusier, about CIAM, about the struggle that we are all involved in: in order to make himself, to make up his mind. This boy might think he is justified in building it if someone asked him, because so much work has gone into it. But ultimately people have to live in it.

Colin St John Wilson: I see the thing Aldo showed as a projection of a certain kind from which one could derive certain constructive aspects, or not. And it is very difficult to reject it in this way. I didn't see it as a plan but as an image of simultaneous thinking which obviously has some constructive faces to it.

Van Eyck: I said that he would build such a thing in such dimensions as he was asked to build, which is not much at all.

Coderch: I think a great many people have been working with great care. I think that there is something dangerous in it – that the young people believe that this is the way, that this is the normal way. They are wrong, I think.

Wewerka: Stop talking about it! I don't understand you! It's a question of dimension, you know, scale. What are you talking about? There are some fantastic points in it. I mean, at any rate it is worth more than there ever was in Holland, you know.

Van Eyck: It's a very important country. We have five buildings there that are much better than everywhere else.

(The discussion goes on to deal with the question raised by Coderch: the capacity of the architect to grasp large number, and his moral responsibility in accepting that kind of commission.)

Van Eyck: I have to assume that Kavafis talks about the great yes and the great no. There is also the man that didn't enter the fight, and the man that did. Now of course, the man that didn't, that is the swine; and the man that did is a very nice chap, for the same reason – but he had a different reason. And there is the chap that entered the fight and he is absolutely right and moral – and the chap who entered the fight and who wasn't. That is to say that the two categories won't help you yet. The fact that you say: 'there is society and there is ZUP,[6] so I enter ZUP' hasn't made you either moral or immoral yet. Nor has it damaged you. It doesn't save you yet. I have a question of how much you really believe you can do well, I think that is the limit. The kind of chap I am, I am not the sort of capable of doing this sort of ZUP junk. Sometimes I am a bit jealous of the people who can and do make a good job of it. I just can't. I attack this sort of junk myself and say no. There is a kind of limit and I know – as Coderch very likely knows – that it is relative, but the question is that each person should know whether he is passing that limit. The question for you would be whether you in your heart know that you are doing more than you can do well. That is interesting from one person to another. It's allowed to be over-ambitious, but then you can't talk about high morals. You can talk about a very similar thing which is over-ambitious – it's allowed. I think you can take your hats off to someone who is over-ambitious, but you can't talk about the great yes and the great no. The great yes and the great no is about knowing exactly what is your limit, what is your maximum and not more. It's like getting on a horse, as a child, which is too tall for me. I don't say that you are getting on a horse too high for you, I'm just asking if you think you are. That's what Coderch is asking you. I am asking you, actually, too.

Candilis: Why am I here, with all of you? What am I doing here? Precisely to hear what you have just said. Otherwise I would be somewhere else, do you see? And to me it's all the same whether you build or not.

Candilis, Van Eyck and Wewerka at the Royaumont meeting, September 1962

Letter to the Smithsons after the Royaumont meeting

Handwritten letter by Aldo van Eyck in the Smithson archives at the NAi in Rotterdam, undated but obviously written shortly after 16 September 1962

Well, that was a meeting crowded with contradictions, side issues, evasions, misunderstandings, misinterpretations, construed obstacles and pragmatic banalities alias sentimentalities etc., etc., in my opinion the old anti-architecture lead showing its head round the corner again. Surely we are not going to funk it and mask the funking by means of the teamwork-anti-primadonna-social functionalist groove this time, but by means of the mobility-freedom of choice one (the twin groove indeed, there for the same escape tram !!) That's how I feel.

I am concerned with the configurative process and the way the mind must work so as to be able to make the entire kaleidoscope of factors coincide. In order to do this the factors simply must be defined – fixed, whether you like it or not, right or wrong. Not until we can do so can we cope with the indeterminable with precision. That is why the plans I brought are very valuable. It's no use mistaking the picture

Team 10 meeting at Royaumont Abbey, September 1962; participants taking a breath of fresh air during a break Photo George Kasabov

impact for the content. That is what you did, I think. The plans I showed were made to clarify the very things you attacked like twin Quixotes! (The mill wasn't even there, so you didn't even break your spears, nor the mill!) The victory was yours all through but nothing was defeated. I see little sense in licking your own tail. However, I think more can be gleaned next time, now that that twin groove had guided us right into CIAM's tomb (they seem to have left place for Team 10!). You mad old empire people have 'islanded' yourselves in yet another empirical island floating in two oceans, the one – the past – rendered closed and obsolete and the other – the future – rendered indeterminable and hence impenetrable (i.e. also closed). I have a different time concept which for me renders both oceans transparent and therefore makes of both a single ocean in terms of the temporal span of the present. What you call open I call static, closed – time exteriorized (the next consecutive instant is always as dense as lead).

Don't be, warriors, be pragmatic at the wrong level. Don't run along the twin circumscribed groove like an obsolete toy tram in an avant-garde playroom floor. Don't fight the wrong foe, i.e. your allies. Open the window – keep the one you yourselves opened open – else Team 10 will get stuck in the mire of mobility and that would be a paradoxical way of getting stuck. (CIAM got stuck in a similar kind of way, grounded its own gears down running round in circles). Open the concept of time, i.e. interiorize the mind. Transmutation potential is never possible through what you conceive unless the transformation is there in what you enforce.

If a thing is only viable continually in that his has no form, it is never viable. Things can only change within a fixed form. The time comes that it is no longer viable. Then a new thing is made. The changing may be continuous but the form changes in jumps at intervals – long intervals if the thing is good, has scope for multi-meaning. The future slumbers in the now-form chosen. There is no other way. It's no good shirking the now-form by turning the form later on onto a spook (labelled freedom sentimentally). What you get is static because it is amorphous.

Answer by Peter Smithson
Handwritten letter dated 21 September 1962, Van Eyck Archives

The only thing I can grasp at is that 'the future slumbers in the now-form created'.
I'm no one not to choose and not to believe in what I've chosen. Similarly I cannot believe in something we cannot accept – even though common sense tells me you are always right!! (Better not let Hannie see this!!) In another year we will all know, maybe all changed our minds. This would be hopeful… but we must not change merely to accommodate each other, or we become of no value to each other, & only of value (maybe) to Erskine – the prophet of reasonable action. (He too is usually right, at another level, damn him!)
A confused meeting, but my mind is being working overtime ever since.
Your letter was very clear & very welcome.

How to humanize vast plurality?

Extracts from a talk at the Pacific Congress, University of Auckland, New Zealand, September 1963[1]

We are not concerned any longer with limited plurality but with vast plurality and this is the enigma. This is where we stand with two left hands. We don't know how to humanize plurality, how to humanize number. We know nothing of the aesthetics of number yet. How are people to participate in fashioning their own immediate surroundings within a conceived overall framework? When one says 'city' one implies the 'people' in it, not just 'population'.

Can the architect-urbanist possibly supplement the lack of a comprehensible social pattern; the lack of a collective concept or vernacular; the lack of direct creative participation on the part of the multitudes? Can he do, in short, what he was never asked to do before, but is now left to do?

Should he participate in society's behaviour to the extent that he answers its demands regardless of the nature of the demand? Will what he offers then be a contribution that has value beyond the incidental? Should he ask for more than the banality of actuality?

Should the architect-urbanist say to society: to hell with you or should he say: try my heaven first? Is he justified either way? I really don't know.

Leaving 'home' and going 'home' are difficult matters both ways. Both house and city, therefore, should impart a feeling of going (coming) home whichever way you go. To go in or out, to enter, leave or stay are often harassing alternatives. Though architecture cannot do away with this truth, it can still counteract it by appeasing instead of aggravating its effects. It is human to tarry. Architecture should, I think, take more account of this. The job of the planner is to provide built homecoming for all, to sustain a feeling of belonging.

I would go so far as to say that architecture is built homecoming.

Tree and leaf

Statement written in 1961 and edited as a diagram in 1965[1]

tree is leaf and leaf is tree – house is city and city is house – a tree is a tree but it is also a huge leaf – a leaf is a leaf, but it is also a tiny tree – a city is not a city unless it is also a huge house – a house is a house only if it is also a tiny city

say leaf – say tree – say a few leaves still and many leaves soon – say leafless tree – say heap of leaves – say this tree when I grow up and that tree when I was a child – say one tree, lots of trees, all sorts of trees, trees in the forest – say forest (hear: dark, lost, nest, fire, fairy, owl's hoot, toadstool, tiger, timber) – say orchard, apples, apple pie – say fig tree – say fig leaf – say NUTS! – say house – say city – say anything – but say PEOPLE!

'What we are after is a new and as yet unknown configurative discipline'

Extracts from a talk given at the Australian Architecture Student Association Convention, Perth, May 1966[1]

What I want to show you is the contemporaneousness of all things, the human validity of all solutions, man's effort in all time, projected and telescoped into the present. When I talk about the past, about societies other than our own, we can get to know ourselves, you can meet yourself in other people. To come face to face with the phenomena of human beings is what the study of architecture should really do – give you a sense of values, a sense of what people really are and how they behave, bring you face to face with yourself and your fellow man.

Man has been going at this question of acclimatising and accommodating himself to his environment for so long, and that body of experience is there – to make you feel enthusiastic. I think you should be introduced to the whole phenomenon of the relationship between human beings and the natural surroundings, and the way they nestle into those surroundings and make their environment, in all forms from house to village and city forms – right from the first year. You see fantastic photographs – an aerial view of Peking or Amsterdam, or Adelaide, with their clear form, their different forms of streets and squares, and people – the way they move – and houses – the way they are grouped – terribly exciting. You will say: 'I am an architect' before you are.

I think it was a marvellous suggestion that the student should design a place for himself. Everybody knows what a house is, so there is no extra knowledge needed. The student can extend his experience and go ahead, no analysis necessary except that of his own past and his own desires. It is a very human approach because it is a total thing. But, can you excite a student beyond that sufficiently? I think it is necessary to raise matters with which the individual dwelling inevitably ties up: the other dwellings, work and traffic. And I wonder whether you should wait until you are actually able to conceive of a total urban complex. I think it is better to start earlier, in the very first year. I would not suggest to begin with a large site of a high degree of complexity, but with a quite different approach, a discipline where the one grows out of the other, and is contained in it.

I remember at a CIAM congress all the architects were discussing vast space, emptiness, and in this vast emptiness they discussed how to arrange different elements with a kind of fluent void in between. That was called the continuity of space. I call it blowing away. This continuity of space was what they wanted. They thought it represented some kind of open society. I think this whole concept of urbanism is obsolete. Our country is becoming almost uninhabitable as a result of urbanism being considered as one thing and architecture as another. Architecture and town planning should be a single discipline.

Our schools have taught us to make a house into a good house, a street into a good street, an office building into a good office building, and then try to reorganise all these loose items into something that would become a unity. We have discovered that this is impossible, that we have to redefine these things. We have to see if we cannot conceive of an item, say a house, in such a way that it has an identity, an identity in terms of human meaning, and that when we multiply it, we do not end up with something that has less identity, but more. Not only more but also different, because several things are different from one thing. Several people are different from one person and many people are quite different from a few people – and from a vast number of people. Whatever a vast number of people means, we don't know. That is a horrific difficulty. We know it numerically, we know it quantitatively, but we don't know it qualitatively. The moment we are confronted with enormous quantity, we just stand with two left hands.

So, we have to see if we cannot conceive of a house with such a meaningful potential in its form that when we multiply it we get a structure that coincides with what is necessary for a larger group, and that also incorporates within it almost automatically those functions which a larger group of people would need. That is to say, you could think of an element that, when multiplied, would generate the necessary common space for the amount of people there. When you deal with a quantity of houses that need e.g. a school, the process of multiplication would produce a place or a form which would itself suggest: 'I can be a school'.

What we are after is a new and as yet unknown configurative discipline. It's hard to talk about it because nobody in the twentieth century has made it his. The discipline is still not ours – the art of humanizing vast number hasn't advanced beyond the first vague preliminaries. We know nothing about vast multiplicity – we cannot come to grips with it – not as architects, nor as planners or anybody else. And there's the challenge. No discipline available to us can solve the social form problem vast number poses. We have lost touch with classical harmony and we have not yet got in touch with harmony in motion or the aesthetics of number.[2]

I tell you, I'm no good at teaching you the aesthetics of number because it is unknown. The only way to teach yourself is to be stimulated to do so by those who know that this problem does exist. The best contributions towards revealing the first mysteries of harmony in motion, with which alone we can harmonise vast numbers, have been made by students. I know about it, I talk about it, I read about it, but it isn't sort of under my skin as with the younger generation. The quantitative explosion is a phenomenon of our time that specifically happened in their world, and it is quite obvious they are the people that will be able to find the key, the new configurative discipline.

When a pressman asked me what I thought of the new high-rise housing blocks by the water in Perth, I replied: 'I don't think they behave very nicely in relation to the little red houses, and I don't think all the little red houses behave nicely to the high blocks.' The problem is these are childish categories. You are not going to solve the problems of the future with little red houses and a few high-rise blocks. It's not a question of either or, it is a question of a far richer sequence and scope for the mingling of functions – known and unknown – so that all sizes, quantities and meanings can be familiarized. You can't just add an absolute type of house to another absolute type of street and, after adding a lot more absolute items, call this a city and expect a nice reply.[3]

On Christopher Alexander's *A City is not a Tree*

Statement published in the hardback edition of Team 10 Primer, 1968[1]

I brought forward the leaf-tree, house-city identification at the Team 10 Royaumont meeting in 1962. Christopher Alexander[2] was present at the meeting as a guest and joined the discussion. His subsequently published thesis that a city is not a tree but a semi-lattice is in my opinion neither a valid negation nor a valid affirmation of the truth in mathematical terms.

I tried to replace the current false 'organic' city-tree analogy, because it is based on the sentimental, though well-meant, assumption that, ideally, the man-made city should behave, and hence also be 'planned', according to the same kind of system of ascending dimension and ascending degree of complexity (with a similar one-track reference sequence from small to large – many to few – and part to whole) as the tree's, oversimplified.

The analogy is false the way all such analogies are false – and unpoetic – because it overlooks the real meaning of both city and tree. I replaced it, therefore, by two separate, autonomous though intersuggestive, identifications: leaf is tree – tree is leaf, and house is city – city is house.

By their inclusive ambiguity they preclude that a city is a semi-lattice. Also that a city is chaotic and necessarily so (when we say city, we imply people). Cities, moreover, as Shakespeare said of man, are 'of such stuff as dreams are made on'. The dream, of course, implies infinite cross-reference.

And so does the city. Both are as man is! This is why cities neither should nor can ever reflect the kind of order a tree wrongly suggests. Wrongly, because a tree is not a tree without its inhabitants.

They – the birds, beasts, and insects – see to it that a tree is also a semi-lattice! Still, a city is no more a tree than it is not a tree. That goes without saying, hence also without mathematics.

The enigma of vast multiplicity

Article published in Harvard Educational Review, fall 1969[1]

> *Qu'il nous est difficile*
> *De trouver un abri*
> *Même dans notre cœur*
> *Toute la place est prise*
> *Et toute la chaleur.*
> Jules Supervielle[2]

Man's scope lies within unbelievable extremes. The same is true of his tools. Handmaid or Master, technology assists his doings at every level of intention; constructively or destructively – a kind and a malicious companion both.

The evidence can be read off the face of the globe, for environment reveals whatever occurs there.

We know all this. But do we know – or are we prepared to acknowledge – that, whilst in the past societies responded more or less successfully to the problems limited number posed, ours, today, are no longer able to. Let alone able to respond to the problems – call them perplexities – vast multiplicity poses.

Faced with these, society at large – the magnanimous kind to which we in these parts of the world belong – has little worth showing, beyond the incidental, which bears on them favourably.

Whatever gain is made is soon counteracted by another gain, **FOR OURS IS A SOCIETY OF WASTED GAIN.**

It is also one of bewildering technological ability. That is its familiar hallmark.

But it is another hallmark – a less familiar one – which is the subject of this small presentation: Our pitiful inability to come to terms with greater number and behave with sanity towards environment – that great place where each person and all people must live.

Why parade a lie, why fool ourselves? There is little we can think of that brings us closer to the riddle of greater number.

Society – our kind – deals with greater number and the environmental problems it poses like a halfwit with two left hands. Measured by its behaviour towards the landscapes of the world (and the inner landscape of the mind) and the way it chooses to accommodate itself in them, we cannot escape the charge that it is of the lowest order.

No previous society made quite so little of the knowledge and technology available, or fell so far short of what imaginative concerted action could bring about.

As of old, there are imaginative and constructive efforts made by individuals from which the greater number could benefit. But minimal use is made of them. In fact a blind eye and a deaf ear is turned to what is done on the periphery, towards what is occasionally smuggled in like contraband and then misused by others; twisted into a negative and then turned against what it could affect.

This presentation is a statement of fact. Unavoidably, it is also an indictment. But the truth need not exclude hope.

NOWHERE
Part of New Town Anywhere

Photo Johan van der Keuk[en]

So little from muc[h]

What are authorities, speculators, architects and planners doing everywhere? With expert thoroughness they are busy organizing the meagre. The result is mile upon mile of organized nowhere. With everything too far and to near; too large and too small; too few and too many; too similar and too different.
With everything far, near, large, small, few, many, similar, and different in the wrong – inhuman – way. Wrong in the wrong way, for things can be wrong in the right – nice – way; the way they can be right in the wrong – nasty – way.

THE SLUM HAS GONE – IN SOME PRIVILEGED PARTS OF THE WORLD IT HAS – NOW BEHOLD THE SLUM EDGING INTO THE SPIRIT.

But, in most parts of the world the slum...

much from so little.

SOMEWHERE
Squatters in Hong Kong

Photo Ed van der Elsken

has *not* gone. There, on the periphery of established society, with no economical and no technological means; no rights and no prospects, vast multitudes have built their own habitat.

These two images tell us that the positive and the negative are present in both, though reversed and antipodal.

Squatters' Settlement in Hong Kong Photo Ed van der Elsken

On the one hand, enormous possibilities, but no scope for individual contribution. On the other, negligible possibilities, but enormous scope for spontaneous effort.
The one, hard, rigid, monotonous and impersonal – a scene for inflated life in spite or because of affluence, security and considerable rights. The others flexible, differentiated and reflecting intense personal participation in spite or because of poverty, insecurity and lack of rights.

Taking advantage of a little or taking no advantage of a lot is apparently no paradox – in human terms.

Dogon Village, Mali, Africa Photo Aldo van Eyck

Always and everywhere, whether in Fiji, Greenland, Africa or Italy, people dealt with limited number both accurately and gracefully, extending collective behaviour into adequate and often beautiful built form. Taking from environment as much as they gave, a gratifying balance was sustained.

This we are no longer able to do; not in the same way, nor in any other way.

Aerial photograph of Mekong Delta and aircraft spreading poison

DISTURB THE DELICATE INTRICACIES OF THE LIMITLESS MICROCOSM. TRESPASS INTO THE LIMITLESS MACROCOSM AND FRIGHTEN THE ANGELS. IN BETWEEN, MESS UP THE MISSISSIPPI AND THE MEKONG. IF THIS IS WHAT WE DESIRE IT WILL SOON BE HERE: LIMITLESS MEDIOCOSM. FOR THERE IS A LIMIT EVEN TO THE LIMITLESS. MAN FALLING IN LINE WITH ENTROPY AFTER ALL.

We have already turned the theory of relativity and quantum physics against ourselves. We now split atoms. SOON IT WILL BE STARS. We even have anthropologists and sociologists – of all people – trained especially in great universities so they can spread over the globe and, smiling their way into the quarters of the poorest, gather information for the ministries at home: to be used against those multitudes WHEN THE TIME IS UP AND THEIR TIME FOR ACTION HAS COME.

So beware of them also; the anthropologist, sociologist and their like; beware of their smiles and wiles. They are not all angels.

Ben Tre, Vietnam

mourn

for all th

Ben Tre, Vietnam

also
butterflies

Remember that tanker holding the largest quantity of oil in a single hull and the way it broke in two.

> Never mind the millions enjoying those two coasts on a fine summer's day.
> Never mind the birds.

And that coal hill towering over a little school at its foot.

> Never mind those children.

And those thousands of square miles of other people's jungle chemically defoliated; their rice fields ruined and their soil poisoned.

> Never mind what or who lives in and between those trees.
> Never mind those who live off that soil.

And, lest I forget, Ben Tre. The city '…we had to destroy in order to save it.'

> Never mind the streets, shops, schools, houses and all the small intimate things.
> Oh yes, and never mind the dead.

Remember also the large and little portions of the same kind of thing occurring all over the globe hour by hour.

> Never mind.

FROM LIMITED TOTAL LOSS TO LIMITLESS TOTAL LOSS.

> *The ball I threw whilst playing in the park has not yet reached the ground.*
> Dylan Thomas[3]

Who are we building for, and why?

Statement published in Architectural Design, *April 1970*[1]

The answer to the first question is clearer in Lima than it is elsewhere in the world since Limeños are neither mute as to their aspirations nor are they passive with regard to effecting them step by step. What they wish is implicitly and explicitly demonstrated by what they actually do. The *barriadas* offer an emphatic testimony.[2]

The question as to why one should build in the way implied by this project programme is another and extremely important issue from many aspects – economic, social and political as well as architectural. There are, of course, positive reasons why one should. However, less positive implications which could, but need not, lurk around the corner if misused, must be kept in mind.

Barriada Pampa de Comas, near Lima in 1962

Aerial and ground level view

It would be a grave error if pre-designed and partially pre-constructed urban environments such as this pilot project proposes should counteract the growth and development of the *barriada* idea and practice, instead of stimulating it through the erection of improved dwelling types, construction systems and overall community planning.

The needs and aspirations of the people are revealed in *barriadas* like Comas, San Martin de Porres and Ciudiad de Dios as well as in partially pre-constructed settlements like Ventinilla and Pamplona. Each is, of course, different in its possibilities and lack of possibilities; yet basically there is little or nothing to show that initially people who will buy and extend a dwelling in a pre-designed and partially constructed settlement are different or have substantially different aspirations to those who go to the *barriadas* to build from scratch both their own house and the community they have initiated themselves.

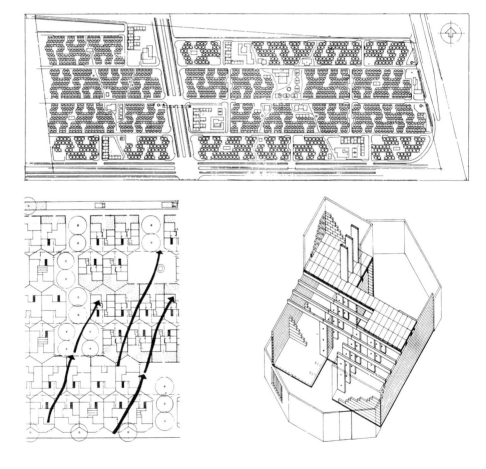

Aldo van Eyck, PREVI public housing scheme, near Lima, general plans and axonometric view of a house.

The Priority Jostle

Intervention at a symposium on housing in developing countries, held at Delft Polytechnic, autumn 1970[1]

The question of why vast multitudes migrate towards cities from rural areas is posed again and again. Many alternative reasons for this universal phenomenon are given as though its very universality points to a single set of reasons or the 'same' reasons must account for vast multitudes doing the same thing! We have just listened to the usual spate of numerical acrobatics; to dark consequences coolly outlined and redeeming solutions smoothly proposed. 'If nothing is done...' or, more ominous still: 'If nothing is done to stop them...'. That is the music murmured. Stop whom? how? why?

Yes, why? Why stop them? 'It so happens'. Dr. Königsberger[2] who knows what he is talking about, reminded the meeting that nothing can stop them and nothing should. That saved the day, although it was probably not what one wanted to hear. But never mind: if the causes are elusive, the solutions perhaps may not be! But that soon proved to be a disappointment also. Different 'experts' have quite different 'first' priorities in mind. To mention just a few: one is a roof and its supports. But what if some people somewhere have reasons to prefer a walled enclosure (without a roof) for lateral protection first or, like many a Paris clochard, simply don't seem to want a roof in the first place? Another expert's 'first' is running water and street lights; then, once the house (presumably a second 'priority') is built, also light inside! This, the message stresses, would counteract the birth explosion more effectively than the pill! There were, of course, some more 1st, 2nd and 3rd priorities less impertinently brought forward by other experts, but let me stick to the 'firsts' I have just mentioned (roof – support and water – light) and look at Lima for a moment.

What if a poor Limeño family, escaping from the burden and oppression of urban slum life, desires to build a house of its own and starts the process, as so many do, by erecting an enclosure – just four walls – to protect, among other things, the material

Aldo van Eyck, a built cluster of his PREVI project, shortly after completion and some years later.
Photos Vincent Ligtelijn (l) and Petra ten Cate (r)

with which to build that very house? As for running water and light, the Limeños leave both behind them voluntarily when they evacuate from the city and go to a *Barriada* to follow their own priorities: a house which is theirs with lots of rooms on land from which they hope they will not be evicted – and a better life and education for their children which, incidentally, implies a proper pair of shoes first.

You see for the sake of that school – often self-built – entered wearing those little shoes (without, no parents would ever send a child to school) – some people are willing to leave running water and electricity behind them. These people establish or join a community willing and able to defend its own first preliminary rights and priorities. One of the latter may be – take heed over there – to erect a nice facade with little behind it. To 'show off' perhaps, which could well mean to suggest – anticipate – the presence (possession) of what is not yet there, but, by God, one day will be. An 'expert' in these matters back from Nigeria has just explained why there is but one modern building in downtown Lagos with timber windows – the American Embassy. 'Africans, you see, prefer steel, though it has to be imported and rusts quickly.' I did hear the burst of laughter that atrocious remark evoked – but missed the joke.

We are often reminded of the United Nations Declaration of Human Rights – the one about each man's inalienable right to food, health, clothes and shelter. I have probably missed some of the great goods proposed during this meeting and got the sequence wrong. Anyway, I should like to propose another, simpler one and call it the Declaration of Delft! It affirms the right of every society to its own priorities as well as the right of each individual to his or hers. Just that; no more.

Whose problems are you trying to solve if they are not your own? Who calls upon a few in the name of all? The Lord? All? Or just you?

Ultimately the condition of the human species cannot be what a small portion of that species has so amply measured out for itself – nor is it necessary or desirable. The discovery of another standard is yet to come: it may be a hundred, it may be hundreds or more years hence, but, sooner or later, people will accommodate themselves to its nature and respond intelligently – tune in – to its prerogatives. It will not be a 'lower' standard, nor will it be a 'higher' one. It will be a different one: an altogether different kind of standard. Whilst not everything desirable is possible, nor everything possible desirable – ecologically speaking, only the possible is desirable. Hence there is still lots of scope for quality which, unlike quantity, is unlimited – boundless – and calls for a different kind – or different use – of intelligence.

Fascism in a snowflake

Statement published in the festschrift Niet om het even, 1986[1]

Divergence within the Team 10 orbit occurs and, occasionally should be resolved if our shared inquiry is to continue. The Smithsons, believe it or not, detected fascism in a snowflake at the Royaumont meeting in 1962, but still fail to consider the damage that faulty verdict – spitefully published – has done. As for the 'snowflake', it so happens that Blom's vision of an urban society or another kind of town ('Noah's Ark' he called it) was certainly the furthest cry imaginable from the irreversible hierarchy, oppression and stifling pathology of fascism because of its exhilarating part-whole, small-large, many-few reciprocity. What even the Smithsons themselves do not deserve should never have been spilt by them on Blom who least deserves it.

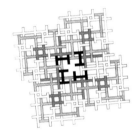

District unit scheme forming the basic pattern of Blom's *Noah's Ark* project, 1962.

Aldo van Eyck with Peter Smithson and Amancio Guedes at the Royaumont meeting.

11
Interiorization

Introduction to chapter 11

Parallel to his struggle with great number Aldo van Eyck continued to investigate the other theme he had brought up in *Forum*: the shape of the in-between, and by extension the idea of 'place' conceived 'in the image of man'. Approaching this concept from different viewpoints, he went into it in *The Child, the City and the Artist*, and developed notions such as 'the interior of space', 'the interior of time', 'Kaleidoscope of the Mind' and 'labyrinthian clarity', which all converged in the idea of interiorization. This idea returned as a kind of leitmotif in his book and would be of decisive consequence for the further development of his work. As *The Child, the City and the Artist* failed to be published, he condensed several of its lines of thought into some substantial articles.

Van Eyck did not use the term 'interiorize' in the current sense of 'incorporate within oneself', but as a way of perception, a mental attitude that subtracts the external shell from things in order to reveal reality as a dynamic unity of coherent energies. When thus perceived in 'the interior of mind', reality is broken open and made accessible. As it becomes transparent and kaleidoscopic, reality is experienced as an interior. This perception applies to both space and time. A full experience of reality presupposes that it is not confined to 'the razorblade instant' of the present. It has to extend into the past and the future, so as to encompass memories and anticipations.

Van Eyck also unfolded his ideas in countless lectures, illuminated with slides he took all over the world. Many were tape-recorded but he only edited a few of them for publication. In one of them, 'The Enigma of Size', which he delivered at Urbino in 1979, he concretized what he meant by 'the gathering body of experience finding a home in the mind'. Showing a broad range of images from the most divergent cultures and ages, he tried to gauge the essential human meaning divided among them in order to accommodate them in 'the interior of mind': the coherence of large and small in Palladio and Ledoux, the simultaneity of inside and outside in Mackintosh and the Alhambra, the threshold between private and public in Djenné, the mapping of the city through the smell and the sound of coffee in Zanzibar, the meshing of building and urban traffic in Pietro da Cortona in Rome, the connection of distant places through association in Angkor, and last but not least, Simon Rodia's 'great ship' in Watts that through its incorporation of a multitude of associations and memories appeals to almost every visitor.

During the 1970s, when he designed and built the Amsterdam Hubertus House, a home for unmarried parents and their children, Van Eyck reflected on the role of contemporary architecture in the historical city centre. He formulated his thoughts in a book published by the Stichting Wonen in 1982. Reacting to certain conservative developments in Dutch architecture, he specified his concept of 'place' and went into the phenomenon of transparency. Assuming that openness is a preliminary condition to closeness, he opposed the interpretation of 'place' as a form of closeness that excludes openness. Remarkably, he recognized a prefiguration of his view of openness being a condition of closeness in the work of the seventeenth-century painter Pieter de Hoogh.

The Otterlo Circles

Second version of the Otterlo Circles diagram, prepared for inclusion in
The Child, the City and the Artist, 1962[1]

Each culture stresses specific aspects – fundamental solutions – which are universally relevant but which, for various specific or random reasons, are emphasized whilst others are repressed. Ultimately man suffers from these limitations, from what is overemphasized at the cost of what is omitted and often forgotten. Now, today, what is specific, what gives meaningful identity, should no longer depend on what is thus arbitrarily omitted or stressed, but on how these specific aspects are absorbed, adapted and combined for the sake of more inclusive solutions which can respond to the nature of the human person as a whole instead of in part.

The three little images united in the first circle hide no real conflict; nor are their properties incompatible. They complement each other, belong together, and reflect equally valid aspects of the human personality. If they are allowed to interact, if their properties are brought together, it should no longer be difficult to resist the lure of false eclecticism, false regionalism and false modernism – three kinds of shortsightedness which continually alternate.

The three images in the first circle do not exclude others equally essential. No limitation is implied. Add San Carlo alle Quatro Fontane or Vierzehnheiligen and we can start reconciling them – the essence, not the form – in a wonderful sequence of possibilities that would really fit man. This is our job: *by 'us' for us.* 'For us' implies each man and all men, the individual and society – hence the second circle.

Get close to the shifting centre of man and build!

The Greek temple represents an order that rests within itself, one that is valid whenever we deal with the singular or with limited multiplicity. Theo van Doesburg's drawing (a 1911 cubist painting or Duiker's sanatorium would be equally appropriate) represents plurality and relativity. The one stands for classical harmony, the other for what I call harmony in motion (the aesthetics of number). House and city can only be understood in terms of both these images today – these two, and a third! The third image, an Indian pueblo for example, represents what I call the vernacular of the heart – the extension of collective behaviour into built form – limited multiplicity successfully tamed.

BY 'US'

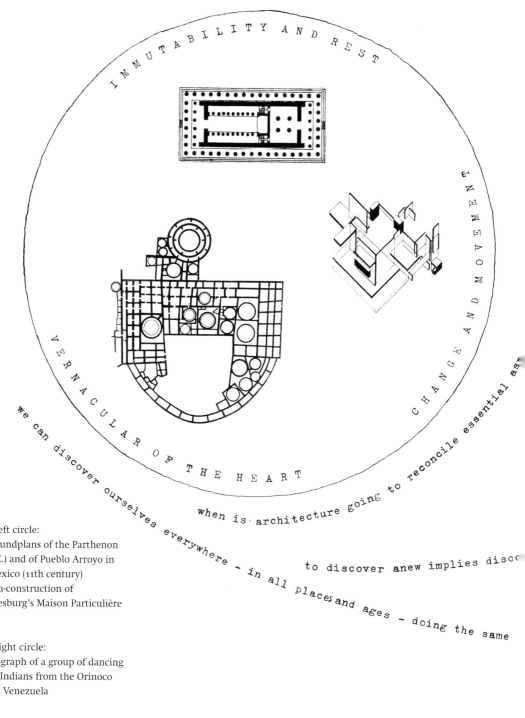

In the left circle:
The groundplans of the Parthenon (438 B.C.) and of Pueblo Arroyo in New Mexico (11th century)
A contra-construction of Van Doesburg's Maison Particulière (1923)

In the right circle:
A photograph of a group of dancing Kayapo Indians from the Orinoco basin in Venezuela

FOR US

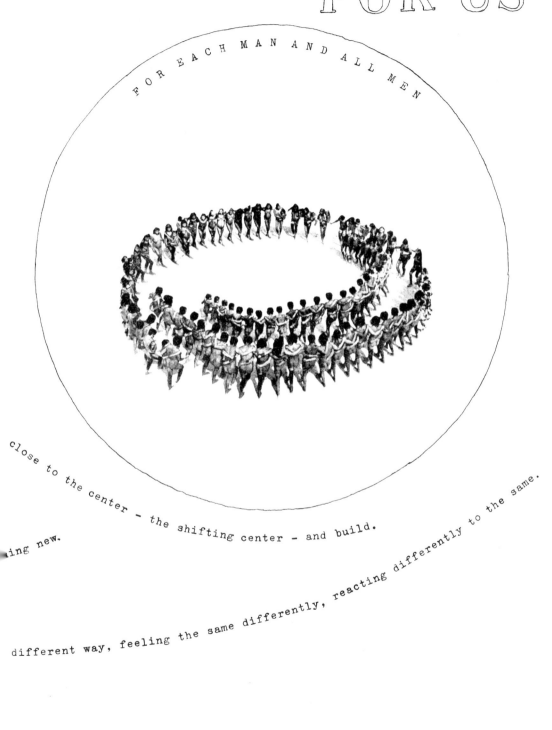

FOR EACH MAN AND ALL MEN

close to the center - the shifting center - and build.

ing new.

different way, feeling the same differently, reacting differently to the same.

Built Meaning

Three statements published in Team 10 Primer, December 1962[1]

It's getting cold again over here – and always when it does I start thinking about how to warm up architecture, how to make it lodge round us. After all, people buy clothes and shoes the right size and know when the fit feels good! It's time we invent the built thing that fits them – us.

We have no time to waste. Better supply the right fruits a little unripe than supply none at all or the wrong sort overripe. Hurry, switch on the stars before the fuses go! (1959)

What you should try to accomplish is built meaning. So, get close to the meaning and build!

Place and Occasion

Shortened version of 'There is a garden in her face' *(1960), first published in 1962*[1]

Space has no room and time not a moment for man. He is excluded.
In order to 'include' him – help his homecoming – he must be gathered into their meaning.
(Man is the subject as well as the object of architecture)[2]

Whatever space and time mean, place and occasion mean more.

For space in the image of man is place and time in the image of man is occasion.

Today space and what it should coincide with in order to become 'space' – man at home with himself – are lost. Both search for the same place but cannot find it.

Provide that place.

Is man able to penetrate the material he organizes into hard shape between one man and another; between what is here and what is there; between this and the following moment? Is he able to find the right place for the right occasion?

No – So start with this: make
a welcome of each door and
a countenance of each window.

Make of each a place; a bunch of places of each house and each city, for a house is a tiny city, a city a huge house.

Get closer to the shifting centre of human reality and build its counterform
– for each man and all men, since they no longer do it themselves.

Whoever attempts to solve the riddle of space in the abstract will construct the outline of emptiness and call it space.

Whoever attempts to meet man in the abstract will speak with his echo and call this a dialogue.

Man still breathes both in and out. When is architecture going to do the same?

Labyrinthian Clarity

Article published in different versions, in 1963, 1965, 1966 and 1967[1]

I have spoken of place, of house and city as bunches of places – both; of the in-between realm as man's home-realm. I have identified the built artefact with those it shelters (the building with that same building entered) – and, having done so, defined space simply as the appreciation of it, thus excluding all frozen properties attributed to it academically whilst including what should never be excluded: man appreciating it!

I have even called architecture *built home-coming*!

With this in mind I have come to regard architecture conceived in terms of 'space' and depending primarily on visibility (visibility taken for granted!) as arbitrary and abstract; only physically accessible and therefore 'closed'.

Space and time must be 'opened' – interiorized – so that they can be *entered*: persuaded to gather man into their meaning – include him.

By virtue of what memory and anticipation signify, place acquires temporal meaning and occasion spatial meaning. Thus space and time, identified reciprocally (in the image of man) emerge, humanized, as place and occasion. (Whatever space and time mean, place and occasion mean more.)

Places remembered and places anticipated dovetail in the temporal span of the present. They constitute the real perspective of space.[2]

What matters is not space but the *interior* of space – and the *inner horizon* of that interior.

The large house – little city statement (the one that says: a house is a tiny city, a city a huge house) is ambiguous and consciously so. In fact, its ambiguity is of a kind I should like to see transposed to architecture. It points, moreover, towards a particular kind of *clarity* neither house nor city can do without. A kind which never quite relinquishes its full meaning.

Call it labyrinthian clarity.

Such clarity (ally of significant ambiguity) softens the edges of time and space and transcends visibility (allows spaces to enter each other and occasions to encounter each other in the mind's interior).

It is kaleidoscopic.
The in-between realm is never without it.
Right-size goes hand in hand with it (and so, of course, does the inner horizon of space).
It harbours bountiful qualities: scope for that which is small yet large – large yet small; near yet far – far yet near; open yet closed – closed yet open; different yet the same – the same yet different; scope for the right delay, the right release, the right certainty, the right suspense, the right security, the right surprise; and, withal, scope for multimeaning.

There is a kind of spatial appreciation which makes us envy birds in flight; there is also a kind which makes us recall the sheltered enclosure of our origin. Architecture will fail if it neglects either the one or the other (to be Ariel means also being Caliban[3]). Labyrinthian clarity, at any rate, sings of both![4]

The Interior of Time

Article written in 1962 and 1966, published in Forum, *July 1967*[1]

Anna was. Livia is, Plurabelle's to be.
James Joyce

As the past is gathered into the present and the gathering body of experience finds a home in the mind, the present acquires temporal depth – loses its acrid instantaneity; its razorblade quality. One might call this: the interiorization of time or time rendered transparent.

It seems to me that past, present and future must be active in the mind's interior as a continuum. If they are not, the artefacts we make will be without temporal depth or associative perspective. My concern with the ultimate human validity of divergent but often only seemingly incompatible concepts of space and circumstantial or incidental solutions found during past ages in different corners of the world is to be understood in the light of the above. The time has come to reconcile them, to gather together the essential human meaning divided among them.

Man, after all, has been accommodating himself physically in this world for thousands of years. His natural genius has neither increased nor decreased during that time. It is obvious that the full scope of this enormous environmental experience cannot be contained in the present unless we telescope the past, i.e. the entire human effort, into it. This is not historic indulgence in a limited sense; not a question of travelling back, but merely of being aware of what 'exists' in the present – what has travelled into it: the projection of the past into the future via the created present – 'Anna was. Livia is, Plurabelle's to be'[2] (who knows, Anna Livia Plurabelle may yet preside over architecture!).

This, in my opinion, is the only medicine against sentimental historicism, modernism and utopianism. Also against narrow rationalism, functionalism and regionalism. A medicine against all the pests combined.

Each culture constitutes a very special case. That surely is a wonderful thing – wonderful in a different way for each different case! To go chasing after historical or anthropological data appertaining to different cultures with the object of propping a preconceived notion of culture is therefore an arbitrary occupation. Toynbee did so industriously. The issue here is not whether it is possible to adventure intellectually into a cultural world not one's own, nor whether it is at all possible ultimately to circumscribe successfully the nature of any special case. I merely want to stress the fact that each case *is* a special case and can only be understood in its own terms. It should by now be possible to acknowledge, *sine qua non*, the intrinsic validity and simultaneous justification of all cultural patterns, irrespective of time and place.

'Western civilization' habitually identifies itself with civilization as such (with what it stands for) on the pontifical assumption that what is not like it is a deviation, less 'advanced', 'primitive' or, at best, exotically interesting – at a safe distance. But western civilization – what a self-assured jingle – is just one special case in an enormous multitude of special cases, each of which carries its own possibilities and deals with them in a way specifically its own. (1962)

Architects nowadays are pathologically addicted to change, regarding it as something one either hinders, runs after or, at best, keeps up with. This, I suggest, is why they tend to sever the past from the future, with the result that the present is rendered emotionally inaccessible – without temporal dimension. I dislike a sentimental antiquarian attitude towards the past as much as I dislike a sentimental technocratic one towards the future. Both are founded on a static, clockwork notion of time (what antiquarians and technocrats have in common). So let's start with the past for a change and discover the unchanging condition of man in the light of change – i.e. in the light of the changing condition he himself brings about. If the lasting validity of man's past environmental experience (the contemporaneousness of the past) is acknowledged, the paralysing conflicts between past, present and future, between old notions of space, form and construction and new ones, between hand production and industrial production, will be mitigated. Why do so many believe they must choose categorically, as though it is impossible to be loyal both ways?

I have heard it said that an architect 'cannot be a prisoner of tradition in a time of change'. It seems to me that he cannot be a prisoner of any kind. And at no time can he be prisoner of change. (1966)

Two kinds of centrality

Statement extracted from the presentation of 'The Wheels of Heaven', Van Eyck's unbuilt ecumenical church project for Driebergen, published in Domus, *May 1965.*

Thinking about such twin phenomena as inside-outside, open-closed, far-near, alone-together, individual-collective, the following twin image came to my mind.
People seated concentrically in a hollow, gazing inwards towards the centre;
and people seated concentrically on a hill, gazing outwards towards the horizon.
Two kinds of centrality. Two ways of being together – or alone.
The images, of course, have ambivalent meanings – though the hill reveals what the hollow may conceal: that man is both centre-bound and horizon-bound (the horizon and the shifting centre, the centre and shifting horizon). Both hill and hollow, horizon and centre, are shared by all seated concentrically either way; both link and both lure.

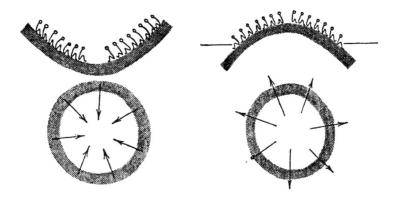

The inner horizon in Wright's Imperial Hotel

Extract from a talk given at the Australian Architecture Student Association Convention, Perth, May 1966[1]

It is not so much space that matters as the interior quality of space. In Japan I saw many contemporary buildings that I had seen in pictures and I remember that I was continually looking upwards, masses of concrete charging through glass, inside, outside, possibly to eliminate the difference between outside and inside. I was surprised when they brought me to Frank Lloyd Wright's Imperial Hotel. It was undersized, slightly smaller than I had imagined. I think all great buildings are a bit undersized. There was no looking upwards here. As you walk up from one floor to another, you carry the horizon of space with you. The horizon is a relative thing, it relates to you, to where you are. It is something which should accompany you as you move through a building. When it does, you will know that something magnificent is happening. That's what I'm trying to put across: the importance of this inner horizon of space which makes you feel at home in the real sense of the word – related. It was extraordinary that none of the Japanese appreciated it, none of them spoke of Wright's hotel. Wright seemed to have discovered the same qualities the ancient Japanese knew about, the same graceful, relaxed presence of horizon wherever you are. What matters is not so much space, but the interior of space – and the inner horizon of that interior.

F.L. Wright,
Imperial Hotel,
Tokyo, 1915–1922,
main lobby,
demolished in 1968

On Frank Lloyd Wright's Imperial Hotel

Extracts from an open letter to The Hon. Eisaku Sato, Prime Minister of Japan, dated 12 January 1968[1]

F.L. Wright, Imperial Hotel, Tokyo, 1915–1922, demolished in 1968

The Imperial Hotel has what unfortunately very few contemporary buildings in and outside Japan have: an interior horizon. I will try to put across what I mean by that. On entering the Imperial Hotel one is, as it were, accompanied. One is subsequently 'received' from space to space and from level to level. This 'interior horizon' can be sensed everywhere. Though it is intangible and cannot be 'perceived' as such, it is there all the time. One takes it with one everywhere as a frame of reference. A sense of whereabouts and emotional correspondence prevails. Each place is deliciously accessible. Architecture can do no more than assist that reassuring feeling of being interiorized. At least it cannot do more until it does *that*, but it seldom does. Very few buildings have succeeded the way the Imperial Hotel has in this respect. Once entered, the spaces there do not remain 'empty'. They accept and receive one; settle round one, as it were. Similarly they 'keep' one as one leaves them. In short they are 'yours' wherever you happen to be. In my opinion, this is why the Imperial Hotel transcends the notion of being just a building in the limited connotation. It is a 'built' environment, imparting, as all human environments should, but seldom do, a sense of belonging...

Let me conclude by conveying to you how, as a foreigner, I relate the Imperial Hotel to the country which accommodates it. Fully aware that my Japanese architect friends are the ones best suited to put across to you what it means to *them* and *their* country, I should like to sum up what I have tried to say: The Imperial Hotel is an extremely meaningful work. As with all things thus meaningful, its meaning cannot be defined or assessed by a single person. Others will no doubt paint a different picture of it, tell a different story. But this will only underline its scope and generosity – the hallmark of all real architecture.

Now, the hotel was built in a country where the quality of such 'real' architecture is overwhelming. It transmits what it received from that country beautifully, and in a way quite its own. It gave back to Japan in a new form what it had learnt from it, revealing at an early stage the extraordinary contemporaneousness of ancient and traditional architecture in that country: its astounding grace. May I say Wright returned that grace graciously, granting the future what neither you in Japan nor we outside it can possibly do without.

The Imperial Hotel is, without doubt, a complex symbol. It also represents the kind of intercultural reciprocity we today need more than anything else. It is even an affirmation of regional and temporal identity and in no way a negation of it (which it could well have been whilst still possessing a high autonomous quality). If it was coca cola, I would say: saké please. But it is not. It is Katsura, Harunobu, Haniwa, Lincoln, Whitman and Iriquoise: It is Asia, America and Europe – east and west. It is past and future. In short, I think it is all that is worthwhile wherever one can find it; and stands for the radiant side of humanity (the side which tends to hide in vulnerable places).

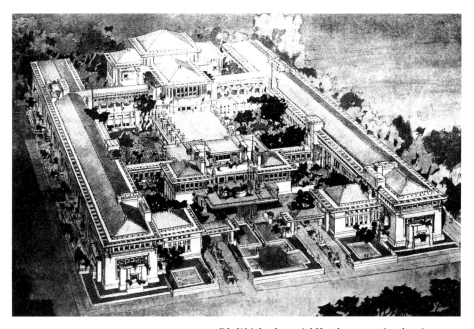

F.L. Wright, Imperial Hotel, perspective drawing, 1920

The Enigma of Size

Lecture given at the ILA&UD in Urbino, 1979[1]

Large hat or small roof?
Photo George Rodger

The sequence of images which follows was selected from a much larger one to fit the occasion. I have used my own photographs because of their emotional proximity. Together they represent what I still imagine architecture to be all about – regardless of either space or time. I know it is currently fashionable to argue that architecture exists above and beyond such matters – that it is, in fact, quite autonomous. That 'Rationalism' could ever be so new as to forsake reason! The images which accompany the comments would, if they were left to speak for themselves, tell the reader what the reader reads into them, which can be different from one to the other and not the same today as yesterday.

Let me look at S. Giorgio Maggiore in Venice for a while.
The 'faults' which Rudolf Wittkower reads into its façade and James Ackerman partially confirms,[2] correspond exactly with what to me are not faults, but signs of genius. Thus, already, S. Giorgio has lots of facades: the readers', each of the historians' and mine! The fun starts when the architect responsible for the whole building – Palladio – is claimed not responsible when it comes to the faults. Since I am not impressed by the arguments brought to bear, I am also not persuaded that Palladio was not responsible for them. Either way, they happen to point straight to the particular qualities I wish to emphasise here.

According to Wittkower, 'S. Giorgio as we see it today does not seem to correspond to Palladio's intentions. The two Orders,' he continues, 'do not rise from the same level. The large half-columns stand on high pedestals while the small pilasters rise almost from the ground. This discrepancy in level, which is particularly unfor-

Andrea Palladio, San Giorgio Maggiore, Venice, 1565 Photos Aldo van Eyck

tunate where the high pedestals cut into the adjoining pilasters, is not the only fault in the facade'.

Wittkower describes the other 'faults' in a note: 'The socles under the aediculae of the outer bays correspond in height to the pedestals of the giant order and are disproportionately high in relation to the aediculae'.

Ackerman in his book at least gives Palladio the credit of trying 'a compromise by starting the orders at different heights'. There is no mention of a fault nor of Palladio not being the author. But Ackerman does come up with another fault – one that underlines Wittkower's second one: 'The base of the lateral half pediment ... continues across the three central bays as a sort of cornice and appears to join the half-pediments into a single, low and broad, temple front behind the pseudo-portico at the centre'. That is indeed a good description, but whereas I am enthralled, Ackerman is not. On the contrary: for he continues, 'since the two halves together constitute all a single order can support, there could be no justification for a cornice between them'.

Now, whatever Palladio's intentions were or were not, whatever changes others made or did not make, the facade of S. Giorgio is a miracle and not in spite of the 'faults', but because of them. It possesses a certain multidimensionality which renders it both grand and gentle. By orchestrating three orders so different in size, kind and meaning, dimensional extremes are brought together and intrinsic conflicts resolved instead of avoided. Discussing the conflict the confrontation of the two orders brings about, Ackerman refers to the Redentore, 'where the stairs hid the trouble'. He tells us that its facade 'represented an optimal solution of an essentially insoluble conflict'. I do not agree, because it is through this very conflict that the facade of S. Giorgio became emotionally inclusive whilst, in the case of the Redentore – wonderful for other reasons – that conflict simply does not exist. There the entrance is 'lifted' to the level of the base from which both orders rise, which is not the same as stairs hiding the trouble. It is strange that neither historian comments on the way the columns of the smaller order in Palladio's earlier facade for S. Francesco della Vigna in Venice rise from a base which, starting halfway up the doorway, divides the latter in two. Perhaps because Palladio's authorship is here undisputed! In S. Giorgio, however, the flat pilasters of the smaller order, intriguingly nestled, rise from entry level and have a very touching detail at their base, where the mouldings merge into those at the base of the pedestals under the giant columns. Delicately, but oh so effective, one thin moulding is drawn – glides – inwards into the depth of the doorway. Thus S. Giorgio's great façade, magnificent from across the water, adjusts itself gently to the physical dimensions of those entering its interior.

The broad horizontality of the suggested temple front, as it were passing through the verticality of the great pseudo-portico; the vertical shift by lifting the large columns into high pedestals while placing the little aediculae on pedestals equally high, but set back a little – these are the interdependent devices – faults! – which were employed to achieve the articulation of altitude and the juxtaposition of very divergent dimensions I find so successful – and relevant today. It is no coincidence that the small entrance detail, which to my mind exemplifies great humanity and thus architecture at its highest level, should occur where the dimensional problems accumulated and the need for a successful solution became acute.

Photo Kalvar Vu

Photo Aldo van Eyck

C.N. Ledoux, Rotonde de Monceau, Paris, 1875–1885
Another detail – sensitive where it matters most. A circular row of doric columns forms a continuous portico. Inside this city-scale order there are tall, appropriately emphasized doorways around lower, relatively modest doors.
It is where the lateral ornaments of the doorways *fuse* into the mouldings which frame the actual doors that Ledoux plays the game of architecture the way it should be played.

Sketch Aldo van Eyck

Photo Aldo van Eyck

483

In Glasgow between bustling Sauchiehall Street and what used to be the Willow Tearooms, there is a wonderful window with mirrors set in plane glass which speaks of both. Two ways of looking into space – two worlds in one: large and small, street and room held in a single surface.
All at once what is there on either side is there side by side.
Charles Rennie Mackintosh

Charles Rennie Mackintosh, Willow Tearooms, Glasgow, 1902–1904
Photo Aldo van Eyck

Photo Vincent Ligtelijn

A house in Gujurat, India
Mirrors, facing the other way this time, adorn a humble doorway. Throwing back evil spirits that dwell outside they also protect the interior Photo Aldo van Eyck

Alhambra, Granada
Jewels of varying size and shape lie set in one stone surface between the same cut edges; wide and angular; small and circular; line-thin. The space above (sky and foliage) continues in them, reflected.
Far back, in the shade of the palace interior, the sky is still there, shining beyond the floor – or in the fountain's spray.

Generalife Gardens, Granada
A hedge, tall and slender, held within a fixed form for centuries – luxury in simplicity: a space survives.

Tiny flowerbeds – no water is wasted, not a drop from cup or kettle – simplicity in poverty. Infinite care for what is fragile and precious in Spain and Peru.

Photos Aldo van Eyck

Photos Aldo van Ey

White lines: a house is drawn in Persia. Landscapes are marked
– rituals follow. And soon there will be places set apart in
which to dwell.

Thus, also, the Karamajon in northern Uganda – cattle folk and dire raiders – seeking lateral protection in the vast savanna, erect circular enclosures inside which smaller ones, likewise circular, and each with its own roof, are made: the rooms and granaries of an extended family.

The men, out in the open with their cattle, carry little stools with them on which they sit, their dark bodies as though suspended just above the ground. Wherever people go space of some kind is defined. It may be the circle they circumscribe when they sit – or just gestures and voices.

Photos Aldo van Eyck

A narrow street in Djenné, a sacred city in the bend of the Niger south of Timbuktu. The presence of the boy on the doorstep reading the Koran draws the area within the semi-circular ridge into the domain of the house. At the same time a large gourd put there to dry temporarily extends the private domain outwards into the public one, almost obstructing the thoroughfare. Yet no passer-by will tamper with the gourd. Transitions between private and public domain property include scope for mutation. Meaning can shift and is taken by degree. Limits are thus not rigid and behaviour responds accordingly.

Like the gourd put in the street to dry, somebody's wool, left to stretch between stones across a corner of the main open space in Yugo Na, a Dogon village, will not be disturbed when, towards evening, people gather from all sides.

For half a *soles*, boys sit down to read strips along a permanent library in Iquitos.
Along the Ucayali – tributary of the Amazon – in Pucalpa, further west, where green bananas are sold in huge bunches, men sit down on plain chairs for a leisurely riverbank shave and haircut. Read or shave the environmental way – the urban way.

And have a drink that way in Zanzibar, where there are no coffee shops. Instead, there is a vendor all in white at almost every street crossing pouring cups of black coffee (with clove or pepper added) from a big copper pot. The cups are stored in the pockets of the vendor's cloak, which he shakes every now and then. Thus in Zanzibar one follows the *sound* of coffee and maps the city in the mind by the *taste*.

Not so in New Orleans. There, special places are frequented. One near the Levee serves coffee and doughnuts only – on a marble-topped table which runs all round the room. On that table, from end to end, there are heavy sterling silver sugar bowls linked together by a long silver chain and multiplied on all sides in mirrors. Those taking no sugar miss something!

Photos Vincent Ligtelijn Photo Francis Strauven

Pietro da Cortona, Santa Maria della Pace church, Rome, 1656–1659
next to the cloister Bramante built in 1500

Contained within Pietro da Cortona's inclusive symmetry there is, on one side, a doorway through which Bramante's cloister is reached. On the other side, below a magic window with sky on both sides, there is a similar 'doorway' through which – believe it or not – no interior space is entered. Instead, just Rome itself – a narrow street leading towards Piazza Navona.

Between the two doorways, along the axis, holding them apart, a semicircular portico penetrates into a small piazza shaped around it symmetrically. For some moments in certain places, but not very often – city is building and building is city; outside is inside and inside is outside; small is large and large is small; part is whole and whole is part. Equipoise through reciprocity – ultimate symmetry.

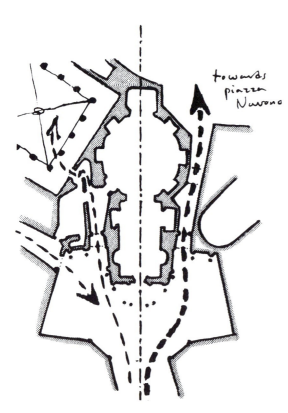

Situation sketch Aldo van Eyck

Photos Aldo van Eyck

Here, fixed in countless memories and identical pictures taken, the symmetry is of quite a different kind. Unlike Santa Maria della Pace and unlike Fatehpur Sikri close by, the Taj is monosyllabic. There is nothing reciprocal or equivocal in its cold distant perfection. But it did soften under my scrutiny as I peopled the foreground photographically and played some little tricks with its axis!

Taj Mahal, Agra, 1632–1647

Angkor Wat Temple, 1113–1150 Photos Aldo van Eyck

Not far from where roots dislodge the walls and windows of Angkor and branches creep across stone faces, children come bringing coloured figures of cloth. As they come along jungle paths from all round to where Buddha sits; as the figures fade where they are hung from the circular awning and new ones are brought from time to time, the circle – small in its setting – which frames and protects the sacred image acquires the dimension of a wider and more intimate horizon – one that includes within its protective radius the villages that lie around. There, in houses made like baskets, small scraps of cloth are sewn together artfully into something that is continually new, gay and never the same.

Sam Rodia, Watts Towers, Los Angeles, 1921–1955

On the other side of the Pacific Ocean, Sam Rodia's great ship, which took him thirty years to build and is known as the Watts Towers, asks to be appreciated in a similar way. Gathered together along the hull, inside or up those incredible masts, there must be a bit of every kind of tile and crockery imported, made, sold, used and discarded in the United States of America. (The truth is in the thought!)
'Look! There's a bit of grandma's teapot!', I heard a child cry out. 'Remember those funny bottles!', 'We used to have plates like that!' There is room for everything aboard this ship – room for everybody. It sails through time and space. Shapes, patterns, textures, samples, ideas, suggestions, associations, memories, prospects, reminders, dreams, wishes – all is there – large, small, low, high, thick, thin, light, heavy, many, few, near, far, dense, loose, pale, dark, rough, smooth, skinny. The world is in it.
It is beautiful in a special way because it is beautiful in every conceivable way.
Anything more generous will be hard to find. There is squalid empty space round it – mud, stones, puddles and litter. Children play there and fight. After the Watts riots, when much in the area was burnt down and wrecked, the Towers (Sam Rodia's ship) was left undamaged. Even the thin staff which stands exposed on its bow was never target for a stone.
Pondering over this extraordinary fact, an idea quite incredible came to my mind: **This miraculous work of art represents no power – no power of any sort.**

Photos Aldo van Eyck

Transparency

Thoughts formulated after the completion of the Amsterdam Hubertus House, 1982[1]

Looking through a wall, a room, or a building – even all at once – is possible, but the question is: which is it to be? When the one, when the other, how, and to what extent? Such questions have been insufficiently considered since the early days of the modern movement, so that qualities like transparency and continuity have become detached, isolated from the meaning of space and enclosure. What has been offered instead is a view straight through, just like that – with emptiness on either side – outside and inside!

What was to be made visible through dematerialization and why, didn't seem to matter – nor what transparency and continuity as such could bring about in human terms. That got lost in the trend – in that style without style. When space vanishes emptiness is all we are left with.

There can be no question of interior quality, nor of enclosure, since there is nothing there – nothing left to 'open'. Can a building be opened towards what is outside, if there is no space to speak of on either side? No inside, no interior and thus no enclosure?

I remember saying once: 'It is not space that counts ultimately, but the interior of space and, above all, the inner horizon[2] of that interior – whether it be inside or outside. See to it, therefore, that this interior horizon is never missing but is always present as one moves through a building (or city), stands or sits, looks up or down – for the gratifying sense of reference it can offer.'

Nor is the horizon outside ever fixed – it shifts up and down as one ascends or descends. The same applies inside a building provided it has an interior horizon. But this, unfortunately, is precisely what is generally lacking – lost at all levels of magnitude from house to city.

Obsessed by movement and hence all too busy with horizontal continuity, the attention of architects has been diverted away from vertical articulation far too long (people after all do close their eyes when asleep!) It is quite pointless to come up with the wrong sort of enclosure (void) as a remedy for the wrong sort of openness (also void). Trying one poison against another as alternating antidotes is certainly not going to save architecture. Vast suburbs and new towns, built here and elsewhere since the last world war, bear ample witness. I wish to skip the loathsome – backlash – monstrosities drawn, published the world over, and now, sadly, also being built. What the Rats, Posts and other Pests are perpetrating is discussed elsewhere.[3]

Open what would otherwise close

What is at stake, what is really needed and must still be sorted out (if what is still to be built is to become more accessible and emotionally able to respond) is a kind of openness in which enclosure is, as it were, innate – included *a priori*. For why should the one exclude the other? Openness, after all, does not necessarily exclude – annihilate – space; though one might have reason to think so! Space can even rest enclosed within it. That both Zonnestraal and Van Nelle have shown, and not so long ago. The time has come to follow that lead – proceed along it patiently.

The meaning of space – that little word with a big meaning – is in the process of being hollowed out, whilst the spaces themselves currently contrived by architects and town planners – (still around?) – are becoming emptier and emptier (or more and more solid!). Space is now just another magic word without effect! That is why I tried to avoid using it for some years (though surreptitiously busy with it all the time). 'Stop talking about space, provide that place,' I protested – taking the edge off it by adding 'start with this for the present'.

Lo and behold, places for this, that and the other came crowding in by the million like a new curse, as void as spaces had become before. That new word (like 'space' before, though there is nothing wrong with either) has dribbled from almost every architect's mouth since. Besides, I failed to foresee that those places would – in Holland – turn out to be quite so cosy. It didn't have to be that way – straight from cold and meagre to snug! But it did show how 'place' too became a magic word without content – and how, without receiving much in return, words are wasted on architects ('language' doesn't really rub off on them). Place, like space, is illusive, and cannot thus be 'provided for', or so it appears. All the same, we cannot do without either the one or the other.

Now, twenty years later, when I say, provide the openness which is being closed so rudely (for the sake of enclosure which was as rudely broken open before), I no longer wish to add 'start with this for the present!' If places cannot be 'provided', who then is going to provide spaces with the kind of openness that makes enclosure possible, if even architects are no longer willing or able to do so? That comes close to being a paradox without becoming one because, sooner or later, architects will stop playing the fool (or foul like the RPP) and start playing the game as before, seeing to it – stage by stage and assiduously – that this time the meaning of openness embraces the meaning of enclosure, instead of negating it. Includes what it cannot exclude without impunity.

'Open what is closed and allow space to enter' therefore refers above all to the mental equipment which alone can bring it about.

To this I should add that I am not disposed to neutralize the significance of openness which makes enclosure possible by adding 'and vice versa'. The reciprocity such a reversal suggests could easily lead to a misunderstanding in spite of the fact that spaces, like people, breathe both in and out – or not at all, in which case they are not spaces in any architectural sense. Openness precedes every space-articulating activity; exists *a priori* and is 'interiorized' by it. Thus openness is rendered measurable once it is properly reconstituted by means of architecture.

However, what people are always so diligently subtracting from virgin – open – exterior space with the help of material and construction, all too often closes in the process. Instead of being 'interiorized', it is rendered empty, and emptiness precludes accessibility. That is why the recent trend towards emptiness (the perforated solid) is so very malicious. It is precisely because constructing in exterior space inevitably entails demarcation, enclosure, separation, and size reduction that I now wish to place special emphasis on the quality which does not survive all this limiting activity without conscious effort: openness. This quality, therefore, demands all the more attention. It is in fact the very thing architects in particular are required to maintain: to reconstitute by means of construction, thus keeping open what (without their special care and competence) would otherwise close.

So open – keep opening – that which if you fail to do so, would sooner or later cease to be space altogether. In the face of such a ghastly prospect, never forget that space can still bring light, and light reveal enclosure.

Whilst constituting light itself (which is filled with it) the spectrum usually manifests itself all round us, only partially – fragmented, through one or more of its colour components at a time. As a composite unity, however, the spectral colours, together and in sequence, form a world within themselves, almost a world apart – both endless and finite. No greater cohesion is imaginable. Painters are its primary interpreters and explorers, meriting our boundless gratitude. They are therefore an indispensable and irreplaceable necessity. Still, now and then, just for a while, the six great colours appear in unison across the sky to confirm the simultaneous presence of sun and rain – fire and water. It is then that we know again that *all things are two*.[4]

Pieter de Hoogh

Varying spatial depth and perceptible distance through transparency.
Beyond a space limit close by, one or several further away.
On this side of a space limit which is further away one or several closer by.
Modulation of spatial depth and perceptible distance from place to place as well as from one place, i.e. both consecutive and simultaneous.

Pieter de Hoogh shows us beautifully what enclosure through openness and transparency can bring about, when he paints an open door or window and a doorway, passage or alley on a single line of view, thus allowing one to see right through several interior and exterior spaces – sometimes even as far as the house gables across the street or canal – and there are always some people articulating the entire depth once more, though in other places. This shows that the kind of openness which brings about the right sense of enclosure does not depend on dematerialization and a lot of glass.

Pieter de Hoogh, *Women beside linen cabinet*, 1663

12
Contemporary architecture and traditional city

Introduction to chapter 12

Van Eyck's identification with the modern tradition did not keep him from fostering an outspoken appreciation of the traditional city, both the vernacular settlements of archaic cultures and the historical Western city. Contrary to his functionalist colleagues in CIAM, he did not consider the traditional city to be an irrational residue of a superseded past doomed to be replaced as soon as possible by a new rational built environment, but as a concretized structure of human relationships, as a unique heritage to be handled with care. As early as 1947, when he was a young civil servant in the town planning section of the Amsterdam Public Works department, he was at variance with the then planned radial traffic breakthroughs while in his playgrounds he clearly showed his appreciation for the old city centre. They were not a negation of but a refreshing contribution to the structure of the existing city. Later, at the end of *The Story of Another Idea*, he stated that 'living is more dignified in a mediaeval city than in one of the new towns', an opinion diametrically opposed to the modern town planning beliefs prevailing in Holland at that time. In one of the following issues of *Forum* he also illustrated the 'other idea' with some contextual interventions, some 'restorations, mutations and newly-inserted elements, brought about in a beloved Dutch town with extreme patience and sensitivity'. He was considering the work of Oudejans and Alberts, two young architects working in Edam, and on this occasion he also rounded on the destructive way both moderns and traditionalists were dealing with urban renewal:

'In this connection it certainly makes sense to look at Alkmaar, Utrecht, and countless other towns.

What gives one the right to so unnecessarily assault the defenceless beauty of the past? It's a job for bombs, not for architects. As long as the creative capacity sticks between sock and sole – which is the case today – one should not defend such irrevocable and senseless acts with the words 'sense of contemporaneity', for that means an entirely different thing.' [1]

Six months later he went deeper into the specific quality of this 'defenceless beauty of the past' when he published a virulent attack on the then proposed project for the Amsterdam town hall. In his criticism he disclosed an original view on the structure of Amsterdam's historical centre. He considered the city a clearly legible legacy of the Dutch civil-democratic tradition. He saw it – and the historic Dutch town in general – as a non-hierarchical structure in which the institutional buildings did not stand out from and dominate their surroundings as authoritarian symbols. All the buildings, large and small, dwellings and monuments, 'largely get by together and not in the first place separately'.

Van Eyck's appreciation for the traditional Dutch town was reinforced in the course of the sixties. As he saw his scepticism regarding the creative potential of modern town planning being corroborated by its concrete results, he gradually distanced himself from the functionalist ambition to bring about entirely new towns while cherishing a growing interest in the qualities and viability of the historical city. In fact, he was one of the first moderns to put forward the quality of the historically developed city as a standard for genuine urbanity. In 1970, when working on the Amsterdam Nieuwmarkt project, he qualified the old city centre as a 'donor', a source of energy for the new urban extensions and, more generally, for the reanimation of contemporary urban planning.

Van Eyck concretized this view from the middle of the sixties, notably in his projects for the Deventer town hall, the Amsterdam Nieuwmarkt and Jordaan quarters, housing projects in Zwolle and Dordrecht, and the Amsterdam Hubertus House. In these projects he considered the urban context to be an essential component of the programme, one of the basic elements of the concept – an approach implying increased attention to the specific character of the building site. For each urban project he carried out a precise investigation into the structure of its environment, acknowledging the existing qualities as well as imagining the desirable but lacking qualities that should be introduced. He devised the simple but pertinent rule of thumb that a new project must never diminish the quality of the environment in which it is built, but must only add quality. A new building, he thought, must behave itself in the urban context in which it settles; it must, through its very form, show appreciation for the specific qualities of this context. Which does not mean that it must imitate its surroundings. It must earn its civil rights by the new qualities it introduces.

Some examples of Van Eyck's contextual approach:
Zaanhof playground, 1948
Deventer town hall competition design, 1966–1967
Housing Palmdwarsstraat, Amsterdam, 1972–1980, with Theo Bosch
Housing Rode Torenplein, Zwolle, 1971–1975, with Theo Bosch

Why not a beloved town hall?

Translation of an article published in De Groene Amsterdammer, *on 14 October 1961*[1]

When I first saw the plans for the new town hall in Amsterdam I could hardly believe my eyes – the world stood still for a moment. That often happens when you suddenly find yourself face to face with something that is beyond comprehension. Later, when I had had some time to let it all sink in, when I had recovered to some extent from the shock, I felt the urge to take up my pen. Until now this urge has not led to action.

Confrontations with things that go beyond extreme limits – either positive or negative ones – often leave you speechless, at a loss for words. Facing that kind of thing, language is sometimes impotent. When I was in St. Louis a few days ago, looking out over the Mississippi, I was thinking of Amsterdam and the Amstel, but also of the shock it gave me to see those plans which threaten to destroy the intimacy that exists between city and river. I thought: I must try to put some thoughts on paper; perhaps the distance I now have in time and space will be an advantage (the sight of one river always makes me think of other rivers). The things human beings prove capable of from one moment to the next and from one place to the next do seem to range between frightening extremes. How pure, homogenous and well-proportioned Amsterdam is – and many cities in Europe are – becomes all the more obvious when you are surrounded by the aggressive chaos of a major American city, and also how difficult it is to keep the forces that went into its making under control – forces that are also at work in Europe.

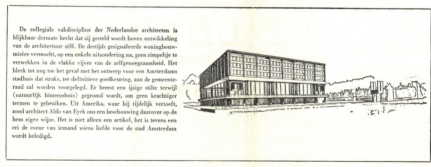

Bird's eye view of the Amsterdam city centre

Man's right to determine his own surroundings in such a way as to allow him the freedom he needs – the freedom to be a man among men – is, I believe, one of the greatest achievements of mankind. I also believe that, to exercise this right, man possesses the creative ability to define total space into room, house, street, square, neighbourhood in such a way as to provide a truly viable environment: i.e. to make each space, small or big, into a nice place to stay.

Without this belief, at any rate, it would not be possible for architects to perform their task properly. And that's why it is impossible to approach this project 'as an architect' because there is in fact no question of a 'building project' in the human sense, and hence not in the architectonic sense either. This plan goes so far beyond the limits of the average weak building project that it is impossible to describe it in normal professional terms. If this project is carried out the result will be a vast no-man's land in the heart of Amsterdam, where no soul will take pleasure in going and where no soul will be able to stay without his human dignity being injured.

Here the citizen will be reduced to being an observer of his own loneliness. It is not even a case of just poor architecture – poor architecture is normally human and tolerable for that reason. The point is how a magnificent city such as Amsterdam is in danger of being locally robbed of the very qualities that make it so habitable, so liveable. Such a brutal blow to the heart of an organism cannot but affect the entire body. This is mutilation – rape, not simple deterioration. The grandeur of Amsterdam's old city centre (I use the term grandeur because those responsible for this attack on Amsterdam no doubt were concerned with 'grandeur', albeit of a very different kind) lies in the wonder of its humane proportions and clear structure. For hundreds of years this humane dimension and structure have accorded with a correspondingly humane life view – being a direct product of it, of course.

The city and the life in it are of the same stuff, have the same climate – and this is something you can no longer say of all cities, however visually attractive they may still be. The old houses along the canals, the canals themselves and the streets connecting them – even the only royal building, the Palace at the Dam – and the enormous churches with their melodious towers, they largely get by together, and not in the first place separately. Nowhere does (did) one thing impose itself at the expense of any other (apart from a few exceptions of recent date); no bombast, no domineering size, no separate objects made autonomous. The stamp of an enterprising middle class is still clearly visible. It is a city where business sense and culture have always gone together. Traces of tyranny are not found here – at least, not until now. But there are plenty of old almshouses for the elderly, the poor and the orphans. A truly beloved tradition!

And now, all of a sudden, this project: Amsterdam has never been confronted with such a merciless proposal as the one which must be decided upon so soon. Its execution would amount to ratifying a general devaluation of feeling, and this is not what Amsterdam, not its past and not its future, deserves. Nor is it what any citizen of Amsterdam deserves – or is it all just to impress the outsider: the Rotterdammer (!), or the provincial visitor, or the German tourist (!) – no councillor, no burgomaster, no bride and groom deserve this. Nor does the old Jewish quarter, with its flea market on the Waterlooplein and the dark memories of the recent past, deserve such treatment. No, this is just unthinkable, I refuse to believe it, it will not happen. It would be the hollow gesture of a frustrated provincial town to carry out such a plan, it would be a manifestation of anxiety, of scorn for all that is human, of small-minded megalomania, of a lack of realism.

Let Amsterdam overcome its inferiority complex by all means, but not by hiding it behind pointless ostentation (really, have those nasty people who behaved like this not yet been defeated?) by propping something upright which as a project is already stone-dead, which no human being can relate to on human terms (they call that a square?) that no one can enter on human terms, (is that an 'entrance'?), where no one can, humanly speaking, reside or work (is that space?), in short, where it is impossible to be a man among men (and this in Amsterdam, of all places!). For no ordinary mortal can retain his identity in the vicinity of such an outrage. A true monarch would smile scornfully, gods would begin to doubt again. Only the vulgar, forever innerly deprived might feel somewhat supported.

The nervous system of a modern city has several focal points – also, but by no means exclusively and certainly not *a priori* in its town hall. Of course a town hall has a specific meaning, *but none other than that*. So why cling to the contrary with such desperate tenacity? And in such a way that even that specific meaning is lost, leaving only a travesty. Isn't this a nasty paradox? Isn't it nonsensical? A good town

J. Berghoef and
J. Vegter, Amsterdam
town hall project,
1961

hall is a serviceable apparatus. This apparatus makes its own specific contribution to the well being of the urban community it serves. It can moreover rely on the affection which its efficacious contribution will earn it. It is what it should be or it is not, but it can never be more and must never be other than that. It has no right to demand more affection than it disinterestedly deserves. Today the community has set sensible limits to the scope of a town hall as a civic apparatus, it is the community that assigns and determines its tasks.

May the apparatus therefore answer with positive deeds the full scope of the competence it has been granted, instead of trying to disguise it, out of sheer impotence, by entrenching itself behind the abstract delusion of a vulgar palace. Is it so aware of its baldness that it needs a wig? Is it so weak that it has to bamboozle the community with gilt-edged splendour, to intimidate, to exact respect under compulsion? Have we reached that stage again? We will not and may not assume this, although the realization of this monstrosity would certainly suggest the contrary. We have no reason to suspect the municipal authorities, nor the architects who drew up the plan, of deliberately intending this. The point is in fact that this plan, perhaps involuntarily (let us assume so) has developed into something which, if executed, will inevitably signify all these negative intentions. So beware, members of the city executive, Amsterdam is unaccustomed to this sort of intervention!

Amsterdam deserves a beloved town hall on a beloved site (nothing wrong with the site), where it will be a pleasure to work, where pleasing and worthy celebrations can be held on occasion, where it is a pleasure to be, to come and go – and for all those reasons pleasing to look at, too. A human place, with a human task: at one with everyday existence, and indeed just as concrete and matter-of-fact.

But there is no trace of any of this in the plan. It is not only appallingly abstract and unreal, it is also appallingly uncertain. It is a plan without proportions, without proportions in the general sense – and therefore obviously also in the architectonic sense. If we did not know that architects were involved we would be inclined to regard the plan as the graphic concretization of mental misbehaviour (now it remains a disconcerting riddle). Everything is systematically wrong with it. May Amsterdam be spared its 'built concretization'!

Let me give a few concrete examples: the insular rectangular site which bears the self-contained building mass makes a sharp cut in the course of the Amstel, degrading the river at the very place where it curves, to the status of a decorative pond (the designer who has no feeling for his fellow man can have no feeling for rivers); this makes the river appear to go on into the Zwanenburgwal, while in reality the space of the Amstel clearly continues along the Munt, Rokin and Damrak – with or without water. The great 'fore-square' is not a place where people will meet spontaneously but a barren plane to keep people at a distance – an empty plane outside as a pendant to the emptiness inside. In no sense is it a space, so it can be neither a square nor a place (buildings and squares must, in order to become real buildings and squares, fill themselves with people and human activity as lungs fill themselves with air, as veins fill themselves with blood). Where there is so much emptiness there is only place for more emptiness – only 'space' for loneliness, The same goes for the insane 'inner court', because there is no such thing here as an inner court. It is an empty, tall shaft – an inbetween-emptiness! As for the entrance, it is the same story all over again: this is not what we understand by 'entrance', i.e. the architectonic score of coming and going. Once 'inside' the visitor will find, to his amazement, that the building simply ceases to exist after he has walked only a few paces. A long introduction leading to nothing. A meaningless introduction.

The enormous hall complex – even on paper – defies every description. A full-size model would immediately convince the Council of the impossibility of carrying out such an idea. Since this is impossible, I must appeal to their imagination. The perspective drawings accompanying the plan aren't that bad, after all – all those little black specks represent people – including yourself!

Let me mention a few other aspects before concluding (the worst is still to come!): the forbidding, huge staircase which no elderly person will dare to set foot on; the grotesque, protruding council-room (in spite of the overwhelming size of the surrounding hallways, it obviously couldn't be incorporated in any other way!) looks like an inflated cigar box (probably symbolic); the eighty-metre-long (eighty metres!) monumental corridor or bridge between the two ends of the U-shaped representative section, with glass on either side from floor to ceiling and, believe it or not, with some odd bench for those who find themselves at a loss or who simply can't go on.

The senseless balcony – hundreds of metres long – surrounding the entire block and designed so as not to afford a view of the Amstel from the inside (this is called a riverside location!); this uninterrupted balcony serves one single purpose: to produce a horizontal articulation in the facade. The result is just the reverse, because the entire ground floor now functions as a sort of pedestal. The Burgomaster's room is just a big cage that has been pushed into the corner, and just as cage-like as the countless other cages, big and small, stacked from one floor to the next, from one end to the other, laced on corridors without end along the entire exterior circumference. The 'Burgerzaal' is a long narrow box for 1200 guests, without a single toilet in the vicinity (in this respect at least comparable to Versailles). Here the tall, paired columns on the window-side are, if not constructively, certainly structurally unacceptable. They are paired columns of which by turns only one will be visible – i.e. a column too many alternated with a column too few. A frightening sensation, that's not the way to treat columns, and certainly not without impunity.

But now, finally, the worst of all, the very worst, because it shows such a gross lack of respect for all those not so highly placed officials who are expected to work there, as well as for all the people who have to be there, hour by hour. I am referring to the office floors unthinkingly piled up on top of all that pseudo-representativeness. Indescribable, this ruthless transition from glooming ostentation to dismal aridity. What a repulsive symbol of harshness towards man, and merciless insensitivity. To look at the ground plans and sections is to disbelieve what you see: what the façades lead one to suspect proves to be true.

Hundreds of civil servants will have to go up the stark staircases and elevators hidden away in elongated vertical service shafts on either side to rush past the 'noble' floor, so that they may do their day's work in one of the three office floors above. 'Let them work but let them not be seen' is the obvious message that this sickening scheme conveys. That is why I consider this a design crime. So here I shall end my negative story. As I said before, everything is wrong with this building, and moreover the ultimate limit of negativeness has been far overstepped. But I do wish to say something else, something that is very close to my heart: painters and sculptors will be expected to contribute to the embellishment of this building, to make it worthy of Amsterdam – in keeping with a time-honoured tradition!

All I can say is this: no one can feel at home in such a building, so no artist either.

I would be deeply disappointed if there were many who find reason to disagree fundamentally with all I have said against the plan, because that would only increase the chances that this piece of cultural misery will be put into effect. My confidence in Amsterdam is still too great to take this possibility very seriously.

Just as we try, for the sake of life itself, to forget the very worst in any sphere, so we must try to forget this plan – pretend we never saw it and take good care that Amsterdam gets what this city, by virtue of its nature, deserves – a beloved, heartwarming town hall on the Amstel where it will be pleasant for all to work, where it will be a delight to go and to be. A building that will derive its distinction, its grandeur, from the very fact that it offers these circumstances, for this is the only kind of grandeur that can truly enhance a building today.

Not a pre-conceived grandeur, but a deserved grandeur. The Amstel, too, would rejoice in this. Let the building be representative – of one thing: of the affection one citizen feels for the other, of the work done by the other in the service of the community. Let it be as Amsterdam always was, still is, and hopefully will continue to be – a human city.

City centre as donor

Explanatory note on the Amsterdam Nieuwmarkt Project, published in Forum, *November 1970*[1]

There are a number of general concepts at the basis of our plan for the Nieuwmarkt neighbourhood. These ideas apply to Amsterdam in particular, but they are also relevant to other old, spatially homogenous urban cores, large and small, in Holland and elsewhere. To regard a city centre as the place where most social, cultural as well as economic activities are concentrated, produced and distributed, is an obsolete nineteenth-century notion.

Today's means of communication render this superfluous, while the increasing size of the economic establishments and all the concomitant accretions render their combination impossible.

We believe that today old city centres – both their spatial reality and their content – are psychologically indispensable for their own sake, simply because they exist in all their multicoloured intensity and enclosure, and because so far no newly-built districts possess these essential qualities in the least, not even in a contemporary version. They are rigid, empty and sterile and are therefore inadequate as places to live. As long as they remain this way, the city centre will continue to function as a donor. Nowadays, however, its donor task is too great for its size. It is therefore absolutely essential not only to keep its size as large as possible, but to ensure that the addition of certain quanta does not have the effect of losing precisely those qualities that, owing to the sterility of the suburbs, make it into a donor.

Breaking open the old city centres to make them more easily accessible to traffic for the convenience of those people who have no choice but to travel there every day, results in the creation of a space where those very concentrations can and probably will occur which, because of their function, are alienated from the existing structure, which have no obvious and direct human relevance and which are therefore emotionally inaccessible. The mutations which take place constantly in every city and which are truly necessitated by changed circumstances will have to be shaped with more imagination, more subtly, more circumspectly, and more organically. The results of this continuous process must always be a reflection of collective behavioural patterns. If society is to safeguard its own identity, everyone alike will have to contribute to the continual changes in the urban environment. This will not be made any easier by the far-reaching changes that are wrought for the benefit of the community, but nor will it be rendered impossible.

A city which dismisses the creative potential and spontaneous initiatives of its inhabitants, which reflects only what people do there and not what they are always doing to it: adding to it and changing it, will end up dismissing its own self – it will die.

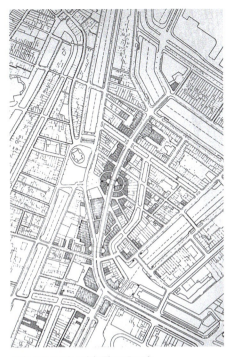

Aldo van Eyck, with Theo Bosch, Nieuwmarkt project, 1970

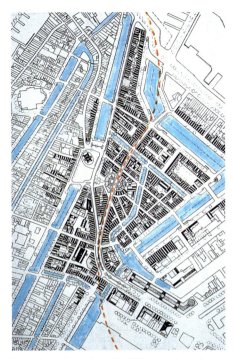

Plan of newly designed buildings and roof plan

Axonometric view of the Nieuwmarkt area after the demolitions necessitated by the planned metro line

The official plan of the Amsterdam City Administration for the transformation of the Nieuwmarkt area, 1953–1959

An experiment to counter urban corrosion

Translation of 'Een experiment tegen aantasting', published in TABK, *November 1971*[1]

Although the adaptation of an old city centre to new circumstances is both desirable and inevitable, it is our opinion that the alterations this sort of 'adaptation' requires need not signify the erosion of the essential meaning of the old city centre as a donor. Additional mutilation of the spatial and social structure for reasons of quantity, which is irreconcilable with their scale and nature, is inadmissible.

On the basis of the conviction that the spatial and social structure (form and function) mutually support and substantiate each other, the further development of the old city centre (in time and space) requires combined attention because the one is to be guaranteed partly by the other (the spatial aspect by the social, and *vice versa*). We would like to point out a number of safeguards against the erosion of old city centres included in the plan and underline them as an example for a new overall approach.

– Preservation and/or adaptation of the variety of functions and their meaningful interweaving.
– No introduction of functions that essentially weaken or destroy either the spatial image or social substance of what already exists.
– No disconnection of the various local functions and no strengthening of the work function to the detriment of dwelling (that proves to be economically weaker).

Variety in this dwelling function too; in this case dwellings for large and small families, singles and the elderly. One important aspect of dwelling in old city centres, which comes out in the present plan, lies in the meaning we think we ought to attach to the existing old houses, even if they are not monuments. We consider it unjust that, as all too often happens, existing houses are protected but not the people who live in them. The clearing of the economically weak out of their neighbourhoods and the accompanying dilapidation of their houses erodes the social quality of an old city centre as a place where everyone should be able to freely choose to continue living. Attractive or not, in good or not-so-good condition, being able or not to meet set standards (which?); this plan is based on the idea that no houses are to be demolished if it is not strictly necessary. Since the advantages and disadvantages of living in a city centre are not the same as for living in the new suburbs, different standards need to apply to homes in the city (regarding access, distance between homes and their division). In this way greater density can also be achieved than is usual for new building in old city centres. Denser housing benefits the seclusion of the public urban space. In principle, we avoided breaking open this seclusion for the purposes of car traffic, concentrated parking or large-scale business premises. It is a negative paradox to 'improve' the movement of traffic and parking to the detriment of that to which one wishes to create access.

Sociocide

Statement likely written about 1971 and published in 1979[1]

Cities are chaotic and necessarily so . They are also kaleidoscopic. This should be accepted as a positive credo before it is too late. Order has no function, this side of evil, other than to make what is essentially chaotic work. Add to this the notion that no abstract norm imposed from above or any other motive, sanitary or speculative, can further justify the wanton destruction of existing buildings or street patterns, nor that which invariably accompanies the demolition of old 'sub-standard' or 'obsolete' housing: I mean the involuntary removal of people from their domicile, be it house, street or neighbourhood. Ultimately, the world today can no longer afford such waste, nor can it afford to overlook the right of people to maintain both the built form and the social fabric of their domicile if that is their choice. Anything else is sociocide – local genocide with only the people left alive.

The fury of renewal

Statement probably written in about 1974 and published in 1986[1]

For several decades now, when it comes to cities and what lies between them, the Netherlands has been overcome by a sort of madness – an almost collective madness (the Netherlands are small but the blind spot is big). Not a single village, city or region has escaped this fury of renewal unharmed.

Things are a little calmer now, and that is at least something! If anyone were to ask me at present what best befits an urban planner, I would say: a bad conscience. Because it is they in the first place who, since the war, have been so expertly engaged in organising the meagre.

In order to reach old city centres they were first partly demolished. Demolish what you want to reach. Take away that which you want to get to... it's even worse than a paradox. Traffic experts designed ring-roads and radial roads on the map of every town and city, large and small. Since then everything that bordered those roads has vanished. There was only one formula for the rolling traffic axis: more of the same. If blockages were the aim, this was certainly the perfect way.

An additional unpleasant side-effect of this is 'slum clearance' – an often sly and crooked business. This does not intended to 'declare uninhabitable' the place where people live and work, but to make it uninhabitable by labelling it as such. Goodbye neighbourhood – goodbye to everything that was there – sociocide.

On breaking through monuments

Translation of some statements made in an interview, published in 1974[1]

What has to be built is stated in the programme: this much space, this many rooms. But the city is dumb, it remains silent. The vulnerable city that you can break without anyone saying 'stop, don't do it'. They say it with regard to isolated buildings, exceptional buildings and monuments. But the understanding that the course of a street can also be a monument is gradually starting to dawn, even without seventeenth-century houses or a halo. It is all about the whole and above all about the people who live in it.

It has never been a human right, but I believe it should become one: the inalienable right of people, of a group of people, to continue to live in their neighbourhood if they so wish. A neighbourhood is not just a certain number of people in a particular place. Take Kattenburg, formerly an individual neighbourhood with its own individual language, its own games, the way it was lived and had grown, with interhuman contacts at every level... and all at once it was swept away with the houses. Swept entirely away. You try to find a word for it. The word sociocide, which I sometimes use, is of course not very accurate, because I don't mean the murder of a community in the physical sense, in the sense of destroying people. The difference with genocide is that the people remain alive, but apart from that everything is gone, all the relationships between the people are gone and all that remain are sad displaced people. If you travel in the world and see how places are cleared completely, it seems that, always and everywhere, the roads need to run where the poor live. It's strange, isn't it? As if the devil were playing with it. It's the vulnerable ones that get the short end of the stick. How on earth would this come about?

The way the Zuiderkerk is now – open – is of course an utter aberration. It was of course never the intention to open up this church. We wanted to close it in again, though differently from in the past, so that it appeared rather mysteriously above the roofs. But the way it is now you have to watch out you don't drive straight into it. We also put in a proposal for an alternative way through! If you are embarked on

The Nieuwmarkt area after the destructions executed in order to dig the metro trench, 1975.

Van Eyck's ironic proposal for an alternative road trajectory through the Nieuwmarkt area, 1970.
Photo Gerhard Jaeger

a breakthrough, you should do it properly. We made a sketch of the Zuiderkerk and I thought, do you know what? We'll make a big hole in it and we'll drive straight through the church, because that's the shortest way to the Dam. What more could they want? Straight through the city in the direction of Zaandam. The unfunny thing about the joke is that they won't do it. Because it's a seventeenth-century monument! They wouldn't go through that. But they would go straight through a monument if it's a neighbourhood with canals and streets and people. Vulnerable people. I am gradually getting sick of the invulnerability of a seventeenth-century monument.

Mutation, insertion, in-fill, accommodate people in what there is: the city has to carry on living like the language, which also changes every day. The language is also one of the few things you can compare the city to. Language as a communication system. There is language in its role as a convention, a sort of imposed norm, such as grammar. If you stick to it well they say, 'that's good Dutch'. But there are people who keep to all the rules of grammar but still speak poor Dutch, because they have nothing to say. And you have people who break the rules and have a lot to say, and for that reason speak good Dutch. The language and its use together form the language. The language is created not only by linguists, writers and poets, but by everyone who uses it. The same applies to the city.

Apart from that you can only compare the city to a dream. In a dream too, everything follows a logic different from the one that occupies your mind during the day: constant mutations, constant leaps. Everything interlocks, much more than you are aware of. The city is chaotic, necessarily chaotic, and kaleidoscopic. Unfortunately it seems too few people accept this. They have trouble accepting chaos as a positive factor. That brings us to a different definition of order. I believe that order can mean nothing other than making chaos possible – making sure that chaos does not choke on itself, does not change from a positive to a negative factor. Every other form of order that attempts to eliminate chaos, complexity and the elusive and never-to-be-defined network of human relationships – a network of such simultaneous complexity that no sociologist can figure it out – is not order at all, but is death itself. Order is what you bestow on chaos so it becomes liveable.

The mute requirements

Statement published in L'Architecture d'Aujourd'hui, *January-February 1975*[1]

It is those *other* requirements – the mute kind – which seldom speak from the client's brief, but nonetheless constitute the real 'countenance' of the site, that can best goad an architect, sensitive to them, towards a design idea which appropriately fulfils the verbalized requirements which do speak from the brief. Buildings, especially within the fabric of old city centres, that misbehave towards what is already there – towards what exists outside – will also misbehave towards what is inside, towards what they are expected to serve in the first place. In short, they must be right irrespective of their specific function. The relationship between a building's interior spatial organization and the exterior urban context to which it is added and hopefully will manage to belong, is not only a formal and spatial one, it is also a temporal one. That is why buildings should have temporal perspective and associative depth – so very different, both, from arbitrary historic indulgence. A building doesn't need to look like its neighbours in order to avoid alienation, but it should take heed. Response through mimicry is faint-hearted, in every way futile. That is why the typology addicts of today are such a liability!

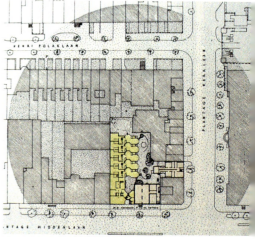

Aldo van Eyck, Hubertus House, Amsterdam, 1973–1978 Photo Aldo van Eyck

You can't build a thing like that for people!

Translation of an article published in the daily newspaper Het Parool, *on 26 June 1981*[1]

I recently received a box full of press views, interviews and reports on the whole 'Stopera' affair, as well as the reports by the Commission for the Old City ('beauty commission').

What strikes one first is that a lot was written – early on, good and unanimous. The suggestion that criticism came too late, which the municipal authorities in particular make, is completely incorrect. *It is simply that no one wanted to read or listen.* In addition, after reading the interviews with and the explanations by the two architects, *Holzbauer* and *Dam*, one is struck by their constant overestimation of themselves and by their adulation of their poor piece of work. They do not give a normal answer to one single question, remark or suggestion from others. All criticism is brushed aside with the aid of clever rhetoric. Or else they lead one to understand that some things have already been incorporated or will be at a subsequent stage.

The praise they constantly lavish on themselves and their masterpiece without the expression of any reasonable doubt washes over everything that comes their way and thus conceals everything unfitting. 'It becomes more refined every time one touches it,' says Dam. 'Fantastic things are still taking shape,' is Holzbauer's opinion. Dam believes that, 'it will make a contribution to the beauty of the city.' Alright. Enough. And also 'It will become more and more sparkling.'

They conceitedly say, 'People are not capable of reading plans'. That's true. But this is followed by, 'They do not have the imagination to see how fine it will become.' *This is indeed unfortunate, because there remains little else for me, who can read plans, to point out that anything but 'sparkling' is going to happen – only an awful mess.* 'We are actually dealers in dreams,' is these gentlemen's opinion of themselves. And to think that their dreams are just illusions. They then add to this, 'But what are drawings?' In other words, even those who can read them cannot discern the miracles that are going to happen. Whereby they demand unlimited confidence.

'We can think up hundreds of variations, just as we have the choice of thousands of sorts of facade cladding.' This statement does not inspire confidence, *because you only think up hundreds of variations when not a single one is satisfactory!* And then that dizzying arsenal of thousands of sorts of facade cladding – it ignores the question of whether one needs 'facade cladding' at all. It is a not uninteresting fact that most buildings in the Netherlands have no cladding, and yet lack nothing!

Let me now briefly go into a few of the architects' more polemical statements. Mr Holzbauer, for instance, says, 'We are not structuralists'. I accept that without question, because in spatial terms the plan is as good as structureless. *'We are not architects who see a building as the sum of smaller elements.'* This in any case tells us something about what they mean by 'structuralists'. And seen from their point of view, of

The bend of the river Amstel where it enters the Amsterdam inner city.

The Stopera by Holzbauer and Dam, carried out in 1982–1986.

course, they are right, because the meaning of all those small and smaller elements (everything extraneous to the grand gesture), which they do not want to sum up, is a reality as large as life.

It is also possible that they do not, or do not want to see this meaning. If you look at it that way, the Stopera plan is not the 'sum of smaller elements', but the miserable result of what they did not see, of what they passed over: all those ordinary, small and smaller, tangible things that together make a building agreeable. Usable, in the sense of bringing it close to the user. *This user – nowadays you are tackled on this point if you dare say it – is just a human being!*

The architects pursue their 'we are not this nor that' to the bitter end, at which point they add, 'We see a building as a large form, an image. Let's say an *objet d'art*. There are too few large buildings in Amsterdam.' And also, 'We are not Hertzbergers.'

Now that really amazes me! They don't want to be Hertzbergers, but I wouldn't be too proud about that, considering the craftsmanship of the music centre in Utrecht, which is beyond the abilities of these two gentlemen, and where there is so much to be found of precisely those things that lie outside their comprehension, which they do not want to 'sum up'. *'We do not think like Hertzberger and Aldo, we think differently'* – I dare say.

Louvre

Another striking statement by Mr Holzbauer of which I ought not to deprive the reader: 'The Dutch at home have an almost neurotic reaction to big things, but hardly have they crossed the border before they are singing the praises of such large complexes as the Louvre with its great 300 metre-long wings.' So, now we know that too.

Literally everything is wrong about this claim about the Dutch. Insofar as the Dutch are averse to big things on home ground, it is not a deficiency or shortcoming ('neurotic'!), but is based simply on their nature. And is in any case their absolute right. No Sun King has ever ruled here! Nor was their any *Kaiserzeit*! The ideas of William the Silent, Hugo the Great, Erasmus and Huygens were not only different, they were far ahead of those of Franz Joseph and his circle. *Their* world was suited to other dimensions.

Anyway, the tendency away from 'big things' in no way indicates a yearning for the small, as is here insinuated. *Is the ring of canals in Amsterdam not big, or just not 'big' enough?* The size and specific *format* of Amsterdam's old centre is founded on an admirable sense of dimension, based on backgrounds, traditions, aspirations, feelings and talents different from those that produced the Louvre. The Louvre is also admirable, but for different reasons. How did it occur to Holzbauer that the Dutch are so full of admiration for all these big things as soon as they get over the border? It is not that 300-metre length that is admired, but what was made of these huge dimensions in the course of a building process lasting more than a century. In any case, monarchs at that time (five of them, from Henry II to Louis XIV) knew very well whom they had to appoint as architect and garden designer. The Louvre is a splendid building, very big indeed, *but without a trace of gigantism*. It is not uniform and not all the same in style: some parts are Renaissance, others Baroque. And although the main dimensions remain the same, the 'size', the scale and the rhythm constantly change.

Talk about large-scale and small-scale has already led to a great many misunderstandings. It is apparent how uncertain people have become on this point from the fact that the opera section of the Stopera is supposed to have the largest backstage and wing area in all Europe, and also the longest opera foyer in the world! These extreme dimensions were never expressly desired. Because the measurements of the stage areas were only recommended after a visit by a German theatre expert. And as far as the gigantic foyer is concerned, the chairman of the 'beauty commission'[2] recently had to admit that he had never realised that it is as long as the Dam is wide.

Pompous

It is the absence of measure, measurelessness, that characterises the Stopera. The big things about it are big in a needless or repellent way – swollen, pompous, ludicrous. And what is small, is small in a repellent way – paltry, mean and cramped. No more unfortunate combination of defects is imaginable in architecture – and in no way does it suit old Amsterdam, where large and small are pleasantly interwoven. But it does alas fit in with the empty excess of Wibautstraat and the Mr Visserplein circuit.

By the way, there has in recent years, and very recently in the Netherlands too, been an increasingly clear and disastrous tendency towards putting the monumental to the fore, towards the 'large form' and often towards a bare sort of classicism too. This is always accompanied by a stinging rejection of any sort of humanist view and of any outside participation. For the building is autonomous, and exists only for its own sake. It is therefore no coincidence that there is increasing interest in *Albert Speer*, friend of the *Führer* and leading architect of the Third Reich. He is 'in', as are the architects who served *Il Duce*. Speer is regularly asked his opinion about today's buildings and architects like to write about him. A gruesome interest. In any case, this wind is blowing again in many countries and here too.

Interest in the Stopera plan is lamentably small, knowledge minimal and well-founded opinion hard to find. That which more or less applies in the worlds of music, dance and sport, i.e. that there it is always a matter of choice between people of quality, does not apply to the genesis of the building. Clients often have such extremes of quality on a single list of candidates, that I can only hope things are different when it comes to choosing a surgeon or pilot rather than an architect! The cost of a good building is not necessarily higher than that of a bad building. On the contrary. But what is much worse is that one cannot escape from a bad building – unlike a bad book, song, painting, performance or competition. It appears all at once and cannot simply be removed. Nor can one simply say, 'Better luck next time'.

The failure in the case of the Stopera cannot of course be blamed on the two architects alone. There is no possible doubt that from the very beginning there was no identifiable client to put his conceptual wishes clearly on the table – neither for the town hall nor for the opera.

The demolition of the whole area around Waterlooplein took place in stages – agonisingly. One can hardly imagine any more reckless and short-sighted mutilation of one of the finest city centres in the world. And let no one forget the assault on the inhabitants. This senseless fury of demolition was not limited to this spot, but reached out brutally in other directions: the whole of the old Weesperstraat disappeared, as did parts of the Nieuwmarkt neighbourhood as far as the Kromme Waal. A little further away Kattenburg disappeared too, lock, stock and barrel. As a result of the tenacious initiatives of the Nieuwmarkt neighbourhood, that part of the old city, despite the underground, was partly saved. Now it's the turn of that desert of clearances alongside the Amstel.

As an urban space and marketplace, the former Waterlooplein lost its function and meaning when it was separated from its original surroundings. In other words, when the old populated neighbourhoods there, just like those along Jodenbreestraat and Weesperstraat, had to make way for broad roads, a circuit and large office buildings. The municipal authorities, always given abominably bad 'expert' advice, must now at last understand and admit that they must not pursue their blunder of the *city-destroying* Wibautstraat as it intends to do with the Stopera. What they should pursue is precisely what, around the Nieuwmarkt, at the last moment turned out to be possible and *constructive for the city*. It was above all the Department of Urban Development (now 'Environmental Planning') that was slow and very poor in its consideration of the what, where, why and how of the eastern part of the city centre. As early as the immediate post-war period they had a blind spot for everything that lay beyond Kloveniersburgwal. Not the least understanding was shown for the superb 'island' structure, more like a sort of aggression.

It is therefore not incomprehensible that, on the basis of this mentality, they used only fossilised, outdated concepts regarding the what, where, why and how of the town hall and opera. They became obsessions just as the underground railway was an obsession. These buildings, preferably two in one, will and must be built! What, where, how and why is no longer relevant. And certainly no feedback, because monkeys can't do that either.

Now it's enough. Enough violence has been done to the inner city. Now virtually every means is permitted to stop the municipal authorities building the Stopera as a lasting scar in this desert. After everything that has taken place there, precisely this spot surely does not deserve a blot on the landscape, nor an architectural death blow.

Nonentity

As far as the opera is concerned, one can in any case say that the basic principle of a new building for opera and ballet is good, as is the site. But, as far as the last point is concerned, that does not mean the opera is good for that location in terms of urban planning. In this respect one might call it over-exploitation of the site, and the same applies to the town hall. The town hall itself was pushed so much into a corner by the intrusive opera that the municipal offices section at least has both internally and externally become an unusable nonentity. *You can't build a thing like that for people!* What's more, this rash of offices means that the world-without-measure of Wibautstraat penetrates further into the city centre.

But first the plan for the opera. In my opinion, no one need doubt that generous facilities for opera and ballet definitely belong on this site. What the trouble is, and the local opera and ballet 'experts' also know this if they just think a little, is that some of the main components are much too big, while the form of others actually hinders certain important performance possibilities. The space next to and behind the actual stage are among the biggest in the world (larger than those of Paris, London, New York and Vienna!).

And then there are the problems of budgetary management, which inevitably ensue from this absurd excess: who will solve them? By what means? Why? This excess creates pressure on the whole urban and national events establishment, which is in danger of being undermined and disrupted. Initiatives in music and dance that are smaller and more modest, but no less important culturally, will find themselves in a tight corner.

It is to be hoped that the Arts Council, and others who have long been convinced of this, will rapidly make their opinions known. To remain silent or keep a low profile can only be interpreted as neglecting one's responsibility, whereby one leaves the municipal authorities in ignorance and wrongs the city of Amsterdam.

Amstel Ditch

Back to the opera building. In contrast to the technical possibilities backstage, there is a lack of good-quality artistic possibilities in front of the stage. *Bijvoet*, an architect of substance who was never shy of improving on his designs, said that everything that is possible in front of the stage at the Carré should in any case be possible in the new opera building too. If only it were true. Anyway, we are now waiting for the comments of those who really know, but are as yet remaining silent.

The entrance hall and foyer, which contain the 'waterfall of stairs' mentioned by the architects, is out of all proportion. *What is more, these spaces are empty and ugly, nothing other than colossal, and neither elegant nor festive.*

There is hardly any trace of spatial development, because around the huge curve of the auditorium itself the eye is focused radially either outwards or inwards. In the first case this means that the opposite side of the Amstel is as it were right under your nose, so that this river is downgraded to a ditch.

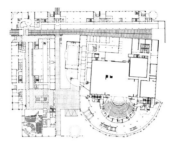
Holzbauer and Dam, Stopera project, 1981, first and second floor

Let the interested reader take up a position in front of the monument on the Dam, facing the Palace. *Let him then, instead of the palace, imagine an enormous 16-metre high curved wall with large openings, bulging about 25 metres towards him, and as wide as... no, not the palace, but the whole of the Dam!* The same reader is now standing on the Amstel, facing the Stopera. Can you see it? The way the brutal counter-bulge of this wall-as-wide-as-the-Dam opposes the bend in the Amstel. It is as if the Amstel were breaking.

And the opera foyer behind it is as long as this bulge is broad! What on earth can be going on there during what, after all, are relatively short intervals, except getting hold of a coffee or a beer and talking a little to the person standing right next to you? Exceptionally regal, is it not, my good sirs, dear architects, all that crockery and all those empty bottles left all over the place? Even half of this foyer is too big, perhaps even a hundredth.

But now the very worst: the town hall part of the Stopera. Buildings do not bring us paradise on earth, but they are able to cause a great deal of woe if every effort is not made to make sure it is pleasant to go there or spend time there.

It seems that no one who has up to now been directly involved has really considered the concept of the town hall and what it might signify instead of the awful existing cliché-ridden image.

What is necessary to make sure that those who spend time there everyday do not do so unwillingly? After all, for so many people to work together in a large building, day in, day out, year after year, is quite simply already half a disaster. In what way might the building be able to help people to be less reluctant to go there, as to the Central Station and the main post office? In short, how do you make sure it does not become a superfluous bastion of bureaucracy? Judging by the brief *and* the town hall part of the Stopera that has now been designed, no one has asked themselves this question. One might almost call it *subhuman*, this perseverance in such indifferent behaviour, or in fact a complete absence of behaviour, and it is certainly *lacking in civilisation*.

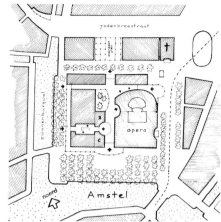

Aldo van Eyck cutting up the Stopera project and joining the pieces into an alternative plan
Photo Izak Salomons

The part played by the Commission for the Old City ('beauty commission') is especially lamentable. I have the official reports in front of me now and I hope never to see anything like it again. Sitting round the table, they discussed with superficial seriousness a variety of secondary external matters without for a moment touching on the heart of the matter. For an hour or so they stood on the sidelines offering design advice, which the reports then call '*strong guidance*'. Each of these gentlemen represents only the shadow of a partial point of view!

When added together, the half-comments made undermine each other, so that all that remains is pure drivel. These gentlemen love sitting in judgement, this comradely patronising approach: '*very good*', '*exciting*', '*forceful*' and '*fine*' alternated with 'I wonder whether...', 'I might have preferred...' and all manner of tiny doubts.

One member did upset this routine twice by actually hitting the nail on the head, even if it was by an indirect stroke. He said, 'At a time when we are awash in aggressive architecture, I am struck by the generous playfulness of the design. Perhaps this façade is a final remnant of this aggressive architecture.' Shortly afterwards he remarks that the brick shell with its bands of stone opposite the glass curtain wall looks like 'a blazer worn with jeans'. In other words, *like a mattress on a bottle of wine*, but words like that do not mix well with 'generous playfulness'. Nevertheless, the first meaningful sound has thus been half expressed.

The chairman of the 'beauty commission' considers the interweaving of the two buildings 'very natural'. When one sees how they clash against each other crookedly inside and almost say farewell to each other outside, this is a statement intended to smother any hint of the opposite view. Who else dares say anything? Another member would like the square to be closed off better on the Amstel side, whereas in fact there is no 'square' there. If there were one, surely one would not want to 'close it off'? The Amstel itself and the houses on the opposite bank do that.

Rudy Uytenhaak, morphological study of the project area, showing that it was a vast urban quarter offering place for several existing large scale buildings: the Munipal Theatre, the Royal Palace, Leidseplein, the Wibaut offices complex and 300 dwellings.

Yet another member wants to 'add some refinement' to the six facade screens that run in a curve and are indeed quite brutal, but most members actually prefer them 'completely in concrete' and not clad in stone. One member finds these screening front buildings 'odd, but possibly interesting'. I am not making this up, it's all there in black and white!

Yet another: 'The council chamber is too small in proportion to the three other elements.' *Why is the truth avoided here, and why does he not say, 'The other elements are too large in proportion to the council chamber?* On the council chamber the report says 'that criticism is concentrated on this component. And that when, in terms of size and shape, this part is precisely the least unreasonable element in the plan.

This sort of group waffling carries on for a while and then all at once comes the approval. Like the Department of Urban Development, this so-called 'beauty commission' was already very much open to doubt. But now they have no credibility left whatsoever. And then they stick their heads in the sand too – it's a nasty mess.

What now? Will eyes at last be opened? After all, that does happen from time to time.

Where, in the eastern part of Amsterdam, will the dividing line be between the worst and the best of what has happened in urban planning? *The worst on one side of the Waterlooplein, the best on the other.* Whether it is the no man's land of Wibautstraat that will continue as far as the Amstel, or the miracle that turned out to be possible between the Zuiderkerk and Kromme Waal (re-establishment of the Nieuwmarkt neighbourhood) that does. *In other words, whether the Stopera-wasteland is permanently withdrawn from the structure of the city centre, or the erosion that has already taken place as a result of demolition and the intended building of alien elements is yet undone by giving this place back to the city centre. Is this actually still an issue?*

By now again refusing to allow the use of this area to be discussed, this duty is once again reneged upon. This, dear Messrs. Polak, Schaefer and Van der Vlis,³ will in any case be to no one's credit. On the contrary.

What a superb opportunity to bring a little closer something of the socio-cultural policy of yesteryear, which now seems a long way off! Considering the special significance of *Wibaut*,⁴ the sad paradox of *Wibautstraat* ought not to be made even sadder by continuing with something that happened there precisely through a lack of social vision. It requires *political courage* to go back on decisions already taken or to change course when it turns out to be wrong. But I see no reason simply to assume that this courage will be lacking in the politicians concerned, as soon as the fixation on '*rather this than nothing*' has been removed and makes way for '*rather nothing than this*'. The road to what is a lot better than nothing, something good, is then once again open and passable.

I would like to know whether the proposed local zoning plan on which the Stopera is based is formally (or even legally) in order. To put it another way, whether there is any approving decision that can be taken, when the actual urban planning work has not been done or turns out to be defective. The Provincial Executive of North Holland should have issued a judgement on this. But unfortunately, despite all objections, they have just recently approved the uses to which the area may be put.

The proposed zoning plan need not be entirely rejected. If it were reduced to the right size, the Stopera might certainly contribute to this place once again becoming a many-sided urban district. The same applies just as much to the old market square. It would be a good thing to let the market start under the trees that I can imagine so well alongside the Amstel. Then there would be an *Amstel Market* – that sounds good, doesn't it?!

As far as the town hall is concerned, parts of it could be located there too: the council chamber and possibly those functions that have a direct public meaning, such as marriage rooms and the registry of births, deaths and marriages. For the huge municipal offices, *which are not necessary on this location at all*, a place outside the area will have to be found. Since Jodenbreestraat, which is after all the remnant of a long superseded and mistaken plan, is three times wider than necessary, this place offers possibilities, possibly combined with an adapted and now vacant Maupoleum. But the municipal offices might also get the place they deserve along Wibautstraat, possibly in one of the gigantic office buildings, since it is no illusion that a general exodus will take place there. Anyway, replacing office staff by other office staff in the proper manner is not the same as roughly chasing away the inhabitants of a neighbourhood for such hard reasons as traffic and offices.

So instead of what does not actually belong on the Waterlooplein (municipal offices) and together with what does belong there but now still occupies an unnecessary amount of space (opera), normal urban life has to be introduced there, as an indispensable constituent of every full urban area. With normal urban streets that *provide access*, that join and connect: Staalstraat, Uilenburgerstraat. Plus all the amenities that go with it such as a few shops, a café, bicycle shed, nursery, neighbourhood centre, playground, etc., etc.

There is no longer any need for an extensive preliminary study of land use. Because this is quite obvious, even though it is insufficiently acknowledged. Nor do the urban planning and spatial issues hold any secrets. Rudi Uytenhaak, an architect who designed some alternatives on the basis of the zoning plan, shows very convincingly how this splendid spot on the Amstel at the heart of Amsterdam could look, as soon as this place is recognised as a rich and full urban area instead of just a building site for a single impenetrable architectural colossus.[5]

It is a large area, but simple in urban planning terms. As is the objective. So one can move forward immediately and at speed. Doubts, hesitation and obscuration have become unnecessary. In the future, the headlines might well be '*Opera shrinks and chases off municipal offices*'. The market stays, plus the council chamber etc., and possibly some housing. And real streets reappear, and thus people too – day and night.

In this aerial photo, the Stopera building has been superimposed to scale on the Dam and its immediate surroundings. Although the buildings around the Dam (Palace, Nieuwe Kerk, Bijenkorf, P&C) cannot really be called small, each of them appears insignificant alongside the gigantic dimensions of the Stopera. One can also see clearly everything that would have to be demolished if the Stopera were to be built on this spot.

The publication of the present article in *Het Parool* (on 26 June 1981), with a photomontage by Izak Salomons showing the size of the planned Stopera by situating it on the Amsterdam Dam, in front of the Royal Palace.

13
Polemics on postmodernism

Introduction to chapter 13

In the course of the seventies a number of a number of trends heading for a break with modern tradition entered the international scene. In Italy Rossi and his *Tendenza* deployed a new rationalism that harked back to the *razionalimo* of the fascist period. They promulgated the autonomy of architecture, detached from all functionality and ideology, an ambition that practically amounted to the reduction of architecture to abstract typologies incorporated in a chill, hierarchical order. Shortly afterwards modern tradition was rejected as a whole by Leon Krier who advocated a radical return to pre-industrial urbanity and therefore came up with a normalized form of handicraft neoclassicism. And in the wake of Venturi, who in 1966 had made a plea for contradiction and complexity in architecture, several kinds of eclecticism soon arose, ironically-intended combinations of forms and fragments from classical and modern tradition which were charted and promoted by Charles Jencks under the label of postmodernism. If some of these developments could, at first sight, be situated in the line of Van Eyck's interest in tradition, and if some of them were probably generated as a response to his appeal to project 'the past into the future via the created present', in fact they all ran counter to the credo he had defended from the start of his career. His interest in the past, in both the classical and the archaic heritage, never did imply a flight from contemporary reality. He always approached tradition from the angle of twentieth-century culture, i.e. from the angle of the twentieth-century avant-garde. From this viewpoint he had manifested himself from the outset as an advocate of true modernism while condemning post-war functionalism as an aberration. From the same position he could now not but react energetically against the tendencies that repudiated the modern tradition.

Van Eyck first turned against the rationalists and the postmoderns in 1976, when he was confronted with their work at two exhibitions in which he participated, the *Dortmunder Architekturausstellung* organized by J.P. Kleinhues and the exhibition *Europa/America,* which took place as part of the 1976 Venice Biennale. Afterwards he seized several opportunities to pursue his offensive. His polemical endeavour culminated in the RIBA Annual Discourse which he delivered in February 1981. On this occasion he bundled his criticism of all the tendencies that he deemed perversions or negations of both the modern movement and the classical tradition. He launched a virulent attack against a number of diverse trends and characters which he lumped together under the label of 'R.P.P.' ('Rats, Posts and other Pests'), from the new rationalists who provocatively reverted to the rigid formalism of the fascist period to the postmoderns who rejected modernism so as to hark back to neoclassicism or neomannerism, and all the variants between them.

In 'The Circle and the Square' Van Eyck reassessed the concept of 'centre' in the context of the contemporary, non-hierarchical view of the world. The fact that reality is not ruled by an intrinsic hierarchy does not mean that the concept of centre ought to be dropped. The new reality is polycentric. Yet, its centres are not fixed, self-contained spots. They should be open centres that enter into interaction with their environment, so as to constitute pivots of asymmetrical equilibrium.

Like that other gift

> *Statement written for the 1976 Venice Biennale, published in* Spazio e società, *December 1979*[1]

With so many architects addicted to a hollow notion of change, and art – even art – hasty and out of breath, we find the builders of today divided into three factions (the third and largest one just picking the crumbs the other two leave behind).

The first lot bundles all those who, because of some lack, real or imagined, have become suspicious of the human faculties which, regardless of time and place, bring about a good building. Placing their shaken confidence in what they crudely imagine science represents, they hope objectivity will bless them with other new and newer methods of design. They are usually flexophiles – and do all sorts of silly things, like turning against the profession of their choice – architecture.

The other lot gathers together all those who (blessed as they already are!), feel art flowing through their enlightened veins. Squinting at the past they rob it of essential material for the next fancy dress. They talk scholastically with a sophisticated air and sometimes carry a slight fascist scent they themselves may well be unaware of.

Thus, people are left to choose from a variety of pests. Not because there are no good buildings left over from the past (or still, occasionally being built today), but simply because there are not enough of them.

It is painfully true of architecture in particular that it is not just good quality which counts, *but a sufficient quantity of such quality*. A good house in Amsterdam is of no use to a family in Venice (or vice versa to avoid any false suggestion).

If making a good building has become too difficult, the dilemma is indeed complete. But is it really all that difficult? Does it really require a genius to avoid the puny?

The past at any rate disproves this generously. It proves (what the present proves sporadically) that it is in the nature of people to deal with environment – hence also to build – adequately and often beautifully; the way they are also given to communicate adequately and often beautifully through language – that other gift.

A message to Mathias Ungers from a different world

Article published in Spazio e società, *December 1979*[1]

This little massage is also for those who, like yourself are given to bending over backwards trying to twist architecture into something which it simply is not: not even in the sense that an apple is not a pear but still a fruit.

Architecture does not mean, nor has it ever meant, nor will it ever come to pass that it may someday mean what people – to sweep them together – like Rossi, that other Aldo, has tried to make it mean; or Tafuri, that italic Rasputin; or the Kriers considerably multiplied creeping over Europe; or Denise contradicting Robert and – recently – Robert himself; or Eisenman-Tigerman-Superman-Simpleman; or the Cooper Union circuit; or the Cornell hedgehogs; or Charles semio-something of London who'll soon be post-post; or you yourself, for that matter with your – or whoever's – OMA ma mix.[2]

Ideas about ideas about ideas about... yes about what? Not about anything as substantial as a useful building? Contrived derivatives just gobbling up forbidden fruits. Perversion rendered distasteful! What strikes me more than the appearance of having been let loose is that the same mechanical notion of time which CIAM, side-stepping the real dimensional of the avant-garde, never overcame, still prevails and accounts for all the awkward posturing vis-à-vis the past. History out history in. In the still so locally limited world of architecture this means: in and out of Rome – a yes or a no to classicism alternating every twenty years or so.

I remember talking about the transparency of time in Otterlo, when CIAM died and Louis Kahn was already spreading incense. At Aix we were really getting somewhere – opening a little window onto a wider world – when Gropius on the very last day started serving his Oh dear industry – happy future – teamwork – no art no-primadonnas kind of gruel. I told him what I thought of him there and then.

Yes bar L.C., Giedion and a few others, CIAM missed the point. But then CIAM and the true avant-garde of architecture did not coincide. Now, although it is probably not the feather you want to stick in your hat, 'the backbenders' certainly deserve credit for the persuasive way they are showing the world what really awful buildings and urban spaces would look like (I always thought that if one was to try making something as ugly as one can following a new trend it would turn out not to be ugly at all). That is how I interpret those pale-coloured two dimensional renderings of buildings and urban spaces many of you have been making. If only they were allowed to speak for themselves! But they are not. Polemics of a strained and awkward kind weigh heavily on these flights of fantasy. 'Flights' in the sense of being carried on the wings of de Chirico or, in more general terms, catching up with surrealism thirty years too late. A drawing, painting, poem, play, films, song etc. can be as intentionally unreal, real or surreal as one wishes and still remain a painting, a poem etc. But no so a building. So actually you are cheating both ways: withholding from a two dimensional medium what belongs to it specifically – autonomy – (pulling it down to the level of social realism) in order to 'illustrate' what it is you wish to saddle architecture with – again autonomy – which does not, should not and cannot belong to it. The kind of autonomy architecture should claim and maintain in order to survive as such – exist – cannot be dissociated from what a building is meant to fulfil in terms of usability and appreciation.

Then, always sustaining this two-way abuse, there is the constant abuse of history – the past selfishly squandered. History, Mathias, to return to the present plight, is not a warehouse for memories, but a gathering body of experience. Memory should not be brought close to a deterministic notion of the past if you want to avoid contaminating its meaning. Memory transcends the clock, it is time humanised (the way occasion is). Without it buildings will have no temporal perspective: something you cannot borrow from a memory warehouse.

Significant discovery, I believe, requires the presence of the past. History is not behind us, because time no longer works that way, not since Joyce, Einstein, Mondrian, Ernst, Le Corbusier and the whole wonderful gang. Time no longer ticks.

And there you go, putting the clock back– starting time ticking again. *Cogito ergo sum* – the prison bars are back.

I got you a deserved prize in 1964 for your Enschede student housing project and, later, saw the one for the Berlin museum. But neither Hadrian nor these projects can account for your recent Lutzowplatz Hotel design. Are you doing Stirling a bad turn or is it vice versa?[3] Anyway, turning co-ordinates by a few degrees, an effective device used to handle well, is not going to redeem that circular shaft from being like hell. I know you like variations on a single theme. So have you tried putting the square inside and the circle outside – like following the limerick, returning from the ride with the lady inside and the smile on the face of the… yes, on whose face, I wonder.[4] Who do you suppose will want to smile down there in that drum or lightwell of yours? Do you care at all? That is the point. You are not going to get the smile off the face of the tiger and back where it belongs in a place like that. If you still like Hadrian then why not a courtyard instead of a shaft.

Why tamper with a fact about which there need be no argument: that it is the architect's job to make pleasant buildings.

Meanwhile we are still on our way and in no hurry. In fact when you get tired of tying history into knots and stop playing tricks instead of playing the game, you will find Team 10 busy with the same inquiry as before, each on his own, most of the time, and in his own way, though luckily never quite alone. What is a good building really like? If that was less obscure, making one would be less difficult and there would be more of them.

You stepped outside our orbit at a certain point, but never a word from you – we were left to notice. Divergence within the Team X orbit occurs and, occasionally should be resolved if our shared enquiry is to continue. Thus for example, Peter and

Alison detected fascism – believe it or not – in a snowflake at the Royaumont meeting in 1962, but still fail to consider the damage that faulty verdict – spitefully published – has done.[5] A little public ceremony will suffice here, but you, Mathias, inside that shaft – in the cage of history – are already beyond reach – unless I am wrong.

Just a closing word about Team X. It has no members, nor has it ever had. Membership was never our line. Does that ring a bell: anyway there is no need to worry: a latecomer like yourself may yet turn out to be the first, last and only member of Team 10.

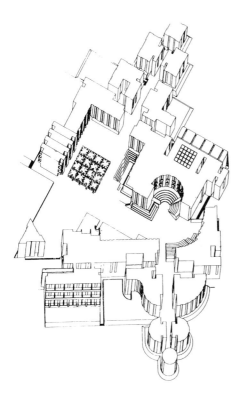

James Stirling, project for the Wissenschaftszentrum at Reichpietschufer, Berlin, 1979

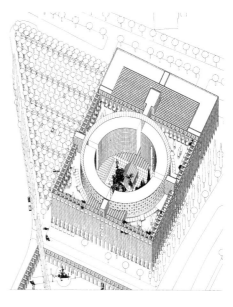

O.M. Ungers, project of Studentenhuisvesting TH Twente, Enschedé, 1964 and project of hotel at Lützowplatz, Berlin, 1979

The Ironbound statement

Address delivered on receiving a honorary doctorate at the New Jersey Institute of Technology,
25 May 1979[1]

Man's scope – our scope – spans disquieting extremes. The same can be said of his tools. Maid or master, technology assists all our doings at every level of intention. Constructive or destructive, it is always by our side – a kind or malicious companion, both.

The evidence of this companionship can be read off the face of the globe, for environment reveals whatever occurs there – like a tell-tale mirror. What we see (if we dare to look) reflected in the mirror – the evidence – is becoming more and more harrowing – even pathological. Indeed, it is befitting today to talk of the pathology of landscape.[2]

Of course you can nod and say: 'Yes, we know, we know!' But do you know – has it really penetrated your consciousness, or are you willing to acknowledge that, whilst in the past societies responded more or less successfully to the problems survival in any given environment poses, ours, those to which you and I belong – the magnanimous ones – are no longer able to? This in spite of bewildering technological and scientific ability – their familiar trademark.

But it is another trademark – a less familiar one now edging in on us – which I want to put before you. I mean our pitiful inability to come to terms with – cope with – vast multiplicity and great quanta no matter of what – and to behave with sanity towards environment, that great and only place there is in which we all live.

No previous society has made quite so little of the experience, knowledge and technology available, or fallen so far short of what imaginative concerted action could bring about. Of course, as of old, there are still imaginative and constructive efforts by individuals from which all could benefit if listened to and applied. But minimal use is made of them. In fact, a blind eye and a deaf ear is turned to what is being done on the periphery – to what is occasionally smuggled in like contraband – only to be misunderstood and misused, twisted into yet another negative.

Whatever gain is made is soon counteracted by another gain, for ours – yours and mine, the presumptuous kind – is a society of wasted gain. Just think of it. Ten years ago, when war was still raging beyond the Pacific, I wrote some lines in big white letters on an exhibition wall in Milan.

Here they are: 'Disturb the delicate intricacies of the limitless microcosm; trespass into the limitless microcosm and frighten the angels. In between mess up the Mississippi and the Mekong. If *that* is what we desire, it will soon be here, for there is a limit even to the limitless.'

Since then, ten years have passed. What is true of the whole is also true of each part, so what is true – painfully true – of environment is also true – painfully so – of most buildings. Now if making a good building (one that is not a bad building) has become too difficult, the dilemma is indeed complete. But is it really all that difficult? Does it really require a genius to avoid the mean and meaningless – or a sage to bypass foolishness? Is there nothing between a fool and a genius – nobody in between to do the job nicely – well?

If behaving with sanity towards environment on whatever dimensional level is no longer within our reach – within reach of the kind of society to which we belong – then surely such societies – ours – thus reasonably gauged, are of a low – primitive – order.

I have just confronted you with a fact which, alas, points towards the only definition of a 'primitive' society that makes sense today: a definition which removes that slight from all those other societies; the kind that never really deserved to be called primitive by that self-assured kind of ours (which behaves towards the landscapes of the world like a half-wit with two left hands).

Whether in Greenland, Africa, America-long-ago or the South Seas, people dealt with limited number both accurately and gracefully, extending collective behaviour into adequate and often beautiful built form. Taking from environment as much as they gave, a gratifying balance was sustained. This we are no longer able to do, not in the same way, nor as yet, in any other way.

Yes, is it really all that difficult or beyond our reach? Do we not belong to the same species as those in Greenland, Africa, America-long-ago and the South Seas? Is our mental equipment not similar? Are we not endowed equally well? Surely we can accomplish what they accomplished in so many different ways. Believe it or not, those little societies and their fast disappearing cultures can by their example still tell us that abilities (hence also possibilities) which we have come to regard as beyond the scope of the human being actually lie within it. And so there is no reason to give up all hope.

For it is in the nature of the human species – all people, you see – to be able to deal with environment, hence also to fashion the spaces they require, adequately – and sometimes beautifully. The way people are also given to communicate with each other through language – speech – that other gift, which, like making spaces, still belongs to their primordial equipment.

It is painfully true of architecture that it is not just good quality that counts but a sufficient quantity of that quality. A good school elsewhere is no use to a child in need of one here. If I have a nice house (or a house at all), it does not mean that millions upon millions of others also have. So let's get moving, bearing this in mind: That today the architect is the ally of every man or no man. Persuade those narrow borderlines – the hard and harsh ones – between inside and outside, between this space here and that space there – to loop generously and gracefully into articulated in-between places and give each space the right interior horizon for the gratifying sense of reference it provides.

Never cease to identify whatever you construct with the people you are constructing it for – for those it will accommodate. Identify a building with that same building entered – hence with those it shelters, and define space – each space built – simply as the appreciation of it. This circular definition has a purpose, for, whilst it excludes all abstract academic abracadabra, it includes what should never be excluded but paradoxically generally is: I mean those entering it, appreciating it – people.

Architecture can do no more, nor should it ever do less, than accommodate people well; assist their homecoming. The rest – those signs and symbols one is worrying about far too much – will either take care of themselves or they just don't matter.

Meanwhile, let us not forget that blight has crept over our field. Keep clear of the entire array of current whimsy-flimsy trends; keep them from nestling in your minds. And do whatever you can to prevent those concerned from being tricked into actually building the vicious soft-coloured absurdities that fill most of today's architectural reviews. Architecture does not mean, nor has it ever meant, nor will it ever come to pass that it could one day mean, what the loathsome five's, sixes and sevens of New York, Minnesota and Chicago[3] or their like are trying to make people believe it means. So beware especially of New York, London and Milan – the worst trend headquarters – where they are still busy bending over backwards trying to twist our profession into something it simply is not. Not even in the sense that an apple is not a pear but still a fruit. That architecture – buildings – should no longer help mitigate inner stress, but should, instead, provoke it, is hardly a conceivable objective.

And yet here it is, flourishing on both sides of both great oceans, escorted by sickening flirtations with absurdity, irony, banality, inconsistency and, of course with ROME, Rome and Rome again – the most obnoxious pests afflicting architecture since Fascist gigantism and Nazi blood-and-earth regionalism in Europe forty years ago. It is worth noting that the new historicists and eclectics, whose habit it is to misquote the past, instead of coming up with a large variety of cocktails, produce – all of them together – little more than a single standard watery monomix. So never mind the Minnesota Six! As for history, that wonderful body of gathering experience, it is there to help – not to be spilt.

What is needed is better functioning – on more levels this time. Just that. For there is no such thing as a solid teapot that also pours tea. Such an object might be a penetrating statement about something (and thus perhaps a work of art), but it is simply not a teapot since it *cannot pour tea*. Neither is there – nor will there ever be – such a thing as a building which is wilfully either absurd, trivial, incoherent, contradictory or disconcerting, that is still a building. Marcel Duchamp invented puzzling objects but they were significantly not buildings!

It will not be long before the earth's face will be like a network of scars. Energy too is spilt and ebbing. Time is ticking faster. Millions have no place to go – no nothing. What can be done that is more effective than trying to save the world? What could an Institute of Technology like this one, for example, do as soon as it is ready to do so? Well, start dissociating technology – setting it free – from that ruthless and naive notion of progress to which it has been falsely tied for so long. For progress means nothing on this side of evil if it does not mean moving towards well-being for all people (and all people means simply that – all people) – and away, to start with, from quite so much waste, pollution, discrimination and unnecessary poverty. I am aware of the fact that many of those present, have, over the years, sacrificed a lot in order that a limited number could study and thus achieve what was still out of reach in their time: scope and space in which to move forward. It would be gratifying if more than just a few of those graduating this morning would in turn wish to share the scope acquired with others not yet as fortunate, so that they too may move.

It would, of course, also be gratifying if, in a future not very distant, those graduating on a morning such as this, would represent the magnificent diversity of your country's people rather more accurately.

I can think of no single word as appropriate and sparkling as the one with which I shall now end: solidarity.

R.P.P. (Rats, Posts and Other Pests)

The 1981 RIBA Annual Discourse, London 12 February 1981[1]

Ladies and Gentlemen,
That so many people – this late afternoon – should have come to hear what yet another architect has to say is quite unexpected. Still to have called upon a conservative-humanist from abroad, known to be rough once in a while, is not without courage nor is it altogether inappropriate in view of all the graphic outpourings currently simulating architecture.

About a year ago I received a letter from the editors of a book, then still in preparation: *Why is British Architecture so Lousy?* It concerned a rather spectacular statement by Leon Krier which was to be included in the book. I was asked to sign the following: 'Although I do not necessarily agree with it, I have no objections to the following statement which I understand was said in the belief of its truth and/or as a fair comment, and with no motive of malice.'

Now for Krier's statement: *'It is difficult to accept that one is an integral part of a monstrous epoch. I will now give you a little list of how untrue, absurd and monstrous the world of contemporary 'architects' is, and I offer you some of the wisdom of those who are still reputed to have been the most intelligent, sensitive and visionary. For this conference I dug out all the crappy literature which I had kept for a long time in an obscure corner of my kitchen cupboard. I re-read L C, Banham, Giedion, the Smithsons, Van Eyck etc, etc. If the result of their utterances had not ended in such a tragedy, we could just have an amusing time.'*

I would have thought that making those pretty drawings, and getting them published as fast as they are drawn, was an amusing and even rewarding pastime. But no! The tragedy of this monstrous epoch apparently casts a shadow too long and dark! However, I did not object to publication – that would have meant censorship – but naturally I did not sign.

The comment I sent to the editors about Krier's gibe brings me to my first point. If what he said was indeed said in the belief of its truth and/or as a fair comment it can best be attributed to *maladjustment* – emotional or intellectual. However, if it was *not* said in that belief then the motive was certainly *one of malice*.

But what of it? Malice, after all, though not agreeable like kindness, can still be a perfectly acceptable motive – if this were not so I'd better sit down straight away! No, the point is whether it's *maladjustment* which was behind the malice. And I'm inclined to believe it is. For it is malice, you see, the malicious kind based on maladjustment, which is behind so much of what the *Rats, Posts and other Pests* say, draw and do, hence also behind all those pretty renderings of urban spaces for Miniature Monarchs.

Whatever it is that K. keeps in his kitchen cupboard, in obscure corners of his head, just sniffing at it will not bring about anything like that which Emmanuel

Owen Williams, Boots Factory, Beeston, 1932

Héré, for example, made in Nancy, or Palmer, Baldwin and Wood in Bath. Nor, I am afraid, would it have, had ours been that revered eighteenth-century instead of this 'monstrous epoch'. How many disenchanted Kriers are there currently creeping over Europe on what today is just a little Grand Tour? How many miles can they still run – didn't I say creep – on Piranesi, Sitte, De Chirico and Marx? And what if they catch up with Albert Speer, if that has not already happened? If there is anything beyond Speer, which is hard to believe... *then let it not be Krier*. As to why British Architecture is lousy; if it is, it would without Krier and Co, have been just *lousy*, but no *so* lousy! We haven't had him in Holland yet – not live... only in print and double Dutch.

And now, Ladies and Gentlemen, I am going to tell you something in all humility which every historian in his right mind is going to affirm sooner or later. At no point in history – bar one horrifying, fortunately localised, exception – was there ever a constellation of notions concerning architecture, so warped and awkward, so cribbed and stereotyped, so ill-behaved and wilfully uncongenial, so useless and unbecoming, *so unreal without ever being surreal*, as that which the Rats, Posts and other Pests, (who from this time forward shall be called RPP) have been construing.

As to that one still fairly recent painful exception I alluded to earlier, the RPP have made it perfectly clear which one that is. Although the RPP are as yet less foul, they are also less local.

Keep clear of them; and, if you can, see to it that next to nothing of what is as rotten as it can be is actually built, lest archaeologists in the future, when all printed pages have disintegrated, reconstruct an inaccurate and unnecessarily unfavourable image of our epoch.

Do we see poets, painters, sculptors or composers allowing themselves to be assailed by a single set of notions; allowing all their periodicals to be filled from cover to cover with exactly the same stuff month after month, year after year? No, nowhere, not in the entire free world. Poets, writers, artists and their like make better use of their intelligence; probably because they are less inclined to *split what they feel from what they think*. I have known many, and found them trying harder to get to the core of the problem than architects and, in general, not as sheepishly; and hence less inclined to trot after the next *trend*.

Architects, after all, didn't *have* to follow Gropius's rigid creed for half a century without as much as a 'Baa-Baa'. And now he's the black sheep. Easy, that, too easy?

Each time I open *AD, Lotus*, or almost any other periodical, I can barely believe my eyes. Has it really come to this – or is it just a bad dream? Such a betrayal – and so soon after that radiant beginning; when was it? 60, 80, 100 years ago? There is no need to decide; nor is it wise to rely on historians. No, it is better to gauge for yourself – it depends on the signs, you see, and you have to find them to feel them. Anyway what the RPP have perpetrated amounts to a violation of sanity. It is in fact treason – just that.

How the mental mechanism of the disenchanted sometimes works is clearly revealed. We shouldn't forget that the steps such people sometimes take are not unprecedented. It isn't the first time either, nor is it that far back – just a bare 50 years; so we are forewarned and should be on our guard.

What bothers me most, and that is putting it kindly, is not so much the pseudo-sophistication and feigned freakishness for their own sakes, for that is just selfishness, but the accusations fortified by half truths and downright untruths, i.e. by fact-twisting, intellectual slander and ransacking the past – *spilling history*. It is the element of foul play, Ladies and Gentlemen, that I wish to condemn. The Rats, Posts

and other Pests have been deceiving students and untold numbers of practising architects who, although unfortunately not producing enough good buildings, are nonetheless still playing the game. They – the RPP – have been doing so for some years now, arresting development, causing delay. Although the RPP hardly build themselves, their odour clings to the buildings others make, perhaps unwittingly. That is why the adverse brainwashing that the periodicals are providing is so very irresponsible. To thus damage a sound and unavoidable profession for the sake of recognition or commercial profit is… yes what is it?

The RPP provide a preview into the antechambers of what might, with the support of the warped notions presented in print, easily slip into the net of a new brand of proto-, or intellectual, fascism. If the general climate is sufficiently conducive, if discontent lurks in too many people's minds, convoluted ideas tend to fill the gap. *That must not happen again.*

To avoid misunderstanding, my worst premonitions are *not* fed by the fact that much of the stuff published flirts more or less obliquely with the formal characteristics we associate with the architecture of power creeds, but by other, familiar symptoms. The false accusations, the trumped up enemy, the distortion and abuse of historical data, twisting the truth to prove your point, turning the clock back, the formation of a kind of 'front' however disparate within, the manipulated influence in schools and editorials, the tendency to *unmask, demystify,* proclaim the *obsolescence* of what has been branded as constituting the cause of the tragedy or – to use Mr K's words – the monstrousness of the epoch.

There is no way of knowing how many RRPs there really are – nor how many of them are here now – given to bending over backwards trying to twist architecture into what it simply is not: *not even in the sense that an apple is not a pear but still a fruit.*

Architecture does not mean, nor has it ever meant – and it has meant many things – nor will it come to pass that it will someday mean, what people[2] (to sweep them onto a single heap) like Tafuri, that *italic* Rasputin, or Rossi, that other Aldo, or the Krier pirates crossing the channel, or Denise contradicting Robert and more recently Robert himself, wish you think it means. People like Eisenman-Tigerman, Superman-Simpleman – or the Cooper Union Circuit, which I thought was the name of a racing car, or Charles Semio-Something of London who, given to sign-spotting, will soon be Post-Post if he isn't already, or delirious OMAMA mix, turned surrealist 50 years too late, and all sorts of other naughty boys like Robert S (in Holland offenders' surnames are abbreviated in the Press), Michael G, Arata I, Hans H, Ricardo B, Mathias U, and – temporarily – Big Jim S(ilver), and finally – although there are many more – old Philip J whose buildings I have from the very beginning disliked most of all.

Notions about notions about… that's what is so nasty… often even good ones originally, but seldom about anything as substantial and down to earth as a *building* – its *use and usefulness.* Instead they just gobble up the forbidden fruits that were never really forbidden – the Puritans!

I find the RPPS' most extravagant fantasies as stale as pornography and certainly as uninventive. And, what is far worse: perversion, even perversion, think of it – is rendered distasteful in their hands. But what really excites my anger more than their little flirtations with absurdity, irony, banality, incoherence, contradictions and ugliness is the wilful inclusion of elements that are intended to be disconcerting, intended to aggravate, to pester. Who could ever have thought that one day, buildings, counter to any conceivable kind of logic, would, instead of assisting people's homecoming by helping to ease inner stress, wilfully provoke it. During the final CIAM gathering at Otterlo in 1959, I remember confessing to those present (you can find it all in the book[3]), that 'I was indulging' to quote myself 'in confusion and symmetry and other really evil matters'. I wanted to tease my stern companions, who found it hard to believe, then, that a more inclusive kind of clarity could well bring a certain kind of formal confusion with it and that symmetry can also bestow gratifying equipoise.

Giancarlo de Carlo's oval windows at Matera were almost unanimously rejected. I remember expounding on how excellently the large oval windows of the Vickers Viscount aeroplanes served their purpose.

This brings me to Robert V's *Complexity and Contradiction in Architecture*, which did not surprise me in the least when it first appeared some years later.[4] It is strange the way architects in particular – as though they belong to a herd – open and close their eyes in unison. To give you an example, you can discover – or rediscover – *Architecture in the Age of Humanism* any time just by taking a train! You don't have to wait for somebody like Wittkower to show you and then rush off to Italy together.[5] Architects didn't *have* to follow what is now supposed to be a poor creed – that of the Modern Movement – for half a century with next to no critical comment and then turn full face as soon as Mr V opens a window onto what, after all, was there all the time. Surely architects, like poets, painters and all sorts of *other* quite normal human beings can think for themselves without being prompted. Of course CIAM at large was traumatically wary of the wicked past, but the RPPS' equally traumatic infatuation with it merely presents the *other side of the same fake coin; one that should be thrown away, not tossed.*

Both then and now, the same mechanical clockwork notion of time prevails, the same awkward posturing vis-à-vis the past. It is still history OUT or history IN. In the minds of architects this all too often means IN and OUT of ROME – or YES or NO to Classicism alternating every 30 years or so. Why this constant unnecessary choosing between imagined alternatives?

Why this blind *either-or* instead of *and-and*? There are more affable kinds of motion than that of a pendulum.

Team 10 – that is certain – behaved far less pathologically towards the past and history than either CIAM or RPP (I'm sorry to have mentioned them together like that – after all!). However, what the Posts and Mods do have in common is that they both stumbled over the past – love-hate complexes can work themselves out in opposite directions – but that's as far as the similarity goes. Although a bit short-sighted, CIAM people were not damn fools.

History, I wrote to Mathias U, a one-time Team-Tenner and now a full-time RPPer, is not a memory warehouse, but a *gathering body of experience*.⁶ Memory should not be brought too close to a deterministic notion of time if one wishes to avoid contaminating its great meaning. *Memory transcends the clock, it is time humanised. Without it buildings will have no temporal perspective, nor the associative depth they require*. But this can't be brought about by arbitrary references and cross-references; by 'quoting', that new design hobby. History, you see, is no longer *behind* us because time no longer works that way, not since Einstein, Joyce, Mondrian and a host of others – not since that Great Gang was around. Time no longer ticks. Yet there go the RPPs, starting it ticking again; putting the clock back, though not to a time or period which ever really existed – *cogito ergo sum* – the prison bars are back, and the tiny windows. My Italian Christian namesake maintains that we (society) deserve no better and should therefore get no better. For that he is acclaimed a hero, but then, he himself can creep through any one of those tiny windows of his.

I remember talking about the *transparency* of time – time humanised – in 1959 at Otterlo when CIAM died and Kahn was already spreading incense. Five years before, at Aix-en-Provence, it had looked as though CIAM was really getting somewhere, opening doors onto a world less embarrassingly local and narrowly international! Wider by far, at any rate, than Atlantic Europe and Harvard yonder. Team 10 was then just fermenting. I remember the last day at Aix very well; how Gropius began to serve his usual dear kind industry – happy future antiprimadonna – teamwork design potion. I told the audience what I thought of that there and then.

I mention this not because of what was said – after all, why shouldn't a man have limited ideas and keep trying to put them across – but because of the thundering, sheeplike applause which followed, as if nothing had been achieved the entire week. That was in 1953. How many years after Dessau and La Sarraz? And how many years after Albert Einstein first published his enlightened theory? 48! *Hearts of Stone!*

While on all sides the wind was blowing firmly, the majority of architects in CIAM didn't really budge. As though afraid, they turned a blind eye and a deaf ear to the great things that were taking place in the field of art, literature and science. It is not a pleasant thing to have to say in retrospect, but that is still the way it is today; those blind eyes and deaf ears are still blind and deaf to what the *Great Gang* brought about. This, I'm afraid, weighs heavily on their insight and courage. They dreaded Surrealism like poison. Art in general – if it was not more or less abstract, in which case it was thought to be objective and hence accurate – was regarded with suspicion.

Economics, on the other hand, about which nobody seems to know anything – was acclaimed a sound and a reliable harbour from which to sail out safely. Well, well, well, and where are we now? 89 years after Gauguin ventured out to the South Seas and painted what he did; 73 years after Picasso turned his great searching eyes to the wonders of African negro art and painted les Demoiselles d'Avignon; 67 years after De Chirico painted the little silent train which, around 1946, first took us, my wife and I, into the open world of constituent contemporary thought.

Initially Team 10 responded to the new dimension. John Voelcker, with whom I talked a lot, certainly did. When I discovered that his name had been struck from the tiny list you'll find on page two of the Primer which was edited and published in England,[7] I was sad and worried. For me, in a way, Team 10 died when that happened. It sideslipped into a groove not far removed from that of CIAM. Still, although I couldn't share its interests in mobility, growth and change, infrastructure and urban scale problems at the cost of actual buildings, there was no better focal point. Of course, there was our own Forum Group at home in Holland named after the review of which we were then editors. The tone is not the same, though the content runs fairly parallel. It would perhaps be good if the differences – the shift of accent – could be ascertained and brought to light. I participated in both groups from the start and know that the Dutch one had no difficulties vis-à-vis the past. In the early 60s the current tear-down-what-you-want-to-reach mania, resulting in much demolition of old city centres, was already being violently criticised by us on every occasion and with very considerable effect.

In retrospect, I can say that Team 10 played a substantial part in my life, though I am sorry to say not an altogether pleasant one. Bringing to bear what occupied me most in the general discussions was always oddly difficult – interests simply didn't coincide. And so I felt alone. There was also uncalled-for brow beating, but then, the London-Berlin axis was never my line. Team 10, I now feel, would have done as well without me.

Let me return to Robert V's book for a while, which I still regard as quite a good one. But how badly it has been digested! Even by V himself! Particularly the misuse/abuse of Mannerism. One thing is certain, *one should not and cannot derive one's own little mannerisms from true Mannerism, which had profound sources.*

Contradiction and *complexity* in architecture, regarded as formal qualities that are thought to be opposed to *coherence* and *consistency* on the one hand, *simplicity* and *clarity* on the other, are not effective medicines against the ailments of mainstream Modern. True Mannerism, for example that of Michelangelo, Giulio Romano and Raphael, although born of inner conflict, mitigated the stress by coaxing harassing paradoxes into significant architectural form with astounding artistry. Emotional extremes, this is the point, were brought together – contained (not *reconciled*) by introducing contrary forms and qualities simultaneously. The audacity of it! Herein lies the lasting *humanity* – that rejected word – of their work, which spans the scope of our emotional reality. Reflecting it, it is also open to it. The RPPs, scorning humanism as they do, should keep their soiled hands off Mannerism. Take the Laurentian Library. It is, among other things, also the highly controlled outcome of inner conflict – Michelangelo's sonnets can tell us more about that – but *it does not transmit distress*. The anguish is kept within the architecture through the language invented

Owen Williams, Boots Factory, Beeston, 1932

to hold it. That is where it was persuaded to settle – where it *rests*. Yes, *rests, thus easing instead of causing anxiety in others*. Its greatness – beauty – lies in its generosity.

But let me descend from these heights to the bottom of the pit where there is no light at all.

Parading stolen feathers and feigning inner stress, the RPP not only play the fool instead of the game, but they also play foul.

Ladies and Gentlemen, I beg you – *hound them down – and let the foxes go*.

It is interesting, is it not, the way all those historicists, eclectics and pastichists are producing hardly more than a single standard mono-mix? The taste is perhaps not always the same, but one does recognise the brand! It is also interesting to note that the best Post Modern is as stale and stereotyped as the worst Modern. *So never mind the Minnesota Six*.[8] What is really required is functionalism – functionalism on more levels – of a broader inclusive kind. RPP makes that abundantly clear. *For there is no such thing as a solid teapot that also pours tea. Such an object might be a penetrating statement about something and thus perhaps still a work of art, but it is simply not a teapot – not one that can pour tea. Nor is there such a thing as a building which is wilfully absurd, banal, ugly, incoherent, contradictory or disconcerting and still a building or architecture*. Such a thing does not exist.

Marcel Duchamp invented many puzzling objects, but they were significantly not buildings – there was a door which closed as it opened and a tiny cage or trap filled with marble sugar lumps. Man Ray made an iron with drawing pins neatly stuck in rows underneath. They knew where to draw the line and what the difference is between a grudge and a work of art.

It is my contention, Ladies and Gentlemen, that Modern architecture at large, CIAM to a lesser degree, *side-stepped the orbit of this century's great avant-garde and failed to move into it or catch the tone*. The mild gears of reciprocity and relativity run gently and quietly – one must listen to hear and watch to see. Thus the message was left unheeded, though the revolutionary ideas the pioneer poets, painters, sculptors, composers, physicists and others managed to put into exhilarating words, forms and formulas did not go unnoticed insofar as they were *applied and misapplied, but seldom understood*.

The dilemma of the Modern Movement in architecture is that it did indeed miss the boat by sidestepping the philosophical implications of what came to light around the turn of the century and since, through the astounding insight, intelligence, audacity and artistry of a relatively small number of people. What they discovered jointly (panorama and -aroma) has not even penetrated the mental fringes of those who now suffer so deeply from the tragedy of this monstrous epoch! Nor has it entered the minds of less burdened architects. There are exceptions like Aalto, Rietveld, Duiker, Van der Vlugt, Le Corbusier and your own Owen Williams who built Boots, surely one of this century's most wonderful buildings and, to my mind, England's finest.

Of those that joined the Great Gang long ago, many were still alive a decade ago. Now only Miró, Chagall and Moore are left – and they will be 90 soon. Great Gang, hear that sound? Gee Gee… not quite the same as R Pee Pee! There was a magnificent show at the Tate last year.[9] Did you all go? Watching those pioneer paintings oil the works, so I suggested to students of the AA that, after a decade or so of trend running, a visit would be well worthwhile and would probably throw some light ahead. GO TO THE TATE AND THINK is what I wrote in huge letters on a banner of paper many yards long.

What those of the Great Gang have done for us is to trace the outline of a *hierarchy that for once and at long last is not irreversible*.[10] Imagine what relief reversibility would bring: tyranny of any kind would soon lose its nourishment. That is my belief – but then I'm a conservative-humanist, even an idealist, somebody who has not given up hope. I am, in short, everything I oughtn't to be according to RPP standards.

It is this very irreversibility which the painters I've just referred to spent their lifetime overcoming – each in a different way – and which is currently being beckoned back; restored in its foulest guise by the RPP: oppressive, mind-splitting, non-reciprocal and anti-relative; in fact pathologically – though not yet politically – already too proto-fascist to be comfortable.

Owen Williams, Boots Factory, Beeston, 1932

The paintings on show at the Tate, together with the statements written by the artists themselves, brought one face to face with what significant enquiry, supreme intelligence and artistry can bring about and why architects just sniffing around must necessarily fail to produce anything parallel to, or as substantial, refreshing and relevant as these paintings. In short, as beautiful.

This reference to the Tate and the AA is taken from a comment I wrote about two prize winning projects for the Toaiseach's residence and state house in Dublin which I helped to judge. The projects by Evans and Shalev, and Wickham and Lavery – both very different – were indeed the best of a few rare islands in a morass of incompetence and RPP trivia.

In the light of the present situation both schemes become quite remarkable. *Negatively*, because, for once, they do not demonstrate what really awful buildings look like – for that is how I interpret most of the fancy drawings so exquisitely printed on both sides of both great oceans. *Positively*, the schemes are remarkable, because they show what really nice buildings look like: *how* such buildings work (how nicely they *work* and how nice they *look*). Also how they manage to belong where they are put. *Nor have they got what they needn't have.* There's a nice one for the AA! Not truly a wicked remark, really, because it would be lost completely on those already beyond help.

People, you see, can't just be left to choose from a variety of pests. Not because there are no good buildings left over from the past or still being built today, but simply because there are not enough of them.

It is painfully true of architecture that it is *not just good quality which counts, but a sufficient quantity of such quality*. A good school in Amsterdam is of no use to a child in London (or vice versa).

If making a good building has become too difficult, the dilemma is indeed complete.

But is it really all that difficult? Does it really require a genius to avoid the awful? The past at any rate disproves this generously. It proves (what the present also proves every now and then) that it is in the nature of people to deal with their environment – hence also to build the enclosures they need – adequately and often beautifully; the way they are also given to communicate adequately and often beautifully through language, *that other gift*. That is what I told the RPP at the Venice Biennale in 1976.

What the two Dublin schemes can tell us in a quiet sort of way is that generosity is the last thing buildings can do without and thus the first thing they should be allowed to have. Generosity, of course, does not necessarily exclude grandeur, although it is certainly not required, but it does exclude *sizelessness* – all forms of gigantism. Hence also the current miniature kind!

My long involvement with the discoveries of the Great Gang, as well as with distant places visited – from Easter Island in the silent South Pacific to St. Lawrence Island in the icy Bering Sea – has never shut me off from Europe as some seem to think. I categorically reject the partitioning of the human effort into that which is supposedly primitive and that which is supposedly not, i.e. supposedly civilised – what a self-assured jingle! Nor do I accept any categorical division between art and folk art – architecture and vernacular. I have always objected to the title of Rudofsky's book: *Architecture without Architects*, since it discriminates both ways, defying all available anthropological data. What differences there are, and there are many, are not that easily pigeon-holed.

I can safely say that I still know of nothing more sustaining than to keep close to that great multicoloured idea – kaleidoscopic is the word – which the Great Gang represented, adding something constituent if I can. And, don't forget, it was they who first opened our eyes to the art and culture of those distant places – distant in space and time. For no concerted body of ideas was ever so mild, penetrating and generous, more suited to lifting burdens and barriers; more suited to counteracting schizophrenia. 'Le monde dans un homme – tel est le poète moderne'! Max Jacob, that wonderful Cubist poet wrote.[11] He would have allowed us to say 'tel est l'architecte moderne' if we deserved it only half as much as the great Cubists.

And now listen to his friend Picasso putting the intrinsic humanity and relativity of cubism and early collages into words: *'L'artiste est un réceptacle d'émotions venues de n'importe où: du ciel, de la terre, d'un morceau de papier, d'une figure qui passe, d'une toile d'araignée. C'est pourquoi il ne faut pas distinguer entre les choses. Pour elles il n'y pas des quartiers de noblesse.* Just think of that: *'pour elles il n'y a pas des quartiers de noblesse.'*[12]

And listen also to the profoundest statement about simplicity imaginable because it sheds light on the meaning of complexity: *'La simplicité n'est pas un but dans l'art, mais on arrive à la simplicité malgré soi, en s'approchant du sens réel des choses.'*

That's Constantin Brancusi,[13] whom I visited so many times.

Cézanne, who started off so much of what we need most, himself probably hardly realised that he had won the battle of probing the enigma of perception in order to rediscover the roots of painting. *'Nature is on the inside,'* he said,[14] *'I do not see it according to its exterior envelope. I live in it from the inside. I am immersed in it. After all, the world is all around me – not in front of me.'* That magnificent statement alone can put any student of architecture on the right track, back onto it.

The number of exhilarating statements of this kind in every medium is large enough to lift us all up and away from doom!

Just two more, by two of the greatest physicists of our time. Werner Heisenberg first: *'We can no longer speak of nature as such. In physics, we are no longer investigating nature itself, but nature subject to our scrutiny – thus man encounters himself – faces himself alone for the first time in history.'*[15]

Now Niels Bohr: *'The world has ceased to be scientific – notions like subject-object, inner-outer world, body-soul no longer fit and lead to difficulties.'*[16]

Do you remember Ferdinand Jelly Roll Morton, that pioneer New Orleans jazzman with diamonds in his teeth? I've quoted him so often, with or without effect, I'll try again: 'OPEN UP THAT WINDOW AND LET THE FOUL AIR OUT.'

Symmetry from the bright side

Manuscript in Van Eyck archive, undated draft for a lecture to be held in Brighton, c. 1984

Let's look at symmetry from the bright side, whilst we are here... of all places. And you are not to assume that the bright side of symmetry means asymmetry. No, no, no, nothing of the sort. Poetry without rhyme doesn't mean free verse, nor does it mean prose, nor does it mean worse or better poetry. Still, by not rhyming love and dove or flower and bower, you are not going to end up with something richer than prose. Likewise by simply avoiding symmetry (asymmetry is all too often just that) better building will not ensue. The bright side of symmetry (let's call it 'Brighton symmetry'!) is that it is able to bring about equipoise. That is what it can do in the first place, often has done and, if we open up its meaning a bit, should again help us to do. In fact, symmetry is the mainstay of equipoise or, conversely, equipoise is symmetry's *raison d'être*. There is partial, reduced and subdued symmetry (hidden asymmetry), there is shifted and multiple symmetry, primary and secondary symmetry, also equivocal symmetry (simultaneously or consecutively ascertained) and alternating symmetry. The latter kinds can sustain multiple meaning, different layers of meaning and seemingly incompatible meanings. When is architecture going to explore and extend the formal language at its disposal not for the sake of the language but for the sake of better, more useful and, if we are lucky, less ugly buildings? Just open *AD, Lotus or Domus* and see for yourself: that's not very difficult and already well worthwhile.

Very rigidly symmetrical organisation of architectural ingredients – i.e. frozen symmetry – stands in the way of equipoise, and of course I mean more than aesthetic equipoise alone (does it ever exist alone or come about just like that?). If this wrong, absolute kind of symmetry excludes equipoise, i.e. balance, the gratifying simultaneous presence of what is expedient but does not easily assert itself simultaneously or coexist in conflict, it will also stand in the way – as all too many current buildings clearly demonstrate – of resolving the enormously divergent and seemingly strident questions we are faced with today, within buildings as well as in their always unique, however typical, exterior context, whether urban or not.

If a school is to be a good school, it probably won't look like the old one down the road, nor will it look like the kind of 'typological' school Aldo R.[1] wants. So it won't have stark thick walls and smallish cut-out windows, or that oppressive central entrance, in fact it won't exemplify the kind of authority that requires punishment. So it will not call upon the kind of symmetry or anything else that creates that kind of climate which Aldo R. and so many others are after. What a good school building requires, if it is to become one, doesn't fit into that sort of formal framework. What any building requires if it is to fulfil its purpose in a gratifying way (which is the only way) cannot be achieved in a building that points in the opposite direction.

On Codussi

Statement first published in L'Architecture d'Aujourd'hui, October 1984[1]

Why, oh why is it that Venice's greatest Renaissance architect – Mauro Codussi – 'belongs' to the Modern Movement – to us – and not to the Rats, Post and others Pests? If I were to build Santa Maria Formosa again, and I would love to, I'd be an innovator, but not an eclectic! It was in my mind all the time (not that there is any direct comparison): that entry from the side; that postponed, at no point frozen, fluid symmetry – a balance gracefully sustained. The space breathes evenly: spreads out and away; whilst beautifully contained, it opens up all the time, because one's attention is kept agreeably on the move in various directions – especially diagonally across. This brings about a sense of articulated depth – a view beyond and transparency. It is in fact a multi-directional central space with a wonderfully subdued axis and, although wide and clear and open, it still eludes definition. Mauro's touch. There's an architect for you.

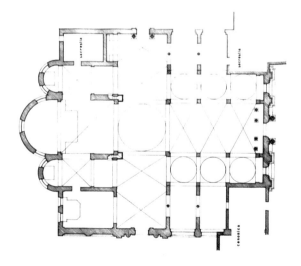

Mauro Codussi, Santa Maria Formosa church, Venice, 1492–1504 Photo Giacomelli

Photo Aldo van Eyck

Photo Francis Strauven

Photo Aldo van Eyck

Mauro Codussi,
Santa Maria Formosa
church, Venice,
1492–1504

Photo Vincent Ligtelijn

The circle and the centre

Lecture at the 1987 Indesem conference at the Delft Polytechnic[1]

Cézanne said: 'Nature is on the inside. I do not see it according to its exterior envelope. I'm immersed in it. After all the world is all around me, not in front of me.'[2]

If you think of that in terms of architecture, we have to be in quest of a horizontal non-hierarchical language. It proves to take a long time but we've got to develop it for the sake of everybody. That is why I find it so terrifying that so many pseudo-architects are making buildings so frontally facing each other that no reconciliation is possible, stressing the hierarchy. They have suddenly forsaken what Cézanne, Duiker, Picasso, Arp and the whole gang of avant-garde have tried to achieve, to discover that new language, that open language, that relative language.

Modern architecture was afraid of the middle because it was afraid of a frozen hierarchical middle. But architecture somehow can't work without the recognition that there is a centre, an open centre. It's not frozen, it is not fixed.

Symmetry means relating a family of forms. Think of symmetry in terms of equilibrium, of a weighing scale. You can weigh bananas with bananas, but also bananas with apples, with bits of gold or anything else. It still has to be in weight. There has to be a relationship between what's here and what's there. There has to be a certain equivalence. Life is so complex, so rich. It is unlikely in a programme for a building to have exactly the same thing happening on both sides. Still the building must be balanced organically. The dynamics of equilibrium is a very strong thing. You bring something to rest within itself, but you're not forcing a reality on this side to be the same as the one on the other side.

The moment you define the circle's centre it looses something. When your attention is fixed on the geometric centre you tend to think of an axis or a segment. If you start with the radials you end up with triangles. Now there is nothing further apart from the spirit of the circle than the spirit of the triangle. The first one so continuous, open and oriented in all directions; the other fixed, just a non-dimensional form. What creates the circle is not the centre but it is in itself the centre.

If you think of a circle in terms of a clock or a wheel with a fixed centre you're thinking mechanistically. I prefer to think of a circle as a disk or a ring. There's no question of a centre. It's just a muscular movement. The wheel, the clock, they perform a never-ending solo. The ring and disk are in a continuous dialogue with what is around them. They somehow seem to breathe. There is a movement, outwards, inwards. The centre is everywhere. The circle interpreted as such is not a frozen form, it breathes like we do and that's what architecture should do.

Open is the hallmark of contemporary architecture. It means many things. It doesn't mean a lot of glass. It means open in spirit.

Aldo van Eyck at INDESEM 87
Photo Jan Kapsenberg

A textile from Thailand, which shows a simple but efficient way to break the hierarchy of a three-part composition. The 2 times 2 spirals at the left are horizontally coupled so that the centre is shifted to the interval at the right. The coherence of the whole is effected by coupling the 2 spirals at the right vertically.

A small Zulu beadwork, a bracelet. This tiny strip is not symmetrically composed around one centre. The little pentagon in the middle is in fact simultaneously part of two different motifs, each with its own symmetry and its own centre. Both motifs are linked in counterpoint.

And just keeping on switching between yesterday and today

Translation of 'En maar tuimelen tussen vandaag en gisteren', a statement published in November 1989[1]

Will the use of concepts and categories that do no more than distort and erode ever give way to simple looking – and, who knows, perhaps also to seeing something? Let's name a few of these fossilised concepts and categories, which are moreover often used in opposing pairs (because they are what mainly concern me): high culture versus primitive culture, and of course art versus primitive or popular art, and, less dire but also unreal: fine art versus applied art. In the meantime, in architectural circles the customary art-with-a-small-or-capital-A lark simply carries on.

What something *is* always has to make way for what it *looks* like – and for that you always need someone who does not look! What penetrates the filters of art criticism is mainly that which does not matter, meaning that which can be 'placed' in compartments old or 'new' (the trend-mafia see to the latter). And that is rarely anything more than hot air!

And then there are the most idiotic series of concepts, abbreviated of course: objective – rational – intellectual – abstract – non-figurative – straight – exact – geometric – structural, as opposed to subjective – emotional – spontaneous – intuitive – figurative – curved – free – organic – surreal... – expressio... etc.

Whereas the nice thing about art is precisely that it makes all these things pointless – superfluous.

Lured from his den

Article published in Archis, *1998, no. 2*[1]

The now universal anyone – anything – anyhow – anywhere escape route amounts, in my view, to doesn't-matter – don't-care – all-the-same-to-me.[2] Since it pulls the rug out from under practically everything, this is hard to take for someone who once composed a book called *Niet om het even – wel evenwaardig*[3] (Not all the same – yet of equal value).

You only have to consider what Ole Bouman[4] recently wrote in *Archis* about the architect, apropos of any – any – any. Was it a forecast of the road ahead for architects, perhaps something already looming into view? Or was it just an inflated caricature of the current situation? Suppose it's true that the individual designing architect soon won't have a leg to stand on and will therefore vanish. If so, he himself bears part of the responsibility for walking straight into that particular trap. The key question seems to be, should Bouman's scenario be seen as a warning or merely as the product of cool, journalistic observation; true or false? Or perhaps just some copy to help fill the magazine? If it's a wish, it's a pathological one – and cynical too. But he doesn't make it clear, and that's what I find unacceptable, for read as a neutral description it's a disgraceful exaggeration of something that is indeed in the air. But the erosion has long been going on – from within, too. Carel W.,[5] for instance, has been demolishing his own basis – and thereby that of his chosen profession – for the last twenty-five years. This too seems to me explainable only in pathological terms. Every new notion he launches in Delft, the BNA[6] or wherever he pops up, and every new harebrained statement he makes, is aimed at undermining the position of the architect and impoverishing the training given at Delft (where his presence seems indefinite).

Architecture and with it the architect are being led astray. This is now actually taking place. But how did it come about? It is a result of the trap he sets and then stumbles into himself at the insidious prompting of the countless pen-wielders who hover around architecture or slouch against it but do not really know what they are writing about. A painful example: in order to disguise the absurdity of historical materialism, to gloss over the dilemma that it is dialectically flawed, many leftist intellectuals, however well-intentioned, are in the habit of appropriating history, i.e. rewriting it with less than a full regard for the truth. All this is justified by dubious new 'concepts of history' such as those disseminated in Delft in publications like 'History now'.[7] 'Historicization of the present' was one of the most destructive slogans. It became the cornerstone of a vacuous 'critical conception of the history and theory of architecture' and was even made the basis of the training. Kees V.[8] formulated this miserable practice at the time as 'This moment, i.e. the present, is constitutive to the questions to be posed of the past.' This amounts to saying that 'historical material' can be distorted in order to shore up a so-called contemporary and relevant argument. It is typical of many post-war radical left-wing mental constructs, such as those propagated by Adorno, Althusser, Baudrillard, Lacan. Derrida, Deleuze and numerous other authors, that they twist existing ideas and facts around to produce the semblance of a valid argument, which then claims an autonomous right to existence and insists furthermore on having a place in the scholarly firmament. The lie thus becomes the truth – e.g. Kees V's 'Art is Society'. Bernard C.[9] presumably absorbed something of this kind while at Groningen from his erstwhile tutor and future doctoral supervisor Ed T.[10] According to Bernard C. (and apparently Ole Bouman too), the present generation of architects dismisses as arrant hypocrisy the theory that we build with the intention of providing a pleasant environment for society. They spurn such 'humanism' and accordingly (as both have written) reject both the *Forum* idea and myself. To the extent that the user of our buildings is indeed, literally, the well-fed consumerist society, this rejection – this cynicism – becomes understandable. I as much as anyone am aware of the malodorous side to the architectural pond. 'Everything functions but man himself', Arp thought. If this is so, rejection, criticism and cynicism are all to be expected. But that doesn't exclude a humane standpoint as a *sine qua non* basis for architecture. On the contrary, it *implies* it. You don't have to be a philanthropist to argue for a person-friendly – humane – architecture. Such a thing as a person-unfriendly or critical-inimical architecture is a priori unthinkable. It's not architecture at all but something else altogether. Even though the human collective does little enough to inspire a love of one's own species, the task remains the same and it's this: to work in a way that achieves something that's positively useful to people, *just as the doctor or the baker on the corner does*. Postmodernism saw things differently and in my view demonstrated near-criminal tendencies – so soon after Albert Speer! – by deliberately allowing in negative qualities. Peter E. and – closer to home – Ben van B. and Adriaan G.[11] also deliberately give room to the destructive, the unpleasant, the unbalanced and the incoherent in architecture. Hence the criminalizing initial-letter surnames, for I totally repudiate what they think they can get away with. *Archis* and its predecessor TABK have eagerly sniffed up every wind passed in the name of Postmodernism or deconstructivism, while ignoring a vast amount of good work done by reasonable architects. On the other hand, *Archis* did choose to publish the Court of Audit, presumably because of its topicality (itself a sensational aspect) albeit accompanied against my express wishes by that arbitrary introduction.

So far my prefatory remarks. Now for the fabrications which Bernard C. committed to paper with regard to the Court of Audit.[12] He sent me his text with the following marginal note, and I quote: '*I understand from Archis that you expect to have a final glance at the text relating to publication of the Court of Audit. Please find it enclosed, I hope you like it. The usual length of a magazine article was in this case barely sufficient. The building could not in my view be published without a bulky introduction to put the principles of the work*

 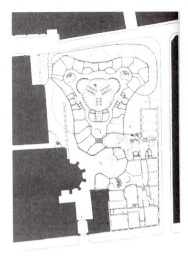

The Court of Audit in The Hague, 1992–1997, Van Eyck's last executed building, designed in collaboration with his wife Hannie Photo Teo Krijgsman

The Court of Audit in its urban context.
On the foreground the 15th century Kloosterkerk and the 18th century mansions facing Lange Voorhout.

Aldo and Hannie van Eyck, Court of Audit, The Hague, 1992–1997, entrance Photos Aldo van Eyck

Inner courtyard on the second floor and one of the winding corridors Photos Teo Krijgsman

Library and Restaurant Photos Izak Salomons

(which have really become totally unfamiliar to the majority of my contemporaries) back on the map. Solely as a building, it makes no sense at the moment for it is too much at odds with the rest. Therefore the article only starts discussing the Court of Audit as such at the end – and even then I am of necessity very short about it.'

What are we in for now? I'm still reeling. We are purported to have put up a building in The Hague which cannot simply be published in the usual way. Yes, that's what we are actually accused of having done! What kind of nonsense is this? We thought we had made a sound piece of work, but suddenly we learn that we are wrong about that, at least if Bernard C. has got it right and not wrong – which is also a possibility! Could he perhaps be mistaken in his contemporaries? On whose behalf does he think he is speaking – after all, his contemporaries are also my contemporaries, aren't they? Surely architecture isn't supposed to go 'in' or 'out' as quickly as high-street fashions. Or are his contemporaries perhaps being misled by his 'bulky introduction'? I wonder. Is the Court of Audit really so much 'at odds with the rest' that it needs that bulky introduction? I think he is deceiving himself. But what do my younger contemporaries think?

I can't go into every distortion that Bernard C. has 'put on the map' in his bulky introduction. None of them throws any light on the Court of Audit. Therefore I would like to discuss just a few points here, even though they have nothing to do with this particular building. As said, Bernard C. has the nerve to posit that I prefer a decentralized city. But that's exactly what I don't prefer, and this is a crucial point. He gets the emphasis wrong, out of incomprehension I hope. What I wrote in *Towards a Configurative Discipline*13 is something else altogether. The only application of a future configurative discipline would be in new towns and urban districts where vast quantities are involved, e.g. huge numbers of dwellings and the things that go with them – lots of everything, in other words. But that doesn't apply at all to the location of the Court of Audit. So no 'identifying device' is necessary there. Why does Bernard C. charge me with ideas he knows are not mine? Moreover, if it is 'a major piece of architecture' as he states, why all this pussyfooting around it, for lack of clarity is the last thing you would usually attribute to buildings in that class. Bernard C. writes that he hopes to find more space for various points in his thesis. I have indeed heard he is going to take his doctorate in Groningen and that his doctoral supervisor will be Ed T. (alias Ed Taverne). And why not? A fine pair they will make when they appear together on the doctoral dais in the spotlight of scholarship. But let me return to my purported preference for the decentralized city.

What is more, and this is silliest of all, neither of the very things he wants to 'put back on the map', namely *the configurative city* and the *identifying device*, is applicable to existing historic cities such as The Hague and they are thus useless for clarifying the 'principles of the work', certainly if he is going to misrepresent the quintessence of the two concepts. I have never spoken of identifying devices in old cities because they already have them (assuming they haven't already been knocked down) and that is why I refer to old inner cities as Donors as long as the new ones or new urban quarters cannot fulfil that role.

In *De Milde Raderen van de Reciprociteit* ('The Mild Gears of Reciprocity'[14] – 1961) I explained that treating polarities like central and decentral as alternatives is a fruitless exercise – 'reciprocity' says it all anyway – or even a fatal one. A little later, in the Dogon issue of *Forum*, Dommo guided us along the many spots he regards as his home – where he 'lives' so that his village is simultaneously his house. That is what I meant by the 'huge house-tiny city' identification, no matter what Alberti (according to Hans van D.[15]) might have meant by it.

What I wrote in *Towards a Configurative Discipline* covers the above. 'It may sound paradoxical, but decentralization of significant city-scale elements will lead to greater appreciated overall homogeneity. Each sub-area will acquire urban relevance for citizens who do not reside there. The urban image – awareness of the total urban cluster (i.e. the city) is then no longer represented by strictly personal place reference, different for each citizen, and a centre common to all, but by a gamut of truly civic elements more or less equally distributed and together relevant to all citizens. Such elements will induce them to go to parts of the city otherwise meaningless to them.'

So I do not speak about the centre of the city but the city being a centre everywhere – i.e. what I intended (and still do) was not a decentralized but a polycentric city. (Why not reprint those early essays so that misquotations and misinterpretations can be checked and, it is to be hoped, eliminated.)

Where Bernard C. missed the point within the scope of a single paragraph, I will now try to put things right as far as possible in a single paragraph of my own.

The Orphanage unmasked. Ed T. 'unmasks' (note terms such as unmask and demythologize which form part of the 'new historiography') the Orphanage as 'an unreal fairy tale whose impact was nevertheless so powerful that it caused Dutch architects to collectively lose their bearings.' What arrogance, to dismiss the actually positive reception of a building, without any commitment and in retrospect, as an aberration!

Dalí and Koolhaas misunderstood. Here Bernard C. begins to slop pure nonsense. He writes that 'at the point where the method culled from the surrealists shakes off the features of humanism to usher in a domain as capricious as it is visionary where literally *anything* goes, Van Eyck pulls out unhesitatingly.' Indeed so, and this is because Bernard C.'s description of surrealism is tantamount to its denial, so you can certainly count me out! Much more is of course possible in surreality than in 'normal' reality, but *not just anything*. 'The paranoid-critical method paves the way for metamorphosis by virtue of its utmost precision' explains Dalí. That is to say not every metamorphosis is truly surreal and hence possible. For my part, Koolhaas is entitled to describe New York as delirious – there is some point to it at least – even without applying that 'utmost precision', but Bernard C. is insensitive to where surrealism begins or ends and so fails to understand why (in his words) I pull out – not of surrealism itself, of course, but of his faulty explanation of it. 'I have seriously tried to keep Rem Koolhaas' name out of this piece,' he writes. So why on earth does he have to drag in not only him but Aldo R., Ed T., Hans v. D etc. as well if it is not to harm?

The surrealists were very precise. Breton's strict regime made it imperative: there was no question of 'anyhow, anywhere, anything'. Thus *'par les lois du hazard'* is not at all the same thing as randomness. Surrealism has preoccupied me since my student days. Bernard C. should think twice before he so casually brushes with it.

As though they fell from the sky. *'When arguing for the configurative city...'* – not city, but discipline! – *'Van Eyck backed it with his pupil Piet Blom's Noah's Ark.'* Piet Blom is *not* my pupil, despite what Bernard C. and others like him invariably maintain, but that doesn't change the fact that Blom was a pupil of no one other than himself. Piet Blom designed his configurative housing projects quite independently. We published them in Forum as they were, as though they fell from the sky. *Not* Noah's Ark but two other designs.[16] Neither of them were 'meritorious utopias', as Bernard C. dubs them, but totally realistic alternatives to the usual arbitrary site layout habitus.

Fascism in a snowflake. It was Blom's Noah's Ark, a later design and not the initial basis for the configurative process, that really drew the fire of the Smithsons and others,[17] with the consequence that a lamentable distance developed between myself and Team 10. Bernard C. turns these events into mere gossip by perfunctorily ignoring the whys and the wherefores of what actually took place. If anything was absolutely not 'fascism in a snowflake' then it was Blom's Noah's Ark. It was a superb piece of open architecture/town planning. Bernard C.'s thoughtless regurgitation of that sorry story is contemptible.

Manning the barricades[18] *'At a practical level as an architect, Van Eyck engaged in the wrong polemics in the wrong place. He let himself be wheedled into manning the barricades.'* As if that were something you did on impulse, and moreover as if it were easy to do. His conclusion, seen from the viewpoint of his generation, can hardly be anything but 'the configurative idea came a cropper'. What came a cropper? In the right place and with the right polemics, with the old inner city as donor and the configurative method inapplicable here, both Rechtboomsloot and Kromboomsloot were completely preserved. It would have been impossible without someone manning the barricades. Belittling things goes along with the practice of unmasking them.

'Of necessity very short.' Meanwhile Bernard C. has barely left himself room to discuss the original subject of his essay, the Court of Audit – and none at all for the interior. It has become trendy to focus on the 'exterior', especially on the 'urban' exterior. But it is the interior of a building that is actually used. That is what it is built for in first place and that is what it needs an exterior for as a consequence. In the case of the Court of Audit, it was the exterior that had to deal with the almost insurmountable demands of the context. We therefore certainly do not neglect the exterior in favour of the interior as Hans van D. has suggested apropos the Moluccan Church, a defect from which in his view all my buildings suffer. I do so 'in the good company of Aalto' he goes so far as to add! So you'd rather have a stuffed exterior with a bit more swank and monummm...? Even a bit BIMmy[19] perhaps, as Ed T. would like it? (I could be mistaken, as he himself has often been!)

What Bernard C. was primarily trying to expose, and it's something for which he is prepared to stage the strangest polemic stunts, is – of all things – my status – and public opinion about it! This occupies an almost obsessive place in his whole argument and it keeps cropping up. It is striking that in order to identify it, he exclusively selected people from the circles around *Archis* who have never cared much for my work. The rest of the world simply doesn't exist; nor does the rest of Holland.

As for me, I'm no longer there. *'A figure with a controversial historical status and no status at all today,'* is how Bernard C. recently portrayed me in *Archis* (1997, no. 11). So I am at least now rid of it, that status, a loathsome concept if ever there was one. There yesterday, gone today. Perhaps that is putting it too mildly, for status is something people stick onto you only to tear it off again when the time seems ripe to 'make a bit of history'. What Bernard C. has robbed me of, and Archis too by being so eager to print it, they can keep it. What is left to me – more or less significance, as the case may be – is a thing of which theoreticians and academics all too often have little grasp. This is why there is endless 'debate' about what has no significance and which I do indeed 'eschew' because it makes me sick and doesn't do architecture any good either. But that doesn't make me an 'absentee', as Bernard C. terms my presence. I can only guess at the cause of all these Oedipal goings-on, at least insofar as it concerns me: as soon as anything one has done stands out way above the insignificant, all kinds of things can happen here – and they're not very nice, either.

In order to put my 'controversial' position on the map, Bernard C. wheels in his future doctoral supervisor Ed T., who then places me 'in an unfavourable light'. 'On one side of the stage' Ed T. positions the duo Oud and J.H. van den Broek who he believes stood for *'an ideological movement that seeks direct communication between architecture and the historical city, with all its noise and visual delight'*. Opposite to them he ranges another duo, *'Van Eyck and Forum'* who *'eschew communication with the city by opting for a fundamentally anti-urban architecture which, thoroughly abstract by constitution, denies the city its true colours.'* The consequences of this would indeed be very bad – to that extent I agree with Ed T. – but his ascribing of this self-invented nonsense to myself and to *Forum* is even worse. Nothing resembling it has ever come from this quarter.

The success of the latter duo had the result that architecture in the Netherlands was, as Bernard C. quotes Ed T., 'offside for quite some time'. That's no laughing matter. So now it is on my conscience that Dutch architecture is offside, just like that! Bernard C. goes on to point out the weaknesses of Ed T.'s interpretation, but only to give him free rein again shortly afterwards.

Apropos of J.H. v.d. Broek and Ernesto Rogers. Ed T. *'expressed a preference for the first ideological tendency, partly as it is allied to the vibrant Italian tradition whose successful exponents through the years have included Ernesto Rogers, Aldo Rossi and Giorgio Grassi.'* I have often had discussions with Van den Broek and he would be very puzzled to find himself ranged alongside Oud and the BIM. You simply cannot come up with such utter nonsense. And as for Rogers, it's just as crass: we sought each other out during CIAM meetings and on other occasions specifically to talk about old cities and their meaning for us all today – because of a lack of others sufficiently interested.

Apropos of Aldo R. The things Bernard C. additionally pulls out of his scholarly bag to establish my historical position but which actually have nothing to do with me are many. For example he wishes to force me, remorselessly and against his own better judgement, into a family relationship with that other Aldo (alias Aldo R.), 'whether he likes it or not'. He adduces such reasons as his own incorrect interpretation of what I mean by an identifying device, which merely demonstrates that I have no such familial connections. By his 'primary elements', Aldo R. means Aldo-R. type buildings (BIM-like): by identifying devices I mean very emphatically 1000 times not that.

Since Bernard C. allows Ed T. to play a very active role in his attempt at 'historic positioning', I wish to state here that I accuse him of giving the development of local post-war architecture an imaginary twist by promoting Oud to the leading role, thereby replacing the misbegotten influence that I and *Forum* are supposed to have had by something more 'positive'. What he calls the 'offside' of architecture in the Netherlands is beyond my comprehension because the criticisms he directs at *Forum* and myself are unrecognizable; in other words, they do not refer to anything I can identify in myself or in *Forum*. Ed T. seems to have suffered a trauma due to myself and *Forum* – and historians with traumas can write strange things! Ed T. apparently does not consider Oud's BIM (Shell) building in The Hague as a regressive eyesore unlike Oud's partner on Ed T's stage: Van den Broek, the whole of '8 en Opbouw' and myself. That he and *Archis* see so much in it – so soon after Albert Speer – and that they moreover have had such a fond eye for the monstrosities of Postmodernism instead of for works which point unambiguously in the opposite direction, such as Zonnestraal, Van Nelle, Rietveld and the great avant-garde of the first half of this century in general, is a blow to me that has been hard to take, I admit. In what kind of background did these people grow up whose names I prefer not to pronounce or write in full, in what lecture halls have they been educated that they should side with the very worst that has ever been built in the name of architecture and with the abhorrent notions that go along with it?

I no longer have a periodical in which I can say everything – I haven't since *Forum* – so I must make do with *Archis*. Not just the generation of Bernard C. but also the next generation, in Delft and elsewhere, are *all of them my contemporaries too*. Things change fast, certainly, but not as fast as some like to pretend. If all of you choose to chase after whatever trend turns up, you, like your predecessors, will keep sidestepping the real issues of architecture. Don't! Begin at the beginning and stay at the beginning. It's fairly obvious what the primary essentials are: the usual shopping list of the reasonably necessary. But this shopping list is varied and colourful, and above all concerns people. Keep that in mind. Even if the list changes, it hasn't changed to such an extent that suddenly none of it matters! Refuse to be deceived by those who buzz around architecture and have no understanding of building as a metier. The shopping list must simply be reinstalled. That means good building, i.e. architecture. There doesn't have to be any more to it than that – on the contrary, it's difficult enough as it is.

Architects wherever you are. Students In Delft and elsewhere: Tolerate no more of this; no more dispiriting nonsense: ignore it. It's time to utter that musical little word NO, first gently, then louder and finally at full chorus. Enough is enough. Give your recently protected title back and then use all three! Better still, start a national association of unchartered architects.

DON'T ASK FOR A RAINBOW. FETCH IT.

Access to the Court of Audit through the old mansion's gate at Lange Voorhout
Photo Vincent Ligtelijn

14

On architects and other artists

Introduction to chapter 14

Aldo van Eyck with Shinkichi Tajiri at the Amsterdam Stedelijk Museum, 1967 Photo Leonard Freed

Aside from his critical positions Van Eyck frequently expressed his appreciation for many of his colleagues and artist friends, for personalities of the previous generation as well as for younger and older contemporaries. According to the themes dealt with in the preceding chapters, these already included articles and passages on Frank Lloyd Wright, Gerrit Rietveld and De Stijl, Brancusi and Miró, Richard P. Lohse and Carola Giedion-Welcker, the Cobra painters Appel, Constant and Corneille, the sculptors Tajiri and Visser, and Van Eyck's former students Verhoeven and Blom.

The present chapter consists of a number of pieces he wrote between 1960 and 1999, not only articles but also lectures, obituaries and introductions to other well-known and lesser-known personalities from the world of art and architecture.

Jaap Bakema, Peter Smithson and Aldo van Eyck at the 1973 Team 10 meeting in Berlin.
Photo Jeffrey Scherer

Blanche Lemco, Sandy van Ginkel, Aldo van Eyck and John Voelcker at the 1959 Otterlo congress.

The last Team 10 meeting, organized by Candilis at his countryhouse in Bonnieux, 1977.
From left to right: Jaap Bakema, Peter and Alison Smithson, Sia Bakema (half-hidden), Georges Candilis, Aldo van Eyck, Amancio Guedes, Karen Axelrad, Manfred Schiedhelm, Giancarlo de Carlo and Ralph Erskine.

On Le Corbusier

Statements made in 1960, 1961 and 1966

About Ronchamp[1]

There is as much biology in a rectangle as there is in a sea shell. If architecture is to be truly natural architecture must not return to the forms of nature. It is of course essential that these could affect the creative impulse, but this does not mean that in translating forms of nature ingeniously into construction they have in consequence been translated into architecture nor that architecture has become natural – 'organic' so to speak. To love nature should, for us at least, imply loving art (architecture) more. To depart from nature is to approach it naturally. Without this art – all human activity for that matter – loses dignity. This is what makes Ronchamp, for instance, rather less, I feel, than it seems.

Owing to the vast potential of its designer it competes with nature, but it does so in nature's own terms, rather than in terms of art and art alone, speculating, unconsciously or not, on the groveling appraisal it will reap from those who, always dumbfounded by the creative ways of nature, have lost all regard for the creative ways of man, i.e. lost that self respect at any rate essential to the artist. In the case of Le Corbusier, so wonderfully close to nature – through contrast – in his earlier work, Ronchamp constitutes a lonely and ageing artist's coup de champagne, to use his own words.

On the Le Corbusier's position in CIAM[2]

It is in the nature of Le Corbusier's personality and genius that he should have supported the potential of the younger generation. His continual regenerative capacity and great humanity lifted CIAM beyond its limited scope from the very beginning. He was CIAM's barely understood banner. His 'rationalism' was fused with both mystery and crystal clarity – a reality none of his Germanic CIAM colleagues managed to live up to, and all too often even suspiciously counteracted.

A classless architect[3]

Le Corbusier is the only classless architect we have ever had. Take any Corbusier building. You can drive up in front of that building and you are a king. You can ride there on a donkey and still you're a king. You belong there even in rags. Everything seems to fit, everything acquires dignity.

On Loos

Translation of a lecture given in Delft on 17 March 1965 to open the exhibition Adolf Loos, set up at the Architecture Department of the Polytechnic[1]

For several decades it has pleased architects to turn the job they are meant to do inside out: the creation of rooms in which it is good to spend time as one goes from one to the other.

It appears they have lost their heart to what they call 'the continuity of space' – to penetration. The result of this sort of music is of course horrible; and that will become more so as this open country becomes even more 'continuous'.

What could be more absurd than so offhandedly making the environment in which you and others live uninhabitable – more absurd than the fact that this has become a sort of 'normal' habit? But what does this actually mean: 'continuity of space', or 'penetration' from outside to inside? (The latter sounds rather impertinent in any case!) No one gains from it: only the glass industry and the oilman. The result is in any case actually the elimination of any real 'continuity', and thus of any 'space', both inside and outside. After all, it is not by accident that a sort of continuous outside is emerging everywhere around us. One cannot get in because the 'inside' is on the outside, nor out, because the 'outside' is on the inside, and because there is no end to it – no end to this continuous outside.

Photo Trude Fleischman

Don't misunderstand me. I am not saying that architects are evil beings (I remain silent on urban planners); but nor am I saying they are darlings. What I am saying is that this mania for continuity is based on a very unfortunate misunderstanding (a misunderstanding that will bring me almost naturally to Loos). The task of the architect is not the creation of the outside, even if it is inside. That's a task for demolishers. His task is the creation of the inside, even if it is outside.

Man has always and everywhere been occupied in bringing closer the universe, in grasping the cosmos with his own measures, in recreating it in his own image, i.e. recreating it into a microcosm. He endeavoured to bring infinity within the scope of the mind, to render mentally accessible what would otherwise remain immeasurable and inexplicable. He also has been occupied in making 'habitable' the interior of his own mind, so as to feel at home in it. He brought inside what was outside, close what was far, making the universe into an interior '(in the form of a basket, a bowl, an urn, a sarcophagus, an house, a temple, a square or a town).

And today, has he all of a sudden stopped doing so? It sometimes looks like that. What is the origin of this aberration, this merciless 'out-siding', this emptying of space, its hollowing out, this turning inside out of everything?

Yes, it is time to bring in Loos, because as an architect he was outstandingly concerned with accommodating the mind. He opened himself with unconditional dedication to authentic human feelings but implacably turned against sham feelings. The material he built with was reality, the reality of man. His insight into this reality is legendary. Arnold Schoenberg, Anton Webern, Alban Berg and Kokoschka, all of whom he supported from the very beginning as an ally and friend, each have their own story about this. As do Peter Altenberg, Bruno Taut, Georg Trakl, Karl Kraus, Maurice Maeterlinck, Ezra Pound and Tristan Tzara, for whom he built a marvellous house in Paris.

Loos approached this material – reality – so directly and at the same time with such subtlety, taking no roundabout routes, that he thoroughly frightened people. He gave short shrift to any form of false illusion – that is always a good thing, but in Vienna at that time it was exceptionally courageous. He tore off masks and undermined taboos.

I was in Vienna recently and people talked about him as if he had still been at work the day before. The way he lashed out at the barriers man throws up against himself, with his pen and tongue and in his work, is unmatched among architects. However, the strictness and control with which he did all this was just as great as the warmth. No one – no architect I can name – ever turned meaningful rage so well into meaningful habitability. But then no one ever made better houses than Adolf Loos. Ladies and gentlemen, believe me, I stand up for what I am saying – this is an extravagant assertion that Loos deserves. He was a phenomenal craftsman, unconditional, unrelenting and consistent, but always kaleidoscopic... polyphonous. He was tender and strong – hard and fragile at the same time. He was packed full of paradoxes and at the same time was as clear as crystal.

This subjugator of the void wrote two collections of criticism: *Ins Leere Gesprochen* and *Trotzdem*. He liked tailors, shoemakers and of course furniture-makers: this says a lot, because Loos was a dandy in the true sense of the word, a Viennese Beau Brummell,[2] mad about London and Paris, especially London. You see: tailors, shoemakers and suchlike, the sort of people Loos writes about, make things that fit well (and that suit the wearer well) and also remain good, staying with the wearer; very directly accompanying and protecting him. Loos approached his work like one of these tailors; as a court supplier who serves every client like a king.

Surely his designs for Alexander Moissi, Josephine Baker and Tristan Tzara are unsurpassable? And also the unbuilt stepped terrace housing that show how he was able to find the right form for everyone – his social commitment is radiated by everything he made.

Listen to what Tzara wrote about him (in the meantime we have, alas, lost Tzara too): 'This great architect, the only contemporary one whose buildings are not photogenic, their shape being a school of profundity and not a way of reaching illusory beauty. For the bias towards the suffering that moves, for a perfection that does not exclude the microbes or the impurities of life.'

Do you remember Tzara's *Forum* motto: '*juste ce qu'il faut de souterrain entre le vin et la vie*'? To think that you will in future no longer be able to 'view' houses, let alone really live in them, and will have to be satisfied with photos. But why should Loos' work be so eminently hard to photograph, or at least its essential qualities? As always, Tzara knew very well what he was writing. I think in the first place because the true experience of space it is not only a matter of visual perception, but much more. Space is a multi-sensory experience because spending time in it is too. The experience of the space assumes spending time there, or in any case an imagining of that spending time, a sensing of how it would be. I said 'multi-sensory' to make it clear to you that the experience of space is not inextricably linked to visibility, nor even to sensory perception in the broader sense.

Listen to what Loos wrote himself:

'*But I say: a real building does not make any impression when couched in an image on a flat plane. My greatest boast is that the interior spaces which I have created completely lose their effect when represented on a photograph; that the inhabitants of my spaces do not recognize their own house in a photographic image, just like the owners of a painting by Monet would not recognize this work at Kastan's. I have to renounce the honour of being published in the architectural magazines. I am denied the satisfaction of my vanity.*'[3]

Experiences encompass associations, memories and anticipation, meaning the temporal in the sense of other, earlier (former) experiences and moments too, and other spaces (that may not be tangibly present). In fact this is rarely the case. But in Loos' work it is always the case!

Now for something else, directly connected to this. I have spoken, slightly, about continuity of space, and the penetration of inside and outside, and mentioned that the absurd literal realisation of this is based on a misunderstanding, a misconception of what simultaneity means. By making a large quantity visible at the same time, the experience is instantaneous, meaning – in the wrong way – the same from moment to moment and from place to place. Not temporal-spatial and thus not spatial. For one does not take anything of one space into the other; nor anything of one moment into the next. Memory and anticipation play no part. Instead of wanting to see a lot of meaningless things at the same time – in that case they *are* indeed photogenic – in Loos' work one experiences a lot of meaningful things, true to life things, successively. It is precisely for this reason that in his work one can truly speak of simultaneity, which one can with few others. And thus also of 'continuity' (!) because it is precisely these experiences that carry on in time and space and merge into one another. In order to read the next page, one will actually have to turn the page. This does not mean that what has just been read has vanished or is forgotten; it is simply no longer 'visible' – you understand what I mean – it remains present in what follows. On repeated reading, that which is to come plays a part page after page.

'Why have architects become so addicted to the lie of literalness?' No, photographing what one has just experienced and will experience later is simply not possible. In Loos' work the 'continuity' lies mainly in the 'succession' of spatial experiences and the 'simultaneity' in the enduring presence of these experiences – and thus also of earlier ones that will come back again.

I have a definition of space that will certainly help you in this respect. It is one which automatically excludes any abstract or academic explanation and equally automatically includes, draws in, that which should and can never be excluded: those who experience the space. The definition is: Space is the experience of it.

If one wants to know whether a suit is good or not one has to wear it. What the wearer experiences when wearing it can be seen in his face or his gait – his behaviour – but not, or to a lesser extent in the suit itself. One cannot photograph what happens in the mind. Feelings simply do not have a visible form. In Loos' work, space, form and material are emotional realities, and their beauty probably reveals itself as a reward to those who experience them as such.

Building in the Netherlands still (the century is well advanced) bears the double stamp of a futile struggle: a struggle – just try to imagine it – between two sorts of rectilinearity – the crooked one even 'straighter' than the straight. On the one hand the now leaner *Nieuwe Bouwen* of yesteryear, sometimes still pure (Elling) but usually rather thin (Van Tijen, Merkelbach, etc.). On the other hand, the direct opposite, which never completely vanished in Delft: the Delft School: cramped, wrong, withered and invariably pathetic. It's a pity we never had a Loos here (Van Doesburg died as early as 1931), no Loos tongue or Loos pen: because the Delft School would never have survived such a massage. And today's remaining, rather pale *Nieuwe Bouwers*? He would just have made them stand in the corner for a while – nothing more – because he was able to keep things under control and to make distinctions.

Messrs Polak and Gonggrijp have written an effective introduction to the catalogue.[4] They focus on things that are very essential to the transformation of space into interior: double multi-meaning, multicentrality, equivalence, shifted symmetry, and so on. They take you through several houses, and repeatedly use the word 'turn'. Of course, they cannot entirely capture or convey in that one word what happens after each 'turn' occurs (what this means for the previous one and will mean for the next one), but you do get a taste of it. So I would say, let's go and call on the photos, and perhaps they will yet let us in to Loos.

University college in Urbino by Giancarlo de Carlo[1]

Article first published in Zodiac, 1966, no. 162[2]

I recall De Carlo's intricate Otterlo essay – a rock-fast house of cards – about the situation of contemporary architecture, as well as the arrows – some poisoned with old CIAM purity – which were aimed at his Matera work during the Otterlo gathering in 1959. I recall also De Carlo's troubled look and the nice way he stood his ground during the harassing discussions. There he sat piling paradox upon paradox with unusual dialectical agility, striving to re-establish the rational approach which according to him became submerged when Theo van Doesburg went to Dessau to oppose Gropius. His listeners glanced sideways at the panels, adjusted their wings and ticked him off 'in severe terms', telling him all sorts of interesting things about 'the new plastic relationships of our epoch'; about an open versus a closed concept, about flexibility and mobility; 'relative space'; regression; the evil past; and, lest I forget, his responsibility as an architect. His critics of course were right in their rather self-assured and optimistic half-right way. Only Smithson tackled De Carlo on a really appropriate level, but the reader can best judge for himself (*CIAM'59 in Otterlo*, edited by Oscar Newman).

De Carlo, who was neither sure nor optimistic, nor even desiring to give that impression, must have felt the weight of his own twin-focus loyalty. He knew how devilishly hard it is to combine positively, let alone reconcile, his task as an architect with his involvement in the socio-political sphere, and what it means to be loyal to both at once; loyal in such a way that the one sustains the other instead of thwarting or distorting it. For even if one is able to tune both spheres to a single overall concept, or envisages a common denominator, the mind is still obliged to change gear as it moves from one to the other – or else damage both gears. Acute social awareness of this kind – direct engagement – tends very easily to dislocate surreptitiously – in fact – a meaningful structure of thought; certainly when that thought structure concerns architecture and one fails to resist its subordination. I have known quite a few architects thus doubly dedicated, but only De Carlo has managed to play the game with his own confusion so intelligently and gracefully, giving Italy, as he now has, a wonderful building which belongs – that is his reward – to old Urbino as much as it does to the new society he envisages.

Of course building for students in Urbino and building for the poor in Matera are not the same thing. But in both cases we have the new and the old, architecture and People. I am inclined to say: send De Carlo down south again and watch the results!

Before saying something about the Urbino building, I should like to refer the reader back to some things that were said at Otterlo about the Matera building, because it seems to me that De Carlo was not as wrong as his critics tried to make him feel he was. The issues involved are important. Wogensky went so far as to say that De Carlo 'through his plastic conception betrayed these people' who, he said, 'had not received an education into the new plastic relationship of our epoch and do not understand the poetry of modern space and movement'. The Matera building, Wogensky said, 'does not open these people's eyes to the whole of the actual situation in the world today' (heaven forbid that buildings should ever set out to do that), 'but rather turns them back to the past and, if anything, hinders them from

Giancarlo de Carlo, housing in Matera, 1956–1957

this realization'. This, I admit, didn't sound as self-righteously CIAMish to me then as it does now. I think Wogensky, maintaining as he did 'that it is not possible to conceive of an architecture which is not based on a relative conception of space – a non-Euclidean space' did not grasp that De Carlo, whilst certainly not disagreeing in principle with a 'relative concept of space' was not only still groping his way towards it (towards 'this new plastic expression' which Wogensky, and with him CIAM, assumed was already at our disposal ready-made) but that he was trying to relate what he had not yet found to *a relative concept of society*. De Carlo was clearly not inclined to identify passively this 'new plastic expression' (of which Wogensky said that it must be made 'understandable to these people if you hope to lead them into the future') with a relative – non-Euclidean – concept of space. It is understandable that Candilis, with his 'open' concept of flexibility, mobility and change in mind, did not wish to accept the rigidity De Carlo had imposed intentionally, because as the latter explained 'the people of Matera simply did not want a contemporary reproduction of the old conditions and consequently deserted the new quarters which endeavoured to reproduce in the modern idiom the plastic complexity and organic freedom of the old city' in favour of their old slum dwellings to which they returned. What they wanted instead, De Carlo said, was 'something far more rigid and formal, something that would give them a feeling of the openness and stability of their future'. As if there were not enough subtle paradoxes in this statement, De Carlo, answering Candilis, added a few more! This was his answer: 'If there is rigidity in this plan and buildings, it is only a formal rigidity, but in terms of the people, the only freedom I felt I could give them was a consciousness of their rights, and the stability of these rights as seen against the background of their lack of rights'. It is all a question of tone. Wogensky talked continually about 'these people', De Carlo simply about the 'People'. Wogensky wanted to educate them and open their eyes to 'the new plastic expression' so as to lead them into the future, whereas De Carlo wished to give them 'a consciousness of their rights and the stability of these rights'. He did of course, rightly or wrongly, betray Wogensky's 'new plastic expression'! But was not Wogensky 'betraying' – what a nasty pompous word – the people of Matera when he called them 'these people'? I think CIAM in-old-age thus betrayed more 'people' than 'these people' for the sake of further exploitation of an already obsolete planning philosophy. De Carlo in his 1959 essay rightly says of CIAM that it has been 'an instrument of progress for the modern movement in the first stage of its life up to the delivery of the charter of Athens, after which it became an instrument of regression, a buzzing beehive where formalism smoothly distilled itself in academics'.[3]

We saw how De Carlo rejected the image of old Matera, denying it contemporary validity, in favour of a formal system of long blocks, whilst at the same time accepting for example roof tiles and bricks 'because they are available cheaply and give a more permanent surface than stucco'. The undertones (they sound like overtones today) are unmistakable! We shall now see how De Carlo took up the thread where it

Giancarlo de Carlo, University college in Urbino, 1962–1966

broke off long ago (when 'de Stijl' entered Bauhaus or when Bauhaus misinterpreted 'de Stijl', Carlo?) and how well he has managed his former inclination towards social realism. For instead of falling into that trap and staying there wasting his loyalty both ways, he has just completed a building which, besides living up to 'the need' as Smithson said to De Carlo at Otterlo, 'for a genuine invention of a formal vocabulary, a new architecture... and a way of life that will suit us all',[4] demonstrates magnificently that old images, whether Urbino or Matera, can still have real contemporary meaning if architects with insight and integrity respond to their message and interpret them in built form for the benefit of the people of today. I think it is significant that of all Italian towns it should be Urbino, the most humanistic and homogenous; and of all Italian architects, Francesco di Giorgio Martini, the most humanistic and functionally imaginative, that have given De Carlo the kind of support no architect, I believe, can do without if he is to make something which belongs to the future. What they reveal, Urbino and di Giorgio in conjunction, like De Carlo's student houses 400 years later, is that unity and diversity are ambivalent; that the one can only be achieved by means of the other and that both together are essential if what we build is to be congenial to people as they really are.

This building somehow makes me wonder when Italy's architects are going to pull themselves together. They can't go on tripping up over the past and flirting with it alternately: they should cut short this almost endless whimsical interlude and go for the real thing; for real freedom after so much fake liberty. It seems to me that past, present and future must be active in the mind as a continuum. If they are not, the artefacts we make will be without it – without temporal depth, associative perspective and hence inaccessible. My own concern with the ultimate human validity of divergent and often only seemingly incompatible concepts of space and building solutions found during past ages in all corners of the world, is to be understood in the light of the above. The time has come to stop combining their exterior attributes, but to gather together the essential and permanent human meaning

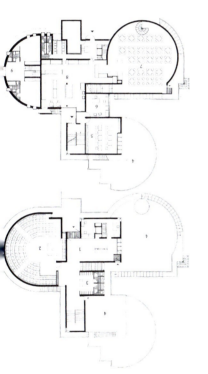
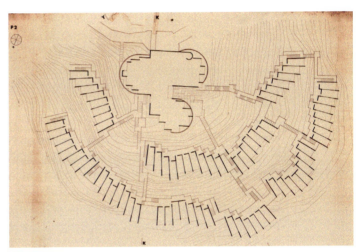

Giancarlo de Carlo, University college in Urbino, 1962–1966

divided among them. People, after all, have been accommodating themselves to environment physically and spiritually for thousands of years. Their natural genius has neither increased nor decreased during all that time (though they fail miserably from time to time to call on this genius). It is obvious that the full scope of environmental experience cannot be contained in the present unless we telescope the past, i.e. the entire human effort, into it. This is not historical indulgence in a limited sense or antiquarian sampling, but simply becoming aware of what exists in the present, of what has travelled into it. The projection of the past into the future via the created present, or, to put in De Carlo's words: 'What I consider as history is the acquisition of an exact knowledge of the problems we, as architects, touch on so that our solutions and our choices are tied to continuous reality and are progressive. History does not concern itself with the past, but with the present and gives direction to the future.'[5]

And now for De Carlo's building.[6] I am not going to describe it verbally, since that would be impossible. It has to be seen to be believed. However let me point out certain properties.

To designate the collective and the individual spheres from the general plan image is not so easy – and rightly so – as it looks. There is a single large building in the centre, a multitude of little cells grouped round it hemispherically, and some radial connectors. Now since I believe in ubiquitous centrality instead of either centrality or its false alternative decentrality, as well as in the ambivalence of the individual and the collective sphere from place to place, I would certainly have questioned the strong polarity which the plan seems to suggest at first sight. The photographs, however, show quite clearly (a visit to the buildings makes this exquisitely manifest) that there is more to it than that. What makes this building so house-and-city-like (hence successful), besides the consistent use of the same constructional vocabulary, materials and colour throughout, is also its major device. It (this device) is at once both places: way of access and communication; both open and closed; both inside and outside; both large and small and has, above all, both individual and collective meaning. It belongs to the 'building' as much as it belongs to the 'site', in fact through it the building *is* the site, the site the building. I am, of course, referring to the continuous system of external and internal covered and uncovered alleys, paths, walls, steps, staircases, seats, balconies, terraces and loggias, which connects, embraces and penetrates all spaces large and small, individual and collective – with what consummate artistry – and at the same time frames both the mild and tangible presence of the steep interior mound (here and there one sees only grass; no sky; nothing built; just grass, breeze-touched) and that vast paradisiacal countryside. De Carlo has simply incorporated a breathtaking sequence of magnificent *vedute* of different size and kind. You can enter them; be part of them, and sometimes even step through their 'built' frames and continue towards another one further down. Sky, skyline and foreground appear together or else in stages as you draw closer. Again, it must be seen to be believed. I don't think I have seen a building that gives more to the countryside (from within) than it takes from it, interiorizing it, articulating it and differentiating it – you would in fact have to go for a very long country walk to take in as much. Students will talk, walk, read and recline, alone and together, everywhere along this ample network of places. It is a huge extended doorstep, an in-between realm coinciding as it were with the building. They will look for sun and shade; light and darkness and find them. In short they will 'people' it (what verb suits a building better?) and join the setting.

There are many factors – all of course immediately allied – which together give the building its city-like quality. De Carlo's attitude towards history has already revealed his relative idea of time. I believe that these factors and the way they are handled reflect the same idea. They show that not only space experience can be qualitatively affected, but that the same is true of temporal experience. The concept of space and time is thus opened, 'interiorized' – gathering man into its meaning. By giving time a spatial quality and space a temporal one, both are 'humanized' i.e. rendered accessible. Places remembered and places anticipated dovetail continually. Yes, in this large-little world in Urbino the people are indeed gathered into the picture – along with the built form and the countryside. Even without people it is 'peopled'. All these qualities are the reward of a definite configurative discipline. I think De Carlo got very close to the enigma of proximity, for everything is far and near in the right way; close also to the enigma of size and number, for everything is large and small, many and few in the right way; and finally, I have already pointed to this, close also to the enigma of unity and diversity, for everything is the same and different in the right way.

Let me give a single example and then leave it at that. The building element containing the large communal spaces is a compound structure made up of superimposed cylindrical drums resting on a complex orthogonal substructure. The articulation of the superstructure is brought about by the cantilevered external staircases, terraces and passageways winding round it. These, this is my point, are clearly part of the overall alley-network that binds, connects, follows and penetrates the different elements throughout the entire complex, whilst the substructure extends the 'smaller' fabric of the alleys and student rooms into this 'larger' structure. By introducing the circle here De Carlo further assisted the idea of unity by means of ingenious contrast. He has avoided arbitrary fragmentation of the large communal spaces as well as avoiding the introduction of oversized rectangular masses as a false alternative. Fragmentation would have deprived the whole of a point of reference by minimizing the plastic difference between the student rooms and the communal spaces in the wrong way; whilst the alternative – large rectangular masses would have centralized the building arbitrarily; caused a distressing dimensional conflict and broken the unity – also the individual-communal ambivalence (the unity's content). Inside, the curved walls interact beautifully with the angular substructure and embrace as they should, quite naturally, many tables, many seats and many people. I cannot mention all the little acts of generosity this building holds in store. They are, besides, meant for the people who live there. Should the reader have wondered at the outset what a relative, open and non-Euclidean concept of architecture is all about, De Carlo's masterpiece in Urbino will, I am sure, have made it quite clear.

The Mirror Master – on Joost van Roojen

Translation of an article published in Forum, *July 1967, pp. 55–70*

When Joost van Roojen[1] takes on a wall or a space, unusual things happen. It is simply that reality gains something very fine – and that is unusual enough! Van Roojen includes all the negative and positive characteristics when he subjects a space to his critical eye. In one way or another he is able to find out the questions the space asks. What is more, he is able to capture it in his answer – that which he ultimately creates. This then gives it something incontestable. One accepts it without being able or wanting to find out the original problem. Van Roojen elicits from the object itself a certain latent identity, which he then gives back to it, internalised and expanded, by means of a series of subtle (and unexpected) changes. The results have something

incontestable, as I said, but also something self-evident. Elusiveness, even strangeness, are not alien to these qualities, because nothing is so surprising as what is self-evident. What is self-evident is in fact always strange and odd!

The fact that specific characteristics and exact data, derived from the object itself, can give it an enhanced identity through the psychological world of the painter – an identity which is no longer tied to either this psychological world or these external characteristics, but despite this still manifests them – is almost unique in the context of what painters bring into being in or on buildings. Van Roojen absorbs even insubstantial or disruptive elements into a clear and at the same time mysteriously nuanced order, but they remain present: in the same way as reflection hides from view what is beneath the water, but does not cover it up.

Van Roojen is a highly individual painter and is exceptionally independent. He treads a no man's land, while the illuminating space that appears in all his work – and this is the remarkable thing – is actually accessible to everyone. When colour, form and dimension open up so gratifyingly, then indeed something very unusual has happened! In Van Roojen's case, it is no mural in the normal sense that takes shape, nor a painterly accompaniment to the architecture, but another reality that lies beyond the reach of the architecture. By way of this detour the idea of space is given a new meaning.

In the glassy hall of the State Road Construction Laboratory in Delft, the large space outside is a prominent presence. It is only by means of what Van Roojen has

Joost van Roojen, murals inside the National Road Construction Laboratory in Delft, 1963
Photos Vincent Ligtelijn

done that this presence assumed a form – by which I mean that the hall became an interior. The changing light – this sounds miraculous – has ended up in the colours. They came into being in this changing light and reflect the characteristics of these changes. One might also say that the nature of the light is always perceptible in the colours. This too is unusual, since up to now colour in painting has only been the 'right' or 'intended' colour in one sort of light. In Van Roojen's work the colours invite the changes in light. What appears to be the same colour used in many different places (in this case green) is in reality actually different everywhere; colours within a single form gradually evolve: it is as if Van Roojen wants to be one step ahead of the whims of the light. I know what it is: in his work, colours are not afraid of time!

Which explains their perspective and luminosity – their space.

Anyone who goes up the big staircase in the hall (or stays standing on the landing) experiences the painting above and the painting below as reflections of each other, and therefore not a continuation of each other.

What is more, the floor between the two storeys has now become the horizon. Anyone who passes a horizon knows he is in space!

And there is more – though one has to be there to believe it: this painting gives the space the joy of its own sunrise and sunset! Every form and colour joins in; not only the little inner suns, each of which is different from the others in colour – while the big sun outside changes colour between sunrise and sunset. So there are similar changes of colour inside and outside: simultaneous and in succession.

The various windows, and also the bits of wall between them, only really assumed any significance when they became part of the painting and the form and dimensions of each one was extended in both directions. It seems to me that colour, form and dimension rarely behave like this in time and space.

And about the painting in the new TH auditorium in Delft, this too: anyone who enters the main auditorium there will probably wonder whether the sun in the hall, which Van Roojen left there 'oval' and unrivalled, has come inside with us* or is shining through the wall between the hall and the auditorium (its stage), and whether it shines out of both sides of the wall. And those two cool lunar circles high above the sun in the hall, inclined slightly diagonally away, and in the evening illuminated, as if by the moon itself, by means of two lamps on the roof outside.

Light, colour and space reflect each other's meaning. Not just like that, of course, but Van Roojen pulls it off. In fact he has always been interested in reflection and therefore has also become a master of mirrors like no other. His colours open up to the light, let it in and become space – this space is his Sahara. He knows the horizon from close up, and knows how to make horizons accessible (there are often a lot of them) – Columbus was not the last! They are moreover transparent, these horizons. They are areas of light of an unprecedented luminosity – and for that matter it is certainly a new luminosity in art. One might even call it the area of light of a line, which is only articulated, made spatial and therefore accessible by the strange reflection of a variety of things from the artist's own world.

The work of Van Roojen will do anyone good who thinks they have a conclusive explanation for the phenomenon of the *fata morgana* (and who possibly regrets it).

* So that the many esteemed listeners will not be distracted or inspired by this illuminated sun, it has disappeared behind a curtain. As if the Polytechnic does not need any light and technology no colour!

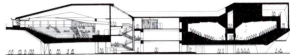

Joost van Roojen, murals inside the Auditorium Building of Delft Polytechnic, 1965.
Photos Con Mönnich

The murals, in the cross-section left, were also intended by Bakema to breach the tectonics of the partition wall between staircase and auditorium.

Joost van Roojen, *Sun with little red moon*, watercolour, 1966

A propos Jan Rietveld[1]

Translation of an article published in Wonen, *1970–71, no. 2.*

If Jan Rietveld has become a builder of detached houses – probably the best in the Netherlands, since none more liveable are made in such varied abundance – it may be partly due to his nature (who is able to establish this in retrospect?), but mostly because he is gradually coming to fulfil the one-sided task society has allotted him – or rather, has saddled him with. He was not given the space due to him as a high-quality architect, but despite this he built spaces for others, for the few, and has done so for no less than 25 years. In some ways it is sad too: that so relatively few people live in all these detached houses. His block of flats in Amsterdam West, alongside the Haarlem road, is the most relevant since Bergpolder, Plaslaan and Nirwana.

Jan Rietveld in the guesthouse Photo Izak Salomons

What I really wanted to say is this: even the schools, theatres, museums and public buildings he did not build because no one has ever asked him to, are, like the detached houses he did build, among the best we have! As to the formation of value judgements, Dutch society proves definitively liable to a certain inertia. In any case, the imminent presence of Jan Rietveld as a professor in Delft will make his potential versatility noticeable there at least. In structural terms, there is one specific aspect of Rietveld's houses that always strikes me in a different way. I would like to limit myself to examining this one aspect (of many) because of the effect it has on liveability.

Although, spatially, building is in the main orthogonal – and certainly in the Netherlands – when entering and leaving a building, and also when spending time in it, our attention is mainly diagonally oriented and this successively in different directions. We do not turn our eyes or head or body simultaneously in fits and starts of 90 degrees like soldiers.

Yet a lot of houses (and other buildings) – too many – hinder the natural course of attention and movement; by among other things always positioning doors, windows and furniture incorrectly in respect of each other. But also by means of an incorrect positioning and relationship between the open and more outwardly-oriented places and those which are more enclosed and inwardly-oriented (assuming there is question of these two kinds of place at all), either in one single space or several spaces running from one to the other.

Jan Rietveld, Weekend house Ameling in Teuven, Belgium, 1968 (with guesthouse added in 1974) Photos Izak Salomons

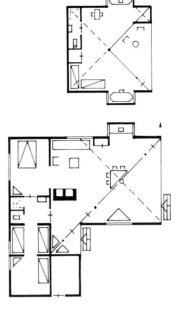

In this way there arises a constant conflict of direction between person and space – between person and house; mental fossilisation and disorientation. People move. Even when they are sitting or standing they turn their eyes, head or body towards something or someone. Spaces should as it were move with them – turn with them – accompany them – follow them. One feels this happening in – and around – Jan Rietveld's houses.

Human experiences are transmitted onto paper by his pencil – sometimes on an envelop or, if I remember rightly, once on the back of a cardboard cigarette packet – and then into a miniature model which he then conjures up out of his pocket at just the right moment.

In connection with the aspect I have referred to, another essential thing is that he succeeds, by building both orthogonally and diagonally in one and the same project, in making the space move and turn with man. The result is never disorienting but often gratifyingly ambiguous. It is a spatial 'ambiguity' that both surprises and reassures; through the fact that walls, facades and spaces turn through 45 degrees, the structure of the building (its orientation) suddenly or briefly converges – and this always at different points – with the diagonally directed attention. The periphery of the space turns towards or away from the people at the right moment.

That's all I want to say here. Qualities that add to liveability are unfortunately impossible or barely possible to photograph – perhaps they can be filmed. It is the experience gained from being present in the space that makes these qualities knowable, and the people who are privileged enough to spend time in one of Jan Rietveld's houses know this.

Jaap Bakema, 1914–1981
'The Moment of Core'

Translation of Van Eyck's words at the funeral of Jaap Bakema on 26 February 1981[1]

I wonder, might Jaap Bakema have been able to build a railway terminus? I think the answer is yes, that too. But he would have got the railway company to the point of leaving out those huge end-buffers. What he did do, what he actually brought about – *in transit* – is indeed astounding. Yet there are limits, even to that; limits to what is possible, limits also to energy. Thus he – Jaap – with so many gathered this late afternoon, is not going to speak. He will not manage that this time round.

Jaap used to quote Bergson, and Sia – his wife – quoting Bergson for him the other day, quoted Jaap: *'Je constate d'abord que je passe d'état en état'*.[2]

Photo Simon Smithson

His curiosity-without-limits must have helped him, when, around half past nine on Friday, he started out again.

For this reason it is not after all so strange – though not therefore understandable – that we shall no longer hear his voice. Even within the span of life it is sometimes impossible to grasp the straight fact that somebody is elsewhere – simply not here. Nevertheless, even though Jaap would not have chosen these words himself, I would like to add another 'passage' to the one from Bergson which he did choose:

'We are of the same making as dreams and our limited lives lie in the midst of sleep.'[3]

What can one say about Jaap Bakema that is not already obvious – such as, for example that he was a great man in his own curious sort of way. It does me good, Ladies and Gentlemen – I can assure you it does – to say precisely this.

We were together in every continent but one – Africa – and about that one we told each other stories. En route to Australia, I remember, Jaap talked and talked about all sorts of things – marvelous things, and the marvel of everything. Then, somewhere over India, we fell asleep. I woke him as we flew over the glistering Irrawaddy delta so he could see what I knew would enthrall him. That was halfway, so there was still time left for talking!

About thirty years ago, as good pathfinders, I shared a hotel room with him. We had just been through the first day of an 8 and Opbouw weekend. After such a long day of talking Jaap was able to literally 'fall' asleep. Around three in the morning a noise like approaching thunder woke me. Then a loud voice soon followed by thundering laughter, again the voice, the laughter and both together – the night shook. My room mate, you see, was apparently building up imaginary events around familiar persons. As the fantasy and absurdity increased, so did the noise, for meanwhile the walls, ceiling and floor of our room started banging and knocking as though a siege had started. Shhhh Shhhhh, I said, you'll wake the entire hotel. 'As if they're not awake by now', he roared laughing towards the climax. All I want to say is this: anyone who has not heard that sound has missed something quite extraordinary. I have heard it, and will therefore miss it.

When Henri Rousseau, Le Douanier, had died, his friend Guillaume Apollinaire wrote a little verse for his grave stone, begging him to allow the lugage friends were sending him to pass through the gates of heaven duty free:
'We shall send you brushes, colours and canvases, so that in your free time you will be able to paint the face of the stars, the way you painted my face.'

We could send Jaap a load of paper and pencils, rulers and something to measure with so that he too can continue to do what he always did.

By definition – on Lucien Lafour

Article published in Forum, *June 1982, and in* Architectural Review, *April 1984*

About 10 years ago Lucien Lafour[1] left Holland with his family in order to settle in Surinam, and 'perhaps' to build something there sooner or later.

I told him, just before he left, that I would write about his tropical firstling for a *good* review!

Various reasons prompted me. In the background there was the fact that out of the way places and societies – call them tribal or archaic – are always beckoning me. Whether in the South Pacific or the Bering Straits, I try to get there. In Lafour's case I was already intimately familiar from afar with the particular country he had gone to, because my mother came from there and my grandfather, who knew all there was to know about it, kept telling wonderful stories about its jungle – rivers, beasts and peoples. And so, ever since, architecture along its widest horizon has kept a firm hold on me, embracing, of course, what is closer by. Then there was the comforting point that writing about a building not yet conceived would in this case incur no risk, for I knew that if Lafour, an appreciated colleague for 20 years, was to build in Surinam, it would turn out the way it did – and that is no small thing.

Those familiar with the perplexities of building in places where conditions are very different will be more surprised than others that it did prove possible after all to get buildings built in Surinam which work well and even belong where they were put. That this should be so – that bringing about anything as 'normal' as appropriate buildings should occasion surprise, says a lot about the sorry state this discipline is now in, regardless of whether or not such buildings happen to be built for other societies, climates and conditions. The question, therefore, as to how many architects are still producing buildings, here or elsewhere, which *belong where they are put, work properly, and haven't got what they needn't have*, is indeed a disturbing one.

In countries like Surinam, caught between the archaic and the modern, people tend to adopt without questioning whatever is made and done in the 'advanced' parts of the world though even there its adequacy will be limited or even questionable.

What the consequences must inevitably be when the present selfish swing towards the 'autonomous' (grand and empty) gesture which takes no account of

Lucien Lafour and Rikkert Wijk, hospital at Mariënburg, Surinam, 1980

straightforward matters, spreads to the largest and poorest part of the world, where the luxury of silly building cannot be afforded, never enters the heads of those responsible.

This presentation, at any rate, shows what can still be achieved when sanity and competence go together. It also shows how appropriate 'modern' buildings can look when they respond well to 'specific local conditions and requirements' which, among other things, could just as well have been those of a temperate or cold climate instead of a tropical one. Lucien Lafour is certainly one of the very few to have evolved an architecture which 'suits' the tropics – and is also satisfactorily contemporary. He gave an impulse which can be carried further, step by step, until people will be heard saying: look, *that's how we do it here* – how we function well in what we build.

Although Lafour was born in Holland – grew up and studied there – it was not until he got to Paramaribo that he managed to bring together the notions about place and use, dimension, light, material and construction, which he had developed over the years. Now that he is back in Holland again and has started a small practice, his

Lucien Lafour and Rikkert Wijk, School in Galibi, Surinam, 1977

The Galibi circles: murals by a local artist who translated traditional motifs of ritual drums into wet mortar.

marked receptivity for what is specific and what is general in divergent situations will enable him to continue building as appropriately and characteristically in Holland as he did in Surinam. And when the time comes I intend to write a little sequel to this – again without risk!

A lot could be said about the different buildings Lafour made whilst in Surinam, but let me comment on just two of them. To begin with the clinic near Paramaribo. Its most characteristic gesture is the way the reinforced concrete verandahs receive people all round as generously as they catch and channel tropical rains from above, for their roofs form gutters across the full width, whilst also supporting the striking canopies, which work like huge lungs.

It must be a real boon, out there in Mariënburg, that ample world underneath, where there is always some breeze. One senses a gratifying understanding between the built form and what is intrinsically local – attuned to the *region* but implying no *ism*! The way sun and shade, openness and enclosure, attention along, through and across, are dealt with to full advantage – in gradation and contrast, diversified and, in places, also adjustable. Without mechanical contrivances a pleasant climate prevails. The structure itself sees to that.

Whilst in the 'sad tropics' there are always countless people patiently, in all sorts of inhospitable places, waiting for what may well not be there, those approaching Lucien's clinic – ill, weary and perhaps apprehensive, will already feel better because of the way the building takes them in – settles round them as they penetrate its shady interior. If this is not a good and beautiful building I don't know another! I even venture to regard it as archetypal for the tropics – and that can mean all sorts of things, since the tropics are as varied as the needs out there – which may be why typologists (or 'typophiles') *are so afraid of archetypes!*

The Galibi Circles

To conclude, just a word about that little school by the shore – and what can be brought about when, through respect, insight and patience, an old Indian lady beyond 80 is found prepared – takes the risk – to transfer the traditional motifs she normally did in dark pigment on her tribe's ritual drums directly and faultlessly into wet mortar – vertically and greatly enlarged. The circles on the wall prepared for the occasion must have looked enormous to her considering the limited reach of her arm. Now that she has died the girl seen working under her guidance – an apprentice – continues to adorn the community's drums. Will she also require an apprentice one day?

In comparison to this breathtaking feat, the forms and motifs the symbolmongers of today are reviving and contriving appear like awkward ghosts nobody likes or fears; like old tales badly retold to deaf ears. But the less selfish, I hope, will be reminded that forms and motifs, which still carry meaning across, do appear from time to time. And when they do, as they did in Galibi, they come, to use Lucien's words, *like precious gifts*. Thus a small modest building became the bearer of great art, and symbolic meaning persists for a while in architecture.

The entire episode in Galibi – what was made, those who did it and how it all came about – that, put together, surely *is what culture is all about* – by definition, I should add.

Joop Hardy, 1918–1983, autumn man between winters

Translation of Van Eyck's speech at the funeral of Joop Hardy, on 8 October 1983[1]

'Self-willed to the very end, Joop died while travelling in the company of his family.' So went the message. Self-willed-travel-company-family: four words that form a concise portrait around which I shall weave a little more. One evening, Wiet, who lived above me on the Keizersgracht, brought Joop Hardy with her. Judging by his behaviour, a demigoddess had only just abducted him. Where did she find someone like that, I thought, but the same thing applied to him as he nestled blissfully at her feet. Years later he told me how it all happened. All at once, there! A woman on a bicycle – wilder and more beautiful than his dreams, but too late – a tram came between them and she was gone! She is the way she looks, he thought, and his definitive decision was made – it coincided with that first appearance and mechanical disappearance.

Photo Henk Kamphuis

I no longer know how the hunt was continued. It was beauty, a lifetime long: also in countless stories, lines of verse, drawings, paintings, spaces and sounds; in books and likenesses in them – in photos: clothes, fabrics, jewels, furniture and objects, that accompany a life – in short, abduction, and transports through worlds of Art – many and frequent: through cultural wealth. This and his habit and gift of taking others with him – to transport them in their turn – were characteristic of him.

Joop Hardy was, like no other, a guide through these salutary worlds, especially through all sorts of singular marginal and in-between areas. He knew the maps and charts of the emotions and found his way in them as if in his own garden. With how many eyes did he see – and how many eyes were opened while he was seeing? Now this fabulous storyteller is no longer there – he talked about the shapes of feeling and the feelings about them – about transformation, in other words – about association and about… signals!

Hardy found the intimacy he sought in a reality he assembled himself; in works of art; in the artistically, sensitively profiled. Whatever touched him as being beautiful immediately became a component of a construction along the broadest horizon. In this way a miraculous interior without boundaries came into being – but also familiar and accessible. He persuaded past and present to merge, for the sake of a gentler awareness of time (time without the sharpness of a knife).

He took care of this ('care' having a particular meaning for Hardy as it had for Rilke): that time was given depth – space – and, by means of associations, perspective too. After all, in time there are no other paths than those that run through space! That is also how time steadily becomes transparent. This is a good thing and Hardy knew that, but the quasi-innovators who had for so many years been operating at Architecture in Delft were just about as receptive to this as grit – and afraid too, scared to death, of this gentler – open – awareness of time, and to the 'space' within it. Paradox or silly misunderstanding? While Hardy as a professor in Delft was persecuted and ultimately ousted by this loathsome collective for his exceptional gifts, at the Academy in Enschede things buzzed, precisely because of his presence as head for a decade or more. His gently anarchic talent for organisation there opened the way to 'intelligent' spontaneity, fantasy and improvisation. One cannot imagine any more painful contrast in education as that between those two schools at that time. As far as Delft is concerned, I would just like to say this: emptiness naturally lacks nothing; its nature also means that nothing can be added to it! The fact that Hardy was treated like an 'animal' by 'people' in the Architecture Department who, themselves nothing, missed nothing, has now in any case been set down in the history of that grubby educational institution.

I just mentioned Hardy's individual organisational talent at Enschede: anarchy interwoven with the absurd and reciprocally nourished and tempered by each other. Hardy found his intimate-creative adventure in the mirror of what was felt, thought and created in times past (and what was added to it in his own time and presence). So, not at a desk, in words on paper, because that just didn't suit him, but in thousands of pictures (illuminations), a soft and restful voice and – above all – people around him who all found something else in this glorious flow of images. Although his knowledge was enormous it was not encyclopaedic, because it was experienced knowledge, having arisen out of sensory involvement in images. It was selected, specific and 'built' like a very special big house: with many meanings and ambiguous, kaleidoscopic but homogeneous; full of changing simultaneity; an imagined museum like a spiral; a suite of mirrored rooms – an image of himself among others.

But above all, and all in all, it was an ode sung to woman from every room, corner and crack – a transformation of matter itself into her. Joop Hardy found the foundations of existence in the female; its intimacy too. On these foundations stood his assembled world, his own construction, containing everything that struck him as beautiful or came across to him as emotion (tenderness). In beauty, Hardy found the intimacy he sought – and the protection. That is why he brought so much of it together – to be able to live in the company of that extended 'family' from day to day. Intimacy along the broadest horizon was typical of him, and also the goal of his 'self-willed' nature. It stretched out – erotically – along this horizon.

But it also coincided with the spectrum, with the elements and the seasons, with night and day, with every alphabet and every language, with signs, signals (his word!) and gestures. The erotic as the pulse of existence, the purpose of breathing and common denominator of his *musée imaginaire* where he spent his time like a northern pasha.

Hardy caught the ordinary (endearing) and the bizarre (absurd) in one and the same hat (the blessings of deliberate perversity). He had it everywhere; in his head, heart and eyes – the corners of his mouth and his nostrils. And also in the way he stood and walked and, not to be forgotten, in his coats, knitted jackets, bags, chests of drawers and suitcases. An end has now come to the expansion of all those Pandora's boxes.

Joop Hardy – an autumn man between winters – appeared more fragile than he actually was – or was he more fragile than he seemed? He was a discerning ascetic in luxury, a connoisseur sold on cultural 'goods', a lover-aristocrat of many forms of beauty. He found it where others did not even look for it. It was attracted to him, overflowed in him and – of course – he enjoyed it, communicated it and again enjoyed the communication – of what, with his calm intensity, he continued to hand on to his students (even when, between the 'loss' of his professorship and his 'return' a year and a half later, he continued unperturbed to give lectures to full auditoria). What's more, I would be astonished if he had aroused feelings of inadequacy and therefore of guilt in others (though perhaps?) – and this a Dutchman!

Because he had a sort of reassuring message, something like 'the non-barbarian is actually a cultivated creature', he was also an engaging moralist. Hardy did not hold out until the 'nineties', but that did not stop him from being '*fin de siècle*' from head to toe! In the calm luxury of his own temperature, as a connoisseur he was, as I have already said, also an ascetic. In him, pleasure and control were related. He loved materials, texture and fine objects, and their sensual presence, almost too much. All this formed part of his everyday fare. Hardy was the living definition of a dandy. He kept his deep emotions behind a veil of imperturbability.

I used to see Hardy so often on the train that in my mind he has become associated with trains. They were carriages full of cultural delicacies, because Hardy was a courier, archivist and ambassador of his own empire.

'*Le monde dans un homme, tel est le poète moderne*', as Max Jacob said. Joop's staggering selection now remains as the residue of a life, without a guardian. The warp of that long and broad woven fabric has gone, because Hardy put very little down in writing. It will therefore largely be dispersed – or rather, after his last autumn, be blown away – in such cases death is in no way appropriate. The voice falls silent and the light goes out. Talking about light, to conclude, Joop liked subdued light and nuances of shadow. To him, literality (which is what we are actually left with now) meant the erosion of reality – handling that one great spider's web too roughly.

'A little, passionately, not at all?'
She casts the snowy petals on the air:
And what care we how many petals fall!
Ernest Dowson, 1896

Dylan Thomas

Translation of a letter to the editor of NRC Handelsblad, *26 September 1986*

'Brute', 'habitual drunkard', 'second-rate talent', 'it's impossible to call him a great poet'.

Imagine that this was a quiz question thought up by Maarten 't Hart[1] specially for CS[2] readers, a week before his book review of *Leven met een bruut*[3] was printed there (13 September 1986). To whom might these phrases apply? Of course to some well-known person. I shall let the cat out of the bag immediately, because I don't think anyone will guess since, except the author of the grotesque descriptions quoted above, no one is made like that.

It will probably amaze you, but it refers to no one other than Dylan Thomas! And as far as the terms used are concerned, they were found amongst similar ones in the review of the new biography that I just mentioned: *Caitlin, Life with Dylan Thomas* by Caitlin Thomas and George Tramlett.

Maarten 't Hart uses Caitlin's words when it suits him, but, as if it were not already enough, adds all sorts of tales and fabrications. He first says, for instance, that Thomas 'was someone who thought that everything is permitted because he was given exceptional talents' which he follows with the observation that 'it is odd that it is only second-rate talents that always think this, who go on to live they way they imagine a genius lives'.

Maarten 't Hart, still kicking the man when he's down, first lets Caitlin say, 'Genius is a terrible thing for people to live with,' and then wonders whether this is actually true, because, 'It certainly did not apply to true geniuses like Bach, Mozart and Verdi' while it does to 'a certain sort of literary figures who have got it into their heads that they have enormous talent. People like Multatuli[4] and this Dylan Thomas. Because you can hardly call Thomas a great poet'. So that's what Maarten 't Hart has to say.

Where does one get such an idea? What's the matter with this Maarten 't Hart, I wonder, that keeps him from 'simply' saying, 'It's impossible to call Dylan Thomas anything other than a great poet'. Why Multatuli is cunningly smuggled in to share indirectly in the punishment is an extra puzzle, to which the readers (and perhaps Geert van Oorschot[5] too) may have more of an answer than me!

Maarten 't Hart has more than one arrow in his child's quiver, but even the most poisonous of them can never hit the intended target because it lies far beyond his range. Here it is, 'If only half of what Caitlin tells us about Thomas is correct, even then the only fitting word for this man is 'brute'.' She herself says, 'He was a scoundrel', 't Hart immediately adds, apparently not realising that a 'scoundrel' is not necessarily a brute and certainly not in this case, even if everything that Caitlin tells is true, and I believe that actually to be the case.

Does 't Hart not know his languages well enough or is he simply a little bit bad himself, picking his bones in public. Diminishing a figure like Dylan Thomas to a second-rate talent like this is in any case an unprofitable business, because of course he does not even succeed in pulling himself up to that lower level. He could hardly have done anything more clumsy than to aim precisely at such a phenomenal talent.

If everything goes well, a talent develops as the result of another's talent – and does so generously and gladly. Thomas' talent was so abundant that a whole generation of poets – in fact a whole language – has been enriched. Here, closer to home, Hugo Claus and Lucebert provided this sort of stimulus. The former recreated *Under Milkwood* so magnificently in Dutch that, alongside Thomas' masterpiece, we now have another, related masterpiece of our own.

To conclude, anyone who ever heard Thomas say '*And death shall have no dominion*' in his distant thunder of a voice – in the flesh or on record – will understand that no badly aimed arrows can any longer harm a great, dead poet. In the same way as Thomas lets the word 'no' swing briefly before he pronounces 'dominion' as a rapid spiral – look, a thing like this happens only very rarely, just a few times in every era. So as not to disappear entirely below the surface of the water, it is advisable never to underestimate or distrust the value of such moments.

Finally, long after it was all past, that life with a 'brute', Caitlin Thomas ended her own masterpiece, *Left-Over Life to Kill*, as follows:

'This is it, this is the finish, a beaten voice said inside me;
and the train started to trundle, and chug, and drone:
Going home, going home, going home;
no home to go to, no home to go to, no home to go to;
going home to no home, going home to no home, going home to no home;
no home no Dylan, no Dylan no home, no Dylan...
And all the mountains I had ever climbed came tumbling down, and crumbled at my feet.
And all the king's horses, and all the king's men, couldn't put Caitlin Thomas together again.'

Shame on you, Maarten 't Hart, shame.

On Van Doesburg, I.K. Bonset and De Stijl

Opening speech for the Van Doesburg exhibition in the Rotterdam Boymans Museum, on 18 December 1988[1]

The war in France had only just finished when I made her acquaintance in Meudon. Nelly[2] was a family friend until her death, even though our houses were far distant from each other. We saw her in Meudon, Zurich or Amsterdam, which she visited regularly, always by taxi. Panting, she ascended the steep stairs of the Binnenkant[3] step by step and after some time went on further by taxi – to Van Eesteren, Sandberg, Baljeu, her niece or another meeting, because she always had a full programme (just as Van Doesburg did whenever he went anywhere) before flying back to Paris or New York.

She was in the habit, believe it or not, of calling me 'My Son' – always – in that hoarse, curiously feminine baritone of hers! As you will understand, I am proud as a peacock of that affectionate caress. Because 'Does', she assured me, would have thought it alright that she should call me that – he didn't want any himself because then you can't choose. 'My Son' – no order of knighthood can match it!

So it is through his wife that I have a special tie with Van Doesburg – more tangible than when he had been just a spiritual father to me, as several of his contemporaries were. For that reason he is always the one who is no longer present, the dead giant. Except Mondrian, the other De Stijl men were still around: Van Eesteren, Rietveld, Oud, Wils, Van der Leck, Vantongerloo, Vordemberge, Huszár, Kok and Cesar Domela. Schwitters, Arp and Lissitsky, also involved in De Stijl, were only just still around.

Theo and Nelly van Doesburg

Nelly never actually spoke of Theo like a widow, but very often of 'Doesburg' without the 'Van', or 'Does', as Van Eesteren did when, shortly before five o'clock, he stuck his head round the door with his disarming Cheshire cat grin (he had persuaded me in Zurich to come and work in the Amsterdam Public Works department) and asked, 'Shall we 'stijl' a little more again?' Meaning chat about that period, which was his oasis.

When Nelly came to Eindhoven to receive the Sikkens Prize posthumously for Theo, I naturally thought it was fine for her, although I considered this late recognition rather dubious. Better late than never is no excuse for just being too late. So in my little speech you might say I turned the prize in her direction: she being the last of the original dadaists, so that the prize still ended up with I.K. Bonset. I am here running ahead of a second, equally contrary trick, which is that, by way of an 'opening', I shall later literally – but nonetheless figuratively – rename the exhibition 'I.K. Bonset, painter and architect. I am doing this as a descendant of De Stijl, to clarify what for many people is the rather obscure and confusing content of the work shown. Because, ladies and gentlemen, behind each of his heteronyms lies the full stature of this kaleidoscopic man.

'Awesome' was the word that rasped deep in Nelly's throat when she spoke of something very good, and that was not just Does and De Stijl, because her eye ranged over an exceptionally wide horizon. When I entered the 'awesome' world of the avant-garde, they were almost all still around. But not all. I realised very clearly that neither Van Doesburg, nor Mondrian, nor Delaunay, nor Klee were any longer around. Neither Joyce nor Schoenberg. Now none of them are around any more (only the shadow of Dalí without Gala). Of this fact I am almost constantly, awfully aware. A few years back it was mentioned in passing in the newspaper that the painter Juan Miró had died. I immediately thought, soon it will be Chagall, the last thread, and then they are all gone; then it's the end of the Great Gang. Before it had come to that, the work of this, the greatest living painter, certainly a hundred years old, was not even shown at De Wilde's little farewell parade at the Stedelijk Museum[4] – farewell! Farewell to whom exactly? To the Great Gang? Just imagine. Such a thing is incredible, isn't it? And yet in the lowest countries so predictable.

When Rietveld was 70, for the occasion I wrote two long pieces about him and the situation around him: *Squares with a smile* and *The ball rebounds*. I shall read part of it out, ending up with the person we are honouring this afternoon. I do not say that lightly, because whichever way you move around the world of that Band of Greats of that time, you will sooner or later bump into Van Doesburg. He is standing on so many corners, and often simultaneously.

> 'Fate has willed that Duiker, Van der Vlugt and Van Loghem died young, leaving Rietveld and Van Eesteren with an enthusiastic but precariously based following. The bridge between this following and de Stijl thus lost three of its pillars (Oud and Van der Leck being unsteady ones). Theo van Doesburg died in 1931 – a leader whose driving force, prophetic insight, intelligence and art together were of such proportions that the dream of his life, prolonged by thirty years, looms often before my eyes, for I am convinced that we would now be in a different position. It is hardly surprising that Rietveld and Van Eesteren were unable to repair the bridge on their own. Indeed this was, constructively speaking, no longer possible.'

At this moment I am thinking for example of *Mécano*, the 'International magazine for mental Hygiene, mechanical Aesthetics and Neo-Dadaism, headed by I.K. Bonset and Theo van Doesburg, with the assistance of all the constructors of the new World-Image. Produced in a curious way, each issue in a different colour and containing many reproductions. Price per year (10 issues) 5 guilders, individual issues 60 cents. For the Netherlands: DE STIJL administration, Leiden. Paris: Librairie Six, 5 ave. De Lowendal 7e.'

Only four issues appeared, very small and square and indeed printed on metallic paper: a red one, a blue one, a green one and one without colour. Nelly had lost her green one and begged me to dig one out there in the Netherlands. An impossible task, but not necessary because my great friend Jan Rietveld was able to find one at the Rinsemas.[5] Which made it a special copy for two reasons. Jan was both the most talented and nicest architect of his generation, and the Rinsemas in Drachten were of the purest Stijl-Merz-Mécano water.

As to that 'mental Hygiene', not long before his death Van Doesburg wrote the following: 'One can to be sure learn more from doctors' laboratories than from painters' studios. The latter are cages that stink of diseased apes. Your studio should have the cold atmosphere of the mountains at 3000 metres. The perpetual snow should be lying there: the cold kills the microbes.'

I shall stay briefly with I.K. Bonset[6] precisely because he leads us to Van Doesburg – the other way round is equally true, but in this case we are after all concerned mainly with the painter and architect. I was fortunate because I never wanted to choose in the world of the avant-garde. The idea of dividing it all up never came to me. We, my wife and I, rode long ago into the world of De Stijl and Surrealism on Giorgio de Chirico's noiseless little train – and I have remained loyal to that fantastic little train. Dalí's *Apparition énigmatique de ma cousine Caroline sur la plage de Rosas* hung real as life above our bed in Zurich, while we devoured *De Stijl* and *Merz*. In my case it has always been *and and*.

At a Max Ernst opening in New York, to his astonishment an art journalist discovered Mondrian among the crowd and stepped jauntily towards him. You can guess all the things he asked. Someone standing nearby heard it and Mondrian's answer too: *'Ah, Max, vous savez, il fait la même chose que moi, mais dans l'autre hémisphère'.*[7] Another related anecdote: in the twenties, at a gathering in Zurich in honour of Van Doesburg, someone thought he could please Van Doesburg by running down Picasso at the table. Van Doesburg immediately stood up and gave Nelly a sign, upon which they left together. So you see, when it came to it, they upheld the great unity – the balance. That is the way the greats act – generous and with solidarity – and that too is 'style'. Do not take De Stijl literally because according to the letter it simply dies – or makes sure it is out of the way – takes flight. Van Eesteren always said: 'De Stijl, you know – style – you can't just get hold of it, but still it's there.' He could really talk fantastically for hours, even in later years, about the De Stijl period and Does – all on the phone. 'I'm just telling you this now,' he always said. He did not want to do any interviews. No tape recorder, nothing written down. I am telling you the following because it's the only sad thing he ever told me. All sorts of things had happened and it was a long time since they had seen each other, when all of a sudden Does and he found themselves standing next to each other waiting for the bus. 'So there we stood. Something had got lost, evaporated. You notice it suddenly. There was no longer any warmth between us.' That warmth is precisely what it's all about – was all about – in De Stijl. Warmth even at 3000 metres. That was so typical of Van Eesteren. So, ladies and gentlemen, there you have De Stijl, its tremendous worth, precisely because it was not a matter of a utopia – no naive belief in an improved, unachievable world, but a reality that was actually achieved. In short, they *made* it, the way they approached their vision and specified it was sufficiently concrete to be able to go further.

In spite of the growing interest in *De Stijl*, today very little of it remains. But it will come back again. For the time being the weak are being briefly the strong: the neo-rationalists or rats, the postmoderns and other pestilences, the RPP. It has gone *wrong*, it went *on the wrong side*. You know the meaning of these words. And there we are again: those who are disappointed, because of what they lack, want what Mulisch wants too: *Gran*.[8] Now, *nota bene*, it is the intellectual trendsetters, the cultural pretenders and the art trend-sniffers who are now on the march – not the others this time, not the political chaps and ordinary people. For them there is no punishment imaginable by those who do not think as they do. Only last week the editor of *Archis* wrote: 'The dance theatre in The Hague is an example of modern architecture, but the utopian optimism of the avant gardes (he knows of several) has been replaced by the latent deathwish of the eighties.'[9] 'Deathwish', but in this case a comfortable one. This wish has been very cleverly thought out, because it makes them rich before they die.

But now back to De Stijl – to the true, intrinsic style, before it went so far and was made understandable by *Til Brugman*,[10] who really understood it all from the start and wrote the following:

'Dressed up with a stand-up collar, as was the fashion at the time but which could be no good for health, and about which Piet Mondrian used to confer with his laundry in order to get them ironed in a soft way. With spindly trousers, which were fashionable at the time but could not be healthy, and about which the tailor had to be interpellated, because being so squeezed could be no good. Topped with a hat, like he would wear all his life. Tall, straight up, his mouth slightly contracted as if he was going to smile. In this way Piet Mondrian walked on Sunday afternoon [from the Amsterdam centre] to the countryside, now and then looking

Cover of *Mécano*, 1922, NO. RED

Cor van Eesteren, Nelly van Doesburg and Til Brugman, The Hague, 1924

Til Brugman's living room in The Hague, designed by Vilmos Huszár in 1924 and provided with furniture by Rietveld.

at the air and talking about all the vicissitudes a man has to endure because those damned other people think so little about how those collars, trousers and other things we just use, have to be. From the Sarphati Park until the last houses left off. Then there were the meadows, the real skies. Then the silence. Sometimes peering briefly over the Amstel, sometimes with a half, rather stiff, swing, a look across the grasslands. 'Very polderish' said Piet Mondrian. 'But very beautiful all the same. See that haze below the sun? Or, might that still be from the city?' And then went and sat on the verge. Looking, looking out over the polderishness. 'See that red cabbage? What tints in the axils and what planes on the leaves! Very cabbagey, but still very beautiful...'

And, back in his studio, he showed his work. In the corner was a suit of armour with red velvet. An incomprehensible suit of armour. 'Very Rembrandtish, but still very beautiful...' And Mondrian rearranged its drape. On the easel was a triptych in bluish-purple tones. Austere, stylised figures of women. 'It's still so womanish. It's not so bad, but I haven't got it yet. Stylisation is nothing. You have to get through it. This is actually still red cabbage, do you see? I have to get to... to style. Style!' On a small easel is a canvas only just started. Light, very light near the purplish-blue figures, to which a hint of red gives a warm feel. This small, light canvas shows a road, diagonally. 'This is still very much what I do not want... What I do want, but not as the last stage. But this road is going in the right direction. Do you see?'

In a fit of great confidentiality Piet Mondrian showed his sketchbook. 'It's very much a rough sketchbook, but still that's the way it will be... Yes, that's how it

should be... Think it's any good?' This rough sketchbook, half-full in 1910, contained the outlines of the oval paintings and tints of the very finest colour. Also, at the end of the used pages, it contained indications of his first abstract, rectangular works. Cautious, though solidly initiated, colour in a single tint, blue, red, yellow. Grey, white and black in between. 'I am becoming primary,' said Mondrian, and shut the book. 'Do you mind?'
Years later his first letter came, from Paris. Lots of news. Piet Mondrian elated. At the end a postscript: 'Til, they have these collars here, you know, those soft, half-height... Paris is well advanced, don't you think? I mean, it has come a long way...'
And in the meantime De Stijl had entered our lives.'

Finally, something about green, my favourite colour. 'Green belongs to nature, not to architecture', was the lesson I heard from my nature-worshipping colleagues at '8 en Opbouw'. For this I teased them with a green slatted chair by Rietveld whose existence I assumed. I never underestimated Rietveld, and thought: he found some sense in red-blue-black with small yellow square ends – indeed, without the De Stijl theory, because that had not appeared yet. So when a green and white slatted chair from 1917 turned up at Christie's and was sold for £90,000, I wasn't at all surprised. And didn't Van Doesburg say very early on that 'nature is a thing, art is something different'? So you have natural green and art(ificial) green. Therefore, in the reconstruction of the Aubette in Otterlo six years ago, I was equally unsurprised to see the three Stijl colours complemented – finally completed. It briefly seemed as if the three missing colours were the actual Stijl colours. By which I only want to say that neither in Mondrian, nor in Van Doesburg, nor in De Stijl is anything missing that is considered essential. They knew what they were doing. And, don't forget, both Van Doesburg and I.K. Bonset and Aldo Camini have altogether had little time to do more, but the same thing happened to others. Think of Seurat, Juan Gris, Rimbaud and Apollinaire... Anyway, there we are. Solemnly, with my hat on, I shall now open for you this magnificent exhibition, *I.K. Bonset, painter and architect*.

Nelly van Doesburg disguised as I.K. Bonset, 1927
Photo Theo van Doesburg

Unearthing the silted-up alphabet of meaningful designing – on Jan Rietveld

Translation of the foreword to a monograph on Jan Rietveld *1, April 1990*

Apart from being the best poker player around Leidseplein, Jan Rietveld was probably also one of the most talented architects of his generation. That certainly means something, when taken together, but by no means everything, because he was clearly what one would call 'a great man'. He followed his own path in his own style and that was doubly eccentric. He moved through life jovial on the outside but well-armoured within – he whistled quietly in threatening situations. Jan was a loner but very much disliked being alone, so in a peculiar way he was still ordinary. He sought conviviality and found female companions with whom he spent a long time and to whom he left a lot – also in built form – when he was given the opportunity: that is why Catharina Uytenboogardt and Meike Wawo Roentoe are also included.

Photo Izak Salomons

He drew a circle around himself within which there was plenty of place for others, but only places of honour. Inside this circumference, with the right people around him and a glass in front of him, he was at home. Introverted but always coming up with a striking remark, he added bizarre verbal appendices to whatever he picked up. They were caricatural verbal hits to which, when the laughter left room for it, an absurd twist or reversal was added. One listener died laughing, another blushed, and yet another sighed, because he sometimes carried on for a long time. Jan Rietveld got on best with writers, painters and suchlike. Among them were his mates. He wasn't keen on architects – with a few exceptions. Between the bulwark of his own flat, the night school and a huge number of cafes, what remained he saw as the 'rest' of the city. The 'rest' of the country consisted of building plots (including former ones) to which he Rovered in dignity, and on the way of course the cafes.

Jan Rietveld was uncomfortable with nature, even though he often talked about the Sahara (where he travelled with us) and the Swedish tundra (with Catharina).

But now for that short step from person to work: Jan Rietveld built little else than detached houses because that was all he was asked to do. The reason for this lies primarily with those who did not ask him anything else. This is sad, and was certainly so for him. After all, in all the houses he built in his lifetime, only a small number of people actually live. Their remote setting has also meant they have remained unknown.

In addition to this is the fact that the Netherlands is not actually much of a villa country and therefore lacks tradition in that area. In any case, for Jan Rietveld the country house tradition did not stretch back any further than the Prins Hendriklaan[2] and what followed it. So it must have been part of him: an affinity with the unity and completeness of the single house, and that was his salvation – as well as his fate, because after all, anyone who can do the one very well cannot do the other!

He reconciled himself to the restriction he had not himself chosen by doing what he *was* asked as well as he did, because there is no one person who has built so many and so varied detached houses in the Netherlands as he did.

In the light of the identification of house with city, his mastery of the part implied he was able to deal with the whole – and he was *at home* in it. He realised that a house, although it is the smallest world-in-miniature of all buildings, is in terms of content the most complete. Neither the block of flats alongside Haarlemmerweg[3] – in my opinion the most relevant after Plaslaan, Bergpolder and Nirwana[4] – nor his superb development of my basic design for a high-rise block of flats at the Martinikerkhof in Groningen, ensued from briefs that he himself had received. In the first case he was appointed to make acceptable someone else's plan, which had been rejected several times. As a result of the Department of Urban Development's fear of heights, his 10-storey plan found no favour, so that one storey had to be removed. It was intended to be more slender than it became.

For the second, I smuggled him in at a later stage so that he would be able to build another large block of flats. After years of outrageous squabbling up there it came to nothing.

But even those schools, theatres, museums and stations that he never built because, for crying out loud, not a soul asked him to, are still the best!

In any case, this book presents a first impression of what was actually built. The idea was that it would be published around the end of the year, together with the exhibition about my work in Berlage's Exchange,[5] which I dedicated to Jan Rietveld.

Now it has happened and so a 'new' pinnacle is unexpectedly added to Dutch architecture. What is more, a second Rietveld has been added, different but just as Rietveldian as the first, so that the spectrum of 'Rietveldianism' – for which there are in fact no words, even though it clearly exists! – has expanded. That's why I have suggested in the course of this piece what it all comes down to. The two Rietvelds (and they alone) had a manifold of it in their short fingers.

It is a good thing to remember that the two Rietvelds were active just as long simultaneously but apart as they were in succession. And in between sometimes together too, although he said little or nothing about that – just like Bijvoet regarding Duiker, he did not claim the credit for anything, not even when he did not need to stretch the truth. For Jan Rietveld, De Stijl worked like a legend-at-first-hand, a warp whose weft he changed, as his father did later.

Jan Rietveld, block of flats 'Westeind' at Haarlemmerdijk, Amsterdam, 1956–1957 Photo Izak Salomons

Entrance hall Photo Vincent Ligtelijn

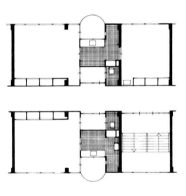

The flats are accessible by way of central interior streets

Jan Rietveld was a realist. So none of his many houses is ever abstract in the sense of being outside, or above everyday reality, but are, each and every one, tailor-made for others. He kept to the matter in hand, gauged people's wishes exactly – even the silent ones – and put down his spatial translation of this on sheets of squared paper or on the back or inside of a little cardboard box, which soon contained a tiny model that he took out of his pocket at the right psychological moment. From the source

607

Photo Jan Versnel

Photo Vincent Ligtelijn

Photo Vincent Ligtelijn

Jan Rietveld, Bots house,
Berkel en Rodenrijs, 1961

– close to the origin – brand new (and already a classic) – ready to live in. Which meant amazement – endearment – agreement on all sides!

Jan was generous. When designing he provided extras attuned to the person in question – intimate ingredients intended for those who discovered them. They play their part right through the austere form (and its seriousness). They are often little Rietveldian peculiarities; disarming surprises; direct hits. After all, Rietveld saw designing as a sort of poker in which he surreptitiously let the other person win (the one he was building for), but then in his own playing style.

I have of course often seen him at work and I learnt a lot from it. Precisely from him, because he managed better than anyone, with a couple of lines and short sentences, to unearth the silted-up alphabet of meaningful designing. This meant he was also unique as a design tutor. He gave only very small tasks, always went straight to the point, was lovable, quick, strict and always on the side of the student.

At the School of Applied Arts in Amsterdam (where we shared a group at the night school) he was at his ease – in his element, for several decades. Not so at Delft Polytechnic. There they didn't know what to do with Professor Jan. He was simply too good to be found good enough and was treated correspondingly. What is more, his time at Delft coincided with the reign of terror of the Projekt Raden and power-hungry crooked-thinkers – meaning the first Durand Prelude (the second followed later from the Rotterdamse Kunststichting). All this upset him and he left of his own accord for his own self-preservation, to devote himself with relief (and how!) to the Rietveld Academy.[6]

Lastly, regarding one particular aspect: when things are built orthogonally (everything at right-angles to each other), this is done in spite of the fact that when one enters a space, or in moving from space to space, the attention – the eye – is directed obliquely – or diagonally. People do not turn their eyes, head or body in jolts through 90 degrees like soldiers. Buildings should, reasonably speaking, react to this by making 'turns' that sufficiently lead the viewer's eyes in order not to cause any disorientation. This is what happens in and around the houses by Jan Rietveld, and it is partly for this reason that he started increasingly and explicitly designing both orthogonally and diagonally (doubly square). By turning walls, partitions and thus automatically also the openings in them by 45 degrees, the orientation of the building converges with the way the attention runs – as if it anticipated it. So the boundaries of the space turn, locally and in less abrupt succession than is possible in a purely orthogonal set-up, towards or away from the viewer. These are perceptions that cannot be photographed – Loos had already spoken about this (they can at best be filmed), but are of course easy to imagine by 'following' – walking through – the superb plans and sections in this book.

If I knew his address I would certainly send him a copy.

On Team 10

Interview given to Clelia Tuscano, Amsterdam 26 September 1991[1]

What are your memories and opinions about Team 10's last meetings in Spoleto, in Toulouse and perhaps in Portugal – a meeting mentioned in Team 10 Meetings[2] *which nobody seems to know anything about?*

Of course they don't, there was no Portugal meeting! The Smithsons wrote to me about it, and so did Guedes. I bet I can still find a letter in which I explain why I wasn't going, even though I was very keen on meeting Guedes again, who was always a very charming man, a very nice person to talk with. Alison had decided, in her authoritarian way, what the theme would be for a Portugal meeting. She had an idea about Portugal and the white architecture of North Africa, an astonishing theory about the white of the South European Mediterranean architecture being transplanted from Africa. Of course there are also white houses in North Africa, but North Africa is basically the colour of sand, so I knew the subject was simply absurd. In that period Alison was becoming more and more interested in culture and history, which originally she was not, both the Smithsons were not. The Smithsons thought in a very straight concept that history lies behind you, but later on, in their own way, they became very interested in history; they studied ancient Greek architecture, Greek towns, ancient Japan, and they suddenly became vastly interested in the possible relevance of what the past means to us, not so much formally but rather intellectually.

What did the others think about the link with the past?

In fact, to begin with, only to begin with, some of the people in Team 10 had the same kind of fear of the past that CIAM had: a feeling that the past was something that had to be overcome and left behind, that it was something from which you had to move away, towards the future. For years I tried to introduce the idea that we'd never get beyond CIAM in any way unless we found away of shaking hands with the past, unless we found a method to deal with the past. Otherwise it wouldn't work.

The trauma we had to get rid of is very similar, strangely enough, to a contemporary one: CIAM and Team 10 were almost completely disinterested in the avant-garde of the twentieth century; they were afraid both of the past and of the relevance of avant-garde art. Of course, people like Giancarlo had a different view, but he is an intellectual, cultivated man, and CIAM wasn't a collection of cultivated people talking about culture, so that was difficult; you could talk about culture with Giedion and with a few others who ventured outside the architect's narrow view that didn't go beyond buildings. That was the trauma of CIAM, and Team 10 followed that up exactly, concerning the vision of the past.

So Alison and Peter Smithson got interested in history.

Both of the Smithsons have capacity, a great intellectual personality; they come from the north of England, and in England the only cultural place was the centre of London, otherwise it was absolutely barbaric. I lived there for a while at the time – it's different now – there was no knowledge of Picasso or Mondrian or Breton… The whole avant-garde didn't exist, 'Corbu' was vaguely known. England hardly participated in the Modern Movement. British are knowledgeable now, they know everything, they have exhibitions of pop art, but they are not inside it.

Americans are different: the United States are like a melting pot where people come from all over the world. New York is an enormous lively place like Paris: the avant-garde wasn't French, but things always referred to Paris. Sometimes they shifted to New York, but never to London.

When you see an exhibition of American pop artists and you run into the absolute power of Warhol and Jasper Johns with his flags, you understand that the British are nothing like that! They look almost naive, it's embarrassing, there's nothing of the clarity of Roy Lichtenstein, or Warhol: just collage, you know, with a bit of war, a bit of anti-bomb, a bit of violence and a bit of surrealism, a bit of sadism and a bit of psychopathology. Everything forbidden in Victorian England is thrown in! The Smithsons belonged to the super British avant-garde in London – though not the real 'avant-garde' – with Nigel Henderson and a few others.[3] They were very eccentric. They were, perhaps, the first people to shake London awake a bit. They really shook up British architecture. England was still frightened of Corbu and frightened of all those mad continental architects who came to England, like Gropius. Peter used to wear a shirt with the Eiffel tower printed on it, or he dressed beautifully as a gentleman while wearing strange red socks, and Alison, she used to wear very provocative clothes, always. They always staged each appearance according to the strength of the meaning their entrance could have, and there's nothing wrong with that, I mean, it's theatre.

And they were always busy with the history of the heroic period, trying to dig into the people before them – Le Corbusier, Mies, Gropius – identifying with the heroic period and measuring everything by that standard. Their main quality lies in the fact that they were able to create history, to make history: they knew what they were going to do, and they knew it was important.

They also proposed themes for discussions, kept records of the meetings and worked out afterthoughts.

Aldo van Eyck interviewed by Clelia Tuscano at his office in Amsterdam Photos Clelia Tuscano

They still do, look at the *Team 10 Meetings* book. But in fact that book is not history. Alison says 'It is my memory' and things seem somehow turned around. To begin with, it starts by saying that all of the people quoted were sent the material and asked to comment, but I didn't even know the book existed until I received it. The basis of Team 10 were these liberal family meetings in which things were discussed in a highly confidential way, because there was nobody looking through the keyhole, so by publishing these tapes she's misusing the privacy of Team 10. It's especially painful for me because every sentence I said is manipulated, and every time I'm mentioned there's some remark: you see a photograph of Alison with a note which says: 'Alison Smithson, Dubrovnik, lunchtime retyping of a Team 10 document Van Eyck put down a lavatory, 1956', or 'Aldo van Eyck, who had at last decided to speak English, said...', but I don't remember having ever spoken anything else!

And what about the ideal city beautifully drawn by Blom that I brought to Royaumont, as described in *Team 10 Meetings*? It was open-ended in a way. The houses were streets and the shops were streets. It was a completely open-minded plan by an idealist who dreamed of a society that works better than ours. There was no reason why it shouldn't be symmetrical in all directions, like a snowflake. It was an ideal city, there was no wind or sea or forest. But the Smithsons and Woods discovered fascism in a snowflake, the lightest and the most beautiful material you can have.[4]

The Smithsons were not so keen on building. Other people would, for instance, need to organize in their head all facts, all emotions necessary to make a building: what they are going to do or not do, the things which you have to bring together, to coordinate and illustrate somehow, also in a mad way. It does not matter the way you gather your ideas as long as the building is not mad. But their concentration has been on the intellectual game, which can be very interesting. They created the rules of the game, very severe new rules; but they are conceptual people, and purely conceptual people have a difficulty: although continuously creating new concepts or judging other people's concepts or making mutations to their own, it's always a concept.

What did Team 10 mean for you then, if it wasn't about ideas?

Team 10 didn't mean everything to me in those days: it was an important element, but it wasn't the five corner stones of the pentagon, as it was for the Smithsons. They tied every fibre in their life to Team 10, and if you make something that important then you can't step outside, you discuss every suggestion done by somebody else. If I'd say together with Bakema: 'Let's have Stirling along in Royaumont!' then you had a terrible fight, or if you said 'Could we not only deal with this subject: it would be wonderful to discuss this' then you had WAR, and 'No, we won't come if you do that!' So we always had trouble with the Smithsons. They were fanatically dedicated, and they always wanted things their way. So, in retrospect, historically you could conclude that they were the strongest members. Well, in a sense they were. The others were too polite, they didn't want to scream or to talk all the time, so we did; we played a duet. And in the morning at breakfast, or in the evening when the official meetings were over, we'd start to play trios or quartets together again, doing a lot of extra discussing.

Team 10 stopped having meetings.

I don't think we should have another Team 10 meeting. If you don't have anything else to say together you don't have to have a meeting, you can also get together casually. For instance, I meet Giancarlo at least once or twice a year, and also Erskine and Herman Hertzberger at his school here in Amsterdam.[5] It's not exactly Team 10, but it is a kind of perpetuation; one talks about and discusses the same things. People run into each other and in that way of course something goes on. That was the best part of Team 10 actually; not the meetings, but the sort of casual in-between meetings: odd letters that went around, a kind of network of letters... Of course, as you say, we were individuals, not some kind of club or sect. Everybody has his own story, his own philosophy, nevertheless there was sufficient overlap, there were sufficient ideas, within all the divergences, that were common and comparable at the time, I suppose. That's the main subject, because what were we coming together for, if not to exchange thoughts about the things we were deeply concerned with?

Could you share with us what you re member of the people in Team 10?

In the beginning some people were very important and then they disappeared. Some of the founding members disappeared straight away, like Geir Grung or Rolf Gutmann. It's interesting to talk about Gutmann, because one of the most fundamental statements out of which the whole Team 10 concept grew was his. Actually, one of the first statements about the tree and the leaf came from Gutmann identifying the house with the city or the part with the whole, identifying the complexity of the plural within the singular, discovering the singularity of the plural.[6] This reciprocity is a concept which should have been at the basis of Team 10, and it was brought forward by Gutmann.

Also Károly Polónyi left, probably for political reasons. I don't know. I forget exactly when it was. But of course it's interesting to find out what Team 10 looked like to somebody coming from Hungary, from behind the iron curtain. It's interesting because although certainly many Hungarian people could read the Team to Primer, he could actually come and tell his point of view. Polónyi had a very high position: he was chief urbanist I think in Budapest and if you were at that level then you could get out of the country, while other people couldn't, so he participated very enthusiastically. As a kind of government official he always had the feeling that the others were building and he was chief town planner, so we were somehow in a different position. You can't exactly say Polónyi was a member, but he was nice, an intelligent man, and he contributed to Team 10 by his presence, because everybody who contributes to a good atmosphere contributes by the mere fact of his presence.

It would be very difficult to formulate what the specific contribution of each of us was. For example, what should I say about Antonio Coderch? Except that he was the most gifted architect of the lot. A great architect. He was very emotional, he didn't argue much, a solitary figure; he was severe, morally severe, but not dogmatic; he was a puritan and catholic. He was a genius architect. He wrote the article 'It isn't geniuses we need now',[7] but he really was a genius, a fantastic architect, an artist. He was a highly complicated person, a modernist in terms of architecture, a great lover of Miró and Lorca and a great friend of them too; on the other hand, he was from a sort of basic Catalan aristocrat family. In Team 10 he gave the impression of being against the people around him, but he probably always came. He didn't say much, but still he was a highly influential person in Team 10.

Once he gave an expo of his housing near the sea, and I took part in the discussion saying: 'Now you've got down to the fact that these are rich houses for rich people, so in the end you have to give a social judgement whether you build for the rich or for the poor.' And he answered: 'This may bean inspiration for the poor houses in future. The houses for the rich are important because they become a kind of example for everybody.' And in Holland it quickly turned out to be that way: if you build a large balcony on a house because you have the money to build it, then, if it's a good building, it becomes a standard for other ones. And that is, in a way, the job of the architect.

Another artist in his own way, although you can completely disagree with what he does, is Pancho Guedes. His buildings are the buildings of an artist. The whole man's behaviour shows an artist: what he paints, what he draws, everything; he does everything all the time; I don't think he ever goes to sleep, Pancho. He would say things like: 'My building is a smiling lion' and that is crazy. He stayed in South Africa and Mozambique, but he was also often in Europe. His buildings are not as good architecturally as the man: he himself is fantastic, he paints, makes sculptures, he does a lot of building himself or with the people. Pancho Guedes has a terrific personality, and I like him because the moment he came, Team 10 woke up. The strange thing is that we all liked him, he was, in a way, the exotic and flamboyant side of the Smithsons; They've got that logic too, they were a bit crazy and provocative, and that was the nice side of the Smithsons; they provoked all of London. We should give the Smithsons a big prize as the 'great enemies'. England is now missing a challenging person that tickles and irritates and makes you wonder if you are doing the right thing. The moral vehemence of both the Smithsons was very useful in sleepy Britain. So I think they deserve a prize for what they've done, and not done, and for their vigour and rudeness!

And what about Doshi?

Doshi came regularly.

Really? It seems he only came once, to the Urbino meeting.

That's very typical of Team 10! If you ask me whom I saw a lot of or whom I appreciated, it's a different story. Doshi is a very good friend of mine; I've been to his architecture school in Ahmedabad and lectured there. I appreciate Doshi enormously; he just sent me some of his beautiful drawings, very colourful. Since Doshi is an old friend of course my memory of Team 10 is of the few times Doshi was there; even if he only attended twice, I have the feeling he was always there, because Doshi is one of the great, very talented architects.

Another man who has real architectural talent is Giancarlo. And he was never afraid of architectural discussion. The architects that are not afraid of architectural discussion wish and hope that there will be discussion about the quality of a building, about the quality of details, but that wasn't always the subject of the discussions within Team 10: instead we often had to discuss urbanism and so on. Of course, you can't say that men like Coderch or Giancarlo are not interested in urbanism, but Team 10 – like CIAM – was in love with big subjects.

In the notes of the meeting in Spoleto, the discussion which follows Giancarlo's presentation of his housing in Terni is very good, but it's about general themes, like the shape of the valleys and hills, the Italian hill town and the 'deck' and the way you move in the buildings, which is very architectural in itself, but it doesn't consider the details of the way concrete is used for instance, or wood or glass.

That's partly due to the fact that Giancarlo's approach always somehow spans the whole scale, and includes territory, history. I remember there was a highly complicated discussion about the Urbino building, and on that occasion I wrote a long essay on Giancarlo, published in *Zodiac*.[8] In that essay I pointed out his sort of double loyalty. On the one hand there's the architecture of his Matera houses and Comasina, which then, in Otterlo, simply looked aggressive (though not so much to me): there were arches, there were oval windows, there's a sloping roof, there's brick: all the contraband forms and materials. But he argued that also in the sense of socialism: the materials were the kind of materials people understood, that were close to them, that were familiar. But on the other hand, as far as the urbanism was concerned, he placed the blocks in a parallel and perpendicular layout; so that the blocks, the actual buildings, followed what some people then called a regressive idiom: his urbanist dialectic was that of CIAM, that of the modern world. So he had this split between architectural idiom and urban theory, a theory which was still very straightforward CIAM. There was a discrepancy between him and us at that time: we tended to use – you might say misuse – Matera as a hill town model, as an example of a casbah, as a small city as a large house. To us Matera was a tightly knit, woven conglomeration of buildings in which a community lived with all the functions mixed. Of course that was something we were looking for after CIAM's technique of separating everything; we wanted this mesh instead. We didn't believe in the four functions – that story was far too simple. That was what we thought, but Giancarlo threw away Matera as a model for the casbah, because he saw it as a symbol of oppression and poverty. In that sense he was of a different mind than we were. We didn't think of a medieval city as an expression of a political system. We knew of course that there was a lot of oppression in feudal times, but it didn't mean anything political to us anymore. We were looking at Matera as an example of a closely knit phenomenon, while Giancarlo was looking at history and seeing poverty.

We just used that one word 'casbah' as an image, as a poetic image. We were referring to any kaleidoscopic society where all the functions are more or less mixed, and I always said the casbah was the final limit. We don't have to literally make a casbah, imitating a period of human history when things were mixed and closely knit, but we need to be a little more 'casbah-istic', by putting things together: and letting things penetrate into each other again. That is what we meant by casbah. In Matera you can say one man's roof is another man's front door, so 'my terrace is your entrance'. If you have to climb up a ladder across someone's terrace, you say 'hello!' and then go up into your house. What excited us wasn't the fact that it could be romantic to do things like this, but the fact that there has to be a kind of communal relationship between people, otherwise it would be impossible to live together. We were interested in other ideas of what community means.

We were looking not only at Matera, but at all kinds of examples in the world, where you can see what private means and what public means. The moment you know that societies all over the world are so different, then you don't have to copy them, but you know things can be different. It supports you.

To Giancarlo Matera was a symbol of oppression. But in Terni things are reversed. He gave up his Matera language and moved into a very, let's say modern idiom; damned, I may be all wrong, he is going to kill me!

In Terni he started building in a modern idiom, yet there he built a casbah; with streets-in-the-air and schools at the level of the streets with houses on top. Terni has a complicated section with children moving over the roofs to school, which is exactly what we were dreaming of in the beginning of Team 10. In between Matera and Terni – that's my story – in between was Urbino, his student college building. At the time, the Urbino building was the only building that reconciled different approaches. There Giancarlo was faithful to the idea of the Matera idiom, and at the same time translated modern architecture into something that was still in many ways very subtle. He used curves, which other architects in Team 10 would not think of. It's a high quality building, intellectually clever, with a certain harshness in the use of concrete, not so much in those tiny pavilions, but in the main central building. The whole building is typical. I mean, there you have a city like a building like a city. All my slogans are there, and also other things, such as the concept of landscape, somehow the building echoes Urbino itself. And it is synthetic, not eclectic. That building is both modern and imbued with the past, isn't it? You notice that Giancarlo knows the past, and he knows a lot about it; he lives today and he has his feet in the past. It's what we were looking for, and exactly what we were against CIAM for. They could not do that, though Aalto had that kind of feeling, but he never came to CIAM. That building is really a generation after CIAM, which is why I enjoyed the presence of Giancarlo. He brought in these elements straight from the beginning. He always provokes. He always claims that the difference between Borromini and Bernini was that one was provoking and one was complaisant. Both were great talents, but one used it to challenge society, which is also typical of Giancarlo, and the other had equal talent but he just went along with society. And it's clear that our kind of personality finds Borromini far more interesting.

You spoke about the link with the past, with the avant-garde, with history. What other themes do you remember that were relevant in Team 10 discussions?

There were of course other highly interesting men in Team 10, for their personality and intellect and passion; one of them was John Voelcker. He really thought about the great problems of urbanism. He was one of the first people, in Aix already, who talked about quantity, number and identity – and in such away that I thought 'hey, now I have a new scale; somebody is tuned rather differently, with a completely other approach...'

Do you think he was both a good architect and a good thinker?

I don't know. He wasn't the kind of person to organize himself to build. He did build several things, but not much. He was younger, a bit younger, and anyway with the kind of ideas he had it wasn't easy to hook on to British building practice. His ideas went very far, though they were not Utopian. John was a quintessential Team 10 thinker. He was urbanistically the best of the Team 10 thinkers, by far. He knew a lot, he was interesting, inclined and open. He was very keen on the theme of the multiplicity of housing, the aesthetics of number. How do you multiply a house a thousand or a million times, or whatever, and still make a habitat avoiding monotony? It is one of the problems of our time, how to tame a vast number. You can't avoid repetition, so you must develop a new aesthetic: the aesthetics of number.

Eventually he left London and started to practice in Sutton Valence, a farming village in Kent. With all his thoughts about cities, London was too much for him in many ways, so he fled to this small village where his theories of people and the penetration of one building into the other could be comprehensible, could become readable.

If you read *Team 10 Meetings* you'll be surprised that one of the leading figures, right through the book from the beginning to the end, is John Voelcker. It's interesting, because in the reprint of the Primer Alison marginalized him. She listed him as a 'guest'. But now she's turned around. In this book John's all over the place. So he's reintroduced. After having thrown him out the Smithsons bring him back again. And Woods, too. Woods and John are everywhere. It's exciting.

Did Voelcker's ideas have anything to do with Woods's ideas about urbanism?

No, I don't believe so, not as far as I can see; with Voelcker I'm just talking about the beginning of Team 10. The dogmatism of Woods turned out to be extreme, intolerable in the end. When Team 10 started out of CIAM, it started well. CIAM seemed to be the final chapter of a one-track mind of narrow rationalism, and Team 10 was the chance to be part of a greater world which could include modern architecture, modern painting, modern thought, modern science, modern formal aesthetics, modern thinking. We didn't want rigidity. Of course we all liked Shad, we couldn't help it. In the first place he was of Irish descent, with all the typical Irish American characteristics. He was irregular, mad or very sober, crying with seriousness about the world with uncontrolled emotionalism. At first we got on very well, but later, and I don't know if that coincided with his illness,[9] he started with his tree story.

You mean the stem-idea?

Yes, the stem. It was a sentimental social idea. It was all right as far as it went, but there was nothing between the lines. It was again a one-track logic. Then Woods wanted to get rid of architecture. He became an anti-architect, because the architect is a formalist, defines the form or defines the way in which people can live, and defining a form one way or another is also choosing for other people, imposing a way of life on other people. In a way of course that's true, but in his thought it became a basic idea. He started being against any material, be it wood or marble, and he started the flexibility story, the need of adapting, but to an extreme degree. Everybody had to discuss with him how the building would adapt to change in time and for different people, and what you should do if your client is anonymous or if you simply have to choose for other people you do not know.

Anyway, there were other interesting people, such as Stefan Wewerka, dadaist and surrealist. He's famous for his strange chairs on one leg. Wewerka made very provocative projects, as mad as a hatter. He was really against architecture. At Royaumont, or in Bagnols, he showed a project that was a 'cloud' he was going to build: absolutely no edge, no walls, no material. It was against all architectural material, against architects, against imposition. Wewerka was a kind of happening, but he was a healthy addition to Team 10.

And Candilis, a charming and highly complex fellow, 'causeur' and story teller. He knows twenty thousands stories, Jewish, Armenian, Turkish, Russian; he comes from all these countries and he has a bit of all of them in him. He is really a Middle Eastern man, saturated with Persian, Iraqi, Mohammedan, Turkish, Greek, Hellenistic culture. He is very Hellenistic in the sense that he is both Greek and oriental. Giancarlo says that Candilis is his only Hellenistic friend.

What about Bakema? He seems to have been a very important nucleus of Team 10, with a very strong personality.

He was. He was the Team 10 post box. Bakema had an unbounded energy and perhaps an unbounded belief in himself. But he wasn't autocratic, he just had this energy. If somebody asked him to talk an hour he talked ten hours. He just had no limits – part of it was generosity and part of it was not quite knowing where to stop. For instance at the meeting in Bagnols, in the beautiful town hall with stone walls and beautiful plaster walls on which we were going to put up our plans and our work, but Bakema had already literally covered every single wall. Downstairs, upstairs and everywhere! Everybody liked him as a person, but he just had no sense of measure at all, and he had that sort of slight... I'm looking for a friendlier word than megalomania, a nicer word. But he somehow gave this feeling.

In other interviews he comes forward as strong and generous, loyal and pleasant; everybody spoke very well of Bakema as a 'steam engine', very powerful and generous. What was he like as an architect?

He had a huge office, and often architects with big offices are managers. Bakema was a terrific manager, but he was also an extremely gifted architect. He had the talent to be an architect. He used to go from one table to the other when the other people in the office had all gone home, and quickly make sketches and notes for about twenty projects. He was an operator, and most operators can't design, but he could, and this was the psychological reason which made him want this big office. Not for the money. No! He was very generous. If somebody needed money, if I needed money when I was younger and I was invited to one of those first meetings – was it in Paris or La Sarraz? – I was just told 'that's O.K.' and he paid for the ticket. He was always like that.

His buildings are rigid, but in his time they weren't. He risked doing things that nobody else risked doing. But he didn't want to be a leader, an intellectual leader. He left that to the Smithsons. About them he felt a combination of great appreciation and sometimes criticism. The appreciation was returned by the Smithsons, but they could make fun of Jaap's plain, ethical, straight-forward architectural thinking: Jaap couldn't think complexly, and to a certain degree I'd agree.

Bakema was a man far more powerful as an individual, for his personality. He was very consistent. You couldn't push him, you couldn't move him off his track. Also with students, he'd work with them in summer schools in Salzburg, in Hamburg, in St. Louis in America, and he'd manage in three months to do a huge project with the students, have a whole book as a result and there was always somebody who immediately started printing it. He was a dynamo, a huge dynamo. One thing he never did was to make enemies. Bakema was reconciling, he would always say: 'Yes, but that is their side of it.' It's true what Peter Smithson said in the memorial speech he gave at the funeral: Smithson in the end said very charmingly 'and beyond and above all he was faithful to his friends'.

What do you think is the best contribution of Team 10?

Usually when people come together they're all personalities, they all want too much, they're all egoists, individualists, but the nice thing in Team 10 was that there was very little of that. There was a kind of brotherly friendship. We did criticize each other, but there was very little personal jealousy. Besides that, I remember they were all people who really appreciated very good buildings. I think the good side of Team 10 was that we didn't want to become dogmatic: if you're going to be more dogmatic than Gropius and Mies, then you're going to loose all of the richness that Giancarlo put into his Urbino building. We were interested in the richer, not the more talented architects. The kind of development we wanted was just a richer functionalism. We were functionalist architects, then: we were for functionalism, for a more inclusive functionalism, which could include the past and learn from the thousands of years of experience people had in building.

Team 10 meeting in Aldo and Hannie van Eyck's garden at Loenen aan de Vecht, 7 April 1974 Photo Peter Smithson

                Jaap Bakema
       Adam Voelcker   Smithson junior
               Manfred Schiedhelm
Giancarlo de Carlo   Val Woods
Reima Pietilä   Georges Candilis
Alison Smithson   Mrs. Richards   Jaap Hillenius
Mme Condilis   Hannie van Eyck   Mies Hillenius
Erik Bakema   Oswald Mathias Ungers
  Frans Hooykaas   Sia Bakema
    Brian Richards   Aldo van Eyck
                  Brita Bakema
       Herman Herzberger

Lucio Fontana apropos Joost van Roojen

Unpublished text, dated 22 April 1993 and written on the occasion of Van Roojen's 1993 exhibition at the Municipal Museum of The Hague.

Since I wrote 'the Mirror Master' in 1967, 25 years have passed. In the meantime, after the 1969 retrospective in the Eindhoven Van Abbe Museum, silence has fallen around the pictorial activities of Joost van Roojen, although he has been continuously busy since then, making both aquarelles and murals. He collaborated with Bakema in Delft, with myself on the playground at the Amsterdam Zeedijk, and recently with Hertzberger, always with exceptional results.

What I experience now when seeing his work of the past 10 years in the Municipal museum of the Hague confirms what I have written at the time. What Joost van Roojen made happen on paper, happens again, still always differently. His world only changes from within – at the inside. He discloses internal seasons and internal continents, both variously related and different. They are mainly other seasons and continents than those which are familiar to us but he brings them forward so that they simply become part of the latter. If that isn't a major contribution, then I think there are no other ones either.

As Heraclites said, one can never step twice into the same river. What is really new is also constant, because it has released itself from time – or coincides with it, which amounts to the same. In the work of Joost van Roojen space has escaped the palpable dimensionality of what is brought about on the white plane. Such a thing is actually a miracle medicine.

In the mid sixties I had a few illuminating discussions with Lucio Fontana, in Joost van Roojen's studio as well as at home. I mention this here, because both, Fontana and Joost van Roojen, activate flat virgin surface – its stubborn two dimensionality – by imparting a wonderful sense of space to where there was none before. On both occasions Fontana referred to Joost van Roojen with admiration. When the latter traces a line (or a double line N.B.!) on a white sheet of paper, enclosing forms or not, the untouched surface in between comes alive; it is rendered ambiguous;

Aldo van Eyck, curved screen in Van Roojen exhibition, 1969 Photo's Aldo van Eyck and Joost van Roojen

Aldo van Eyck, Van Roojen exhibition design in the Eindhoven Van Abbe Museum, 1969 Photos Aldo van Eyck

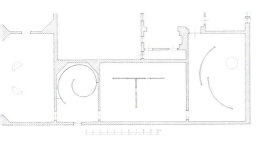

Lucio Fontana, Concetto spaziale 'Attese', 1959 Photo Carlo Cisventi

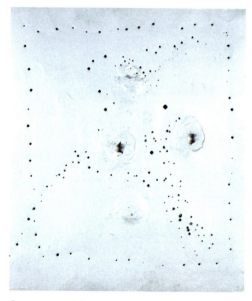

Fontana's hand cutting the surface

Concetto spaziale, 1950

Fontana breaching the surface with hammer and chisel

Joost van Roojen

ambiguous as to what is passive and what is active: the lines, the coloured surfaces or what lies between them untouched. An Enigma is born. Space is drawn out of the surface or brought into it – both at the same time. There is no alternation – and no illusory effect, i.e. nothing is either in front or behind anything else. The surface is rendered gratifyingly transparent. Now when Fontana struck his surfaces, piercing them or slicing into them, their virgin two dimensionality is lifted into... space. Not because of the actual three dimensionality - plasticity – which ensues through the slits or holes in the first place, but, as with Joost van Roojen's lines and transparent coloured surfaces, the untouched ones in between are activated with the same precision and become spatial. That Lucio Fontana and Joost van Roojen should appreciate each others work did not surprise me at all. But what did was not so much that Fontana should have discovered 'another' *concetto spaziale* alongside his own in Joost van Roojen's work, but that he recognized in the latter somebody who – in his own words – had reintroduced landscape into the realm of painting – brought it back in an entirely new dimension. In this way paintings can again become landscapes – are in fact landscapes, sine qua non, as soon as they impart a sense of space within a flat surface. Thus concepts of space coincide with those about landscape – real ones – new ones, but not imaginary. Joost van Roojen, like Fontana (like Mondrian for that matter) bring about space the moment they touch a virgin surface. Therein lies the magic of their art. Both orchestrate varying degrees of density, so that their surfaces breathe – come alive: they are rendered transparent – indefinite by means of very precise definition.

If the art world had responded to Joost van Roojen's achievement the way Lucio Fontana did, it would have been the richer for it. It is what the semi-blind world of art does not 'see' which constitutes the true reality of art at any given time as much as what it does happen to see. There is art and 'other' art.

On Charles Rennie Mackintosh

Interview by Richard Murphy, published in C.R. Mackintosh, the Architects' Architect, *Bellow, London, 1993.*

We decided to go north that winter, my wife and I. It was December 1959. I had been working on the orphanage without a break for too long, so we headed for Scotland with the Callanish standing stones as our ultimate destination. The start from Edinburgh's Waverley Station was as good as could be: asking for tickets to Kyle of Lochalsh, the lady in the ticket office exclaimed, 'Dearies, you'll have the islands all to yourselves'– pure poetry, that! On Skye we kept running to avoid cloud breaks between shafts of sunshine for a fortnight, so when finally we got to Glasgow on the way back – nicely tanned – we were well disposed to take in the work of an architect who represents all this and more, and who, reaching for extremes, turned them into exquisite buildings: Mackintosh of course – CRM. I remember climbing that steep slope and, turning into Renfrew Street, being 'struck' by what I saw. Like Michelangelo he accomplished a reconciliation of emotional extremes in architectural terms, thus mitigating inner stress by bringing together formal qualities and aspects deemed incompatible. Struck also by the way CRM, on the threshold of the modern movement, yet still within the nineteenth century, had, taking the past with him into the present without doing it again ... pointed to the future. Having taken the building in on three sides we passed through what Leon K. calls 'the miserly meanness of the main entrance'. And there was Mr Jefferson Barnes – later the school's director as well as a terrifically nice man, who responded enthusiastically to our enthusiasm. He was one, the very first, to recognize the value of the school (beyond the question of its particular formal style as a period piece) for what it actually is: a superbly well-adjusted environment for art students.

Photo T. and R. Annan

CRM reconciled incompatibles by sidestepping all the artificially construed formal barriers and academic categories which still bedevil the architectural scene – blocking the minds of too many architects. He shifted across the familiar panorama of architecture like a true magician, taking with him what he wanted – little – and inventing the rest. An arch non-academician and non-eclectic both. On this rests his modernity – full and early. But it is also why people like Leon K. and Stanley T., cannot get on with him. Their silly pollutions of the school's incomparable front elevation demonstrated as much.

You were quite damning at the symposium on how art historians have done Mackintosh great injustice.

Indeed I was. Except for the monograph on the Glasgow School of Art (GSA), all the major works on CRM present a biased judgement founded on the erroneous notion that contrary qualities are also incompatible – worlds apart – and to be kept that way. A senseless judgement due to senseless choices – once again it's *or* instead of *and*. In the case of CRM, whose mind and work eludes simplistic categorization and generalization, what is straight, undecorated, geometric and rational has strength, is sound, and is consequently masculine, while what is curved, decorated, organic and emotionally founded is soft and weak and therefore feminine; just think of it! So these authors simply split CRM down the middle. Theirs is a dead-end dialectic – like splitting the alphabet into a set of vowels and a set of consonants in order not to use both within a single word – which would be indeed worse than Welsh, which sounds marvellous! Fixing a gender onto aspects and qualities regarded as contrary is bad enough, but far worse if there is an unwarranted preference for a single direction.

But what if, on top of all this, it is to be taken literally and a real sinner is found, for that is how it is, believe it or not. Had CRM followed his own sound, strong and masculine inclinations and resisted the lure of his wife's decorative feminine ways, his stature as precursor, heralding the modern movement, would, they contend, have been greater than it was. How I resent this mental witch-hunt. It is all the more shameful because, lurking behind juxtapositions like straight, curved, strong, weak, and masculine, feminine, there is still the nasty and predictable extension: right – wrong. Without Margaret, CRM would have been a great architect – more purely modern – is their point.

But the truth is quite different: CRM extended the scope of architecture's formal language before it was reduced by the 'moderns' in their search for 'purity'. That he was able to reach beyond the modern movement is due to the very same qualities which, the various authors went out of their way to explain, kept him from becoming one of them – hence 'historically' more important. The irony of it is that his relevance now is all the more certain because of these qualities, not in spite of them.

Take the huge studio windows and the enigmatic brackets slanting inwards towards them. They do not reveal what they'll be like inside against the sky: terrific transmitters of light into studios. More beautiful 'big' windows that are still windows I have never come across. Nor, incidentally, a more appropriately proportioned main entrance through which to slip in and out of an art school than the one located between their windows, the one Leon K. cannot stand.

Did you always know about CRM?

Quite early anyway, but I wasn't 'struck' until that winter. In the CIAM world, remember, people like CRM were forbidden fruit. Team 10 later turned the same blind eye towards whatever was not flat, plain and pure. 'How are you, Aldo, and how's Mackin*slosh*?', a postcard from the Smithsons enquired. Reactions were similar if I mentioned, say, Horta or Gaudí, Palladio, Romano or Ledoux. Not to mention reference to archaic or tribal architecture.

Over the last twenty-five years appreciations of Mackintosh have advanced from abject neglect to his being embraced as a stylist. While his architecture and spatial contributions still await discovery, 'Mockintosh' decoration has become designer kitsch round town.

There you are: Mockintosh's or Mackinslosh's decoration – but Mackintosh didn't 'decorate' anything. What he did was 'elaborate'– not decorate, and for the most part locally. These extremely effective elaborations cannot be lifted from where they occur. They are essential and inevitable. Nor is there more of it than is required to 'complete' the story, though without revealing every secret. High-level restraint, I call that. Each elaboration is given its own place, whether square or rose.

Can you expand a little on your perception of Mackintosh's handling of space?

CRM was a true organizer of interior spaces. He composed them in sequence, articulating the latter so as to bring about the right continuity – not too much, nor too little. As you move through the building there is, everywhere, just the right sense of proximity and distance and everything from the smallest to the largest item is just the right size. Spellbound is the word; that's what I was when I went up the school's great central staircase for the first time. Its generous stride and bracing openness take you up with such ease that you want to go down again in order to go up once more. Actually, the same goes for Leon K.'s 'miserly cottage door' through which I had just passed. It makes you want to enter and re-enter again and again, which is as it should be, surely.

You highlighted a telling detail from a Mackintosh tea room in your GSA installation.

You mean those little mirrors set in plain glass right across the tea room facade along Sauchiehall Street. Yes, indeed, I have expanded on that particular 'elaboration' no end of times over the years, always using the photograph I took on that first occasion. So I did once again for my little installation for the GSA exhibition.

'More beautiful "big" windows that are still windows I have yet to come across.'
Photo Wilson Steel

Entrance Photo T. and R. Annan

North and West facades Photo Bryan and Shear

The gallery Photo J.W. Goodchild

The main staircase Photo Bryan and Shear

Van Eyck's installation *in situ*

Thanks to these mirrors what is there on either side is all at once there side by side: I mean – exterior and interior – street and room (city and building) – large and small – all simultaneously present as they are held within the surface of that window. As for the little 'Tea Room' window I installed in the GSA, it opened on to another – different – 'street' in the school's interior. It brings to mind what was lost when the fire doors appeared later on every floor.

CRM, you see, knew what art is all about, what the prerogatives are; thus also what the pulse of an art school should be. So what he came up with next to so much else, was certainly no corridors, but streets with *interior urbanity* along which the school's various localities are gathered and all and sundry occurs.

The generosity and warmth of this great unifying device (with miraculous staircases playing their part) is unique and surely CRM's most revolutionary and enduring single gesture (another opportunity never came his way). But also his most intrinsically 'modern' one in that the stigma of authority is absent and nothing hierarchical is sensed. A core for people 'multilateral' in spirit.

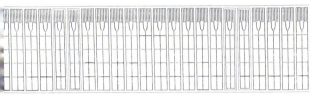

Van Eyck's drawing of the first floor window of Willow Tea Room

Proposal:
- Retrieve what was lost, so the 'streets' will be there again.
- Replace the fire doors!
- Do so step by step – floor by floor, the inner ones first. Thus, at each stage – as the streets open up – there will be every reason for celebration.
- And remember: he was a master in the use of 'iron', glass and transparency. So there's your cue. As for the new doors: they must remain open unless emergency requires them closed.

Willow Tea Room facade Photo Vincent Ligtelijn 1983

GSA is a gentle building if ever there was one – its strength lies in its generosity. There is also no school more spirited. In fact, with architecture way down in the dumps, *there is no better 'school' for us all*. Nor was there ever a better architect – that's saying an awful lot, but it's all right: he shares that tribute with others, though not that many.

How on earth did he do it? Or, what brought about a building which has no equal when it comes to the way each window and each door – each bit of wood, stone, iron or glass – each tile (and every rosebud) – every place and every dimension whomever it accommodates must be the better for it – and gratefully bewildered.

Leon Krier was critical of the school's small entrance, which signalled for him that it was a private not a public building.

Critical is not the right word. He simply demonstrated physical distaste of the building, which is telling us something about Leon K.'s private self but nothing about the building. However, his black ill-humoured intervention pointed to the current semi-professional malady I call RPP (Rats, Posts and other Pests). And so did Stanley T., author of that other exterior pollution which was just as black and silly as Leon K.'s.

The school happened to be the subject of renewed assessment – hence also scrutiny, so its exterior disfigurement was, on that score alone, a gross impropriety. Only temporary, it was argued, but the mental scar is not.

Stanley T. calls what he did 'only plastic surgery', which turned out to be just another self-portrait nobody wants. The GSA is wasted on despoilers of this sort. I questioned whether I should contribute at all, in that particular building, with them around, you remember. Sometimes too divergent levels should be kept apart.

Do you think Mackintosh is inescapably Scottish?

I was waiting for that! The Dutch, you know, never stop highlighting Mondrian's Dutchness (he himself soon gave up spelling his name the Dutch way, with a double a). The truth is that Holland looks more like Mondrian than Mondrian like Holland. The same goes for CRM's Scottishness.

Although, I suppose, as an outsider, I do associate him with Scotland, but not with a Celtic emphasis. None the less, he is a 'twilight' architect if ever there was one. Twilight standing for day and night; the way an eclipse stands for sun and moon and what they in turn stand for. Mackintosh was close to all that, so he took it in his stride – the entire panorama – the full panaroma.

Has Mackintosh informed your own work?

Something would be amiss if he hadn't. Fabulous architecture, where and whenever, is mental nourishment – but that goes for fabulous art in general. I was aware of CRM's presence during the final stage of the orphanage; it was approaching completion at the time. From the start, I wanted a non-hierarchical configuration of spaces strung along an articulated interior street. The GSA was therefore an encouraging confirmation of what I had done. What if I'd seen the GSA a few years earlier? Well, that would have done no harm! Since CRM's personal touch is intoxicating, I tried to keep clear of it (bar a few lamps!). In fact, I always resist reacting directly in architectural terms to strong formal impact; though of course, not the meaning or message it may convey.

Why do you think Mackintosh ran out of commissions?

He was simply too good at it – and to fall in line or go along with one like him is not everybody's ability or choice. Your question stings a bit. Since the Scots and Dutch are not quite the same, there must have been another reason why I, incidentally, was not asked to build more than I have. Not a single public building ever came my way – let alone on a site it could easily have spoilt – until recently, when a small art centre did on just such a site!

Is there anything more you would like to add?

Architects are there to render service. To do otherwise consciously is nothing less than treason – intellectual cowardice. I refer to the cynicism with which this era's great avant-garde in art and science is currently being ridiculed by the RPP. And thus also CRM, who anticipated so much more than the architects of the modern movement's second generation were prepared to absorb. CRM took the lonesome road in the opposite direction to that of today's regressive spoilsports. He is still far ahead. Finally: what he did could not have been done without lots of encouragement and intelligent criticism; not if the buildings were to be good ones, and they were very, very good.

So here's to Margaret, who stood by her husband so long and so well, playing her part in what is surely a miraculous achievement.

On Josep M. Jujol

Preface to a monograph on Josep M. Jujol published in 1996[1]

With architecture and meaning drifting apart – believe it or not – this little volume comes as a message from another more enlightened world. It was to have appeared in 1979 for the hundredth anniversary of Jujol's birth, but no publisher could be found willing to take the risk – not even in Barcelona. The authors had everything ready: texts, plans, diagrams, their own photographs and layout. Since this first pioneering effort floundered several attractive books on Jujol have become available. What makes the present one, which is a modest version of the one the authors originally intended, so timely and gratifying, is what the authors bring to bear about their singularly endowed subject and, indirectly, why his work is so relevant today.

In fact the opening paragraphs put the reader on the right track straight away: in Jujol's world a detail's scope reaches beyond its actual size! Expanding on this pivotal statement the authors tell us that Jujol the architect made spaces in accordance with their use, whilst Jujol the painter bestowed upon them unexpected moods. His decorations, we read, impart an ambiguous dimension, thus escaping from their usual isolation. In other words, Jujol's decorations are not merely something added which could just as well, or better, be subtracted, but a vital spatial ingredient. Such decorations are in fact *elaborations* which strengthen the physical place-quality of the spaces made: refining their appreciated human context. Jujol thus literally prepared his spaces for human use – still, after all, the architects primary job. How painfully different, this, when contrasted with the current sick wish to minimise the value of architectural detail and belittle attention for place-quality on the grounds that this detracts – from the 'big' central concept. *Bigness*, the latest magic word, is even expected to render architecture no longer necessary – obsolete. The obvious truth, of course, points to the exact opposite and is one which Jujol in particular substantiated so well: that only through architecture can oversize be successfully tamed – humanised. Architects are obliged to subdue *Bigness* (whatever it means) – gigantism and oversize. That too is their specific job.

Did Jujol drop those plates in order to put them together again over the curved surfaces of the world's most beautiful public seat? With this question the authors, at any rate, introduce the notion of a more inclusive –'surrealist' they call it – rationale; one which Jujol drew upon continually in one way or another. The solutions he

Josep M. Jujol, ceramic works at Gaudí's Park Güell, Barcelona, 1911–1913

Photos Vincent Ligtelijn

Josep M. Jujol, wrought iron balustrades in the facade of Gaudí's Casa Mila, Barcelona, 1907–1910

came up with are as startling as they are ingenious; the result of what I like to call 'hendecagonic' thinking [2]– the unexpected efficacy of the unusual.

Little did we know that it was Jujol who had contributed such astonishing elaborations to some of Gaudí's masterpieces. The authors make it quite clear that Jujol was no minor Gaudí, but a small giant next to a large one – an appropriate paradox about relative size!

635

Josep M. Jujol, wall lamp from the Mañach factory, 1916–1918

Josep M. Jujol, Torre de la Creu, San Joan Despi, 1913–1916

Josep M. Jujol, Casa Planells, Barcelona, 1923
Photo Vincent Ligtelijn

A Superlative Gift – on Lina Bo Bardi

Article on the Brazilian architect Lina Bo Bardi (1919–1992), published in 1997[1]

Whether you approach it from below or along Paulista[2] – see it from afar, like a nucleus standing above the tunnel, in that enormous space or see it as you pass close by, opening onto that same space from above, the MASP[3] is simply not just another fine building but already a phenomenon.

On that extreme gradient and with so much metropolitan vehemence milling round it, along it and underneath it, what Lina Bo Bardi built there is quite beyond belief until you see it with your own eyes. What seems impossible actually acquires tangible – *concrete* – shape. An amazing feat, for the building is indeed both there and not there, *giving back to the city as much space as it took from it*. An impossible site if ever there was one – all the more so because it was destined to remain open – not built upon. The gesture is a breathtaking one, and royal too, for not only did she keep the city open at that spectacular point, she also constructed an enormous space for people. *Her people*, for that is how she saw them.

Photo Lew Parella

But this is not all, there is still more to it since her generosity and audacity were all inclusive. Responding to the vast space below, literally spanning it and almost doubling it, there is that great interior accommodating a miraculous sea of paintings – a *kaleidoscopic* spectacle exemplifying each individual item and at the same time transcending the painter's name, culture, period or style.

It is on this final interior gesture that I should like to dwell, since it is not always readily understood and hence, unfortunately, vulnerable. That not everybody sympathizes equally with the way the paintings were originally presented is, however, not surprising. The presentation, being unique, is consequently also abnormal. And what is abnormal – in this case by default, due to its uniqueness – is also vulnerable in the sense that it risks being changed or dismantled altogether, which would be an unspeakable loss. The problem is at any rate now acute.

If seen, however, for what it is – a final gesture completing the building's other superlative feature, of which I have already spoken – it should no longer be so difficult to come to terms with what may seem excessive – even exorbitant – because it stands alone. The point is that these two outstanding gestures – the exterior one and the interior one – are interdependent, belong together, tuned as they are to the

Lina Bo Bardi, Museo de Arte de São Paulo ('MASP'),
São Paulo, Brazil, 1957–1968

The pinacoteca on the upper floor

same mental key: Lina Bo Bardi's *uncompromising – simultaneous – solidarity with people, art and architecture.*

In a sense – wrong sense – paintings on walls tend to be seen as windows onto another world, but this denies the tactile reality of their painted surface i.e. the physical existence of something actually made – with paint and brush, stroke after stroke – *in space.*

A painting – each painting – constitutes its own painted reality no matter what it depicts. That reality will come across best if the painting is returned to where it was painted, which is also where the painter was when he painted it. The truth being that its essential two-dimensionality *cannot breathe fully when fixed – locked – to a wall.*

Yes, paintings everywhere seem to belong to the walls onto which they are indeed *fixed* – as if they were born there. A ubiquitous dilemma for sure. We are no longer aware of the fact that the imposed union is a false one; not in accordance with what paintings really are. The dilemma is indeed so general that the impact of the MASP solution comes as a shock on first encounter, contrary as it is to what one has wrongly become accustomed to. Even after becoming familiar with it and having assimilated the very substantial advantages, the impact is still overwhelming: inevitably with so many great paintings, evocatively presented in a single space. Of course the uniqueness of the MASP presentation renders it all the more *extra*-ordinary.

Since cubism we began to look in a different way; to see things spatially, hence also paintings – and sculpture – no matter from what period. Lina Bo Bardi, imbued as she was with day-to-day reality, history and the spirit of the twentieth-century avant-garde, knew exactly what she was doing. With penetrating insight she cleared the age-old painting-versus-wall conflict opening an unfortunate dilemma in her own wonderful way.

It is difficult and painful to visualize all the countless paintings on countless walls in countless rooms, halls and museums waiting to move back into space where they can again vibrate, breathe as it were. The way they did in the MASP, where what was until recently, *the world's most beautifully presented collection of paintings and sculpture will, hopefully, be reinstalled without compromise.* Any other solution would mean partitions with several paintings on each facing each other from all sides across voids – and people once again shifting sideways from painting to painting. Terrible thought.

Painted as they were during a relatively short time span – about 500 years – and in a small part of the world – Europe – the paintings brought together in the MASP appeared, due to the way they were presented, to be gratifyingly affiliated, transcending period, culture and individual genius. It is as if they all belonged to a single complex family – one that is remarkably coherent and diverse. To sense the homogeneity of what is thus presented in the MASP is very moving.

And so, with the walls on which the paintings were previously doomed to hang, gone – hence also the flat surface, arbitrary texture and colour immediately behind and around them also gone – we are left with paintings in space where they were originally painted – *on an easel.* The whole lot together – here and now – and all at

The public square covered by the MASP building

The MASP seen from the São Paulo centre

Pinacoteca

once *contemporaneous*. You are made aware of the fact that the appreciation of art, like its 'history', is again *allowed to move* on, expand, through spontaneous confrontation and unexpected juxtaposition, for that is what the intended *simultaneity* of the presentation brings about: *unity embracing a diversity* far beyond established categories. But it also reflects the vigour and enthusiasm with which the paintings were acquired – brought together from afar.

You are contemplating a particular painting. Your eyes are focussed on its *painted surface*. Momentarily they may focus on another painting nearby and then back. If the paintings are not contemporaneous, it will be as if time is compressed. But if their nature and qualities appear in dire contrast, they may even merge in the mind! No amount of specific factual knowledge will deter the truly *kaleidoscopic* experience as you make your way from painting to painting up, down and across the space from end to end. The paintings – all of them – must again be allowed to face one way, whilst their history – who painted them, when, where and whatever else is worth knowing – looks the other way. Another great idea, this, because there is no interference, either visual or mental, if none is desired. The paintings are left to speak for themselves, unlabelled, one by one or together, no longer burdened by established evaluation and academic categorisation.

Looking, say, at the Matisse or Gauguin's Fisherman, your eye may well fall on Mantegna's St. Jerome, or even further back on a Lautrec, Rembrandt's self-portrait or even Léger's Dish of Pears.

Going for a walk among the paintings in the MASP is certainly mind invigorating. Keeps your appreciation moving, and hopefully, having done away with preconceptions, your judgement also.

Just call to mind Renoir's Bather. It was, of course painted with the girl, the painter and his easel, standing all three in space, and so was his Victorious Venus or Degas's dancers when they were modelled in clay before being cast in bronze. The difference between painting and sculpture is considerable, but not on every level, one notices at the MASP.

Just imagine Matisse, his canvas on a wall, painting with his studio *behind his back* – and now look at the painting – unthinkable! Matisse was not showing you a plaster torso on a table through a window in a wall. MASP has a 'real' Matisse for you! And many more paintings that have become more real due to Lina's unique presentation. And then Cézanne, imagine him out in the open, immersed in what was around him, tackling that very reality with paint and brush on canvas. He too was not making yet another pseudo-window in a wall, opening onto what was never there.

As to Bosch's Temptation of Saint Anthony: standing in front of it, as I was all of a sudden, was an amazing sensation. The phantasmagoria – hell approaching – with every detail sharply delineated – is not somewhere else beyond the surface, but there *on it* – oh so real. Had there been a Mondrian in MASP as one of the family, it would have looked marvellous anywhere.

I would like to conclude by diverting the reader's attention for an instant to another masterpiece of architecture elsewhere in this city, which, like the MASP, combines a similar range of superlatives: Pompéia,[4] and conclude by paying a personal tribute to the lady who actually managed to bring it off – supreme architecture – more than once in her lifetime. I had the extreme pleasure of spending an afternoon with Lina Bo Bardi 25 years ago, having that morning just undergone the shock of experiencing the museum for the first time and witnessing all those paintings *populating* that enormous hovering space the way she had thought best (from end to end and right across) for the first and *only* time. For, alas, when I was there again last year, it was already no longer as it had been. And this year – *now* – *it has all gone*. A terrible sight. Let us hope temporary. I shall only come back a fourth time, if everything is restored in Lina's original grand manner, including the lovely falling water round the lower structure and a solution more in keeping for the stairway, which once scooped me up from the street straight into the interior's amplitude. *Let the MASP remain a marvellous exception to the wrong rules and practice.*

15
Retro and Prospect

Introduction to chapter 15

Aldo van Eyck circa 1995 Photo Peter Zonneveld

The work of Aldo van Eyck was assigned a central place at the 1997 Kassel Documenta, which was conceived on the basis of the theme 'Politics – Poetics'. The cluster of curved panels displaying his ideas and projects occupied the rotunda of the Fredericianum. Guest curator Catherine David had invited him on account of his critical position towards the prevailing rationalist models and his interest in the heritage of non-Western cultures. She had asked him to reveal his views by means of his projects – the playgrounds, the Sonsbeek pavilion, the housing project for Lima and the Hubertus house – and to relate them to his anthropological interests.

In the text he included (and which he slightly reedited one year later for an exhibition of his own work in the Rotterdam NAi) Van Eyck again, and for the last time, drew attention to the themes that continued to preoccupy him: the problem of number and the negation of this problem by the 'posts', the radiant message of the Great Gang and the aesthetic heritage of archaic cultures which, he believed, were to provide the necessary inspiration for the development of the configurative discipline.

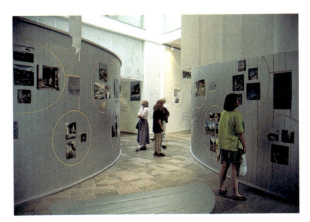

Van Eyck's contribution to the 1997 Kassel Documenta
Photos Vincent Ligtelijn

The radiant and the grim

Statement included in Van Eyck's contribution to Documenta X, Kassel, 1997[1]

My position has not changed since the 60s, 70s and 80s, nor for that matter has the overall situation, other than that is has worsened. So falling back on the past was all right with me – in Kassel as it is here in Rotterdam. The truth is that the entire world of art and architecture has failed to contribute in any substantial way since, let's say 1968, when Milan Triennale chose as general theme *Il Piu Grande Numero*. Next to nothing has been done to awaken the kind of sensibility with which vast multiplicity and quanta are to be reasonably humanized. With even awareness of the necessary still missing and 800,000 dwellings waiting to be built in this country the prospect is certainly a very bleak one.

It is for this reason that the title I used in Milan for my personal contribution then: *Rimpiangi anche tutte le farfalle* (Mourn also for all butterflies) is appropriately used again here as well as Dylan Thomas's 'the ball I threw whilst playing in the park has not yet reached the ground'.[2]

The radiant and the grim face to face

The RADIANT is represented here by the first half of this century's avant-garde: that Great Gang of artists and scientists who together opened the mind to a more relative world in which all things are seen to exist side by side, thus permitting continual metamorphic change.

The GRIM, which took over all too soon, is represented by the Post Modern Disaster – PMD – that rude, convoluted, and above all, mindless interlude which witnessed architects not only playing the fool but also playing foul, reinstalling the same suffocating time-worn hierarchy whilst building the silliest buildings the world has ever seen. Nor is the PMD and its Decon-Virtual wake a thing of the past.

To represent the Great Gang, just two specimens from among countless others are shown here: a small paper cut-out by Hans Arp and a single sentence by Franz Kafka. In Arp's cut-out, a mountain, a table, two anchors and a navel are fraternally brought together through the corporal reduction of the homo sapiens. Kafka's little sentence – equally significant –

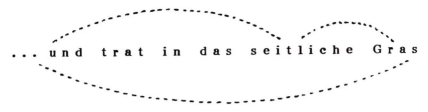

...und traten ins seitliche Gras[3]

(... and stepped into the sideward grass)

does away with the irreversible time worn subject-object hierarchy by allowing the adverb – *seitlich* – to become an adjective: thus in turn subject and object to become gratifyingly equivalent, due to a single – radical – grammatical innovation.

Both Arp and Kafka suggest a horizontally structured – relative – order of things in an open world which is what the Great Gang stood for, *'Pour elles'* (all things) *'il n'y a pas des quartiers de noblesse. C'est pourquoi il ne faut pas distinguer entre les choses'*. Picasso too knew what he was talking about.

However, decades before the Grim set in and Albert Speer was once again contemporary, architects – but for a few – were already drifting away from the spirit of the avant-garde, when CIAM gathered for the first time after the war in 1947. From then on their work became evermore dispirited, thus paving the way for the PMD. I told them so then and there.

Nor was advantage taken of the wonderfully expanded horizon of artistic appreciation which the Great Gang of painters, sculptors, writers, poets and composers had brought about when, in their creative quest, they discovered the enormous tribal world of archaic art, music and thought. What they found – because they were ready for it – lay beyond the orbit of the architect's appreciation. In fact a blind eye and a deaf ear is still turned to what the others had found and made their own almost a century ago.

Hans Arp, *Mountain, Table, Anchors, Navel,*
Oil on cardboard with cut-outs, 1925

Pueblo bowl from Arizona. The interior of this pre-Columbian bowl is decorated with a pattern of parallel lines. Instead of following the concentric contours the lines cross the bowl form side to side. They are as it were projected vertically into the hollow of the bowl. When viewed non-perpendicularly, the lines express the curvature of the bowl and produce a different image from every angle. Photos Aldo van Eyck

Architects took no notice of the incomparable genius with which archaic cultures all over the world embellished whatever they make. For sheer versatility, variety and formal inventiveness the design capacity of 'primitive' tribal people is unrivalled.

They alone, the world over, excelled in repetition and variation of element and theme, in serial composition, counterpoint, syncopation, shifting symmetry, multi-centrality and, perhaps most relevant for us today, in the ability to deal with form and counterform as equivalents and, above all, to open the centre by avoiding a single or central dominant. Nor are geometric and non-geometric design ever separate categories.

What had inspired the others in the Great Gang should have inspired architects as well, faced as they then already were with the onslaught of plurality in general. Had they been more fully aware of the real nature of the problem, they too would have opened their eyes and benefited from the breathtaking example of tribal design and architecture – but they did not. Looking toward and away from Rome and Classicism every 30 years or so instead is not going to assist architecture in coming to terms with vast multiplicity and the menace of uniformity, monotony and oversize.

A new configurative discipline, not yet ours, was actually on its way. Mondrian, Vantongerloo, Sophie Täuber and Richard Paul Lohse were pioneer configurative artists. Their work points towards an aesthetic of number, but sadly saw no real follow-up by either painter, sculptor or architect after they died, except for the one made some 30 years ago around Forum and several young architects working independently, like Piet Blom: but all too soon this initiative side-tracked into an additive formalism wrongly dubbed 'structuralism' by others, which in turn led to a smug reduction of scale. I opposed this foolish interpretation of *Forum's* central theme from the start. Meanwhile, however, the creative achievement of the tribal world could still help to point the way by its breathtaking example because what until then was unknown or, at any rate was thought to lie outside the accepted scope of human ability, was all at once shown to lie within it! The knowledge that what they are able to do in their way, we can still learn to do in our way, is not merely stimulating but brings with it what has almost gone:

HOPE.

The formal vocabulary with which people hitherto successfully imparted order and harmony to the singular and particular cannot help them to harmonise the plural and the general. To accomplish this, the basic principles of a new configurative discipline are still to be discovered. Disclosing the formal conditions implied may yet lead to the right articulation of the plural.

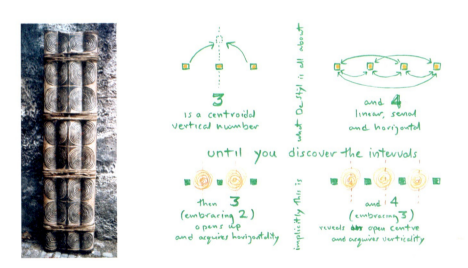

A shield from West Irian in New Guinea. Three convex boards, a wide board in the middle with a narrower one on either side, are tied together by four bundles of string to form an elementary structure in which the skilful detailing has produced a polycentric form. The central board has a groove carved along its entire length; this may be regarded as the main axis of the design. At the same time, however, the two 'valleys' between the planks also present themselves as axes, namely of the spiralling rondels painted on the boards. These rondels bring the lateral boards into relation with the central board, thereby forming two halves of a binary design. Photo Aldo van Eyck

Short biography

Aldo van Eyck was born in Driebergen, Holland, on 16 March 1918. At the age of one and a half he moved with his parents to England. From October 1919 to July 1935 he resided in London where his father, the poet P.N. van Eyck, earned his living as a foreign correspondent of the *Nieuwe Rotterdamse Courant*, a major Dutch newspaper.

He got a classic but unconventional education at King Alfred School in Hampstead (1924–1932) and Sidcot School in Somerset (1932–1935), two progressive schools where art and literature occupied pride of place.

In 1935, after the Van Eycks returned to Holland, Aldo started studying Architecture at the Senior Technical School (MTS) of the Royal Academy of Visual Arts in The Hague. In 1938 he moved to Zurich in order to complete his architectural studies at the Eidgenössische Technische Hochschule, where he graduated in 1942. During his studies he took a particular interest in the lectures of the art historian Linus Birchler on Baroque architecture and the classical design course of the Beaux-Arts veteran Alphonse Laverrière.

At the ETH he also got acquainted with Hannie van Roojen, a Dutch fellow student which he married in 1943. They stayed in Zurich during the war and would have two children: Tess (born in 1945) and Quinten (born in 1948). At the end of their studies they became close friends with Carola Giedion-Welcker, one of the first art historians engaged in an in-depth study of modern art. She introduced the young Van Eyck in the world of the twentieth-century avant-garde and brought him in touch with such artists as Arp, Vantongerloo, Tzara and Brancusi. This experience proved to be of fundamental importance for his world view and cultural ideology.

In 1946 Aldo van Eyck settled with his young family in Amsterdam, where Cor Van Eesteren engaged him as a designer in the Urban Development section of the Public Works department (1946–1951). There he was assigned to design a number of public playgrounds, a project that enabled him to start the experimental development of his form language. Continuing this project after the start of his own practice in 1951, he designed some 700 playgrounds during the next 25 years, gradually evolving a network of places that injected new life into the urban fabric.

The start of the playground project coincided with his involvement in the Cobra movement (1948–1951). He became friends to Appel, Constant and Corneille, and actively took on their defense. He made the lay-out of the two Cobra exhibitions, in Amsterdam (1949) and in Liège (1951).

In 1947 he became a member of the Dutch CIAM group 'de 8 en Opbouw' which appointed him as a delegate to international CIAM. Within CIAM, both in national and international meetings, he took a fundamentally critical stand right from the start. In 1954 he belonged, with Jaap Bakema, Georges Candilis, Alison & Peter Smithson and John Voelcker to the founders of Team 10, the group of angry young architects who rejected the established analytical method of CIAM and proposed a new design approach based on 'patterns of human association'. Aldo van Eyck proved to be one of the most inspired members of this group. He developed a personal version of the Team 10 ideology, a view he was to expound in the Dutch architectural review *Forum*, notably in 1959–1963, when he was a member of its editorial staff, with Apon, Bakema, Boon, Hardy, Hertzberger and Schrofer.

After having achieved some minor projects (houses, schools and exhibitions), Van Eyck gave his ideas a fully elaborated form in the Amsterdam Orphanage (1955–1960), 'a house like a tiny city'. This building earned world-wide admiration and was paradigmatic for a new design approach, the so-called configurative discipline which was developed by such architects as Piet Blom, Joop van Stigt and Herman Hertzberger.

Subsequently Van Eyck condensed his ideas in some particularly pregnant designs: his prize-winning but unexecuted competition project for a protestant church in Driebergen (1963), the catholic Pastoor van Ars church in the Hague (1964–1969) and the Sonsbeek Pavilion in Arnhem (1965).

From the end of the sixties he went to apply his approach in the context of historical towns, first in his competition design for the Deventer town hall (1966, another prize-winning but unexecuted project), and then in the renovation projects for the Amsterdam Nieuwmarkt and Jordaan quarters (1970), and for the inner cities of Zwolle (1971–1975) and Dordrecht (1975–1981) – all of them urban housing projects which he developed and executed in association with Theo Bosch (1971–1983). His most striking building of that period was the Hubertus House in Amsterdam, a home for single parents and their children (1978–1981) which achieved a remarkable integration of a colourful functionalist language within an eclectic context.

From 1983 Van Eyck worked in association with his wife Hannie. Their projects show a further liberation from CIAM rationalism and a passionate exploration of new possibilities in the fields of structure, form and colour. The major works they achieved, a church for the Moluccan community of Deventer (1983–1992), the ESTEC complex in Noordwijk (1994–1989) and the Auditor's Office in The Hague (1992–1997), embody a union of biomorphic forms and flowing space.

Throughout his career Van Eyck developed an active anthropological interest. As a result of his broadly oriented reading he acquired an uncommon knowledge of the most diverse non-Western, archaic cultures. He travelled extensively in order to get more closely acquainted with these cultures. He was a collector and a connoisseur of 'primitive' art from all continents which, together with classic and modern Western art, formed his major source of inspiration.

Aldo van Eyck died in Amsterdam on 14 January 1999.

Teaching

Van Eyck started teaching in 1951. He taught art history at the Enschede Art and Industry Academy (1951–1954), architectural design at the Academy of Applied Art (1950–1966) and the Academy of Architecture (1954–1959), both in Amsterdam. From 1966 to 1985 he was professor at the Delft Polytechnic.

In the meantime he also fulfilled numerous teaching commitments in the USA. He was Visiting Professor at the University of Pennsylvania, Philadelphia (April–May 1960); at Washington University, St. Louis (September 1961 – January 1962); at Harvard University, Cambridge Mass. (March–April 1963); and at Tulane University, New Orleans, March–May 1965; during this last period he also gave lectures at Columbia University, New York; Cornell University, Ithaca; McGill University and the École d'Architecture, Montreal; Rice University, Houston, Texas; and the University of California, Berkeley.

Moreover he was Paul Philippe Cret Professor of Architecture at the University of Pennsylvania, Philadelphia, from 1979 to 1982.

In between he was also visiting lecturer at Trondheim University (December 1958) and at the Architectural Association School, London (July 1964); visiting Critic at the American Academy in Rome (October-November 1965); and Visiting Professor at Reid Hall in Paris (July 1966), at Singapore Polytechnic (July–August 1967), and at the Zurich ETH (1977–1978).

Exhibitions of his own work

Dortmunder Architekturausstellung, Museum am Ostwall, Dortmund, May–June 1976
Venice Biennale, exhibition Europa-America, July 1976
National Museum of Athens, September 1983
RIBA, London, 1990
Berlage Stock Exchange, Amsterdam, 10 November 1989 – 2 January 1990
Vleeshal, Middelburg, May 1992
Documenta X, Kassel, 21 June – 28 September 1997
NAi, Rotterdam, March–May, 1998
4a Bienal Internacional de Arquitetura in São Paulo, 19 Nov. 1999 – 25 Jan. 2000

Honours and awards

Prizes

Sikkens Prize, with Constant in 1960, with Joost van Roojen in 1961
Architecture Prize of the City of Amsterdam, 1964, for the Municipal Orphanage
Rotterdam-Maaskant Prize, 1982
Wihuri International Prize (Finland), 1982
Royal Gold Medal, RIBA, London 1990
Fritz Schumacher Prize, 1992
Ikea Prize, 1992
Wolf Prize, 1998

Honorary doctorates

New Jersey Institute of Technology, 1979
Tulane University, New Orleans, 1979
University of Nova Scotia, Halifax, 1985
Technical University, Delft, 1990

Honorary memberships

Staatlichen Kunstakademie Düsseldorf, 1979
Royal Academy of Belgium, 1981
American Institute of Architects (FAIA), 1981
Bund Deutscher Architekten (BDA), 1982
Royal Incorporation of Architects of Scotland (RIAS), 1985
International Academy of Architecture (Sofia-Paris), 1987
Royal Institute of British Architects (RIBA), 1987
Officer in the Order of Oranje-Nassau, 1990
Order of Science and Art of the Austrian Republic, 1992

Principal projects and buildings

1944

Interior design of tower room in the house of Prof. W. Loeffler, Zürichbergstrasse, Zurich, 1944 (dismantled in 1973).

1947

Approximately 730 children's playgrounds in Amsterdam, for the Public Works Department, 1947–1978.

1948

Interior of own apartment, third floor of Binnenkant 32, Amsterdam (dismantled in 1965).

Development plan for the village of Nagele, Noordoostpolder. Participation in design process as member of a team formed from members of 'de 8' (1948–1951) and Opbouw (1952–1953), built 1954–1958.

1949

Layout of first 'Exposition Internationale d'Art Expérimental' (the 'Cobra Exhibition', organized by the Dutch Experimental Group) in Stedelijk Museum, Amsterdam, 3–28 November, 1949.

1950

'Landmark' at entrance to 'AHOY'' marine exhibition, Rotterdam, 1950.

1951

Dutch contribution to the ninth Triennale of Milan, 1951 in collaboration with J. Rietveld, (awarded a gold medal).

Layout of second 'Exposition Internationale d'Art Expérimental' in Palais de Beaux-Arts, Liège, 6 October – 6 November 1951.

64 dwellings for the elderly, Jan Bottemastraat, Amsterdam-Slotermeer. Design 1951–1952, built 1953–1954; in collaboration with J. Rietveld.

Damme House, Herman Gorterstraat 16, Amsterdam. Design 1951–1952, built 1953–1954; in collaboration with J. Rietveld.

1952

Blue-Purple Room with painting by Constant, part of 'Mens en Huis' exhibition in Stedelijk Museum, Amsterdam, 21 November 1952 – 5 January 1953.

1954

Three schools in Nagele, Noordoostpolder. Design 1954–1955, built 1955–1956, in collaboration with H.P.D. van Ginkel.

1955

Municipal Orphanage, Amstelveenseweg Amsterdam. Design 1955–1957, built 1957–1960.

Winning design in limited competition for Open-Air School, Amsterdam. Design 1955–1956, not built.

1958

Congress Building project, Jerusalem. Design 1958, not built.

Own house project, 'Viertorenhuis', Baambrugge. Design 1958–1960; planning permission withheld, not built.

1962

Limited competition for design of housing estate in Buikslotermeer. First design 1962, second design in collaboration with J.B. Bakema 1963, neither design executed.

Layout of Carel Visser and Joost van Roojen exhibition in Zonnehof, Amersfoort, 2 November – 9 December 1962.

1963

'The Wheels of Heaven', winning design in limited competition for Protestant Church, Driebergen. Design 1963–1964; not built.

Roman Catholic Church for Pastoor van Ars Parish, Aaltje Noorderwierstraat 4, Loosduinen, The Hague. Design 1963–1966, built 1968–1969.

1964

Conversion of 18th century house to own home, Loenen aan de Vecht. Design 1964, executed 1964–1965.

1965

Sculpture pavilion for Sonsbeek Exhibition, Arnhem. Design 1965–1966, built 1966. Demolished in 1966, reconstructed in 2006 in the sculpture garden of the Kröller-Müller Museum, Otterlo.

1966

Conversion of Maas House, Vreeland. Design 1966, executed 1967.

Winning design in limited competition for Deventer City Hall. Design 1966–1967; not built.

1967

Layout of Tajiri exhibition in Stedelijk Museum, Amsterdam, 28 April – 11 June 1967.

Extension to Martin Visser House, Eikendreef 2, Bergeyk. Design 1967, built 1968–1969.

Layout of Mijnden camping site and design of two washroom/toilet buildings, Loenen aan de Vecht. Design 1967, built 1969.

Alfred Schmela House and Art Gallery, Mutter-Eystrasse, Dusseldorf. Design 1967–1969, built 1969–1971.

Verberk House, Herungerweg, Venlo. Design 1967–1970, built 1970.

1968

'The greater number', contribution to Fifteenth Triennale, Milan, 1968.

1969

Layout of Joost van Roojen exhibition in Van Abbemuseum, Eindhoven, 7 March – 20 April 1969.

Limited competition, PREVI housing development, Lima, Peru. Design 1969, built 1972–1976.

1970

Winning design in limited competition for Nieuwmarkt urban development scheme, Amsterdam. Design 1970 in collaboration with Th. Bosch, P. de Ley, G. Knemeijer, D. Tuinman; executed in modified form.

1972

Layout of Carel Visser exhibition in Stedelijk Museum Amsterdam, 18 March – 30 April 1972.

Winning design in limited competition for extension to Provinciaal Overijssels Museum, Zwolle. Design 1972 in collaboration with Hannie van Eyck, detailed 1974–1975; not built.

1973

House for single parents and their children (the 'Hubertus House'), Plantage Middenlaan 31, Amsterdam. Design 1973–1975, executed 1976–1978. Conversion of existing premises nos. 33 and 35, 1979–1981. Interior in collaboration with Hannie van Eyck.

1974

G.J. Visser House, Retie (Belgium). Design 1974–1975, built 1975–1976.

1980

'Padua' Psychiatric Clinic, Boekel. Design 1980–1981, built 1988–1989, in collaboration with Hannie van Eyck.

1983

Design and layout of an exhibition on own work and ideas, National Museum of Athens, September 1983, in collaboration with Hannie van Eyck.

Protestant church for Moluccan community, Deventer. Design 1983–1985, built 1991–1992, in collaboration with Hannie van Eyck.

1984

Conference centre, library, restaurant and offices for the European Space Agency (ESTEC), Noordwijk. Design 1984–1986, built 1987–1989, in collaboration with Hannie van Eyck.

1989

Design and layout of Carel Visser exhibition, Kröller Müllermuseum, Otterlo, March–April 1989.

Design and layout of an exhibition on own work and ideas, Berlage Exchange Building, Amsterdam, 10 November 1989 – 2 January 1990, in collaboration with Hannie van Eyck.

1990

'Tripolis' office complex, adjacent to Municipal Orphanage, Amsterdam. Design 1990–91, built 1992–1994, in collaboration with Hannie van Eyck.

Visual Arts Centre project, Middelburg. Design 1990–1991, in collaboration with Hannie van Eyck, not built.

1992

Auditor's Office building, Lange Voorhout, The Hague. Design 1992–1994, built 1996–1997; in collaboration with Jaap Hillenius (colour design for the façades).

1994

Limited competition for a museum in Nijmegen. Design 1994, not built.

1995

Design for a jetty in Tessaloniki, Greece.

1997

Design and layout of an exhibition on own work and ideas, Documenta X, Kassel, 21 June – 28 September 1997.

Writings by Aldo van Eyck

This list covers most of Van Eyck's writings, as well his published articles as a number of texts (lectures, letters and notes) which are published for the first time in the present edition. The texts are listed in chronological order according to their date of writing (if known) or their earliest date of publication. As a rule, republications are recorded next to their original. All the published articles are listed between inverted commas.
Van Eyck wrote many of his articles in both a Dutch and an English version. These articles are listed by their English title, while their Dutch version is mentioned separately. The articles of which Van Eyck only wrote a Dutch version are listed by their original Dutch title, followed by its English translation, enclosed in square brackets. The titles of the writings which are included in the present volume are indicated in purple. The other, non-included writings amount to duplications or explanatory notes to projects.

1947

Report concerning the interrelation of the plastic arts and the importance of cooperation, report for CIAM 6, Bridgwater 1947.

Architectuur-Schilderkunst-Beeldhouwkunst en hun betekenis voor de Nieuwe Bewustwording, Dutch version of report for CIAM 6, Bridgwater 1947.

Intervention at CIAM 6, Bridgwater, manuscript, 13 September 1947.

1948

On Brancusi, Sert and Miró, letter to the Giedions, 28 October 1948, manuscript in Giedion archive, Zurich.

1949

'Wij ontdekken stijl' [**We discover style**], in *Forum*, 1949, no. 2–3, pp. 115–116.

'Inrichting van een torenkamer voor prof. W.L. te Zürich', in *Forum*, 1949, no. 2–3, p. 90.

1950

'Een appèl aan de verbeelding' [**An appe(a)l to the Imagination**], Amsterdam 12 January 1950; manifesto for the Experimental Group Holland Cobra.

'Bij het "teken" van de tentoonstelling', in *Forum*, 1950, no. 6–7, pp. 202–203.

On the function of a UNESCO art review, letter to Sigfried Giedion, presumably written in September 1950, manuscript in Van Eyck archive.

'Kind en stad' [**Child and City**], in *Goed Wonen*, October 1950, no. 10, pp. 152–153.

1951

Statement against rationalism (intervention at CIAM 6, Bridgwater 1947), in S. Giedion, *A decade of New Architecture*, Zurich 1951, p. 37, and in S. Giedion, *Architecture, you and me*, Harvard 1958, pp. 77–78; German version in S. Giedion, *Architektur und Gemeinschaft*, Hamburg 1956.

Constant and the Abstracts, translation of 'Constant en de abstracten', opening speech for the Constant exhibition in Galerie Le Canard, Amsterdam, 16 February 1951; stencil in Van Eyck archive.

On the Hispano Suiza factory, letter to J.H. van den Broek and J. Bakema, 11 June 1951, translation of manuscripts in Van Eyck and Bakema archives.

'Over de Nederlandse inzending' [**On the Dutch contribution** (to the 1951 Milan Triennale)], in *Forum*, 1951, no. 9, pp. 244–245; Italian translation in *Domus*, September 1951, no. 261, pp. 6–7.

Corneille and the Realists, opening speech for the Corneille exhibition in Martinet & Michels gallery, Amsterdam, 7 November 1951; translation of untitled manuscript in Van Eyck archive.

1952

'Kinderspielplatz in Amsterdam', in *Bauen und Wohnen*, 1952, no. 1, p. 28.

Corneille versus clocks, opening speech for the Corneille exhibition in 'Het Venster', Rotterdam, 5 January 1952; translation of untitled manuscript in Van Eyck archive.

Statement on Lohse [**Lohse and the aesthetic meaning of number**], in *Forum*, 1952, no. 6–7, p. 186; and in *Forum*, 1959, no. 7, p. 223.

'P.W. en de kinderen van Amsterdam', in *Forum*, 1952, no. 6–7, pp. 194–198.

Corneille as a landscape painter, translation of untitled and undated manuscript in Van Eyck archive, presumably written in 1952.

Note on the experience of the elementary in the desert, translation of untitled and undated manuscript in Van Eyck archive, presumably written in 1952.

1953

'Bouwen in de Zuidelijke Oasen' [**Building in the southern oases**], in *Forum*, 1953, no. 1, pp. 28–38.

'Naar aanleiding van een weekendbijeenkomst van de Nederlandse CIAM-groep ter bespreking van het probleem: Wapenfabriek Hispano Suiza' [**Thoughts after a weekend discussion of the Dutch CIAM group concerning the problem of the armaments factory Hispano Suiza**], in *Forum*, 1953, no. 3, p. 91.

'Een ruimte door kleur begrensd', in *Forum*, 1953, no. 3, pp. 92–93.

Voor een spatiaal colorisme [**Spatial Colourism**], Amsterdam 1953 (in cooperation with Constant).

'**Aesthetics of Number**', statement made at CIAM 9, Aix-en-Provence, 1953; first published in *Forum*, September 1959, no. 7, p. 223.

'Enkele conclusies betreffende de structuur en realisering van het dorp Nagele', report of a three-day excursion to the Noordoost-Polder, 14, 15, 16 May 1953; stencil, in cooperation with H.D. van Ginkel.

1954

'**Statement on Habitat**', Doorn declaration drawn up in cooperation with J. Bakema, H. Hovens Greve, P. Smithson J. Voelcker and H.D. Van Ginkel; stencil dated 31 January 1954, first published in *Forum*, September 1959, no. 7, p. 231.

Letter to the Smithsons on the guideline for CIAM 10, undated manuscript in Van Eyck archive, written shortly after 20 September 1954.

'**Orientation**', alternative version of the guideline for CIAM 10, stencil (October 1954).

1955

On the cooperation between the arts, translation of an untitled typescript for a panel discussion at the Amsterdam Stedelijk Museum, June 1955.

1956

'Over binnen- en buitenruimte' [**On inside and outside space**], in *Forum*, 1956, no. 4, p. 133.

'Huis aan de Herman Gorterstraat te Amsterdam', in *Forum*, 1956, no. 4, p. 118.

'Woningen voor bejaarden te Amsterdam' (Slotermeer), in *Forum*, 1956, no. 4, pp. 130–133.

'**Lost identity**', grid presentation of the Amsterdam playgrounds for CIAM 10 in Dubrovnik, 1956; reprinted in M. RISSELADA & D. VAN DEN HEUVEL, *Team 10 (1954–1981) – in search of a Utopia of the Present*, NAi Publishers, Rotterdam, 2005, pp. 56–57.

'**Nagele, village in the N.E. Polder**', grid presentation for CIAM 10 in Dubrovnik, 1956; reprinted *ibidem*, pp. 58–59.

1957

'**A tribute to Carola Giedion-Welcker**', introduction to a lecture by Carola Giedion-Welcker in the Stedelijk Museum, Amsterdam on 8 February 1957, on the occasion of the opening of an exhibition of work by Paul Klee, published in *Forum*, 1959, no. 9, pp. 321–322.

Postcard to Bakema on the dissolution of Dutch CIAM, translation of handwritten postcard in Bakema Archive, dated 19 February 1957.

'Scholen te Nagele', in *Forum*, 1957, no. 7, pp. 243–245.

'Het kind en de stad' [**When snow falls on cities**], in *Goed Wonen*, 1957, no. 10, pp. 207–212.

On garden and landscape art, translation of an untitled and undated manuscript in Van Eyck archive; draft for a lecture, probably given in 1957.

1958

'De bal kaatst terug' [**The ball rebounds**], in *Forum*, 1958, no. 3, pp. 104–111.

'Kwadraten met een glimlach' [**Squares with a smile**], in *De Groene Amsterdammer*, 17 May 1958.

'Drei Schulhäuser in Nagele, Nordost-Polder, Holland', in *Werk*, May 1958, no. 5, pp. 170–173.

'De ruimte achter het oog' [**The space behind the eye**], undated typescript in Van Eyck archive, probably written in 1958.

1959

'Child and City', in A. Ledermann, A. Trachsel, *Playgrounds and Recreation Spaces – Spielplatz und Gemeinschaftzentrum*, Niggli, Teufen 1959, pp. 38–45.

'Dag beeld' [**Good morning, sculpture**], in *De Groene Amsterdammer*, 2 May 1959.

On the relationship between architecture and art, translation of an untitled statement in *Forum*, 1959, no. 6, p. 176.

'het verhaal van een andere gedachte' [**The Story of Another Idea**], in *Forum*, 1959, no. 7, special issue.

Talk at the Otterlo Congress, transcription and partial translation of tape recording made on 11 September 1959, Bakema archive, NAi, Rotterdam.

Introduction to 5 projects, in *Forum*, 1959, no. 9.

The CIAM City and the Natural Cycles, sketch proposal for an intended but unpublished Forum issue, fall 1959; Van Eyck archive.

'Dag en Nacht' [**Day and Night**], undated manuscript in Van Eyck archive, intended to be included in *The CIAM City and the Natural Cycles*, intended but unpublished Forum issue, fall 1959.

1960

'**Hello Shinkichi!**', in exhibition catalogue *Tajiri*, 2 March- 2 April 1960, Stedelijk Museum, Amsterdam.

'Aquarium' [**Aquarium design by Jan Verhoeven**], in *Forum*, 1960–61, no. 2, pp. 69–71 and 79.

'Tussen hier en daar, nu en straks' [**Between here and there, now and later**], in *Forum*, 1960–61, no. 3, pp. 107–117.

'**There is a garden in her face**', in *Forum*, 1960–61, no. 3, p. 121.
Italian version, 'Luogo e occasione', in *L'architettura*, 1961, no. 7, p. 395.

'Overwegend vuile was' [**Dirty linen, mostly**], in *Forum*, 1960–61, no. 4, pp. 150–156.

'Three schools in Nagele', in *Architects' Year Book*, no. 9, August 1960, p. 140–143.

Remarks on pictures of the old and the new Municipal Orphanage, in *Goed Wonen*, November 1960, no. 11, pp. 319–331.

Letter to Giedion on the dissolution of CIAM, undated manuscript in Van Eyck Archive, written shortly after 10 December 1960.

1961

'**Is architecture going to reconcile basic values?**', in O. Newman, CIAM *'59 in Otterlo*, Stuttgart 1961, pp. 26–35.

'Children's Home, Amsterdam' and 'Congress Building in Jerusalem', *Ibidem*, pp. 29–35.

'**The moment of realization**', talk at the conclusion of the Otterlo congress, *Ibidem*, pp. 216–217.

'Binnenhuiskunst' [**Interior Art**], lecture given on 6 February 1961 at the Royal Academy of Fine Arts in The Hague, in stencilled collection of 1961 lectures, The Hague (1961).

'Raadsel van de tijd' [**The Enigma of Time**], written in 1961 after a visit to Duiker's Zonnestraal sanatorium, but only published in *Forum*, July 1976, p. 51.

'The medicine of reciprocity tentatively illustrated', in *Forum*, 1960–61, no. 6–7, pp. 237–238 and 252.
'De milde raderen van de reciprociteit', *Ibidem*, pp. 205–206.
English version republished in *Architects' Year Book,* no. 10, London 1962, pp. 173–178.
Dutch version republished in H. Heynen, A. Loeckx et al., eds., Dat is architectuur, 010 Publishers, Rotterdam, 2001, pp. 343–346. Shortened German version, 'Kindergarten in Amsterdam', in *Baumeister*, June 1961, pp. 530–543; and 'Kinderhaus in Amsterdam', in *Werk*, January 1962, pp. 16–22.
Danish translation, 'Gensidighedens medecin forsgevis illustretet', in *Louisiana Revy*, 1961, no. 2, pp. 25–27.

'**Visser is a winged digger**', in *Forum*, 1961, no. 6–7, p. 238.
'Visser is een gevleugelde delver', *Ibidem*, p. 206.

About the Economist project, undated letter to the Smithsons, probably written in July 1961; Smithson archive, NAi.

'**After a heavy snowstorm**', brief for a 12-day student project at Washington University, St Louis, fall 1961, in *Team 10 Primer, Architectural Design*, 1962, no. 12, pp. 572–573.

'**Tree is leaf and leaf is tree**', statement written at Washington University, St Louis, fall 1961; included in chap. 5 of *The Child, the City and the Artist*, first published in *The Situationist Times*, October 1963, no. 4, p. 80.

'Architecture of the Dogon', in *Architectural Forum*, September 1961, pp. 116–121.

'Waarom geen dierbaar stadhuis?' [**Why not a beloved town hall?**], in *De Groene Amsterdammer*, 14 October 1961.

1962

The Child, the City and the Artist, typescript of a book written on commission of the Institute of Urban Studies of the University of Pennsylvania, with a grant from the Rockefeller Institute, 1962.

'**Place and Occasion**', in *Progressive architecture*, September 1962, p. 155; slightly modified and enlarged version of 'There is a garden in her face' (1960). At the same time a shortened version was included in *The Child, the City and the Artist* (at the end of chap. 2). This definitive version was published in *Architectural Design*, December 1962, p. 600; in *Situationist Times*, October 1963, p. 79; in Team 10 Primer (paperback edition, 1965, p. 43; hard cover edition, 1968, p. 101) in *Via 1 – Ecology in Design*, Philadelphia, 1968, p. 90; and in *Aldo van Eyck – Hubertus House*, Stichting Wonen, Amsterdam, 1982, p. 49.

'Home for Children in Amsterdam', in *The Indian Architect*, August 1962.

'The things that really matter', in *Werk*, May 1962, no. 5, p. 108.

'De vormgeving van speeltoestellen en de inrichting van speelplaatsen' [**On the design of play equipment and the arrangement of playgrounds**], lecture given at Marcanti theatre in Amsterdam, typescript (1962).

'**The fake client and the great word "no"**', in *Forum*, August 1962, no. 3, pp. 79–80.
'De verkapte opdrachtgever en het grote word "neen"', *Ibidem*.
English version reprinted under the title 'Notes in passing' in *Arts & Architecture*, November 1962, pp. 9, 11.

'**Steps towards a configurative discipline**', in *Forum*, August 1962, no. 3, pp. 81–94.
'De straling van het configuratieve', *Ibidem*, pp. 81–89.

English version republished in J. Ockman, ed., *Architectural Culture in 1943–1968 – a documentary anthology*, Columbia Books of Architecture, Rizzolo, New York, 1993, pp. 348–360.
Dutch version republished in *Panorama van de avant-gardes*, Arnhem 1981, pp. 162–169.

'**The pueblos**', in *Forum*, August 1962, no. 3, pp. 95–114.
'De Pueblos', *Ibidem*, pp. 95–113.

On Blom's *Noah's Ark*, translation of untitled manuscript in Van Eyck archive, 1962.

Discussion of the problem of number at the Royaumont Meeting, September 1962, proceedings summarized from the original transcript of the meeting's tape recordings.

'Toespraak bij de uitreiking van de Sikkensprijs 1962' [**Speech for the award of the 1962 Sikkens Prize**], manuscript (November 1962), published in *Niet om het even – wel evenwaardig*, Rotterdam-Maaskantstichting, Rotterdam 1986, pp. 34–35.

'Gensidigheden – menneskeligt og arkitektonisk', in *Arkitekten*, December 1962, no. 24, pp. 451–457.

'**Wheels or no wheels, man is essentially a pedestrian**', in *Team 10 Primer*, *Architectural Design*, 1962, no. 12, p. 574; paperback edition, 1965, p. 17; hard cover edition, 1968, p. 51–53.

Various passages in *Team 10 Primer*, *Architectural Design*, 1962, no. 12, special issue, edited by Alison Smithson, pp. 559–560, 564–565, 570, 572, 579, 590–591, 593, 594–595, 598, 601–602. Reprinted in paperback 1965. Hard cover edition with several additions: Studio Vista, London 1968, pp. 6, 12, 15, 20, 21, 22, 27, 30, 31, 32, 33, 35, 41, 43, 44, 45, 59, 73, 83, 89, 95, 96, 98, 99 100–104.

1963

'Kindertehuis in Amsterdam', in *Bouwkundig Weekblad*, 1963, no. 1, pp. 25–30.

'The Pueblos', in *Ecistics*, April 1963, pp. 240–241.

On Rykwert's *Idea of a town*, in *Forum*, 1963, no. 3.

'Switch on the stars before the fuses go – Organized Nowhere: The Boredom of Hygiene – Reconciling False Alternatives: The Inbetween Realm – Beyond Visibility', in *Report '63, a record of the Pacific Congress organized by the students of the school of architecture*, University of Auckland, New Zealand, September 1963, pp. 37–45.

'Beyond Visibility – About Place and Occasion – The Inbetween Realm – Right-size – Labyrinthian Clarity', in *The Situationist Times*, October 1963, no. 4, pp. 79–85.

1964

'Aldo van Eyck speaks: extracts from an address delivered at Auckland, Christchurch and Wellington', in *New Zealand Institute of Architects Journal*, February 1964, pp. 3–6, and March 1964, pp. 25–26.

Contribution to symposium 'Gestaltungsprobleme der Gegenwart', in *Werk*, March 1964, no. 3, p. 114.

'Het interieur van de ruimte', in *Wijsgerig perspectief op Maatschappij en Wetenschap*, September 1964, no. 1, pp. 16–23.

1965

'Adolf Loos' [**On Loos**], introduction to an exhibition held in Delft, in *Delftse School*, April 1965, no. 12; republished in *Niet om het even – wel evenwaardig*, Rotterdam-Maaskantstichting, Rotterdam 1986, pp. 120–121.

'The Wheels of Heaven', in *Domus*, May 1965, no. 426, pp. 1–6; and in J. Donat, ed., *World Architecture 3*, Studio Vista, London 1966, pp. 123–129.

'Tree is leaf and leaf is tree' [**Tree and leaf**], handwritten diagram, in *Domus*, May 1965, no. 426; and in J. Donat, ed., *World Architecture 3*, Studio Vista, London 1966, p. 120

1966

Report of a talk given at the Australian Architecture Student Association convention, held at Perth in May 1966, [**What we are after is a new and as yet unknown configurative discipline**], in *Building Ideas*, vol. 3, no. 4, September 1966, pp. 10–14.

'**Labyrinthian Clarity**', in J. Donat, ed., *World Architecture 3*, Studio Vista, London 1966, pp. 121–122; and in *Forum*, July 1967, p. 51;
republished under the title 'The Interior of Space' in *Via*, 1968, no. 1, pp. 91–92.

'**University college in Urbino by Giancarlo de Carlo**', in *Zodiac*, 1966, no. 16; in J. Donat, ed., *World Architecture 4*, Studio Vista, London 1967, pp. 50–57; and in *Architects' Year Book*, no. 12, Elek Books, London, 1968, pp. 150–160.

1967

Japanese translation of 'Place and Occasion, Labyrinthian Clarity, Otterlo Circles, Hill and Hollow Image, Childrens Home, The Singular embracing the Plural, Protestant Church', in *Kenchiku Bunka*, January 1967, no. 243, pp. 94–98.

'Paviljoen Sonsbeek 1966', in *Forum*, July 1967, pp. 24–25.

'Anna was, Livia is, Plurabelle's to be', in *Forum*, July 1967, p. 28; republished under the title '**The Interior of Time**' in *Via*, 1968, no. 1, pp. 93–94.

'Dogon: mand-huis-dorp-wereld', (in collaboration with P. Parin and F. Morgenthaler), in *Forum*, July 1967, pp. 30–50; with shortened English version in gray insert, pp. 7–9.

'Raadsel van de tijd' (1961) [**The enigma of Time**], in *Forum*, July 1967, p. 51.

'**The Otterlo Circles**' (2), in *Forum*, July 1967, p. 52; and, in a slightly enlarged version, in *Via*, 1968, no. 1, p. 95.

'The sailor's nostalgia' (1960), in *Forum*, July 1967, p. 52; republished without title in *Via*, 1968, no. 1, p. 92.

'Het interieur van de ruimte' (1962–1964) [**Place and Occasion**], in *Forum*, July 1967, p. 54.

'De Spiegelmeester' [**The Mirror Master**] (about Joost van Roojen), in *Forum*, July 1967, pp. 55–59.

'Pavilion, Arnheim, a place for sculpture and people', in *World Architecture 4*, London 1967, pp. 59–60; and in *Domus*, March 1968, no. 460, p.2.

1968

Statement on Christopher Alexander's *A City is not a Tree,* in A. Smithson, ed., Team 10 Primer, hardback edition, Studio Vista, London, 1968, p. 98.

Open letter to the Hon. Eisaku Sato, Prime Minister of Japan, to save the Imperial Hotel of F.L. Wright, 12 January 1968.

'Hello Shinkichi!' (2), in *Domus*, March 1968, no. 461.

'Kaleidoscope of the Mind: Place and Occasion – The Interior of Space – The Interior of Time – The Otterlo Circles', in *Via*, 1968, no. 1, *Ecology in Design*, (University of Pennsylvania), pp. 90–95.

A Miracle of Moderation: **Design Only Grace, Open Norm; Disturb Order Gracefully, Outmatch Need – Basket, House, Village, Universe – The small brought about by the large – Some Comments on a significant Detour – Lacking the Spirit of Ecology'** (in collaboration with P. Parin and F. Morgenthaler), *Ibidem*, pp. 96–125.

'*Image of Ourselves*: Another Miracle – The Snow Image again – The Boredom of Hygiene – The Fake Client and the Great word "No"' (extracts from The Child, the City and the Artist), *Ibidem*, pp. 125–135.

These three contributions to *Via*, 1968, no. 1, were republished in 1976 at Eidgenössische Technische Hochschule, Zurich, under the title '*Miracles of Moderation*'.

'A Miracle of Moderation' was also published by G. Baird and Ch. Jencks in *Meaning in Architecture*, London 1969, pp. 170–213; and in French translation in *Le Sens de la Ville*, Seuil, Paris 1972.
'The Interior of Time' was published in German translation under the title 'Das Innere der Zeit' by G.R. Blomeyer and B. Tietze in *In Opposition zur Moderne*, F. Viewig & Sohn, Braunschweig-Wiesbaden 1980 (Bauweltfundamente 52).

1969

'The Child, the City and the Artist', in *Byggekunst*, 1969, no. 1, pp. 16–17.

'Bewoonbaar of onbewoonbaar', in *Gemeentelijk Jaarboek 1969*, The Hague 1969, pp. 19–31.

'The Enigma of Vast Multiplicity', in *Harvard Educational Review*, 1969, no. 4, pp. 126–143. Reprinted in *School House*, Stylos, Delft 1970.

'Juror's Statement', in *Our Environment*, catalogue of the 59th Annual Exhibition of the Associated Artists of Pittsburg, March-April 1969.

1970

'Who are we building for, and why?', in *Architectural Design*, 1970, no. 4, p. 189.

Description of own entry for Low Cost Housing competition, Previ, Lima, in *Architectural Design*, 1970, no. 4, p. 205.

'A propos Jan Rietveld', in *Wonen*, 1970–1971, no. 2, pp. 5–8.

'Stadskern als donor' [**City centre as donor**], in *TABK*, September 1970, no. 20, pp. 469–470; and in *Forum*, November 1970, no. 4, pp. 20–27.

'The Priority Jostle', intervention at a symposium on housing in developing countries, held at Delft Polytechnic, autumn 1970, typescript, published in *Spazio e Società*, December 1979, no. 8, pp. 55–57.

1971

'Waarborg voor behoud van verscheidenheid van functies en hun vervlechting – een experiment tegen aantasting' [**An experiment to counter urban corrosion**] (concerning the housing project in Zwolle, designed in association with Theo Bosch), in TABK 1971, no. 22, pp. 556–560.

Order and chaos, statement likely written about 1971, published in *Spazio e Società*, December 1979, no. 8, p. 78

'Sociocide' [**Sociocide**], statement likely written about 1971, published in *Niet om het even – wel evenwaardig*, Rotterdam-Maaskantstichting, Rotterdam 1986, p. 137.

1972

'Wonen in de binnenstad van Zwolle' (in collaboration with Th. Bosch, P. de Ley, G. Knemeijer), in *Stedebouw en volkshuisvesting*, 1972, no. 1, pp. 18–22.

1974

'Enkele overwegingen die tot de gestalte van het huis hebben geleid', in *Jaarverslag 1974 Hubertusvereniging*, pp. 19–22.

Open letter to the Mayor and Aldermen of Amsterdam (8 July 1974, concerning Nieuwmarkt, with Th. Bosch), in *Wonen-TABK*, 1974, no. 15, pp. 1–2.

'De scrupules van bouwmeester Aldo van Eyck' [**On breaking through monuments**], interview by W. Rothuizen in *Haagse Post*, 14 December 1974, pp. 54–58.

1975

'In search of Labyrinthian Clarity', explanatory notes on his own work, in *L'Architecture d'Aujourd'hui*, January-February 1975, no. 177, pp. 14–30.

Open letter to the Mayor and Aldermen and Council of the City of Amsterdam (3 March 1975, with Th. Bosch, concerning Nieuwmarkt), in *Wonen-TABK* 1975, no. 7, pp. 2–3.

'Dank je wel, Pjotr', in *B-nieuws*, 1975, no. 34, p. 615.

1976

'Roman Catholic Church in The Hague', in *Lotus International*, 1976, no. 1, pp. 109–114. Spanish translation, 'Una Iglesia Católica en La Haya', in *Arquitectura*, 1997, no. 311, pp. 84–87.

Short explanatory notes (in German) on his own work, in *Dortmunder Architekturheft* no. 3, Dortmund, 1976, pp. 11–31.

'**Like that other gift**', text for the architecture exhibit of the Venice Biennale, July 1976. Published in Italian under the title 'Come l'altro dono', followed by a selection of earlier texts in Italian version, in F. Raggi, *Europa/America – Architetture Urbane, alternative suburbane*, Venice 1978; and in *Spazio e Società*, December 1979, no. 8, pp. 60–61.

Intervention in the debate 'Quale movimento moderno?' at the Venice Biennale, on 1 August 1976, Italian version in F. Raggi, *Europa/America – Architetture Urbane, alternative suburbane*, Venice 1978, p. 179.

1978

Investigation of the effect of changes in climate and culture on the design process (in cooperation with F. Burke, S. Jhaveri), ETH Zurich 1978.

'Haus für ledige Mütter und ihre Kinder, Amsterdam 1975–78', in *Deutsche Bauzeitung*, 1978, no. 11, p. 42.

1979

'Imagination and Competence' (on the PREVI housing project for Lima, Peru), in *Spazio e Società*, December 1979, no. 8, pp. 43–57.

'The Priority Jostle' (contribution to a symposium at Delft Polytechnic in 1970), *Ibidem*, pp. 56–57.

'Triennale di Milano 1968 "Il grande numero"', *Ibidem*, pp. 58–59.

'The Ironbound statement', key address delivered for the 1979 Commencement of the New Jersey Institute of Technology, *Ibidem*, pp. 62–63.

'A message to Mathias Ungers from a different world', *Ibidem*, pp. 63–64

'The Enigma of Size', *Ibidem*, pp. 65–77; and in *Signs and Insights*, Annual Report ILA&UD 1979, Urbino 1980, pp. 42–53.

'When snow falls on cities' [**Order and chaos**], in *Spazio e Società*, December 1979, no. 8, p. 78.

1980

'Errata corrige', in *Spazio e Società*, March 1980, no. 9, p. 113.

'Over het verhaal van een andere gedachte', in *Wonen-TABK*, 1980, no. 15, p. 7.

1981

'What is and what isn't architecture – à propos of Rats, Posts and Other Pests (R.P.P.)', in *Lotus International*, 1981, no. 28, pp. 15–20.

'"Het ogenblik van Core" – Jaap Bakema, 1914–1981' [**Jaap Bakema, 1914–1981 – 'The Moment of Core'**], in *Forum*, juli 1981 (1980–81, no. 3), p. 3.

'R.P.P. (Rats, Posts and Other Pests)', the RIBA Annual Discourse, in *RIBA Journal*, April 1981, no. 4, pp. 47–50; and, prefaced by a letter to Dr. Papadakis, in *AD News Supplement*, 1981, no. 7. Dutch translation in *Forum*, 1980–81, no. 3, pp. 25–29, under the title 'Omtrent die massieve theepot'. Shortened German translation under the title 'Die Transparanz der Zeit' in *Archithese*, 1981, no. 5, pp. 32–34.)

'Zo iets bouw je toch niet voor mensen!' [**You can't build a thing like that for people!**], in *Het Parool*, 26 juni 1981.

'Ex Turico Aliquid Novum', in *Archithese*, 1981, no. 5, pp. 35–38.

'Transparancy and colours', in *L'Architecture d'Aujourd'hui*, October 1981, no. 217, pp. 72–79; and in *Progressive Architecture*, March 1982, p. 78.

1982

'En wel per definitie', on the work of Lucien Lafour, in *Forum*, June 1982 (1982–82, no. 3), p. 27. English version, **'By Definition'**, in *Architectural Review*, October 1984, no. 1052, p. 62; corrected version in *Architectural Review*, April 1985, no. 1058, p. 72.

'Building a house: Still the gentle gears – 33 Plantage Middenlaan – **Transparancy** – The gift of colour', in H. Hertzberger, A. Van Roijen-Wortman, F. Strauven, *Aldo van Eyck*, Stichting Wonen, Amsterdam, 1982, pp. 38–95.

1983

'Ax Bax', in collected documentation for the exhibition on A. van Eyck in the National Museum of Athens, September 1983.

Pamphlet on the Elgin Marbles, *ibidem* and in *Forum*, 1983, no. 3, pp. 8–9.

'Joop Hardy 1918–1983, herfstman tussen winter **man between winters**], funeral address for Joop Hardy on 8 October 1983, folder published by the Architecture Faculty, TH Delft 1986; also included in J. Hardy, *Cultuurbeschouwing*, collected lectures given at the Technical University of Delft from 1981 to 1983, Amsterdam 1987, pp. 313–317.

1984

'Wasted Gain' (The Ironbound Statement, 1979), 'The Declaration of Delft' (The Priority Jostle, 1970), 'Low Cost Housing in Lima, Peru' (1979), 'Mothers' House, Amsterdam' (1982) in D. Lasdun, *Architecture in an Age of Scepticism*, Heinemann, London, 1984, pp. 234–253.

'Un nouveau centre de gravité', comments on the design for a staff restaurant and conference facilities for ESTEC, Noordwijk; 'A propos de non espaces, de roses et de Codussi', comments on the design for a church for the Moluccan community in Deventer, in *L'Architecture d'Aujourd'hui*, October 1984, no. 235, pp. LXXXI-LXXXII, and 21–22.

'Restaurant and conference facilities for ESTEC', in *Architectural Design*, 1984, no. 11–12, pp. 80–83.

'Open brief aan het bestuur van de afdeling Bouwkunde', in *B-nieuws*, 24 October 1984, p. 1.

1985

'About Non Space, Roses and Coducci' in *Architectural Review*, January 1985, no. 1055, pp. 14–17.

'Typology (typologically)', answer to an inquiry, in *Casabella*, January-February 1985, p. 112.

'Architetture e pensieri', in *Casabella*, October 1985, no. 517, pp. 4–21.

1986

'A last Resort', programme for the international student competition held by the Royal Institute of British Architects, folder issued by the RIBA, London 1986; also published in *Architectural Review*, July 1986, no. 1073, pp. 55–56.

'Cobra (Luik en Stedelijk)' [**Looking back on the Cobra exhibitions in Liège (1951) and Amsterdam (1949)**], in *Niet om het even – wel evenwaardig*, Rotterdam-Maaskantstichting, Rotterdam 1986, p. 46.

'Avondje Limbo in de Lage Landen' [**An evening of Limbo in the Low Countries**], in *Niet om het even – wel evenwaardig*, Rotterdam-Maaskantstichting, Rotterdam 1986, pp. 52–54.

'Toespraak bij de uitreiking van de Sikkensprijs 1962', 'Speelplaats Zeedijk', 'De Roze Po', 'Het project van Ton Bruynèl', 'Omtrent het aantal potloden', 'In de leegte gesproken', 'Kleine tafelspeech', and various other commentaries and reprints in *Niet om het even – wel evenwaardig*, Rotterdam-Maaskantstichting, Rotterdam 1986.

'Dylan Thomas', letter to the editor, *NRC Handelsblad*, Cultural Supplement, 26 September 1986.

1987

'The circle and the centre', in *Indesem '87*, Delft University Press, Delft, 1988, pp. 184–185.

On Van Doesburg, I.K. Bonset and DeStijl, opening speech to the Van Doesburg exhibition in the Rotterdam Boymans Museum, 18 December 1988, translation of manuscript in Van Eyck Archive.

1989

'De architectuur van de gestolde toegankelijkheid', in *Eikenheuvel* (house journal of Huize Padua, Boekel), August 1989; and in *Traverse*, 20 September 1989.

'Padua – Local symmetry winking', in *Aldo & Hannie van Eyck: recent work*, Beurs van Berlage 1989, pp. 19, 27.

'En maar tuimelen tussen vandaag en gisteren' [**And just keeping on switching between yesterday and today**], in catalogue newspaper for the exhibition 'Aldo van Eyck in de Beurs van Berlage', 1989.

1990

'Preface' [**Unearthing the silted-up alphabet of meaningful designing – on Jan Rietveld**], in P. Salomons and S. Doorman, *Jan Rietveld*, 010, Rotterdam, 1990.

'De interpretatie van de openbare ruimte in het Plan-zuid van Berlage aan de hand van het ontwerp voor een plein aan de Apollolaan', mimeograph, 1990, Van Eyck Archive.

'Verandert Delft voor of na Albanië?' [**Will Delft change before or after Albania?**], in *Architectuur/Bouwen*, 1990, no. 11, pp. 45–50.

'Milano, Atene, Amsterdam', in *Spazio e Società*, October-December 1990, no. 52, pp. 6–17.

1991

'Everybody has his own story' [**On Team 10**], interview given to Clelia Tuscano (on 26 September 1991), in M. RISSELADA & D. VAN DEN HEUVEL, *Team 10 (1954–1981) – in search of a Utopia of the Present*, NAi Publishers, Rotterdam, 2005, pp. 328–331.

1993

'Architectuur', letter to the editor in *Haagse Courant*, 21 January 1993.

'Remembrance of a good friend' and 'The Royal Gold Medal Address', in *Quaderns d'Arquitectes*, 1993, nr. 3, pp. 110–145.

On C.R. Mackintosh, interview given to Richard Murphy, in *The Architects' Architect*, Bellew Publishing Company, London 1993, pp. 47–57.

1995

'Vanuit die kastanjes', explanatory note to Nijmegen Museum competition project, in *Vijf ontwerpen voor een nieuw museum in Nijmegen*, LaVerbe, Nijmegen, 1995, pp. 38–41.

1996

Explanatory note his Thessaloniki pier project, in S. LEBESQUE, ed., *Between sea and city: eight piers for Thessaloniki*, NAi Publishers, Rotterdam, 1996, pp. 29–44.

On Josep M. Jujol, preface to Vincent Ligtelijn and Rein Saariste, *Josep M. Jujol*, 010 Publishers, Amsterdam, 1996

Letter to Vittorio Gregotti, in *Casabella*, 1996, no 630–631, pp. 116–117.

1997

'Church for the Moluccan Community of Deventer', in *Zodiac*, September 1996-February 1997, pp. 194–197.

'A Superlative Gift' – about Lina Bo Bardi, Sao Paulo Art Museum, Sao Paulo 1997.

'The radiant and the grim', typewritten Statement included in his contribution to Documenta X, Kassel, June 1997

1998

'Tecnología y arquitectura integrados con el ambiente' (Spanish version of 'Wasted Gain', 1979; 'The Priority Jostle', 1970; and 'Low Cost Housing in Lima, Peru', 1979) in J. Villamón, *Grandes Maestros de la Arquitectura*, Colegio de Arquitectos del Perú and Universidad Ricardo Palma, Lima, 1998, pp. 43–56.

'Lured from his den', in *Archis*, 1998, no. 2, pp. 19–25.
'Uit de tent gelokt', *Ibidem*, pp. 19–26.

1999

Revised version of 58 explanatory notes to own projects, in V. Ligtelijn, ed., *Aldo van Eyck, Works*, Birkhäuser, Basel/Boston/Berlin, 1999.

Publications on Aldo van Eyck

A select bibliography edited and completed by F. Strauven in Spring 2007 during his stay as a Mellon Senior Fellow at the Canadian Centre for Architecture in Montreal.

1947

J.B. BAKEMA, 'Bridgwater 1947. Het 6ᵉ CIAM-congres, indrukken en feiten', in *Bouw*, 29 November 1947, pp. 389–397.

1950

C. DOTREMONT, 'L'Affaire Appel', in *Le Petit Cobra*, no. 3, spring 1950.

1951

H. SALOMONSON, 'Bij het interieur van Aldo van Eyck', in *Goed Wonen*, February 1951, no. 2, pp. 25–27.

H. HARTSUYKER, 'Kinderspielplätze in Amsterdam', in *Werk*, 1951, no. 11, pp. 335–336.

1952

S. GIEDION, 'Historical Background to the Core', in J. TYRWHITT, J.L. SERT, E.N. ROGERS, *The Heart of the City*, Lund Humphries, London 1952, pp. 17–25.

R. BLIJSTRA, 'Waar het kind zijn stad ontdekt', in *Vrij Nederland*, 23 August 1952, p. 5.

1955

CORNEILLE, 'De mannen van de Hoggar', in *Het Parool*, 7 January 1955.

J. VOELCKER, 'Polder and Playground', in *Architects' Yearbook* 1955, no. 6, pp. 89–94.

1958

P. BAKKUM, 'Meervoudige opdracht tot het verkrijgen van een ontwerp voor de bouw van een openluchtschool voor het gezonde kind', in *Bouwkundig Weekblad*, 1958, no. 76, pp. 437–448.

1960

J.J. VRIEND, 'Verzet tegen materialistisch bouwen', in *De Groene Amsterdammer*, 27 February 1960.

J. WEEKS, 'The Children's House, Amsterdam', in *Architectural Design*, May 1960, no. 5, pp. 179–180.

M. VAN BEEK, 'Verzoening tussen Palladio en Mies van der Rohe – Het nieuwe Burgerweeshuis te Amsterdam van Aldo van Eyck', in *De Tijd-Maasbode*, 2 July 1960.

H. HARTSUYKER, 'Spielplatz Zeedijk in Amsterdam', in *Werk*, August 1960, no. 8, p. 293.

R. BLIJSTRA, 'The Amsterdam Municipal Orphanage', in *Delta*, autumn 1960, no. 3, pp. 55–56.

J.J. VRIEND, 'Het weeshuis van Aldo van Eyck', in *De Groene Amsterdammer*, 17 September 1960.

J.B. BAKEMA, 'Gewoonte en gewoon – Nogmaals het weeshuis van Aldo van Eyck', in *De Groene Amsterdammer*, 8 October 1960.

J.J. VRIEND, 'Het ongewone is zeer gewoon' (answer to Bakema), in *De Groene Amsterdammer*, 15 October 1960.

F. OUDEJANS, 'Het Burgerweeshuis nu in een nieuw tehuis onder 336 koepels', in *Goed Wonen*, November 1960, no. 11, pp. 331–333.

'Aldo van Eyck, maison d'enfants, Amsterdam, Pays-Bas' in *L'Architecture d'Aujourd'hui*, September – December 1960, no. 921/92, pp. 168–169.

1961

L. KAHN, Statement on Van Eyck, in O. Newman, CIAM '59 in Otterlo, Stuttgart 1961, p. 214.

J.J.P. OUD, 'De melodie van de ruimte', in *De Groene Amsterdammer*, 18 March 1961.

B. ZEVI, 'Convitto di Aldo van Eyck. Parlare con la propria eco non è dialogare', in *L'Espresso*, 3 September 1961.

J.H. VAN DEN BROEK, 'De Sikkensprijzen 1960 en 1961', speech delivered in the Stedelijk Museum, Amsterdam, September 1961; stencil.

K. WIEKART, 'De duofenomenen van Aldo van Eyck', in *Vrij Nederland*, 7 October 1961.

J. VAN GOETHEM, 'Casa dei Ragazzi ad Amsterdam', in *L'architettura, cronache e storia*, October 1961, no. 72, pp. 386–402.

1963

S. VINKENOOG, *Karel Appel*, Bruna, Utrecht 1963, pp. 56–61, 65–78, 167–169.

B. KROON, 'Bruisend van ideeën? Niets nieuws bij! Laat mij maar bouwen, zegt Aldo van Eyck', in *De Tijd*, 16 February 1963.

H.R. HITCHCOCK, 'A letter from Rome' (1 September 1962), in *Zodiac*, 1963, no. 11.

N. KURAKAWA, 'New movements of Architecture and Urbanism in the World', in *Kenchiki Bunka*, 1963.

R. MAXWELL, 'Frontiers of inner space', in *Sunday Times Magazine*, 29 September 1963, pp. 7–14.

1964

H. HERTZBERGER, 'The Permeable Surface of the City', in J. Donat, ed., *World Architecture 1*, Studio Vista, London, 1964, pp. 194–202.

A.H.T. VERCRUYSSE, 'Het kinderhuis', in *Tijdschrift voor architectuur en beeldende kunsten*, March 1964, no. 7, pp. 161–163.

'Juryrapport meervoudige opdracht verleend door de Prof. dr. G. van der Leeuwstichting' (2 April 1964), in *Mededelingen Prof. dr. G. van der Leeuwstichting*, 1964, pp. 1182–1211.

'Zes "kerken in ontwerp"', jury report of a limited competition for the project of a church, organized by the Prof. dr. G. van der Leeuwstichting, in *Bouwkundig Weekblad*, 1964, no. 15, pp. 165–180.

Mr. A.J. D'AILLY, 'Geef Aldo van Eyck een speciale uitnodiging om aan de open prijsvraag deel te nemen', in *Het Vrije Volk*, 10 November 1964, p. 5.

1965

J. RYKWERT, Introduction to Van Eyck's 'Wheels of Heaven' project, in *Domus*, May 1965, no. 426.

J. VOELCKER, 'Team X', in *Arena*, June 1965, pp. 11–14.

J. SCHROFER, 'Een kwestie van verhoudingen', in *Bouwkundig Weekblad*, 18 June 1965, no. 12, pp. 213–217.

An., 'Van Eyck kerk', in *Architectural Review*, August 1965, no. 822, pp. 81–82.

J.A. WELLS-THORPE, 'Van Eyck Church', in *Architectural Review*, November 1965, no. 825, p. 318.

1966

R. VENTURI, *Complexity and contradiction in architecture*, Museum of Modern Art, New York 1966, pp. 14, 19, 84 and 86.

W. RÖLING, 'Rond en recht in harmonie – beeldenpaviljoen in Sonsbeek door Aldo van Eyck', in *Museumjournaal* 1966, no. 5, pp. 127–29.

H. HERTZBERGER, W. RÖLING, 'Aldo van Eyck 1966', in *Goed Wonen*, 1966, no. 8, pp. 11–15.

P. FIERZ, 'Die AIA/ACSA Konferenz in Cranbrook USA', in *Werk*, 1966, no. 8.

1967

G. BEKAERT, *In een of ander huis*, Lannoo, Tielt-The Hague, 1967, pp. 90–92.

J.H. MULDER, 'Op de drempel', public lecture at Amsterdam University, 8 November 1966, in *Bouw*, 4 February 1967.

Ch. SCHEEN, 'De Stedebouw en de Structuren', in *Delftse School*, 1967, no. 16.

M. VAN REGTEREN ALTENA-ZAHLE, 'Arkitekten Aldo van Eyck', in *Arkitekten* (Denmark), 1967, no. 6, pp. 133–137.

1968

L. VAN MARISSING, 'Aldo van Eyck: "Ik zeg wel eens: een stad is een droom"', in *de Volkskrant*, 9 March 1968.

1969

D. HIGHLANDS, 'The environmental spirit', in *Carnegie Magazine*, April 1969, no. 4, pp. 123–127.

'Meervoudige opdracht schetsontwerp nieuw stadhuis te Deventer', in *Bouwkundig Weekblad*, 1969, no. 18, pp. 393–412.

G. BEKAERT, 'De architectuur in Nederland aan de kunstgeschiedenis overgeleverd', in *TABK*, 1969, no. 15, pp. 373–381.

1970

L. VAN DEN BERGH, 'Aldo van Eyck: "Een kind is geen economisch kwantum; er wordt een minimum aan zorgen aan besteed." – Uit een duikelrek worden geen vlinders geboren', in *Vrij Nederland*, 27 June 1970.

P. BLOM, 'Aldo moet het worden', in *De Tijd*, 9 October 1970.

P. RESTANY, 'Dall'Olanda: una casa per una collezione – intervento di Aldo van Eyck in un edificio di Rietveld', in *Domus*, October 1970, pp.16–20.

L. SCHIMMELPENNINK, 'Het ontwerp van Van Eyck leent zich het best om uit te groeien tot een voor de buurt aanvaardbaar plan', in *TABK*, 1970, no. 22, pp. 517–519.

1971

R. BROUWERS, 'Woningbouw in de binnenstad van Zwolle door bureau Van Eyck & Bosch', in *TABK*, 1971, no. 22, pp. 554–560.

L. KAHN, Statements on Van Eyck in a conversation with R. Wemischner, 17 April 1971, in R.S. URMAN, ed., *What Will Be Has Always Been – The Words Of Louis Kahn*, Rizzoli, New York, 1986, p. 113.

1972

'Da vedere a Dusseldorf', in *Domus*, October 1972, no. 515, pp. 30–34.

W.G. OVERBOSCH, 'Aldo van Eycks Pastoor van Arskerk', in *Mededelingen Prof. dr. G. van der Leeuwstichting*, no. 43, Amsterdam 1972.

1973

Ch. JENCKS, *Modern Movements in Architecture*, Penguin, Harmondsworth 1973, pp. 311–318.

R. BROUWERS, 'Een mirakel in de Jordaan. Een plan voor de bouw van woningen en winkels van Aldo van Eyck, Theo Bosch, Lucien Lafour en G. Knemeijer', in *Wonen-TABK*, 1973, no. 1, pp. 9–21.

M. VAN ROOY, 'De bewoonbaarheid van Nederland hangt af van een lijstje telefoonnummers', in *NRC Handelsblad*, Cultural Supplement, 2 March 1973.

F. STRAUVEN, 'Symboliek in het werk van Charles Rennie Mackintosh', in *Wonen-TABK*, October 1973, no. 20, pp. 5–21.

1974

W. STOKVIS, *Cobra, geschiedenis, voorspel en betekenis van een beweging in de kunst van na de Tweede Wereldoorlog*, De Bezige Bij, Amsterdam 1974, pp. 114–123, 130 and passim.

A. SMITHSON, 'How to read and to recognize Mat Building', in *Architectural Design*, September 1974.

R. BROUWERS, 'Begint in Zwolle binnenstadsvictorie?', in *Wonen-TABK*, 1974, no. 22, pp. 1–3.

1975

B.B. TAYLOR, ed., 'Team 10+20', special issue of *L'Architecture d'Aujourd'hui*, January-February 1975, no. 177.

K. FRAMPTON, 'The Vicissitudes of Ideology', in *L'Architecture d'Aujourd'hui*, January-February 1975, no. 177, pp. XLIX-L, 66.

P. GONGGRIJP, 'Open brief aan Aldo van Eyck', in *B-nieuws* (Architecture Faculty newspaper, Technical University of Delft) 1975, no. 30, p. 532.

P. SMITHSON, 'Aldo van Eyck's church at the Hague', in *Architectural Design*, June 1975, no. 6, pp. 344–350.

A. SMITHSON, 'Team 10 at Royaumont', in *Architectural Design*, November 1975, pp. 664–689.

Ch. JENCKS, 'The Rise of Post Modern Architecture', in *Architectural Association Quarterly*, October-December 1975, pp. 3–9.

1976

A. LUCHINGER, 'Strukturalismus – eine neue Strömung in der Architektur', in *Bauen und Wohnen*, 1976, no. 1, pp. 5–11.

'Aldo van Eyck', in *Dortmunder Architekturheft* no. 3, (catalogue *Dortmunter Architekturausstellung*, 12 May – 7 June 1976), Dortmund, 1976, pp. 11–31.

P. L. NICOLIN, 'Aldo van Eyck: la trama e il labirinto – the web and the labyrint', in *Lotus International*, 1976, no. 1, pp. 105–108.

J. ROOS, 'Praten met Aldo van Eyck', in *Het Parool*, 11 November 1976.

T. NEELISSEN, *De vuurvogel*, NOS TV broadcast, prod. Max Appelboom, recorded in winter 1976–77.

O. BOHIGAS, 'Once Arquitectos', in *La Gaya Ciencia*, Barcelona 1976, pp. 227–252.

1977

O. BOHIGAS, 'Aldo van Eyck or a New Amsterdam School', in *Oppositions*, 1977, no. 9, pp. 21–36.

F. CORREA, 'Aldo van Eyck, una conversacion biografica', in *Arquitecturas bis*, November 1977, pp. 1, 17–21.

P. GONGGRIJP, 'Dank je wel Aldo', in *B-nieuws*, 1977, no. 27, pp. 638–639.

1978

J. JOEDICKE, 'Zur Entwicklung der heutigen Architektur', in *Bauen+Wohnen*, 1978, no. 7–8, pp. 269–274.

M. SCHIEDHELM, ed., 'Team 10 in Bonnieux' (1977), in *Deutsche Bauzeitung*, 1978, no. 11, special issue.

1979

J. DEN HOLLANDER, 'Moederhuis Amsterdam – kleurige toverbal als architectuurmanifest', in De Architect, April 1979, no. 4, pp. 78–83.

H. VAN DIJK, 'Vertrouwen op de regenboog', in *NRC Handelsblad*, Cultural Supplement, 20 April 1979, p. 3.

I. SALOMONS, 'Het "moederhuis" provocerend origineel', in *Het Parool*, 7 May 1979.

P. GOULET, 'Une bouffée d'air frais – Foyer pour des enfants et leurs mères', in *Architecture Intérieure*, November–December 1979, no. 147, pp. 121–124.

G. DE CARLO, 'Questioni – Questions', in *Spazio e società*, December 1979, no. 8, pp. 46–47.

1980

G.R. BLOMEYER & B. TIETZE, *In Opposition zur Moderne – Aktuelle Positionen in der Architektur*, Vieweg, Braunschweig 1980.

K. FRAMPTON, *Modern architecture; a critical history*, Thames & Hudson, London 1980, pp. 271–279.

A. LUCHINGER, *Structuralism in Architecture and Planning*, K. Krämer, Stuttgart 1980.

A.M. VOGT, *Architektur 1940–1980*, Propyläen, Munich 1980, pp. 72–73.

J. FURSE, 'Aldo van Eyck', in M. Emanuel, *Contemporary Architects*, Macmillan Press, London 1980, pp. 843–845.

J. TAYLOR, 'The Dutch Casbahs', in *Progressive Architecture*, March 1980, no. 3, pp. 86–96.

F. STRAUVEN, 'Plaats voor wederkerigheid', in *Wonen-TABK*, 1980, no. 8, pp. 11–32.

J. MAULE MCKEAN, 'Rainbow House', in *Building Design*, 13 June 1980, pp. 24–26.

U. BARBIERI, 'Labyrinth and Square. The architectural story of Aldo van Eyck', in *Dutch Art and Architecture Today*, 1980, no. 7, pp. 33–42.

J. DE HEER, K. VOLLEMANS, 'Postscriptum of Voorbij het laatste woord over de laatste stad (ook andere formaties kunnen dat)', in *Raster*, 1980, no. 12, pp. 129–145.

D. GRINBERG, 'Modernist Housing and its Critics', in *Harvard Architectural Review*, Spring 1980, pp. 147–159.

1981

J. VAN DE BEEK, ed., *Aldo van Eyck, projekten 1948–1961*, Academie van Bouwkunst, Groningen 1981.

P. BLUNDELL JONES, 'I'm just a hardboiled functionalist', in *Architects' Journal*, 18 February 1981, p. 293.

I. SALOMONS, 'Prof. Aldo van Eyck verknipt het Stopera-plan: "Niet te laat om te luisteren"', in *Het Parool*, 21 April 1981.

F. STRAUVEN, 'A place for reciprocity: home for one parent families' in *Lotus International*, 1981, no. 28, pp. 20–40.

A.M. VOGT, 'Mutmassungen über Aldo van Eyck', in *Archithese*, 1981, no. 5, pp. 31–32.

P. KEMPTER, 'Haus für alleinstehende Mütter', *ibidem*, pp. 39–40.

I. SALOMONS, 'Het moederhuis: licht en ruimte', in *Forum*, July 1981 (1980–81, no. 3), pp. 20–24.

I. SALOMONS, 'Amsterdams Stoperaverdriet', *Ibidem*, pp. 10–17.

G. BROADBENT, 'The Pests strike back', in *RIBA Journal*, November 1981, pp. 31–34.

1982

H. HERTZBERGER, A. VAN ROIJEN-WORTMAN, F. STRAUVEN, *Aldo van Eyck*, Stichting Wonen, Amsterdam, 1982.

W. CURTIS, *Modern Architecture since 1900*, Phaidon, Oxford, 1982, pp. 290–291, 347–348.

A. SMITHSON, ed., *The Emergence of Team 10 out of CIAM: Documents*, London, 1982.

D. J. TELTSCHER, *Team 10's Contribution to the Idea of Community*, Master Thesis, M.I.T, Cambridge, Mass., 1982.

S. FRANK, 'van Eyck, Aldo', in A.K. Placzek, ed., *Macmillan Encyclopedia of Architects*, vol. 4, Collier Macmillan, New York and London, 1982, pp. 283–284.

H. HERTZBERGER, 'Het 20ste-eeuwse mechanisme en de architectuur van Aldo van Eyck', in *Wonen-TABK*, 1982, no. 2, pp. 10–19. English and Italian translations in *Spazio e Società*, December 1983, no. 24, pp. 80–97.

R. BROUWERS, 'Moderne Beweging zet met Van Eyck in Finland de tegenaanval in', in *Wonen-TABK*, 1982, no. 22, pp. 2–3.

P. BUCHANAN, 'Mothers' house, Amsterdam', in *Architectural Review*, March 1982, no. 1021, pp. 23–33.

S. DOUBILET, 'Weaving chaos into order', in *Progressive Architecture*, March 1982, pp. 74–77.

1983

J. VAN DE BEEK, ed., *Aldo van Eyck, projekten 1962–1976*, Academie van Bouwkunst, Groningen 1983.

H. VAN DIJK, 'Forum', in *Architectuur en Planning – Nederland 1940–1980*, 010 Publishers, Rotterdam, 1983, pp. 146–165.

E. BOESCH-HUTTER, 'Aldo van Eyck: Turmzimmer, 1946', in *Archithese* 1983, no. 1, pp. 25–26.

J. VAN GEEST, 'Assaulting grimness', in collected documentation for the Van Eyck exhibition in the Athens National Museum, 1983. Dutch version, 'Een roepende in de polder', in *Forum*, 1983, no. 3, pp. 9–16.

G. CANDILIS, S. & D. ANTONAKAKIS, G. DE CARLO, contributions on A. van Eyck, in collected documentation for the Van Eyck exhibition in the Athens National Museum, September 1983.

1984

H. KLOTZ, *Moderne und Postmoderne – Architektur der Gegenwart 1960–1980*, Vieweg, Braunschweig 1984.

TH. NOVIANT, *Une Eglise catholique à La Haye*, dissertation Unité Pédagogique 8, Paris, 1984.

H.M. TROMP, 'The essential architect: Aldo van Eyck', in *Holland Herald*, 1984, no. 4, pp. 14–22.

C. MATHEWSON, 'Multiple Meaning in Equipoise', in *Dichotomy* (Detroit Students' Journal), 1984, no. 1, pp. 1–15.

C. MATHEWSON, 'Defining Space as the Appreciation of Space Entered', in *Dichotomy* (Detroit Students' Journal), 1984, no. 2, pp. 33–61.

1985

L. DOUMATO, *Aldo van Eyck*, Vance Bibliographies, Monticello, Ill., 1985.

F. STRAUVEN, 'Aldo van Eyck als ontwerpleraar', in *Wonen-TABK*, 1985, no. 1, pp. 19–24.

P. BUCHANAN, 'Aldo van Eyck – New Amsterdam School', in *Architectural Review*, 1985, no. 1, pp. 14–17.

O. LASER, E. VARGAS, 'Ein Grundriss ist keine Autobahn', in *Arch+*, 1985, no. 1, pp. 56–60.

I. SCHEIN, 'Amsterdam: Renaissance de Nieuwmarkt', in *Techniques et Architecture*, April-May 1985, pp. 72–83.

C. MATHEWSON, 'The Architecture of Aldo van Eyck', in *Crit*, Summer 1985, no. 15, pp. 54–64; shortened reprint under the title 'The Defining of Space as a Design Objective', in *Crit*, fall 1989, no. 23, pp. 58–62.

'The Netherlands: Paradise of Modern Architecture', in *Space Design*, August 1985, no. 251, pp. 5–64.

A. SCHIMMERLING, 'Amsterdam, modestie et audace – note sur la rénovation des quartiers Nieuwmarkt et Jordaan', in *le carré bleu*, 1985, no. 3–4, pp. 7–16.

V. GREGOTTI, 'Un amico indisciplinato' – 'A rebellious friend', in *Casabella*, October 1985, no. 517, p. 6.

S. BRANDOLINI, 'La semplicità dell'avanguardia' – 'The simplicity of the avant garde', in *Casabella*, October 1985, no. 517, pp. 16–18.

Questions (CERAA, Brussel), October 1985, no. 7, special edition on Amsterdam and A. van Eyck, with contributions by B. Vellut, R. Matthu and F. Parmentier.

B. BAINES, 'La quadrature de Aldo', in *Parallèles*, no. 2 (supplement to *Questions*, no. 7), October 1985, pp. 16–21.

J. BURNEY, 'Taking a leap in the dark', in *Building Design*, 25 October 1985, p. 5.

C. MAGNANI, 'Il Concorso dello IACP di Venezia per Campo di Marte alla Giudecca', in *Casabella*, November 1985, no. 518, pp. 5–16.

I. FRANCE, 'Hubertusvereniging: a transition point for single parents', in *Women and Environments*, Winter 1985, no. 1, pp. 20–22.

1986

Niet om het even – wel evenwaardig, van en over Aldo van Eyck, Festschrift on the occasion of Van Eyck being rewarded the 1982 Rotterdam-Maaskantprijs, Van Gennep, Amsterdam 1986; including numerous contributions by Van Eyck himself and 26 interviews by F. Strauven, namely with Felix Schwarz, Richard P. Lohse, Hein Salomonson, Jan Rietveld, Constant, Corneille, Alechinsky, Tajiri, Carel Visser, Dick Cassée, Peter Schat, Martin Visser, Georges Candilis, Peter Smithson, Piet Blom, Joop van Stigt, Jan Verhoeven, Herman Hertzberger, Theo Bosch, Lucien Lafour, Pjotr Gonggrijp, Gerrit Smienk, Joseph Rykwert, Yap Hong Seng, Hannie van Eyck and Jaap Hillenius.

Redisegnare Venezia: diece progetti di concorso per la riconstruzione di Campo di Marte alla Giudecca, Marsilio, Venezia, 1986.

L. LEFAIVRE, 'Order in the Children's Home', in *Forum*, 1986 (31), no. 1, pp. 3–7 (with Dutch translation).

P. BLUNDELL JONES, 'Modernism betrayed' (report on Van Eyck's Tanner lectures in Cambridge on 21 and 22 April 1986), in *Architects' Journal*, 7 May 1986, pp. 24–25.

B. HATTON, 'The Flying Dutchman' (report on Van Eyck's Tanner lectures in Cambridge), in *Building Design*, 9 May 1986, p. 2.

1987

F. STRAUVEN, *Het Burgerweeshuis van Aldo van Eyck, een modern monument*, Amsterdam 1987.

H. HERTZBERGER, *Bewaar het weeshuis*, protest newspaper demanding preservation of the Municipal Orphanage, with contributions from all over the world, Amsterdam 1987.

H. HERTZBERGER, 'SOS per l'orfanotrofio di Aldo van Eyck', in *Casabella*, April 1987, pp. 32–34.

J. BAKKER, 'Aldo Van Eyck on His Work', in *Canadian Architect*, August 1987, no. 8, pp. 32–33.

1988

A. VAN DER WOUD, 'Niet om het even...wel evenwaardig', in *Archis*, January 1988, no. 1, p. 54.

P. BUCHANAN, 'Nederlandse architectuur is spoor bijster', in *Architectuur/Bouwen*, June-July 1988, pp. 63–67.

G. BEKAERT, 'Entre pragmatisme et radicalisme, une tradition moderne à la fois solide et mouvante', in *L'Architecture d'Aujourd'hui*, July 1988, no. 257, pp. 96–105.

I. SALOMONS, 'Architectuur van ongekende dimensies' (on Estec), in *Het Parool*, 11 August 1988.

F. CORREA, 'Le Tercera Generación (II)', in *El Croquis*, November 1988, no. 36, pp. 4–13.

1989

H. VAN DIJK, 'The demise of structuralism', in *Architecture in the Netherlands-Yearbook 1988–1989*, Deventer 1989.

I. SALOMONS, 'Estec under construction' in *Architecture in the Netherlands – Yearbook 1988–1989*, Deventer 1989.

J. DE HEER, 'Het centrumloze labyrint', in *Oase*, 1989, no. 23, pp. 10–21.

J. VAN DE BEEK, reply to De Heer in *Oase*, 1989, no. 25, pp. 22–23.

E. MIK, 'Aldo van Eyck: ruimte moet blijmoedig zijn', interview in *De Tijd*, 3 March 1989, pp. 30–36.

H. SELIER, 'Berlage Instituut in Burgerweeshuis', interview with H. Hertzberger, in *De Architect*, October 1989, pp. 46–49.

W. VAN HEUVEL, 'Formes, Textures, Couleurs', in *Techniques et Architecture*, October 1989, pp. 99–101.

J.B. KLASTER, 'Het lastige geweten van de architectuur', in *Het Parool, Kunst*, 4 November 1989, p. 1.

I. SALOMONS, 'Gebouwde ruimte veelzijdig als leven zelf', *ibidem*, p. 3.

F. STRAUVEN, 'Aldo van Eyck: An outline of his ideas, the meaning of his work', in catalogue newspaper for the exhibition 'Aldo van Eyck in de Beurs van Berlage', Amsterdam, November 1989.

P. BUCHANAN, 'Architect Ludens – The architecture of Aldo and Hannie van Eyck', in *Aldo en Hannie van Eyck: recent werk*, Beurs van Berlage, Amsterdam 1989, pp. 3–14 (with Dutch translation); and in *Architectural Review*, February 1990, no. 1116, pp. 35–57.

L. LEFAIVRE & A. TZONIS, 'Dragon in the Dunes', in *Aldo en Hannie van Eyck: recent werk*, Beurs van Berlage, Amsterdam 1989, pp. 22–26, with Dutch translation; French version in *le carré bleu*, 1990 no. 1. Spanish version in *Arquitectura viva*, September – October 1990, pp. 42–44. Also reprinted in *A + U*, April 1991, no. 247, pp. 68–74.

M. VAN ROOY, 'Klein dak of grote hoed', in *NRC Handelsblad, Cultureel Supplement*, 17 November 1989, p. 9.

M. DE BOER, L. DE CARLO & E. MASOERO, 'I nuovi edifici dell'Estec', in *Spazio e Società*, July-December 1989, pp. 8–27.

E. KOSTER, 'Alternatief functionalisme in low-tech en barok' (about ESTEC and Padua), in *De Architect*, December 1989, pp. 42–54.

H. VAN DIJK, 'De bal opnieuw geworpen', in *Archis*, December 1989, no. 12, pp. 12–14.

1990

'Verbeelde Orde', *Oase*, 1990 no. 26–27, special edition on Aldo van Eyck, with contributions by G. Hoving, E. Terlouw, H. Engel, E. van Velzen and J. Meuwissen.

H. ENGEL, 'Het verlangen naar stijl – Tussen de biologie van een rechthoek en de geometrie van een kreeft', in *Oase*, 1990 no. 26–27, pp. 26–45.

E. TERLOUW, 'Le musée imaginaire – Het verhaal van een andere gedachte', in *Oase*, 1990 no. 26–27, pp. 6–25.

E. VAN VELZEN, 'De parallelle stad – Aspecten van het stedebouwkundig werk van Aldo van Eyck', in *Oase*, 1990 no. 26–27, pp. 46–63.

J. MOLENAAR, 'Architectuur achter de zintuigen van de waarnemer – ESTEC en Padua, twee nieuwe werken van Aldo en Hannie van Eyck', in *Archis*, 1990, no. 1, pp. 32–41.

P. BUCHANAN, 'Forum Fellowship', *Architectural Review*, February 1990, no. 1116, special edition on recent work by A. & H. van Eyck, H. Hertzberger, Th. Bosch, P. de Ley, L. Lafour and R. Wijk.

H. SLAWIK, 'Het Burgerweeshuis', in *Deutsche Bauzeitung*, February 1990, no. 2, pp. 84–88.

C. MATHEWSON, 'Europäisches Raumfahrtzentrum ESTEC', in *Bauwelt*, 9 March 1990, p. 415.

'Van Eyck takes the Gold Medal', in *Architects' Journal*, 21 March 1990, no. 12, pp. 9–10.

'Royal Gold Medal for Aldo van Eyck', in RIBA *Journal*, April 1990, p. 7.

V. VISCONTI, 'Diabolico Maestro', in *L'Architettura*, April 1990, pp. 314–318.

J. WELSH, 'Gold Standard', in *Building Design*, 22 June 1990, pp. 20–24.

J. WELSH, 'Slings and arrows', in *Building Design*, 29 June 1990, p. 2.

P. DE SANTIS, 'La trasparenza', in *Dossier di Urbanistica e Cultura del Territorio*, Maggioli, Rimini, June 1990, pp. 40–42.

'Van Eyck slams the profession', in *Architects' Journal*, 4 July 1990, p. 13.

D. SHARP, 'Holland's Bright Star', in *World Architecture*, September 1990, vol. 2, no. 4, p. 92.

1991

H. HERTZBERGER, *Lessons for Students in Architecture,* 010 Publishers, Rotterdam, 1991, pp. 126–128.

A. SMITHSON, ed., *Team 10 Meetings: 1953–1984*, Rizzoli, New York, 1991.

A. CIRÉ & H. OCHS, eds., *Die Zeitschrift als manifest*, Birkhäuser, Basel, 1991, pp. 184–190.

E. VAN VELZEN, 'De restauratie van het Burgerweeshuis', in *Archis*, 1991, no. 5, pp. 2–3.

1992

W.J. VAN HEUVEL, *Structuralisme in de Nederlandse Architectuur*, 010, Rotterdam, 1992.

Aldo en Hannie van Eyck met Karel Appel in Middelburg, brochure published for presentation of the project Centrum Beeldende Kunst Middelburg, with contributions by Appel, Van Eyck and I. Salomons, Middelburg, May 1992.

J. SHACK, 'Color in Architecture', in *The Structurist*, 1991–92, no. 31–32, pp. 109–115.

C. DAVIES, 'Window to another world', in *Architectural Review*, April 1992, no. 1142, pp. 46–50.

E. VAN VELZEN, 'Een cultureel centrum voor Middelburg', in *Archis*, 1992, no. 5, pp. 10–11.

S. LEBESQUE, 'Rietveld, Van Eyck, Koolhaas' in *Vrij Nederland*, 28 November 1992, pp. 56–58.

H. VAN BERGEIJK, 'Architectuur van bewustwording', in *De Architect,* December 1992, no. 12, pp. 52–61.

J. BOSMAN, 'CIAM after the War: a Balance of the Modern Movement', in *Rassegna*, December 1992, no. 52, pp. 6–21.

F. STRAUVEN, 'The Dutch Contribution: Bakema and Van Eyck', in *Rassegna*, December 1992, no. 52, pp. 48–57.

B. HOUZELLE, 'L'île Souterraine, Eglise moluque, Deventer', in *Techniques et Architecture*, December 1992 – Jan 1993, pp. 64–65.

1993

J. BUCH, *Een eeuw Nederlandse architectuur 1880–1990*, NAi Publishers, Rotterdam, 1993, pp. 303–316, 323–25; English version, *A Century of Architecture in the Netherlands 1880–1990,* NAi Publishers, Rotterdam, 1994.

P. DE SANTIS, *Aldo van Eyck*, dissertation, Università La Sapienza, Rome, 1993.

J.R. PRATLEY, *Relativity and Architecture*, dissertation, Plymouth School of Architecture, Plymouth, 1993.

H. VAN DIJK, 'Laugier's garden', in *Architecture in the Netherlands – Yearbook 1992–1993,* NAi, Rotterdam, 1993, pp. 58–59.

P. FAWCETT, 'van Eyck, Aldo', in R.J. Van Vynckt, ed., *International Dictionary of Architects and Architecture*, vol. 1, St. James Press, Detroit and London, 1993, pp. 932–934.

F. STRAUVEN, 'Shifting Symmetry', in *Archis*, Febr. 1993, no. 2, pp. 17–25.

M. PAWLEY, 'Money, time and details', in *World Architecture*, March 1993, no. 22, pp. 22–23.

S. BRANDOLINI, 'Passionate Practitioner', in *World Architecture*, March 1993, no. 22, pp. 24–27.

P. PRAGNELL, 'Cerchi magici e foreste incantate'–'The extraordinary familiarity of ESTEC' in *Spazio e Società*, January-March 1993, pp. 18–27.

J. BOSMAN, 'CIAM en de naoorlogse moderne architectuur', in *de Architect,* 1993, no. 4, pp. 30–43; German version in *Werk, Bauen+Wohen*, April 1993.

S. BRANDOLINI, 'La chiesa blu di Deventer di Aldo van Eyck', in *Casabella*, October 1993, no. 605, pp. 60–70.

M. CASCIATO, 'Forum: architettura e cultura nei primi anni sessanta', in *Casabella*, November 1993, no. 606, pp. 48–53, 69–70.

1994

F. STRAUVEN, *Aldo van Eyck – relativiteit en verbeelding,* Meulenhoff, Amsterdam 1994.

A. LUCHINGER, 'Aldo van Eyck', in M. Emanuel, ed., *Contemporary Architects*, 3rd edition, St. James Press, New York and London, 1994, pp. 993–995.

M. MAAS, 'De kasbah valt aan diggelen', in *De Volkskrant*, 18 Febr. 1994, p. 5.

W. VAN HEUVEL, 'Aldo de vuurvogel', in *Cobouw*, 15 March 1994, p. 13.

M. VAN ROOY, 'Haal de regenboog', in *NRC Handelsblad*, 1 April 1994, Cultural Supplement, p. 5.

H. HEYNEN, 'Poëzie van het bouwen', in *De Standaard*, 30 April/1 May 1994, p. 4.

G. BEKAERT, 'Aldo van Eyck, poète et "structuraliste"', in *L'Architecture d'Aujourd'hui*, June 1994, no. 293, pp. 24–25.

C. BOEKRAAD, 'het verhaal van een andere gedachte', in *Architectuur/Bouwen*, 1994, no. 6–7, pp. 14–17.

F. STRAUVEN, 'Aldo van Eyck *1918', in *Baumeister*, 1994, no. 11, pp. 20–23.

1995

C. ST JOHN WILSON, *The Other Tradition of Modern Architecture: The Uncompleted Project*, Academy Editions, London, 1995.

W. RÖLING, 'Aldo van Eyck – relativiteit en verbeelding', in *Amsterdamse Boekengids*, January 1995, no. 1, pp. 30–32.

1996

F. STRAUVEN, *Aldo van Eyck's Orphanage – A Modern Monument*, NAi, Rotterdam 1996; with an introduction by Herman Hertzberger.

F. STRAUVEN, 'L'orphelinat d'Aldo van Eyck – un monument moderne' in *eaV (Revue de l'Ecole d'architecture de Versailles)*, 1996, no. 2, pp. 68–81.

B. STRUIJK, *Van Burgerweeshuis tot Garden Court*, BeAver Communication Support, Ede, 1996.

1997

I. SALOMONS, *Met kleur gebouwd – De Algemene Rekenkamer in Den Haag*, Rijksgebouwendienst, Den Haag 1997.

D.L. JOHNSON & D. LANGMEAD, *Makers of 20th Century Modern Architecture*, Greenwood Press, Westwood, CT, 1997, pp. 94–97.

H. VAN DIJK, 'Ultimos magisterios, Aldo van Eyck, Herman Hertzberger y Rem Koolhaas', in *Arquitectura Viva*, May–June 1997, pp. 27–31.

J.-C. GIRARD & M. BAERTSCHI, *Aldo van Eyck, Eglise du Pasteur van Ars à La Haye*, dissertation Ecole Polytechnique Fédérale de Lausanne, September 1977.

B. COLENBRANDER, 'A tradition resumed – rethinking Aldo van Eyck', in *Archis*, November 1997, no. 11, pp. 42–49.

C. GRAFE, 'Configuratie van versmolten ruimtes', in *De Architect*, December 1997, pp. 60–69.

1998

F. STRAUVEN, *Aldo van Eyck – the Shape of Relativity*, Architectura & Natura, Amsterdam 1998.

'Aldo van Eyck', *Kunstschrift*, 1998, no. 1, special issue, with contributions by M. Haveman, L. Oosterbaan & E. van Uitert, B. Hulsman, W. Denslagen and M. Van Rooy.

'Aldo van Eyck', in *20 Jaar Rotterdam-Maaskantprijs*, Stichting Rotterdam-Maaskant, Rotterdam, 1998, pp. 34–37.

O. BOUMAN, 'The General Chamber of Audit as an arena of colliding visions', in *Archis*, February 1998, no. 2, pp. 18–29.

H. ENGEL, 'The irritant principle of renewal', in *Archis*, February 1998, no. 2, pp. 26–30.

E. TAVERNE, 'Vicissitudes', in *Archis*, 1998, no. 3, p. 61.

H. VAN DIJK, 'Eighty years of avant-garde. What now?', in *Archis*, 1998, no. 3, pp. 74–75.

G. GINEX, 'Van Eyck in Olanda', in *Domus*, July–August 1998, p. 120.

M. VAN ROOY, 'Built with colour – The General Audit Office in the Hague', in *World Architecture*, September 1998, p. 85.

R. PEREZ DE ARCE ANTONCICH, 'Ecos del Team Ten', in *ARQ*, 1998, no. 11, pp. 36–41.

S. VON MOOS, 'Baukunst und "Infant Joy"', in *Neue Zürcher Zeitung*, 31 October/1 November 1998, no. 253, p. 49.

J. BOSMAN, 'Eyck, Aldo van', in V. M. Lampugnami, ed., *Lexikon der Architektur des 20. Jahrhunderts*, Gerd Hatje, Ostfildern-Ruit, 1998, p. 102.

1999

V. LIGTELIJN, ed., *Aldo van Eyck, Works*, Birkhäuser, Basel/Boston/Berlin, 1999; with introductory articles by V. Ligtelijn, P. Smithson, H. Hertzberger, H. Engel and F. Strauven; simultaneously published in a Dutch and a German version..

L. LEFAIVRE & A. TZONIS, *Aldo van Eyck, Humanist Rebel, Inbetweening in a Post-War World*, 010 Publishers, Rotterdam, 1999.

W. WILMS FLOET, 'Burgerweeshuis, Amsterdam', in U. Barbieri and L. van Duin, eds., *Honderd jaar Nederlandse Architectuur 1901–2000*, SUN, Nijmegen, 1999, pp. 247–256.

M. KOURNIATI, 'Team X Primer 1954–1962 : la narration de l'expérience d'un groupe', in *Villes, espaces et territoires : travaux de l'EHESS 1999*. Paris : EHESS, Programme de recherches interdisciplinaires « Études urbaines », 1999, pp. 12–23.

M. RICHARDSON, 'Aldo van Eyck, 1918–1999', in *Architects' Journal*, 21 January 1999, pp. 20–21.

F. STRAUVEN, 'Aldo van Eyck', obituary, in *The Independent*, 21 January 1999.

S. VON MOOS, 'Aldo van Eyck, 1918–1999', in *Archithese*, 1999, no. 1, pp. 72–73.

R. ROOS, 'Aldo van Eyck 1918–1999', in Trouw, 16 January 1999; with testimonials by R. Koolhaas and H. Hertzberger.

L. FERNÁNDEZ-GALIANO, 'El laberinto y la vida', in *Arquitectura Viva*, January-February 1999, p. 112.

A. LÜCHINGER, 'Architekt einer humanen und poetischen Baukunst', in *Schweizer Ingenieur & Architekt*, 19 February 1999, pp. 4–7.

P. BUCHANAN, 'Aldo van Eyck, 1918–1999', in *Architectural Review*, March 1999, p. 15.

M. EMERY, 'Aldo van Eyck, 1918–1999', in *L'Architecture d'Aujourd'hui,* March 1999, p. 18.

M. SPENS, 'Aldo Van Eyck: The Shape of Relativity', in *Architectural Design*, March-April 1999, no. 3–4, p. 14.

H. HERTZBERGER, 'Die kaleidoskopische Idee', in *Werk, Bauen + Wohnen*, 1999, no. 5, pp. 56–57.

J. WELSH, 'Life after death', in *World Architecture*, May 1999, pp. 38–39; and in *RIBA Journal*, May 1999, no. 5, pp. 12–13.

R. MATTHU, 'In memoriam Aldo van Eyck', in *Aplus* (Brussels), April-May 1999, no. 157, pp. 30–31.

R. MATTHU and F. STRAUVEN, 'Aldo van Eyck, dichter onder de architecten' – 'Aldo van Eyck, poète parmi les architectes' in *Aplus* (Brussels) June-July 1999, no. 158, special issue.

A. CUNNINGHAM, 'Aldo van Eyck 1918–1999', in *Docomomo*, June 1999, p. 5.

T. SCHMIEDEKNECHT, 'Projected Space and Labyrinthine Clarity', in *Architectural Design*, 1999, no. 7–8, pp. 98–100.

I. CURULLI, 'Come, Quanto, Quale Blu?', in *Spazio e Società*, July-September 1999, pp. 24–33.

L. LEFAIVRE, 'Rebel with a cause', in *Architecture* (N.Y.), September 1999, p. 81.

L. LEFAIVRE & A. TZONIS, 'Aldo van Eyck, humaniste révolté', in *AMC*, September 1999, pp. 60–67.

V. LIGTELIJN, ed., *Aldo & Hannie van Eyck – The Ball I threw*, catalogue newspaper for the exhibition 'Aldo & Hannie van Eyck' at the 4a Bienal Internacional de Arquitetura in São Paulo, 19 November 1999 – 25 January 2000.

V. LIGTELIJN, 'Aldo van Eyck e seu estilo', in *4a Bienal Internacional de Arquitetura de São Paulo*, São Paulo, 1999, pp. 32–33.

A. GOZAK, 'The rainbow is my favourite colour', in Architektyrni Vestnik (Moscow), 1999, no. 50, pp. 48–52.

2000

E. MUMFORD, *The CIAM Discourse on Urbanism, 1928–1960*, MIT Press, Cambridge, Mass., 2000.

H. HERTZBERGER, *Space and the Architect – Lessons in Architecture 2*, 010 Publishers, Rotterdam, 2000, pp. 198–199.

C. VAN HOUTS, *Karel Appel*, Contact, Amsterdam/Antwerpen, pp. 110–113, 128–129, 143–157, 160–162.

W. WANG, 'Orphanage', in K. Frampton, ed., *World Architecture, a Critical Mosaic 1900–2000*, vol. 3, China Architecture and Building Press – Springer Verlag, Vienna, 2000, pp. 166–167.

N. CHASIN, 'He's Been With the World: Aldo Van Eyck's Ethnographic Gambit', in *Architecture and Ideas (AI)*, 2000, no. 1, pp. 24–41.

G. OLIVER, 'Aldo van Eyck – Works', in *Architectural Research Quarterly* (Cambridge), 2000, no. 2, pp. 185–187.

W. PEHNT, 'Auf der Schwelle zwischen Haus und Stadt', in *Frankfurter Allgemeine Zeitung*, 5 May 2000.

M. SCIMEMI, 'Peruvians make Lima', in *Architektur Aktuell*, September 2000, pp. 102–104.

R. SKINNER, 'Dutch Treat – The Van Eycks in New Zealand', in *Formulation Fabrication – The Architecture of History*, proceedings of the 17th annual conference of the Society of Architectural Historians, Australia and New Zealand, Wellington, 2000, pp. 287–296.

2001

A. PEDRET, *CIAM and the Emergence of Team 10 Thinking, 1945–1959*, PhD dissertation, MIT, Cambridge, Mass., 2001.

H. SARKIS, ed., Le Corbusier's Venice Hospital and the Mat Building Revival, Prestel, Munich/New York, 2001; with contributions by P. Allard and E. Mumford.

C. VERMEULEN & A. WILDRO, *Analyse en in situ onderzoek van de speelplaatsen van Aldo van Eyck in Amsterdam 1947–1978*, dissertation Gent University, Ghent 2001.

V. LIGTELIJN, 'Aldo van Eyck and the configurative process', in *The Architecture Annual 1999–2000, Delft University of Technology,* 2001, pp. 172–180.

2002

G. GINEX, *Aldo van Eyck – L'enigma della forma*, Testo & imagine, Universale di Architettura, Rome, 2002.

L. LEFAIVRE & I. DE ROODE, eds., *Aldo van Eyck: the playgrounds and the City,* Stedelijk Museum, Amsterdam, 2002; with contributions by R. Fuchs, L. Karsten, L. Lefaivre, A. Novak, I. de Roode, E. Schmitz and F. Strauven.

L. LEFAIVRE, M. BOTERMAN, S. LOEN & M. MIEDEMA, 'A psychogeographical bicycle tour of Aldo van Eyck's Amsterdam playgrounds', in *Archis,* 2002, no. 3, pp. 129–135.

R. DETTINGMEIJER, 'De kerk uit het midden: van godshuis tot "een of ander huis"', in *Bulletin Koninklijke Nederlandse Oudheidkundige Bond,* 2000, no. 1, pp. 1–15.

R. OXMAN, H. SHADAR & E. BELFERMAN, 'Casbah: a brief history of a design concept', in *ARQ,* 2002, no. 4, pp. 321–336.

F. STRAUVEN, 'Aldo van Eyck – Modern Architecture and Dogon Culture', in *Lotus international,* September 2002, no. 114, pp. 120–131.

2003

P. DE SANTIS, *Aldo van Eyck: scritti e architettura*, Florence, 2003.

R. MCCARTER, 'Louis I. Kahn and Aldo van Eyck: Parallels in the other tradition of modern architecture', in *PTAH,* 2003, no. 2, pp. 3–14.

A. COCCO & E. FOULON, 'Les mutations de l'orphelinat d'Aldo van Eyck', *Le Visiteur,* Spring 2003, pp. 30–47.

H. PLUMMER, 'Aldo van Eyck, Roman Catholic Church', in *Architecture and Urbanism,* November 2003, pp. 268–271.

2004

F. STRAUVEN, 'Aldo van Eyck', in G. Postiglione, ed., *One Hundred Houses for One Hundred European Architects of the Twentieth Century*, Taschen, Keulen, 2004, pp. 112–115.

N. CHASIN, 'van Eyck, Aldo', in *Encyclopedia of 20th-Century Architecture*, Fitzroy Dearnborn, New York and London, 2004. Vol 1, pp. 428–430.

M. VERBEECK, *De vormgeving van het aantal in de stedenbouw – het configuratieve denken van Aldo van Eyck en Piet Blom, een wisselwerking*, dissertation Gent University, Ghent 2004.

2005

N. COLEMAN, *Utopias and Architecture*, Routledge, London/New York, 2005, pp. 196–256.

R. MCCARTER, *Louis I Kahn*, Phaidon, London/New York, 2005, pp. 217–219, 425–426,

C. SECCI, *La notion d'identité chez les architectes du Team 10 (1947–1962)*, Ph.D. dissertation, Paris 8 University, Paris, 2005.

M. RISSELADA & D. VAN DEN HEUVEL, *Team 10 (1954–1981) – in search of a Utopia of the Present*, NAi Publishers, Rotterdam, 2005; with contributions (related to Van Eyck) by J. Bosman, M. C. Boyer, G. Damiani, K. Frampton, V. Ligtelijn, L. Molinari, F. Strauven and C. Tuscano.

L. LEFAIVRE, 'Puer ludens', in *Lotus international*, 2005, no. 124, pp. 72–85.

2006

B. B. TAYLOR, 'Aldo van Eyck, Nikolaas Habraken et le débat sur l'habitat', in J.-L. BONILLO, C. MASSU, D. PINSON, *La modernité critique. Autour du CIAM 9 d'Aix-en-Provence 1953*, Imbernon, Marseille, 2006, pp. 181–190.

A.P. DE OLIVEIRA LEPORI, *El Taller de Proyectos como Laboratorio: Memoria y Lugar*, Ph. D. dissertation, Universidad Politecnica de Cataluña, 2006.

K. JASCHKE, 'Mythopoesis of Place and Culture: Aldo van Eyck, Herman Haan, and the Dogon', in *Team 10 – Keeping the language of Modern Architecture Alive*, Proceedings of a Conference organized by the Faculty of Architecture Delft University of Technology, 5–6 January 2006, Delft 2007.

A. BETSKY, 'Het dwaalhof, Sonsbeekpaviljoen Aldo van Eyck', in *Bouw*, 2006, no. 5, pp. 12–14.

A. BOKERN, 'Labyrinthische Klarheit', in *Werk, Bauen + Wohnen*, 2006, no. 6, pp. 74–75.

M. KOURNIATI, 'Team 10 1953 – 1981. In Search of A Utopia of the Present', in *Les Cahiers du Musée National d'art Moderne*, October 2006, no. 97, pp. 99–101.

2007

R. LABRUNYE, 'La réception d'une icône de l'architecture « autre » : l'orphelinat d'Aldo van Eyck', in *fabricA*, Landrhaus, Ecole d'architecture de Versailles, 2007, no. 1, pp. 7–29.

Acknowledgements

While preparing this publication we encountered considerable support and often direct help from various individuals and organizations, to whom we would like to express our gratitude.

Our thanks are due in the first place to Mrs. Hannie van Eyck, the architect's widow, who gave us unlimited access to her archives, and entrusted us with the copyright of Van Eyck's texts; and to Mrs. Tess Van Eyck-Wickham, the architect's daughter, who supported our project from the outset and provided precious inside information.

We also met with much sympathy and support in our respective academic communities, notably from Bart Verschaffel, head of the Department of Architecture & Urban Planning at Ghent University, and Max Risselada, head of the architectural analysis section of the Architecture Faculty at Delft Technical University. The team of typists the latter put at our disposal was of considerable help in the initial stage of our project.

Research was carried out in several libraries and collections, especially at Delft Technical University, the Netherlands Architectural Institute in Rotterdam and the Canadian Centre for Architecture in Montreal. Our appreciation goes to the staff of these institutions, in particular to Chris Smeenk, former head of the Delft Architecture Faculty Library, to Mariet Willinge, head of the NAi collections and Christel Leenen, head of the NAi library, to Mirko Zardini, director of the CCA and Renata Gutman, head of the CCA library.

In addition to documents from the Van Eyck archive we included some texts from other sources. We express our thanks to Andres Giedion for allowing us to publish some letters by Van Eyck to his parents; and to Clelia Tuscano and Richard Murphy for agreeing with the republication of the interviews they made in 1991 and 1993, respectively.

We owe special thanks to Gregory Ball who meticulously checked Van Eyck's English texts and conscientiously translated his Dutch ones. He also made the final editing of the introductions and notes. We extend our thanks to Eleni Gigantes who friendly took on additional editing of numerous fragments.

We are also grateful to a number of friends and scholars who willingly helped to complete our historical information, and to trace the origins of the quotes which punctuate Van Eyck's texts, notably Arnaud Dercelles (curator of the Fondation Le Corbusier in Paris), Bruno Maurer (curator of the Giedion Archives at the Zurich ETH), Marijke Küper (with respect to Rietveld), Evert van Straaten (as to Van Doesburg), Jonneke Jobse (with respect to Baljeu and *Structure*), Jeroen Schilt (as to Architectura et Amicitia), Herman Hertzberger (on the *Forum* period), Pjotr Gonggrijp, Michiel Polak and Izak Salomons (concerning the early Delft period).

The illustrations were drawn in the first place from the Van Eyck archive, but in addition we could rely on some friends, colleagues and institutions for completing our visual material. We extend our thanks to Max Risselada and Dirk van den Heuvel, who kindly allowed us to reproduce a considerable number of images published in their *Team 10 – in search of a Utopia of the present,* and to Gijs de Waal who was most helpful in supplying this material in digital format.

We also owe special thanks to Johanna Lohse who provided us with digital images of two paintings by her father and gave us free admission to reproduce them; to Izak and Paul Salomons (for the material on Jan Rietveld); to Wies van Moorsel (with respect to Til Brugman); to Joost van Roojen and to Lucien Lafour and Rikkert Wijk (for their helping to trace the images of their own work).

In our search for images we also met with generous help from staff members in several institutions. We like to extend our thanks in particular to Carolien Provaas, assistant at the Nederlands Fotomuseum in Rotterdam; to Ramses van Bragt, head of the Archival Collection at the Netherlands Institute for Art History in The Hague; to Cecile van der Harten, head of the Image Department at the Amsterdam Rijksmuseum; to Hans Schouten, responsible of the Audiovisual Service of the Architecture Faculty at Delft University of Technology; to Hetty Wessels, curator of the Reproduction Department at the Amsterdam Stedelijk Museum; to Marion Bouwhuis of the AKI-ArtEZ Archive in Enschede; and to Babette Wijsman of Aviodrome in Lelystad.

We owe special thanks to Gijs Snoek for his recording of the lecture given by Aldo van Eyck at INDESEM 67, and to Cees Sterrenburg who transferred the audio tape to a DVD.

Finally we want to extend our gratitude to SUN publishers, in particular to Henk Hoeks who assumed our project from the outset and continued to support it with unusual patience, to Sjef van de Wiel and Wouter van Gils who diligently looked after the budget side, and to Sabine Verschoor who took care of bringing the whole collection of texts into publication.

Editors' notes

Introduction

1 For these notes and Van Eyck's projects themselves, see his *Works*, edited by Vincent Ligtelijn and published by Birkhäuser in 1999.

Chapter 1
Looking back on his student years in Zürich

Ex Turico aliquid novum

1 'Ex Turico aliquid novum' ('Something new from Zurich') is a variant of the Latin saying 'Ex Africa semper aliquid novum' ('There is always something new coming from Africa'), which was itself a translation of a phrase from Aristotle's *History of Animals*.
2 The present text is a shortened version of the letter published in *Archithese*. The last part, which bears on a subject that is largely dealt with in chapter 13, has been left out.
3 The Limmat is the river that runs through Zurich. At the end of the nineteenth century the Swiss democracy was reputed to be an oasis of freedom, both intellectually and politically. Especially Zurich harboured refugees and students from all over Europe and became a cradle of revolutionary ideas. The university and the ETH were centres of advanced research while the Zurich cafés were the setting for an uninhibited political debate. All kinds of ideologies, from socialism to liberalism, from anarchism and Marxism to Zionism, were freely discussed in an open atmosphere which was seminal to future politic protagonists such as Lenin, Radek and Rosa Luxemburg. This open ideological climate also proved to be conducive to ground-breaking developments in science and art. Einstein began to reflect on relativity in the late 1890s when he was still studying at the ETH. And in the middle of the First World War, in 1916, Hugo Ball started Cabaret Voltaire in the back theatre of a Zurich café which soon became a focus of modern art and where performances by Tzara, Hennings, Arp and Huelsenbeck gave birth to the Dada movement. For the ideological climate in Zurich round 1900, see Lewis S. Feuer, *Einstein and the Generations of Science*, Basic Books, New York, 1974.
4 The Rütli meadow is a sloping patch of grass on the western shore of the Urnersee where the representatives of the three forest cantons around

the lake – Uri, Schwyz and Nidwalden – met on 1st August 1291 in order to swear an oath of mutual defence against Habsburg repression, thereby laying the foundations of the Swiss Confederation as it stands today.

5 The Neubühl Siedlung in Zurich-Wollishofen was a project by the Swiss Werkbund, designed by Max E. Haefeli, Werner M. Moser, Rudolf Steiger, Carl Hubacher, Emil Roth, Paul Artaria and Hans Schmidt. The settlement ranks among the most important achievements of Swiss functionalism between the wars.

6 Inflammation of the cornea.

7 The Cantonal Hospital, situated opposite Zurich Polytechnic, was designed in 1939–1942 by W. Moser, M. Haefeli, R. Steiger *et al.*, and built in 1942–1951. With regard to this building Van Eyck extolled a statement by Steiger in Archithese, 1980, No. 2, p. 50: 'From the outset we consciously intended to dispel the impression of something powerful and massive. Such an impression easily arises in the design of hospitals. The patient should in no way get the unpleasant feeling of being a sick man caught in a big and cluttered machine. That will not be the case when he can recognize in the building, on the outside as well as on the inside, the kind of dimensions he is familiar with in his private daily environment.'

8 For Van Eyck's polemics with the Post Moderns, see chapter 13.

9 Van Eyck is referring to the two small blocks of flats built by Alfred Roth, Emil Roth and Marcel Breuer in 1935–36 for Sigfried Giedion at 17 and 19 Doldertal, a valley avenue on the east side of Zurich. The Giedion family lived in an old villa at Doldertal 7.

10 Van Eyck is referring to the Villiger house in Bremgarten built by Max Bill in 1943, an elementary wood skeleton structure. On Bill (1908–1994), constructivist painter, sculptor and architect, see E. Hüttinger, *Max Bill*, Hatje, Zurich 1977, and S. von Moos, *Max Bill and 'simple' architecture*, Lars Müller, Baden, 1996.

11 'Red because I am young'. Alfred Roth gives a moving account of his friendship with Mondrian in *Begegnung mit Pionieren* (Birkhäuser, Basel 1973). After he asked Mondrian for a painting 'with red and a little blue and yellow', the latter did a fine composition dominated by a red square, explicitly dedicated to his 'dear friend and colleague Alfred Roth'.

12 All-in.

13 Hans Fischli (1909–1989) studied at the Bauhaus in Dessau and worked as an architect, painter and sculptor. His works include the Gwad social housing in Wädeswil (1943), the Pestalozzi children's village in Trogen (1944–1949) and the Bucheg kindergarten in Zurich (1946). See K. Jost, *Hans Fischli*, Zurich, 1992.

14 Hans Hofmann (1897–1957) was a tradition-oriented architect who built numerous residential complexes and specialised in exhibition design. He was responsible for the Swiss pavilions at the world exhibitions in Cologne (1928), Barcelona (1929), Liège (1930) and Brussels (1935).

15 First prize or financial compensation. In Switzerland it was normal practice to award commissions for public buildings solely on the basis of competitions. The competing firms made much use of promising younger architects for this purpose and went talent-spotting at the annual Diplomarbeiten show at the ETH.

16 Eliminated.

17 Tower room.

18 Professor Wilhelm Löffler, whose house was built in 1929 by Friedrich Hess, a convinced adept of *Blut und Boden* architecture.

19 In *Bauen + Wohnen*, 1948, no. 2, and in *A Decade of New Architecture*, Girsberger, Zürich 1951.

20 Extras.

21 Organ grinder in Nestroy's play *Einen Jux will er sich machen*.

22 A play by Von Kleist.

23 A may-beetle couple in *Maybeetle Wedding*, a play by J.V. Widmann.

24 'You had a second arrow in your quiver', a phrase from *Wilhelm Tell*, a play by Friedrich Schiller. The remark is made by the Habsburg governor after the protagonist succeeded in shooting the apple from his son's head. Tell admits that the second arrow was intended for the governor in case the first one had hit his son.

25 Café Select was and still is situated on the Zurich Limatquai.

26 A herringbone forest frottage.

27 Carola Welcker (1885–1979), was one of the first classically trained art historians to concentrate entirely on the essential meaning of contemporary art. She studied in Munich under Heinrich Wölfflin and gained her doctorate in 1922 under Paul Clemen in Bonn with a dissertation on Bavarian rococo sculpture. In Zurich, where she settled with Giedion whom she had married in 1920, she became close friends with Hans Arp who introduced her into the world of the twentieth-century avant-garde. For an overview of her ideas, see C. Giedion-Welcker, *Schriften 1926–1971*, Dumont, Cologne, 1973.

28 Introductory speech, in fact a flamboyant homage, delivered in Amsterdam Stedelijk Museum, early March 1957; first published in Forum, 1959, no. 9, pp. 321–322. See chapter 5 of the present book, 131–135 .
29 Richard Paul Lohse (1902–1988), constructivist painter and major exponent of 'concrete art'. Starting from Mondrian's Boogie-Woogies, he carried out a systematic pictorial study of strictly orthogonal colour grids.
See R.P. Lohse, *Modular and Serial Orders*, Waser Verlag, Zürich, 1984
30 Swiss Werkbund.
31 'That's terrific, but in this combination! Of all people with Lohse, the rationalist!'
32 'Yes, but he is indeed an inspired artist.'
33 'What carries Lohse beyond the foundation of highly-developed systematics and methodical consistency is the genuine poetical sensibility he is filled with.' Carola Giedion Welcker in *Richard Paul Lohse Festschrift*, Niggli, Teufen, 1962.
34 'Max, you know, he is doing the same thing as I do, but in the other hemisphere.'
35 'Terrific!'
36 'Aldo is indeed half Dutch and half Spanish – keep that in mind.' In fact, Aldo van Eyck's maternal grandmother, Guilermina de Gouvea, was of Portuguese descent.
37 Konkretion I (1945) and Konkretion III (1947)
38 The Van Doesburg house is in rue Charles Infroit 29, Meudon; the Arp house in rue des Châtaignes 21, Clamart.
39 Sophie Täuber (1889–1943), painter, sculptor and textile designer, participated in the Zurich dada movement and married Arp in 1922. They settled in Paris and collaborated on several projects, notably the interior design of the Aubette in Strasbourg (1927–1929). In 1942 the couple fled for the Nazi's to Zurich where, due to an accident, Sophie died on 13 January 1943.
40 'woe, our good kaspar is dead. who'll carry now the burning banner in his pigtail wig. who'll crank the coffee-mill. who'll entice the idyllic deer. at sea he confused the boats by addressing them as parapluie and the winds by calling them father of the bees. woe woe woe our good kaspar is dead. holy ding-dong, kaspar is dead. the hay fishes rattle in the tower bells when his christian name is uttered...' etc., a dadaist poem from *Der Vogel Selbdritt* (1920) by Arp.
41 'Just the necessary substrate between wine and life', dedication by Tristan Tzara to Tess van Eyck on 23 November 1945, in the *Sixième Cahier* in the *Habitude de la Poésie* series published by Guy Levis Mano. Aldo van Eyck used this phrase on several occasions, notably when he published his Amsterdam orphanage in *Forum*, 1961, no. 6–7.
42 'The eye always fresh for the return of things'.
43 After making the acquaintance of the work of Dudok, Rietveld and Duiker during a stay in Holland in 1929, Felix Schwarz (b. 1917) had become a passionate admirer of Dutch functionalism and took a subscription to *de 8 en Opbouw*. While Schwarz opened Van Eyck's eyes to modern Dutch architecture, the latter introduced the former to English poetry. In 1952 Schwarz participated as a Swiss CIAM delegate in the CIAM congress at Sigtuna. In 1956 he set up a firm with Rolf Gutman. Their work includes the Sibir Factory in Schlieren (1953–1958), the Promenade School in Bremgarten (1962–1963), the Municipal Theatre in Basel (1964–1975), the transformation of the Zurich Schauspielhaus (1973–1977) and the renovation of the Wil Concert Hall (1978).
44 Herman Gorter (1864–1927) and Henriëtte Roland Holst (1869–1952) were both famous Dutch poets and figureheads of socialism. Gorter made his name with symbolist and 'sensitivist' poetry, after which he revealed himself as a doctrinaire socialist theorist. H. Roland Holst was inspired by William Morris and Dante. She held a humanitarian-socialist conviction and expressed her ideals in passionate, compelling verse. Both were editors of the review *De Nieuwe Tijd*.
45 Lotte Schwarz: *Tagebuch mit einem Haus*, Verlag Girsberger, Zurich, 1956.
46 Sober.
47 Van Eyck launched this slogan in *Architectural Design News Supplement*, 1981, no. 7.
48 Rolf Gutman (b. 1927) can be considered a founding member of Team 10. He wrote, with Theo Manz, a fundamental paper for the Sigtuna 1952 CIAM meeting, he participated in the 1953 CIAM Congress at Aix-en-Provence, in subsequent CIAM X Committee meetings and the 1956 CIAM Congress at Dubrovnic.
49 For the 1962 Team 10 Royaumont meeting, see chap. 10, pp. 425–439.
50 Paul Parin, Fritz Morgenthaler and Goldy Parin-Matthey: *Die Weissen denken zuviel – Psychoanalytische Untersuchungen bei den Dogon in Westafrika*, Zürich, 1963; *Fürchte deinen Nächsten wie dich selbst – Psychoanalyse und Gesellschaft am Modell der Agni in Westafrika*, Frankfurt, 1971.
51 See chapter 9, p. 189.
52 *Minotaure*, 1933, no.2.
53 See note 1.
54 Cable railway.

55 Linus Birchler (1893–1967) was professor of art and architectural history at the ETH. He approached his subject matter in terms of antithetic pairs, which he illustrated with double slide projections. Born and raised in Einsiedeln, he nourished a frank admiration for the Baroque.
56 Self-evident.

Chapter 2
Advocate of the avant-garde in postwar CIAM (1947–1953)

Introduction to chapter 2

1 S. Giedion, *Architecture you and me*, Harvard University Press, Cambridge, Mass., 1958, p. 28.
2 Community planning, in particular neighbourhood planning, was developed before the First World War by the New York planner Clarence Perry. Working in the context of the New York Community Center Movement, he conceived the city as a cluster of independent neighbourhoods of a limited size, geared to pedestrian traffic, each with its own centre and public facilities. This concept was applied in Radburn (1928) and Chatham (1931), both designed by C. Stein and H. Wright. Unlike the abstract, monofunctional *'Rationelle Bebauungsweisen'* then embraced by CIAM, the neighbourhood unit was an organic combination of habitation and complementary functions. On Perry, see L. Mumford, 'Neighborhood and Neighborhood Unit', in *Town Planning Review*, Jan. 1954 (also included in his collected articles *The Urban Prospect*, New York 1968); and L. Mumford, *The City in History*, New York 1961, pp. 568–573 ('The suburb as neighborhood unit').
3 For a more circumstantial account of the preparatory discussion for CIAM 6, see E. Mumford, *The CIAM Discourse on Urbanism* 1928–1960, M.I.T Press, Cambridge, Mass., 2000, pp. 168–179.
4 There were two CIAM groups in Holland, 'de 8' for the Amsterdam members and 'Opbouw' for the Rotterdam members. In the thirties the two groups jointly published the review *de 8 en Opbouw*.
5 S. Giedion, in *A Decade of New Architecture*, Girsberger, Zurich, 1951, p. 30.
6 As A. van Eyck was later to recall in *The Story of Another Idea*. See chapter 7, p. 221.
7 See S. Giedion, *A Decade of New Architecture*, Girsberger, Zurich, 1951, pp. 33–35.
8 Ibid, p. 37. In his account Giedion situates Van Eyck's intervention after Le Corbusier's. However, Van Eyck repeatedly pointed out that it happened the other way round. In his opinion there would not have been much point in saying what he did after Le Corbusier's lyrical speech.

Report concerning the interrelation of the plastic arts and the importance of cooperation

1 Report written in two versions, Dutch and English, during the summer of 1947, typed on tracing paper. It was not published but printed copies were sent to Giedion and distributed among CIAM members.
2 **Hans Arp**
Concrete art aims to transform the world. It aims to make existence more bearable. It aims to save man from the most dangerous folly: vanity. It aims to simplify man's life. It aims to identify him with nature. Reason uproots man and causes him to lead a tragic existence. Concrete art is an elementary, natural and healthy art, which causes the stars of peace, love and poetry to grow in the head and the heart. Where concrete art enters, melancholy departs, dragging with it its gray suitcases full of black sighs.
English version from: H. Arp, 'On My Way – Poetry and Essays, Wittenborn, New York, 1948, p. 72.
3 By 'grace' Van Eyck meant the beauty of natural behaviour and movement in animals and mankind, in the flight of a bird or in a gracious gesture. He particularly referred to the lifestyle evoked in the plays of William Saroyan, notably *Sweeney in the Trees*, *The Time of Your Life* and *Beautiful people*.
4 **Arnold Schoenberg**
The artist does not do what the others take to be beautiful but only that what is necessary to him.
Original German quote from A. Schoenberg, *Harmonielehre*, 1911, p. 495.
5 **Constantin Brancusi**
Simplicity is not a goal in art. One arrives at simplicity in spite of oneself, by approaching the real sense of things.
Original French quote in C. Giedion-Welcker, *Moderne Plastik*, Girsberger, Zurich, 1937, p. 11.
6 The crucial importance of the imagination was part of the legacy Aldo van Eyck inherited from his father, the poet and philosopher Pieter Nicolaas van Eyck (1887–1954). In his fundamental essay 'Critical Research and Imagination' P.N. van Eyck advanced imagination as the most important human faculty of cognition, the faculty that enables man to condense the essence of his personal

experience into a meaningful form. For a more circumstantial account of his views, see
F. Strauven, *Aldo van Eyck –The Shape of Relativity*, Amsterdam 1998, pp. 49–56.

7 **Vordemberge-Gildewart**
The absolute artistic expression is averse to virtuosity. That's the reason of its impopularity (1931).

8 **Hans Arp**
The works of concrete art should remain anonymous in the great workshop of nature, just like the clouds, the mountains, the seas, the animals, the human beings. Yes, men should go back into nature! The artists should work in community like the artists in the Middle Ages
Original French quote in C. Giedion-Welcker, 'Jean Arp', *Horizon*, October 1946, no. 82, p. 234.

9 **Hans Arp**
Everything functions, only man himself does not.

10 **Hugo Ball**
The human beings bleed from their gnarls.

11 **Wassily Kandinsky**
Every epoch takes a face peculiar to itself, full of expression and force. So, 'yesterday' transforms into 'today' in all spiritual fields, but art moreover possesses the exclusive quality of becoming 'tomorrow' in the present. Creative and prophetic force.
Original French quote in W. Kandinsky, 'Art Concret', xxe Siècle, Paris March 1938, no. 1.

12 A central idea in the philosophy of Henri Bergson. See for example his 1911 conference 'La perception du changement' in *La pensée et le mouvant* (1934), English translation *The Creative Mind*, Greenwood, Westport, 1968.

13 **Henri Bergson**
Whether matter or mind, reality appears as continuous change. It becomes or dissolves, it is never something finished.
Translated from German quote in C. Giedion-Welcker, *Die neue Realität bei Guillaume Apolinaire*, Bentelli, Bern, 1945, p. 10.

14 **Piet Mondrian**
The culture of particular form is approaching its end. The culture of determined relations has begun.
Original English quote from his article 'Plastic Art and Pure Plastic Art' in J.L. Martin, B. Nicholson, N. Gabo, *Circle*, London, 1937, p. 47.

15 **Gerrit Rietveld**
For the coming style that which people have in common is more important than their differences.
Originally, 'Voor de nieuwe vormgeving is dat, wat eender is in alle mensen, belangrijker dan hun verchillen', a quote from Rietveld's short article 'industriële vormgeving' in *Open Oog*, 1946, no. 1. *Open Oog* was an 'avant garde journal for visual design', published by Brusse in Rotterdam. It was edited by Brusse, Jaffé, Kloos, Rietveld and Stam, assisted by Braque, Bill and Le Corbusier. Only two issues appeared, the numbers 1 and 2 of 1946. (With thanks to Marijke Küper, who provided this information.)

16 **Georges Vantongerloo**
We need space in order to locate things. Space, which we cannot do without but we are unable to define, is inseparable from life.
Quoted by C. Giedion-Welcker, in *Moderne Plastik*, Girsberger, Zurich, 1937.

17 **Max Jacob**
The world in one man, that's the modern poet.
Quoted from M. Jacob, *Art poétique*, Emile-Paul, Paris 1922.

18 **Eric Gill**
Holiness is not a moral quality at all, it is above and beyond prudence, it is loveliness itself, it is the loveliness of the spirit.'
Quoted from E. Gill, *Art*, John Lane The Bodley Head, London, (1935) 1946, p. 130.

Intervention at CIAM 6, Bridgwater 1947

1 Van Eyck made this intervention on the penultimate day of the congress, after Richards and Giedion had been countered by Arthur Ling. See introduction. The text of this manuscript indeed overlaps with the edited version published four years later. It is included here because its more colloquial language contains some ideas and connotations which were lost in the editing.

2 For Giedion's lecture, see his *A Decade of New Architecture*, Girsberger, Zurich, 1951, pp. 34–35.

3 This last paragraph, which Van Eyck wrote in French, was translated by the editors.

Statement against rationalism

1 Van Eyck edited his intervention at the 1947 Bridgwater congress in September 1951 for Giedion, who published it in *A Decade of New Architecture*, Girsberger, Zurich, 1951, pp. 37. Later Giedion also included it in *Architecture you and me*, Harvard University Press, Cambridge, Mass., 1958, pp. 77–78.

2 Given his scepticism about the work of his CIAM colleagues, Van Eyck obviously means: CIAM should be first and foremost an affirmation of this new consciousness.

3 'The natural flow of existence' is a notion derived from Bergson, notably his 1911 conference 'La perception du changement' in *La pensée et le mouvant* (1934), English translation *The Creative Mind*, Greenwood, Westport 1968.

We discover style

1 In this article, written in Dutch and published in *Forum*, 1949, no. 2–3, pp. 115–116, Van Eyck formulates nearly the same ideas as in 'Statement against rationalism'. Yet here he focuses on the prospect of discovering style – a prospect he outlined in his report for CIAM 6 but which he did not touch upon in his intervention at the congress. The affirmative and optimistic 'we discover style' was obviously meant as an appeal to his CIAM countrymen. Before its publication, on 15 January 1949, Van Eyck read out the text of this article in a lecture for Poorters club, the student association of the Amsterdam Academy of Architecture.

2 'The new architecture' is a translation of the Dutch expression 'het nieuwe bouwen', which designates, like the German 'Neues Bauen', modern architecture conceived as an avant-garde movement.

3 'From chair to city', in Dutch 'van stoel tot stad' an alliterative expression that Bakema adopted 15 years later as the title of his book *Van stoel tot stad*, W. De Haan, Zeist 1964.

4 When Van Eyck quotes from this article in 'The Ball rebounds' (*Forum*, 1958, no.3) the first part of the sentence reads: 'The new architecture has its roots in a "new" reality'.

5 Originally, *Vom Vorbildlichen zum Urbildlichen. Es kann nicht überstürzt werden. Es muss wachsen, es soll hinauf wachsen, Und wenn es dan einmal an der Zeit ist, jenes Werk, desto besser! Wir mussen es noch suchen. Wir fanden Teile dazu, aber noch nicht das Ganze. Wir haben noch nicht die letzte Kraft, denn uns trägt kein Volk.* Quoted from Paul Klee, in *Über die moderne Kunst*, Bern 1945 (address to the 'Kunstverein' at Jena, given on 26 February 1924).

6 Originally, *La simplicité n'est pas un but dans l'art, mais on arrive à la simplicité malgré soi, en s'approchant du sens réel des choses.* Constantin Brancusi, quoted by Carola Giedion-Welcker, in *Moderne Plastik*, Girsberger, Zurich 1937, p. 11.

On Brancusi, Sert and Miró

1 'Pep' was the nickname of Sigfried Giedion. It was probably borrowed from the name of a watercolour by Paul Klee, *Der Vogel Pep* (1925), which was itself inspired by a poem by Christian Morgenstern. 'C.W.' was the way Carola Welcker, Giedion's wife, liked to be called by her friends.

2 'Bird, project to be enlarged so as to fill the vault of heaven', title given by Brancusi to his sculpture which is better known as *Bird in Space* (1932–1943). Van Eyck responds to a passage in 'Constantin Brancusis Weg', an article by C.W. he had just received. C.W. asked him for an English translation for publication in *Horizon*, a London based avant-garde review that appeared from 1939 to 1949. Van Eyck had two years previously translated one of C.W.'s articles on Arp for the same review, but this time he was too busy with professional work to oblige.

3 Van Eyck means the 'Cidade dos Motoros' or 'Motor City' (1944), a project by Sert and Wiener for an aircraft engine factory with housing facilities to be constructed on reclaimed marshland twenty-five miles northwest of Rio de Janeiro in Brazil. Van Eyck had set down his thoughts on this project in a five page handwritten note. His main criticism was that the planned housing facilities in this 'city' were entirely determined by the demands of the factory. It comprised dormitory housing for 9000 single male workers, with no room for privacy, so that the development of normal relationships or family life would be excluded. The Spanish architect J.L. Sert (1902–1983), who fled to the U.S.A. in 1939, was a co-founder of the American CIAM Chapter and he was elected president of CIAM in 1947.

4 A quote from 'The Dead', the last chapter of Joyce's *Dubliners*.

5 Peter Watson, the publisher of *Horizon*.

On the function of a UNESCO art review

1 Undated manuscript in Van Eyck Archives. As appears from the last sentence, the letter was written before the congress that was intended to take place in London. Early 1950 it was indeed decided to hold CIAM 8 in London but in the end it took place in Hoddesdon, 20 miles north of London, from 7 to 14 July 1951. At the end of August 1950 Van Eyck had presumably been informed by Van Eesteren of the plan, conceived by Giedion, Herbert Read and himself, to set up a UNESCO art review. In this letter Van Eyck frankly expresses his opinion on the function of such a review. He reasserts the ideas he expounded in his report for CIAM 6 and stresses the fundamental role of art in society. Remarkably, he endeavours to persuade Giedion of the views he (Van Eyck) shares with C.W in order to make the UNESCO review into a platform for these views. Shortly afterwards Van Eyck was asked to write an article for the new review. But as its plans were abandoned, the article was never published. Later,

in 1962, Van Eyck incorporated the text into the first chapter of *The Child, the City and the Artist*.

2 'Pep' was the nickname of Sigfried Giedion. It was probably borrowed from the name of a watercolour by Paul Klee, *Der Vogel Pep* (1925), which was itself inspired by a poem by Christian Morgenstern.

3 A home-made concept which occurs here for the first time and goes on to occupy a central place in Van Eyck's thinking. A dual phenomenon results from the interaction of two opposites which are reconciled, becoming complementary halves that reinforce each other and form a dynamic unity. Later, in 1962, to avoid any suggestion of dualism, Van Eyck renamed this concept 'twin phenomenon'.

4 Herbert Read (1893–1968), literary critic, political thinker, art historian and apologist of avant-garde art, can be considered a kindred spirit of C.W.'s. Like C.W. he was profoundly aware of the communicative and persuasive power of visual art. He believed that human concepts primary originate through aesthetic experience, and that they are only afterwards formulated theoretically.
In *Education through Art* (1943) he propounded as the general purpose of education: 'to foster the growth of what is individual in each human being, at the same time harmonizing the individuality thus educed with the organic unity of the social group to which the individual belongs'. Van Eyck possessed a copy of this book dedicated to him by the author on 18 December 1945.

5 With this paradox Van Eyck summarizes an essential implication of his relativistic view. The essential core of a thing, its identity, is not simply that which remains constant; it is 'what is constant and constantly changes'. In other words, things do not have a purely spatial but a spatio-temporal identity, an identity that takes a different form according to the space-time context in which it occurs. In order to grasp the identity of something it has to be studied in many different frames of reference.

6 'Nachwuchs', a term used by Giedion and other Swiss CIAM members, means the younger people of the coming generation who are expected to succeed the older.

On the Dutch Contribution

1 This short article was published in Forum, 1951, no. 9, pp. 244–245. An Italian translation appeared in Domus, Sept. 1951, no. 216, pp. 6–7. The present English translation is partly based on an English draft version, written in May during the installation of the Dutch stand in Milan. Van Eyck designed this stand in collaboration with Jan Rietveld, son of Gerrit Rietveld. The images were selected in consultation with members of 'de 8' and covered the development of Dutch modern architecture from Berlage to 1950. Yet Van Eyck introduced his own accents. He reduced the post-1945 work to a minimum and drew special attention to the work of Rietveld. The exhibition ran between Rietveld's 1918 red-blue chair, mounted as a wall sculpture, and his 1942 perforated aluminium chair. The stress placed on De Stijl and the recognition given to Rietveld had at that time an unmistakably polemic character. The functionalists of 'de 8 en Opbouw' tended to dismiss De Stijl as a bygone episode and were not inclined to take Rietveld all too seriously on account of his alleged lack of technical knowledge.

2 See note 5 of 'About a Unesco art review'.

3 The passage between brackets does not appear in the Dutch text but was imported from the English draft.

4 Quoted from Rietveld's short article 'industriële vormgeving' in *Open Oog*, 1946, no. 1.

On the Hispano Suiza factory

1 Letter written to Van den Broek and Bakema after it became known that they had accepted a commission from the multinational Hispano Suiza company to design a gun factory for warplanes. This act appeared to be fairly contradictory to Bakema's openly avowed conviction that architecture should express a political viewpoint, that it should voice the protest of the creative against the negative, particularly against the willingness to destruction that surfaced again in the Cold War. In February 1951 Bakema had written an open letter to the Minister of Reconstruction on behalf of 'de 8 en Opbouw', complaining that the quality of reconstruction was suffering on account of the new arms race.

2 Van Tijen and Maaskant designed the Fokker factory that made the aircraft for which the Hispano Suiza guns were intended.

3 The Hoddesdon congress started on 7 July 1951. In fact illness prevented Van Eyck from carrying out this intention. This illness, which resulted from his second Sahara journey in February and March, also kept him from participating in CIAM 8. He did not post the letter until 22 July.

4 Some core concepts of Bakema's architectural discourse.

5 'Het Venster', meaning 'the window', was the name of this cultural centre.
6 *Katholiek Bouwblad*, 14 April 1951, p. 213.
7 Subsequently, Bakema agreed to place the affair on the agenda of the next meeting of Dutch CIAM. The question was discussed at a special two-day meeting on 22 and 23 September 1951. The prominent members of 'de 8' and 'Opbouw' expressed their views but failed to reach unanimous conclusions. Their statements reveal how little agreement there was among the Dutch CIAM group on fundamental principles. The discussion kept dragging on for four more meetings until May 1952 when the Opbouw members reached the conclusion that a conflict only existed for a CIAM architect if the form of the space itself had to express an unacceptable intention.
8 The publication of this laconic statement by Aldo van Eyck in a special CIAM issue of *Forum* (1953, no. 3) formed the conclusion of the debate on the Hispano Suiza affair. It was preceded by a ten-page pictorial of the completed factory, without any mention of its function.

Lohse and the aesthetic meaning of number

1 Statement published in a special CIAM issue of *Forum* (1952, no. 6–7, p. 186), between the Rotterdam Pendrecht project and the Amsterdam Frankendaal project. In his introduction to the Pendrecht project Bakema relates that after presenting the first version of this project to CIAM 7 at Bergamo in 1949, he received a warm reaction from Richard P. Lohse 'who recognized in the structure of the Opbouw plan much of what he was trying to achieve in his own work'. In fact, since 1943 Lohse had endeavoured to build up visual themes with the potential 'to expand or to contract in every dimension'. He aimed to combine formally identical basic elements into themes that recurred in several variations; themes that could take on the role of the individual visual elements usual until then, and furthermore were capable of combining into a *'Gesamtthema'*. Still, compared to Lohse's paintings, the Pendrecht projects appeared to turn out much more repetitive, verging on monotony. In order to show this, Van Eyck published a colour reproduction of *Konkretion III* accompanied by one of Lohse's texts and the present statement. In the last paragraph he expresses barely concealed criticism of Bakema's go-aheadness, while pointing out the meaning Lohse's work *could* have in town planning.
2 Published in *Forum*, 1959, no. 7, p. 223.

Chapter 3
Cobra

Introduction to chapter 3

1 For Cobra, see W. Stokvis, *Cobra*, Amsterdam 1974; and J.C. Lambert, *Cobra*, Antwerp, 1983.
2 In addition to the opening speeches included in this chapter mention must be made of the introduction he wrote for the 1960 exhibition of Tajiri which is incorporated in the fifth chapter of the present book.

An Appe(a)l to the Imagination

1 Translation authorized by Van Eyck for the English edition of the monograph by F. Strauven. In the original Dutch title *'een appèl aan de verbeelding'*, *'appel'* refers not only to Appel but also means both 'apple' and 'appeal'. The manifesto, written in the form of an open letter to Appel, was printed on a horizontal poster of 63 by 47 cm, along with the favourable recommendations of the expert committee and a number of impressive declarations of sympathy: from all the architects and some engineers of the Public Works Department, including Van Eesteren and Mulder, from an office clerk and a cleaning lady, from various figures in Dutch cultural circles, including J.P. Mieras, the chairman of the Society of Dutch Architects, J.J.P. Oud, John Raedecker, Adriaan Roland Holst and Jan Sluyters. Below these endorsements, which were repeatedly interspersed with the line 'but the municipal executive knew better', there appeared a number of statements from 'the heroes of the upside-down world' who attacked Appel's work. These were printed, literally, upside down. Van Eyck signed the manifesto in the name of the Dutch Experimental Group (postal address; Binnenkant 32, Amsterdam), pasted it up in various public places and sent it to a variety of notables, artists, politicians, institutions, newspapers and magazines at home and abroad.
2 A statement by Mrs Luns at a meeting of the City Council.

Constant and the Abstracts

1 Translation of a transcript by Hans Rooduyn, the owner of *Le Canard* gallery.

2 From 1950 to 1952 Constant lived with his little son Victor in Paris.
3 Heinz Trökes (1913–1997) was a German expressionist painter who became involved in Cobra through his friend Karl Otto Götz.
4 'Creatie' was an 'association for the promotion of absolute art', founded in 1950 by Willy Boers and Ger Gerrits. It was a dissident faction of the 'Vrij Beelden' association which had been set up in 1949 to defend abstract art against traditional figurative art. Van Eyck held his speech at *Le Canard* a day after the opening of a *Creatie* exhibition at the Fodor Museum.
5 A.C. Willink (1900–83) was a Dutch adherent of Surrealism who developed a personal version of Magic Realism.

Corneille and the Realists

1 Translation of a manuscript, Van Eyck Archives.
2 See note 4 in the Opening speech for the Constant exhibition.
3 'De Realisten' was an association of artists founded in 1947 by Nicolaas Wijnberg and Hans van Norden. Starting from German Expressionism, they wanted to develop an expressive figurative art. The foundation of the group was a reaction against the exhibition policy of Sandberg, the director of the Amsterdam Stedelijk Museum who showed a preference for abstract art and the young experimental group. Five days before Corneille's vernissage at Martinet & Michels, the Stedelijk Museum had opened an exhibition called 'Realisten uit zeven landen' (Realists from seven countries).
4 Herman Justus Kruyder (1881–1935) was a major exponent of Expressionism in the Netherlands.
5 Van Eyck refers to the adherents of Richard N. Roland Holst (1868–1938), before the war a professor and director of the Amsterdam National Academy. He had founded a special studio of Monumental Art where he trained painters to produce monumental murals that expressed a socialist view of life.
6 'De Kring' was and still is the artists' society located near Leidseplein in Amsterdam.

Corneille versus clocks

1 Translation of a manuscript from the Van Eyck Archives. In this dadaist performance Van Eyck rejects the current mechanical understanding of time in favour of a vital experience of time inspired by the philosophy of Bergson.

Corneille as a landscape painter

1 Undated manuscript in Van Eyck archives, presumably written in 1952.

Looking back on the Cobra exhibitions in Liège (1951) and Amsterdam (1949)

1 *Niet om het even – maar evenwaardig*, Amsterdam 1986, p. 46. Van Eyck made the layout of the Cobra exhibitions in Amsterdam's Stedelijk Museum (3–28 November 1949) and the Palais des Beaux-Arts in Liège (6 October – 6 November 1951).
2 'No, my dear, it will be a real event, with people from everywhere.'
3 Constant painted the gigantic canvas *Barricade* to mark the entrance of the exhibition, Appel the almost equally large *Mens en dieren* (People and Animals) which confronted the visitor on entering the third room, Brands the narrow, floor-to-ceiling canvas *Neergeschreven drift* (Penned Passion) for the sixth room, and Corneille painted up a wooden cube he had dug up in the museum storehouse.

An evening of limbo in the Low Countries

1 *Niet om het even – maar evenwaardig*, Amsterdam 1986, pp. 52–53.
2 The event took place on 14 December 1951.
3 Dr C. van Emde Boas.
4 The country of fear.
5 'Exquisite Corpse'.
6 *Zwart*, a bibliophile volume, with poems by Hugo Claus, a preface by Christian Dotremont, and illustrations by Karel Appel and Pierre Alechinsky, published in 1978 by Landshoff, Bentveld-Aerdenhout. The title, 'Zwart', means 'Black'.
7 Translation of a handwritten note in the Van Eyck archives, undated but presumably written in 1952.

Spatial Colourism

1 In November 1952 Aldo van Eyck collaborated with Constant on an experiment with space and colour, 'a space bounded by colour' carried out in the Amsterdam Stedelijk Museum. Van Eyck designed an accessible half-cube round a square painting by Constant who had just returned from London where his work had taken an abstract turn. The two halves of the half-cube's interior were painted in deep purple and bright blue; These colours did not accentuate the two halves but brought about a flattening of the space, giving it a two-dimensionality akin to the plane space of Constant's painting. The colours of the space en-

velope and those of the painting interacted so as to bring about a new space-colour unity. Van Eyck and Constant considered their experiment a success and recorded its results in a publication. They produced *Voor een spatiaal colorisme*, a portfolio containing a miniature reproduction of Constant's painting, a coloured fold-out of the half-cube and a new colour composition by Constant providing an interpretation of the interaction between his painting and Van Eyck's coloured interior space. Next to these pictures they included the present manifesto. Afterwards Constant published a slightly different version of the text alone under his own name, in *Forum*, 1953, no. 10, pp. 360–61.

Chapter 4
Playgrounds

Child and City

1 *Goed Wonen*, 1950, no. 11, pp. 152–153
2 This conversion was the first executed project by Jan Rietveld, with whom Aldo van Eyck collaborated from 1951 to 1954. for Van Eyck's appreciation of his colleague's work, see chap. 14, pp. 586 and 587.
3 Rietveld's staircase offers Van Eyck the opportunity to intimate his relativistic view. By instituting multiple viewpoints, architecture can contribute to a richer perception of reality.

When snow falls on cities

1 *Goed Wonen*, 1957, no. 10, pp. 207–212. This English version is based on analogous passages in original English texts, notably the first chapter of *The Child, the City and the Artist*, and 'Lost Identity', Van Eyck's grid presentation of the playgrounds at CIAM 10 in Dubrovnic, 1956.

After a heavy snowstorm

1 Published in *Team 10 Primer*, *Architectural Design*, 1962, no. 12, pp. 572–573. Hardback edition, Studio Vista, London, 1968, p. 45. Van Eyck was visiting professor at Washington University in St Louis from September 1961 to January 1962.

Wheels or no wheels, man is essentially a pedestrian

1 *Team 10 Primer*, in *Architectural Design*, 1962, no. 12, p. 572; in the 1965 paperback edition on p. 17. In the 1968 hardback edition on pp. 51–53. Van Eyck's statement appeared in the chapter on 'Urban Infrastructure' and was a reaction against the Smithsons' one-sided preoccupation with the motor car.

On the design of play equipment and the arrangement of playgrounds

1 Translation of a typescript, Van Eyck archives, undated but judging by Van Eyck's mention of almost 400 playgrounds having been designed, the lecture was given in 1962. Marcanti is a variety theatre in Van Galenstraat, Amsterdam.

Chapter 5
Art and architecture in the fifties

Introduction to chapter 5

1 Municipal Museum.
2 On Sandberg and the Stedelijk Museum, see Ad Petersen and P. Brattinga, *Sandberg – a documentary*, Kosmos, Amsterdam 1975.
3 Quoted from the catalogue leaflet of the 1969 exhibition of *Liga Nieuw Beelden* in the Amsterdam Stedelijk Museum.
4 For the ideas developed in *Structure* and their context, see Jonneke Jobse, *De Stijl Continued – The Journal Structure (1958–1964)*, 010 Publishers, Rotterdam 2005.

On the cooperation between the arts

1 Van Eyck wrote this text in June 1955 in preparation for his participation in a panel discussion with Constant and Gerrit Rietveld in the Amsterdam Stedelijk Museum. The panel discussion was organized on the occasion of the exhibition *Architectuur en Beeldende Kunst* (Architecture and Plastic Art) which took place in the museum from 18 June to 18 July 1955. The aim of the exhibition, the first one organized by the Liga Nieuw Beelden, was 'to raise the problem of the relationship between architecture and art in a visual way' by presenting a number of spaces created as a result of the collaboration of architects with different kinds of artists. Van Eyck did not participate in this exhibition. With thanks to Jonneke Jobse who provided this information. In the Baljeu archives she found a preparatory document for the said panel discussion, containing the present text by Van Eyck along with shorter notes by Constant and Rietveld.

2 The Jordaan is the name of the elongated neighbourhood west of Amsterdam city centre, originally a working class area.

3 Amsterdam's Weesperstraat was until 1949 a radial street comparable to Vijzelstraat and Leidsestraat, but during the fifties the street was stripped of its original buildings to be broadened into an approach road for motor car traffic.

On inside and outside space

1 Article published in *Forum* (1956, no. 4, p. 133) next to the housing project for the elderly in Slotermeer that Van Eyck carried out in collaboration with Jan Rietveld.

On garden and landscape art

1 This lecture was probably given in connection with the exhibition by Roberto Burle Marx which took place in the Amsterdam Stedelijk Museum from 18 February to 18 March 1957.

2 This was, in fact, the planning method applied in the Amsterdam Extension Plan. The municipal town planning office defined the situation, the outline and the dimensions of the buildings, after which architects were commissioned to design plans and façades.

3 Van Eyck means the western part of the Amsterdam Extension Plan, the Slotermeer and Slotervaart neighbourhoods, which were being carried out during the fifties.

A tribute to Carola Giedion-Welcker

1 Tribute made in English on 8 March 1957 and published in *Forum*, 1959, no. 9, pp. 321–322.

2 'Ordovico Viricordo' is an expression found in Joyce and is used here by Van Eyck as a kind of regal greeting, a form of address understandable to initiates. The expression comes from *Finnegans Wake*, the concluding passage of Chapter 8: 'Teems of times and happy returns. The seim anew. Ordovico or viricordo. Anna was, Livia is, Plurabelle's to be.' (James Joyce, *Finnegans Wake*, Faber & Faber, London 1939, p. 215) 'Ordovico' means 'according to the system of Vico', *i.e.* his view of history as a cyclic process in which certain situations and archetypes recur endlessly. 'Viricordo' is a near-anagram and a typical Joycean wordplay, charged with many meanings. It blends the return (*ricorso*) of the archetypal character (*viri*) with the notion of remembering (*ricordo*). 'Anna, Livia, Plurabelle': – the little river running through Dublin, the Liffey (Livia, Allalivial), takes several shapes (Plurabelle).

3 An allusion to the exhibition *'Opdracht'* (meaning 'commission'), held in the Amsterdam Stedelijke museum from 5 May to 16 June 1956 and organized by the *Vereniging van Beoefenaars van de Monumentale Kunsten* (Society of Practitioners of Monumental Arts).

4 Brancusi's 'Table of Silence', 'Gate of the Kiss' and 'Endless Column', carried out between 1935 and 1938 in Tîrgu Jiu, near his birth place in Rumania, constitute a memorial to the First World War.

5 *'Just the necessary substrate between wine and life'*, dedication by Tristan Tzara to Tess van Eyck, the architect's daughter, on 23 November 1945, in the *Sixième Cahier* in the *Habitude de la Poésie* series published by Guy Levis Mano.

6 *Transition* was an avant-garde literary review published in Paris from 1927 to 1938 by Eugene and Maria Jolas.

7 A quote from Lewis Carroll, *Through the Looking Glass* (1872), chap. 4.
'The time has come,' the Walrus said,
'To talk of many things:
Of shoes – and ships – and sealing-wax –
Of cabbages – and kings –
And why the sea is boiling hot –
And whether pigs have wings.'

8 A quote from *Finnegans Wake*, *cit.*, p. 213. On her way back to Zurich C.W. responded with a letter (dated 10 March 1957) which begins as follows: *'Lieber Feuervogel, Nun sitze ich schon wieder 'retrospektiv' auf der Rückfahrt und denke an die Joyce'schen und Brancusi'schen Blitzsplitter von Aldo's Schleuder, die mich mit einbezogen und mir nahe gingen. Ich habe mein Passé und Pourquoi auf charmante weise erfahren – dabei nach lebendig und gleichseitig von Aldo destilliert auferstanden. Quelle chance d'avoir un fils fabulant et foudroyant like Aldo!'* (Van Eyck archives)

The ball rebounds

1 Article written on the occasion of Gerrit Rietveld's 70th Birthday and published in *Forum*, 1958, no. 3. Intended to be published in May 1958, when Utrecht's Centraal Museum opened a retrospective exhibition of Rietveld's work, it was in fact included in the March issue of that review. The present English text is a translation of the *Forum* article, completed with a number of passages from the manuscript which were apparently censored by the editors of the review.

2 Mondrian quoted by Til Brugman in her article 'Piet Mondriaan omstreeks 1910' in the catalogue

of the 1946 Mondrian exhibition in the Amsterdam Stedelijk Museum. Til Brugman (1888–1958) was a Dutch writer and language prodigy, author of novels, dadaist grotesques and sound poems. In 1908 she became friends with Mondrian, through whom she was to get involved in *De Stijl*. For some time she acted as an unseen assistant to the review, editing and translating articles by several authors. Later she also translated Giedion's *Space, Time and Architecture* into Dutch. For the context of this quote, see Van Eyck's opening speech to the 1988 Van Doesburg exhibition in chapter 14, pp. 599–604.

3 Van Eyck quotes from his article 'Over de Nederlandse inzending' (On the Dutch contribution), see p. 51. The last sentence, between brackets, is extracted from 'Wij ontdekken stijl' (We discover Style), see p. 43.

4 Jan Engelman (1900–1972) was a Dutch poet who entered the public eye in 1932 by publishing *De Tuin van Eros* (The Garden of Eros), a collection of erotic poems. He was also active as an essayist and critic, which earned him the nickname of 'the Art Pope of Utrecht', Utrecht being the city where he was born and bred. As an art critic he displayed affinities with the Realists, which Van Eyck criticized in his introduction to the 1951 Corneille exhibition. In his review of the 1946 Mondrian exhibition at the Amsterdam Stedelijk Museum Engelman had called Mondrian 'de candide zwakzinnige uit New York' (the candid mental defective from New York). 'Engel', in Dutch, means 'angel'.

5 A year later the wallpaper was removed at the instigation of the Amsterdam architect Hein Salomonson.

6 Lucebert (1924–1994), both poet and painter, was a member of Cobra in 1949. As a poet he soon ranked as the most outstanding exponent of the 'Vijftigers', the experimental Dutch poets of the fifties. In 1953 a literary critic labelled him as 'de keizer der Vijftigers' (the emperor of the Vijftigers). When Lucebert was awarded the Amsterdam Poetry Prize in 1954 he adopted that role and came dressed as an emperor and escorted by halberdiers to the presentation ceremony at the Stedelijk Museum. He was expelled by the police before the mayor could hand him the certificate.

7 'We have found parts of it, but not the whole thing. We don't yet have the eventual strength because we are not backed by the people', quoted from Paul Klee, *Über die moderne Kunst*, Bern 1945 (address to the 'Kunstverein' at Jena, given on 26 February 1924).

8 These statements have to be understood in the context of the pantheistic world-view Van Eyck had developed since his youth, notably through the poetry of Blake, the philosophy of Spinoza and the historiography of Vico. For an introduction to the sources of Van Eyck's thinking, see F. Strauven, *Aldo van Eyck – The Shape of Relativity*, Amsterdam, 1998.

9 A mentality that originated in 1929 at the Frankfurt CIAM Congress, which was dedicated to *die Wohnung für das Existenzminimum*.

10 'Over binnen- en buitenruimte' (On inside and outside space), see p. 126.

11 'Nieuwe Zakelijkheid', the Dutch translation of the German *'Neue Sachlichkeit'* can be considered a synonym of 'Nieuwe Bouwen' or functionalism. The term was introduced in the Netherlands by J.B. van Loghem in 1932, with the publication of his book *bouwen – nieuwe zakelijkheid*.

12 A quote from Hugo Ball, borrowed from C. Giedion-Welcker, 'Urelement und Gegenwart in der Kunst Hans Arp', in *Werk*, 1952, no. 5, pp. 164–73.

13 From Spinoza, *Short Treatise* II, 2.

14 T. Van Doesburg, 'Dadaïsme' in *Het Vaderland*, 3 Februari 1923, p. 2. With thanks to Evert van Straaten, who traced the origin of this quote.

15 In *'Over de toekomstige bouwkunst en haar architectonische mogelijkheden'* (on the future art of building and its architectonic possibilites), 1921, Oud had stated: 'Ornament is het universeel geneesmiddel voor bouwkundige impotentie' (Ornament is the universal medicine for architectural impotence). Reprint in J.J.P. Oud, *Ter wille van een levendige bouwkunst*, The Hague-Rotterdam, 1962, p. 24.

16 Kloos' Rijnlands Lyceum in Wassenaar, designed in 1938 and built in 1939, was published in *de 8 en Opbouw*, 1940, no. 9, pp. 89–98.

17 This paragraph was left out of the published version in *Forum*.

18 Oud's work took a neo-classic turn when he designed the headoffice of the Bataafse Import Maatschappij (BIM), built in The Hague in 1937–42. After the war he continued working in the same retrograde manner, notably in his design of the National Monument on the Dam in Amsterdam (1946–56). On the occasion of an exhibition on Le Corbusier in the Amsterdam Stedelijk Museum in the spring of 1958 Oud published a review in *De Groene Amsterdammer* (12 April 1958) that turned out to be rather critical of the post-war work of his Swiss colleague.

19 W. van Tijen, 'Het bureau Van den Broek en Bakema', in *Forum*, 1957, no. 6, pp. 167–189.
20 The artist does not do what the others take to be beautiful but only that what is necessary to him. Original German quote from A. Schoenberg, *Harmonielehre*, 1911, p. 495.
21 *I.e.* the Schröder House, Prins Hendriklaan 50, Utrecht (1924).
22 Quoted from Rietveld's short article 'industriële vormgeving' in *Open Oog*, 1946, no. 1.
23 Hans Jaffé (1915–1984) presented his PhD on De Stijl at the University of Amsterdam in 1956. His dissertation, *De Stijl 1917–1931*, was published the same year by Meulenhoff in Amsterdam.
24 Van Eyck quotes from Rietveld's article 'Nieuwe zakelijkheid in de Nederlandse architectuur', published in *De Vrije Bladen*, 1932, no. 7; reprinted in M. Küper and I. van Zijl, *Gerrit Rietveld 1888–1964*, exhibition catalogue Centraal Museum, Utrecht, 1992, pp. 32–39.
25 'League of New Plasticism', see the introduction to the present chapter.
26 Van Eyck refers to Martin Visser, one of the first admirers and promotors of the Dutch experimentalists. He had his house built in Bergeijk by Rietveld in 1955–1956. Later, in 1967, Visser asked Van Eyck to extend the house with an exhibition room.
27 Van Eyck refers to the house Rietveld built in 1951 for the Stoop family in Velp.
28 Rietveld built the sculpture pavilion for the Sonsbeek exhibition near Arnhem in 1955. In 1966 Van Eyck would build another pavilion on the same spot. Both pavilions were demolished but reconstructed in the grounds of the Kröller-Müller museum, Rietveld's in 1965, Van Eyck's in 2006.
29 The Dutch Pavilion in the Venice Biennale gardens was built by Rietveld in 1953–1954.
30 The Verrijn Stuart summerhouse, a house with a curved plan and a thatched roof built in 1940–1941 on a finger of land in the Loosdrecht lakes.
31 *De 8 en Opbouw*, 1941, no. 8, pp. 106–107.
32 A et A (Architectura et Amicitia) is a Dutch society of architects, founded in 1855 and mainly concerned with the cultural aspects of architecture. In the course of its existence it took important initiatives in the fields of education, building regulation and preservation. It regularly organized seminars and published important reviews such as *Wendingen* and *Forum*. (On the history of A et A, see Jeroen Schilt and J. van der Werf, *Genootschap Architectura et Amicitia*, 010, Rotterdam, 1992.) In February 1956 A et A devoted a seminar to the issue of 'form and content' and invited Annie Romein-Verschoor (1895–1978), Marxist historian and distinguished Dutch intellectual, to give the introductory lecture. Her lecture and the subsequent discussion were published in *Forum*, 1955–1956, no. 12, pp. 393–399 and 427–428 (with thanks to Jeroen Schilt who provided this information). In the course of her lecture Annie Romein-Verschoor expressed some scepticism about contemporary artists 'who try to resolve the eternal problem of form and content on an irrational basis'. Apparently hinting at Cobra, she stated that those who complain of being hindered by rationality mostly prove 'to be small, limited intellects'.
33 This paragraph was left out of the published version in *Forum*.
34 The Fokker jet assembly halls in Schiphol were built in 1945–53 by H.A. Maaskant.
35 The first postwar joint meeting of 'the 8' and 'Opbouw', which took place on 28 June 1947 in the rotunda on top of the Van Nelle factory in Rotterdam.
36 See chap. 2, p. 43. Remarkably, in this version Van Eyck specifies 'reality' as 'a new reality'.
37 M.J. Granpré Molière (1883–1972), professor of architecture at Delft Polytechnic from 1924 to 1952, was the founder and the leader of the so-called Delft School, the traditionalist movement in Dutch architecture. Being a convinced Catholic, he based his thinking on the philosophy of Thomas Aquinas and developed an explicitly hierarchical view of the world, in which the lower was subordinated to the higher and everything was ultimately subordinate to a Prime Mover. He saw this hierarchy as the most appropriate model for the organization of a harmonious society. He fiercely opposed the rationalization and uniformization of architecture, caused by industrialization and social levelling. Still, due to his erudition and acuity, he made a great impression on his younger modernist opponents, notably Van Tijen, Bakema and Van Eyck. In Van Eyck's view Molière was obviously holding 'the wrong stick', i.e. his hierarchical, subordinative worldview, his Ruskinian submission to tradition and his total misunderstanding of the new consciousness. With 'the right end of the stick' he indubitably meant Molière's rejection of unilateral rationalism and functionalism, his view of architecture as a bearer of meaning and his plea for a poetic approach to architecture and town planning.
38 The garden village of Vreewijk (1915) in Rotterdam south is generally considered the most successful work by Molière.

39 In his apologia of the Delft School ('Delft en het Nieuwe Bouwen' in *Katholiek Bouwblad*, 1947, no. 13) Molière compared architecture to the art of organizing a dinner. Just as a good dinner cannot be reduced to mere feeding, but must also be a relief to the spirit, so architecture should not be reduced to mere utility and material confort.

40 Passage re-edited in accordance with the manuscript.

41 This is the final paragraph of Rietveld's article 'Nieuwe zakelijkheid in de Nederlandse architectuur', see note 24.

Squares with a smile

1 *De Groene Amsterdammer*, a weekly newspaper, published this article a week after the opening of the Rietveld exhibition at the Utrecht Central Museum. For this account, written for a general public, Van Eyck borrowed several passages from 'De bal kaatst terug' ('The Ball rebounds'), published in *Forum* two months before.

2 In his youth Aldo van Eyck was familiar with poets such as Geerten Gossaert, Jacques Bloem, Martinus Nijhoff, Adriaan Roland Holst and William B. Yeats, who were all friends of his father. Later he was friendly with Til Brugman, Lucebert, Hugo Claus and Bert Schierbeek.

3 On Annie Romein-Verschoor, see note 32 to 'The Ball rebounds'.

4 Quoted from Rietveld's short article 'industriële vormgeving' in *Open Oog*, 1946, no. 1.

5 In fact the article referred to, 'The Ball rebounds', was published in March, while the present article appeared in May.

6 Van Eyck means Jan Engelman (1900–1972), a Dutch poet who entered the public eye in 1932 by publishing *De Tuin van Eros* (The Garden of Eros), a collection of erotic poems. See note 4 to 'The Ball rebounds'.

7 Van Eyck quotes from Rietveld's article *'Nieuwe zakelijkheid in de Nederlandse architectuur',* published in *De Vrije Bladen*, 1932, no. 7; reprinted in M. Küper and I. van Zijl, *Gerrit Rietveld 1888–1964*, exhibition catalogue Centraal Museum, Utrecht, 1992, pp. 32–39.

8 'League of New Plasticism', see the introduction to the present chapter.

9 An allusion to the exhibition *'Opdracht'*, held in the Amsterdam Stedelijke museum from 5 May to 16 June 1956 and organized by the *Vereniging van Beoefenaars van de Monumentale Kunsten* (Society of Practitioners of Monumental Arts).

10 Rietveld built the sculpture pavilion for the Sonsbeek exhibition near Arnhem in 1955.

11 The Dutch Pavilion in the Venice Biennale gardens was built by Rietveld in 1953–54.

12 The Verrijn Stuart summerhouse, a house with a curved plan and a thatched roof built in 1940–41 on a finger of land in the Loosdrecht lakes.

The space behind the eye

1 Undated typescript in the Van Eyck archives. This statement was possibly a reaction to the exhibition Kleur (Colour), organized by the Liga Nieuw Beelden in the Amsterdam Stedelijk Museum from 8 november to 8 December 1958. Van Eyck's quote 'without light no colour' appears to be a paraphrase of a statement in the catalogue leaflet: 'Kleur is licht. Als het licht verdwijnt, verdwijnt ook de kleur' (Colour is light. When the light disappears, colour also disappears).

On the relationship between architecture and art

1 The enquiry, issued by the Liga Nieuw Beelden (League of New Plasticism) on the occasion of its exhibition *verbondenheid der kunsten* (solidarity of the arts) in October 1959, focused on the different ways art and architecture could possibly 'go together': cooperation (between autonomous architecture and autonomous works of art), synthesis (architecture and works of art considered as clearly separated elements and joined into a mutually stimulating polarity) or integration (construction of an entirely new entity, merging art and architecture into an indivisible unity). Quoted from the introduction by Hartsuyker, in *Forum*, 1959, no. 6, p. 175.

Good morning, sculpture

1 Article published on the occasion of an exhibition of Carel Visser, in the De Jong Lithographic Printing House in Hilversum. Carel Visser (born in 1928) is considered one of the major Dutch constructivist sculptors. His work from the fifties and sixties mainly consists of assemblages or stackings of identical elements, both geometrical and biomorphic. From the start he was intuitively concerned with the question of how to link individual things and how to shape their relationship, a concern that fitted in closely with Van Eyck's preoccupation with the in-between. After they became friends in 1953, Van Eyck told him about Brancusi and he went to visit the artist in Paris.

Apart from numerous sculptures of mating birds, Visser also made the iron 'family' (1955) which he gave on loan to Van Eyck. On Visser, see J.L. Locher, *Carel Visser*, Van Dooren, Vlaardingen, 1972.

Visser is a winged digger

1 Introduction to a photographic survey of Visser's bird sculptures, which Van Eyck included next to the publication of his Orphanage in Forum, 1961, no. 6–7. Van Eyck wrote both a Dutch version and this English one.

Hello Shinkichi

1 Article written in English and published in the catalogue of a Tajiri exhibition which ran from 2 March to 2 April 1960 at the Amsterdam Stedelijk Museum. Shinkichi Tajiri (born in Los Angeles in 1923) is an American-Dutch artist of Japanese origin, active as sculptor and painter, photographer and film-maker. After the Second World War he studied in the studios of Zadkine and Léger in Paris. He participated in Cobra and settled in the Netherlands. Most of his early work is marked by the traumatic experiences he went through as a voluntary American GI during the war. He endeavoured to counteract the horror he witnessed with both aggressive and vitalist expressions. On Tajiri, see H. Bavelaar and E. Barents, *Shinkichi Tajiri. Sculptor,* Sdu/Openbaar Kunstbezit, The Hague, 1990; and M. Vleugels, ed., *9 rue d'Odessa – the Tajiri Genealogy*, Stichting Pensioenfonds, Heerlen, 2001.

2 Aldo van Eyck recalls a memory from his secondary school days at Sidcot, a Quaker school in Somerset, England. As a boy he had a soft spot for reptiles, lizards and other 'quasi surrealistic Hieronymus Bosch creatures'. He found them on his speleological excursions in the caves of the Mendip Hills, near the said school.

3 I.e. the first Cobra Exhibition, November 1949.

4 'A game with shabby remnants', Hugo Ball, Tagebuch, 12 June 1916, in *Die Flucht aus der Zeit*, Munich, 1927.

5 'The artist is a receptacle of emotions coming from anywhere: from the sky, the earth, a scrap of paper, a passing figure or a spider's web. That is why one should not discriminate between things. For them there are no quarters of nobility' quoted from Christian Zervos, 'Conversation avec Picasso', in *Cahiers d'Art*, 1935, VII-X, pp. 173–178.

6 *Robber Symphony* is a 1936 surrealist film by Friedrich Feher. *The Beggar's Opera* is a satirical opera written in 1728 by John Gay. Conceived as a persiflage of the then prevailing Italian opera, it substituted the usual aristocratic characters and dignitaries by criminals and prostitutes.

7 Tajiri was married to Ferdi Jansen (1927–1969), an artist who acquired a reputation through her 'hortisculptures'.

Speech for the award of the 1962 Sikkens Prize

1 The Sikkens Prize, set up in 1959 by the Sikkens Paint factory, was intended 'as a mark of recognition for an artist whose work had achieved a synthesis of space and colour'. The first time, in 1959, it was awarded to Gerrit Rietveld. Van Eyck got the prize twice, in 1960 with Constant for their joint 'spatial colourism' experiment of 1952, in 1961 with Joost van Roojen for their collaboration on the playground at the Amsterdam Zeedijk (1956–1958). In 1962 the prize was awarded to the editors of the review *Structure*, whose ambition it was to continue the tradition of De Stijl. Van Eyck, being the recipient of the previous prize, was asked to introduce the new prizewinners.

2 After Cobra, Constant's work took an abstract turn. Then he abandoned painting and joined *the Internationale Situationiste*. In 1958 with Guy Debord, he launched the programme for a 'Unitary Urbanism', in fact it was the programme of his 'New Babylon' project on which he had embarked two years before, a utopian city that would enable modern man to lead a nomadic existence and affirm himself thoroughly as a 'homo ludens'. After the publication of 'Unitary Urbanism' (in *Forum*, 1956, no. 6) Constant and Van Eyck went in different directions but this did not prevent them from mutual appreciation.

3 Obviously a reaction to 'Unitary Urbanism', the first sentence of which reads: 'The starting point of unitary urbanism is the changing nature of our aspirations and activities'.

4 I.e. The Amsterdam Orphanage.

5 When Baljeu founded the review *Structure* in 1958, he had secured the cooperation of a number of kindred spirits from different countries: his fellow-countryman Dick van Woerkom, Charles Biederman (USA), Jean Gorin (France), Anthony Hill, Kenneth and Mary Martin (England). The Swiss Max Bill and Richard P. Lohse also occasionally lent their cooperation. In view of its international orientation this Amsterdam-based review was edited in English. In May 1962 the work of the group was presented in the exhibition 'Experiment in Construction' at the Amsterdam Stedelijk Museum. Data derived from: Jonneke

Jobse, *De Stijl Continued – The Journal Structure (1958–1964)*, 010 Publishers, Rotterdam 2005.

6 J. Baljeu, *Mondrian or Miró*, De Beuk, Amsterdam 1958.

7 'The world in one man, that's the modern poet', quoted from Max Jacob, in *Art poétique*, Emile-Paul, Paris 1922.

8 This paragraph was written in English.

9 In *Structure*, 1962, no. 2.

10 'Pataphysics' was invented by the French writer Alfred Jarry (1873–1907) who defined it as 'the science of imaginary solutions, which symbolically attributes the properties of objects, described by their virtuality, to their lineaments' (quoted from Jarry's *Gestes et opinions du docteur Faustroll, pataphysicien, roman néo-scientifique*, written in 1898 and posthumously published in 1911). The pataphysical science is perpetuated in the Collège de Pataphysique in Paris and the London Institute of Pataphysics.

11 In 1951 the Dutch government decided to reserve 1.5% of the cost of every new public building for the incorporation of plastic art (sculpture, murals, mosaics etc.).

12 See P. Mondrian, 'Natuurlijke en abstracte realiteit', 'trialogue' published in *De Stijl*, June 1919 – August 1920, particularly the last three sections in *De Stijl*, 1920, nos. 8, 9 and 10; and P. Mondrian, 'De realiseering van het Neoplasticisme in de verre toekomst en in de huidige architectuur' (the realization of Neoplasticism in the distant future and in present architecture), in *De Stijl*, 1922 nos. 3 and 5.

13 Mondrian quoted by Til Brugman in her article 'Piet Mondriaan omstreeks 1910' in the catalogue of the 1946 Mondrian exhibition in the Amsterdam Stedelijk Museum. For Til Brugman, see also Van Eyck's opening speech for the 1988 Van Doesburg exhibition in chapter 14.

14 For Jan Engelman, see note 4 of 'The Ball rebounds' in the present chapter.

Chapter 6
The beginning of Team 10 and the end of CIAM

Introduction to chapter 6

1 On the end of CIAM and the development of Team 10, see Van Eyck's 'Story of Another Idea' (chap. 7 of the present book), A. Smithson, *The Emergence of Team 10 out of CIAM*, Architectural Association, London, 1982; and *Team 10 Meetings 1953–1984*, Rizzoli, New York, 1991; F. Strauven, *Aldo van Eyck – the Shape of Relativity*, Architectura et Natura, Amsterdam, 1998; E. Mumford, *The CIAM Discourse on Urbanism, 1928–1960*, MIT Press, Cambridge, Mass., 2000; M. Risselada and D. van den Heuvel, *Team 10, 1953–81*, NAi Publishers, Rotterdam, 2005.

2 The interim congress at Sigtuna took place from 25 to 30 June 1952. Its participants included a number of younger members such as Wogensky, Candilis, Bakema, Van Eyck, Van Bodegraven, Korsmo, Schwarz and Norberg-Schulz. Partly because leading veterans such as Le Corbusier, Gropius and Giedion were absent, the younger contingent played a considerable role in the discussions. Also present was the Swedish historian Gregor Paulsson, who had already outlined the ecological meaning of 'habitat' at the 1951 Hoddesdon congress.

3 See chap. 2 of the present book.

4 For Patrick Geddes and his Valley Section, see Volker M. Welter, 'Post-war CIAM, Team X and the influence of Patrick Geddes', in *CIAM, Team 10, the English Context*, Faculty of Architecture, TU Delft, 2001, pp. 87–110.

5 See note 1 to 'Statement on habitat'.

6 At the UNESCO Headquarters, on 30 June 1954.

7 'Draft Framework 4', a document reproduced by A. Smithson in *The Emergence of Team 10 out of CIAM* (cit., pp. 38–41) and by M. Risselada and D. van den Heuvel in *Team 10, 1953–81* (cit., pp. 48–49) but erroneously dated '1956'. It was in fact written round about the end of September 1954.

8 A reproduction of this letter, dated 31 October 1954, is included in *The Emergence of Team 10 out of CIAM, cit.*, pp. 36–37.

9 When preparing the final version of the Instructions for CIAM 10, P. Smithson wrote in a letter to Bakema (incorrectly dated "Sunday 15.10.'54", but probably Sunday 14.11.1954): 'We still feel that the "Suplement Hollandaise" [sic] is at the same time too detailed & too vague. I, personally, question the fundamental validity of isolating any aspects of a problem & codifying them in this way. We empirical radicals (the bloody English!) feel terribly, & I hope, creatively, against analysis which may not be relevant to the nature of the enquiry, or of presupposing that say the disciplines of "number" or "growth" are the most important things at this time, or if they are essential to the discipline of built form *at all*. I have good & rational (National?) doubts, while remaining your obedient servant.'

10 The first quotation is from a letter from Le Corbusier to Sert on 23 July 1956, and the second from the 'Message de Le Corbusier adressé au X Congrès CIAM à Dubrovnic' of the same date appended to that letter; both are included in the provisional report CIAM 10 Dubrovnik 1956, pp. 23–30 (Bakema archives, NAi Rotterdam).

11 'Summary of a talk which Merkelbach, Van Eyck and Bakema had with Van Eesteren about CIAM ', in the provisional report CIAM 10 Dubrovnik 1956, p. 33.

12 Quoted from the minutes of a discussion between Bakema, Van Eyck, Hovens Greve and Hartsuyker on 31 January 1957 (Bakema Archives, NAi, Rotterdam).

Statement on Habitat

1 The Doorn meeting took place from 29 to 31 January 1954 in 'De Paddesstoel', the parental home of Lucia Hubrecht, the then spouse of Daniel van Ginkel. The Dutch group consisted of Bakema, Van Eyck, Van Ginkel and Hovens Greve. They had invited Wogensky, Candilis, Lasdun, Voelcker and Gutman. Of these only Voelcker showed up. Remarkably, the Smithsons were not invited, but Peter Smithson arrived in place of Lasdun. So the Doorn meeting was attended by Bakema, Van Eyck, Van Ginkel, Hovens Greve, Peter Smithson and Voelcker.

2 In the original draft of this declaration, handwritten by Peter Smithson and reproduced in *The Emergence of Team 10 out of CIAM* (cit., pp. 28–32), one reads *human relations*, but crossed out and 'corrected' as *human associations*. Peter Smithson, obviously at the suggestion of his Dutch fellow team members, initially wrote 'relations', but preferred to substitute it by 'associations'. However, these terms cannot be considered synonyms, especially not in the way they were understood by the two parties. The Smithsons used 'association' in the sense of a society or a group of people organized in a particular way and at a particular place. For Bakema and Van Eyck 'relation' meant the (spatial or mental) connection between people, between things, or between people and things. Another symptom of the initial discord was that Alison Smithson would subsequently brush aside the Doorn declaration as agreed upon in Doorn. In her *Team 10 Primer* (1962 and 1968) she replaced that declaration with the text she had tabled in advance with her husband in preparation for the Doorn meeting.

Letter to the Smithsons on the guideline for CIAM 10

1 Letter written as a response to the Smithsons' 'Instructions to groups, draft framework 3' after this document had been discussed at a joint meeting of Team 10 with Giedion and Le Corbusier at the latter's apartment in Paris on 14 September 1954. The letter is undated but according to Bakema's 20 points letter, dated 20 September 1954, it was sent shortly afterwards.

2 In fact, this passage from the Doorn declaration did not appear in the Smithsons' preparatory text for the Doorn meeting which they were subsequently to present as the Doorn Manifesto.

3 After CIAM 9 it was decided to organize CIAM 10 in Algiers, but because of the outbreak of the Algerian war of independence in late 1954, this location was abandoned. In September 1955, at an interim congress at La Sarraz, it was decided that CIAM 10 would take place in Dubrovnic.

4 Van Eyck refers to points 12, 13 and 14 of Bakema's 20 points list (see the introduction to this chapter). Point 14 reads: 'The need for change is not an attempt to escape from the necessary construction of order, but for the moment we have to recognize it as the most important base of it'.

5 This theme had been introduced in 1952 by the Dutch CIAM member Wim van Bodegraven at the interim congress in Sigtuna.

6 Bakema's point 5 reads: 'The idea of full life is a great thing that is growing in such little daily activities as washing, eating, working, recreation, sleeping.'

7 Van Eyck appears to interpret the notion of 'doorstep' in a much broader way than the Smithsons themselves intended when they advanced it at CIAM 9 in Aix-en-Provence. Rather than limiting it to the transition between the house and the street, Van Eyck extended its meaning to cover every significant relation between man and man, and between man and things.

Orientation

1 After Bakema and Van Eyck sent their remarks and suggestions concerning draft 3 of the guideline for CIAM 10, the Smithsons mailed a draft 4 of the said guideline which appeared to only casually incorporating some of the Dutch ideas. So Van Eyck decided to rework the instructions himself in order to articulate his and Bakema's views properly.

2 Quoted from Mondrian's article 'Plastic Art and Pure Plastic Art' in J.L. Martin, B. Nicholson, N. Gabo, Circle, London, 1937, p. 47. By reintroducing this quote, Van Eyck not only recalls his stand at CIAM 6 in 1947 but also draws attention to the cultural and aesthetic meaning of the notion of 'relation' that Team 10 was introducing, 30 years after Mondrian, in the field of architecture and urbanism.
3 'Just the necessary substrate between wine and life', dedication by Tristan Tzara to Tess van Eyck, the architect's daughter, on 23 November 1945, in the Sixième Cahier in the Habitude de la Poésie series published by Guy Levis Mano.

Nagele grid for CIAM 10

1 Nagele was a new village on the newly reclaimed Northeast Polder, designed by the Amsterdam CIAM group 'de 8'. Van Eyck played a decisive role in the development of the project, notably in the early conceptual phase (1948) and the final design (1954). The village images incorporated in the couple's silhouette refer to the different social and religious backgrounds the immigrants would bring along.

Talk at the Otterlo Congress

1 Transcription and partial translation of Van Eyck's talk, as tape-recorded by Herman Haan at the Congress. (The Otterlo tapes are deposited at the NAi, Rotterdam.) Van Eyck spoke alternately in English and French. The French passages were translated and integrated into the English. This condensed reproduction of the spoken version brings to light some aspects that were left out in the edited version.
2 Wendel H. Lovett (born 1922) was an architect from Seattle who was proposed as a participant in the Otterlo congress by the former American CIAM Chapter. Two days before Van Eyck's talk he had presented his work: a detached house for one family facing Lake Washington. This project had been severely criticized by Peter Smithson and more moderately by Van Eyck. See O. Newman, CIAM '59 in Otterlo, K. Krämer, Stuttgart, 1961, pp. 48–49.
3 After this introduction Van Eyck presented the design of his Amsterdam Orphanage which was under construction at that moment.

Is architecture going to reconcile basic values?

1 Published by Oscar Newman in CIAM '59 in Otterlo, K. Krämer, Stuttgart, 1961, pp. 26–29. As this version was edited two years after the Otterlo congress, Van Eyck had the opportunity to formulate his thoughts more carefully and to add some of the ideas he developed in the meantime, notably his idea that a city should be a large house while a house should be a tiny city. He actually first formulated this idea in the 'door and window' number of Forum, issued in August 1960.
2 Van Eyck is refering to the Torre Velasca in Milan by Belgiojoso, Peressutti and Rogers, presented by the last-mentioned at the Otterlo congress, where it was severely criticized by Peter Smithson. See O. Newman, CIAM '59 in Otterlo, K. Krämer, Stuttgart, 1961, pp. 92–97.
3 When the Smithsons advanced the notion of 'doorstep' at CIAM 9, they meant by this no more than the extension of the house into the public realm, the transition between home and street, a rather subordinate factor to link their first level of association to the second. But Van Eyck immediately drew a connection with Buber's idea of the Zwischen introduced by Gutman and Manz at the Sigtuna congress.
4 The text goes on to discuss the Amsterdam Orphanage.
5 Published by Oscar Newman, op. cit., pp. 216–217.

Letter to Giedion on the dissolution of CIAM

1 Personal reaction to an open letter written by Giedion on behalf of the former CIAM Council and sent out on 10 December 1960, handwritten document in the Van Eyck Archives.
2 At the conclusion of the Otterlo congress the radical core of Team 10 (Bakema, Van Eyck, the Smithsons and Voelcker) decided to continue organizing meetings among themselves and those they were to invite, but no longer do this under the name of CIAM. Since Team 10 constituted the last vital force in the thirty-one-year-old organization, this act meant its certain demise – a fact that was directly acknowledged by the professional press. In October 1959 Architectural Design noted that 'the Death of CIAM was formally announced at Otterlo, Holland, this September'. In February 1960 the Architectural Review printed a photograph of the Smithsons, Voelcker and Bakema holding a placard featuring in big capitals 'C.I.A.M.' the death of which was sealed by a cross sign, a fact

enacted by Blance Lemco and Van Eyck lying underneath it. The article left no doubt about Team 10's responsibility for the failure of CIAM's 'resurrection move' and also quoted those who deeply regretted the state of affairs, notably Ernesto Rogers and Kunio Maekawa, who were of the opinion that the support of CIAM was still badly needed by those who wanted to commit themselves to progressive architecture. And in October 1960 Kenzo Tange stated in the *Japan Architect* that the decision to drop CIAM had been taken without his knowledge, after he had left Otterlo. He felt that CIAM should 'remain organized under the same name as before' and believed that it would continue to develop, albeit 'no longer centred around Europe but around other areas'. These messages did not fail to affect the old CIAM guard. Instigated by Gropius and Sert, Giedion drew up an open letter to voice the viewpoint of the former CIAM Council. In this letter, circulated on 10 December 1960, Giedion summed up the achievements of CIAM and stated that since 1953 the Council had planned to hand over the helm to the younger generation. He pointed out that the representatives of this generation – Team 10 – had been eager to develop their activities under the name of CIAM until the last La Sarraz conference, but that in Otterlo a minority fraction within Team 10 had decided to distance itself from CIAM. Referring to the reaction of Kenzo Tange, he stated that the majority of those present in Otterlo thought otherwise and expressed the hope that CIAM would continue to be 'a positive workable platform', in particular with regard to 'the vast areas coming only now into the orbit of the contemporary evolution' (published in Architectural Design, January 1961, p. 5; Architectural Review, March 1961, p. 154; and in Forum, 1960/61, no. 5, p. 189). Bakema responded with an open letter (published in *Forum*, 1960/61, no. 5, p. 189; and in Architectural Review, April 1961, p. 226) stating that Team 10 had in no way abolished but simply withdrawn from CIAM, and that those who wished to continue 'should certainly do so'. Aldo van Eyck reacted to Giedion with the present personal letter.

3 Wilhelm Schütte (1900–1968), a German architect who settled in Vienna after the Second World War. He worked for Ernst May in Frankfurt (1925–1930) and Russia (1930–1934), and played an active role in CIAM from 1947. Schütte had delegated Eduard Sekler to Otterlo.

4 When Team 10 was instituted at the Paris Council meeting in July 1954, it was placed under the supervision of an Advisory Group composed of Sert, Giedion, Le Corbusier, Gropius and Tyrwhitt. When Bakema finally sent out the Team's instructions for CIAM 10, the Advisory Group, or at least its American resident contingent, voiced its dissatisfaction in a letter to all CIAM groups. Its criticism was silenced by Le Corbusier who took up the defence of Team 10 in an open letter. 'The elements established by Team 10 are reasonable and perfectly acceptable' he wrote. Only then were the new ideas of Team 10 taken seriously.

5 In 1947 Giedion had asked Barbara Hepworth to participate in CIAM 6, but she declined the invitation. She felt 'that the gulf between architects and sculptors is a very large one and that it can only be bridged by a change of heart in the architects. I felt that that the question to be asked should not be "should the architect and sculptor collaborate from the beginning?" but "why do the architects and sculptors not collaborate from the beginning!" … During my last exhibition I found there was a keen sense, among all kinds of people, of the part that sculpture plays in life, except among the architects. They all stood with their backs to the sculptures and bewailed their lot, or chattered about new materials.' (As quoted by Giedion in *Architecture you and me,* Harvard, 1958, pp. 73–74.)

6 In the first version of *The Story of Another Idea*, distributed to the participants of the Otterlo congress, Van Eyck had qualified Gropius as 'the dullest character who ever aspired to fame', a passage which in the *Forum* version mailed to the subscribers was replaced by 'a persevering art pedagogue rather than an artist'.

7 I.e. the story of an other idea, in *Forum*, 1959, no. 7; see chapter 7.

8 In *Forum*, 1960, no. 3; see chapter 8.

About the Economist project

1 The first few years after the Otterlo congress were probably the happiest period in the life of Team 10. The group deliberately restricted itself to ten members, the 'family' as Alison Smithson called them, who now (in 1961) consisted of Bakema, Van Eyck, Candilis, Woods, the Smithsons, Voelcker, Erskine, Grung and Soltan. They held 'family meetings' twice a year and occasionally organized a larger meeting with a careful selection of invited guests. They decided to set out their ideas in a publication, the *Team 10 Primer,* which was to be edited by Alison Smithson. The letters they wrote to each other at that time reveal a particularly optimistic mood. In one of

them (a handwritten note on the minutes of the Paris meeting in early January 1961) Alison Smithson suggests buying and restoring the Villa Savoye at Poissy – with or without public backing – and to set it up as a 'family house'. Van Eyck's present letter, expressing his appreciation for the Smithsons' Economist complex, is undated but is likely to have been written after the 'family meeting' of early July 1961 at the Smithson's home in London. At that time the project was in the course of being worked out. It would be carried out between September 1962 and June 1964.
2 The Economist complex was to be built in St James Street, next to the neo-classical Boodle's club.

Chapter 7
The new start of Forum: The Story of Another Idea

Introduction to chapter 7

1 For Van Eyck's memories of this friend, see 'Joop Hardy, autumn man between winters' in chapter 14.
2 That the author was Van Eyck was not immediately apparent. It was only mentioned on the last page, at the end of the list of illustrations. The manifesto was put forward as a collective statement by the new editorial team.
3 Giedion had selected these quotes from the reports of pre-war CIAM congresses in order to summarize 'CIAM's attitude towards Housing and Urban development from 1928 to 1953'. This summary was meant as an introduction to the planned *Charte de l'Habitat*. See S. Giedion, 'Prolegomena pour une Charte d'Habitat' in CIAM 10 Dubrovnic 1956 (stencilled preliminary report), pp. 51–60.

The Story of Another Idea

1 Originally, *'Poser la question de l'Habitat moderne c'est poser le problème de l'art de vivre aujourd'hui. Cet art existe-t-il ?'*, quoted from Le Corbusier, 'Introduction au Congrès', mimeograph in CIAM 9 files, Bakema archives, NAi.
2 The original version specifies 'the Netherlands' instead of 'the western world'.
3 Dr. G. Scott Williamson was co-founder and director of the pioneering Health Centre in Peckham near London, a combination of a preventive medical institute and a social club, equipped with extensive sporting and recreational facilities. The seat of the centre was built in 1934–36 by Owen Williams. Scott Williamson was invited as guest speaker to CIAM 8. The present quote is the beginning of his lecture, as published in the mimeographed report of the congress. In *The Heart of the City*, the official report of the congress, published by Tyrwhitt, Sert and Rogers in 1952, this passage was left out.
4 Quoted from 'CIAM Dissolution', a note written by the Smithsons in March 1957 and included by A. Smithson in *The Emergence of Team 10 out of CIAM*, AA London, 1982, p. 77.
5 John Voelcker, 'CIAM 10, Dubrovnic, 1956' in *Architects' Yearbook 8*, London 1957, pp. 43–52.
6 Van Eyck argues that urbanism is the only discipline among the contemporary arts and sciences to have ignored the essential renewal of the twentieth century, an accusation that in the Dutch context could be targeted in the first place at none other than Van Eesteren. Having been an assistant to Van Doesburg, he had been in a position to draw inspiration from one of the original wellsprings of the new consciousness.
7 Van Eesteren had presented his Amsterdam General Extension Plan at the Athens congress of 1933 as a prototype of 'the functional city'. Unlike Le Corbusier's 'Ville Radieuse', Van Eesteren's plan was far from a project of urban morphology. However, what Van Eyck appears to pose as an alternative is not the said Corbusian concept, which he appreciated for its poetic connotations rather than for its concrete form, but an image of a quite different order. This is clear from the illustrations. The aerial photo of a row development in Slotermeer is not contrasted with a *Unité d'habitation* but with a lively pavement *trattoria* in an unnamed Roman street.
8 In fact, the following quotes from pre-war congresses were selected by Giedion in order to sum up the merits of CIAM. See the introduction to this chapter.
9 Translation of the original French version by Van Eyck.
10 A quote from Van Doesburg's *Klassiek-barok-modern* (1918), De Sikkel, Antwerp 1920, p. 28, translated by Van Eyck.
11 Originally, 'Die soziologischen Grundlagen der Minimalwohnung für die städtische Bevölkerung', in *Die Wohnung für das Existenzminimum*, Frankfurt, 1930. Translation by Van Eyck.
12 This qualification of Gropius appeared in the pre-publication of the first *Forum* issue, prepared for

the participants in the Otterlo congress. On the insistence of Bakema, in the version eventually circulated to the subscribers it was replaced by 'a persevering art pedagogue rather than an artist'.

13 In response to Gropius' gesture, Van Eyck drew up a list of avant-garde artists who died during the war, including Mondrian, Klee, Joyce, Jacob, García Lorca, Delaunay, Sophie Täuber, Malevich, Béla Bartók and Anton Webern. He also proposed the congress to send a message to a prominent survivor, Kurt Schwitters, who had turned sixty two months earlier and was currently living in the British Lake District, where he was working on his final Merzbau, a 'Merzbarn'.

14 Originally, *Rationelle Bebauungsweisen*, Julius Hoffmann Verlag, Stuttgart, 1931.

15 The original French version of the Athens Charter was published by Le Corbusier in 1941. The quotes are borrowed from the points 1, 2 and 77.

16 Originally, '*Die hohe Einsicht wohnt nicht in den einzelnen Kammern, sondern im Gefüge der Welt. Ihr entspricht ein Denken das sich nicht in abgesonderten und abgeteilten Wahrheiten bewegt, sondern in bedeutenden Zusammenhang, und dessen ordnende Kraft auf dan kombinatoischen Vermögen beruht*', a quote which Van Eyck derived from the contribution by Gutman and Manz to the interim congress at Sigtuna.

17 Van Eyck quotes from Giedion's lecture as it was reproduced in the provisional report of the Hoddesdon congress. This original version is slightly different from the edited version in Tyrwhitt, Sert and Rogers, *The Heart of the City*, London 1952.

18 In his introductory lecture, reproduced in the provisional report of the Hoddesdon congress.

19 During the open session on 11 July 1951.

20 Ibid.

21 From his lecture 'The Human Scale at the Core', on 10 July 1951. On Scott Williamson, see note 3.

22 This phrase is a translation of Bakema's original Dutch version: '*het moment waarop wij ons bewust worden van vollediger leven door het ervaren van betrekkingen waarvan we het bestaan niet kenden*', published in *Forum*, 1952, no. 6/7, p. 170. The version published by Tyrwhitt, Sert and Rogers in *The Heart of the City* (London 1952, p. 67) reads: 'the moment we become aware of the fullness of life by means of cooperative action'.

23 Quoted from Bakema, 'Relationship between Men and Things', in Tyrwhitt, Sert and Rogers, *Op. cit.*, pp. 67–68.

24 A chapter in Tyrwhitt, Sert and Rogers, *Op. cit.*, pp. 165–168, compiled from the 'Propositions' of the Commissions 1 and 6, respectively chaired by Le Corbusier and Emery.

25 'Summary of a talk which Merkelbach, Van Eyck and Bakema had with Van Eesteren about CIAM' in CIAM 10 Dubrovnic 1956, provisional report, unpublished mimeograph, p. 33.

26 A statement by Martin Buber in *Urdistanz und Beziehung*, Lambert Schneider Verlag, Heidelberg, 1951. The German original reads as follows: '*Kunst ist weder Impression naturhafter Objektivität, noch Expression seelenhafter Subjektivität, sie ist Werk und Zeugnis der Beziehung zwischen der substantia humana und der substantia rerum, das Gestalt gewordene Zwischen.*'

Martin Buber (1878–1965) was a Jewish philosopher and theologian. Departing from German culture and imbued with Hasidic mysticism, he developed his own philosophy of dialogue, which displayed close affinities with existentialism. In *Ich und Du* (1923) he viewed human existence in terms of reciprocal I-Thou relations, as opposed to the impersonal and objectivizing I-It relations of rationalism. Actively involved in the political development of the young state of Israel, he advocated a form of non-authoritarian socialism.

27 Rolf Gutman and Theo Manz, 'Überlegungen über das Wesen des Thema's', in CIAM – *les documents de Sigtuna 1952*, unpublished report.

28 Originally, '*Il faut envisager le problème de la simultanéité et de la durée. CIAM est l'affirmation d'une nouvelle conception du temps dans l'architecture*', a statement which includes a reference to Bergson and his discussion of relativity in *Durée et simultanéité*, Paris, 1922.

29 Wim van Bodegraven, 'Time as an essential factor in planning', in CIAM – *les documents de Sigtuna 1952*, unpublished report. In his contribution to the Sigtuna congress the Dutch architect Van Bodegraven pointed out that the major extension plans being implemented in Amsterdam and elsewhere threatened to disrupt the organic coherence of the city as a whole. In order to prevent the growing cities from degenerating into unstructured conglomerates, he stated that the time dimension had to become an essential factor in modern town planning. As a possible procedure he proposed the development of an urban structure based on a rhythmic, sinusoidal movement which could 'continue in time and simultaneously in various dimensions'.

30 Notably the Algerian group headed by Emery and the Moroccan groups Gamma and Atbat, respectively headed by Ecochard and Candilis, who

brought up the problem of building *'pour le plus grand nombre'*. Gamma presented its housing projects for the new districts of Casablanca, in fact new types of urban fabric inspired by the traditional courtyard housing in the old Medina's. Candilis addressed the problem with some plastically articulated medium-rise blocks which were conceived as a vertical piling of courtyard dwellings. CIAM-Alger brought its fascinating *Bidonville Mahieddine* grid, presenting an Algerian squatter settlement as a meaningful example of habitat.

31 By inserting this verse from the Gospel of Matthew in this context Van Eyck conveys his accord with Candilis, who used a French version of it as a motto for his manifesto 'Habitat for the Greatest Number', published as a folder grid in *L'Architecture d'Aujourd'hui*, December 1953, no. 50–51.

32 Originally, *'Il faut que la vie passe avant tout et les feuilles du printemps s'ouvrent devant les feuilles de l'automne de l'année précédente qui se replient tranquillement et parfois tombent'.* Quote from a letter by Le Corbusier to Bakema, dated 18 November 1958 (FLC D3(19)145. With thanks to Arnaud Dercelles of the Fondation Le Corbusier, who provided this information.

33 A hint at Werner Moser.

34 Jules Supervielle (1884–1960), French poet born in Montevideo, Uruguay. Inspired by the pampas of his native country, his poetry deals with human loneliness and relatedness. The quoted verse is derived from *Naissances* (1951) and can be translated as follows: How difficult it is for us to find shelter, even in our heart. All the space is taken, and so is all warmth.

35 Franz Boas, *Primitive Art*, New York, 1955 (1927), p. 1.

36 More precisely, Alison and Peter Smithson, Howell and Voelcker, 'Draft Framework 3' of 'Instructions to Groups', September 1954.

37 'With the Athens Charter the corridor street disappeared. Now it is the corridor space that must disappear.' Candilis first coined the notion *'espace corridor'* in his article 'L'Esprit du plan masse de l'habitat' in *L'Architecture d'Aujourd'hui*, December 1954, no. 57, p. 1: *'Les espaces libres cessent d'être des espaces corridors entre volumes bâtis'.*

38 The Pendrecht (1949, 1951) and Alexanderpolder (1953, 1956) projects were the results of a continuous research of Opbouw (the Rotterdam CIAM group and notably its most inspired member Bakema) into the structure of the neighbourhood and the housing unit. Pendrecht was carried out in a rather different way by Lotte Stam-Beese, who worked as a town planning official at the Rotterdam Urban Development Department. She was also responsible for the entirely different development of Alexanderpolder (1961–70).

39 *'De steden zullen dorpsgewijs bewoond worden'* was Blom's first urban design project. He completed it in June 1958, at the end of his second year of study at the Amsterdam Academy of Architecture.

Chapter 8
Forum 1959–1963: from the shape of the in-between to configurative design

Introduction to chapter 8 by the editors

1 The notion of the 'dual phenomenon' first appears Van Eyck's 1950 letter to Giedion on the function of a UNESCO art review (see p. 48). Its roots can be traced back to the poetical intuitions of his youth and his understanding of avant-garde art. Van Eyck uses the term 'dual phenomenon' (in Dutch 'duofenomeen') until the publication of 'The Medicine of Reciprocity' (in *Forum*, April–May 1961). The term 'twin phenomenon' first appears in 'Steps towards a Configurative Discipline' (in *Forum*, August 1962). Later, he declared he had renamed the concept in order to avoid any suggestion of dualism. His decision was probably inspired by the crucial importance of the twin-relationship in Dogon culture, which he became acquainted with during his journey to Mali, in early 1960.

2 Blom's next project, a housing scheme for Slotermeer, was published in *Forum*, February 1961, the Orphanage in *Forum*, April–May 1961.

3 In English 'configuration' is considered the equivalent of the German *Gestalt*, i.e. 'an organized whole that is more than the sum of its parts'. In this sense it can be found in different contexts, in both art and social science. It constitutes the core concept of an important movement in American anthropology, the so-called Configurationist School formed by Edward Sapir, Ruth Benedict and Margaret Mead. On the other hand, Hans Arp conceived several of his compositions as *Konfigurationen*.

4 Bakema was no doubt inspired by N.J. Habraken who brought this idea to the fore in his book *De dragers en de mensen*, first published in 1961.

5 Notably 'Under Milk Wood' by Hans Tupker (in the 1961 August issue), the Craneveld exten-

sion plan by Joop van Stigt (in the 1962 October issue), and the Pestalozzi village projects by Blom and Van Stigt (in the first issue of 1963). The 'posthumous' 1967 issue opened with 'a study in configuration', an account of four configurative projects respectively by R. Blom van Assendelft, J. Koning, J. Stroeve and H. Tupker.

6 The term 'structuralism' was introduced in the architectural discourse by Herman Hertzberger in 1966, when he presented his competition project for the Valkenswaard town hall. The term was first endorsed by Arnaud Beerends (in TABK, 1969, no. 1) and later by Arnulf Luchinger (in Bauen+Wohnen, 1974, no. 5).

Day and Night

1 Unpublished manuscript, which Van Eyck rewrote and extended in 1962 to make the sixth chapter of The Child, the City and the Artist.

Aquarium design by Jan Verhoeven

1 Van Eyck was tutor of architectural design at the Amsterdam Academy of Architecture from 1954 to 1959. His teaching would have a far-reaching importance for students such as Piet Blom, Joop van Stigt and Jan Verhoeven. In 1958 he assigned a group of third-year students to design an aquarium building, asking them 'to give form to the relation between man and animal'. Jan Verhoeven made a particularly complex design, giving evidence of an uncommon spatial imagination. Van Eyck published this assessment in Forum, July 1960, a special issue dedicated to architectural education.

Between here and there, now and later

1 The 'door and window' issue of Forum was composed by Hardy and Van Eyck. While Hardy enlarged on the theme in a kind of écriture automatique, Van Eyck worded his view on the in-between in this dense poetical statement. The Dutch version ran over ten pages and was interspersed with numerous pictures. The English version which Van Eyck wrote at the same occasion was included at the end of the issue. Remarkably, both versions appear to be rather different. The Dutch one revolves around 'het gemoed', a specific Dutch notion meaning the interior of man as the seat of both thinking and feeling. In the English version this notion is missing. Apparently Van Eyck did not find an equivalent with the same emotional value. He got rid of the notion altogether and entirely rewrote the opening paragraphs. Reflecting more expressly on the meaning of space and time, he came to introduce the notions of place and occasion, which henceforth were to occupy an important place in his thinking. However, a few years later, in The Child, the City and the Artist, notably in chapter 7, he obviously adopted the notion of 'mind' as an equivalent for 'gemoed'. In light of this, we include the present more literal translation of the Dutch original. Van Eyck's own English version is included hereafter under the title 'There is a garden in her face'.

2 A verse by the seventeenth-century English poet Thomas Campion. The first stanza of the quoted poem reads as follows:
There is a Garden in her face,
Where Roses and white Lillies grow;
A heav'nly paradice is that place,
Wherein all pleasant fruits doe flow.
There Cherries grow, which none may buy
Till Cherry ripe themselves doe cry.

3 The mutual identification of house and city can be traced back to Alberti and Palladio. In De Re Aedificatoria (I, IX, 4–5) Alberti asks: 'If, as the philosophers maintain, the city is some large house, and the house is in turn like some small city, cannot the various parts of the house be considered little dwellings?' The philosophers he refers to are most likely Plato and Aristotle. (See Plato, Laws III, 679–680, and The Statesman 259 b; Aristotle, Politics I, 1252.) A hundred years later Palladio states the idea in a more affirmative way, in I Quattro Libri (1570), II, cap. XII, where he discusses the factors to be considered in the choice of a site for a villa: 'Finally, in choosing a place to build a villa, the same matters must be considered as in building a city; for the city is nothing other than a large house, and conversely the house is a little city.' Remarkably, Van Eyck did not know these precedents when he formulated the idea. He rediscovered it on his own while designing the Amsterdam orphanage, as a result of his thinking in terms of reciprocity.

4 'Counterform' is a neologism introduced by Van Eyck in order to make a clear distinction between architectural form and the form of life it shelters. The idea is that architecture should not be a servile reflection of social form, not a 'three-dimensional expression of human behaviour' as Bakema stated in the same Forum issue, but should encompass it with a counterform, an autonomous architectonic form rooted in its own tradition. It is only by virtue of its (relative) autonomy that architec-

tonic form is capable of contributing to the quality of the life it shelters.
5 Senmut, an ancient Egyptian courtier living in the fifteenth century B.C., was the architect of the Mortuary Temple at Deïr-el-Bahari.

'There is a garden in her face'

1 See note 1 to the previous text.
2 Published in *Forum*, August 1960, no. 3, p. 121. In the opening paragraphs Van Eyck simultaneously introduces the notions of space and time, which lead directly to the concepts of place and occasion, which henceforth are to take an important place in his thinking. The present text was repeatedly reedited under the title 'Place and Occasion', slightly modified in *Progressive Architecture*, September 1962, and noticeably shortened in *The Child, the City and the Artist*. The shortened version was first published in *Architectural Design*, December 1962 (see 'Place and Occasion' in chapter 11).
3 Senmut, an ancient Egyptian courtier living in the 15th century B.C., was the architect of the Mortuary Temple at Deïr-el-Bahari.

Interior Art

1 Mimeograph, part of a collection of lectures held at and edited by the Royal Academy of Art in The Hague in 1961. In this lecture Van Eyck dwells more circumstantially upon the ideas he condensed in 'between here and there, now and later' and 'There is a garden in her face'.

Dirty linen, mostly

1 In *Katholiek Bouwblad*, 1960, no. 3, its chief editor Jan Beerends had saluted the new *Forum* as 'the rebirth of romanticism' which he felt to be characteristic for the new spirit of the age. Identifying romanticism as Dionysian, he contrasted it with classicism which he identified as Apollonian.
2 Marius van Beek (1921–2003), sculptor and critic, reacted to *The Story of Another Idea* with an article entitled 'Faalt de hedendaagse architectuur?' (Does contemporary architecture fail?) published in the Utrecht newspaper *De Tijd*, on 26 September 1959.
3 In the fifties both *Katholiek Bouwblad* and *De Tijd* were outspokenly traditionalist. *Katholiek Bouwblad* was founded as a platform for Granpré Molière and kindred spirits.
4 Beerends found a number of romantic elements in the work of Kropholler and Kromhout, two traditionalist followers of the Amsterdam School.
5 Willem van Tijen (1894–1974), an eminent exponent of the second generation of Dutch functionalists, achieved fame through the Rotterdam flat buildings he carried out in the thirties. During the war he tried to bring about a reconciliation between functionalism and the traditionalism of the Delft School. After this attempt failed, he advocated a further development of functionalism, but in a less rigid, more mature and 'supple' form. Although he acknowledged the early work of Bakema as a realization of this view, he could not agree with the course taken by the new *Forum* team. In a letter (dated 9 August 1960) he set himself up as a spokesman of his generation in order to formulate his criticism. He stated that the new *Forum* had in no way introduced 'another idea', but at most a personal, somewhat different variant of what he had been trying to achieve in his working circles for years. He accused *Forum* of being unclear and vague, particularly of approaching architecture in an emotional and literary way. He branded the casbah idea as the very opposite of architecture, as a product of individualism and looseness that would result in chaos and confusion.
6 See pp. 136.
7 In a letter to Van Eyck and in the review *x functie*. With '8' Van Tijen was referring to the former Amsterdam CIAM group 'de 8'.
8 St Thomas Aquinas and St John of the Cross respectively.
9 Beerends started his article, refered to in note 1, by paraphrasing 'a negro from Mozambique', a verse by the Dutch poet Remco Campert: 'at least a human being of flesh and blood, with the warmth and the limberness of an animal, with the pride of a king, with the candour of a child'.
10 In a letter to Bakema, published in *Forum*, November 1960, p. 133.
11 Rietveld closed his letter quoted in the previous note as follows: 'It can be a good thing sometimes to seek courage in the understandable enjoyment of taking one's sparrow for an eagle'.
12 Following the example of the Surrealists, Van Eyck uses the term 'illumination' instead of 'illustration'.
13 Oud's letter, published in Forum (1960/61, no. 4, p. 128) reads as follows: 'Dear colleagues, perhaps the enclosed project can enlarge your examples of casbah. True, it stems from 1917 (it was published

in the first issue of *De Stijl*), but whatever is kept in a good vessel does not sour. Yours sincerely.'
14 Hammel, Klunder and Witstok were three young Rotterdam architects who reacted positively and with high expectations to *The Story of Another Idea*, but raised a number of questions concerning the published projects.
15 The Zone Project by John Voelcker, Pat Crooke and Andrew Derbyshire was published in *Forum* 1960, no. 1, pp. 18–27. Its original CIAM grid was reproduced by M. Risselada and D. van den Heuvel in *Team 10 – in search of a Utopia of the present*, NAi Publishers, Rotterdam, 2005, pp. 34–37. For an overall picture of this project, see *The Child, the City and the Artist*, p. 206.
16 See p. 327.
17 Published in *Forum* 1960, no. 1, pp. 30–31.
18 In this and the following paragraphs Van Eyck anticipates the configurative discipline he was to expound two years later, in *Forum*, August 1962. See 'Steps towards a configurative discipline', on p. 327.

The enigma of time

1 Early 1961 the *Forum* team conceived the plan of composing a special issue on the work of Duiker. However, when the editors visited Duiker's Zonnestraal sanatorium near Hilversum they felt rather disconcerted about the derelict state of this functionalist masterpiece. A set of pictures was taken by the photographer Violette Cornelius and Van Eyck wrote the present text. Still, after some discussion the team decided to resort to old documents in order to present the building in its pristine clarity. The compilation of the number (issued in January 1962) was entrusted to Jelle Jelles, a young Delft architect who had come into possession of the Duiker archives. Van Eyck did not publish his text until five years later, in the posthumous *Forum* issue of July 1967. At that moment the state of the sanatorium had become even worse. Only 35 years later Zonnestraal was restored in its original state by H.J. Henket, one of Van Eyck's former Delft students.

The medicine of reciprocity tentatively illustrated

1 Original English text published in *Forum*, 1960/61 no. 6–7 (and in *Architects' Yearbook*, Elek, London, 1962), slightly reedited and enlarged with two passages translated from the Dutch version, 'de milde raderen van de reciprociteit' (the mild gears of reciprocity), published in the same Forum issue.
2 For Herman Hertzberger these remarks formed a point of departure for reflection on 'flexibility and polyvalence' in *Forum* 1962, no. 3, pp. 115–118.
3 For the notion of 'dual phenomenon' or 'twin phenomenon', see the introduction to this chapter and F. Strauven, *Aldo van Eyck – the Shape of Relativity*, Amsterdam 1998, pp. 459–466.
4 Paragraph translated from the Dutch version.
5 Paragraph translated from the Dutch version.

The fake client and the great word 'no'

1 Senmut, an ancient Egyptian courtier living in the fifteenth century B.C., was the architect of the Mortuary Temple at Deïr-el-Bahari.

Steps towards a configurative discipline

1 Jelly Roll Morton (1885/90–1941) was a famous jazz pianist and composer. The quote is borrowed from his *Buddy Bolden's Blues* (1939):

Thought I heard Buddy Bolden say:
'You're nasty, you're dirty, take it away.
You're terrible, you're awful, take it away.'
I thought I heard him say.

I thought I heard Buddy Bolden shout:
'Open up that window and let that bad air out.
Open up that window and let the foul air out.'
I thought I heard Buddy Bolden shout.

I thought I heard Judge Fogarty say:
'Thirty days in the market, take him away.
Get him a good broom to sweep with, take him away.'
I thought I heard him say.

2 Van Eyck refers to two projects by Blom: 'the cities will be inhabited like villages' (1958), published in *Forum* 1959, no. 7, pp. 244–47; and a housing scheme for Slotermeer (1960), published in *Forum*, 1960–61, no. 5, pp. 181–189. He commented on these plans in 'Dirty linen, mostly' (in the November 1960 issue of *Forum*), see p. 302.
3 Van Eyck uses the term 'multiply' in order to avoid any confusion with the usual additive arrangements. Instead of being linearly juxtaposed the urban components are configurated in clusters that include place for common facilities.
4 The Zone Project (1952) by John Voelcker, Pat Crooke and Andrew Derbyshire was published in *Forum* 1960, no. 1, pp. 18–27. Its original CIAM grid

was reproduced by M. Risselada and D. van den Heuvel in *Team 10 1953–81, in search of a utopia of the present*, NAi Publishers, Rotterdam 2005, pp. 34–37.

5 For an overall picture of the megastructures by Tange, Maki, Ohtaka and Kurokawa, see chapter 11 of *The Child, the City and the Artist*.

6 Van Eyck refers to Blom's 'Noah's Ark', a vast urban project situated between Amsterdam and Haarlem. But contrary to what he announces here, this project would never be published in *Forum*. Yet he included it in *The Child, the City and the Artist* (see pp. 202) and presented it to Team 10 at the Royaumont meeting in 1962.

7 Van Eyck had been interested in the aesthetics of number since his Zurich years. He got to know it through the paintings of Richard Paul Lohse. See chapter 1 and 2.

8 K. Tange, *A plan for Tokyo, 1960: towards a structural organization*, Tokyo, 1961, p. 26; also published in The Japan Architect, April 1961. For an overall picture of this plan, see *The Child, the City and the Artist*, pp. 211.

9 K. Tange, Ibidem, pp. 9 and 26.

10 F. Maki and M. Ohtaka, *Some thoughts on collective form; with an introduction to group-form*, Washington University, Saint Louis, 1961.

11 Paul Goodman, *Communitas*, Random House, New York, 1947, pp. 12–13.
Paul Goodman (1911–1972) was an American novelist, essayist and social critic. In *Communitas* he made a critical investigation into contemporary planning models in order to advance a new kind of city planning based on a community concept.

12 Van Bodegraven, 'Time as an essential factor in planning', see note 27 to *The Story of Another Idea*, on p. 708.

Chapter 9
Forum 1962–1967: the Vernacular of the Heart

Introduction to chapter 9

1 Van Eyck found the writings of Griaule and his school in the Paris Musée de l'Homme. Besides Griaule's *Dieu d'eau – entretiens avec Ogotemmêli* (1948) of which he obtained the 1966 edition, he purchased Geneviève Calame-Griaule's 'Notes sur l'habitation du plateau central nigérien' (1955) in an offprint of the *Bulletin de l'Institut Français d'Afrique Noire*, and Montserrat Palau Marti's, *Les Dogon*, P.U.F., Paris, 1957.

2 Up to and including 'The medicine of reciprocity' (in *Forum*, April-May 1961), Aldo van Eyck used the term 'dual phenomena'. The term 'twin phenomena' first appears in 'Steps towards a Configurative Discipline' (*Forum*, August 1962), and in the almost simultaneously published reedited version of the first-mentioned article in *Architects' Yearbook*, no. 10, London 1962, p. 173–178.

3 In 1962 Van Eyck started teaching at the Delft Polytechnic. In the course of 1963 he was visiting professor at Harvard University, he made a journey around the world and he received two major commissions: the project for the church at The Hague and the invitation to participate in the limited competition for the Driebergen church. Hertzberger was designing the students' house in Amsterdam and the Montessori School in Delft.

4 In the meantime, Van Eyck tried to publish his Dogon story as a separate book. He made a book project, composed of the essays by Parin, Morgenthaler and himself, and including a large number of photographs. The Amsterdam publisher Allert de Lange showed interest but was not prepared to commit himself without the cooperation of a foreign colleague. He abandoned the project after it was declined by the Swiss Verlag für Architektur.

5 Remarkably, the colophon of this posthumous issue, dated July 1967, says that it completes Volume XVII, 1963, of *Forum*, 'which thus consists of four issues'.

6 See chapter 10 of *The Child, the City and the Artist*. The first section of this chapter was published as a short article in *Architectural Forum*, September 1961, pp. 116–120.

7 At the end of 1966 Van Eyck was contacted by Rolf Eric Sauer, then a student at University of Pennsylvania, with the request to write a contribution on 'the spirit of ecology in design' for the said publication.

8 In fact a substantial prepublication of the book of the same name, issued thirteen years later by Princeton University Press.

The Pueblos

1 Stanley A. Stubbs, *Bird's-Eye view of the Pueblos*, University of Oklahoma Press, 1950, pp. 96–97.

2 Ruth Underhill, 'Workaday Life of the Pueblos' in W.W. Beatty, *Indian Life and Customs* – 4, Department of the Interior, Bureau of Indian Affairs, Phoenix, Arizona, December 1954, pp. 84–85.

On Rykwert's *Idea of a Town*

1 Translation of a passage extracted from Van Eyck's Dogon article in *Forum*, July 1967, p. 35

A Miracle of Moderation

1 Van Eyck wrote his three-part carrying essay in 1967, incorporating some passages from the Dogon chapter in *The Child, the City and the Artist*, completed in 1962. Parin and Morgenthaler wrote their essays in 1961. The set was first published in *Forum*, July 1967, Van Eyck's carrying essay in Dutch, the essays of his Swiss friends in their original German version. The *Forum* issue included an insert with the English translation of the Dutch texts. For this insert Van Eyck wrote an English version of his essay, which he subsequently enlarged for the English publication of the whole set, under the title 'A Miracle of Moderation' in *Via 1 – Ecology in Design*, Philadelphia, 1968, pp. 96–125. For this version, which is reproduced here, the essays by Parin and Morgenthaler were translated by Jared Sparks. The whole set was thereupon included by Jencks and Baird in Meaning in Architecture, Barrie & Jenkins, London, 1969.
2 A. van Eyck, 'Bouwen in de Zuidelijke oasen', in *Forum*, January 1953, no. 1, pp. 28–38.
3 *Minotaure*, revue artistique et littéraire, June 1933, no. 2, a special issue titled 'Mission Dakar-Djibouti, 1931–1933.'
4 Van Eyck's sojourn in Dogonland covered about a month between 19 February and 25 March 1960.
5 Paul Parin, Fritz Morgenthaler, and Goldy Parin-Matthey, *Die Weissen denken zuviel; psychoanalytische Untersuchungen bei den Dogon in Westafrika*, Atlantis Verlag, Zurich, 1963. French translation: *Les blancs pensent trop*, Payot, Paris 1966.
6 Paul Parin, Fritz Morgenthaler and Goldy Parin-Matthey, *Op.cit.*, p. 31.
7 Joseph Rykwert, *The Idea of a Town, Forum*, 1963, no 3, special issue; extended and published as a book by Princeton University Press in 1976.
8 A. van Eyck, introduction to Rykwert's *The Idea of a Town, Forum*, 1963, no. 3.
9 See p. 716.
10 Here and in the following sections Van Eyck tends to idealize Dogon culture in a way he wanted to correct at an advanced age. When he learned about initiation practices such as female circumcision he felt it to be too high a price for achieving social harmony.
11 Marcel Griaule, *Dieu d'eau – entretiens avec Ogotemmêli*, Editions du Chêne, Paris, 1948; Geneviève Calame-Griaule, 'Notes sur l'habitation du plateau central nigérien', in *Bulletin de l'Institut Français d'Afrique Noire*, 1955, no. 3–4, pp. 477–499.
12 A. van Eyck, 'The Pueblos', in *Forum*, August 1962, no. 3, pp. 95–114.
13 Marcel Griaule and Germaine Dieterlin, 'The Dogon of the French Sudan', in Daryll Forde, ed., *African Worlds – Studies in the Cosmological Ideas and Values of African Peoples*, Oxford University Press, London, 1954, pp. 83–110.
14 Marcel Griaule, *Dieu d'eau – entretiens avec Ogotemmêli*, Editions du Chêne, Paris, 1948.
15 Montserrat Palau Marti, *Les Dogon*, Monographies ethnologiques africaines, Presses Universitaires de France, Paris, 1957, pp. 57–58.
16 Quote from a letter by Morgenthaler to Van Eyck, dated 21 June 1961, completed with a quote from another letter, dated 30 December 1964.
17 Paul Parin, Fritz Morgenthaler and Goldy Parin-Matthey, *Op.cit.*, p. 68.

Chapter 10
The Problem of Number

Introduction to chapter 10

1 In 'Steps towards a configurative discipline', see chapter 8.
2 So as to neutralize the hierarchy between these two categories which Louis Kahn had advanced at the Otterlo congress in 1959.
3 Tupker's project 'Under Milk Wood' had been published in *Forum*, August 1961, no. 8.

Differentiation and unity through rhythm

1 'Three Schools in Nagele' in *Architects' Year Book* no. 9, August 1960, pp. 140–143. Partly reprinted in Alison Smithson, ed., *Team 10 Primer*, in *Architectural Design*, December 1962, pp. 590–591. A preliminary German version had been published in *Werk*, May 1958, no. 5, pp. 170–173.

On Blom's *Noah's Ark*

1 The manuscript appears to be part of a preliminary draft for 'de straling van het configuratieve', i.e. the Dutch version of 'Steps towards a Configurative Discipline', published in *Forum*, August 1962. The present passage was left out of the published version.

Discussion of the problem of number at the Royaumont Meeting, September 1962

1 Team 10's first larger meeting after the Otterlo congress took place from 12 to 16 September 1962 in the Royaumont abbey, north of Paris, and was devoted to the 'reciprocal urban infrastructure/ building group concepts'. Team 10 had invited some twenty guests, including Christopher Alexander, José Coderch, Giancarlo de Carlo, Amancio Gueddes, Guilermo Jullian de la Fuente, Kishu Kurokawa, Colin St John Wilson, James Stirling and Stefan Wewerka.

2 A report of the meeting was published by Alison Smithson in *Architectural Design*, November 1975, and in *Team 10 Meetings*, Rizzoli, New York, 1991. This was however a heavily reduced and often biased representation of the discussions. As to the debate on Blom's Noah's Ark project, all passages suggesting appreciation by the participants were left out. The present report of Van Eyck's contribution was summarized from the transcript of the whole meeting's tape recordings. A copy of this full transcript, made by Clarissa Woods shortly after the conference, can be found in the Bakema archives at the NAi in Rotterdam. Even so, the present report is a far from complete version of Van Eyck's exposition and the subsequent discussion, which cover 47 pages in the transcript. Digressions, unclear passages and detailed descriptions were left out.

3 In fact, Van Eyck's argument contained an implicit criticism of certain projects presented at the meeting, notably the design for Toulouse-le-Mirail by Candilis and the diagram for a village in India by Alexander, both of which were based on a tree structure.

4 Here Van Eyck continues to explain the project in detail for six pages. This description, the understanding of which requires detailed plans, has been left out here.

5 In an unrecorded intervention, pronounced during the changing of the tapes, Alison Smithson had obviously criticized Blom's project in that it would allow a Gestapo-like control over all urban activities.

6 'ZUP' is the acronym of 'Zone à Urbaniser en Priorité', a town planning concept introduced in France at the end of the 1950s in order to tackle the housing shortage by means of large-scale developments. During the 1950s and 1960s the firm of Candilis, Josic and Woods received numerous commissions to design ZUP areas.

How to humanize vast plurality?

1 In 1963 Van Eyck was invited by the Architectural Students' Society of the University of Auckland, New Zealand, to participate as a guest speaker in the Pacific Congress which took place from 2 to 7 September of that year. Van Eyck's lectures were published by Dick Scott in *Report '63 – a record of the Pacific Congress*, Auckland, 1963. He discussed most of the themes which he had developed until then: the in-between, place and occasion, the problem of number and the importance of vernacular building tradition. The texts published in the *Report* largely correspond to passages from his *Forum* articles and *The Child, the City and the Artist*. The new passages which are reproduced here are indicative of Van Eyck's doubts about the possible approach to great number. For an account of Van Eyck's stay and interventions in Auckland, see R. Skinner, 'Dutch Treat – The Van Eycks in New Zealand', in *Formulation Fabrication – The Architecture of History*, proceedings of the 17th annual conference of the Society of Architectural Historians, Australia and New Zealand, Wellington, 2000, pp. 287–296.

Tree and leaf

1 Van Eyck wrote the first version of this statement in autumn 1961 when he was visiting professor at Washington University in Saint Louis, and incorporated it into chapter 5 of *The child, the City and the Artist* (1962) and into his contribution to *Situationist Times*, October 1963, p. 80. The slightly different text of the present version was first published in the 1965 paperback edition of Team 10 Primer. The present handwritten diagram was first published in *Domus*, May 1965. As Van Eyck explained in *The child, the City and the Artist*, the purpose of this statement was not to establish an analogy between a city and a tree, but to confront two images that identify part and whole. The twin images house-city and tree-leaf both disclose a wealth of multiple meanings, they both evoke a number of twin phenomena which can be mutually suggestive.

'What we are after is a new and as yet unknown configurative discipline'

1 In 1966 Van Eyck, Buckminster Fuller, John Voelcker and Jaap Bakema were invited by the Australian Architecture Student Association to participate in its convention, held at Perth in May of that year. The theme was: difficulties and op-

portunities in architectural education. A report of the convention was published in *Building Ideas*, vol. 3, no. 4, September 1966. The present passages were partly extracted from that report, partly from the 1968 hardback edition of *Team 10 Primer*. Only the latter were edited by Van Eyck.
2 This paragraph was first published in the 1968 hardback edition of *Team 10 Primer*, on p. 12, and slightly reedited by Van Eyck for publication in Strauven's *The Shape of Relativity*, on pp. 404–405.
3 This paragraph was first published in the 1968 hardback edition of *Team 10 Primer*, on p. 6.

On Christopher Alexander's *A City is not a Tree*

1 A. Smithson, ed., Team 10 Primer, Studio Vista, London, 1968, p. 98. The statement was reedited as a note to 'A Miracle of Moderation' in *Via*, 1968, no. 1.
2 In the early sixties, Christopher Alexander, schooled in both architecture and mathematics, endeavoured to develop a computer-aided design method based on the factorial analysis of 'misfits'. In 1962 he stayed in India, where he applied his method in the project for a village, derived from a study of existing villages near Ahmedabad. On the proposal of Doshi he was invited to participate in the Royaumont meeting where he presented the said village project. This project, in fact a complex diagram, clearly displayed a tree structure, a hierarchical layout that was actually inherent to the method Alexander held at that time, 'a hierarchical nesting of sets between sets' (see his *Notes on the Synthesis of Form*, Cambridge, Mass., 1964). In his talk at the Royaumont meeting Van Eyck took a stand against tree structures in town planning, while arguing that in 'Noah's Ark' Blom had managed to overcome this kind of hierarchy by interweaving the different levels of association and the mutual identification of part and whole.
Alexander entered into discussion with Van Eyck on this matter without reaching agreement. Still, three years later he returned to the problem in order to explicitly dismiss the tree structure himself, namely in his article 'A City is not a Tree' (published in *Architectural Forum*, April 1965, pp. 58–62 and May 1965, pp. 58–61). As an alternative to the 'tree' he now proposed the 'semi-lattice', a non-hierarchical structure of relations that corresponds to the complex relational patterns in traditional cities. He did not however refer to his discussion with Van Eyck in any way.

The enigma of vast multiplicity

1 This article is an edited version of the statements which Van Eyck prepared for his contribution to the 14th Milan Triennale in 1968, an event co-organized by Giancarlo de Carlo and entirely devoted to the theme of *'il grande numero'*. Van Eyck joined his statements into a violent indictment of Western society's inability to house itself in adequately. This inability is strikingly contrasted with the wealth of built environments that originated from a direct participation of the inhabitants, squatter constructions in Hong Kong as well as a Dogon village. The article was published in *Harvard Educational Review*, autumn 1969, no. 4, pp. 126–143.
2 Jules Supervielle (1884–1960), French poet born in Montevideo, Uruguay. Inspired by the pampas of his native country, his poetry deals with human loneliness and relatedness. The quoted verse is derived from *Naissances* (1951) and can be translated as follows: How difficult it is for us to find shelter, even in our heart. All the space is taken, and so is all the warmth.
3 A quote from Dylan Thomas's poem 'Should lanterns shine'.

Who are we building for, and why?

1 'Footnote' which Van Eyck joined to his entry for the experimental PREVI project in Lima, Peru.
2 See *Architectural Design*, 1963, no. 8 and 1968, no. 8.

The Priority Jostle

1 Published in *Spazio e Società*, December 1979, no. 8, pp. 55–57.
2 Otto H. Königsberger (1908–1999), architect of German origin, specialized in housing in developing countries. In 1957, having been active in India and Ghana, he became head of the Department of Development and Tropical Studies at the Architectural Association School of Architecture in London.

Fascism in a snowflake

1 *Niet om het even – wel evenwaardig*, festschrift published on the occasion of Van Eyck's receipt of the 1982 Rotterdam Maaskant Prize, Van Gennep, Amsterdam 1986, p. 87.

Chapter 11
Interiorisation

The Otterlo Circles

1 The present text is a slightly reedited version of a passage from chap. 7 of *The Child, the City and the Artist* (1962), and was first published in *Via 1, Ecology in Design*, 1968, p. 95, after a shortened version had appeared in *Forum*, July 1967, p. 52.

Built Meaning

1 Alison Smithson, ed., *Team 10 Primer*, in *Architectural Design*, December 1962, pp. 559, 560 and 564; in the 1965 Paperback reprint on pp. 2, 3 and 7; in the 1968 hardback edition on pp. 21, 22 and 31. The other texts by Van Eyck which can be found in the Primer were extracted from previously published articles or *The Child, the City and the Artist*.

Place and Occasion

1 For *'There is a garden in her face'*, see chapter 8. This shortened version was published in *Architectural Design*, December 1962, as a contribution to the first edition of *Team 10 Primer*, albeit with some mistakes, which were corrected in the 1965 paperback edition. 'Place and Occasion' was also published (with some minor modifications) in *Situationist Times*, October 1963, p. 79; in *Via 1 – Ecology in Design*, Philadelphia, 1968, p. 90; and in *Aldo van Eyck – Hubertus House*, Stichting Wonen, Amsterdam, 1982, p. 49.
2 In the version published in *Via 1 – Ecology in Design*, *cit.*, the sentence between brackets was left out.

Labyrinthian Clarity

1 This article constitutes a concise summary of the ideas Van Eyck developed in chapter 3, 4 and 5 of *The Child, the City and the Artist*. A short preliminary version appeared in *Situationist Times*, October 1963, pp. 84–85, an enlarged one in the 1965 paperback edition of *Team 10 Primer* (on p. 14) and in *World Architecture 3*, Studio Vista, London 1966, pp. 121–122. The definitive one, which is reproduced here, appeared in *Forum*, July 1967, p. 51. It was published under the title 'The interior of Space' in *Via 1 – Ecology in Design*, Philadelphia, 1968, pp. 91–92.
2 In the 1965 paperback edition of *Team 10 Primer* the last sentence reads: 'Memory and anticipation, in fact, constitute the real perspective of space; give it depth'; in *World Architecture 3*: 'They are the depth of space; its essential perspective'.
3 In *World Architecture 3* this sentence reads: 'To gratify Ariel means gratifying Caliban also, for there is no man who is not both at once'. Ariel and Caliban are two antagonistic characters in Shakespeare's *The Tempest*. Ariel is the airy spirit characterized by lightness, quickness and grace. Caliban is the embodied earth spirit and represents the animal instincts of primitive man.
4 In *World Architecture 3* the article concludes with the following paragraph: 'Neither centralized nor decentralized but *centred* in every place and every stage of multiplication, with the interior horizon of space as constant companion – that surely is our real home! It is also what Labyrinthian Clarity can bring about – house and city a bunch of place both. Architecture need do no more than assist man's homecoming'.

The Interior of Time

1 Condensed edition of passages from chapter 4 and 7 of *The Child, the City and the Artist* (1962), completed with a conclusion written in 1966; published in *Forum*, July 1967, p. 28 and in *Via 1 – Ecology in Design*, Philadelphia, 1968, pp. 93–94; a shortened version appeared in *Aldo van Eyck – Hubertus House*, Stichting Wonen, Amsterdam, 1982, p. 47.
2 A quote from James Joyce's *Finnegans Wake*, namely the concluding passage of chapter 8.

The inner horizon in Wright's Imperial Hotel

1 Passage from the transcription of the tape-recorded talk, edited by Van Eyck. He visited F.L. Wright's Imperial Hotel in Tokyo at the end of September 1963, during a tour in Japan organized by Fumihiko Maki, after his participation in the Pacific Congress of the Architectural Students' Society of the University of Auckland. As Van Eyck stated later, it was his wife Hannie who drew his attention to the inner horizon that they experienced in this building.

On Frank Lloyd Wright's Imperial Hotel

1 Open letter in favour of the conservation of Wright's Imperial Hotel, which was threatened with demolition at the time. The initiatives taken by Van Eyck's and others were not able to prevent Wright's 1922 masterpiece being pulled down soon afterwards.

The Enigma of Size

1 Lecture given in the summer of 1979 at the 4th Residential Course of the International Laboratory for Architecture and Urban Design at Urbino, organized by Giancarlo de Carlo. The text, illustrated with prints of Van Eyck's slides, was published in *Spazio e società*, December 1979, no. 8, pp. 65–77, and in *Signs and Insights*, Annual Report ILAUD Urbino 1979, Urbino 1980, pp. 42–53.
2 Van Eyck refers to Wittkower's *Architectural Principles in the Age of Humanism*, Tiranti, London, 1962, pp. 89–97, and Ackerman's *Palladio*, Penguin, Harmondsworth, 1966, pp. 140–146.

Transparency

1 The present piece is an extract from *Aldo van Eyck – Hubertus House*, Stichting Wonen, Amsterdam, 1982, pp. 81–83.
2 A notion originated by Hannie van Eyck, the architect's wife, during a visit to Frank Lloyd Wright's Imperial Hotel in Tokyo. See 'The inner horizon in Wright's Imperial Hotel' in the present chapter.
3 See chapter 13.
4 (Note by Van Eyck) There is a German saying 'all good things are three'. Why on earth three, I wonder!

Chapter 12
Contemporary architecture and traditional city

Introduction to chapter 12

1 Translation of a statement in *Forum*, 1959, no. 9, on the black page facing p. 285.

Why not a beloved town hall?

1 Van Eyck expressed his views on the Dutch city from the other side of the ocean, when he was a visiting professor at Washington University in Saint Louis. The plan for building a new Amsterdam town hall dated from before the Second World War. In 1936 the city authorities had held a competition for a project located on Frederiksplein. After three years of deliberation, the jury selected the project by Berghoef and Vegter, a retrograde, mediaeval-style, monumental complex. After the war the said architects were commissioned to design a new project, located on Waterlooplein. The result, a modernized, square form of classicism, was under discussion in 1961. Van Eyck's critique, which was published on the front page of the weekly newspaper *De Groene Amsterdammer*, is said to have greatly contributed to the rejection of the project by the Amsterdam Municipal Council.

City centre as donor

1 The present translation was authorized by Van Eyck for publication in his *Works*, edited by Vincent Ligtelijn in 1999.

An experiment to counter urban corrosion

1 Explanatory note on the housing project near the Rode Torenplein in the old centre of Zwolle by Van Eyck and Bosch, published in TABK, November 1971 no. 22, pp. 558–559; a note addressed to the Commission of Experimental House-Building at the Dutch Ministry of Housing and Town Planning,

Sociocide

1 Published in *Spazio e Società*, December 1979, no. 8, p. 78.

On breaking through monuments

1 Statements summarized from an interview by William Rothuizen, published in *Haagse Post*, 14 December 1974.

The mute requirements

1 The first publication in *L'Architecture d'Aujourd'hui* (1975, no. 177, p. 29) contained some misprints which were corrected in an enlarged version published in *L'Architecture d'Aujourd'hui*, October 1981, no. 217, pp. 72–79 and *Progressive Architecture*, March 1982, p. 78. The present version was slightly adjusted to the manuscript of the author.

You can't build a thing like that for people!

1 After the Amsterdam Town Hall project by Berghoef and Vegter was definitively abandoned by the City Council in 1964, a new international competition was organized in 1967. From the 804 entries the jury selected the project by the Viennese architect Wilhelm Holzbauer, a project that was treated to sharp criticism in Dutch architectural circles. However, Holzbauer was commis-

sioned to develop his plan, but nevertheless the project was shelved due to budgetary problems in about 1970. Parallel to the Town Hall project Amsterdam had for a long time also nurtured the plan for an opera house. Ever since the early sixties, plans were being drawn up by the architects Bijvoet and Holt, but at the end of the seventies this project too arrived at an impasse. Then, in 1979, Holzbauer launched the idea of combining the Town Hall and the opera into one new project. After the city authorities agreed, Holzbauer collaborated with Bijvoet and Holt on a first sketch plan that was made public in October 1979. In spite of the sharp criticism that this plan was also subject to, Holzbauer continued to develop this 'Stopera' project (as it was soon called in Amsterdam parlance), this time in collaboration with Cees Dam, Holt's son-in-law, to whom the now deceased Bijvoet had devolved his rights. When they submitted their 'definitive plan' in mid-April 1981, it was violently attacked by a group of 80 architects, among them Soeters, Uytenhaak, Blom, Röling, Salomons, Hertzberger and Van Eyck. They organized a press conference where Van Eyck declared that it would be possible to make a better plan within a fortnight. A few days later, turning his words into action, he set to work with Izak Salomons, then architecture editor of the daily newspaper *Het Parool*. They cut up the Stopera plan and joined the pieces to form a project for an urban area that was publicly accessible and permeable from several sides. Publication of this alternative proposal in *Het Parool* (on 21 April 1981) meant that Dam and Holzbauer, who scornfully announced that they were at their critical colleagues' disposal and were prepared to hear their suggestions, were kept to their word. Two months later Van Eyck published the present article. His critique and counterproposals are said to have urged the Stopera architects to transform their plans in some way. They introduced an open north-south connection and an interior street. The protest action continued but could not prevent the Stopera being built between 1982 and 1986. On the Stopera question, see I. Salomons, 'Amsterdams Stopera-verdriet', in *Forum*, 1980/81, no. 3, pp. 10–17 (with English summary), and M. van Rooy, *De Stopera – een Amsterdamse geschiedenis*, Thomas Rap, Amsterdam 1986.

2 The official aesthetic advisory committee in Dutch municipal planning administration.
3 The Amsterdam mayor and the aldermen responsible for urban renewal and town planning.
4 F.M. Wibaut (1859–1936), Dutch social-democratic politician. From 1914 to 1931 alderman of the city of Amsterdam, he became famous for his successful socialist housing policy.
5 Uytenhaak's proposals were published in *Forum*, 1980/81, no. 3, pp. 18–19.

Chapter 13
Polemics on postmodernism

Introduction to chapter 13

1 On Granpré Molière, see note 37 to 'The ball rebounds' in chapter 5.

Like that other gift

1 Van Eyck included this statement in his contribution to the *Europa/America* exhibition which took place from 1 August to 10 October 1976 as part of the Venice Biennale. In response to the crisis which afflicted architecture at that time he presented a number of images from all over the world, showing how people everywhere prove to be able to house themselves in a meaningful way. In accordance with the Otterlo circles, his selection, in addition to images from archaic cultures, also included examples from both the classical and the modern traditions, notably the Santa Maria Formosa church by Codussi, the Glasgow School of Art by Mackintosh and the Zonnestraal sanatorium by Duiker.
Van Eyck wrote this statement as a reaction to the self-assured formalism that manifested itself at the Venice exhibition, from the rigid formalism of Rossi to the neoclassical monumentality of Bofill. At the Forum discussion that took place after the opening, Van Eyck inveighed strongly against postmodern ideas and trends, against the cynicism of Tafuri and Rossi, against the craving for gigantic monumentality and trendy collages of fragments borrowed from Giulio Romano and Giorgio de Chirico. See F. Raggi, ed., Europa/America, La Biennale di Venezia, Venice 1978.

A message to Mathias Ungers from a different world

1 O.M. Ungers participated in the Team 10 meetings at Urbino (1966), Toulouse-le-Mirail (1971), Berlin (1973) and Rotterdam (1974). Soon afterwards his work took a neo-rationalist turn. After taking notice, Van Eyck wrote the present 'message',

published in *Spazio e società*, December 1979, pp. 63–64.
2 Van Eyck successively takes aim at Aldo Rossi, Manfredo Tafuri, Leon and Rob Krier, Denise Scott-Brown, Robert Venturi, Peter Eisenman, Stanley Tigerman, Charles Jencks and OMA.
3 Ungers' hotel project at Lutzowplatz in Berlin was situated near to the *Wissenschaftszentrum* which James Stirling was to build at Reichpietschufer.
4 The limerick to which Van Eyck alludes reads: There was a young lady of Niger,/ Who smiled as she rode on a tiger;/ They returned from the ride/ With the lady inside,/ And the smile on the face of the tiger.
5 Van Eyck is referring to the Smithson's attack on Blom's 'Noah's Ark' project at the Royaumont meeting, published by Alison Smithson in *Architectural Design*, November 1975. For a more complete report, see 'Discussion of the problem of number at the Royaumont meeting' in chapter 10.

The Ironbound statement

1 Published in *Spazio e società*, December 1979, no. 8, pp. 60–63. The New Jersey Institute of Technology is situated in Newark, at that time a rather underdeveloped agglomeration. 'Ironbound' is one of its industrial districts, mainly populated by migrant families from Portugal and other Southern European countries. In those days the students of the Institute of Technology mainly came from the financially weaker layers of the white population. In his concluding remark Van Eyck alluded to the small number of coloured people among the graduates.
2 A term coined by Pjotr Gonggrijp, one of Van Eyck's former Delft students who dedicated himself, among other subjects, to an ecological analysis of the Dutch landscape.
3 The New York Five were R. Eisenman, M. Graves, Ch. Gwathmey, J. Hejduk and R. Meier, who set themselves up as radical formalists in 1972 by publishing the book *Five Architects*. The Chicago Seven were L. Booth, S. Cohen, S. Tigerman, B. Weese, J.I. Frees, G. Horn and H. Jahn, a group formed in 1978. Ten years before another group had become notorious under the same name: seven men who were arrested in 1968 because they were suspected of planning a disturbance at the National Democratic Convention in Chicago. The Minnesota Six could not be traced and were probably a hoax. In *Lotus*, 1981, no. 28, p. 15, Van Eyck explained: 'As for the Minnesota Six, like the New York Five and the Chicago Seven, they don't exist'.

R.P.P. (Rats, Posts and Other Pests)

1 Published in RIBA *Journal*, April 1981, no. 4, pp. 47–50; and, preceded by a letter to the editor, Dr. A.C. Papadakis, in *Architectural Design News Supplement*, 1981, no. 7, pp. 15–16. At almost the same time a similar article was published in *Lotus*, 1981, no. 28, p. 15–19, under the title 'What is and what isn't architecture – apropos of Rats, Posts and other Pests'. A shortened German version was published in *Archithese*, 1981, no. 5, pp. 32–34, under the title 'Die Transparanz der Zeit'.
2 Here Van Eyck successively takes aim at Manfredo Tafuri, Aldo Rossi, Leon and Rob Krier, Denise Scott-Brown, Robert Venturi, Peter Eisenman, Stanley Tigerman, Charles Jencks, OMA, Robert Stern, Michael Graves, Arata Isozaki, Hans Hollein, Ricardo Bofill, Oswald Mathias Ungers, James Stirling and Philip Johnson.
3 O. Newmann, *CIAM' 59 in Otterlo*, Karl Krämer, Stuttgart, 1961.
4 R. Venturi, *Complexity and Contradiction in Architecture*, Museum Modern Art, New York, 1966.
5 *Architectural Principles in the Age of Humanism*, a book published by Rudolf Wittkower in 1949, engaged the interest of the rising generation of English architects in the Italian renaissance, notably the work of Palladio.
6 See 'A message to Mathias Ungers from a Different World' in the present chapter.
7 In the first editions of *Team 10 Primer* (Architectural Design, 1962, no. 12 and the 1965 paperback edition) John Voelcker was listed as a Team 10 Member. In the 1962 hardback edition Alison Smithson left out his name. Voelcker died in 1972.
8 See note 3 to 'The Ironbound statement' in the present chapter.
9 'Abstraction: Towards a New Art. Painting 1910–20', an exhibition held at the Tate Gallery in 1980.
10 (Note by Van Eyck) Pjotr Gonggrijp suggested that it is not hierarchy as such which causes the trouble but the irreversibility which so often accompanies it.
11 Max Jacob, in *Art poétique*, Emile-Paul, Paris 1922.
12 Quoted from Christian Zervos, 'Conversation avec Picasso', in *Cahiers d'Art*, 1935, VII-X, pp. 173–178.
13 Quoted by Carola Giedion-Welcker, in *Moderne Plastik*, Girsberger, Zurich 1937, p. 11.
14 The origin of this quote could not be traced. A close reference can be found in M. Merleau-

Ponty, *L'Oeil et l'esprit* (1960): '« La nature est à l'intérieur », dit Cézanne. Qualité, lumière, couleur, profondeur, qui sont là-bas devant nous, n'y sont que parce qu'elles éveillent un écho dans notre corps, parce qu'il leur fait accueil.'
15 Quoted from Werner Heizenberg, in *Das Naturbild der heutigen Physik*, Rowohlt, Hamburg, 1955, pp. 18.
16 Quoted from Niels Bohr, *Atomic Physics and Human Knowledge*, New York, 1958.

Symmetry from the bright side
1 Aldo Rossi

On Codussi
1 Statement written on the occasion of the publication of the Deventer Moluccan Church project, published in *L'Architecture d'Aujourd'hui*, October 1984, no. 235, pp. LXXXII; and in *Architectural Review*, January 1985, no. 1055, p. 15. Mauro Codussi (1440–1504) ranks as the most important Venetian architect of the Quattrocento. His works include the churches of San Michele in Isola (1468–71), Santa Maria Formosa (1492) and Giovanni Grisostomo (1497), the clock tower at the Piazza San Marco (1496–1500) and the Palazzo Vendramin-Calergi (1502-). Remarkably, the description Van Eyck made of Santa Maria Formosa also applies to the Moluccan church he built in Deventer.

The circle and the centre
1 Published in *Indesem '87* (6–10 April 1987), Delft University Press, Delft 1988, pp. 184–185.
2 The origin of this quote could not be traced. A close reference can be found in M. Merleau-Ponty, *L'Oeil et l'esprit* (1960): '« La nature est à l'intérieur », dit Cézanne. Qualité, lumière, couleur, profondeur, qui sont là-bas devant nous, n'y sont que parce qu'elles éveillent un écho dans notre corps, parce qu'il leur fait accueil.'

And just keeping on switching between yesterday and today
1 Statement published in the newspaper-like catalogue to the exhibition 'Aldo van Eyck in de Beurs van Berlage' which ran in Berlage's Stock Exchange from 10 November 1989 to 3 January 1990.

Lured from his den
1 Van Eyck wrote this piece as a reaction to a discussion of his latest building, the Court of Audit in The Hague, in *Archis* magazine (1997, no. 11). The author, the art historian Bernard Colenbrander, had hung his story on the concept of the 'identifying device' which Van Eyck had advanced in his 1962 essay 'Steps towards a Configurative Discipline'. Van Eyck tells the author that he has misunderstood this concept and points out the resulting misinterpretations. He also goes into a number of issues which the author had brought up rather inconsiderately: the reception of the Orphanage, Surrealism, the projects by Blom, the fight over the Amsterdam Nieuwmarkt project, the alleged connections between J.J.P. Oud and J.H. van den Broek, and the author's imputing to him an affinity with Rossi.
2 Van Eyck alludes to the 'anyhow' conference that took place at the NAi in Rotterdam in June 1997.
3 *Niet om het even – wel evenwaardig*, festschrift on the occasion of Van Eyck's receiving the Maaskant Prize, Rotterdam Maaskant foundation and Van Gennep, Amsterdam 1986.
4 Ole Bouman was editor in chief of *Archis* from May 1996 to April 2004. In his editorial of July 1997 he discussed the *Anyone, Anywhere, Anyway, Anyplace, Anywise, Anybody and Anyhow conferences*.
5 Carel Weeber (b. 1937), architect and engineer, supporter of a rationalist and pragmatic architectural practice, from 1969 to 1975 professor and from 1976 to 1977 dean at the Architecture Department of Delft Polytechnic, where he took up an antagonistic position towards Van Eyck.
6 The BNA is the Society of Dutch Architects, which was presided over by Weeber from 1992 to 1998.
7 A report written in 1973 by the 'History working party' at the Delft Architectural Department, a group composed of six young assistants headed by Weeber.
8 Kees Vollemans, lecturer in art history and the leading ideologue of leftist radical thinking at the Delft Architecture Department in the seventies.
9 Bernard Colenbrander
10 Ed Taverne, Professor of architectural and town planning history at Groningen University from 1981 to 2002.
11 Successively Peter Eisenman, Ben van Berkel, and the landscape architect Adriaan Geuze.
12 For a comprehensive documentation on this building, see Van Eyck's *Works*, edited by V. Ligtelijn, pp. 264–277.
13 See 'Steps towards a Configurative Discipline' in chapter 8.

14 The English version of this article was actually published under the title 'The medicine of reciprocity tentatively illustrated', see chapter 8.
15 Hans van Dijk, editor in chief of *wonen-TA/BK* from 1982 to 1985, and of *Archis* from 1986 to 1990.
16 Piet Blom was only tutored by Van Eyck in 1956–1957 when he was a first year student at the Amsterdam Academy of Architecture. In that year he made projects in a free, expressive manner. Independently of Van Eyck's teaching but inspired by his work, notably the Nagele schools, Blom started working on the basis of systematic geometrical patterns from 1958. The two projects Van Eyck is referring to are: 'the towns will be inhabited like villages' (published at the conclusion of *the story of another idea*, in *Forum*, September 1959) and 'thing – counter thing', published in *Forum*, February 1961. Blom made these projects in his second and third years, for others tutors, the last of whom disqualified his approach. Van Eyck did not direct these projects but recognized them in 1962 as 'the first radiance' of the configurative discipline. Although announced, Blom's 'Noah's Ark' project was never published in *Forum*.
17 See 'Discussion of the problem of number at the Royaumont Meeting', in chapter 10.
18 This paragraph bears on the Amsterdam Nieuwmarkt project (1970–1984). Contrary to the official plans, which amounted to complete demolition and the construction of an urban motorway, Van Eyck's plan aimed at the preservation and the reconstruction of the neighbourhood, in fact one of the oldest cores of the city. While working on this project, he formulated his view on the 'city centre as donor' (see chapter 12). Van Eyck and Theo Bosch, whith whom he formed a firm in 1971, considered the local residents rather than the City Council as their real clients. They regularly took part in the neighbourhood meetings and supported the residents' interests in their plans and in public manifestations.
19 Van Eyck refers to Oud's almost neoclassically shaped headquaters of the Bataafse Import Maatschappij (BIM) built in The Hague in 1937–1942.

Chapter 14
On architects and other artists

On Le Corbusier

1 Extract from an article on the Nagele Schools, in *Architects Year Book*, no. 9, London 1960, pp. 140–142. Later in life Van Eyck thoroughly adjusted this view. After visiting Notre Dame du Haut at Ronchamp, he deemed it to be one of Le Corbusier's masterpieces.
2 Extract from the English version of *the story of another idea*, issued in mimeographed format at Washington University, Saint Louis, in 1961.
3 Extract from a talk given at the Australian Architecture Student Association Convention, Perth, May 1966, typewritten transcription, partly corrected by Van Eyck, p. 25.

On Loos

1 The Loos exhibition was borrowed from the Eindhoven Van Abbe Museum where it had been put up in 1964 by its new director Jean Leering, who had freshly graduated at Delft Polytechnic. In 1962, when still a student, he had collaborated with his friends Pjotr Gonggrijp and Michiel Polak on the organization of the exhibition 'Autonomous Architecture', an event that marked a break with the traditionalism of the Delft School. Van Eyck's lecture was published in *Delftse School*, April 1965, no. 12, pp. 269–273. The present translation is partly based on the slightly enlarged version which Van Eyck published in *Niet om het even – wel evenwaardig*, Amsterdam 1986, pp. 120–121.
2 George Bryan Brummel (1778–1840), an innovator of men's fashion in Regency England, ranks as the prototype of the dandy. He was immortalized in literature by Barbey d'Aurevilly and Clyde Fitch.
3 Originally, *'Ich aber sage: Ein rechtes bauwerk macht im bilde, auf die fläche gebracht, keinen eindruck. Es ist mein grösster stolz, dass die innenräume, die ich geschaffen habe, in der photographie vollständig wirkungslos sind. Dass die bewohner meiner räume im photographischen bilde ihre eigene wohnung nicht erkennen, genau wie der besitzer eines bildes von Monet das werk bei Kastan nicht erkennen würde. Auf die ehre, in den verschiedenen architektonischen zeitschriften veröffenticht zu werden, muss ich verzichten. Die befriedigung meiner eitelkeit ist mir versagt.'* Extract from Loos's article 'Architektur' (1910), included in *Trotzdem*, Innsbruck, 1931.

4 Pjotr Gonggrijp and Michiel Polak each wrote a short introduction which was printed on the backside of the exhibition's poster.

University college in Urbino by Giancarlo de Carlo[1]

1 Giancarlo de Carlo (1919–2005), member of CIAM since 1952, was invited by Team 10 to participate in the meetings at Otterlo (1959), Bagnols-sur-Cèze (1960), Royaumont (1962), Paris (1963) and Berlin (1965). After having organized the meeting at Urbino in 1966, he was mentioned as a Team 10 member by Alison Smithson in the 1968 hardback edition of the Primer.
2 Subsequently also published in J. Donat, ed., *World Architecture 4*, Studio Vista, London 1967, pp. 50–57; and in *Architects' Year Book*, no. 12, 1968, pp. 151–160.
3 Quoted from De Carlo's 'Talk on the Situation of Contemporary Architecture', published by O. Newman in CIAM '59 Otterlo, K. Krämer, Stuttgart, 1961, p. 86.
4 Quoted from Smithson's reaction to De Carlo's talk, ibidem, p. 91.
5 Ibidem, p. 88.
6 The Collegio del Colle student village on a hill to the southwest of the historic city centre, designed in 1962–63 and built in 1965–66.

The Mirror Master

1 Joost van Roojen (born in 1928), a self-willed and subtle Dutch painter who collaborated with Van Eyck on the Amsterdam Zeedijk playground in 1956, a work for which they jointly received the Sikkens Prize in 1961 (see p. 169 of the present book). Van Eyck designed the layout of Van Roojen's exhibitions in Amersfoort (1962) and Eindhoven (1969).

A propos Jan Rietveld

1 Jan Rietveld (1919–1986) trained as an architect in the firm of his father Gerrit Rietveld, and had been friends with Van Eyck since the late forties. They collaborated for a few years and, with some other friends, went on a memorable journey through the Sahara in 1951. From 1950 Jan Rietveld taught at the Amsterdam Rietveld Academy, and from 1971 to 1980 he was professor at Delft Polytechnic. For his first executed project, see 'Child and City', on p. 40.

Jaap Bakema, 1914–1981 'The Moment of Core'

1 The original Dutch version was published in *Forum*, July 1981. Bakema died on 20 February 1981.
2 'I find, first of all, that I pass from state to state', a quote from Bergson's *Creative evolution*, 1913.
3 A quote from Shakespeare's *The Tempest*.

By definition

1 Lucien Lafour (born in 1942) was taught by Van Eyck at the Amsterdam School of Applied Arts. In 1970, having worked with Piet Blom and Van Eyck & Bosch, he went to Surinam where he built up a design practice, from 1977 in collaboration with Rikkert Wijk. In 1981 both came back to Amsterdam, where they continued their practice.

Joop Hardy, 1918–1983, autumn man between winters

1 The original Dutch version was printed in a folder, published by the Architecture Department of the Delft Polytechnic in March 1986; it was reprinted in J. Hardy, *Cultuurbeschouwing* (collected lectures given at the Delft Polytechnic from 1981 to 1983), Amsterdam, 1987, pp. 313–317. Hardy studied at the Academy of The Hague, and was taught by Johannes Itten in Zurich and Paul Citroen in Paris. He was art editor of the weekly newspaper *Vrij Nederland*, and from 1959 to 1963 editor of *Forum* with Van Eyck, Bakema, Hertzberger and Apon. From 1950 he was lecturer at the Academy of Art and Industry in Enschede, from 1969 to 1983 director of the same institute. From 1969 to 1983 he was professor at the Architecture Department of the Delft Polytechnic.

Dylan Thomas

1 Maarten 't Hart (born in 1944) is a Dutch novelist and literary critic.
2 The Cultural Supplement of the *NRC Handelsblad*, one of the major Dutch newspapers.
3 'Life with a brute'.
4 Multatuli (1820–1887), author of *Max Havelaar*, ranks as a major figure in Dutch literature.
5 Geert van Oorschot (1909–1987), major Dutch publisher who issued the work of writers such as Multatuli, Couperus, Ter Braak, Reve and Hermans.

On Van Doesburg, I.K. Bonset and De Stijl

1. Translation of Dutch manuscript in Van Eyck Archive.
2. Nelly van Doesburg (1899–1975, born Petronella van Moorsel), avant-garde pianist and Van Doesburg's wife from 1921 until his death in 1931. She was actively involved in De Stijl movement and participated as a pianist in dada performances. After 1931 she lead her own busy life and actively devoted herself to the promotion of Van Doesburg's artistic legacy. See: Wies van Moorsel, *Nelly van Doesburg 1899–1975*, SUN, Nijmegen 2000.
3. 'Binnenkant 32' was Van Eyck's Amsterdam home address from 1947 to 1965.
4. Edy de Wilde (1919–2005) succeeded Sandberg as director of the Amsterdam Stedelijk Museum in 1963. When he retired in 1985 he put together a farewell exhibition called *La Grande Parade*.
5. Evert and Thijs Rinsema (1877–1947) were two artistically inspired shoemakers living in Drachten (Friesland). Van Doesburg got to know them when he was mobilized as a soldier during the First World War and involved them in De Stijl movement.
6. 'I.K. Bonset' was the pseudonym Van Doesburg adopted for publishing his experimental poetry.
7. 'Max, you know, he is doing the same thing as I do, but in the other hemisphere.'
8. Harry Mulisch (born 1927), the celebrated Dutch novelist and essayist. In 1982 he published *Opus Gran*, a set of poems that reflected his recurrent dream of a gigantic mythical city incorporating memories of ancient Egypt, Jerusalem and Rome alongside fragments of Speer's Berlin project.
9. Hans van Dijk in *Archis*, 1988, no. 4, p. 43.
10. Til Brugman (1888–1958), Dutch writer and language prodigy, author of novels, dadaist grotesques and sound poems. In 1908 she became friends with Mondrian, through whom she was to get involved in De Stijl. For some time she was as a hidden cooperator to the review, by editing and translating articles by several authors. Later she also did the Dutch translation of Giedion's *Space, Time and Architecture*. The testimony quoted by Van Eyck is an extract from her article 'Piet Mondriaan omstreeks 1910' in the catalogue of the 1946 Mondrian exhibition in the Amsterdam Stedelijk Museum.

Unearthing the silted-up alphabet of meaningful designing – on Jan Rietveld

1. Paul Salomons and Simone Doorman, *Jan Rietveld*, 010, Amsterdam 1990. On Jan Rietveld, see note 1 to 'A propos Jan Rietveld' in the present chapter.
2. The street in Utrecht where Gerrit Rietveld built the Schröder house in 1924.
3. The block of flats which J. Rietveld built in 1956 in collaboration with P.A. Bloemsma at Haarlemmerdijk in the Slotermeer district, Amsterdam.
4. The blocks of flats in Plaslaan (1938) and Bergpolder (1934) in Rotterdam by Van Tijen and Maaskant, and the Nirwana flats (1930) by Duiker in The Hague.
5. Exhibition held from 10 November 1989 to 2 January 1990.
6. The Amsterdam School of Applied Arts, housed in a building by Gerrit Rietveld since 1967, was renamed 'Rietveld Academy' in 1968.

On Team 10

1. Published by M. Risselada and D. van den Heuvel in *Team 10 – in search of a utopia of the present*, NAi Publishers, Rotterdam, 2005, pp. 328–331. Interview included by courtesy of Clelia Tuscano.
2. Alison Smithson (ed.), *Team 10 Meetings 1953–1984* (Delft/New York, 1991), a book that had just appeared at the time of the interview.
3. They were involved in the Independent Group, a group of radical young artists within the London Institute of Contemporary Arts. Founded in 1952, it was responsible for the formulation, discussion and dissemination of many of the basic ideas of British Pop art and of much other new British art in the late 1950s and early 1960s.
4. The passage on Blom was left out in the version published in *Team 10 – in search of a utopia of the present, cit.*
5. The Berlage Institute, founded in 1990 by Herman Hertzberger, was initially located in Van Eyck's reconverted Orphanage.
6. See the statement by Gutman and Manz in *The Story of Another Idea*, in chapter 7, p. 221.
7. Jose Antonio Coderch, 'No son genios lo que necessitamos ahora', in *Domus*, November 1961.
8. See 'University College in Urbino by Giancarlo de Carlo' in the present chapter.
9. Shadrach Woods died of cancer on 31 July 1973.

On Josep M. Jujol

1 Vincent Ligtelijn and Rein Saariste, *Josep M. Jujol*, 010 Publishers, Amsterdam, 1996.
2 During the development of his ESTEC project (1984–89), Van Eyck devised what he called a 'hendecagonic order', based on an eleven-sided column.

A Superlative Gift

1 On Lina Bo Bardi, see Marcelo Carvalho Ferraz, ed., *Lina Bo Bardi*, Charta, Milano,1994; and Olivia de Oliveira, *Subtle Substances of the Architecture of Lina Bo Bardi*, Romano Guerra, São Paulo and Gustavo Gili, Barcelona, 2006.
2 One of the main avenues of São Paulo.
3 The Museu de Arte de São Paulo (MASP), built by Lina Bo Bardi in 1957–1968.
4 The Pompéia Factory transformed into a socio-cultural centre in 1977.

Chapter 15
Retro and Prospect

The radiant and the grim

1 Typewritten text included in the Documenta X exhibition at Kassel (June-September 1997).
A Dutch version was made for the exhibition on Van Eyck's ideas and work held on the occasion of his 80th birthday at the Rotterdam NAi in 1998.
2 A quote from Dylan Thomas's poem 'Should lanterns shine'.
3 Fragment from F. Kafka, 'Kinder auf der Landstrasse' in *Betrachtung*, Rohwolt, Leipzig, 1913. The whole sentence reads: 'Gegen abend sah ich einem Herrn mit einem Stock langsam spazieren gehn, und ein paar Mädchen, die Arm in Arm ihm zugegenkamen, traten grüssend ins seitliche Gras.' (Towards the evening I saw a gentleman with a walking-stick slowly going on a walk, and a couple of girls, who came towards him arm in arm, stepped into the sideward grass.)

Illustration credits

The editors and the publisher wish to thank the photographers, already mentioned in the captions, and those who could not be traced until now.

Van Eyck archive
pp. 13, 18 (l and r), 52, 60, 61, 65, 77 (l), 78, 79, 85, 97, 102, 103, 105 (r-top), 106, 107, 114, 117 (bottom), 126, 145 (l and r), 146, 147, 157, 163 (top), 166, 181, 184 (top), 200, 229, 421 (top), 450, 451, 452, 456, 457, 459, 569 (r-top), 570, 621, 644, 647 (bottom)

Van Eyck collection
pp. 2, 17 (l and r top), 20, 21 (l-middle and l-bottom), 31, 43, 69, 70, 82, 83 (r), 84 (l and r), 86-95, 104, 109, 127 (l and r-top), 130, 160, 170, 280-285, 313 (all), 314 (all), 315, 316 (all), 320, 321 (all), 322, 323 (all), 347, 374-417, 422, 453, 460, 483 (r-top and bottom), 439 (l-top and bottom), 440, 486, 487 (all), 488, 489, 491, 492, 493 (all), 501 (l-bottom and r), 509 (all), 513, 514 (all), 522 (r), 550 (l-top and r-top), 553 (top and bottom), 558 (l-top and r-top), 622 (l and r), 623 (all), 648, 649 (all).

A number of pictures were graciously provided by some individuals and institutions:
– Dirk van den Heuvel and Max Risselada, *Team 10*, (Rotterdam, 2005): pp. 184 (bottom), 207, 213 l-top, r-top and r-middle, 307 (r-bottom), 308 (all), 439, 463 (r), 569 (l-top and bottom), 575, 576 (bottom), 578 (all), 579 (all).
© gta-Archiv/ETH, Zurich: p. 41
© Richard Paul Lohse Foundation, Zurich: pp. 19 (l-bottom and r-bottom), 57, 250 (l-bottom)
© Keystone Zurcher James Joyce Stiftung: p. 132
© NAi, Rotterdam: pp. 141 (l) (KLM aerocarto); p. 141 (r) Collection Spies; p. 150 (Collection Granpré Molière); 158 (r-top and l-bottom) (Archive G.Th. Rietveld), 504 (Collection Berghoef), 512 (Collection Theo Bosch), 516 (top) (Collection Nielsen)
© Nederlands fotomuseum, Rotterdam: pp. 110, 240 (3x) (Collection Ed van der Elsken); 29, 216 (Collection Violette Cornelius)
© AKI-ArtEZ: p. 594
© Archive Rijksmusem, Amsterdam: p. 497
© Archive Stedelijk Museum, Amsterdam: pp. 603 (r), 624 (top)
© Aviodrome, pp. 503, 516 (bottom), 557 (bottom)
© RKD, The Hague, Photocollection: pp. 585 (l-top and r-top); Archief Theo van Doesburg, Schenking Wies van Moorsel: 599, 603 (l), 604

The remaining illustrations were borrowed from:
– ANP foto: pp. 123, 582, 625
– Archive Bakema: p. 307 (l-top and l-bottom)
– Archive Piet Blom: p. 424 (all)
– Archive Instituto Lina Bo e P.M. Bardi: pp. 637, 638 (all), 640 (all)
– Archive Jujol: pp. 634, 636 (l-top and r-top)
– Archive Lucien Lafour and Rikkert Wijk, architects: pp. 590, 591, 592 (all)
– Archive Rietveld-Schröder: pp. 137, 153
– Archive Joost van Rooijen: pp. 585 (bottom), 622 (middle)
– Archive Paul Salomons: pp. 586, 587 (r), 605, 607 (top and r), 608 (top and bottom)
– Archive Stedelijk Museum Schiedam: p. 74
– Archive Nic Tummers: pp. 421 (bottom), 424 (l-bottom)
– Galerie van de Loo, Munich: p. 65
– KLM aerocarto: pp. 14 (top), 324 (middle)
– Kunstmuseum Winthertur: p. 173
– Municipal Archive Amsterdam: pp. 61, 63, 78, 105 (l-top), 111 (l and r), 116 (l top and r-bottom), 117 (top and middle), 501 (l-top)
– Municipal Archive Utrecht: p. 143
– Municipal Museum The Hague: p. 171 (bottom and top)

- Moderna Museet Stockholm: p. 133
- Museum Kröller-Müller: p. 163 (bottom)
- N.L.R. mij. Meteoor: p. 222 top
- Photo Bräm, Zurich: p. 17 (l and r-bottom)
- Photo Lunte Zurich: p. 17 (l-top and r-top)
- Photo Etienne Bertrand Weill, Paris: p. 21.

Illustrations and pictures borrowed from:
- Bardi, P.M., *The tropical gardens of Burle Marx* (New York 1964): p.129
- Bastlund, K., Jose Luis Sert, Architecture, City planning, Urban Design (London 1967): p. 46
- Catalogue, *Arp,* Museo Correr, Venice (8-4/16-7-2006): p. 83
- Catalogue, *Fontana,* Stedelijk Museum Amsterdam (29-4/12-6-1988): pp. 624 (l-bottom and r-botttom), 625 (l-top).
- Catalogue, *Piet Mondriaan,* Haags Gemeentemuseum (18-12-1994/30-4-1995): p. 173
- Catalogue, *Tajiri,* Stedelijk Museum, Amsterdam (2 -3/ 2-4-1960): p. 165
- Dupin, J., *Joan Miró,* (Cologne 1961): pp. 47 (r-top), 173 (r-top)
- The Glasgow School of Art, *Charles Rennie Mackintosh and the Glasgow School of Art* (Glasgow 1961): pp. 626, 629 (all)
- Grohmann, W., *Paul Klee* (Stuttgart 1954): pp. 47 (bottom), 49 (r-top), 135
- Janneke Jobse, *De Stijl continued* (Rotterdam 2005): p. 174
- Kelemen, P., *Medieval American Art* (New York 1944): p. 270 (top)
- Lotte Schwarz, *Tagebuch mit einem Haus* (Zürich 1956): p. 23 (middle and bottom)
- Murray Grigor and Richard Murphy, *The Architects' Architect: Charles Rennie Makintosh* (Glasgow 1993): p. 630 (all)
- Newman, O., CIAM *'59 in Otterlo* (Stuttgart 1961): pp. 204, 207 (r-top), 576 (top)
- Sartoris, Alberto, *Encyclopédie de l'Architecture Nouvelle* (Milan 1957) pp. 538, 539, 544, 546.
- Ungers, O.M., *Oswald Mathias Ungers, Architektur 1951–1990* (Stuttgart 1991): p. 532

The Publisher has made every effort to contact all those with ownership rights pertaining to the illustrations. Nonetheless, should you believe that your rights have not been respected, please contact SUN Publishers, Amsterdam.

Aldo van Eyck at INDESEM 67 – *international design seminar* – at the Department of Architecture of the Delft Polytechnic, 1967. Intro of a lecture as registered on the DVD accompanying this publication.

Portrait Aldo van Eyck from ± 1970, by Ab Koers
How to start – how to end?
   I think one thing is obvious, obvious to me. That is, the time has come to stop the freezing, silly notions into organized emptiness and to call that organised emptiness a city, and then just go whistling for population.
   When I say 'city' I do not mean population, and I do not mean a built form. When I say 'city' and when you say 'city' – when every human being says 'city' – it means the people that live there.

Dancing Kayapó Indians from the Orinoco Basin, Venezuela
Today, this is my first picture.
   Talking about people, that's clarifying a bit, that's right. Talking about people, I would say – and that's why I show you this picture – today the architect is the ally of all men or nobody. Our concern therefore is with people.
Next slide.

Little boys with toy rifles on Waterlooplein, Amsterdam, shown 'accidentally', photo by Ed van der Elsken
With people and people again!

Rotating children, photo by Violette Cornelius
But there is something wrong with that picture. They talk with their hands up. When I talk, I talk with my hands down. That is a funny mistake.

Rotating children shown upside-down, photo by Violette Cornelius
That's it, that's the way we talk: we talk while we rotate. Architecture of course is except being for one person, also for two people. That's to say, unless you talk about a 'monologue interieure', it is for a dialogue. You see the way the shadow passes. It's for dialogue and these children are talking while they rotate. Believe it or not, I have made enough children's playgrounds to be able to tell you that children can discuss while rotating.

Rotating children, photo by Violette Cornelius
You have no idea what people can do. Please don't underestimate, I mean by this: please don't underestimate human capacities. Both to the good and evil.
Next slide please.

Little boys with toy rifles on Waterlooplein, Amsterdam, photo by Ed van der Elsken

There again, you can discover the first little boys I took. They may now. Again, just the difference and the mystery of the difference, between one person and more people. Actually they are all shooting, they all have made little rifles. As they pull the trigger you have a sort of shoot-outs.

Black screen

And now the projector light goes out … They are imitating us already … The time has come of course to look at them. Let's have the next slide. It's just people, I'm talking about people!

Actually I'm showing you some slides, a series of images, which introduce what I want to say. I showed you the children upside-down, which is not the way up, as you want them. You see them never upside-down, either in New Zealand or in Holland, while they are rotating. But here you have another photograph which may perplex you – in other words it does.

The negative of the eclipse

This photograph is representing something else. It is not representing one man or many people, one person or all people. As I said: the architect is the ally of all men or of no men – but in what light?

This actually is a negative of an eclipse, which symbolizes for me the simultaneous presence of the sun and the moon. In that sense the simultaneous presence of night and day.

Black light, you know. The sun amidst black light, as you all know. What I want to say with this, is that we don't conceive of what we make, of what we do in terms of the natural cycles.

Eclipse

We do not make night-cities, we do not make winter-cities, we do not make rain-cities, we do not make stone-cities. We do not make cities for old people, we do not make cities for young people – we just make cities for businessmen!

Time has come to make cities for people, that's why I started with people – people! That is to say, we should make things that can be peopled. 'People' that's a wonderful verb – I thought it was. So there we are, this just stands for the things that are beyond our rational understanding. We all know the sun, I think we do, but we have forgotten about the moon. I'll show you some pictures in a minute which pay tribute to the moon. By the moon I mean the stars and by the moon I mean all the things which are valuable, the sun included. When I say moon, I mean sun. When I say sun, I do not necessarily mean moon – that's the poverty of our civilisation. Next slide, please.

'Moth-Butterfly', photo by Brassai
That's another image which is quite perplexing. Is that a moth or a butterfly – a little moth? I'm not sure it's a moth. Is it a moth or a butterfly? I mean, is it night or day, is this animal-insect outside or inside? Am I outside, is it inside? What is inside, outside, actually? You know? I don't know. I would say we don't know. I would say that architects have been concerning themselves horrifically for thirty or forty years in creating outside for people – even inside. I thought that his job, the job of the architect and the job of the urbanist – same thing, same thing – the job of the urbanist-architect, was to create inside, even outside. Next slide.

Beach in Portugal, photo by Carel Blazer
That's enigmatic, that's of course another thing. I want to say something about what I call the in-between realm. You can have thousands of images for the in-between realm, but this is a very simple one. Because here, I have shown this before, you have a magnificent transition between two great phenomena. One is the ocean, the other is the land. They're both vast. Irrespective what size they may both be, they are always vast. Vastness is not concerned with measurable size. Still it is vast. And here you see people walking almost on the transition between great phenomena. If you take off your shoes and walk along that last thin sheet of water between land and ocean, you know, then you will have a strange – I do, I don't know what you do – a very particular sensation. What is that sensation? I would say that sensation is merely that you are in both places at the same time.

You somehow know the horrific, almost horrific difficulty you have as a sailor. Simply imagine being a sailor. Well if you are sailing you are always longing for the opposite. Sailors always long for the opposite because they usually find neither. The sailor is always dreaming of the land, this landward yearning for the sea – a seaward yearning for the land. But he is always nowhere, his home is always somewhere else. Why?

There is nothing wrong with the sailor, nothing wrong with Popeye, nothing at all. What is wrong is that we continue the sailor's nostalgia, and always try to be somewhere else. Never at home anywhere. I would say that the architects today have become great experts in the creating of nowhere, wherever it is. Just nothing at either side of nothing, a continuous exterior with you outside always, whatever side you may be. As I said before: experts at creating of the meagre, experts at organising the hollow, experts at constructing at enormous costs of the society, that which is utterly inaccessible, because it is both hollow and solid. Now hollow and solid mean exactly the same thing in human terms. The only thing is that you can fill hollowness with more hollowness. And the only thing inside a solid is just solid. Architects just create solids which you cannot enter. If you do so, you just get a hollow, which is the same thing. So why take the trouble?

That wonderful image of the in-between realm brings me to the idea that architecture, if it is anything at all – it's not as much as we think it is – but if it is anything at all – and I think it is – it's just to assist to man's homecoming. We don't necessarily have to assume that people always try to be somewhere else. It will never be at home, that you never could go inside of yourself, that you never feel that you are somebody somewhere. Really, the difficulty of trying to persuade yourself that you are somebody somewhere, knowing so very well that you are nowhere nobody, is just terrific. You can't have that feeling all your life. Here is another simple image.

Child with dog on doorstep, photo by Ernst Haas
It is a doorstep. It could be anywhere, perhaps in Bolivia? And obviously everybody knows what this image means, it is the immediate doorstep. This is not the transition between land and ocean, but the transition between equally incredible truths, realities. It is a transition between something which is inside, probably cool and safe and small. And something that is outside, and probably very hot and less safe – not necessarily, but I assume less safe or larger and more complex. And between those two you see an image of a child.

Just imagine that child sitting on the other doorstep here. If that child sits on that doorstep, obviously there would be only two possibilities. Either it moves back into the house or it risks the larger world outside. And it may not be in a state where it can do either the one or the other. The result is a kind of strange paralyses having to choose between false alternatives.

Architects are always building at great costs for society as I said before, places in which it is impossible to choose what you want to do. Where you want to retreat, where you want to be alone or together. In this particular case having extended the doorstep here, there is – within the public domain, within this larger world, this adventurous world, this magnificent world, which is enticing the child outwards to risk to widen his horizon – there is another doorstep. And here of course, still feeling sitting on a solid mass of her own house, but also sitting on a solid mass which belongs to the city, there is an alternative. It is so clear, the only thing is: why can we not start and persuade the narrow borderline between two realities at the cost of all our lives? A large world of which we are afraid and a small world of which we are also afraid, I assume. Our interior world and the world outside – why cannot we persuade these horrific borderlines to loop generously into articulated in-between realms in which it is good to live? Why can't we ask the contractor to make that for us? And provide them the drawings and use our technology just to arrive at that?

The time has come to create an architecture in which it is possible to linger.

That's all I have to say. I can say more, but we just can go home. An architecture in which it is possible to linger. When I say 'make an architecture in which it is possible to linger', it means not to construct that very thing which causes schizophrenia. You have to choose between silly, false alternatives. I think, this is a magnificent simple example made of mud. Imagine somebody choosing a place in which you can still feel the safety of the cool world inside and the other outside. That's a too long story, so: next slide please!

Hat-Roof, photo by George Rodger
Oh yes, there is another story about which I want to talk, and that's about cities. That's to say, about the large and the small. That's one of the main subjects that can deal with urbanism or with cities. Urbanism is just crap, I mean 'cities'.

This is my image, my beginning, my first image, after the one you saw with the eclipse and the one with the child upside-down. This is the symbol of the city, because we don't know whether that is a large hat or a small roof. As long as you don't know whether a thing is large or small, it probably is both. The same with a thing which is not both large and small: at the same time it has no size. That which is large, without being small, is neither large nor small: it has no size. If it has no size, it has no human size and it has no right size. If a thing is small without being large, of course it's neither large nor small either.

Whether these people are carrying a roof or are wearing a hat together, gives you a strange idea of collectivity. A communal hat if you like. O.K. O.K. I don't know what it is. Why should you? I will not find out what things really mean. Because if I do, half the meaning is lost!

Actually this brings me to the question of the city: the city is a large house – the city is a large house and the house is a small city.

I'm trying to discourage, I'm trying to render relative whatever preconceived notions you may have as to what is large and what is small. As to what is many and what is few. As to what is different and to what is the same. Because in our cities, the cities we know – I'm not talking about the old cities but about those new concoctions, gentlemen called 'urbanists' make for us. In those emptinesses, perpetuated built emptinesses, everything is too far and too near, too small and too large, too different in the wrong way and too much the same in the wrong way, which is the same in the wrong way. In the right way, of course, it's different, this strange concern with difference and with the same. It is wonderful that things should be the same, as long it is the same in the right way. Which is not the way of saying it is different in the right way.

I give you this picture in order to destruct. Later on I will give you far more pictures of the same problem to show you that a house and a city are equally complex. Obviously you can tell me that the sort of ménage of a house is a smaller one than that of the city. But I am not concerned here as anybody with right senses – which I thought I am tonight – concerned with quantitative difference. I don't care that a house is more simple than a city, why should I? Because after all, those they serve, those both house and city serve, are obviously equally complex. And that's the people I started with.

In terms of people there is no difference in complexity between the house and the city. Qualitatively there is no difference, but you are told there is. The whole educational system is based on the fact that a small thing is more simple than a big thing. You start making a tiny thing, then making a big thing. You start with a part and you throw them together and at the end you are supposed to be able to integrate them. And then you do the whole thing, which is one pilfering nonsense – build, you know.

This image is my personal symbol for the equal identity of house and city: of hat and roof. The smallest roof we know is a hat. Let's have the next picture.

Otterlo-circles
I can't possibly do that without looking at my text. I'm terribly interested in the question of large and small, and I'm very terribly excited – always have been – by the idea of the past and the future. Now you know that wherever you go, people are always talking about change. Architects are as usual, absolute change-addicted. They are change-addicted. Other people are addicted more to valuable things, but we are addicted to change.

Now I have heard it said that 'an architect cannot be the slave of tradition'. That an architect cannot be the slave of tradition in a period of change, is that what is said. I don't know who said it, but it has been said many times, by many people. I don't know what a period of change means of course. I thought that a period means change. But a period of change is something very special in the eyes of an architect. I would say that the architect should be a prisoner at no time, a slave at no time. And at no time should he be the prisoner of change: to discover the old anew, always implies discovering something new!

I think this question of time, I want to talk about that in one moment, is more difficult. Because it concerns me terribly and it makes me rather stiff. I'm sorry about that, but I'll use a piece of paper.

You see, modern architecture is so fanatically concerned with change, with what is different in our time, what is different in this period, that they have lost all sight on what is the same in this period. That is to say, what is the same in all people, in all times.

As the past is gathered into the present – it is a question of gathering the past into the present – this enormous gathering body of experience finds a home in the mind. That's the way it does find a home; the present then acquires a kind of temporal depth. That is to say it loses its horrible hard razor-edge accurate instantaneity. I have always called this the interiorisation of time. It means you are giving temporal depth to the present. Or, if you like: time rendered transparent. It's this delicious transparency which gives us a feeling of a continuum.

It seems to me that past, present and future are active in the mind's interior. Somewhere there is an interior in that mind. That's why I talk about interiorisation of time, and interiorisation of the mind. I think past, present and future are active in the mind's interior as a continuum. And if they are not, if the past, present and future are not active in the mind as a continuum – what we make will be without it, without that idea of continuum. That's to say without temporal depth. If anything is without temporal depth it's without associative perspective. And it is associative perspective that we cannot miss. You see, my concern always with the ultimate human validity of different but often seemingly incompatible concepts of space, or circumstantial incidental solutions found during the past ages wherever in the world, must be understood in the light of the above.

I think the time has come to combine not the exterior attributes of all the efforts of men, but to gather the essential meaning which divide among them.

Man after all has been dealing physically and spiritually with the environment for thousands of years, you know. He really has. He's been busy with this thing for thousands of years, and I actually think his natural capacity has neither increased nor decreased during that period.

It's obvious that the full scope of this incredible environmental experience cannot be understood, cannot be contained in the present unless we telescope – you cannot contain this enormous experience man has in terms of environment, unless we telescope the entire past into the present. Let's say the entire human effort.

Somehow it must be there in your heart. You can't just have it in a book, it must be there. It is not a question of knowledge so much; it is a question of an intuitive feeling of belonging to this whole thing. This of course is quite different. It does not mean historical indulgence, in a limited sense. It's not a question of travelling back. It is not a question of antiquarism, but merely of becoming aware of what exists in the present. What has travelled into it.

Left Otterlo circle
These things exist in the present. It is not a question of that these things do not exist in the present. The Parthenon, Van Doesburg's drawing, the Pueblo's village, whatever you like, they exist in the present. They have travelled into us. They have managed to travel into your mind. That's to say, I'm concerned with the contemporaneousness of the past.

I think, that by now, which also my little sketch tries to tell you, we should be able to acknowledge sine qua non the intrinsic validity of simultaneous justification of all cultural patterns. Every culture is a special case. Western civilisation, you know, 'Western Civilisation', is habitually identified with civilisation as such, with what civilisation stands for. But why on the pontifical assumption that what is not like western civilisation is either less advanced, barbaric, or at best exotically interesting for a holiday? Western civilisation is a horrific self-assured jingle, but western civilisation is just one special case. Western civilisation is interesting of course – all civilisations are interesting – it's one interesting special case among a multitude of special cases, and each of which carries its own possibilities and deals with them in a way, specifically its own.

I just want to say that, to tell you that, because it is the only way of course, to open your mind. Make it into an interior to allow the past to be telescoped into it. This sketch says nothing else. It says the time has come to reconcile things we have regarded as being incompatible.

How long we have it regarded as anything that could possibly stand as image for immutability and rest, as the Parthenon can. It takes a long time to see that this is relevant. It does not belong to the past. Quite apart from the fact is that you can see it in Greek shops to bits. Or with the Turks. But it is still there. And why it is still there? Because classical harmony is reality. It does not belong to the Greeks or the Romans or the Renaissance. Classical harmony is simply a law. It is just a way we behave and things behave, in smaller number. If you want to persuade a small number of things to harmonise, to rest within themselves, all you can do is to be imbued with the rhythm that the classical harmony was concerned with.

As far as limited number is concerned, classical harmony will do the job. It's a thing which is not static, as everybody thinks it is, it is dynamic. It is highly dynamic. It is not a question of being static or dynamic, it is very dynamic, but it is always going to be interpreted in a new way.

But this goes to immutability and rest. And we all know that in the 20th century they did not like this. They regarded it as being static; as being immobile; as being closed in itself; as being closed, not open ended. And of course a great period of ours has come to do it in a terrible amount. Not in terms of mechanics so much as in terms of relativity. That is the great sort of spiritual effort of our time. I would say: the idea of relativity. And relativity is not divergent of this. I want to make many images for relativity, but I have chosen this particular sketch by Van Doesburg.

Maison Particulière, Van Doesburg

It could have been a Mondrian, it could have been a formula by Einstein, it could have been $E = mc^2$, it could have been a Picasso painting of 1911, it could have been many things, it could be any bit of Finnegan's Wake.

But there it is, as a kind of symbol of change and movement. Of the continuum if you like, of the fourth dimension: the Non-Euclidian concept of everything. Just a different behaviour, a different movement. You can both regard these of course as being highly sophisticated efforts, creations of the mind, of a single person, within a particular person in a culture.

Left Otterlo circle

And there is a third little drawing here which is enigmatic. I don't know but these two, anything between these two – and there are hundreds, you can have hundreds of images – I just chose these two.

This third one is very difficult. If these two images are somehow results of concepts of a single person, working with others of course in a certain context and period, the other is what I call 'the vernacular of the heart'.

Pueblo Arroyo
The other is a small Pueblo village. It could be any other, hundreds of drawings. And this one somehow suggests that you can build. A man can conceive the Parthenon and several people can make it. Let's say a contractor can make it, if you like. This thing, i.e. Van Doesburg, also can be conceived by one man, or a small group of people. It can also be built by a contractor, but this thing – a city – cannot. It cannot be conceived in our terms by one man, nor can it be built by anybody. Cities are not built. A city is not a huge building, in spite of the fact that I say that the city is a large house. It is a large house, but it is not built. Nor drawn. Nor executed according a plan – what is a city?

What is a city? Actually a city has been compared to all kinds of things. A city has been compared quite recently, and often actually, to a tree. Why is a city compared to a tree? Alexander said it's not a tree, which is the same thing. I don't agree with Alexander because he says a city is not a tree. Well that is just quibbling. A city is a tree or not a tree, it means the same thing. I'll tell you why it means the same thing, because an analogy is always false. A city is not a tree or is a tree, never mind. But why people say that a city is a tree is obvious, it is a dream. I'll tell you why it is a wrong dream. It is not a real dream but just a fake dream. It is a dream because people think that a tree is an organic thing. It grows, it develops from small to large as it grows, it has very small members, leaves. It has twigs, it has branches, it has limbs and it has a trunk, and it even has roots, but architects tend to forget that.

So it is a beautiful example, something which is organic, something which has a kind of logical functional sequence of ascending dimensions, from the smallest to the largest. In which architects forgot leaves as being houses, and twigs with many leaves on, as being streets. And if you go on like that, you get the whole thing and that is the city?

Identification of tree with leave
I believe that any kind of analogy which suggests that a leaf has anything to do with a house, and a twig has anything to do with a street, and a tree has anything to do with a city, is just a false analogy. It is just like opening a door. It is just comparing small with small and medium size with medium size. It is running around the rule, when I'm saying this thing has small things and big things, and that thing is huge and huge. It has no sense. And that's why I'm telling you that an analogy is a false thing, it is unpoetic. And what is unpoetic simply is a lie. What has no poetry in it, is just a lie!

Tree is leave and leaf is tree...
Therefore I tried to some saying like 'a house is a leaf'. I have said 'a leaf is a tree', which is quite different. I have said a house is a city, which is not confounding the physiological reality of a tree, nor the built reality or the created reality of the house or the created reality of a city. But it is confounding everything which has to do with size. One is simply assisting your ridiculous preconceived idea of what is small and what is large.

Identification of tree with leave
And if I say: a house is a city and a leaf is a tree, then I'm making the fool. I'm playing the fool with all the arbitrary concepts you may have as to what is small and to what is large; as to what is simple and to what is complex. And also as to what is part and what is whole. A house is not a part of a city. As a matter of fact, the city is part of my house. When I'm in my house, the city is part of it.

Actually, there are as many Londons as there are Londoners. And there are as many Londoners as Parisians wanting to go to London. There is not one place, there are many places! It is a different place every time I go there. It is my city, not yours. It is yours too, I mean – sorry!

The Dancing Kayapó Indians
And here you see of course what it's all for, this is what I started with. This is a batch of people. The little boy I showed you in the beginning with one person, here we again have a batch of people. And I said 'for each man and all men'. The architect – I say it again and again before I leave you – the architect is the ally of all men or no men. You made your choice when you chose to become an architect. If you want to change that choice, then, leave it!

Now, what you are going to do about it? If society has no form – has society got a form? I leave it to you. If society has no form, that society will be rather wicked, won't it? Let's say, if society has no comprehensible form – if it has no comprehensible form, can its counter form be built? Can we at least conceive, or can society conceive what its counter form would look like? That's to say like a jacket: fits it well? Can society, no: can we – when I say 'we' I don't mean we-bloody architects!

BY 'US' FOR US
I mean US, which last, you know. And I mean US again. That's FOR US – BY 'US', always the same. Architects often talk about 'we and they'. I always say: who the hell is 'they'? Yesterday I shouted: I'm 'they'. You are talking about 'we and they', but I don't know who 'they' are!'. All we really have is WE. It's always WE, make it WE, WE-WE, WE-WE-WE-WE!
O.K. I think that's enough with that picture. I got hundreds more.

Portrait Aldo van Eyck from ± 1964, by Alechinsky.

Index

*Italic numbers
refer to illustrations.*

Aalto, Alvar 545, 562, 617
Ackerman, James 480, 482, 717
Adorno, Theodor 556
Aken-Aton 233
Alberti, Leon Battista 560, 710
Alberts, Ton 500
Albini, Franco 259
Alechinsky, Pierre 76, 83, 677, 696
Alexander, Christopher 385, 430, 431, 447, 664, 715, 716, 736
Altenberg, Peter 572
Althusser, Louis 556
Amba 397, 398
Apollinaire, Guillaume 35, 132, 134, 589, 604
Apon, D.C. 216, 217, 651, 723
Appel, Karel 60–63, 76, 81, 83, 84, 137, 145, 569, 650, 670, 679, 682, 695, 696
Aquinas, Thomas 151, 700, 711
Aristotle 174, 175, 688, 710
Arp, Hans 13, 20, 21, 31, 32, 34, 35, *43*, 83, 100, 133, 134, 415, 552, 556, 599, 646, 647, 650, 688–693, 699, 709
Artaria, Paul 15, 209, 688
Asam, C.D. and E.Q. 25
Asplund, Gunnar 238
Axelrad, Karen 569

Bach, Johann Sebastian 597
Baird, George 664, 714
Bakema, Jaap 30, 31, *41*, 53–55, 141, 145, 147, 149, 150, 152, 156, 180–185, 187, 198, 216–219, 223, 231, 239, 241, 245, 247, 249, 254, 256, 257, 262, 276–278, 295, 298, 305, *307*, *308*, 309, 351, 433–435, 438, *569*, *585*, 588, 619–622, 650, 651, 655, 658, 659, 660, 666, 670, 671, 680, 693–695, 700, 703–711, 715, 723
Baker, Josephine 572
Bakunin, Michael 22, 132, 140
Baljeu, Joost 123, 172–175, 599, 697, 702, 703
Ball, Hugo 34, 134, 166, 688, 692, 699, 702
Baldwin, Thomas 538
Banham, Reyner 537
Bartók, Béla 707
Baudrillard, Jean 556
Bayer, Herbert 209
Beerends, Jan 710, 711
Belgiojoso, L. *204*, 705
Ben Hamou, Mabrouk 86
Benedict, Ruth 346, 709
Berg, Alban 572
Berghoef, J. *505*, 718
Bergson, Henri 13, 31, 37, 132, 202, 588, 692, 696, 708, 723
Berlage, H.P. 31, 51, 606, 656, 668, 678, 694, 721, 724
Biederman, Charles 174, 175, 702
Bijvoet, Bernard *14*, *138*, *311*, 520, 606, 719
Bill, Max 15, 16, 211, 689, 692, 702
Birchler, Linus 25, 650, 691
Blake, William 12, 699
Bloem, Jacques 701
Blom, Piet 219, 268, 276, 278, 305, 306, 309, 328, 332, 420, 421, 423, 429, 432–434, 436, 463, 561, 569, 612, 649, 651, 662, 672, 677, 684, 709, 712–716, 719–724
Blom van Assendelft, R. 710
Boas, Franz 252, 709
Bo Bardi, Lina 637–641, 669, 725
Bodon, A. 141
Boers, Willy 696
Bofill, Ricardo 540, 719, 720
Bohr, Niels 425, 548, 721

Bonset, I.K. 22, 599–601, 604, 668, 724
Boon, G. 216, 651
Booth, L. 720
Borromini, Francesco 302, 617
Bosch, Hieronymus 641, 702
Bosch, Theo 501, 509, 651, 655, 665, 672, 673, 677, 679, 718, 722, 723
Botticelli, Sandro 432
Bottoni, Piero 243
Bouman, Ole 555, 556, 681, 721
Bramante, Donato 490
Brancusi, Constantin 13, 20, 32, 42, 45–47, 49, 64, 100, 132–134, 202, 232, 548, 569, 650, 657, 691, 693, 698, 701
Braque, Georges 20, 692
Brattinga, P. 697
Brecht, Bertold 18
Breton, André 346, 561, 611
Brinkman, Michiel *14*, *138*
Breuer, Marcel 15, *209*, 689
Brugman, Til 177, 602, *603*, 698, 699, 701, 703, 724
Brummel, George Bryan 722
Brummell, Beau 572
Brunelleschi, Filippo 302
Brusse, Kees 692
Buber, Martin 204, 218, 243, 244, 705, 708
Buckminster Fuller, Richard 715
Burle Marx, Roberto 122, 128, *129*, 698

Calame-Griaule, G. 389, 391, 713, 714
Camini, Aldo 604
Campert, Remco 711
Campion, Thomas 275, 291, 293, 710
Candilis, Georges 180, 181, 245, 257, 262, 276, 328, 437–439, 569, 577, 619, *621*, 650, 676, 677, 703, 704, 706, 708, 709, 715
Castañeda, Pedro 353

Cézanne, Paul 13, 64, 132, 199, 249, 548, 552, 641, 721
Chagall, Marc 131, 545, 600
CIAM passim
Citroen, Paul 723
Claudius-Petit, Eugène 262
Claus, Hugo 83, 598, 696, 701
Clemen, Paul 689
Coderch, José Antonio 184, 437–439, 614, 615, 715, 724
Codussi, Mauro 550, 551, 719, 721
Cohen, S. 720
Colenbrander, Bernard 556, 559–564, 681, 721
Constant 60, 61, 64–67, 68, 70, 76, 81, 96, 97, 145, 166, 169, 171, 569, 650, 653, 654, 658, 677, 695–697, 702
Corneille, Pierre 61, 68–75, 81–83, 145, 152, 302, 569, 650, 658, 670, 677, 696, 699
Corot, J.B. 68
Cosimo I 236
Couperin, François 302
Courbet, Gustave 68, 70
Crooke, Pat 712
Cros, Charles 134

Da Cortona, Pietro 466, 490
Dalí, Salvador 13, 18, 66, 81, 560, 600, 601
Dam, Cees 515, 516, 521, 719
Dante 690
David, Catherine 645
Dean, Christopher 433
Debord, Guy 702
De Broglie, Louis 425
De Carlo, Giancarlo 184, 207, 541, 569, 575–581, 610, 612, 615, 616, 617, 619–621, 663, 715, 716, 718, 723, 724
De Chirico, Giorgio 530, 538, 543, 601, 719
Degas, H.G.E. 641
De Hoogh, Pieter 466, 497
Delacroix, Eugène 50, 68
Delaunay, Robert 134, 600, 708
Deleuze, Gilles 556

Della Francesca, Piero 302
Demeter 302
Denis the Pseudo-Areopagite 151
Derbyshire, Andrew 712
Derrida, Jacques 556
Descartes, René 40, 42, 231
De Smet, Gustaaf 68
De Stijl 22, 28, 35, 51, 60, 64, 100, 123, 124, 136, 137, 139, 142–145, 149, 150, 154–156, 177, 198, 209, 227, 303, 304, 569, 578, 599–602, 604, 606, 668, 694, 697, 699, 700, 702, 703, 712, 724
De Wilde, Edy 600, 724
Dieterlin, Germaine 714
Di Giorgio Martini, Francesco 578
Dogon 24, 346–349, 371, 373–416 passim, 453, 488, 560, 661, 663, 685, 684, 690, 709, 713, 714, 716
Domela, Cesar 599
Domela Nieuwenhuis, F. 22
Dommo 398, 399, 404, 406, 407, 411, 560
Doshi, B.V. 615, 716
Dotremont, Christian 83, 670, 696
Dowson, Ernest 596
Dudok, Willem 690
Duiker, Jan 14, 16, 22, 51, 138, 139, 310, 311, 467, 545, 552, 600, 606, 660, 690, 712, 719, 724

Ecochard, Michel 245, 708
Einstein, Albert 132, 202, 236, 425, 531, 542, 688, 735
Eisenman, Peter D. 530, 540, 556, 720, 721
Elling, P.J. 141, 574
Emery, Pierre-André 245, 682, 708
Engelman, Jan 70, 137, 155, 177, 699, 701, 703
Ernst, Max 13, 16, 18, 19, 133, 531, 601

Erskine, R. 207, 275, 441, 569, 613, 706
Euclid 199, 202, 577, 581, 735
Evans, Eldred 546

Feuer, Lewis S. 688
Fischli, Hans 16, 18, 689
Fontana, Carlo 237
Fontana, Lucio 622–625
Forbat, Fred 209
Freed, J.I. 720

Gabo, Naum 145, 156, 692, 705
Galileo 151
García Lorca, Federico 18, 153, 614, 708
Gasser, Hans Ulrich 18
Gaudí, Antoni 628, 635
Gauguin, Paul 253, 542, 641
Geddes, Patrick 181, 703
Gerrits, Ger 696
Geuze, Adriaan 556, 721
Giacometti, Alberto 13, 20
Giedion, Sigfried 12, 16, 28–31, 40, 42, 46–48, 54, 182, 208, 217, 218, 231, 236, 237, 245, 253, 530, 537, 610, 657, 660, 670, 689, 691–694, 699, 703–709, 724
Giedion-Welcker, Carola 12, 13, 18–20, 31, 46, 122, 131–135, 209, 211, 569, 650, 659, 689–694, 698, 699, 720
Gill, Eric 39, 692
Gonggrijp, Pjotr 574, 673, 674, 677, 720, 722, 723
Goodman, Paul 337, 713
Gorin, Jean 174, 702
Gorter, Herman 22, 690
Gossaert, Geerten 701
Götz, Karl Otto 696
Goya, Francesco 67
Granpré Molière, M.J. 150, 151, 700, 711, 719
Grassi, Giorgio 563
Graves, Michael 540, 720
Griaule, Marcel 346–348, 373, 383, 389, 391–395, 713, 714
Gris, Juan 604

739

Gropius, Walter 28, 210, 211, 226, 227, 530, 539, 542, 575, 611, 620, 703, 706, 707, 708
Grung, Geir 613, 706
Guedes, Amancio 436, *463*, *569*, 610, 614, 715
Gutman, Rolf 24, 180, 181, 218, 243, 244, 257, 613, 614, 690, 704, 705, 708, 724
Gwathmey, Charles 720

Haan, Herman 685, 705
Habraken, N.J. 348, 685, 709
Hadrian 531
Haefeli, Max E. 689
Hammel, P. 305, *306*, 309, 712
Hansen, Oskar *184*, *200*, 275
Hardy, Joop 216, 274, 275, 594–596, 651, 667, 707, 710, 723
Hartsuyker, H. 670, 700, 704
Hatseput 300, 325
Heisenberg, Werner 425, 548, 721
Hejduk, J. 720
Hegel, G.W.F. 426
Henderson, Nigel 611
Henket, H.J. 712
Hennings, Emmy 688
Hepworth, Barbara 209, 706
Héré, Emmanuel 538
Hertzberger, Herman 216, 217, 274, 277, 348, 517, 613, 621, 622, 651, 667, 671, 672, 675, 677–679, 681–683, 710, 712, 713, 719, 723, 724
Hess, Friedrich 16, 689
Hill, Anthony 702
Hippodamus 233
Hobbema, Meindert 74
Hofmann, Hans 16, 689
Hokusai, K. 50
Hölderlin, Friedrich 302
Hollein, Hans 540, 720
Holt, G.H.M. 719
Holzbauer, Wilhelm 515–517, *521*, 718, 719
Horn, Lex 70
Horta, Victor 628

Hovens Greve, H. 185, 256, 658, 704
Howell, Bill 180, 181, 245, 257, 709
Hubacher, Carl 689
Hubrecht, Lucia 704
Huelsenbeck, Richard 688
Huszár, Vilmos 22, 599, *603*
Hüttinger, E. 689

Ibsen, Henrik 18
Isozaki, Arata 540, 720
Itten, Johannes 723

Jacob, Max 39, 173, 547, 596, 692, 703, 708, 720
Jaffé, Hans 144, 692, 700
Jahn, H. 720
Jansen, Ferdi 168, 702
Jarry, Alfred 134, 175, 703
Jefferson Barnes, H. 626
Jelles, Jelle 712
Jencks, Charles 528, 530, 540, 664, 673, 714, 720
Jobse, Jonneke 697, 702, 703
Johns, Jasper 611
Johnson, Philip 540, 720
Jolas, Eugene and Maria 698
Jorn, Asger 83
Joyce, James 12, 46, 132–134, 202, 474, 531, 542, 600, 693, 698, 708, 717
Jujol, Josep M. 634–636, 669, 725
Jullian de la Fuente, Guillermo 715
Junger, Ernst 230

Kafka, F. 646, 647, 725
Kahn, Louis 184, 206, 432, 530, 542, 671, 673, 684, 685, 714
Kandinsky, Wassily 35, 68, 131, 134, 227, 692
Karsten, Charles 141
Kavafis, Konstantinos 439
Kekovis-Syrier 83
Kirchner, Ernst Ludwig 68

Klee, Paul 13, 18, 45, 47, 49, 60, 122, 132–135, 139, 202, 227, 372, 600, 659, 693, 694, 699, 708
Kloos, J.P. 140, 141, 692, 699
Klunder, H. 305, *306*, 309, 712
Knpobo *350*, 351
Kok, Antony *150*, 599
Kokoschka, Oscar 572
Königsberger, Otto H. 461, 716
Koning, J. 710
Koolhaas, Rem 560, 561, 680–682
Korsmo, A. 703
Kraus, Karl 572
Krier, Leon 16, 528, 530, 537, 538, 540, 626–628, 632, 720
Kromhout, W. 302, 711
Kropholler, M. 302, 711
Kropotkin, Pjotr 140
Kruyder, H.J. 68, 696
Kurokawa, Kisho 332, 713, 715

Lacan, Jacques 556
Lafour, Lucien 590–593, 666, 673, 677, 679, 723
Lambert, J.C. 695
Lasdun, Denys 667, 704
Lautréamont 167
Lavery, Desmond 546
Le Corbusier 16, 30, 42, 54, 55, 133, 141, 144, 153, 182–184, 202, 210, 211, 223, 228, 231, 232, 238, 245, 309, 436, 438, 530, 531, 537, 545, 570, 611, 684, 691, 692, 699, 703, 704, 706–709, 722
Ledoux, Claude-Nicolas 436, 466, 483, 628
Léger, Fernand 20, 28, 131, 133, 641, 702
Lehning, Arthur 22
Lemco, Blanche 181, *184*, 245, 247, *569*, 706
Lenin, V.I. 688
Levis Mano, Guy *21*, 690, 698, 705
Lichtenstein, Roy 134, 611
Lissitzky, El 22, 66, 599

Löffler, Wilhelm 17, 689
Lohse, Richard Paul 13, 16, 19, 30, 31, 56, 57, 250, 569, 648, 658, 677, 690, 695, 702, 713
Loos, Adolf 140, 571–574, 609, 663, 722
Lovett, W.H. 201, 436, 705
Lucebert 137, 274, 598, 699, 701
Luxemburg, Rosa 688

Maaskant, H.A. 694, 700, 724
Macdonald, Margaret 633
Mackintosh, Charles Rennie 466, 484, 626–633, 668, 673, 719
Maekawa, Kunio 706
Maeterlinck, Maurice 572
Maillart, Robert 49
Maillol, Aristide 81
Maki, Fumihiko 332, 336, 713, 717
Malevich, Kasimir 66, 68, 708
Malraux, André 200
Mantegna, Andrea 641
Manten, G. 351, 356
Manz, Theo 24, 218, 243, 244, 690, 705, 708, 725
Martin, Kenneth and Mary 702
Marx, Karl 538
Matisse, Henri 122, 641
May, Ernst 436, 706
Mayakovsky, Vladimir 141
Mead, Margaret 346, 709
Meier, R. 720
Merkelbach, Ben 141, 241, 574, 704, 708
Merleau-Ponty, M. 720, 721
Michelangelo 235, 236, 543, 626
Mieras, J.P. 695
Mies van der Rohe, Ludwig 209, 212, 611, 620, 670
Miller, Henry 67
Miró, Joan 13, 19, 28, 46, 47, 60, 122, 172, 173, 175, 436, 545, 569, 600, 614, 657, 693, 703
Moholy Nagy, Laszlo 209, 227

Moissi, Alexander 572
Mondrian, Piet 13, 16, 19, 22, 31, 35, 36, 42, 49, 51, 60, 66–68, 70, 122, 124, 132, 134, 136, 137, 143, 144, 155, 173, 177, 182, 189, 202, 218, 227, 232, 249, 303, 531, 542, 599–604, 611, 625, 632, 641, 648, 689, 690, 692, 698, 699, 703, 705, 708
Moore, Henry 545
Morgenstern, Christian 693, 694
Morgenthaler, Fritz 24, 347–349, 373, 374, 385, 396, 407, 414, 663, 664, 690, 713, 714
Morton, Jelly Roll 327, 548, 712
Morris, William 690
Moser, Werner 15, 689, 709
Mozart, W.A. 597
Mulder, Jacoba 100, 695
Mulisch, H. 602, 724
Multatuli 597, 723
Mumford, Eric 683, 684, 691, 703
Mumford, Lewis 691

Nestroy, J.N. 18, 689
Neumann, Balthasar 25, 302
Newman, Oscar 575, 660, 671, 705, 720, 723
Nijhoff, Martinus 701
Norberg-Schulz, Christian 703
Nouveau, Germain 134

Ohtaka, Masato 332, 336, 713
Opbouw 30, 54, 123, 139–142, 147, 149, 150, 180, 183, 219, 254, 563, 588, 604, 650, 654, 691, 694, 695, 700, 709
Oud, J.J.P. 22, 139–141, 275, 303, 304, 562, 563, 599, 600, 695, 699, 711, 722
Oudejans, Har 500

Palladio, Andrea 466, 480–482, 628, 670, 710, 720
Palmer, John 538

Papadakis, A.C. 666, 720
Parin, Paul 24, 347–349, 373, 374, 376, 385, 663, 664, 690, 713, 714
Parin-Matthey, Goldy 690, 714
Paulsson, Gregor 703
Peressutti, E. 204, 237, 705
Permeke, Constant 68
Perry, Clarence 691
Petersen, Ad 697
Pevsner, Antoine 20, 66, 145, 156
Picasso, Pablo 35, 50, 67, 122, 134, 166, 202, 542, 548, 552, 601, 611, 647, 735
Pietilä, R. 260, 621
Piranesi, G.B. 538
Planck, Max 425
Plato 710
Polak, Michiel 574, 722, 723
Polak, Wim 524
Polónyi, Károly 207, 614
Pound, Ezra 572
Pueblo Indians 277, 278, 342, 343, 346, 347, 349, 351–370, 371, 385, 391, 433, 467, 469, 648, 662, 713, 714, 734, 736

Radek, Karl 688
Rasputin 530, 540
Read, Herbert 48, 693, 694
Rembrandt 603, 641
Renoir, Auguste 641
Richards, J.M. 29, 30, 692
Rietveld, Gerrit 22, 35, 38, 123, 136, 137, 139, 141, 143–148, 150–158, 177, 275, 302–304, 545, 563, 569, 599, 600, 603, 604, 690, 692, 694, 697, 698, 700–702, 711, 723, 724
Rietveld, Jan 51, 52, 82, 102, 103, 104, 126, 127, 586, 587, 601, 605–609, 654, 664, 668, 672, 677, 680, 694, 697, 698, 723, 724
Rilke, R.M. 594
Rimbaud, Arthur 132, 199, 604
Rinsema, Evert and Thijs 601, 724

741

Risselada, M. 659, 668, 685, 703, 712, 713, 724
Rodia, Simon 466, *493*
Rogers, Ernesto 54, 184, *204*, 207, 208, 563, 670, 705–708
Roland Holst, Adriaan 695, 701
Roland Holst, Henriette 22, 690
Röling, Wiek 672, 681, 719
Romano, Giulio 543, 628, 719
Romein-Verschoor, Annie 148, 155, 700, 701
Rooduyn, Hans 695
Rossi, Aldo 528, 530, 540, 549, 561, 563, 719, 720, 721
Roth, Alfred 15, 16, 184, 208, 209, 689
Roth, Emil 15, 689
Rousseau, Henri 20, 68, 134, 589
Ruskin, John 700
Rykwert, Joseph 349, 371, 372, 384, 385, 662, 671, 677, 714

Salomons, Izak 525, 674, 675, 678, 679, 681, 719
Salomonson, Hein 141, 670, 677, 699
Sandberg, W.J. 122, 599, 696, 697, 724
Sapir, Edward 709
Sato, Eisaku 487, 664
Sauer, Rolf Eric 713
Schaefer, Jan 524
Schiedhelm, Manfred 569, *621*, 674
Schierbeek, Bert 701
Schiller, Friedrich 16, 689
Schilt, Jeroen 700
Schlemmer, Oskar 209, 227
Schmidt, Hans 15, 209, 689
Schönberg, Arnold 31, 32, 132, 143, 202, 572, 600, 691, 700
Schrofer, Jurriaan 216, 651, 672
Schütte, Wilhelm 208, 706
Schwarz, Felix 16, 20, 22–24, 677, 690, 703
Schwarz, Lotte 23, 690

Schwitters, Kurt 22, 69, 70, 133, 134, 166, 167, 599, 708
Scott, Dick 715
Scott Brown, Denise 530, 540, 719, 720
Scott Williamson, George 223, 238, 707, 708
Seghers, Hercules 74
Sekler, Eduard 706
Senmut 291, 293, 300, 325, 711, 712
Sert, José Luis 28, 30, 46, 54, 55, 183, 208, 237, 241, 657, 693, 704, 706, 707, 708
Seurat, Georges 64, 132, 604
Shakespeare, William 16, 447, 588, 717, 723
Shalev, David 546
Sitte, Camillo 538
Skinner, R. 683, 715
Skopas 25
Sluyters, Jan 695
Smithson, Alison and Peter 143, 180–187, *200*, 201, 204, 212, *213*, 218, 223, 224, 245, 247–249, 256–259, 275, 332, 339, 420, 421, 431, 435–438, 440, 441, 463, 532, 537, 561, 569, 575, 578, 610–613, 615, 618, 620, *621*, 628, 650, 658, 659, 661, 662, 664, 673, 675, 677, 679, 682, 697, 703–707, 709, 714–717, 720, 723, 724
Soeters, Sjoerd 719
Soltan, Jerzy 706
Speer, Albert 518, 538, 556, 563, 647, 724
Spinoza, Baruch 140, 699
Stam, Mart 141, 692
Stam-Beese, Lotte 709
Steens, Charlie 351
Steiger, Rudolf 209, 689
Stein, C. 691
Stern, Robert 540, 720
Stirling, James 212, 531, *532*, 540, 613, 715, 720
St. John Wilson, Colin 433, 436, 438, 681, 715
Stokla, J.M. 309

Stokvis, W. 673, 695
Stroeve, J. 710
Stubbs, Stanley 346, 355, 713
Supervieille, Jules 230, 251, 448, 709, 716

Tafuri, Manfredo 530, 540, 719, 720
Tajiri, Giotta F. 168
Tajiri, Ryu Vinci 168
Tajiri, Shinkichi 76, 123, 164–168, 568, 569, 655, 660, 664, 677, 695, 702
Tange, Kenzo 276, 278, 332, 335–339, 706, 713
Tanguy, Yves 18
Täuber, Sophie 20, 45, 83, 100, 648, 690, 708
Taut, Bruno 572
Taverne, Ed 556, 559–563, 682, 721
Team 10 24, 111, 179–184, 208, 217, 218, 241, 245, 255, 257, 258, 276, 339, 341, 348, 420, 438, 440, 441, 447, 463, 470, 531, 532, 541–543, 561, 569, 610–621, 628, 651, 659, 661, 662, 664, 668, 673–675, 679, 684, 685, 690, 697, 703–707, 712–717, 719, 720, 723, 724
't Hart, Maarten 597, 598, 723
Thomas, Caitlin 597, 598
Thomas, Dylan 153, 197, 279, 458, 597, 598, 646, 668, 716, 723, 725
Tigerman, Stanley 530, 540, 626, 632, 720
Toulouse-Lautrec, Henri de 641
Trakl, Georg 572
Tramlett, George 597
Trökes, Heinz 64, 696
Tupker, Hans 420, 709, 710, 714
Tyrwhitt, Jacqueline 670, 706–708
Tzara, Tristan 13, 20, 21, 133, 191, 312, 572, 573, 650, 688, 690, 698, 705

Underhill, Ruth 346, 370, 713
Ungers, Oswald Mathias 530–532, 540, 542, *621*, 666, 719, 720
Uytenboogaardt, Catharina 605
Uytenhaak, Rudy 523, *525*, 719

Van Beek, Marius 302, 711
Van Berkel, Ben 556, 721
Van Bodegraven, Willem 244, 340, 703, 704, 708, 713
Van den Broek, J.H. 53, *123*, 141, 149, 309, 562, 563, 658, 671, 694, 700, 721
Van Dijk, Hans 560–562, 722, 724
Van Emde Boas, C. 696
Van Gogh, Vincent 68, 74, 137
Van der Leck, Bart 22, 139, 149, 303, 438, 599, 600
Van der Leeuw, C.H. 15
Van der Vlis, Michael 524
Van der Vlugt, Leendert C. 14–16, 22, 35, 51, *138*, 139, 149, 545, 600
Van der Werf, J. 700
Van Doesburg, Nelly 20, 22, 599–601, *603*, *604*, 724
Van Doesburg, Theo 22, 35, 66, 133, 134, 139, 140, 143, 144, 155, 199, *201*, 209, 226, 227, 438, 467, 468, 574, 575, 599–604, 668, 690, 699, 703, 707, 724, 734–736
Van Eesteren, Cornelis 22, 28, 41, 139, 141, 149, 150, 152, 183, 209, 210, 211, 239, 241, 303, 309, 343, 436, 599–*603*, 650, 693, 695, 704, 707, 708
Van Eyck, Hannie 7, 12, 16, 20, 31, *83*, *85*, 347, 441, *557*, *558*, *621*, 650, 651, 656, 668, 677–679, 683, 717, 718
Van Eyck, P.N. 650, 691
Van Eyck, Tess 21, *84*, 104, 650, 690, 698, 705
Van Eyck, Quinten *84*, 650

Van Ginkel, Sandy 185, 247, 256, 569, 654, 658, 704
Van Loghem, J.B. *138*, 139, 600, 699
Van Norden, Hans 69, 70, 696
Van Oorschot, Geert 597, 723
Van Roojen, Joost *123*, 169–171, 349, 582–585, 622–625, 653, 655, 663, 702, 723
Van Rooy, M. 673, 678, 681, 682, 719
Van Stigt, Joop 651, 677, 710
Van 't Hoff, Robert 22
Van Tijen, Willem 30, 141, 148, 149, 210, 302, 303, 574, 694, 700, 711, 724
Vantongerloo, Georges 13, 20, 22, 38, 303, 599, 648, 650, 692
Van Woerkom, Dick 171, 172, 174, 175, 702
Vegter, J. *505*, 718
Venturi, Robert 528, 530, 540, 541, 543, 672, 720
Verdi, G. 597
Verhoeven, Jan 289, *290*, 569, 660, 677, 710
Vico, J.B. 698, 699
Visser, Carel *123*, *160–163*, 349, 569, 655, 656, 660, 677, 701, 702
Visser, Martin 145, 655, 700
Voelcker, John 180, 181, 184, 185, *200*, 218, 225, 245, 247, 249, 256, 257, 262, 263, 275, 305, 430, 431, 437, 543, *569*, 617, 618, 651, 658, 670, 672, 704–707, 709, 712, 715, 720
Vollemans, Kees 555, 556, 675, 721
Von Hoddis, Jacob 134
Von Kleist, Heinrich 16, 689
Von Moos, Stanislaus 13, 14, 682, 689
Vordemberge-Gildewart, Friedrich 33, *44*, 599, 692

Warhol, Andy 611
Watson, Peter 693

Wawo Roentoe, Meike 605
Webern, Anton 572, 708
Weeber, Carel 555, 721
Weese, B. 720
Wewerka, Stefan 432, 436, 438, *439*, 619, 714
Wibaut, F.M. 524, 719
Wickham, Julyan 546
Widman, J.V. 689
Wiener, P.L. *46*, 693
Wijk, Rikkert *591*, *592*, 679, 723
Wijnberg, Nicolaas 70, 696
Williams, Owen 538, 544–546, 707
Willink, A.C. 66, 696
Wils, Jan 22, 599
Wittkower, Rudolf 480, 482, 541, 718, 720
Witstok, N. 305, *306*, 309, 712
Wogensky, André 184, 242, 245, 576, 577, 703, 704
Wölfflin, Heinrich 689
Wood, John 538
Woods, Shadrach 181, 245, 257, 437, 612, 618, 706, 715, 724
Wright, Frank Lloyd 153, 477–479, 569, 664, 717, 718
Wright, H. 690

Yeats, W.B. 12, 701

Zadkine, Ossip 81, 131, 702
Zernike, Frits 297
Zervos, Christian 702, 720
Zur Linden, Otto 134

Colofon

Aldo van Eyck, *Writings*, consisting of two volumes, *The Child, the City and the Artist* and *Collected Articles and Other Writings*, was issued in 2008 by SUN Publishers, Amsterdam.
The text was set in Swift and the graphic design was done by Bart de Haas, The Hague.
The lithography was carried out by All-Print (Fred Vermaat) in Wijchen and VS Graphics (Ben van Schaijk) in Berghem.
The books were printed on Arctic Volume 100 g/m² by Drukkerij Wilco, Amersfoort, which was also responsible for the binding of both volumes and the production of the slip case.
The DVD joined to this publication was composed by Vincent Ligtelijn and Cees Sterrenburg.

The present publication was made possible thanks to the financial support of

Stimuleringsfonds voor Architectuur / Netherlands Architecture Fund

Prins Bernhard Cultuurfonds / Prins Bernhard Fund

Faculty of Architecture of Delft University of Technology

TUDelft
Delft University of Technology

and some private persons who wish to remain anonymous.

The production of the DVD was sponsored by the Faculty of Architecture of Delft University of Technology.

On the slip case: Aldo van Eyck, Tree and leaf (see Collected Articles and Other Writings, p. 443)

© SUN Publishers, Amsterdam 2008
and the Editors
ISBN 978 90 8506 262 2

On the editors

Vincent Ligtelijn, architect, studied at the then Delft Polytechnic, under Aldo van Eyck among others. After graduating he became a member of Van Eyck's teaching team at the said institute. Until 2005 he taught and conducted research in the field of architectural design at the Faculty of Architecture of Delft University of Technology. He published a monograph on the Catalan Modernista architect Josep M. Jujol (in cooperation with Rein Saariste) and edited *Aldo van Eyck, Works*, issued in 1999 by Birkhäuser, Basel and Thoth, Bussum.

Francis Strauven, architect and historian, studied at the Brussels Sint-Lucas Institute and took his PhD at Leuven University. Until 2006 he was professor of Architectural Theory and History at Ghent University. He published monographs on several Belgian architects and was co-editor of the *Repertorium of Architecture in Belgium 1830–2000*. His research into the ideas and work of Van Eyck, carried out in concert with the architect, resulted in the monograph *Aldo van Eyck – the Shape of Relativity*, published in 1997 by Architectura & Natura, Amsterdam.